| Topic | Author | Abbreviated Title | Kaleido-scope (pages) | Those Who Can, Teach (chapters) | Foundations of Education (chapters) |
|---|---|---|---|---|---|
| Curriculum | Adler | *The Paideia Proposal* | 166–172 | 4, 8 | 4, 14 |
| | Elkind | *The Cosmopolitan School* | 108–115 | 2, 4, 6, 11 | 10, 11, 12, 13, 14, 16 |
| | Haycock | *Closing the Achievement Gap* | 210–216 | 4, 5, 9, 11 | 11, 12, 16 |
| | Hirsch | *Seeking Breadth* and *Depth in the Curriculum* | 173–177 | 4, 8, 11 | 4, 13, 14, 16 |
| | Nord | *The Relevance of Religion to the Curriculum* | 185–189 | 4, 7, 11 | 3, 9 |
| | Peddiwell | *The Saber-Tooth Curriculum* | 152–157 | 4 | 14 |
| Ethics of teaching | Strike | *The Ethics of Teaching* | 325–329 | 7 | 4, 9 |
| Finance | Miles | *Putting Money Where It Matters* | 381–386 | 10 | 8, 16 |
| Gender issues | Bailey | *Shortchanging Girls and Boys* | 449–453 | 3 | 10 |
| | Woods | *Hostile Hallways* | 77–80 | 3, 7 | 6, 9 |
| | Kirby | *What Does the Research Say about Sexuality Education?* | 202–209 | 3 | |
| Harassment | Woods | *Hostile Hallways* | 77–80 | 3, 7 | 6, 9 |
| Home schooling | Lines | *Home Schooling Comes of Age* | 145–151 | 7, 11 | 9 |
| Homework | Hofferth & Jankuniene | *Life After School* | 140–144 | 3 | 10, 11 |
| Inclusion | Kluth, et al. | *"Our School Doesn't Offer Inclusion"* | 459–463 | 2 | 12 |
| | Merritt | *Clearing the Hurdles of Inclusion* | 454–458 | 2 | 12 |
| Instruction | Tomlinson | *Mapping a Route Toward Differentiated Instruction* | 467–472 | 4 | 14 |
| Law and the teacher | McDaniel | *The Teacher's Ten Commandments* | 330–342 | 7 | 9 |
| Multicultural education | Banks | *Multicultural Education in the New Century* | 435–438 | 2, 4 | 11, 12 |
| | Minicucci, et al. | *School Reform and Student Diversity* | 443–448 | 2, 4, 11 | 11, 12, 16 |
| | Ravitch | *A Considered Opinion* | 432–434 | 2, 4 | 11, 12 |
| | Stotsky | *Multicultural Illiteracy* | 439–442 | 2, 4, 9 | 6, 11, 12 |

# Kaleidoscope

# Kaleidoscope

## Readings in Education

### Tenth Edition

**Kevin Ryan**
*Boston University*

**James M. Cooper**
*University of Virginia*

Houghton Mifflin Company    Boston   New York

*Sponsoring Editor:* Sue Pulvermacher-Alt
*Senior Development Editor:* Lisa Mafrici
*Project Editor:* Jane Lee
*Editorial Assistant:* Talia Kingsbury
*Senior Production/Design Coordinator:* Jodi O'Rourke
*Senior Designer:* Henry Rachlin
*Manufacturing Manager:* Florence Cadran
*Marketing Manager:* Nicola Poser

Printed in the U.S.A.

Library of Congress Catalog Card Number: 2002109665

ISBN: 0-618-30583-1

1 2 3 4 5 6 7 8 9–MV–07 06 05 04 03

# Contents

# Part Four: Curriculum and Standards

# Part Five: Instruction

# Part Six: Foundations

# Preface

When we were children, one of our favorite toys was the kaleidoscope, the cylindrical instrument containing loose bits of colored glass between two flat plates and two mirrors so placed that shaking or rotating the cylinder causes the bits of glass to be reflected in an endless variety of patterns. We chose *Kaleidoscope* as the name of this book because it seems that education can be viewed from multiple perspectives, each showing a different pattern or set of structures.

## Audience and Purpose

This is the tenth edition of *Kaleidoscope: Readings in Education*. It is intended for use either as a supplemental book of readings to accompany any "Introduction to Education," "Foundations of Education," or "Issues in Education" textbook, or as a core textbook itself.

Today is a time of unprecedented educational debate and reform in the United States. It is our hope that this collection of seventy-four high-interest selections will help readers participate in these national discussions in a more informed way.

The book's wide range of sources and writers—from the classic John Dewey and Carl Rogers to the contemporary Diane Ravitch, Elliot Eisner, Linda Darling-Hammond, and David Elkind—makes it highly flexible and responsive to a broad variety of course needs.

The material we have selected for *Kaleidoscope* is not technical and can be understood, we believe, by people without extensive professional backgrounds in education. The articles are relatively brief and come from classroom teachers, educational researchers, journalists, and educational reformers. Some selections are summaries of research. Some are classic writings by noted educators. Some are descriptions of educational problems and proposed solutions. And, we hasten to add, we agree with some articles and do not agree with others. Our aim is to present a wide variety of philosophical and psychological positions to reflect the varied voices heard in education today.

## Coverage

*Kaleidoscope* is divided into nine parts. Part One concentrates on teachers, with articles ranging from personal reports by teachers to an article about what constitutes great teaching. Part Two contains selections about students, dealing with topics from the changing nature of childhood in the United States to child abuse. Part Three looks at schools and describes some of their current problems as well as a number of recent recommendations for developing more effective schools. Part Four examines curriculum issues and deals with the classic question: "What is most worth knowing?", but also has a number of articles dealing with a major contemporary curricular concern—the movement for higher curricular standards. Part Five focuses on instruction and includes selections on cooperative learning, multiple intelligences, constructivist learning, differentiated instruction, assessment, and research on effective teaching. Part Six contains articles on the foundations of education that discuss the historical, philosophical, psychological, and legal roots of contemporary education. Part Seven contains articles on contemporary educational reform efforts in the United States, with particular attention given to the national concern over school choice. Part Eight examines various aspects of how educational technology is affecting or is likely to affect teaching and learning. Finally, Part Nine focuses on various social issues affecting education in the United States today, with particular attention to ethnic and linguistic diversity as well as gender issues and special education inclusion efforts.

## Features of the Revision

Given that over 35 percent of the selections are new to this edition, *Kaleidoscope* covers current topics such as multicultural education, standards-based education, professional development of teachers, teacher reflection, technology, assessment, brain research, inclusion, school reform, and curriculum reform.

***New: Education Classics.***   In this edition, we have designated several articles as *Education Classics*. These articles, marked with special icons, provide readers with a grounding in some of the ideas that have stood the test of time and shifts in educational priorities over many years. As we explain in the postnotes for these articles, they were chosen because the article's author has been highly influential or is well-known or because the article addresses an enduring idea or controversy in American education.

***New: Curriculum and Standards Section.*** Curriculum has been a mainstay of past editions of *Kadeidoscope,* but we have revamped the section, giving more prominence to what we believe is the major curricular issue facing today's educators: content standards and their accompanying high-stakes testing and assessment. In addition, the effects of the movement to increase students' academic achievement are reflected in a number of articles in other sections.

***Diversity and Social Issues Section:*** In the previous edition, we inaugurated a section on diversity, and with this edition we are broadening the section to include additional social issues. The articles in Part Nine examine such topics as multiculturalism, inclusion, immigration, the role of parents, and issues of gender in the classroom.

***New:*** Companion web site, *Kaleidoscope Online,* accompanies the printed version of the tenth edition. It offers several articles from *Kaleidoscope,* annotated and enhanced with links to more information and critical thinking questions, as well as several new articles that are unique to *Kaleidoscope Online.* An article review form and a student response form are also included.

## Special Features of the Book

To facilitate understanding of the selections in this book, the tenth edition of *Kaleidoscope* includes a number of especially helpful features.

▶ Each of the nine major sections is introduced by a section-opening overview to place the readings into a broader context.

▶ The end of each reading features a postnote and several discussion questions. The postnote comments on the issues raised by the article, and the discussion questions prompt readers to do some additional thinking about the major points made in the reading.

▶ *New* "Terms to Note." Key terms are called out on pages where they appear, providing alert students valuable additions to their educational vocabularies and reminding them that a glossary of these terms is included at the end of the book.

▶ The Glossary of key terms at the end of the book is especially useful to those students taking their first course in education or those using this book as a primary text. A detailed subject index also appears at the end of the book.

▶ The Article Review Form, found at the end of the book, will help you to analyze and discuss the articles in the text.

▶ The Student Response Form, also at the end of the book, is your opportunity to comment on each of the readings and to suggest new readings or topics for the next edition. We sincerely hope that you will take the time to complete this form and mail it back to us. Your comments will be invaluable to future students and us as you help us to select the best readings.

▶ The Correlating Table, arranged alphabetically by topic, relates each *Kaleidoscope* selection to specific chapters in both *Those Who Can, Teach,* tenth edition, by Kevin Ryan and James M. Cooper, and *Foundations of Education*, eighth edition, by Allan Ornstein and Daniel Levine. We hope this chart will serve as a handy cross-reference for users of these books. This chart is printed on the inside covers of the text for easy reference.

## Acknowledgments

We are especially grateful to a number of reviewers for their excellent recommendations and suggestions, most notably:

Dr. Veronica P. Stephen, *Eastern Illinois University*
Christy Gonzales, *California State University–Stanislaus*
Robert Fitzgerald, *South Florida Community College*

In addition, we would like to offer a special note of thanks to the many users of this book who have been kind enough to share with us their impressions of it and their suggestions for how we might improve it in subsequent editions. We hope this tradition will continue as you complete and return the Student Response Form or send us your comments via the Houghton Mifflin web site, http://education.college.hmco.com/students

Kevin Ryan and James M. Cooper

# Kaleidoscope

# Teachers

B eing a teacher today has special drawbacks. It is difficult to be a teacher in an age that mocks idealism. It is difficult to be a teacher without the traditional authority and respect that came with the title in the past. To be a teacher in the midst of a permissive time in childrearing, when many students are filled with anti-authoritarian attitudes, causes special strains. It is punishing to work at an occupation that is not keeping up economically. It is painful to be part of a profession that is continually asked to solve deep social problems and to do the essential job of educating children and then regularly criticized for its failings. A good case can be made for discouragement, even for self-pity.

This negativism, or at least acknowledgment of the negative, obscures the fact that teaching is one of the truly great professions. These passing conditions ignore the greatness that resides in the teacher's public trust. Many adults struggle with the question: Am I engaged in significant work? Teachers always know that they are engaged in crucial, life-shaping work.

# The Influence of Teachers

### Mihaly Csikszentmihalyi and Jane McCormack

The ordered pattern of human energy that we call a social system can run into trouble in many different ways. It can, for instance, be broken up by the invasion of more numerous and desperate people, as happened to innumerable civilizations from the Sumerians to the Romans. Its economy can be made obsolete by the discovery of new trade routes, as happened to the Venetian Republic when the Atlantic became the main avenue for commerce; or by the development of a new technology, as when plastics undercut the production of leather, on which the affluence of Uruguay depended. Powerful nations have been destroyed by natural catastrophes, by changes in the ecology, or by epidemics that decimated the population and sapped its will to live.

**TERM TO NOTE**
Social system

In addition to such external dangers, every society faces an internal threat to its continuity. Appearances to the contrary, such seemingly powerful and enduring entities as "state," "nation," and "culture" are in reality quite vulnerable. If just one generation of young people were to grow up rejecting the language of their parents, the values of their community, or the political commitments of their elders, the nation to which they belong would be changed in irreversible ways. A social system can survive only as long as people are willing to support it.

At the time this article was written, Mihaly Csikszentmihalyi was a professor in the Department of Psychology at the University of Chicago, and Jane McCormack was a clinical psychologist in private practice in Chicago. Mihaly Csikszentmihalyi has since retired and is living in Claremont, CA. "The Influence of Teachers," by Mihaly Csikszentmihalyi and Jane McCormack, *Phi Delta Kappan*, February 1986, pp. 415–419.
© February 1986 by Phi Delta Kappa, Inc. Reprinted by permission of authors and publisher.

If there is such a thing as "America," with its peculiar dreams, its unique political and economic patterns, its values and habits of lifestyle, it is because generation after generation of fathers and mothers have passed on to their sons and daughters some distinctive information that makes these offspring think and behave differently from youngsters growing up elsewhere. If this information were no longer transmitted successfully, "America" as we know it would no longer exist. Neither words carved in stone nor constitutions and laws written on paper can preserve a way of life, unless the consciousness of people supports their meaning.

At first glance, it might seem that such a "danger" is too far-fetched to worry about. After all, how likely is it that a majority of young Americans in a given generation will turn their backs permanently on the example of their elders? Moreover, a certain rebelliousness in adolescents is normal, even desirable. We expect teenagers to reject the ways their parents dress and talk, to despise the music their parents enjoy, and to ridicule the values their parents hold. But this is only a passing phase. By the time these youngsters move into young adulthood, they retain—in the guise of new lifestyle fashions—only the most superficial traces of their former rebelliousness. In all important respects, children end up repeating the pattern of their parents' lives.

All of this is true. But there are also times when, instead of disappearing in the course of maturation, the customary rebelliousness of adolescence leads to permanent changes in the ways young people see the world. The outcome is often an irreversible transformation of the society. The young people of most "underdeveloped" nations are obvious examples; fascinated by the miracles of western technology, they are no longer interested in learning the traditions of their cultures—which, as a result, will eventually become extinct.

Many western sociologists and psychologists consider this a positive trend. The spread of "modernization" through education is, they believe, a welcome advance over the superstitious nonsense on which preliterate traditions were based. To a certain extent, they are right—for, without constant experimentation and change in ways of living, human society would become rigid and closed to the possibility of further evolution.

On the other hand, it is also clear that not all change leads to improvement. Sometimes a population gets used to an easy way of life and forgets the technological or moral skills that allowed it to survive in the past. If conditions then take a turn for the worse again, that population may no longer be able to cope with the challenge. Some scholars claim, for example, that the Appalachian settlers once had a vigorous and complex material culture. They were masters of many crafts and technologies that were state of the art in the 17th and 18th centuries. But by now the memory of those skills has decayed, and the way of life in Appalachian communities today is more primitive than it was a few centuries ago—not only in relation to the rest of the world, but in absolute terms as well. Why did this regression take place? We could list many reasons, but one factor was clearly essential: over time, young men and women no longer felt that it was worthwhile to learn what their parents had known.

Indeed, if we were to look at history from this point of view, we might discover that many of the great changes that have befallen the human race had as their source an erosion of belief, or will, or interest that undermined the younger generation's inclination to follow in the footsteps of its elders. Sometimes this reluctance to follow the elders yields positive outcomes; liberating new ideas can arise out of a stagnating culture. But probably more often,

when youths reject the messages passed on to them by their elders, important information that has proved its value in helping the society to survive is lost as well.

A timely example is the so-called "sexual revolution" of the last 30 years. During this period messages concerning the physical dangers of sexual promiscuity were quickly discredited. It is true that the "wisdom" of the elders on this score was quite garbled and often hypocritical. Yet their moralistic warnings were based on thousands of years of experience with disease and psychic disintegration. They may not have had a scientific understanding of the situation, but they had a pretty clear idea of what eventually happens to individuals who indiscriminately satisfy their sexual needs.

Yet entire cohorts of young people dismissed the warnings as "repressive victorian morality." With the hubris of a generation that believed itself to be emancipated from the weakness of the past, that felt in control of its destiny because it was privy to the magic of science, the sexually liberated stepped boldly into a new world of ultimate self-indulgence—only to discover there some of the ugly realities that had forced their ancestors to counsel self-discipline. It was not ignorance that made the Victorians praise sexual restraint after all, but knowledge of the dangers of venereal diseases and of the dislocations prompted by illegitimate births. As it turned out, our liberated contemporaries were the ignorant ones—ignorant of the painfully accumulated experiences of previous centuries.

It is bad enough when a culture fails to communicate to its youngsters those facts (such as the need for sexual restraint) that bear on its chances for physical survival. But a more subtle and dangerous loss of information occurs when the elders cannot pass on to the young convincing goals that make living worthwhile. When this occurs, the younger generation is left in an emotional morass. Without meaningful goals, the behavior of young people can easily become self-destructive.

This lack of meaningful goals most likely accounts for the unprecedented surge of social pathology in the U.S. over the past 30 years. The worst explosion in teenage suicide (a 300% increase in barely a generation) has occurred among white, middle-class boys—the privileged heirs to the richest society the world has ever known. Vandalism, crime, drug use, and venereal diseases all show similar gains. Clearly, the material affluence of suburbia is not enough to make young people happy. It is not even enough to make many of them want to go on living. What youngsters need, more than anything else, is purpose: meaningful goals toward which to channel their energies.

**TERM TO NOTE**
Social pathology

But how does one learn about meaningful goals? The simple answer is, "from other people." Certainly, books that enshrine past wisdom help. And personal experiences might move us to confirm our purpose. But the most pervasive and effective information about what makes life worth living comes from older people with whom children and adolescents interact—assuming, of course, that the elders have some useful information to impart. In any given instance, they may not. By and large, however, it is safe to assume that the older generation—simply by virtue of the fact that it has weathered the hazards of existence—can help those who have less experience to set worthwhile goals.

If this is the case, the hitch in transmitting information between generations these days becomes readily apparent. Typical American adolescents spend only five minutes a day alone with their fathers, and half of this time is spent watching television. Moreover, typical American adolescents spend only about 40 minutes a day alone with their mothers, an hour a day with both parents, and about 15 minutes a day with other adults—for a total of about two hours a day in the company of mature individuals. But almost all this time is spent unwinding from the tensions of school or work and in such repetitive maintenance activities as eating, shopping, or cleaning. Very little information of any moment is passed on in these routine interactions.

By contrast, the same teenagers spend more than four hours each day with their friends. This is time spent outside of school and beyond the influence of elders, and it is during this time that most of the information vital to teenagers' lives is exchanged. But values and goals that develop in peer groups—exciting and novel though they may be—have not passed the test of time and thus are of unknown survival value. To round out the picture, most teenagers spend from four to five hours each day alone, left to their own devices—and perhaps two additional hours with the media, which essentially means "in front of the television set." Although scholars have argued that television is a conservative socializing influence, we have not found a single youngster in the course of our research who claims to have derived a meaningful goal from watching television.

Of course, in describing the network of relationships that define adolescence, we left out a crucial element: the roughly three hours each day that teenagers spend with their teachers. This is the single most important opportunity for them to learn from adults in our culture—a culture that has essentially delegated the upbringing of its young to educational institutions.

Unfortunately, the transmission of adult goals in classrooms takes place under far from ideal circumstances. In the first place, teachers, tend to be outnumbered, by a ratio of at least 20:1. Second, regardless of how much real or theoretical authority teachers have, they are isolated and cannot participate in the kinds of spontaneous interactions that generate internally binding norms and values. Thus the values of the peer group become real to the students, because those are the values that they help to develop and are able to experience directly.

Moreover, because school attendance is compulsory, the school cannot count on the loyalty of students. Our research shows that, of all the places teenagers hang out, the school is the one place they least wish to be. Moreover, when they are in school, the classroom is the one place they most strongly wish to avoid. They far prefer the cafeteria, the library, or the hallways.

Since the audience is a captive one, the teacher's task of passing on the central goals of the culture (and thus a sense that life has meaning and worth) becomes exceedingly difficult. In fact, when they are listening to teachers' lectures, students' levels of alertness and motivation are about as low—and their levels of passivity are about as high—as they get all day.

Yet, despite these obstacles, teachers do manage (almost miraculously) to make a positive difference in the lives of many students. When we asked teenagers to tell us who or what influenced them to become the kinds of people they are, 58% mentioned one teacher or more. However, 90% mentioned their parents, and 88% mentioned peers.

At first glance, these figures do not seem to give teachers a great deal of weight. That 30% more teenagers should mention peers than teachers as having shaped their lives is a thought-provoking commentary on the relative influence of the two groups. Moveover, these students saw only about 9% of all the teachers whom they had encountered in the course of their school careers as having made a difference in their lives. In other words, at least 91% of the teachers left no memorable mark. But, considering the difficult circumstances under which teachers usually struggle, even these meager figures inspire some hope.

What distinguishes those teachers who, despite all the obstacles, are able to touch students' lives, giving them shape and purpose? Or, to phrase the question in more general terms, What makes an adult an effective carrier of cultural information?

Psychological theories of modeling, which describe how young people imitate and internalize the behavior of their elders, suggest that, for a teacher to have an impact on the behavior of students, the teacher must be perceived as having control over resources that the students desire. According to social learning theory, an influential teacher is one who can reward and punish or who has outstanding command of a particular field of knowledge.

**TERM TO NOTE**
Social learning theory

Because adolescents wish to identify with adults who have status and power, they will choose as models those teachers who are strong, powerful, or extremely skilled.

Our interviews with adolescents, however, suggest that this picture of what motivates a teenager to let a teacher influence his or her life is much too simple. Clearly, an adult who attracts the attention of a young person strongly enough to make a difference must possess a "resource" that is attractive to the young. But this resource is not what psychologists have assumed it to be. The obvious traits—power and control, status and expertise—do not move most teenagers. When adolescents try to explain why particular teachers have helped to shape who and what they are, this is the kind of thing they say:

> Mr. R. has really interesting classes because he's so full of pep and energy when he's teaching. It's not like the boring lectures you get in other classes when you listen to some guy drag on. He really gets into it, he's interesting, and it's fun to learn that way. It's easy to learn, because you are not bored.

Most often, the teenagers described influential teachers in terms of their ability to generate enthusiasm for learning through personal involvement with the subject matter and skill in teaching it. Such responses far outnumbered mentions of power, status, or intelligence. Adolescents respond to teachers who communicate a sense of excitement, a contagious intellectual thrill. When excitement is present, learning becomes a pleasure instead of a chore. Thus teachers' involvement with subject matter translates into effective learning for students.

But involvement with subject matter does not come at the expense of involvement with the students. On the contrary, teenagers see influential teachers as exceptionally approachable—"easy to talk to" and ready to listen when students have difficulty understanding the material.

> Mrs. A. was the best teacher I ever had. . . . When you had problems, you could always go to her. Other teachers just yell at you

when you don't understand something; they tell you to bring a note home to your parents.

Mr. M. has the ability to create an atmosphere where you don't feel scared to ask a question. Even if you *feel* dumb, he doesn't make you look dumb by asking the question in class or by saying, "I really don't understand."

Mr. N. was a teacher you could really talk to. He *listened* to you, and he helped you to learn because he didn't shoot you down when you asked a question.

The most obvious consequence of teachers' nurturant attitudes is that students gain the self-confidence necessary for perseverance in learning: "Mr. J. was always kind and helpful. . . . He'd go over things as many times as you needed, which really helped you learn."

But many more teenagers saw nurturance as important because, in one teenager's words, "It shows you that the teacher really cares, and just seeing that makes *you* want to learn." The teacher's investment of psychic energy proves to students that learning is worth *their* time and effort. The teacher's enthusiasm and dedication are the main vehicle for socializing the young into meaningful academic experiences. To paraphrase Marshall McLuhan, the medium of education is the message; the attitude of the instructor toward teaching is what is being conveyed to the students.

In addition to caring about students and about the subjects they teach, influential teachers are remembered for taking the trouble to express their messages in unusual, memorable ways.

Mr. C. is such a fantastic teacher because he has a special way of thinking that catches your attention. He makes brains *go,* he makes brains *think*, and he says things in a way that you just can't forget them.

Mr. J. was influential because he gave us a lot of unusual assignments to do—it was never just "read Chapter 2 and answer the questions at the back of the book." When we were studying about Africa, he came up with the idea of having us do some research

on what it would be like to take a trip there. We had to go to a travel agency and find out all kinds of things because he wanted us to come in and tell him where we'd go and what we'd *see* there. We even had to tell him what it would cost to travel around Africa in a boat, a plane, a car, and on a bicycle. . . . He *really* opened your eyes, and his class wasn't like any class I've ever had before.

This ability to engage the attention of students by presenting material in an original way is often seen as an expression of a teacher's creativity. But to label such behavior as "creative" could be misleading, because that term implies that only exceptionally gifted teachers have the capability. It seems more probable that a teacher who presents material in an original manner is not necessarily highly creative but simply more willing to spend time thinking about how best to convey information to a specific audience. In other words, creativity—like nurturance and involvement—is probably a reflection of a teacher's enthusiasm for teaching.

Perhaps the most important accomplishment of influential teachers is that they are able to transform the usual drudgery of the classroom into an enjoyable experience. Teenagers typically say about the classes of such teachers, "You learn a lot because it doesn't seem like work; it's something you really *want* to do." One adolescent expressed this idea in a particularly pointed way:

What made Mrs. R. influential was that she made it *fun* to learn. . . . When something is fun, it's not like learning. I mean, I learned *a lot* in her class, but things would stick in my head. In other classes, things don't stay in my head; they just fly out!

Another student made a statement that highlights an important outcome of effective teaching:

Mrs. A. was influential because her [English] class was a lot of fun. . . . After all these years, I found out for the first time that I really *liked* English—it was really fun—and I've kept up my interest even though I'm not doing as well as other kids.

When teaching is effective, students not only enjoy the class but also learn to enjoy the subject matter. Only after a student has learned to love learning does education truly begin. Having caught a teacher's enthusiasm for the ordered pattern of information that constitutes "English," or "mathematics," or "chemistry," the student is ready to pursue the subject for its own sake, without threats or bribes from adults.

Past studies of teacher effectiveness have often noted that good teachers are "warm," "accessible," and "enthusiastic." But such traits are almost always lumped with the *expressive* dimensions of teaching. They are seen as characteristics that a teacher ought to possess to be popular with students, not as task-relevant traits. Indeed, they are seen as hindrances to the serious purpose of teaching. A recent article on research related to course evaluations reflects this widespread misunderstanding of the teaching process. This research suggests that jokes and theatrics, along with well-chosen materials and well-delivered lectures, are often of major importance to achieving high course ratings. In order to obtain higher ratings, an instructor should make his or her course one that students enjoy attending.

Most scholars in the field assume that enthusiasm, a sense of humor, and the ability to make learning enjoyable are dubious gimmicks to be used only by those teachers who wish to cater to their students' foibles. But this attitude is built on a mistaken view of what young people need most from their teachers. They don't need just information; they need *meaningful* information. They don't need just knowledge; they need knowledge that makes sense and inspires belief. They need knowledge that helps them understand why learning and living are worthwhile.

But how can young people believe that the information they are receiving is worth having,

when their teachers seem bored, detached, or indifferent? Why would teenagers trust knowledge that brings no joy? Indeed, teenagers are following a perfectly sound

survival strategy when they ignore information that has no relevance to the central business of life, which is enthusiastic involvement with enjoyable activities. To the extent that teachers cannot become joyfully involved in the task of teaching, their efforts will be largely in vain. Their message will be eliminated from the stream of cultural evolution as well, because the younger generation will have no interest in retaining it.

This obvious connection between enjoyment and education has been missed in the past because we have viewed the learning process in terms of the stimulus-response model developed by the behavioral psychologists. Most educational psychologists have tried to look at what happens in schools according to rules developed to describe the behaviors of dogs, pigeons, or rats in laboratories. The educational process has been broken into tiny learning steps, and we have spent our time analyzing the "laws" of learning related to relationships among these microscopic units. Teacher trainers and developers of educational software for computers have all been guided by the assumption that, if the structural units of, say, mathematics are correctly sequenced and rewards are provided at appropriate points in the sequence, students will "learn mathematics."

We believe that it is more useful to see the learning of a complex system of information—be it trigonometry, music, or chemistry—as an outcome of a conscious commitment to the particular domain of knowledge. Of course, the steps of learning proceed piecemeal, according to the laws of effect specified by behaviorist theories. But to understand why mastering a new skill in computation will reward one person but not another requires knowledge of the motivational systems involved.

All complex learning that requires concentrated effort over time depends on intrinsic moti-

vation. If an individual doesn't *like* to do math, he or she will never become a real mathematician. Extrinsic motives—the ones manipulated through the so-called operant rewards and punishments that are administered by outsiders to increase the desired behaviors—can cause students to cram for tests, pass them, and meet professional standards of knowledge. But extrinsic motives alone are not enough to cause students to identify with a body of knowledge and internalize it. And unless young people come to "love" mathematics (or music, physics, poetry, psychology, or any other discipline)—unless they try to make the body of knowledge their own—it is premature to speak of genuine learning. Knowledge that is not the outcome of intrinsic motivation is very fragile. It needs external inputs of energy, in the form of rewards and punishments, if it is to be maintained. Such knowledge remains static, because it lacks intrinsic incentives to grow. Only a student who wants to know something for its own sake can be said to be really learning.

The same is true of the much more complex process of learning to become an adult member of society. To grow up to be an "American" means to accept with enthusiasm the values, habits, and patterns of behavior that set this culture apart from others, that give it a particular historical identity and evolutionary significance. If young people fail to encounter adults who are enthusiastically involved with the culture, they cannot be expected to replicate the patterns of that culture in their own lives. If the adults who represent mainstream values to the young are bored, listless, and disinterested, their way of life will be rejected by the coming generations. And this would be a catastrophe comparable to those visited on past generations by wars or by the bubonic plague.

## POSTNOTE

When this article first appeared, in February of 1986, the United States was facing forecasts of a deep shortage of teachers. Reports and commentaries predicted classrooms without teachers. But the authors of this article discuss a much more serious and dangerous possibility: youth without meaningful contact with adults. When this happens, society begins to crumble. Its sustaining values no longer make sense to the young. The social glue no longer sticks.

Because of the decline in the power of the family, teachers are increasingly being called upon to act as transmitters of values. They must not only teach content but do it in a way that inspires the young to "buy into" the values of the culture. For this reason, the authors believe that the affective elements of teaching are of enormous importance.

## DISCUSSION QUESTIONS

1. What are the forces that currently diminish the power of parents and teachers to affect the values of the young?

2. In the view of these authors, what are the skills or qualities of "the effective teacher"?

3. Are these authors suggesting that the main job of teachers is to socialize children into society's core values? Why? Why not?

# Reflection Is at the Heart of Practice

Simon Hole and Grace Hall McEntee

The life force of teaching practice is thinking and wondering. We carry home those moments of the day that touch us, and we question decisions made. During these times of reflection, we realize when something needs to change.

A protocol, or guide, enables teachers to refine the process of reflection, alone or with colleagues. The Guided Reflection Protocol is useful for teachers who choose to reflect alone. The Critical Incidents Protocol, which we developed through our work with the Annenberg Institute for School Reform at Brown University, is used for shared reflection. The steps for each protocol are similar; both include writing.

**TERM TO NOTE**
Guided Reflection
Protocol

## Guided Reflection Protocol

The first step in guided reflection is to collect possible episodes for reflection. In his book *Critical Incidents in Teaching: Developing Professional Judgement* (1993), David Tripp encourages us to think about ordinary events, which often have much to tell us about the underlying trends, motives, and structures of our practice. Simon's story, "The Geese and the Blinds," exemplifies this use of an ordinary event.

Simon Hole is a fourth grade teacher at Narragansett Elementary School in Narragansett, Rhode Island. He has written a book entitled *Reflection: The Heart of Changing Practice* (Teachers College Press, 2002). Grace Hall McEntee is cofounder of Educators Writing for Change. She may be reached at Box 301, Prudence Island, RI 02872 (e-mail: Gmcente@aol.com). From Simon Hole and Grace McEntee, "Reflection Is at the Heart of Practice." *Educational Leadership*, May 1999, pp. 34–37. Reprinted by permission of the Association for Supervision and Curriculum Development. Copyright © 1999 by ASCD. All rights reserved.

### Step One: What Happened?

Wednesday, September 24, 9:30 A.M. I stand to one side of the classroom, taking the morning attendance. One student glances out the window and sees a dozen Canada geese grazing on the playground. Hopping from his seat, he calls out as he heads to the window for a better view. Within moments, six students cluster around the window. Others start from their seats to join them. I call for attention and ask them to return to their desks. When none of the students respond, I walk to the window and lower the blinds.

Answering the question What happened? is more difficult than it sounds. We all have a tendency to jump into an interpretive or a judgmental mode, but it is important to begin by simply telling the story. Writing down what happened—without analysis or judgment—aids in creating a brief narrative. Only then are we ready to move to the second step.

### Step Two: Why Did It Happen?

Attempting to understand why an event happened the way it did is the beginning of reflection. We mush search the context within which the event occurred for explanations. Simon reflects:

It's not hard to imagine why the students reacted to the geese as they did. As 9-year-olds, they are incredibly curious about their world. Explaining my reaction is more difficult. Even as I was lowering the blinds, I was kicking myself. Here was a natural opportunity to explore the students' interests. Had I stood at the window with them for five minutes, asking questions to see what they knew about geese, or even just listening to them, I'd be telling a story about seizing the moment or taking advantage of a learning opportunity. I knew that even as I lowered the blinds. So, why?

Searching deeper, we may find that a specific event serves as an example of a more general category of events. We need to consider the underlying structures within the school that may be a part of the event and examine deeply held values. As we search, we often find more questions than answers.

Two key things stand out concerning that morning. First, the schedule. On Wednesdays, students leave the room at 10:00 A.M. and do not return until 15 minutes before lunch. I would be out of the classroom all afternoon attending a meeting, and so this half hour was all the time I would have with my students.

Second, this is the most challenging class I've had in 22 years of teaching. The first three weeks of school had been a constant struggle as I tried strategy after strategy to hold their attention long enough to have a discussion, give directions, or conduct a lesson. The hectic schedule and the need to prepare the class for a substitute added to the difficulty I've had "controlling" the class, so I closed the blinds.

There's something satisfying about answering the question Why did it happen? Reflection often stops here. If the goal is to become a reflective practitioner, however, we need to look more deeply. The search for meaning is step three.

## Step Three: What Might It Mean?

Assigning meaning to the ordinary episodes that make up our days can feel like overkill. Is there really meaning behind all those events? Wouldn't it be more productive to wait for something extraordinary to happen, an event marked with a sign: "Pay attention! Something important is happening." Guided reflection is a way to find the meaning within the mundane. Split-second decision making is a crucial aspect of teaching. Given the daily madness of life in a classroom, considering all the options and consequences is difficult. Often, it is only through reflection that we even recognize that we had a choice, that we could have done something differently.

Like a football quarterback, I often make bad decisions because of pressure. Unlike a quarterback, I don't have an offensive line to blame for letting the pressure get to me. While it would be nice to believe that I could somehow make the pressure go away, the

**Guided Reflection Protocol (For Individual Reflection)**

1. *Collect stories.* Some educators find that keeping a set of index cards or a steno book close at hand provides a way to jot down stories as they occur. Others prefer to wait until the end of the day and write in a journal.

2. *What happened?* Choose a story that strikes you as particularly interesting. Write it succinctly.

3. *Why did it happen?* Fill in enough of the context to give the story meaning. Answer the question in a way that makes sense to you.

4. *What might it mean?* Recognizing that there is no one answer is an important step. Explore possible meanings rather than determine the meaning.

5. *What are the implications for practice?* Consider how your practice might change given any new understandings that have emerged from the earlier steps.

fact is that it will always be with me. Being a teacher means learning to live within that pressure, learning from the decisions I make and learning to make better decisions.

Our growing awareness of how all events carry some meaning is not a new concept. In *Experience and Education* (1938), John Dewey wrote about experience and its relationship to learning and teaching: "Every experience affects for better or worse the attitudes which help decide the quality of further experience" (p. 37). He believed that teachers must be aware of the "possibilities inherent in ordinary experience" (p. 89), that the "business of the educator [is] to see in what direction an experience is heading" (p. 38). Rediscovering this concept through the examination of ordinary events creates a fresh awareness of its meaning.

The search for meaning is an integral part of being human. But understanding by itself doesn't create changes in classroom practice. The last phase of guided reflection is more action oriented and involves holding our practice to the light of those new understandings.

### Step Four: What Are the Implications for My Practice?

Simon continues:

My reaction to the pressure this year has been to resort to methods of control. I seem to be forever pulling down the blinds. I'm thinking about how I might better deal with the pressure.

But there is something else that needs attention. Where is the pressure coming from? I'm sensing from administration and parents that they feel I should be doing things differently. I've gotten subtle and overt messages that I need to pay more attention to "covering" the curriculum, that I should be finding a more equal balance between process and product.

Maybe they're right. What I've been doing hasn't exactly been a spectacular

success. But I think that what is causing the lowering of the blinds stems from my not trusting enough in the process. Controlling the class in a fairly traditional sense isn't going to work in the long run. Establishing a process that allows the class to control itself will help keep the blinds up.

Cultivating deep reflection through the use of a guiding protocol is an entry into rethinking and changing practice. Alone, each of us can proceed step-by-step through the examination of a particular event. Through the process, we gain new insights into the implications of ordinary events, as Simon did when he analyzed "The Geese and the Blinds."

Whereas Guided Reflection is for use by individuals, the Critical Incidents Protocol is used with colleagues. The goal is the same: to get to the heart of our practice, the place that pumps the lifeblood into our teaching, where we reflect, gain insight, and change what we do with our students. In addition, the Critical Incidents Protocol encourages the establishment of collegial relationships.

### Critical Incidents Protocol

Schools are social places. Although too often educators think and act alone, in most schools colleagues do share daily events. Stories told in teachers' lounges are a potential source of rich insight into issues of teaching and learning and can open doors to professional dialogue.

Telling stories has the potential for changing individual practice and the culture of our schools. The Critical Incidents Protocol allows practitioners to share stories in a way that is useful to their own thinking and to that of the group.

Three to five colleagues meet for the purpose of exploring a "critical incident." For 10 minutes, all write a brief account of an incident. Participants should know that the sharing of their writing will be for the purpose of getting feedback on what happened rather than on the quality of the writing itself.

Next, the group decides which story to use with the protocol. The presenter for the session then reads the story while the group listens carefully to understand the incident and the context. Colleagues ask clarifying questions about what happened or why the incident occurred, then they discuss what the incident might mean in terms of the presenter's practice. During this time, the presenter listens and takes notes. The presenter then responds, and the participants discuss the implications for their own practice. To conclude, one member leads a conversation about what happened during the session, how well the process worked, and how the group might change the process.

The sharing of individual stories raises issues in the fresh air of collegial support. If open dialogue is not already part of a school's culture, however, colleagues may feel insecure about beginning. To gain confidence, they may choose to run through the protocol first with a story that is not theirs. For this purpose, Grace offers a story about an incident in the writing lab from her practice as a high school English teacher.

### Step One: What Happened?

We went into the computer lab to work on essay drafts. TJ, Neptune, Ronny, and Mick sat as a foursome. Their sitting together had not worked last time. On their single printer an obscene message had appeared. All four had denied writing it.

The next day Ronny, Neptune, and Mick had already sat together. Just as TJ was about to take his seat, I asked him if he would mind sitting over at the next bay of computers. He exploded. "You think I'm the cause of the problem, don't you?"

Actually I did think he might be, but I wasn't at all certain. "No," I said, "but I do want you to sit over here for today." He got red in the face, plunked down in the chair near the three other boys, and refused to move.

I motioned for him to come with me. Out in the hall, I said to him quietly, "The bottom line is that all of you need to get your work done." Out of control, body shaking, TJ angrily spewed out, "You always pick on me. Those guys. . . . You. . . ." I could hardly hear his words, so fascinated was I with his intense emotion and his whole-body animation.

Contrary to my ordinary response to students who yell, I felt perfectly calm. I knew I needed to wait. Out of the corner of my eye, I saw two male teachers rise out of their chairs in the hallway about 25 feet away. They obviously thought that I, a woman of small stature, needed protection. But I did not look at them. I looked at TJ and waited.

When he had expended his wrathful energy, I said softly, "You know, TJ, you are a natural-born leader." I waited. Breathed in and out. "You did not choose to be a leader; it was thrust upon you. But there you are. People follow you. So you have a tremendous responsibility, to lead in a positive and productive way. Do you understand what I am saying?"

Like an exhalation after a long in-breath, his body visibly relaxed. He looked down at me and nodded his head. Then he held out his hand to me and said, "I'm sorry."

Back in the room, he picked up his stuff and, without a word, moved to the next bay of computers.

### Step Two: Using the Critical Incidents Protocol

At first you'll think that you need more information than this, but we think that you have enough here. One member of the group will take the role of Grace. Your "Grace" can answer clarifying questions about what happened or why it happened in whatever way he or she sees fit. Work through the protocol to figure out what the incident might mean in terms of "Grace's" practice. Finally, discuss what implications the incident in the writing lab might have for her

1. *Write stories.* Each group member writes briefly in response to the question: What happened? (10 minutes)

2. *Choose a story.* The group decides which story to use. (5 minutes)

3. *What happened?* The presenter reads the written account of what happened and sets it within the context of professional goals. (10 minutes)

4. *Why did it happen?* Colleagues ask clarifying questions. (5 minutes)

5. *What might it mean?* The group raises questions about the incident in the context of the presenter's work. They discuss it as professional, caring colleagues while the presenter listens. (15 minutes)

6. *What are the implications for practice?* The presenter responds, then the group engages in conversation about the implications for the presenter's practice and for the participants' own practice. A useful question at this stage might be, What new insights occurred? (15 minutes)

7. *Debrief the process.* The group talks about what just happened. How did the process work? (10 minutes)

practice and for your own as reflective educators. Then, try an event of your own.

We think that you will find that whether the group uses your story or someone else's, building reflective practice together is a sure way to get to the heart of teaching and learning.

## REFERENCES

Dewey, J. (1938). *Experience and education.* New York: Macmillan.

Tripp, D. (1993). *Critical incidents in teaching: Developing professional judgement.* New York: Routledge.

## POSTNOTE

A common complaint of teachers is that they don't have enough time to do all the things that they either need or want to do. There just doesn't seem like the day has enough hours to do everything that needs doing. When time is precious, making the time to reflect on one's teaching seems extravagant. After all, there are so many more pressing items. On the other hand, if teachers are asked if they want to improve their teaching, it's hard to imagine one saying, "No." The authors of this article make the case that teacher reflection is the key component for improving our teaching. And, if you think about it, improving your teaching without seriously reflecting on it is virtually impossible.

Reflective teaching involves a process of examination and evaluation in which you develop the habits of inquiry and reflection. By describing two structured ways of reflecting, one individually and one with colleagues, the authors give us useful protocols for conducting a reflective process. The use of journal writing, observation instruments, simulations, and videotaping can also help you examine teaching, learning, and the contexts in which they occur. Comparing your perspectives with those of fellow students, professors, and school personnel will broaden your interpretations and give you new insights. As you reflect on your experiences, you will come to distrust simple answers and explanations. Nuances and subtleties will start to become clear, and situations that once seemed simple will reveal their complexities. Moral and ethical issues are likely to be encountered and thought about. By practicing reflective teaching, you will grow and develop the attitudes and skills to become lifelong students of teaching—you will become an effective, professional teacher.

## DISCUSSION QUESTIONS

1. What do you see as the primary benefits of reflecting on your teaching? What concerns do you have about it?

2. What case do the authors make for reflecting on ordinary, as opposed to special, events? Do you agree?

3. Are you more likely to use an individual or cooperative form of reflection? Why?

# *The Heart of the Matter*

Robert Fried

When you get right down to it, every teacher faces one existential question: "What am I here for—to journey with young people into the great world of knowledge and ideas or to shepherd a bunch of mostly unwilling students through the everyday rituals of instruction and assessment?" Who among us has not sought the former and suffered through the latter time and again in our teaching?

Just maybe it's time to face this issue head-on and resolve to no longer accept an answer that defines a teacher as a "classroom manager," or "deliverer of instruction," or "assertive disciplinarian," or "keeper of the grade book."

The alternative to such roles is to assert that one is a passionate teacher: someone truly enamored of a field of knowledge, or deeply stirred by issues and ideas that challenge our world, or drawn to the crises and creativity of the young people who come into class each day—or all of these. To be a passionate teacher is to stop being isolated within a classroom, to refuse to submit to a culture of apathy or cynicism, to look beyond getting through the day.

Only when teachers bring their passions about learning and life into their daily work can they dispel the fog of passive compliance or surly disinterest that surrounds so many kids in school. I believe that we all have it within us to be passionate teachers and that nothing else will quite do the trick.

In too many classrooms, we see the sound and smoke of note-taking, answer-giving, homework-checking, test-taking, and the forgetting that so quickly follows. And in the end, there is creativity for a few, compliance for most, rebellion for some, but not much fiery engagement of the mind and spirit.

What counts is students' willing engagement. They have to want to see where their ideas and energies might take them, to follow their curiosity and intuition to useful places. They have to get unshy about being smart—to stop using their brains to put each other down or to get around doing the work we assign them. Today's students need help from teachers who are more than well-prepared or genial or fair. They need teachers who have passions.

Passion itself isn't the goal of education. It's a bridge that connects us to the intensity of young people's thoughts and life experiences—things that they too rarely see as part of school. Once that connection has been made, we can help transfer passions about ideas into habits of hard work and discipline that will remain with students even when peers cajole them to "take it easy." It's not the whole story, of course, but passion is at the heart of what teaching should be if we want to be mentors for young people who sorely need (but rarely seek) heroes of the mind to balance the heroes of brute strength and exotic fashion that surround them in the media.

Yet as I look into hundreds of classrooms, watch all kinds of teachers working with a bewildering variety of students, when I ask myself what makes the greatest difference in the quality and depth of student learning—it is a teacher's passion that leaps out. More than knowledge of subject matter. More than variety of teaching techniques. More than being well-organized, or friendly, or funny, or fair.

Passionate people are the ones who make a difference in our lives. By the intensity of their

Robert Fried is the author of *The Passionate Teacher— A Practical Guide*, published by Beacon Press. Reprinted with permission from *Teacher Magazine*, Vol. 7, Issue No. 2, October 1995. By permission of Robert Fried, author of *The Passionate Teacher: A Practical Guide* (Boston: Beacon Press, 1995).

beliefs and actions, they connect us with a sense of value that is within—and beyond—ourselves. Sometimes that passion burns with a quiet, refined intensity. Sometimes it bellows forth with thunder and eloquence. But in whatever style a teacher's passion emerges, students know they are in the presence of someone whose devotion to learning is exceptional. It's what makes a teacher unforgettable—this caring about ideas and values, this fascination with the potential for growth within people, this fervor about doing things well and striving for excellence.

Passion may just be the difference between being remembered as a "pretty good teacher" who made chemistry or algebra "sort of interesting"—or being the person who opened up a world of the mind to some students who had no one else to make them feel that they were capable of doing great things with test tubes, trumpets, trigonometry, or T. S. Eliot.

How, then, is a teacher "passionate"?

You can be passionate about your field of knowledge: in love with the poetry of Emily Dickinson or the prose of Marcus Garvey; dazzled by the spiral of DNA or the swirl of Van Gogh's cypresses; intrigued by the origins of the Milky Way or the demise of the Soviet empire; delighted by the sound of Mozart or the sonority of French vowels.

You can be passionate about issues facing our world: active in the struggle for social justice or for the survival of the global environment; dedicated to the celebration of cultural diversity or to the search for a cure for AIDS.

You can be passionate about children: about the shocking rate of violence experienced by young black males; about including children with disabilities in regular school activities; about raising the low rate of high school completion by Latino children; about the insidious effects of sexism, racism, and social class prejudice on the spirits of all children; about the neglect of "average" kids in schools where those at the "top" and "bottom" seem to get all of the attention.

To be avowedly passionate about at least some of these things puts one apart from those who approach each day in a fog of fatigue, or who come to work wrapped in a self-protective cocoon. The passion that accompanies our attention to knowledge, values, and children is not just something we offer our students. It is a gift we grant ourselves, a way of honoring our life's work, our profession. It says: "I know why I am devoting this life to children."

Let's distinguish passionate teaching from mere idiosyncrasies. Lots of teachers have pet peeves or fixations: points of grammar, disciplinary practices, eccentricities of diction. These may, indeed, make them memorable to their students (for better or worse). But the passions I am speaking about convey much more.

What impresses me about truly passionate teachers is that there is no particular style of teaching, much less a common personality type, that epitomizes them. What unites them are the ways they approach the mission of teaching. They organize their curricula and their daily work with students in practical ways that play to their own strengths.

But how do we make passionate teaching happen? How do we shove aside all the stuff we're supposed to do and make room in our lesson plans for things we feel strongly about?

We may want to ask our students to study in depth the Cuban Missile Crisis, rather than surveying the entire Cold War history. Or study the ecology of one small nearby pond instead of covering all the chapters in the biology text. Or learn a lot about Emily Dickinson and leave other 19th-century poets to be discovered later in students' lives. Language arts teachers in an urban middle school may decide that learning to write good, clear, convincing prose is so vital to students' future success that they enlist colleagues in science and social studies and math to teach writing across the curriculum.

A high school history teacher in a rural New Hampshire town brought her intense interest in archaeology into the classroom by taking her students out into the woods in search of a long-forgotten graveyard. After watching her begin to carefully restore the site, they pitched in to clean and prop up the headstones. A week later, the class traveled to the local historical society to search for the records of the people whose graves they had tended. Each student became a 200-year-old former resident of the town and shared his or her life story in a presentation for the townspeople.

As passionate teachers, we share our commitment to active learning by showing, not just telling. We are readers, writers, researchers, explorers of new knowledge, new ideas, new techniques and technologies, new ways of looking at old facts and theories Our very excitement about these things helps young people reach beyond their social preoccupations and self-centeredness. When we are no longer learning, we no longer teach because we have lost the power to exemplify for young people what it means to be intellectually active. Even though we may still be able to present them with information, we have

become simple purveyors of subject matter, "deliverers of educational services," in the jargon of the field.

Students need us, not because we have all the answers but because we can help them discover the right questions. It's not that we always know what's good for them but that we want to protect them from having to face life's dilemmas in ignorance or in despair. Those adults to whom young people look for advice on serious life issues know how important they are to kids' futures. For all teachers, the recovery of passion can mean a recovery of our dynamic and positive influence in the lives of children.

This, I argue, is what education *is*. There simply is no education without a commitment to developing the mind and the character of learners. And in our time and culture, perhaps as never before, that commitment must be a passionate one if we want young people to heed that calling.

## POSTNOTE

The passion a teacher has for the subject that he or she teaches is often not discussed in teacher education programs. Hollywood, however, frequently employs passionate teachers as the protagonists in films: Robin William's character in *Dead Poets Society*, Maggie Smith's in *The Prime of Miss Jean Brodie*, and Richard Dreyfus's in *Mr. Holland's Opus* display fire and passion in their teaching.

Some of our most memorable teachers are probably the ones who cared deeply and passionately about what they taught. Equally or perhaps more important are caring and passion for one's students. Teachers who care about their students—and let those students know it in various ways—are often the ones who affect their students the most.

## DISCUSSION QUESTIONS

1. Think of two or three of the best teachers you've ever had. What was it that made them so good? How were they alike or different?

2. Have you ever had a really good teacher who didn't have passion for his or her subject?

3. Can passion for the subject be learned, or is it something one just has or doesn't have? Why do you think so?

# 4

# *The Great Teacher Question: Beyond Competencies*

Edward R. Ducharme

I begin this essay by defining a great teacher as one who influences others in positive ways so that their lives are forever altered, and then asking a question I have asked groups many times. How many teachers fitting that description have you had in your lifetime? It is rare for anyone to claim more than five in a lifetime; the usual answer is one or two.

I ask this question of groups whose members have at least master's degrees, often doctorates. They have experienced anywhere from eighty to one hundred or more teachers in their lifetimes and usually describe no more than 2% of them as great. Those voting are among the ones who stayed in school considerably longer than most people do; one wonders how many great teachers those dropping out in the 9th or 10th grade experience in their lifetimes. My little experiment, repeated many times over the years, suggests that the number of great teachers is very limited. They should be cherished and treasured because they are so rare; we should do all that we can to develop more of them.

This paper is purely speculative; no data corrupt it; no references or citations burden it. It began as I sat with a colleague at a meeting in 1987 in Washington; we were listening to a speaker drone on about the competencies teachers need. I asked my friend: "How would you like to write a paper about qualities great teachers have that do not

**TERM TO NOTE**
Teacher competencies

lend themselves to competency measurements?" The proposed shared writing exercise did not get much beyond our talking about it the next couple of times we saw each other, but I have continued to speculate on these qualities as I have read, taught, studied, talked with others, and relived my own learning experiences.

The remarks result from years of being with teachers, students, and schools; of three decades of being a teacher; of five decades of being a learner. There is no science in the remarks, no cool, objective look at teaching. These are personal reflections and observations to provoke, to get some of us thinking beyond numbers, test scores, attendance rates, and demographics, to reflect on the notion of the Great Teacher.

I am weary of competencies even though I recognize the need for specific indicators that teachers possess certain skills and knowledge. I believe, however, that good teacher preparation programs do more than a reasonable job on these and are doing better and better. Three conditions lead me to believe that most future graduates of teacher education programs will be competent. First, the overall quality of teacher candidates is improving; second, there is a great deal more known about helping to develop people to the point where they are competent; third, the level of the education professoriate has improved dramatically. Thus, I think that *most* preparation programs will be graduating competent teachers. We should begin to worry about what lies beyond competency.

My interests extend beyond competencies to qualities that I see from time to time as I visit classrooms. Few teachers possess even several of the qualities I will describe—no great teacher lacks all of them. In the remainder of this paper, I will name and describe the qualities and show

Edward R. Ducharme is a writer and consultant, living in Brewster, Massachusetts. From "The Great Teacher Question: Beyond Competencies" by Edward R. Ducharme in *Journal of Human Behavior and Learning*, Vol. 7, No. 2. Copyright © 1991. Used with permission.

what these qualities might look like in prospective teachers.

## 1. Penchant for and Skill in Relating One Thing with Another with Another and with Another

John Donne, the 17th century English poet and cleric, once wrote "The new science calls all into doubt." He was referring to the Copernican contention that the earth is not the center of the universe, that humankind may not be the cynosure of divine interest, countering beliefs that the old Ptolemaic system of earthcenteredness had fostered.

Donne saw relationships among things not readily apparent to many others. He recognized a new truth cancelled another belief, one that had affected attitudes and actions among his fellow Christians for a long time, and would have a dramatic effect. He knew that if something held eternally true were suddenly shown to be false, conclusively false, then other things would be questioned; nothing would be steadfast.

Many of us do not see the implications and relationships among seemingly unrelated events, people, places, works of art, scientific principles. Some great teachers have the ability to see these relationships and, equally important, help others see them. Donne saw them. His collected sermons evidence the intellectual force of great teachers.

I once took a course in which John Steinbeck's *The Sea of Cortez* and *The Grapes of Wrath* were among the readings. *The Sea of Cortez* is Steinbeck's ruminations on the vast complexity and interrelatedness of life under the water; *The Grapes of Wrath,* his ruminations on the complexities of life on land, on what happens when a natural disaster combines with human ineptness and lack of concern, one for the other. The professor used a word not much in vogue in those ancient days: ecology. He defined it as the "interrelatedness of all living things." He raised

questions about the relationships of these issues to the problems of New York City and its schools, as we sat in class in Memorial Lounge at Teachers College, Columbia.

E. D. Hirsch, in *Cultural Literacy: What Every American Needs to Know,* has a series of provocative listings under each letter of the alphabet. His point is that in order to grasp the meanings of words on pages, readers must know things not part of the page. Hirsch's book contains pages of items. Under the letter C, he lists caste, cool one's heels, *Crime and Punishment,* coral reef, and czar. One would "know" such things by studying sociology, language, literature, biology, and history or, perhaps equally often, simply by living for a period of time and reading newspapers, watching movies, and so forth. Hirsch's point is that when one hears a sentence like "He runs his business as though he were the czar," one would think of autocratic, harsh rule, tyranny, Russia, lack of human rights. Some might think of how the word is sometimes spelled tsar and wonder why. Others might think of the song about the czar/tsar from *Fiddler on the Roof,* while a few would think the person incapable of pronouncing the word tsar. Hirsch has in mind one kind of "relating one field to another": that which occurs when one sees a known reference and makes the associative leap.

Edna St. Vincent Millay, in her poem on Euclid's geometry, also drew associations from seemingly unrelated things. She saw the design and texture in poetry related to the design and texture of a geometric theorem. The quality described here is the same quality that Donne and Steinbeck manifested: seeing the interrelatedness of things.

What does that quality look like in prospective teachers? Sometimes it is the person who sees the connections between sociological and educational themes; sometimes, the person who wants to introduce students to the variety of language by teaching them about snowflakes and the vast number of words Eskimos have for them; sometimes, the person who understands mathematics through music, in fact, it may be the person who says mathematics is a kind of music or that music is a kind of mathematics.

## 2. Lack of Fondness for Closure or, Put Another Way, Fondness for Questions over Answers

Many of us are constantly on the lookout for answers to questions. For example, we might give a great deal to know the answer to the two-part question: What makes a great teacher and how do we produce one? Of course, the answer to the first part of the question depends on who is answering it. For someone in need of specific guidance at some point in life, the great teacher may be the one pointing the way to a different kind of existence, the one making the individual feel strong. To another person, confident about life, the great teacher may be the one raising questions, challenging, making the person wonder about certitudes once held dearly.

I teach Leadership and the Creative Imagination, a course designed as a humanities experience for doctoral students in educational administration. In the course, students read twelve novels and plays, discuss them effectively, and write about them in ways related to the leadership theory literature, their own experience, and the works themselves. In the fall semester of 1987, I had what has become a redundant experience. A student in the course stopped me in the hall after class one night in November. She said that she had taken the course because her advisor had said it would be a good experience for her. And, said she, she had truly enjoyed the early readings and the discussions. But now she found the readings troubling; they were causing her to question things she does, ways she relates to people, habits of thinking. She said that she was losing a sense of assuredness of what life was all about. The books, she said, just kept raising questions. "When do we get answers?" she asked.

We talked for awhile, and I reminded her of a point I had made repeatedly during the first couple of classes: there are two kinds of books,

answer books and question books. Writers of answer books raise provocative questions and then provide comfortable, assuring answers. Then there are the writers who raise the provocative issues—"Thou know'st 'tis common,—all that lives must die, passing through nature into eternity," (if you get the source of that, Hirsch will like you)—and then frustrate the reader looking for facile answers by showing that the realization in the statement prompts questions: Why must all that lives die? What does it mean to pass through nature into eternity? What or when is eternity? Are we supposed to know that all that lives must die?

The predisposition to raise questions is present in all of us to varying degrees. In young, prospective teachers, the predisposition takes on various shades and hues. They ask questions like: Why do some children learn more slowly than others? Tell me, why is that, whatever that may be, a better way to do it? But how do I know they learned it? In more mature prospective teachers coming back for a fifth year and certification, it might look different: Why is this more meaningful than that? Why should we teach this instead of that? Why does my experience teach me that this is wrong? What happens next? How do I know if this is right or wrong?

Persons with fondness for questions over answers recognize that most "answers" to complex questions are but tentative, that today's answers provoke tomorrow's uneasiness. As prospective teachers, they show a disrespect for finite answers to questions about human development, the limits of knowledge, the ways of knowing, the ways of doing. They itch to know even though they have begun to believe that they can never really know, that there is always another word to be said on every subject of consequence. Often, to answer-oriented teacher educators, these students are seen as hindrances instead of prospective great teachers. In truth, they stand the chance of provoking in their future students the quest to explore, to question, to imagine, to be comfortable with the discomfort of never "really knowing," of lifelong pursuit of knowledge.

## 3. Growing Knowledge, Understanding, and Commitment to Some Aspect of Human Endeavor; for Example, Science, Literature, Mathematics, or Blizzards

In the last several years, the point that teachers must know something before they can teach it has been made ad nauseum. We have admonitions from the Carnegie Forum to the Holmes Group to Secretary Bennett to the person on the street to all the teachers in the field who prepared with BS degrees in education all belaboring the obvious need for knowledge, albeit with a slightly different twist than the argument had the first twenty times around: teachers must have a bachelor's degree in an academic major before being admitted to a teacher preparation program.

But we all know that to know is not enough. Merely holding a bachelor of arts does not answer the question of the relationship between teacher and knowledge. What answers the question?

Teachers are rightfully and powerfully connected with knowledge when, even early in their learning careers, they begin to make metaphors to explain their existence, their issues and dilemmas, their joys and sorrows, from the knowledge they are acquiring. I speak not of that jaded notion of students being excited by what they are learning. I get excited watching a baseball game, but it doesn't have much meaning for me the next day. I mean something including and transcending excitement. Great teachers are driven by the power, beauty, force, logic, illogic, color, vitality, relatedness, uniqueness of what they know and love. They make metaphors from it to explain the world; they are forever trying to understand the thing itself, always falling a bit short yet still urging others on. They are the teachers who make learners think what is being taught has value and meaning and may actually touch individual lives.

This quality shows itself in a variety of ways in prospective teachers. Often, it is hidden because that which captures the imagination and interest of a student may not be part of the course, may have no way of being known. I have never forgotten a young woman in a class I taught fifteen years ago. She was a freshman in one of those horrible introduction to education courses. For the last assignment, each student in the class had to teach something to the class. This young woman, who had spoken, but rarely and only when challenged during the semester, asked if the class might go to the student lounge when her turn came. I agreed; we went as a group. There was a piano in the room and she proceeded to play a piece by Chopin and explain to the class why it was an important piece of music. I suspected—and subsequent discussions with her bore out my thought—that this young woman saw the world through music, that she could explain almost anything better if she could use music as the metaphor, the carrier of her thoughts.

Most of us do not have students in our classes capable of playing a piece by Chopin, but we all have students who understand the world through a medium different from what the rest of the group may be using. Experience has taught many young people to hide this quality because it is not honored in classrooms.

## 4. A Sense of the Aesthetic

The development of the aesthetic domain in young people is critical to their growth and development; it is a fundamental right. The ability to grasp the beautiful makes us human; to deny that to young people is to deny their humanity. Great teachers often have an acutely developed sense of the aesthetic; they are unafraid to show their fondness for beauty in front of young people; they do so in such a manner as to make the young people themselves value beauty and their own perceptions of it.

**TERM TO NOTE**
Aesthetic

For many young people, the world is a harsh and barren place, devoid of beauty. But in every generation, there are those who emerge spiritually changed from their schooling experiences, eager to face what is at times a hostile world. The changes are sometimes the result of a teacher with a sense of the aesthetic, one able to see beyond the everydayness and blandness of institutional life.

In a world stultified by the commercial definitions of beauty, individuals preparing to teach with this embryonic sense of the aesthetic are rare. Our own jadedness and mass-produced tastes make it difficult for us to recognize this quality in students. What does it look like? In its evolutionary phases, it might be an impulse to make the secondary methods classroom more attractive; it might be a choice of book covers; it might be in the selection of course materials for young people; it might be in the habits of an individual. I'm uncertain as to its many forms, but I am quite certain that when we see it we should treasure its existence and support its development.

## 5. Willingness to Assume Risks

There are teachers who say the right things, prescribe the right books, associate with the right people, but never take risks on behalf of others, beliefs, and ideas, never do more than verbalize. They are hollow shams.

The quality of risk-taking of great teachers is subtle, not necessarily that which puts people on picket lines, at the barricades, although it might be. The quality is critical to teacher modeling, for great teachers go beyond the statement of principles and ideas, beyond the endorsement of the importance of friendships, as they move students from the consideration of abstract principles to the actualization of deeds.

The 1960s and 1970s were filled with risk-taking teachers. While neither praising nor disparaging these obvious examples, I urge other instances for consideration inasmuch as the "opportunity" for collective risk-taking is a rare occurrence in the lives of most of us. While it was not easy to be a risk-taker then, it wasn't very lonely either. Other instances, some more prosaic, abound: teachers in certain parts of the country who persist in teaching evolution despite pressure to desist, teachers who assign controversial books despite adverse criticism, teachers who teach the Civil War and the Vietnam War without partisanship or chauvinism. These quiet acts of risk-taking occur daily in schools and universities; they instruct students of the importance of ideas joined with actions.

I recall my high school art teacher who took abuse from the principal because she demanded the right for her students to use the gymnasium to prepare for a dance. He rebuked and embarrassed her in front of the students for "daring to question [my] authority." His act prompted some of us to go to the superintendent to complain about him; we got the gym. But we also each had a private interview with the principal in which he shared his scorn and derision for us for having "gone over [my] head to the superintendent." We learned that acting on principles is sometimes risky, that we had to support a teacher who took risks for us, that actions have consequences, that a "good" act like defending a brave teacher can lead to punishment. But her risk-taking led us to risk-taking on behalf of another person and the resolution of a mild injustice.

Detecting this quality in the young is difficult. The young often appear cause-driven and it is hard to distinguish when students are merely following a popular, low-risk cause and when they are standing for something involving personal decisions and risk. We might see it in its evolutionary form in some quite simple instances. Many teacher educators suffer the indignity of seeing their ideas and principles distorted by the wisdom of the workplace, of having their students grow disenchanted with what they have been taught as they encounter the world of the school: "We'll knock that Ivory Tower stuff out of you here. This is the *real* world." Of course, we all know some of it should be knocked out, but much of it should remain. It is a rare student who during practical, internship, and early years of teaching remains steadfast to such principles as: all student answers, honestly given, merit serious consideration; or worksheets are rarely good instructional materials. It is risky for young pre-professionals and beginning professionals to dispute the wisdom of the workplace and maintain fidelity to earlier acquired principles. Perhaps in these seemingly small matters lies the quality to be writ large during the full career.

## 6. At-Homeness in the World

Great teachers live effectively in what often seems a perverse world. Acutely aware of life's unevenness, the disparities in the distribution of the world's goods, talents, and resources, they cry out for justice in their own special ways while continuing to live with a sense of equanimity and contribute to the world. They demonstrate that life is to be lived as fully as one can despite problems and issues. They show that one can be a sensitive human being caring about and doing things about the problems and issues, and, at the same time, live a life of personal fulfillment. They are not overwhelmed by the insolubility of things on the grand scale, for they are able to make sense of things on the personal level.

**TERM TO NOTE**
At-homeness

I once had a professor for a course in Victorian poetry. In addition to his academic accomplishments, the professor was a fine gardener, each year producing a beautifully crafted flower garden, filled with design and beauty.

We were reading "In Memoriam," the part in which Tennyson refers to nature, red in tooth and claw. All of a sudden, the professor talked about how, that morning, while eating his breakfast, he had watched his cat stalk a robin, catch it, and devour part of it. He related the incident, of course, to the poem. (Clearly he had the quality alluded to earlier, the sense on interrelatedness of things.) I am uncertain what I learned about "In Memoriam" that morning, but I know I learned that this man who earlier in the semester had pointed out the delicate beauty of some

of Tennyson's lyrics had integrated death into his life while remaining sensitive to beauty, to love. It was partly through him that I began to see that the parts of life I did not like were not to be ignored nor to be paralyzed about. All this in the death of a bird? No, all this in a powerful teacher's reaction to the death of a bird in the midst of life.

And what does at-homeness in the world look like in prospective teachers? I am quite uncertain, very tentative about this one. Perhaps it shows itself in a combination of things like joy in life one day and despair over life the next as the young slowly come to grips with the enigmas of life, its vicissitudes and sorrows. The young are often studies in extremes as they make order of life, of their lives. As a consequence, one sees a few students with vast energy both to live life and to anguish over its difficulties. But one cannot arrive at the point of my professor with his lovely garden and dead robin simultaneously entertained in his head without a sense of the joyful and the tragic in life, without a constant attempt to deal with the wholeness that is life, without a sense of being at home in the world.

All prospective teachers have touches of each of these qualities which should be supported and nurtured so that their presence is ever more manifest in classrooms. But a few students have some of these qualities writ large. Buttressed by programs that guarantee competency in instructional skills, these individuals have the potential to become great teachers themselves, to be the teachers who take the students beyond knowledge acquisition and skill development to questioning, to wondering, to striving. We must, first, find these prospective teachers, help them grow and develop, treasure them, and give them to the young people of America, each one of whom deserves several great teachers during thirteen years of public schooling.

And what has all this to do with the preparation of teachers? Surely, preparing teachers to be competent in providing basic instruction to as many students as possible is enough of a major task. Clearly, the raising of reading scores, of math achievement levels, of writing skills, of thinking processes are significant accomplishments. Of course, all these things must be accomplished, and teacher preparation programs around the country are getting better and better at these matters.

But we must have more; we must have an increase in the presence of greatness in the schools, in the universities. Love for a teacher's kindness, gratitude for skills acquired, fondness for teachers—these are critically important. But equally important is the possibility that students will encounter greatness, greatness that transcends the everydayness of anyplace, that invites, cajoles, pushes, drags, drives, brings students into the possibilities that questions mean more than answers; that knowledge is interrelated; that there is joy to be had from beauty; that knowledge can affect people to the cores of their being; that ideas find their worth in actions; that life is full of potential in a sometimes perverse world.

## POSTNOTE

Ducharme's article is provocative in its challenge to go beyond competence to reach for greatness in our teaching. The characteristics that he suggests embody greatness in teaching are difficult to challenge because they ring true. They also are formidable if we dare to want to become teachers who possess these characteristics.

In an effort to ensure that prospective teachers will be "safe to practice," many teacher educators focus their instruction on the knowledge and skills (competencies) new teachers will need to function effectively in classrooms. It may be a rare instance where the focus of teacher education is on what it will take to become a *great* teacher, not merely a *competent* one.

## DISCUSSION QUESTIONS

1. Is a particular kind of teacher preparation needed to produce great, rather than just competent, teachers? Or does a prospective teacher need to earn competence before greatness can be achieved? Explain your answers.

2. Think of the great teachers you have had. Did they possess the characteristics Ducharme describes? Briefly discuss what made these teachers great.

3. Can you think of any other characteristics that great teachers possess that were not identified by Ducharme? If so, what are they?

# Selecting "Star" Teachers for Children and Youth in Urban Poverty

## 5

## Martin Haberman

No school can be better than its teachers. And the surest and best way to improve the schooling of the approximately 12 million children and youth in poverty is to get better teachers for them. The strategy for doing this is not mysterious and has been evolving for more than 35 years.

The premise of the strategy is simple: selection is more important than training. My calculated hunch is that selection is 80% of the matter. The reason is that the functions performed by effective urban teachers of students in poverty are undergirded by a very clear ideology. Such teachers not only perform functions that quitters and burnouts do not perform, but they also know why they do what they do. They have a coherent vision. Moreover, it is a humane, respectful, caring, and nonviolent form of "gentle teaching" that I have described elsewhere.[1] My point here is that teachers' behaviors and the ideology that undergirds their behaviors cannot be unwrapped. They are of a piece.

Nor can this ideology be readily or easily taught in traditional programs of teacher preparation. Writing a term paper on Piaget's concept of conservation or sharing with other student teachers such problems as why Ray won't sit down will not provide neophytes with the ideological vision of "star teachers." This ideology, while it is open to development, must be selected for. What can be taught are the functional teaching behaviors that are built on the foundation of this belief system. And like the ideology, the teaching behaviors are not typically learned in traditional programs of teacher education but on the job, with the benefit of a teacher/coach, a support network, and some specific workshops.

There are four dimensions of excellence that programs claiming to prepare teachers for children of poverty can and should be held accountable for: 1) the individuals trained should be adults; 2) they should have demonstrated ability to establish rapport with low-income children of diverse ethnic backgrounds; 3) they should be admitted as candidates based on valid interviews that reliably predict their success with children in poverty; and 4) practicing urban teachers who are recognized as effective should be involved in selecting candidates.

My colleagues and I have identified three related truths that grow out of the recognition that selection is the heart of the matter where teachers for the urban poor are concerned: 1) the odds of selecting effective urban teachers for children and youth in poverty are approximately 10 times better if the candidates are over 30 rather than under 25 years of age; 2) there is no problem whatsoever in selecting more teachers of color, or more males, or more Hispanics, or more of any other "minority" constituency if training begins at the postbaccalaureate level; and 3) the selection and training of successful urban teachers is best accomplished in the worst schools and under the poorest conditions of practice.

This last truth requires some comment. States routinely give out teaching licenses that are deemed valid for any school in the state.

**TERMS TO NOTE**

Ideology

At-risk

Star teachers

Burnout

At the time this article was written, Martin Haberman was a Distinguished Professor in the School of Education, University of Wisconsin, Milwaukee. Martin Haberman, "Selecting 'Star' Teachers for Children and Youth in Urban Poverty," *Phi Delta Kappan*, June 1995. Copyright © 1995 by Phi Delta Kappa. Reprinted by permission of author and publisher.

The most reasonable basis for awarding such licenses would be to prepare teachers in the poorest schools and assume they will be able to deal with the "problems" presented by smaller classes, more and better materials and equipment, and safer neighborhoods if they should ever be "forced" to teach in more advantaged schools. Traditional teacher education makes almost the reverse assumption: create professional development centers (the equivalent of teaching hospitals) and then assume that beginners will be able to function in the poverty schools to which city school districts typically assign them. "Best practice" should not be thought of as ideal teaching under ideal conditions but as effective practice under the worst conditions.

## Functions of "Star" Urban Teachers

By comparing the behaviors and undergirding ideologies of "star" urban teachers with those of quitters and failures, my colleagues and I have identified 14 functions of successful teachers of the urban poor that are neither discrete behaviors nor personality attributes. Instead, these functions are "midrange" in the sense that they represent chunks of teaching behavior that encompass a number of interrelated actions and simultaneously represent beliefs or commitments that predispose these teachers to act. "Stars" are those teachers who are identified by principals, supervisors, other teachers, parents, and themselves as outstanding. They also have students who learn a great deal as measured by test scores and work samples. Between 5% and 8% of the staff members who now teach in urban poverty schools are such "star" teachers. The quitters and failures with whom their functioning is compared constitute a much larger group: 30% to 50%, depending on the particular district. In a continuing series of interviews with a population of star urban teachers every year since 1959, we have found that the 14 functions

have remained stable. What has changed in some cases are the questions needed to elicit interviewees' responses related to these functions.

The structured interview we use has been developed to select beginning teachers who can be prepared successfully on the job. This means that they can function at satisfactory levels while they are learning to teach. The highest success rate for selecting such exceptional neophytes has been achieved by combining both the interview and the opportunity to observe the candidates interacting with and teaching children in the summer prior to their assuming the role of beginning teacher. When the interview is combined with such observation, there is less than a 5% error rate. Use of the interview alone raises the error rate to between 8% and 10%.

Compare these figures with the fact that approximately 50% of newcomers to urban schools who were prepared in traditional programs quit or fail in five years or less. And these "trained" beginners are only the very small, self-selected group who choose to try teaching in an urban school and not a representative sample of those currently being prepared to teach. It boggles the mind to imagine what the failure rate would be if a truly representative sample of those now graduating from traditional programs of teacher education were hired as first-year teachers in the largest urban school districts.

In the rest of this article, I will briefly outline the seven functions that the star teacher interview assesses (and the additional seven for which we have never been able to develop interview questions). In order for a candidate to pass the interview, he or she need not respond at the level of a star teacher. The interview predicts applicants' potential functioning from "average," through "high," to "star." A zero answer on any of the functions constitutes a failure response to the total interview. The interview is couched in behavioral terms; that is, it attempts to determine what the applicant would do in his or her class and why. (Readers should note that merely reading about these functions does not constitute preparation to conduct an interview.)

## The Dimensions of Effective Teaching

1. *Persistence.* Many urban teachers honestly believe that most of their students (all in some cases) should not be in their classrooms because they need special help; are not achieving at grade level; are "abnormal" in their interests, attentiveness, or behavior; are emotionally unsuited to school; or are in need of alternative schools, special classes, or teachers trained to work with exceptional individuals. In some urban districts and in individual urban schools many teachers perceive 90% of their students to be not "normal."[2]

Effective urban teachers, on the other hand, believe it is their responsibility to find ways of engaging all their students in learning activities. The continuous generation and maintenance of student interest and involvement is how star teachers explain their jobs to themselves and to others. They manifest this persistence in several ways. They accept responsibility for making the classroom an interesting, engaging place and for involving the children in all forms of learning. They persist in trying to meet the individual needs of the problem student, the talented, the handicapped, and the frequently neglected student who falls in the gray area. Their persistence is reflected in an endless search for what works best with each student. Indeed, they define their jobs as asking themselves constantly, "How might this activity have been better—for the class or for a particular individual?"

The persistence of star teachers demonstrates several aspects of their ideology: teaching can never be "good enough," since everyone could always have learned more in any activity; teaching inevitably involves dealing with problems and problem students, and such students will be in every class, every day; and better materials and strategies can always be found. The basic stance of these teachers is never to give up trying to find better ways of doing things. The quip attributed to Thomas Edison,

"The difference between carbon and diamonds is that diamonds stayed on the job longer," might describe these teachers as well.

2. *Protecting learners and learning.* Star teachers are typically involved in some life activity that provides them with a sense of well-being and from which they continually learn. It might be philately, Russian opera, a Save the Wolves Club, composing music with computers, travel, or some other avocation from which they derive meaning as well as pleasure. Inevitably, they bring these activities and interests into their classrooms and use them as ways of involving their students in learning. It is quite common to find teachers' special interests used as foci that generate great enthusiasm for learning among the students. The grandiose explanation for this phenomenon is that people who continually experience learning themselves have the prerequisites to generate the desire to learn in others. A more practical explanation would be that we teach best what we care most about.

In any event, star teachers frequently involve their students in learning that transcends curriculum, textbooks, and achievement tests. Their commitment to turning students on to learning frequently brings them into noncompliance with the extremely thick bureaucracies of urban schools. Stars do not view themselves as change agents, per se, but they do seek ways to give themselves and their students greater latitude within the traditional curriculum.

Consider the following episode. The teacher has succeeded in truly involving the class in a learning activity. It might be an environmental issue (What happens to our garbage?); a biological study (How does a lie detector work?); or the production of a class play dealing with violence in the neighborhood. Imagine further that the intense student interest has generated some noise, the use of unusual equipment, or a need for extra cleaning of the classroom. The principal learns of the activity and requests that it be discontinued. The principal also instructs the teacher to stick with the approved texts and to follow the regular curriculum. At this point the lines are clearly drawn: continuing a genuine learning activity in which the students are thriving versus complying with the directive of a superior and following a school policy.

The way star teachers seek to work through such a problem is in direct opposition to the reaction of quitters and failures. Star teachers see protecting and enhancing students' involvement in learning activities as their highest priority; quitters cannot conceive of the possibility that they would diverge from the standard curriculum or that they would question a school administrator or a school policy.

To the uninitiated, such struggles over red tape may seem atypical. Experienced star teachers, however, find themselves involved in a continuous, day-to-day struggle to redefine and broaden the boundaries within which they work. One reason they so often find themselves at odds with the bureaucracy of urban schools is that they persist in searching for ways to engage their students actively in learning. Indeed, their view that this is their primary function stands in stark contrast to the views of teachers who see their primary function as covering the curriculum.

Star teachers try to resolve their struggles with bureaucracy patiently, courteously, and professionally. They seek to negotiate with authority. Quitters and failures perceive the most professional response to be unquestioning compliance.

**3.** *Application of generalizations.* Some teachers have 30 years of experience, while others have one year of experience 30 times over. One basis for professional growth is the ability to generate practical, specific applications of the theories and philosophies. Conversely, successful teachers can also reflect on their many discrete classroom activities and see what they add up to. If you ask stars to give examples of some principle they believe in (e.g., "What would an observer see in your classroom that would lead him/her to believe that you believe all children can learn?"), they are able to cite clear, observable examples. Conversely, if a star is asked to offer a principle or make a generalization that accounts

for a series of behaviors in which he or she engages, the star is equally able to move from the specific to the general.

The importance of this dimension is that teachers must be able to improve and develop. In order for this to happen, they must be able to take principles and concepts from a variety of sources (i.e., courses, workshops, books, and research) and translate them into practice. At the same time, stars can explain what their day-to-day work adds up to; they have a grasp not only of the learning principles that undergird their work but also of the long-range knowledge goals that they are helping their students achieve.

At the other extreme are teachers who are "concretized." They do not comprehend the difference between information and knowledge; neither do they see any connection between their daily lessons and the reasons why children and youth are compelled to go to school for 13 years. Indeed, quitters and failures frequently respond to the question, "Would you give an example of a principle in which you believe that guides your teaching?" with, "I don't like to generalize" or "It's wrong to make generalizations."

The ability to derive meaning from one's teaching is also a function of this ability to move between the general and the specific. Without this ability to see the relationship between important ideas and day-to-day practice, teaching degenerates into merely "keeping school."

**4.** *Approach to "at-risk" students.* Of all the factors that separate stars from quitters and failures this one is the most powerful in predicting their future effectiveness with urban children of poverty. When asked to account for the large numbers of at-risk students or to suggest what might be done about cutting down on the number of at-risk students, most teachers are well-versed in the popular litany of causes. The most common causes cited are poverty, violence, handicapping conditions, racism, unemployment, poor housing, lack of health care, gangs, drugs, and dysfunctional families. But while the quitters and failures stop with these, the stars also cite irrelevant school curricula, poor teaching, and overly bureaucratic school systems as additional causes.

Since quitters and failures essentially blame the victims, the families, and the neighborhoods, they do not come up with any measures that schools and teachers can or should take to improve the situation. Indeed, they say such things as "You can't expect schools to be all things to all people" or "Teachers can't be social workers, nurses, and policemen." Stars also see all the societal conditions that contribute to students' problems with school. But they are able to suggest that more relevant curricula and more effective teaching strategies are things that schools and teachers could try and should be held accountable for. Star teachers believe that, regardless of the life conditions their students face, they as teachers bear a primary responsibility for sparking their students' desire to learn.

**5.** *Professional versus personal orientation to students.* Stars expect to find some youngsters in their classrooms that they may not necessarily love; they also expect to be able to teach them. Stars expect that some of their students will not necessarily love them, but they expect these students to be able to learn from them. They use such terms as caring, respect, and concern, and they enjoy the love and affection of students when it occurs naturally. But they do not regard it as a prerequisite for learning.

Quitters and failures, on the other hand, cannot and do not discriminate between the love of parents for their children and the love of teachers for their students. They regard such love as a prerequisite for any learning to occur. They also believe that the children should feel a similar sort of love for their teachers. Consequently, it is not uncommon for quitters and failures to become disillusioned about their work in poverty schools. Once they realize that the children do not love them or that they cannot love "these" children, they find themselves unable to function in the role of teacher. For many quitters and failures, this love between students and teachers was a major reason for seeking to become teachers.

Star teachers have extremely strong, positive feelings toward their students, which in many cases might be deemed a form of love. But these feelings are not the primary reasons that stars are teachers, nor are these feelings the basis of their relationships with their students. Indeed, when their students misbehave, star teachers do not take it as a personal attack. Neither do they maintain class order or inspire effort by seeking to instill guilt. Genuine respect is the best way to describe the feelings star teachers have for their students.

**6.** *Burnout: its causes and cures.* Star teachers in large urban school systems are well aware that they work in mindless bureaucracies. They recognize that even good teachers will eventually burn out if they are subjected to constant stress, so they learn how to protect themselves from an interfering bureaucracy. As they gain experience, they learn the minimum things they must do to function in these systems without having the system punish them. Ultimately, they learn how to gain the widest discretion for themselves and their students without incurring the wrath of the system. Finally, they set up networks of a few like-minded teachers, or they teach in teams, or they simply find kindred spirits. They use these support systems as sources of emotional sustenance.

Without such organizational skills—and lacking the awareness that they even need such skills—failures and quitters are literally beaten down by the system. The paperwork, the conflicting rules and policies, the number of meetings, the interruptions, the inadequate materials, the lack of time, large classes, and an obsessive concern with test scores are just some of the demands that drive the quitters out of the profession. Moreover, quitters and failures are insensitive to many of the conflicting demands that every large, impersonal organization makes. And worst of all, they don't believe a good teacher "should" ever burn out. They believe that a really good person who really wants to be a teacher should *never* be ground down by any bureaucracy. This set of perceptions leads them to experience feelings of inadequacy and guilt when they do burn out. And unlike stars, who use their support networks to offset the expected pressures, quitters and failures respond to the pressures by feeling that they probably should never have become teachers.

**7.** *Fallibility.* Children and young people cannot learn in a classroom where mistakes are not allowed. One effective way to ensure that we find teachers who can accept the mistakes of students is to select those who can accept their own mistakes. When teachers are asked, "Do you ever make mistakes?" they answer, "Of course, I'm only human!" or "Everyone makes mistakes." The difference between stars and quitters is in the nature of the mistakes that they recognize and own up to. Stars acknowledge serious problems and ones having to do with human relations; quitters and failures confess to spelling and arithmetic errors.

## Functions Beyond the Interview

Thus far I have outlined seven teaching functions for which we have been able to create and validate interview questions. While the actual questions we use in the interview cannot be shared, I have described above the goals of the questions. It is noteworthy that there are seven additional functions for which we have never been able to develop interview questions but which are equally powerful in discriminating between stars and quitters. These functions and brief explanations follow.

▶ *Organizational ability:* the predisposition and ability to engage in planning and gathering of materials.

▶ *Physical/emotional stamina:* the ability to persist in situations characterized by violence, death, and other crises.

▶ *Teaching style:* the predisposition to engage in coaching rather than directive teaching.

▶ *Explanations of success:* the predisposition to emphasize students' effort rather than ability.

▶ *Basis of rapport:* the approach to student involvement. Whose classroom is it? Whose work is to be protected?

▶ *Readiness:* the approach to prerequisite knowledge. Who should be in this classroom?

For children in poverty, schooling is a matter of life and death. They have no other realistic options for "making it" in American society. They lack the family resources, networks, and out-of-school experiences that could compensate for what they are not offered in schools. Without school success, they are doomed to lives of continued poverty and consigned to conditions that characterize a desperate existence: violence, inadequate health care, a lack of life options, and hopelessness. The typical high school graduate has had approximately 54 teachers. When I ask successful graduates from inner-city schools, "How many of your teachers have led you to believe that you were particularly good at anything?" the modal response is none. If graduates report this perception, I wonder what those who have dropped out would say?

I recognize that getting better teachers is not a reconstructive change strategy. Indeed, I may well deserve the criticism that I am offering a Band-Aid solution by finding great people who are merely helping to shore up and preserve bad systems.

As I listened to the great change experts of the 1950s, I bet myself that they would not succeed, and I set myself the modest task of doing whatever I could to save young people in schools as they are currently constituted by getting them a few better teachers. After 35 years the movers and shakers seem further behind than ever. School systems serving poor children have become more rigid, less financially stable, more violent, and further behind their advantaged counterparts.

During the same period the school districts using my selection and training methods have become a national network. We now know how to recruit and select teachers who can succeed with children in poverty. The number of such teachers in every urban school system will continue to grow. So, too, will the impact these star teachers are making on the lives of their students.

Mark Twain once quipped, "To do good things is noble. To advise others to do good things is even nobler—and a lot easier." I fail to understand why *talking* about the reconstruction of urban schools in America is noble work, while what star teachers and their students *actually accomplish* in these schools is merely a palliative. In my own admittedly naive view, it seems that the inadequate nostrums of policy analysts and change agents are being given more attention than the effective behaviors of people who are busy making schools work better. A society that values ineffectual physicists over effective plumbers will find itself hip-deep in insoluble problems.

## NOTES

1. Martin Haberman, "Gentle Teaching in a Violent Society," *Educational Horizons,* Spring 1994, pp. 131–36.
2. Charles M. Payne, *Getting What We Ask For: The Ambiguity of Success and Failure in Urban Education* (Westport, Conn.: Greenwood, 1984).

## POSTNOTE

Our nation's noble tradition of offering education to all Americans, independent of gender, race, religion, or social class, has been an inspiration to people around the world. Over the years, too, it has brought millions upon millions of individuals into the American mainstream and in the process strengthened our nation. But while the achievements are many, our failures to provide quality education to the children of the poor, particularly the urban poor, have also been many. Urban education remains one of the nation's thorniest problems and, while the proposals, programs, and schemes have been many, large numbers of urban children year-in and year-out receive an inferior, future-crippling education. Haberman cuts through many of the nostrums and identifies the primary need of our urban schools: "star teachers." We have the star teachers. We, as a nation, have the resources. Do we have the will?

## DISCUSSION QUESTIONS

1. Which of Haberman's seven "dimensions of effective teaching" do you believe is most important? Why?

2. Which of these seven dimensions is least important in middle-class schools? Why?

3. Does reading this article make you more or less eager to teach in urban schools? Why?

# 6  ⌂ CLASSIC *Creating a High-Quality Teaching Force*

Arthur E. Wise

Teacher quality is on the national agenda as never before. We finally recognize that the teacher is the single most important school-based determinant of student learning. That fact accords not only with every parent's common sense, but also with research. How do we ensure that every classroom has a qualified teacher?

## Building a System

For the past decade, the teaching profession has been hard at work building a system of quality assurance that will increase the likelihood that every child is taught by a caring, competent, and qualified teacher. We are now noticing the results.

The seven elements of this system did not exist until the mid- to late 1980s. The medical profession took 30 years—from 1890 to 1920—to develop and implement an analogous quality-assurance system. The education profession also will need time to fully integrate the following seven features.

▶ *Advanced certification.* The first element is the National Board for Professional Teaching Standards (NBPTS). The Board was created in 1987 by the teaching profession, with help from the Carnegie Corporation, businesses, and the federal government, to provide advanced certification to accomplished teachers—a type of recognition never before available to teaching

Arthur E. Wise is president of the National Council for Accreditation of Teacher Education (NCATE). From Arthur E. Wise, "Creating a High-Quality Teaching Force," *Educational Leadership*, December 2000/January 2001, pp. 18–21. Reprinted with permission of the Association for Supervision and Curriculum Development. Copyright © 2001 by ASCD. All rights reserved.

professionals. Previously, once teachers began their careers, they had no widely accepted mechanism for achieving professional and public recognition. The Board certification creates new career options for teachers and encourages excellent teachers to remain in the classroom. The Board also generated a consensus definition of accomplished teaching and an accepted means for measuring it, giving the lie to those who maintained that accomplished teaching is too idiosyncratic to be measured. Many institutions are revising their master's programs to be consistent with the Board's standards and assessments.

**TERMS TO NOTE**

National Board for Professional Teaching Standards (NBPTS)

Licensing

Interstate New Teacher Assessment and Support Consortium (INTASC)

▶ *Licensing standards.* Building on the experience of the NBPTS, California and Connecticut launched an initiative to develop model state-licensing standards that states could use to reform the teacher-licensing process. Known as the Interstate New Teacher Assessment and Support Consortium (INTASC) and now operated by the Council of Chief State School Officers, these standards help states develop systems that assess the knowledge and skills of graduates as a condition for attaining a license. Not long ago, teachers were given a license merely on the basis of seat time and graduation, without having to demonstrate knowledge, skill, or the ability to teach.

▶ *Curriculum standards.* Beginning in the mid-1980s, a number of national professional associations began to develop standards for preK–12 students. The National Council of

Teachers of Mathematics, working with committees of school and university faculty, created a national professional consensus about what students should know and be able to do at various ages and grade levels. Other associations followed suit. For the first time in history, professional associations have a comprehensive set of expectations across the full range of the curriculum. So profound is this development that it has come to be called the standards movement.

▶ *Alignment.* There is a growing consensus to align the standards for accreditation, initial licensing, and advanced certification. Before 1990, accreditation and licensing authorities did not coordinate their activities, and, of course, the NBPTS did not exist. The result was a cacophony of standards and expectations —effectively meaning that there were no standards. In 1995, the National Council for Accreditation of Teacher Education (NCATE) began to incorporate INTASC's model state-licensing principles into its standards and continues to do so in the 2000 standards. Thus, NCATE and the states hold colleges of education accountable for producing candidates who have the same knowledge and skills that the states require for licensing individual candidates. This symmetrical relationship will strengthen accreditation and licensing. Additionally, NCATE has aligned teacher preparation standards with national standards for preK–12 students and with National Board standards for advanced certification. This alignment will revolutionize the quality-assurance system.

**TERMS TO NOTE**
Curriculum standards
National Council for Accreditation of Teacher Education (NCATE)
Professional development schools

▶ *Accreditation.* Until the late 1980s, NCATE and the states did not collaborate in the review of teacher preparation programs. As of 2000, 45 states and the District of Columbia have integrated NCATE's professional review of colleges of education with their own reviews, thereby strengthening the evaluations of teacher preparation in a growing number of institutions. Although NCATE accreditation remains voluntary in most states, a substantial number of new institutions are seeking NCATE accreditation. Seventeen states now require NCATE accreditation for their public institutions, and many states now use NCATE standards, whether or not they require institutions to gain NCATE accreditation. New York, Maryland, and Alaska have recently passed legislation requiring accreditation.

▶ *Professional development schools.* One of the most promising ideas for strengthening teacher preparation—professional development schools (PDSs)—did not even take shape until the late 1980s. Like the teaching hospital in the field of medicine, the PDS is designed to more fully integrate academic and clinical preparation for beginning teachers. Policymakers and educators recognize that beginning teachers and teacher candidates require more support than the truncated clinical experience of a four-year undergraduate program affords. As many as 1,000 PDSs now operate. To help support this new structure, NCATE is working with 20 pilot institutions to set new expectations for clinical practice. States and institutions are using NCATE's draft standards for professional development schools.

▶ *State standards boards.* Until 1990, only three states had experimented with professional standards boards—boards made up mainly of members of the profession charged with establishing and implementing standards for teacher licensing. As of 2000, 12 more state legislatures created independent professional state standards boards. Unlike state boards of education, which have myriad other responsibilities, professional state standards boards have as their overriding concern the implementation of standards and assessments that will result in high-quality teachers in their states.

## Making A Difference

The teaching profession has been hard at work developing the elements of the new systems of teacher development and quality assurance, all of which include NCATE involvement or leadership. Is there evidence of progress?

A recent study by Educational Testing Service (ETS) shows that NCATE-accredited institutions produce proportionally more-qualified teachers than nonaccredited institutions. ETS examined 270,000 candidates who took the PRAXIS II licensing exam between 1995 and 1997 in the content area that they planned to teach and who had also taken the Scholastic Aptitude Test (SAT). ETS divided the candidates into three groups: graduates of NCATE-accredited institutions, graduates of non-NCATE institutions, and candidates who had never entered a teacher-preparation program.

Of all the candidates who took the PRAXIS II licensing exam, designed by ETS and administered in 37 states and the District of Columbia, graduates of NCATE-accredited institutions significantly outperformed those from unaccredited institutions, and both groups significantly outperformed those who had never prepared as a teacher but who took the exam.

The ETS study provides some quantitative evidence that this reform is making a difference. As we continue to implement the reform, we can anticipate that the quality of the teaching force will rise.

## The Choice We Have

The seven elements of the teaching profession's new quality-assurance system were developed because the existing traditional systems clearly do not provide the level of quality assurance that the public and policymakers now demand. But the system needs support; its development can move quickly or slowly depending on the degree to which university leaders, policymakers, and education professionals develop the kind of trust that now exists between the state and the quality-assurance mechanisms of other established professions.

The movement to professionalize teaching is growing at the same time that other powerful forces are making an impact on education. Among these are the impending shortage of teachers, the integration of technology into schools, and the movement to deregulate schooling through charter schools and vouchers. What are the likely effects of these trends on the movement to professionalize teaching?

A shortage of teachers in some specializations and geographic areas could jeopardize the movement to increase teacher quality. The most popular policymaker response is to deregulate entry into teaching to produce an adequate supply of "teachers" in the classroom. This response has two effects. First, it yields a supply of unqualified teachers, almost all of whom are assigned to poor and minority schoolchildren. The result, all too often, is low-quality instruction for those children who most need high-quality, well-prepared teachers. Second, deregulation sets in motion a chain of events that lowers the overall quality of the teaching force because it reduces the incentive for quality preparation. Why work hard to prepare when easy routes are available and compensation and treatment are the same?

We can reconcile professionalization with the growing demand for teachers in one of two ways. First, assuming little structural change in schooling, we can increase salaries and incentives to the level necessary to attract and retain sufficient numbers of candidates. This is a classic market solution to labor shortages in every field and discipline.

Second, we can differentiate the teaching force. In a differentiated staffing structure, with corresponding levels of compensation, qualified teachers supervise those without proper qualifications. This is already occurring in a rudimentary way—such as when teachers certified by the National Board receive mentoring assignments.

A teacher team might include Board-certified teachers, fully licensed teachers, beginning interns, teacher candidates, and those with little or no preparation. Individuals would have distinct titles and different pay scales. This structure provides a career ladder for highly qualified teachers who stay in teaching, and it gives districts a way to fulfill staffing needs with integrity. The structure rewards those teachers who invest time, money, and effort in their own professional development. Many school districts currently pay the same salary to qualified and unqualified personnel, creating a disincentive for individuals to prepare.

A differentiated staffing structure allows for different and appropriate levels of compensation, thus keeping the overall expenditure on salaries in check. Most important, it provides for accountability by ensuring that the responsibility for every child's instruction is in the hands of qualified personnel. It also provides training for less-qualified personnel.

In addition, a truth-in-labeling law would recognize qualified, competent, well-prepared individuals. Only those who have met a state's requirements for a teaching license would be known by the title *teacher*. Others whom school districts must hire to fill classrooms would get another designation. Already in Texas, parents must be notified if their children are taught by an unlicensed or out-of-field teacher for more than 30 consecutive days. In Florida, parents must also be notified when teachers are assigned out-of-field. Other states could follow suit.

Just as patients know the difference between health-care professionals and health-care workers—for example, the differences among a doctor, a nurse practitioner, a nurse, and a nurse's aide—the U.S. public has a right to know who has prepared to teach and who has not. This information, when made public, will give us a clearer picture of who is teaching in our nation's schools and help us decide how much we want to invest to attain teacher quality for our children.

Next, the integration of technology is clearly impending. Although technology has altered some classrooms, it has had minimal, if any, impact on the structure of the teaching force. How might technology influence the professionalization of teaching? At one level, technology can enhance the effectiveness of qualified teachers. At another level, technology raises questions about the most effective use of teachers' time, the proper substitution of technology-mediated instruction, the management of noninstructional activities, and the proper mix of teachers and technology experts. In other words, technology could lead to a restructuring of the teaching force; teachers would be responsible for student learning but would draw on other personnel as appropriate for tasks requiring other kinds of expertise. Technology can enhance teacher quality through a growing differentiation of the teaching force.

Finally, how might the deregulation of schooling through vouchers and charter schools intersect with the movement to professionalize teaching? Generally, the proponents of the deregulation of schooling favor the deregulation of teaching. In some cases, proponents have legislated to allow unprepared personnel into charter schools. Most states do not require licensure for private school teaching, although most private school teachers are licensed. Thus, the deregulation of schooling at first seems incompatible with professionalization.

Paradoxically, the deregulation of schooling could and should demand a stronger state role in ensuring that teachers are qualified for their work. Most professionals other than teachers work in private settings, yet the state maintains a strong interest in the quality of those professionals. Accreditation and licensing are the norms in medicine, law, and other professions because the state wishes to ensure that these professionals are qualified. If schooling is deregulated, there should be an even stronger state interest in ensuring the quality of personnel. Thus, deregulation could potentially strengthen the movement to professionalize teaching.

### Ensuring Quality

The current mixed strategy of simultaneously regulating and deregulating teaching will not raise the overall quality of the teaching force. This dysfunctional system will increase inequality between the educational haves and have-nots. As teacher shortages grow, more unqualified people will fill classrooms. However, if we choose to support the movement to strengthen the teaching force, we can build a system that is suited to today's needs for high student achievement.

## POSTNOTE

This article by a leading voice in the reform of teacher education was selected as a Classic because it offers a compelling vision of change for the teaching profession. Frank Newman, former president of the Education Commission of the States, characterized the first wave of educational reform in the mid-1980s as one in which teachers were the *objects* of change. The second wave of reform, he asserted, would be one in which teachers were the *agents* of change.

The move toward increasing teacher professionalism makes teachers agents of change. There is growing agreement among policymakers that more educational decision making should be granted to teachers and other professional educators. However, many policymakers are reluctant to trust teachers to make more educational decisions. The tension between those who support steps to make teaching a true profession and those who push for standardization, accountability, and inexpensive labor will continue through the next decade.

## DISCUSSION QUESTIONS

1. Of the seven features of a quality-assurance system that the author mentions, which do you think is the most promising for ensuring a highly-qualified teaching force?

2. What are the forces or factors that work against the creation of a system for ensuring high-quality teaching?

3. How would you evaluate the author's suggestion for a differentiated staffing structure? What are the advantages and disadvantages of such a system?

# Developing an Effective Teaching Portfolio

Kenneth Wolf

E ducators have used student portfolios to assess student performance for many years. Recently, they have turned their attention to portfolios for teachers.[1]

Why the interest in teaching portfolios? Although portfolios can be time-consuming to construct and cumbersome to review, they also can capture the complexities of professional practice in ways that no other approach can. Not only are they an effective way to assess teaching quality, but they also provide teachers with opportunities for self-reflection and collegial interactions based on documented episodes of their own teaching.

Essentially, a teaching portfolio is a collection of information about a teacher's practice. It can include a variety of information, such as lesson plans, student assignments, teachers' written descriptions and videotapes of their instruction, and formal evaluations by supervisors. If not carefully thought out, however, a portfolio can easily take the form of a scrapbook or steamer trunk. The "scrapbook" portfolio is a collection of eye-catching and heart warming mementos that has strong personal meaning for the portfolio owner. The "steamer trunk" portfolio is a larger container filled to the brim with assorted papers and projects.

Unfortunately, these kinds of portfolios do not allow for serious self-reflection, and others

**TERMS TO NOTE**
Portfolio
Artifacts
National Board for Professional Teaching Standards (NBPTS)

cannot examine them in an informed way. They do not illustrate an underlying philosophy of teaching, and they provide no information about instructional goals or teaching context. They do not explain the contents of the portfolio or connect them to intended instructional outcomes. Perhaps most important, such portfolios contain no written reflections by the creators on their teaching experiences.

A teaching portfolio should be more than a miscellaneous collection of artifacts or an extended list of professional activities. It should carefully and thoughtfully document a set of accomplishments attained over an extended period. And, it should be an ongoing process conducted in the company of mentors and colleagues.

## Why Develop a Portfolio?

Teachers create portfolios for a variety of reasons. In teacher education programs, students develop portfolios to demonstrate their achievement. Later, they may present these portfolios at job interviews. Experienced teachers construct portfolios to become eligible for bonuses and advanced certification. And, some administrators have invited teachers to become architects of their own professional development by having them create portfolios based on individual growth plans.

In Colorado, for example, teachers are preparing portfolios in many different settings. In the Douglas County School District south of Denver, teachers submit portfolios to demonstrate their teaching excellence. Those who meet district standards receive annual performance bonuses. Some teachers also are striving to earn national recognition by preparing portfolios for

At the time this article was written, Kenneth Wolf was an assistant professor at the University of Colorado at Denver. From Kenneth Wolf, "Developing an Effective Teaching Portfolio." *Educational Leadership*, March 1996, pp. 34–37. Reprinted by permission of the Association for Supervision and Curriculum Development. Copyright © 1996 by ASCD. All rights reserved.

the National Board for Professional Teaching Standards. And soon, Colorado will require all educators, including administrators, to develop portfolios in order to renew their professional licenses.

## Selecting the Contents

A portfolio might include items such as lesson plans, anecdotal records, student projects, class newsletters, videotapes, annual evaluations, letters of recommendation, and the like. It is important, however, to carefully select the contents of the finished portfolio so that it is manageable, both for the person who constructs it and for those who will review it.

While the specific form and content of a portfolio can vary depending upon its purpose, most portfolios contain some combination of teaching artifacts and written reflections. These are the heart of the portfolio. The introductory section, in which the teacher broadly describes his or her teaching philosophy and goals, and the concluding section, which contains evidence of ongoing professional development and formal evaluations, provide a frame for these artifacts and reflections. (Figure 1 provides a suggested outline for organizing a teaching portfolio.)

Here's (in part) how Susan Howard, a preservice elementary school teacher at the University of Colorado at Denver, described her philosophy of teaching:

> Visitors to my classroom would see a supportive, risk-free environment in which the students have an active voice in their learning and in classroom decision making. Students would be engaged in a variety of individual and collaborative work designed to accommodate their diverse learning styles. Curriculum would combine basic skills, authentic learning, and critical thinking. Finally, visitors also would see parental involvement demonstrated in a variety of ways. . . .
>
> Students should help establish class rules, have a vote in the topics for the year,

---

### TABLE OF CONTENTS

**I. Background Information**
- Résumé
- Background Information on Teacher and Teaching Context
- Educational Philosophy and Teaching Goals

**II. Teaching Artifacts and Reflections**
   Documentation of an Extended Teaching Activity
- Overview of Unit Goals and Instructional Plan
- List of Resources Used in Unit
- Two Consecutive Lesson Plans
- Videotape of Teaching
- Student Work Samples
- Evaluation of Student Work
- Reflective Commentary by the Teacher
- Additional Units/Lessons/ Student Work as Appropriate

**III. Professional Information**
- List of Professional Activities
- Letters of Recommendation
- Formal Evaluations

---

**FIGURE 1**
How to Organize a Teaching Portfolio

and have a voice in as much of their learning as possible. I believe it is important to use a variety of presentation styles and provide a range of learning experiences to support students' diverse learning styles. . . .

In my classroom, language arts would pair phonics with literature enrichment. Math would combine basic skills and application. Science and social studies would emphasize application and problem-solving exercises while targeting basic area knowledge.

I would invite parents to share information about hobbies, skills, jobs, and cultures. I would communicate with them frequently, and would encourage them to become involved in their child's learning in as many ways as possible.

Artifacts (unit plans, student work samples) are essential ingredients in a teaching portfolio, but they must be framed with explanations. For example, Linda Lovino, a high school English teacher from the Douglas County School District, included surveys of students, parents, and colleagues in the portfolio she submitted for the Outstanding Teacher Program. She commented in her portfolio on what she learned from these surveys:

I felt validated when the client surveys indicated that my students and their parents feel I use a variety of teaching strategies and methods, and that I am knowledgeable in my subject area. Although I received high ratings from over 80 percent of parents and students on the statements, "The teacher effectively communicates information regarding growth and progress of my child," and "The teacher effectively motivates the student," the remaining 20 percent of the respondents gave me a "neutral" rating.

I feel these areas are essential to being an outstanding teacher. Therefore, I am currently researching and developing methods that might help me better motivate students and assess their progress.

Each artifact also should be accompanied by a brief statement, or caption, which identifies it and describes the context in which it was created. This often can be done in one or two sentences. Figure 2 shows the kinds of captions Colorado educators include in their license renewal portfolios.

---

**Title:** Weekly Classroom Newsletter

**Date:** March 15, 1996

**Name:** John Stanford

**Description of context:** Students write, edit, and publish this weekly newsletter in writer's workshop.

**Interpretation:** This newsletter is one way that I keep parents informed about classroom events. It is also an example of how I engage students in meaningful learning activities.

**Additional Comments:** Parents have told me how they use the newsletter to talk with their children about what is happening in school. I also learn more about what my students find important or newsworthy in class each week!

*This is an example of the kind of captions Colorado teachers use in License Renewal Portfolios.*

---

**FIGURE 2**
Sample Portfolio Caption

Reflective commentaries are another important part of the portfolio. These commentaries do more than describe the portfolio contents; they examine the teaching documented in the portfolio and reflect on what teacher and students learned.

Valerie Wheeler, a middle school teacher from Boulder, included an account of a unit she taught on communicable diseases in the portfolio she submitted to the National Board for Professional Teaching Standards:

> The primary goal for teaching about communicable diseases is to educate students about their own role in leading a safe and healthy life. . . . When young people are informed, chances are they will act in ways that protect their own and others' health.
>
> The day I introduced this topic to my students, we used the entire period to discuss the meaning of the term "communicable disease." Together, we brainstormed questions about disease—its history, status, and future.
>
> As in most class discussions, students eventually began to share relevant personal or family experiences. The energy and participation level was high, and by the end of class, two themes had emerged: Students wanted to know more about the most common communicable diseases, and they wanted to know more about AIDS.
>
> Because student understanding is enhanced by prior experiences, I assigned each student to write a brief history of his or her own health.

In addition to the written account, Valerie included a videotape of her teaching along with samples of her teaching materials and her students' work. These included a newspaper article about the rights of tuberculosis patients, which her students had read and annotated; a letter they wrote to the mayor about the confinement of TB patients; thank you letters to guest speakers from the local AIDS center; and photographs of a quilt the class made after reading about the AIDS quilt.

## Developing Your Profile

There are many approaches to developing a teaching portfolio. The following one involves articulating an educational philosophy and identifying goals, building and refining the portfolio, and framing the contents for presentation to others.

▶ Explain your educational philosophy and teaching goals. Describe in broad strokes the key principles that underlie your practice. These principles will help you select goals for your portfolio.

▶ Choose specific features of your instructional program to document. Collect a wide range of artifacts, and date and annotate them so you will remember important details when assembling the final portfolio. Consider keeping a journal for written reflections on your teaching.

▶ Collaborate with a mentor and other colleagues. This is an essential, but often overlooked, part of the process. Ideally, your mentor will have experience both in teaching and in portfolio construction. And consider meeting at regular intervals to discuss your teaching and your portfolio with a group of colleagues.

▶ Assemble your portfolio in a form that others can readily examine. While any number of containers will work, the easiest to organize and handle seems to be a loose-leaf notebook. (Electronic portfolios may soon replace notebooks.)

▶ Assess the portfolio. Assessment can range from an information self-assessment to formal scoring by the National Board for Professional Teaching Standards. Such assessments are tied to specific performance standards. (The Douglas County School District in Colorado has identified three categories, each of which contains specific criteria, for assessing outstanding teachers: assessment and instruction, content and pedagogy, and collaboration and partnership.)

## A Means to an End

Portfolios have much to offer the teaching profession. When teachers carefully examine their own practices, those practices are likely to improve. The examples of accomplished practice that portfolios provide also can be studied and adapted for use in other classrooms.

Too often, good teaching vanishes without a trace because we have no structure or tradition for preserving the best of what teachers do. Portfolios allow teachers to retain examples of good teaching so they can examine them, talk about them, adapt them, and adopt them.

Finally, it is important to remember that the objective is not to create outstanding portfolios, but rather to cultivate outstanding teaching and learning.

### NOTE

1. L. S. Shulman, (1988), "A Union of Insufficiencies: Strategies for Teacher Assessment in a Period of Reform," *Educational Leadership* 46, 3: 36–41.

## POSTNOTE

Portfolios are playing an important role in the assessment of both beginning and experienced teachers in many parts of the country. Many school districts expect to see a prospective teacher's portfolio as part of the job application process. The National Board for Professional Teaching Standards requires experienced teachers to prepare a teaching portfolio as part of the assessment for national board certification. Both state licensing and accreditation processes are moving away from a focus on courses and experiences; instead, they are putting more stress on what teacher education graduates actually know and are able to do. Developing your own portfolio will also give you valuable practice that will let you help students, in turn, prepare their own portfolios.

## DISCUSSION QUESTIONS

1. How does the notion of developing a teaching portfolio as part of your teacher education program strike you? What would be the advantages? Disadvantages or limitations? What works or evidence would you want to put into such a portfolio?

2. How structured or open-ended should the requirements for a teaching portfolio be? That is, should everyone have to submit evidence that certain proficiencies have been met, or should the contents of the portfolio be left to the discretion of the teacher education student?

3. Portfolios are being urged by educators to play a major role in assessment and evaluation. Do you see a drawback, or downside, to the new emphasis?

# *8*    *Lessons of a First-Year Teacher*

## Molly Ness

When I graduated from college, I joined Teach For America and so committed the next two years of my life to teaching in one of the nation's most underresourced school districts. Now part of the Ameri-

Corps service program, Teach For America has a clear mission: to give every child—regardless of race, ethnicity, background, or religion—the opportunity to attain an excellent education. Founded a decade ago, Teach For America places more than 800 college graduates every year in impoverished school districts in such urban areas as Baltimore, Los Angeles, and New York City and in such rural areas as the Mississippi Delta and the Rio Grande Valley. Teach For America teachers fill vacancies in districts that suffer from teacher shortages, most often taking the most challenging placements in the most difficult schools.

Corps members go through an intensive five-week training program before they are placed in schools. In that training, they focus on theories of education, holding children to high expectations, practical ways of becoming an effective teacher, and leveling the playing field for students who lack the educational opportunities that children from better backgrounds take for granted. Corps members are hired directly by school districts, and many complete state credentialing programs during their two years of service. Upon the completion of their two-year commitment, more than 60% of corps members continue teaching, while the others change paths and move on to graduate school or to other forms of employment.

At the time this article was written, Molly Ness was a second-year teacher at Roosevelt Middle School, Oakland, Calif. Molly Ness, "Lessons of a First-Year Teacher," *Phi Delta Kappan*, May 2001. Copyright © 2001 by Phi Delta Kappa. Reprinted by permission of the publisher.

In my first year of teaching, I was assigned to Roosevelt Middle School in East Oakland, California, an extremely overcrowded school with an annual teacher retention rate of just 60%. The student body is 50% Asian, 25% Latino, and 25% African American. Roosevelt is located in a rough area that is notorious for drug use, and gangs are an ever-present force. Most of my students were not native speakers of English. Indeed, in that first year, my students spoke 10 languages, including Arabic, Cambodian, Spanish, Vietnamese, and Chinese. Many were recent immigrants, and I was expected to teach them conversational and written English, as well as the state-mandated social studies curriculum.

Although I had been told before I began my Teach For America commitment that I was about to experience a harsher reality than anything I had previously known, I still believed that teaching was a 9-to-3 job and that I could leave my work at school and keep my personal and professional lives totally separate. I thought I could bring my students into my classroom, shut the door, and leave the problems of their inner-city community outside. I believed that I could instill the love of learning in my students and that they would somehow be able to forget all the turmoil they faced in their lives.

I vowed that my passion and enthusiasm for my children and for teaching would never diminish. I would never allow myself to suffer emotionally, as many first-year teachers do. I would stay positive and avoid the disillusionment that so many teachers feel. I would enter my classroom every day with the same energy and passion I started with in September. It wouldn't matter if it was a gloomy Thursday in late October or if I had been battling the flu for two weeks. I would never become the "worksheet teacher." Rather than slide grammar worksheets under my students' noses, I would have them build the pyramids out of sugar cubes. I set high expectations not only for my students, but for myself as well.

In one swift transformation, I graduated from college, packed my belongings, and drove across the country to start life anew in an entirely unfamiliar environment, without the comforts of family, friends, and home. It was an exciting adventure at first—relocating, getting my first real job, and having the responsibilities of adult life.

But by early November, the excitement had worn off, and the reality had begun to sink in. I was living in a new city, far from my home and with no connections to my past. Maintaining a positive learning environment in an otherwise depressing place was an endless challenge: the constant planning, the discipline, the paperwork, the headaches of the district bureaucracy. I felt underappreciated by my administration and abused by my students. I would come home from school, sit on my couch, and think, "I can't go back tomorrow." I felt drained. And gradually I felt that I was letting my students down; nothing I was doing in my classroom could ever be enough to make life fair for them. I was becoming the worksheet teacher that I swore I would never be. I felt that I had lost myself in this process of trying to serve my students. And so I started asking the really hard questions, about myself, about my life, and about my commitment.

Often I feel that Teach For America is too eager to dismiss the frustrations we teachers inevitably feel about our lives and our jobs. It sometimes seems as if I am just supposed to grin and bear it through the two years. Then I can pause to reflect on my experience and say, "That was an impossibly difficult experience, but I am a richer person because of it."

Given the passion and dedication of most corps members, it seems taboo to question your commitment to Teach For America and to your students. But, in fact, I question my commitment nearly every day. I have a vivid memory of calling a friend in Los Angeles, a corps member placed in Compton, to ask, "Will you quit with me?" At first I thought that doubting my commitment made me a bad person, that some omniscient Teach For America presence was frowning down on me. In fact, maybe all this questioning of my commitment is actually a positive force that makes me push to achieve more in my classroom.

When I went home for the winter break that first year, I wasn't sure exactly what to tell my friends and family about my Teach For America experience. Should I focus on the good or the bad of teaching? Should I tell them how I teach 97 students who speak little or no English? Should I tell them how there are never enough markers or scissors or even textbooks to go around? Should I tell them of my 12-year-old student who is now serving time in juvenile hall for armed robbery? Or maybe I should tell them about my 13-year-old student who cannot spell *dog* because he is a victim of social promotion.

Slowly I realized that I was mouthing platitudes that were simply untrue to the experience. I could barely make sense of the tension of opposites I felt in my life: Did I want to quit and get out, or did I want to devote all my life and energy to the vision of Teach For America? How should I characterize the way I felt, cynicism or optimism? Should I dwell on the bad experiences or dismiss them in light of the positive ones?

I began to reflect on my initial impressions of teaching. I remembered feeling overwhelmed on first entering the classroom. How would I ever begin to teach these children English and social studies? More important, how could I teach them that education could be their way out of poverty and into a better future? How could I teach them to be upstanding citizens and to practice civility in their everyday lives? How could I teach them conflict resolution, responsibility, and self-respect? When I told my father about my worries, he told me, "Do your best. You have been handed an unrealistic situation. All that anybody can ask you to do is your best. Don't beat yourself up over what you cannot accomplish."

For a long time, I believed my father's advice. I believed that I did face an unrealistic situation at Roosevelt Middle School. I believed that it was unrealistic to think that a first-year teacher could handle such a difficult placement, in such an underresourced school, with so little support.

But after a while, I came to realize that my father had it backwards. My situation was realistic—and that was exactly the problem. Far too many of our nation's children attend overcrowded schools like Roosevelt that cannot provide adequate materials, instruction, or attention. Too many of our children receive a subpar education, which seems to ensure that the cycle of poverty will not soon be broken. Too many teachers are thrown into classrooms with minimal support. In such circumstances, teachers do not receive enough concrete incentives to make teaching a lifelong profession. Our best teachers are often lost before they even start to achieve success in the classroom. It is no secret that teachers are overworked, underpaid, and underappreciated; I am living proof of that.

Upon completing my first year of teaching, I struggled to make sense of the lessons that I had learned. I truly believe that I have learned more about the world in a year of teaching than I did in several years of college.

I have learned that children are unbelievably resilient. My students have been handed immeasurable challenges and have tackled them with the courage, grace, and strength that many adults fail to demonstrate. I have learned how to make personal sacrifices for the sake of a greater good. I have learned that many people in the world today would rather let schools in places like Oakland be forgotten than try to solve the problems head-on. I have learned that it is rather easy to be idealistic in thoughts and words, but much harder to keep that idealism alive in actions every day. I have realized that not enough people in our society today devote their lives, their energy, and their souls to making this world a little better than they found it. I have learned the meaning and value of humility. And last, I have learned that I am only one person, but my power as a teacher will extend further than I could ever have guessed.

## POSTNOTE

*Teach For America* is one of those ideas that has a great deal of surface appeal. It is a quick and rather painless way to get into a classroom after going through only a brief training. The program is filled with bright and idealistic people like Molly Ness, the author of this article. And, of course, we are sure that it is a great idea for some people. On the other hand, it leads many young, potentially gifted teachers into a swamp that they are totally unprepared to handle. And while this may be enormously disappointing to the young teachers involved, what about the students? What about the third grader who only has one "third grade" and that is spent with a teacher who is not up to the task? What about the minority high school freshman who needs a solid basis in geometry if he or she is ever to fulfill a dream of becoming an engineer? While their ill-prepared teacher is crashing and burning, so are their opportunities.

What makes teacher preparation difficult (along with most professional training) is that the trainees all have different needs, different background experiences, and different learning styles, and are going out to apply what they learn in vastly different environments. A certain amount of seemingly unnecessary information and overtraining is part of all professional training. On the other hand, quick-fixes and crash programs may be extremely costly for both prospective teachers and particularly their future students.

# DISCUSSION QUESTIONS

1. Have you ever had a teacher who was clearly incompetent? What were the causes? What were the effects?

2. What was the advice the author received from her father? Do you believe it was the right advice? Why or why not?

3. Which of the problems encountered by the author do you believe you might be vulnerable to? What can you do about it now?

**9**

# Finding Allies: Sustaining Teachers' Health and Well-Being

## Patricia Houghton

If we hope for wonderful schools for our children, then we must be concerned with the mental health and well-being of our teachers. I have often heard teachers criticized for being concerned about their own comfort and happiness as educators or even for taking care of themselves. As teachers, however, we can be effective only if we are able to maintain our own health and energy levels. Roland Barth offered a telling analogy:

> Consider the common instructions given by flight attendants to airline passengers: "For those of you traveling with small children, in the event of an oxygen failure, first place the oxygen mask on your own face and then— and only then—place the mask on your child's face." The fact of the matter is, of course, that the adult must be alive in order to help the child. In schools we spend a great deal of time placing oxygen masks on other people's faces while we ourselves are suffocating.[1]

Nel Noddings writes that "teaching requires tremendous amounts of physical and psychic energy."[2] When we as teachers can maintain a high level of energy, we can be powerful educators. We may even have the strength and the ability to change schools for the better. The question is, How do we achieve and maintain the levels of mental and physical energy that are required to sustain ourselves as teachers?

I have been searching for the answer to this question for years. I have examined my own

Patricia Houghton is a teacher and a teacher educator at the University of Puget Sound, Tacoma, Wash. Patricia Houghton, "Sustaining Teachers' Health and Well-Being," *Phi Delta Kappan*, May 2001. Reprinted with permission of Patricia Houghton.

teaching, watched other teachers, observed wonderful and not so wonderful schools, and read a variety of literature related to this topic, and I continue to talk and think about these issues with others. In my search for the answer to this question I traveled to New York City to speak with Deborah Meier, the founder of the Central Park East Schools in Harlem, and to observe her schools. She advised me to find *allies.* To be great teachers and have an impact on the system of education or the schools in which we teach, we must have the support of others. There are endless resources we can tap: colleagues, students, parents, professional organizations, other schools, universities, and—ultimately—ourselves.

## Colleagues as Allies: Building Positive Communities of Support

During the difficult and discouraging times of teaching, it is often hard for me to recognize all the progress that my students and I are making and how much we are growing. Sometimes I stumble on the good that I had been unable to see, as I write in my journal or speak with colleagues—as I take the time to be reflective. My friend Tricia and I made a ritual of meeting each week while we were student teaching. We would begin to tell each other how hard—even terrible—the week had been. Yet soon enough, we were pointing out the good we heard in the other's story, the growth the other had missed. We began to see for ourselves that there were a lot of wonderful things happening in our classrooms. It took the telling of our stories to find the good. It took the other person to point out what we ourselves were unable to see. We need others to help us solve problems and to console, understand, celebrate, and appreciate ourselves and our students.

We as teachers tend to isolate ourselves. But the job of teaching is too big and too complex to do alone. We need one another. Even though collegial support is so vital to the lives of teachers, it can be hard to find. My friend Lori was telling me about a conversation among teachers in the staff lounge. It went something like this:

*Teacher A:* How was your field trip?
*Teacher B:* It was wonderful. We had a great time. Everything was great!

Lori had been on the same field trip and knew that there had been many complications and that everything had *not* been great. Many teachers have a tendency to make things sound better than they really are. The first step in building communities of teachers as allies may be just to be honest. When one person takes the risk to tell how he or she really is, it can create an atmosphere in which it is safe for others to do the same. We cannot support one another if we feel the need to hide behind a façade.

Joseph Featherstone recommends that teachers form groups to break the isolation. Such groups could meet to talk directly about teaching issues, or they could be a way for teachers just to get to know one another. "Sometimes people need to socialize before they feel able to bring up real problems."[3]

Pam Grossman and Sam Wineburg led a group of high school teachers as they read and discussed "literary and historical works and plan[ned] an interdisciplinary humanities curriculum." These teachers also helped one another improve their teaching methods. Teachers showed videos of their own classrooms, thus "opening up the act of teaching to question, comment, and elaboration by a group of supportive peers."[4] Membership in this group helped move these teachers from isolation to collaboration.

The most successful schools and programs that I have observed are characterized by teachers who support one another in a variety of ways. For example, the Central Park East Schools

in Harlem were designed to allow teachers to work closely with one another. In a staff meeting at CPE II, I heard the teachers talking about how to help a new teacher who had just joined them and another teacher who had broken her toe. Other items that were discussed included the school picnic to be held at Central Park the next day, integrating science with the Harlem Meer (a body of water on the north side of the park) project, a phone tree for parents, and how to manage the number of students in the bathroom at once. The director spoke with the teachers. He did guide the discussion, but the teachers all spoke and gave input. He did not make the final decisions about anything; rather, he was a facilitator. The feeling that teachers had ownership of their school was evident when one teacher answered the phone as if she were in her own home. It was clear that staff members were working together.

Many of us already know that increased interactions with our colleagues do not always help us to be healthier. Early in my teaching career, I discovered that my attitude about students became much more negative when I began eating lunch with some of the other teachers. Their negativity was contagious, and I began to think of the relationship between teachers and students as *us* against *them.* It is important that we choose positive staff members to associate with and learn from and that we strive to be positive ourselves.

## Students as Allies: Building Honest, Mutual Relationships

Our students are a valuable source of support that we often overlook. When I began my teaching career, I was cautioned not to smile for months in order to gain students' respect. One teacher suggested that I not be honest with my students about being a first-year teacher or about my age because they might respect me less. Others believed that it was important not to let students know you were unsure of something when teaching and that it was best to "bluff" instead. I found that these suggestions distanced me from my students and did not make the job of teaching easier or make me a better teacher.

In order to enlist our students as allies, it is important to be human, real, and honest with them. When I began teaching, there was so much I did not know. There is still so much that I want to learn. I was fortunate to have a clear sense of purpose as a teacher and my own philosophy of teaching. I was less knowledgeable about the subject matter. I was to teach students about Canada, Latin America, earthquakes, volcanoes, and how their own bodies worked. I knew little about these subjects. During one lesson about the respiratory system, students asked question after question while I was trying to explain how the respiratory system worked. I was having quite a hard time teaching the lesson, so I stopped and explained, "I am really excited that you are so interested in this lesson. I know how to teach, but I don't know very much about the respiratory system. I have spent a lot of time this past week trying to learn more about it so I could teach you, but it is hard for me to teach this and answer questions along the way. I was wondering if you could save your questions for the end? I probably won't be able to answer them, but I can ask Mr. Flak [another science teacher] or do some research to find the answers for you."

We had all been sitting on the rug when I said this. One of my students, Theressa, got up on her knees and exclaimed, "You know, no other teacher would ever tell us that they didn't know something. They'd just pretend." It was clear that Theressa was very proud of me for being honest with the class. She was letting me and the rest of the class know that she respected me for my honesty. I have been able to develop strong relationships with my students because of this type of honesty.

If we strive to keep ourselves distant from our students, we will tend to feel that we only give—receiving nothing in return. This is because we are not creating an environment that is reciprocal. Susan Florio-Ruane, a former teacher education professor of mine, says that when she was a teacher she sometimes began the day feeling like a wet, full, dripping sponge. By the time she left the classroom at the end of the day, she often felt like a sponge that had been sucked dry—hard and empty. Many of us can relate to this feeling all too well. Yet if we can tap into our students' energy, we may not end each day feeling dry and depleted. There can be a flow between us so that when we give, we also receive. We can receive only if we are open to what our students have to offer. It seems that we as teachers often forget to look for what our students do have to offer.

One night I was feeling quite troubled as I was trying to plan for the next day's math lesson. I was teaching third-graders about fractions. I came to a point where I felt completely hopeless. How on earth could I teach this lesson to 31 students? Their skill levels varied so greatly. I felt that the task was impossible. In the midst of these feelings of despair came what felt like a revelation: *my students could help one another!* I realized that I did not have to be the only teacher in that classroom. I could facilitate the process of students teaching and helping one another. My thoughts about teaching have not been the same since. It is not an us against them kind of game. We can do this together.

Each of us has to decide for ourselves if we want to build connections with students. In my observations of schools in which staff members and students seem happy, healthy, and productive, there is always a sense of closeness between the teachers and the students. At Seattle Public Alternative School #1, the connection between teachers and students is of primary importance. The courses offered are designed in such a way that teachers and students connect over common interests. Each teacher offers courses in an area of personal interest, such as sailing or environmental studies. Students then choose courses that are of interest to them. Thus the teacher and the student have something in common that can bring them together in a learning partnership.

At Gig Harbor (Washington) High School and Central Park East Secondary School, the staff members feel so strongly about building relationships with their students that they have advisory periods on a regular basis. Students are assigned advisors upon entering high school and see these adults weekly throughout their high school careers. The advisory periods acknowledge that students need to have adults in the school who know them and that teachers need time to get to know their students.

## Parents as Allies: Joining Forces with Students' Families

Feeling alone as a teacher can be a source of stress. The more supported we feel, the healthier we are likely to be. I have been fortunate to receive help and encouragement from the parents of my students. They are a wonderful resource. Working with them has made my job easier and much less stressful. I also feel certain that a positive relationship between parents and teachers helps students do better in school. The praise and encouragement I have received have helped give me energy to push onward when I am tired and discouraged. It saddens me when teachers view parents as a hindrance. I understand that it is sometimes hard to find the time and energy to meet with parents who have concerns, and it can be easy to feel threatened or criticized when parents don't understand or like your teaching methods. However, the benefits of working with parents can far outweigh any possible negatives.

To help parents get more involved in helping their children to be more successful, we need to tell them how they can help. Within a week of my arrival in a new state to begin my first teaching job, the school had an orientation session and barbecue for students and parents. My excitement about the coming year bubbled over, although I was simultaneously overwhelmed and scared. I confided my conflicting feelings to many of the parents as we talked. Parents responded by reaching out. One grandmother gave me a big hug and said, "You're going to be just fine, just fine, honey." Another mother heard me laughing and telling someone that I was still sleeping on the floor because I didn't yet have a bed. She approached me and said that she would keep her eyes out for a bed at the thrift store where she worked. I learned quickly that allowing others to give is a way to build community and gain support. I did not keep these families at arm's length by trying to maintain a "professional" relationship. We treated one another as people—able to step outside the roles of teacher and parent.

Throughout the year, I found that the parents and I worked as a team to educate their children. We supported one another. If I was having difficulty with a student's attitude or behavior or was concerned about a child's reading, writing, or math skills, I was able to reach out to the parents and ask for help. There were many times that I called, visited, or met with parents at school to ask them to speak with their child about a problem we were having or to suggest that they have their child work on skills each day at home.

Many times the greatest help I received was when parents were candid with me. They shared some of the troubles they were having at home. This helped me to understand where their child was coming from, and I was often able to support the child and the family. One mother, Callie, was having a hard time getting her daughter to come to school. Angela would throw temper tantrums in the morning. I began to support Callie by calling in the morning and talking with Angela. I often told Callie, "You really need to get Angela to school. I know it's hard, but you're the mom. You just need to get her here, and I'll do the rest," Callie told me that she needed this support and encouragement. I needed Callie's help as well. It was hard for me to teach Angela when she was absent so often. By getting Angela to school, Callie helped me tremendously, making my job easier. Most important, together we were able to help Angela.

## Professional Groups as Allies: Entering Larger Conversations

Being a member of a professional organization and attending professional conferences can be a source of inspiration and support for teachers. These organizations and conferences allow teachers to connect with other colleagues, share ideas, and learn about new methods, materials, literature, and so on. Breaking outside of one's individual school or district can be refreshing and lead to a sense of hope. There are times when we feel alone in the school where we teach because we are unable to find others who share a common philosophy. Organizations or conferences can give us a chance to get our souls fed by others who are like-minded and to have our own beliefs affirmed.

Making a presentation or sharing personal expertise at a conference or as a member of an organization can be personally rewarding. This is particularly important if we do not feel valued in the school where we teach. I have also seen that it can be quite energizing for teachers to work with university students during their field experiences or student teaching. Taking on leadership roles such as these helps us gain some ownership over our profession. Becoming involved in these ways can elicit a sense of worth. People burn out when they don't feel valued and when their work is unrewarding.

Taking on leadership roles within our own schools can also be a way for us to feel empowered. While this option may not always seem available, there are always ways to have a positive impact on other staff members. It may be just by providing coffee in the morning and encouraging others to join in. I found it rewarding to leave articles or inspirational poems or stories in other teachers' mailboxes. As a new teacher, I shared my excitement over a reading workshop that I was implementing in my classroom. I never tried to push my ideas on anyone; I just shared what was happening in my classroom over lunch. Soon, a few of the veteran teachers asked me to help them set up a reading workshop.

It may seem strange in an article about the health of teachers to recommend doing *more* as a way to be healthy. But it is important for us to take an active role in the leadership of our schools or in professional organizations if we are to overcome the feelings of helplessness that sometimes overtake us. I have felt frustrated and even angry about all that I cannot change or cannot easily change within the schools where I teach. Looking at what I *do* have the power to affect has helped me to feel more hopeful. There is much that we can do.

## Other Settings as Allies: Seeing Alternatives

Getting outside of one's own classroom is very important. Observing the classrooms of effective colleagues in our own schools, throughout the district, and in other districts can open up many possibilities we might not otherwise have considered. Observing other teachers and other schools can help us to stop and rethink the cycle we are in. Actually seeing things done differently can guide us to new places in our teaching.

Another benefit of observing other teachers is that we often discover that they have problems, too. In many cases, we feel inadequate because things don't always go smoothly in our classrooms or our students don't seem interested in the subject at hand. Finding out that all teachers have challenging days can help us be less critical of ourselves and of our students. The complex job of teaching does not always go smoothly.

## Professional Literature as an Ally: Nourishing Our Inner Teacher

A helpful way to cope when feeling uninspired, alone, overwhelmed, lost, or inadequate is to read literature by or about teachers and teaching. Reading good books can be a source of inspiration, direction, and comfort. When I was reflecting on my first three years of teaching, I realized that I turned to a book about teaching every August before school started. I didn't do this consciously, but I was drawn to these books because I needed something to help prepare me for the coming year. The sustenance I received from these books was powerful.

The August before my first year of teaching. I was feeling apprehensive about some of my teaching ideas and how they would be perceived by others. I was committed to creating a community of learners in a classroom that was student-centered rather than teacher-centered. I wanted students to feel a sense of belonging and a sense of ownership over *our* classroom. For these reasons, I had decided not to decorate the classroom before the students arrived. I would not put up posters or arrange the desks because I had decided that the students should be involved. Although I firmly believed this was a good idea, I began to worry that others would think I was strange or, worse, lazy. I then read William Ayers' book *To Teach: The Journey of a Teacher.* Instantly I felt I had an ally. Someone understood and affirmed what I was doing. Ayers did not talk specifically about decorating the classroom, but he did write about the importance of the environment in which one teaches.

> Questioning everything in the environment, from the bottom up, is an important task for teachers. We cannot necessarily change it all, but we can certainly become aware of the messages, the hidden as well as the obvious, the commonplace as well as the gaudy. We can peel the cover back a bit, peek underground, disclose the undisclosed—at least for ourselves. And in telling what is untold, we can become stronger in shaping our own environments, until they become places that more fully reflect what we know and value. . . . We can become better at creating what we intend for ourselves and for our students. If I am aiming to create a classroom where kids are eager to be, where they hate to leave, where I have to finally whisk them out the door, what would I do?[5]

Ayers' philosophy was much like my own. I had a wonderful feeling that someone was telling me that it was okay not to decorate the room before the students arrived. The book affirmed what I was doing, and I planned on using it as a reference if others questioned my choice. These ideas were in writing—in a book. It was a source of validation. Reading Ayers' book helped me step into my first year of teaching with a stronger hold on my beliefs about teaching. It helped me start the year believing that I had a friend beside me, and it helped me feel much more confident.

This experience may have been what led me to another book the following August. I read Lucy Calkins' *Living Between the Lines.*[6] Prior to my third year of teaching, I read "*My Posse Don't Do Homework,*" written by LouAnne Johnson.[7] The book was the story of her experiences as a teacher in a "tough" urban school. As I read, I was amazed by the similarities between Johnson's struggles and my own. Reading the book was much like sitting down to have a conversation with a fellow teacher about the joys and challenges and even the heartbreaks we face as educators. I also gained some great teaching ideas as I "watched" her solve problems. Reading these books in August and continuing to read wonderful books about teaching throughout the school year has helped inspire and sustain me.

## Universities as Allies: Pursuing Further Education

A valuable step I have taken on this journey to achieve a greater level of mental health, energy, and well-being has been to take a year off from teaching to spend as a full-time learner. Spending a year as a graduate student allowed me to focus on building myself up as a professional. I was able to devote more of my energy to my own mental health and was able to return to the classroom reenergized. The university was a place for me to find all the allies I have mentioned. I had more time to get in touch with myself as an ally as I spent hours thinking and reflecting on my teaching practice and writing in a journal. I had hours to spend with colleagues, discussing issues that I am passionate about and solving problems together. I had greater access to colleagues in other schools and districts. I had more time to attend professional conferences and to observe a variety of schools, thus expanding my network of support. And, of course, I had the privilege of being immersed in wonderful literature, some of which reaffirmed previous beliefs and some of which opened me up to new ways of thinking.

A colleague of mine chose to pursue her master's degree while teaching. She was quite intimidated by the notion of returning to the university. It was hard for her to imagine being able to find the time to devote to being a student as well as a teacher. She discovered that, although she had more demands on her time, she had more energy for teaching. Her coursework at the university caused her to be more excited about teaching and allowed her to build connections with other educators. Spending time in an intensive learning program for yourself can be a way to dedicate time to your own well-being and to renew yourself and your energy supply for teaching.

## Self as Ally: Befriending Ourselves

In order to be successful and healthy teachers, we must first and foremost be allies to ourselves. We can begin by teaching ourselves to think in new ways. It is easy to lose hope when teaching students who are far behind academically, who have no books at home, and who are not getting many of their physical and emotional needs met. I have spoken with several teachers who feel a sense of despair because their students are so far behind in school or have troubling home situations. It may be necessary for us to focus only on what we *can* do and to do that to the

best of our ability. We must let go of those things we cannot control. Judith Deiro writes about six teachers who have "healthy connections" with their students. One way in which these teachers "ease their stress level and cope with the demands of the job" is to detach. This is not to say that the teachers do not deeply care about their students, but rather "that they do not assume responsibility for students' well-being."[8]

There are limits to what we can give to our classrooms and our students. We are responsible for taking care of ourselves physically and emotionally. During my first year of teaching, I would stay up late working on plans and reading students' work. I realized midway through the year that pushing myself so hard was actually causing me to be a less effective teacher. I was tired and frustrated instead of rested and energetic. I have learned that I can never really do enough. There is always more to do. I have to stop at some point in order to be healthy.

I have therefore created a system that works for me: I work for a certain amount of time and then go home. I try not to take my "teaching bag" home anymore so that I have a space in my life that allows another aspect of my self to grow and thrive. A colleague of mine used to joke that he just took his box full of teaching stuff for a ride each evening. He couldn't find the energy to work on it when he finally got home, but he continued to take it for a ride! If we are to be friends to ourselves, we must set limits for what we can give to our teaching and be sure to meet our own needs as well.

Another way in which I have relied on myself as an ally has been to keep a journal. Writing in my journal has been an outlet for the vast array of emotions that I feel as a teacher. I can write about and celebrate my successes. I can work through frustrating situations that arise in my classroom and in my school or system. Things often become clearer for me as I put down on paper what is happening and what I am feeling. The process of writing forces me to slow down and reflect, which often enables me to gain a new perspective.

One powerful way to help ourselves is to be mindful of all that is beautiful and glorious about being a teacher. There is much to celebrate in what we do. It is essential to work toward self-improvement, but it is also critical to forgive ourselves for mistakes we make along the way. A field instructor of mine in college encouraged us to focus on what students *can* do rather than to look at their deficiencies. She also helped us as preservice teachers to focus on our own capabilities. I find both of these activities necessary, if I am to enjoy teaching.

## Taking an Active Role in Our Well-Being

Taking care of ourselves and getting support from colleagues, students, parents, professional organizations, observations, and reading are all ways to sustain ourselves as teachers. Yet even if we surround ourselves with allies, we may find that it is nearly impossible for us to be healthy in a given teaching situation. I have come to realize that there are some places where I cannot be the type of teacher—or even the type of human being—that I want and need to be. Ultimately, achieving wellness as an educator may require understanding what one absolutely needs in order to be good at one's job. I know that I have to be in a place where I can teach according to my philosophy. I have to teach in a situation that is conducive to my getting to know students on a personal level. Without these bare necessities, I am miserable and feel professionally ineffective.

The schools I have visited in which teachers show little or no signs of burnout are those in which teachers share a common philosophy and are given the encouragement and the environment that enable them to teach according to their beliefs. These schools are also places in which teachers take an active role in decision making. At the Seattle Country Day School, staff members make virtually every decision that affects them as teachers. When a new library assistant was hired, the current librarian was allowed to advertise the position and to interview and choose the person to fill it. Teachers at the school are given personal budgets to buy supplies for their classrooms. They are trusted to act as professionals, and they live up to these expectations. It is obvious that the teachers feel ownership of their school. Settings like these are conducive to being a healthy teacher. If we are teaching in situations where we are not valued or respected in such ways, we may find it difficult to sustain the levels of energy and health we need to be successful.

Teaching can be frustrating, challenging, and even infuriating. It can also be rewarding, meaningful, joyous work. I have often said to friends that teaching is too hard a job unless you have a passion for it. If we don't have a good answer to the question "Why do you teach?" we may not ever be able to achieve wellness in this profession. A passionate sense of purpose is essential.

What is it that you can do to be healthy as a teacher? How can you achieve and maintain the level of energy that is required to sustain yourself in this profession? We each need to answer these questions for ourselves. The suggestions I have put forth here are meant as guidelines to help you think about what it is that you need to be healthy and how you can meet those needs. We owe it to ourselves and to our students to take our own well-being seriously.

## NOTES

1. Roland Barth, *Improving Schools from Within: Teachers, Parents, and Principals Can Make a Difference* (San Francisco: Jossey-Bass, 1990), p. 42.

2. Nel Noddings, Foreword to Judith A. Deiro, *Teaching with Heart: Making Healthy Connections with Students* (Thousand Oaks, Calif.: Corwin, 1996), p. vii.

3. Joseph Featherstone, "Getting a Life: A New Teacher's Guide," in William Ayers, ed., *To Become a Teacher: Making a Difference in Children's Lives* (New York: Teachers College Press, 1995), p. 230.

4. Pam Grossman and Sam Wineburg, "Creating a Community of Learners Among High School Teachers," *Phi Delta Kappan*, January 1998, pp. 350–53.

5. Williams Ayers, *To Teach: The Journey of a Teacher* (New York: Teachers College Press, 1993), p. 53.

6. Lucy McCormick Calkins with Shelley Harwayne, *Living Between the Lines* (Portsmouth, N.H.: Heinemann, 1991).

7. LouAnne Johnson, *"My Posse Don't Do Homework"* (New York: St. Martin's, 1992).

8. Deiro, p. 77.

## POSTNOTE

For those readers who have yet to experience their first year of teaching, this one is a keeper! Like the first year in many occupations (medicine, sales, the law), teaching often has a taxing "break-in" period. It is complicated by the fact that new teachers are shocked by the strangeness of something that is quite familiar: being in school. The issue, and the problem, is that new teachers are in an entirely different role. Being on "the other side of the desk" can be a world away. One of the most difficult aspects of the work for many new teachers is being "in charge." They know about school. They know their subjects. They know what their students should be doing. They don't, however, know how to get them to do it. They have not had much experience being the boss or "the responsible person." Neither have they had much experience with directing others or with what would be called in the military, "giving orders." Necessity, however, is still the mother of invention and most new teachers adapt in time. This fine article is rich with insights and sources of support for struggling new teachers. Don't lose it!

## DISCUSSION QUESTIONS

1. As a student, did you have any "memorable experiences" with new teachers? Describe.

2. If and when you become a new teacher, what do you believe will be your most vulnerable areas?

3. Which ideas and suggestions in this article appeal most to you and which do you plan to put into practice?

# Calling in the Cosmos

Margaret Metzger

## 10

Dear Christine Greenhow,

You have asked one of the hardest questions about teaching or perhaps about any profession. You have asked how a teacher moves from competence to excellence. I could postpone an answer by saying that your question is premature; you have been a student teacher for only a few weeks, and your task now is to learn the basic skills of teaching. But I admire your thinking about the larger questions. You are not getting mired in the panic of inexperience. So let me try to answer as best as I can.

How does a teacher move from competence to excellence? Partially it's just experience. If you expect excellence immediately, you degrade the craft of teaching. You would not expect to do brain surgery during your first month in medical school.

My advice is to be gentle with yourself. Teaching is an art form. All art, done with integrity, is excruciatingly difficult. You are just learning. As my mother, a gifted math teacher, bluntly told me during my first year of teaching, "For the first three years of teaching, new teachers should pay the schools for the privilege of practicing on the children. If you struggle enough, you'll get better."

You are struggling to improve. I watch you searching for the perfect assignment, the perfect classroom activity, the perfect lesson plan. Perhaps you are looking for answers in the wrong

At the time this article was written, Margaret Metzger had been a teacher of English at Brookline High School in suburban Boston for over twenty-five years. Metzger, Margaret, "Calling in the Cosmos," Part I of "Maintaining a Life," *Phi Delta Kappan*, January 1996. Copyright © 1996 by Phi Delta Kappa. Reprinted by permission of publisher and author, a teacher at Brookline High School, Brookline, MA.

places. Instead of seeking just the right tidbit of knowledge or pedagogy, I suggest that you look at the larger picture. Think about what it means to be educated.

It seems to me that the missing ingredient in the lessons you teach is the subtle and explicit message that education is important. Students must be dedicated to their own growth, enthusiastic about academic work, and willing to take intellectual risks.

You must convince adolescents that being educated will enhance their lives. Students need to know, believe, and accept the idea that what they are doing is important. They are becoming educated adults; they are not just playing school. Christine, I know that you value your own education. You enjoy your intellectual life. You are in this profession because you believe that education matters. Now you must convey those values to the students.

My colleague Liz Kean teases me about how I convey the importance of education to my students. "Kids think your class is the most important event since the discovery of ice cream," she says. "You insist that what they are doing is important, that it matters in the great scheme of the universe. Even during routine work, you 'call in the cosmos.'"

I have never seen the concept of "calling in the cosmos" addressed in the research literature on teaching. Perhaps the ideal is too lofty or too unquantifiable to be included in teaching theory. Still, all the outstanding teachers I have known at Brookline High School, at Harvard, and at Brown University regularly "call in the cosmos," even if they would never use this silly term.

**TERM TO NOTE**

Cosmos

Strong teachers convey to their students a passion for a particular discipline, theory, or idea.

But these teachers go beyond their own enthusiasm for the subject; they convince their students that learning has intrinsic value. When you are in their classes, you believe that the material matters.

Let me give you a concrete example of calling in the cosmos. Please remember that I developed this lesson after a decade of teaching. I want you to think about calling in the cosmos as an ideal, not as a requirement for a new teacher. When you first begin to teach, you can barely think about yourself, the students, and the material simultaneously, much less the cosmos. This sample is meant only to clarify the concept, not to intimidate you.

On the first day of some literature classes, I hand out a copy of Plato's "Parable of the Cave" (sometimes called "The Allegory of the Cave"). We read it, diagram it on the board so that everyone understands where the characters are standing in relation to one another, and then act it out (complete with bicycle chains and a candle on a desk to represent the fire). This makes for a dramatic beginning, but the most important part of the lesson is my introduction.

I say to the class, "I am giving you this reading as an intellectual gift, in honor of the work that we will do together this year. I first read Plato when I was your age, more than 35 years ago. As a high school sophomore, I wrote a paper on 'The Parable,'—and received, to my delight, an A. So when my college professor passed out 'The Parable,' I smugly assumed that I understood it. Yet when I reread Plato's work, I realized that I had changed my mind in three years and now understood it in a new way. I wrote another paper and again did well.

"I have been reading 'The Parable' every year of my life, and I keep changing my mind about its meaning. It has become a benchmark of my own intellectual growth. At different times, I identify with different characters in the story. More important, I understand that the tale contains a great truth about the world. Things happen in my life, and I say to myself, 'Ah, here it is again—a Parable-of-the-Cave experience.' I hope that you will think about this reading for years and years and that it will help you understand the world. We will also look for Parable-of-the-Cave experiences in the literature we read this semester. I teach you this work by Plato not as I now understand it, but as an introduction—a first exposure. I hope you receive this reading as a gift."

Sometimes I follow Plato's "Parable" with Maurice Sendak's *Where the Wild Things Are*. Particularly when I am dealing with stuffy advanced classes, we sit on the floor and I hold the book up as kindergarten teachers do. Then we talk about archetypes and language and imagination. I tell them to watch for Sendak's and Plato's ideas in Homer, Twain, Dante, and Shakespeare.

That first-day introduction contains many elements that I use to "call in the cosmos." Authentic material in any discipline moves beyond schoolwork to a larger context. I show my students that other authors and ordinary people like me think about literature. I include students in the society of educated people throughout history. Finally, I try for an almost liturgical tone because I believe that education is a sacred act.

High school teaching requires energy and drama. But flash without substance is mere gimmickry. Therefore, teach what is important. Don't claim that something is important if it isn't. Be truthful with students about whether you are required to teach particular material or whether that material will lead to more interesting ideas.

You can always call in the cosmos simply by telling students the "big reasons" for learning. Why do we learn to write? To gain personal and academic power. We need to be able to write a college essay, to complete an insurance form, to compose a love letter. Why do we read literature? To enlarge our puny vistas. Literature shows us other people, other cultures, other times and ideas. Why should we educate ourselves? Tell your students about Seneca, who believed that education should produce a free people who are responsible for their own thinking and can examine their own world critically.

Emphasize *how* to learn, rather than *what* to learn. Students may never need to know a particular fact, but they will always need to know how to learn. Teach students how to read with genuine comprehension, how to shape an idea, how to master difficult material, how to use writing to clarify their thinking. A former student, Anastasia Koniaris, wrote to me: "Your class was like a hardware store. All the tools were there. Years later I'm still using that hardware store that's up there in my head. At Harvard they just tell us to learn stuff; they never stop and explain how to learn anything." Empower your students to learn.

Empowering students is not just a faddish notion. Include students in the process of teaching and learning. Every day ask such basic questions as: What did you think of this homework? Did it help you learn the material? Was the assignment too long or too short? How can we make the next assignment more interesting? What should the criteria for assessment be? Remember that you want students to take ownership of their learning.

For every assignment, explain the larger purpose. Students are entitled to know why they should do the work, even when it comes to something as insignificant as studying a spelling list. "You must know how to spell correctly because people who can spell make judgments about those who can't. Spellers think correct spelling is an indication of intelligence and character. I don't want anyone else to assume you aren't intelligent just because you can't spell. So, let's learn these blasted words. Not all learning is fun or even interesting; sometimes we just have to memorize."

Explain common knowledge. High school students need guidance regarding academic and cultural conventions. For example, they need to know that it is not appropriate to call Thoreau "Henry," that educated people recognize the name Hamlet, that footnotes are done in a certain fashion, that in the U.S. it is a sign of respect to look the teacher in the eye.

Although the curriculum is important, students are most fascinated with one another. Instead of deploring peer pressure, try to establish a community of learners. Despite the high school's emphasis on individual learning, much success in adulthood depends on the ability to work with others. Students must respect one another's intellectual and cultural differences. Students must learn to work collaboratively, to accept editing from peers, to discuss various ways of solving a problem, to share both their knowledge and their confusion. Adolescents, like all of us, hunger for exciting work within a community.

You, too, are a member of the community of learners. Do your own assignments. Talk to students about the things you've been reading. Show students drafts of your writing. Promise not to bore your students by giving them busywork or by wasting class time; in return, expect students to teach you by writing interesting papers and giving you new insights into life and literature.

Students want to be part of a classroom community, but they also want to be part of the larger community. Much of high school seems disconnected from real life and thus irrelevant to them. Whenever possible—and I hope you're able to do this far more frequently than I have ever managed—connect classroom learning to the outside world.

During my first semester of teaching, a particularly recalcitrant student refused to learn any grammar or mechanics, and his writing was unreadable. At the end of the course, I asked my students to write to their elementary school principals to arrange visits to their former schools. The boy demanded that I proofread and fix his letter. "Why?" I asked. "You've never cared about correctness."

"I know," he replied, "but if it's full of mistakes my old principal will think that I'm dumb, and maybe he won't let me visit."

"Okay," I said. "Now you're ready to learn mechanics." He did.

Despite all your best intentions and hardest work, Christine, in the end the students must decide whether they are ready to give up ignorance and take the scary step into knowledge. Like parenting, teaching makes us humble. There is only so much a teacher can do. A teacher can present learning experiences, but each student must ultimately take responsibility for becoming educated.

A former student, Chris Hummel, told me that when he read Martin Luther King's *Letter from a Birmingham Jail,* he decided to become educated. Chris described his thinking in this way: "So this is what it means to be well-educated. King sat in a jail, and all those references and quotes were right at his fingertips. He could see his predicament in larger terms because he had read all those authors. I want to have a mind like that."

Keep providing opportunities to think and good role models. Challenge students to think carefully about their assumptions by giving them interesting materials, questions, and alternatives. Don't just call in the cosmos, but question it.

Useful research has been conducted lately on learning styles and frames of intelligence. Read that research. The basic axiom to keep in mind is that students should think for themselves. Your job is to teach them how to think and to give them the necessary tools. Your students will be endlessly amazed at how intelligent they are; you do not need to show them how intelligent you are.

Calling in the cosmos means asking the big questions. Be careful, though, not to stereotype students' lives. Adolescents are prickly about condescension. Do not ask them questions that you would not ask an adult: What was your most embarrassing moment? How do you deal with family problems? Instead, ask students about issues that arise out of literature: When is it necessary to surrender? What is the use of solitude? How does language reveal character? What is the difference between forgiving and forgetting?

Even your least academic students want to discuss big ideas; you just need to explain the ideas more simply. Do not water down material for less academic students. They need more rigorous teaching, not less, because they are behind.

Every day, make thorough and precise lesson plans. But remember that you can always abandon your plans to take advantage of the teachable moment. Once my class was reading *King Lear,* and a thunderstorm crashed down just as we encountered the lines: "Blow, winds, and crack your cheeks. Rage, blow." I took the students outside, and we screamed Lear's lines into the storm. I love moments like that!

For the final calling in of the cosmos, I help students envision their own futures. During the last week in all my classes, my students write letters to themselves that I mail to them 10 years later. They can write about whatever they wish: predictions for the future, accounts of daily life, a list of friends. I suggest that they write down the most important knowledge that they possess. "What do you know that, if you didn't know it, would make you someone else?" Then I read a few letters that former students have written to me after they have received their 10-year-old letters.

This assignment affirms that students have important things to say at this stage of their lives—things that they will want to know 10 years from now. I am affirming the importance of the examined life.

Christine, as a beginning teacher you cannot reach all these goals right away. Even my most benign suggestions are fraught with dangers. For example, it sounds easy enough to explain to students why they ought to do something. But brand-new teachers often have no idea why they are doing something—beyond the fact that they have 180 days to fill. It takes a long time for teachers to develop the philosophical underpinnings for everything they do in the classroom.

Teaching thinking, creating communities, and engaging students in their own education are standards I have set for myself. But as I teach, I keep raising my standards. Joseph MacDonald, a professor at Brown University, helped me to clarify my thinking about that metaphor. Instead of my thinking of standards as ultimate goals, he suggested that I think of them as the banners held by the standard bearers at the head of an army. You never quite reach them, but they tell you where you are going, and they lead you forward.

You are not going into battle (though on some days teaching seems so). You are going into joy. For when you teach well, when classes sing, you will feel great jubilation. Treat your students as adults, walk beside them as they educate themselves, and they will respond with respect—even joy. They will lead you. I wish you a good journey.

Sincerely,
Margaret Metzger

## POSTNOTE

Survival in the classroom is usually very much on the mind of new teachers. For many, their first experiences as teachers truly test their mettle. But, overwhelmingly, teachers survive. They learn to cope and get past whatever blocks they encounter in their first experiences. That is the good news. The bad news is that too many of us settle in just a little further up the scale than survival—at "adequacy" or "competency." This author is interested in something more. She wants "excellence," and in this selection (the first part of a four-part article) she lays out some goals and strategies for teachers.

Our junior and senior high schools, which have been repeatedly identified as the soft underbelly of our educational system, are the places where many of our students, too, settle for adequacy. Many settle for even less, doing only what they are driven to do. As a twenty-five-year veteran of life in a demanding high school, Margaret Metzger tells us that we must be "standard bearers" for these children who have quit on themselves as students. There are few greater missions in education today.

## DISCUSSION QUESTIONS

1. What is your personal response to the author's call to move from competence to excellence?

2. Have you yourself been taught by teachers who could rally students mired in low expectations?

3. What teaching tips or perspectives in this article do you believe are of most value to you?

# Letter from a Teacher

John C. Crowley

Dear Bill:

Well, your baptism by fire is about over. You have passed through that vague state appropriately mislabelled as "Student Teacher." Soon you will return to the more familiar and secure world of the college campus.

I hope your teaching experience was of some value. Throughout the time we worked together I made repeated plans to sit down with you and have a long talk—a "tell it like it is" type session. Unfortunately, except for between-class chats and noontime gab sessions, our talks never did get down to the nitty-gritty. So, with due apologies for a letter instead of a talk, this will have to do.

If you leave here feeling to some degree satisfied and rewarded, accept these feelings. You have worked diligently and consistently. For your part you have a right to feel rewarded. Teaching offers many intangible bonuses; feeling satisfied when a class goes well is one of them. The day teaching no longer offers to you the feelings of satisfaction and reward is the day you should seriously consider another profession.

Mingled with these feelings is also one of discouragement. Accept this too. Accept it, learn to live with it, and be grateful for it. Of course certain classes flopped; some lesson plans were horror shows; and some kids never seemed to get involved or turned on. This is not a phenomenon experienced only by student teachers. We all encounter this. The good teacher profits

from it—he investigates the reasons for the failure and seeks to correct himself, his approach, or his students. And in so doing, the good teacher further improves and gets better.

Bad teachers develop mental calluses, blame it on the kids, and sweep the failures under the rug. Always be discouraged and unsatisfied; it's the trademark of a good, professional teacher.

I don't know if you plan to make teaching your career—perhaps, at this point, you don't know yourself—but if you do, I'm sure you will do well; you have the potential. In the event you do elect a teaching career, I would offer these suggestions:

1. Develop a philosophy for yourself and your job. Why do you teach? What do you expect of yourself and your students? Do not chisel this philosophy on stone. Etch it lightly in pencil on your mind, inspect it frequently. Do not be surprised that it changes—that can be a good sign. Be more concerned with the reasons for a change rather than the change itself. Unless you base your teaching on a foundation of goals and ideals, you are wasting time. If you as the teacher-model cannot show a solid basis of beliefs, how can you expect your student-imitators to develop any definite beliefs?

**TERMS TO NOTE**

Philosophy
Professional teacher

2. Do not be just "a teacher," be a professional teacher. Teaching is the most rewarding, demanding, and important job in the world. We deal with the minds of men and the future of the world. It is not a task to be taken lightly. Demand professionalism of yourself and your associates. Do not shut yourself up in a classroom, isolated from and ignorant of the real world. Be prepared to teach at any time, in any

John C. Crowley was a high school teacher in Massachusetts. He died shortly after the publication of this letter. "Letter from a Teacher" by John C. Crowley. From the *Massachusetts Teacher* (Sept.–Oct. 1970), pp. 2, 34, 38. Copyright 1970 by the Massachusetts Teachers Association. Reprinted by permission.

place, to anyone. Ferret out ignorance with the zeal of a crusader and the compassion of a saint. Teach as if the fate of mankind rested squarely upon your shoulders and you'll know, in part, what I mean.

3. Always be a learner. Never assume you know all the answers or enough material to teach your class. Read constantly. Do not become an encapsulated specialist. Vary the material. Talk to others. Most of all, learn to listen to your students . . . not to what they say but to what they mean.

A good teacher learns as much from his students as he teaches to them. Do not discourage dialogue. Do not be so dogmatic as to accept only your own views. Do not use the textbook as a mental crutch.

Any fool can break a book up into 180 reading assignments and still manage to keep one section ahead of the students, but such a fool should not assume the title of teacher. At best, he would be a grossly overpaid reading instructor.

4. Develop the feeling of empathy. Try to feel how the student feels. Do not lapse into the warm complacency of a seating chart, names without faces. Do not accept the cold facts of a rank book, marks without personality.

**TERM TO NOTE**
Empathy

See the girl in the second row, homework undone because her parents fought all night. She couldn't even sleep, let alone concentrate on homework. Does that deserve an "F"?

Or the boy in the back of the room. Bad teeth, poor complexion, shabby clothes. No known father, a promiscuous mother, and a cold-water flat in a bad part of town. Of course he acts up and appears rebellious; wouldn't you? How have we alleviated his problems by assigning detention time and writing a bad progress report? How does it feel to sit in a class day after day hungry, ill, knowing that when the last bell rings it will be back to the sewer?

Is it any wonder that Jacksonian Democracy, the English morality plays, or Boyle's Law leaves these kids cold? But if they are to eventually move into society we must reach them, and the first step comes when we, as teachers, understand them.

I am not advocating that you become a "softy." Do not rationalize every failure with some outside cause. But be prepared to evaluate a student on the basis of your understanding of him and his problems. A grade is something more than a mathematical total and an average. Before assigning a grade, look closely at the particular student and ask yourself, "Why?"

5. Finally, alluding to the misadventures of Don Quixote, I would counsel—"Do not be afraid of windmills!" As a conscientious, professional teacher you will find your path constantly bestraddled with windmills of one type or another.

These may come in the form of other teachers, guidance departments, administrators, department heads, school committees, parents, or heaven knows what. They will obstruct, criticize, belittle, and attack you for a variety of reasons and motives. If you think you are right, do not back down! Always be willing to go as far as necessary to defend your convictions and beliefs. Do not avoid experimentation for fear of mistakes or criticism!

If we accept the status quo and maintain a conservative view toward change, we will not progress. In fact, we'll probably regress. We have an obligation, as educators, to constantly seek better ways of doing things. If that means putting our own heads on the chopping block, so be it. Either we stand for something or we stand for nothing. If we stand for something it should be so important that any sacrifice to preserve and further it is worthwhile. And, as educators, we are under a moral and ethical responsibility to stand for something.

Well, I hope these words of advice have proved helpful. Repeating an earlier statement, you have a great deal of potential and I personally hope you put it to use as a teacher.

I know of no other job that compares with teaching. We need every promising candidate who comes along. It goes without saying of course that should you need a letter of recommendation I will be only too glad to supply it.

Having participated in your student teaching experience I also feel morally obliged to assist you should you, at some future date, require and want such assistance. It's there for the asking.

With confidence in the nature of man, I remain

Very truly yours,
Jack Crowley

## POSTNOTE

"With confidence in the nature of man, I remain . . ." This letter, one of the last Jack Crowley wrote before he died, is overflowing with one of life's rarest commodities—wisdom. His closing, though, speaks to a value that stands behind the huge edifice of education. "Confidence in the nature of man" captures the hope and conviction that must undergird the teacher's work. Without this confidence, teachers may find their goodwill eroding. The phrase also reminds us that as teachers, we must be dedicated to more than the status quo. We must try to bring human nature to a higher level.

## DISCUSSION QUESTIONS

1. What are your reactions to the suggestions Jack Crowley makes to Bill, the student teacher?

2. How would you feel if you received such a letter from your supervising teacher? Why?

3. What attitudes toward teaching and toward students does Jack Crowley reveal in this letter?

# Students

## PART TWO

Education is one of life's most complex activities. So much is involved. There are the knowledge, attitudes, values, and skills to be learned; there is the process of instruction; there is evaluation; there is the management of the learning environment. To teach well, to be an effective educator, demands so much of our attention that an essential element in the teaching-learning process may be lost: the student.

The entire purpose of teaching is to make some positive change in students. They are the main event, but sometimes we teachers lose focus. We become so involved in the knowledge to be conveyed or in the process of instruction that we often lose sight of our students. We need to remind ourselves continually that the entire enterprise of education fails if the student is ill served. And we need to remind ourselves constantly that each student has a different set of needs, preferences, and goals.

One thing that should help us stay attuned to the student is the fact that modern life regularly requires us all to become students. No longer is the term *student* reserved for a relatively few young people receiving formal education. With the explosion of education in the last quarter century, people continually move in and out of student status. A knowledge- and information-oriented society such as ours requires continuous education. Whether it is acquiring computer literacy or learning how to run cooperative learning groups, we all return to being students from time to time. Having to struggle with new information or trying to master a new skill may be the best thing we can do to improve our teaching.

# 12 Who Is This Child?

Robert D. Barr

During my spring vacation, I visited my grandson Sam's first-grade classroom in Eugene, Oregon—home of author Ken Kesey, the University of Oregon's Fighting Ducks, and a T-shirt that proudly proclaims, "Me Tarzan, Eugene." Eager to start the day, Sam and I traded a couple of high-fives and sallied forth. He carried his books and an authentic Mighty Morphin Power Ranger lunch box; I carried a note pad and wore a sappy grin. This was the essence of grandparenting: a bright spring day in Oregon and off to school, hand-in-hand with Sam.

On arrival, Sam threw down his things and yelled over his shoulder, "Watch my stuff," as he ran off to join his friends in a soccer game. Almost immediately, I felt a small arm slide around my waist. Surprised, I looked down into the face of a little girl. "Who is this child?" I wondered. She flashed me a ragged smile that was missing half a dozen teeth. "I am from Chicago," she said and buried her head in my side. Suddenly uneasy, I looked around for some other adult. Having served on teacher licensure boards in two states and having sat through a dozen or so hearings to revoke the certification of child molesters, I was well aware of the taboos governing interactions between old guys like me and this small child.

As I tried to disentangle myself, she looked up at me with huge, longing eyes. "We don't have a father in our family," she said in her small voice. Then, as if repeating from a script,

she whispered, "My father is a deadbeat dad. He ran away because he couldn't pay his bills." She blew her bangs up out of her eyes and sighed. "They found him, though. He is somewhere, I forgot . . . maybe in Portland, but I don't know where that is." She stared up at me with moist eyes. "But it's all right. My mom says we don't need him." Once again she burrowed into my side.

The longing and need of this small child caught me off guard. Her yearning for affection was almost palpable. And suddenly I knew this child—not her name or her address, but her identity. In her ragged dress, with her dirty fingernails, she carried the staggering weight of research predictability, of statistical probability. I had pored over the data far too long; I knew where she came from, where she was bound, and where her sad journey would end. I knew that a deep yearning for denied love can soon wither into anger—perhaps even hate—and that one generation will impose its tragic story on the next.

Was there even a chance that this small child would one day graduate from the University of Oregon School of Law and walk crisply into the world, clad in a Brooks Brothers pin-striped jacket and miniskirt, swinging an Armani briefcase? More likely, she was a teenage parent in the making. I could envision a burned-out, unemployed 28-year-old, recovering from a messy second divorce and pregnant with her third child. Yes, I thought, I knew this child.

Just then a bell rang, setting off a wild rush to classes. My little friend gave me a final squeeze, waved goodbye, and skipped away. Sam ran up laughing—and, after he had gathered his things, we walked hand-in-hand into the school.

Still troubled by my encounter with the little girl, I watched her up ahead as she turned into

At the time this article was written, Robert D. Barr was Professor of Secondary Education, Boise State University, Boise, Idaho. He is the co-author, with William H. Parrett, of *Hope at Last for At-Risk Youth* (Allyn and Bacon, 1995). Barr, Robert D., "Who Is This Child?" *Phi Delta Kappan*, January 1996. Copyright © 1996 by Phi Delta Kappa. Reprinted by permission of author and publisher.

a classroom. When I came abreast of that particular classroom door, I paused and looked in. What I saw was a teacher kneeling to hug the little girl and to say, "Melody, it's so good to see you! I'm so glad you made it to school today!" The teacher held the little girl at arm's length and gave her a thousand-watt smile that lit up the entire classroom. Then she took the little girl's hand and walked her to a desk. "Won't we have a great time today?" the teacher asked. "We'll paint today and sing—and of course we'll read some books." Bathed in the warmth of the teacher's care, the little girl seemed almost to glow.

Watching this touching tableau reminded me that researchers often jump to hasty conclusions, overgeneralizing from far too little data. I knew all the grim predictions that could be derived from the research literature, but I also knew the power of a good school and of caring and demanding teachers. I knew that schools could make a difference, could transform the lives of children, could overcome the deficiencies of the home and the dysfunctions of the family. I knew about resilient children and about the power of education, done well, to transform.

With a sigh of relief, I turned back to Sam, who was impatiently tugging at my hand. "Come on, Bob," he said. "We're gonna be late for class." With a final wave at the little girl, this 55-year-old researcher—now filled with hope—headed once again into a first-grade classroom.

## POSTNOTE

This brief, poignant article reminds us of the potential power of education to make a difference in the lives of children. While statistical norms and stereotypical images tempt us to form expectations that can lead to self-fulfilling prophecies, this article helps us to see that each child is an individual with potential to overcome the circumstances that place him or her at risk of not succeeding in life. For many of these children, education is their best chance to beat the odds and improve their lot in the world, but only if educators take it upon themselves to provide the extra care and love these children need.

## DISCUSSION QUESTIONS

1. The author uses the term resilient children. What do you think he means by it? What research can you find on the topic?

2. What are some of the factors that put children at risk for failure? What role can/should schools play in addressing these risk factors?

3. What did you learn from the way the teacher greeted Melody?

# 13

**CLASSIC** *Leaving No Child Behind*

Marian Wright Edelman

We are living at an incredible moral moment in history. Few human beings are blessed to anticipate or experience the beginning of a new century and millennium.

How will we say thanks for the life, for the earth, for the nation, and for the children God has entrusted to our care? What legacies, principles, values, and deeds will we stand for and send to the future through our children to their children and to a spiritually confused, balkanized, and violent world desperately hungering for moral leadership?

How will progress be measured over the next thousand years if we survive them? By the kill power and number of weapons of destruction we can produce and traffic at home and abroad, or by our willingness to shrink, indeed destroy, the prison of violence constructed in the name of peace and security?

By how many material things we can manufacture, advertise, sell, and consume, or by our rediscovery of more lasting non-material measures of success—a new Dow Jones for the purpose and quality of life in our families, neighborhoods, and national community? By how rapidly technology and corporate merger-mania can render human beings and human

work obsolete, or by a better balance between corporate profits and corporate caring for children, families, and communities?

By how much a few at the top can get at the expense of the many at the bottom and in the middle, or by our struggle for a concept of enough for all Americans? By the glitz, style, and banality of too much of our culture, or by the substance of our struggle to rekindle an ethic of caring, community, and justice in a world driven by money, technology, and weaponry?

The answers lie in the values we stand for and decisions and actions we take today. What an opportunity for good and evil we Americans personally and collectively hold in our hands as parents, citizens, public school leaders, and as titular world leader in the post-Cold War and post-industrial era on the cusp of the third millennium . . .

**TERM TO NOTE**

Values

A thousand years ago the United States was not even a dream. Copernicus and Galileo had not told us the earth was round or revolved around the sun. Gutenberg's Bible was not printed, Wycliffe had not translated it into English, and Martin Luther had not tacked his theses on the church door. The Magna Carta did not exist, Chaucer's and Shakespeare's tales had not been spun, and Bach's, Beethoven's, and Mozart's miraculous music had not been created to inspire, soothe, and heal our spirits. European serfs struggled in bondage while African empires flourished in independence. Native Americans peopled our land free of slavery's blight, and Hitler's Holocaust had yet to show the depths human evil can reach when good women and men remain silent or indifferent.

A thousand years from now, will civilization remain and humankind survive? Will America's

---

Marian Wright Edelman, founder and president of the Children's Defense Fund (CDF), has been an advocate for disadvantaged Americans for her entire professional career. Under her leadership, the Washington-based CDF has become a strong national voice for children and families. The mission of the Children's Defense Fund is to "Leave No Child Behind." Marian Wright Edelman's article is excerpted from *The State of America's Children Yearbook 1996*, published by the Children's Defense Fund. "Stand for Children: Leave No Child Behind," from *The State of America's Children Yearbook 1996*, Children's Defense Fund. Reprinted with permission.

dream be alive, be remembered, and be worth remembering? Will the United States be a blip or a beacon in history? Can our founding principle "that all men are created equal" and "are endowed by their Creator with certain inalienable rights" withstand the test of time, the tempests of politics, and become deed and not just creed for *every* child? Is America's dream big enough for every fifth child who is poor, every sixth child who is black, every seventh child who is Latino, and every eighth child who is mentally or physically challenged?

Protecting children is the moral litmus test of our humanity and the overarching moral challenge in our world and nation where millions of child lives are ravaged by the wars, neglect, abuse, and racial, ethnic, religious, and class divisions of adults. In the last decade, UNICEF reports, 2 million children have been killed, 4.5 million disabled, 12 million left homeless, more than 1 million orphaned or sundered from parents, and some 10 million have been traumatized by armed conflicts throughout the world.

In the United States since 1979, more than 50,000 children have been killed by guns in our homes, schools, and neighborhoods in a civil war on our own young. Although we are the world's leading military power, we stand by silent and indifferent as a classroomful of children are killed violently every two days from guns. About every day and a half, gun violence kills as many children as the children killed in the tragic Oklahoma City bombing.

In the richest nation in history, we appear unashamed that a child dies from poverty every 53 minutes, that children are the poorest group of Americans, and do not express outrage as political leaders of both parties propose policies to make them poorer. We talk about family values but turn our backs on real needs of families for jobs and decent wages and child care and health care. We tolerate a child welfare system that abuses and neglects children already abused and neglected by their families. While we bemoan a few child victims of abuse like Susan Smith's young sons and beautiful Elisa

Izquierdo in New York City, we do not mend our cracked child welfare system that lets an abused child die every seven hours.

How much child suffering, death, and neglect will it take for you, me, religious, civic, school, and political leaders to stand up and cry out "enough" with our hearts and voices and votes to protect our young who are our sacred trust and collective American future?

## A Mass Movement

When Jesus Christ invited little children to come unto him, He did not invite only rich, middle-class, white, male children without disabilities, from two-parent families, or our own children to come. He welcomed all children. There are no illegitimate children in God's sight. James Agee eloquently reminded: "In every child who is born under no matter what circumstances and of no matter what parents, the potentiality of the human race is born again, and in him, too, once more, and each of us, our terrific responsibility toward human life: toward the utmost idea of goodness, of the horror of terrorism, and of God."

Yet every day too many of us fail our terrific responsibility toward our own children and millions of other people's children who are America's and God's potentiality.

It is not just poor or minority children who are afflicted by the breakdown of moral, family, and community values today. The pollution of our airwaves, air, food, and water; growing economic insecurity among middle-class children and young families; rampant drug and alcohol abuse, teen pregnancy, and domestic violence among rich, middle-class, and poor alike; AIDS; random gun and terrorist violence; resurging racial intolerance in our places of learning, work, and worship; and the crass, empty materialism of too much of our culture threaten every American child.

Every day in America, 2,660 children are born into poverty and 27 die from poverty. And every day 7,962 children of all races and classes are reported abused or neglected, and three die from abuse; 15 die from firearms and 2,833 drop out of school; 2,700 get pregnant; and 790 are born at low birthweight. We are first in the world in military and health technology but 18th in the industrialized world in infant mortality.

But it is poor children who suffer most. What kind of country permits this? A poor one? An undemocratic one? An uncaring one? A foolish one? One that ignores the biblical injunction to "defend the poor and fatherless and do justice to afflicted and needy"?

Our failure to place children first as parents, communities, corporate, civic, cultural, educational, and political leaders is our Achilles' heel and will be our future undoing. Indeed the present unraveling of our family fabric is a portent of what is to come if we do not correct course and regain our moral moorings.

The stresses and strains of making a living leave too many parents too little time with their children. Too many affluent parents are more preoccupied with material than with eternal things—with fun rather than faithfulness in providing the family rituals, continuity, and consistent companionship children need to grow up healthy, caring, loving, and productive.

Parenting itself is not a valued calling and people who care for children get the least support in America. Too many neighbors look out just for themselves and take little or no interest in each other's children. Too many business people seem to forget they are parents and family members and treat children as consumers to whom they can market excessively violent, sexually charged messages and products they would not want their own children to see or use. And too many faith communities fail to provide the strong moral leadership parents and communities need to meet their shared responsibilities to children.

What you stand for and do now as educational leaders—and encourage our political leaders to stand for during the final years of the century—will shape our nation's fate and our children's futures in the next century and millennium. It is time to call the moral question about whether America truly values and will stand up for children not just with words but with work; not just with promises but with leadership and investment in child health, early childhood education, after-school programs, and family economic security; not just with a speech or photo opportunity, but with sustained positive commitment to meet every child's needs.

## POSTNOTE

This article by a lifelong advocate for children earns Classic status because it both outlines the problems and calls upon the nation to act. Marian Wright Edelman has for years been America's conscience for children's welfare. As the founder and president of the Children's Defense Fund, she has forcefully reminded Americans that, as a nation, we have turned a blind eye and a deaf ear to the worlds of many of our children, particularly our children of color. She has worked tirelessly with presidents, congressional representatives, governors, and bureaucrats to better children's lives. In this article, she once again appeals to our consciences. Although the United States is the richest country in the world, it has the highest poverty rate for children among industrialized countries. Our health care system permits millions of children to fall between the cracks. About a million verified cases of child abuse occur each year. Guns kill more children in America than in all of Europe. How can this be? Who is looking out for the children?

## DISCUSSION QUESTIONS

1. What reasons can you give for the sad state of so many children living in the United States?

2. What steps would you recommend to help remedy the problems experienced by children that Edelman identifies in the article?

3. Who besides Edelman can you identify as children's advocates? What actions have they taken to improve children's lives in America?

# 14

# Problem Students: The Sociocultural Roots

## D. Stanley Eitzen

Although many of today's students are a joy to work with in the classroom, some are not. Some children are angry, alienated, and apathetic. A few are uncooperative, rude, abrasive, threatening, and even violent. Some abuse drugs. Some are sexually promiscuous. Some belong to gangs. Some are sociopaths. Why are some children such problems to themselves, to their parents, to their teachers, and to the community? Is the cause biological—a result of flawed genes? Is the source psychological—a manifestation of personalities warped by harmful experiences? My strong conviction is that children are *not* born with sociopathic tendencies; problem children are socially created.

Now you might say, "Here we go again; another bleeding-heart liberal professor is going to argue that these problem children are not to blame—the system is." Well, you are partly right. I am politically liberal, and as a social scientist I embrace a theoretical perspective that focuses on the system as the source of social problems. However, I do recognize that, while human actors are subject to powerful social forces, they make choices for which they must be held accountable. But I also believe that it is imperative that we understand the social factors that influence behavior and impel a disproportionate number of children in certain social categories to act in socially deviant ways.

Children of this generation manifest more serious behavioral problems than children of a generation ago. I believe that four social forces account for the differences between today's young people and those of 15 years ago: the changing economy, the changing racial and ethnic landscape, changing government policies, and changing families. Moreover, these structural changes have taken place within a cultural milieu, and they combine with one another and with that culture to create the problem students that we face today. We must understand this sociocultural context of social problems in order to understand problem students and what we might do to help them.

## The Changing Economy

I begin with the assumption that families and individuals within them are shaped fundamentally by their economic situation, which, of course, is tied directly to work. I want to consider two related features of the changing economy: 1) the structural transformation of the economy and 2) the new forms of poverty.

### Transformation of the Economy

We are in the midst of one of the most profound transformations in history, similar in magnitude and consequence to the Industrial Revolution. Several powerful forces are converging to transform the U.S. economy by redesigning and redistributing jobs, exacerbating inequalities, reorganizing cities and regions, and profoundly affecting families and individuals. These forces are technological breakthroughs in microelectronics, the globalization of the economy, capital flight, and the shift from an economy based on the manufacture of goods to one based on

D. Stanley Eitzen is a sociologist and an emeritus professor at Colorado State University, Fort Collins. Eitzen, Stanley, "Problem Students: The Sociocultural Roots" from *Phi Delta Kappan*, April 1992. Copyright © 1992 by Phi Delta Kappa. Reprinted by permission of author and publisher.

information and services. I want to focus here on the significance of the last two factors.

The term *capital flight* refers to investment choices to maximize profit that involve the movement of corporate funds from one investment to another. This activity takes several forms: investment overseas, plant relocation within the U.S., and mergers and buyouts. These investment choices, which are directly related to the shift from manufacturing to services, have had dramatic and negative impacts on communities, families, and individuals.

Across the country such capital flight has meant the loss of millions of well-paid industrial jobs as plants have shut down and the jobs have migrated to other localities or the companies have shifted to other types of work. Similarly, there has been a dramatic downward tug on organized labor and wages. . . . Although many new jobs have been created by the shift to a service economy, . . . the large majority of these jobs are "bad" jobs—with much lower pay and fewer benefits than the manufacturing jobs that were lost. . . .

This is the first generation in American history to have more downward social mobility than upward. Downward mobility is devastating in American society, not only because of the loss of economic resources, but also because self-worth is so closely connected to occupational status and income. Individual self-esteem and family honor are bruised by downward mobility. Those affected feel the sting of embarrassment and guilt. Moreover, such a change in family circumstances impairs the chances of the children—both as young people and later as adults—to enjoy economic security and a comfortable lifestyle.

Some families find successful coping strategies to deal with their adverse situations. Others facing downward mobility experience stress, marital separation and divorce, depression, high levels of alcohol consumption, and spouse and child abuse. Children, so dependent on peer approval, often find the increasing gap in material differences between themselves and their peers

intolerable. This may explain why some try to become "somebody" by acting tough, joining a gang, rejecting authority, experimenting with drugs and sex, or running away from home.

## Poverty

One especially unfortunate consequence of capitalism is that a significant proportion of people—13.5% in 1990 and rising[1]—are officially poor. (Of course, many additional millions are just above the official government poverty line but poor nonetheless.) Poverty in the 1980s declined for some categories of the population (whites and the elderly) and *increased* for others: racial minorities, fully employed workers (the working poor), households headed by women, and children.

There is an important historical distinction that we must draw regarding the poor. Before 1973 the poor could hope to break out of poverty because jobs were generally available to those who were willing to work, even if the prospective workers were immigrants or school dropouts. The "new poor," on the other hand, are much more trapped in poverty because of the economic transformation. Hard physical labor is rarely needed in a high-tech society. Moreover, those few available unskilled jobs now offer low wages and few, if any, benefits or hopes of advancement. This situation diminishes the life chances of the working class, especially blacks, Hispanics, and other racial minorities who face the added burden of institutional racism.

Consequently, poverty has become more permanent, and we now have a relatively permanent category of the poor—the underclass. These people have little hope of making it economically in legitimate ways. This lack of opportunity explains, in part, their overrepresentation in the drug trade and in other criminal activities. Moreover, their hopelessness and alienation help us to understand their abuse of

---

[1]The proportion of Americans living in poverty reached 14.5% by 1995.—Eds.

alcohol and other drugs. All of these conditions stem from the absence of stable, well-paid jobs. A further consequence of this state of affairs is that it undermines the stability of families.

Poverty is especially damaging to children. Poor children are more likely to weigh less at birth, to receive little or no health care, to live in substandard housing, to be malnourished, and to be exposed to the health dangers of pollution. Let me provide one example of this last point. Poor children are much more likely than others to be exposed to lead from old paint and old plumbing fixtures and from the lead in household dust. Sixteen percent of white children and 55% of black children have high levels of lead in their blood, a condition that leads to irreversible learning disabilities and other problems. Children suffering from exposure to lead have an average I.Q. four to eight points lower than unexposed children, and they run four times the risk of having an I.Q. below 80.

We are currently experiencing a resurgence of racial antipathy in the U.S. This is clear in various forms of racial oppression and overt acts of racial hostility in communities, in schools and universities, and in the workplace. We can expect these hateful episodes to escalate further if the economy continues to worsen.

Racial and ethnic minorities—especially African-Americans, Native Americans, and Latinos—are also the objects of institutional racism, which keeps them disadvantaged. They do not fare as well in schools as white children, their performance on so-called objective tests is lower, the jobs they obtain and their chances for advancement are less good, and so on. They are negatively stereotyped and stigmatized. Their opportunities in this "land of opportunity" are drastically limited. They are blamed for their failures, even when the causes are structural. Is it any wonder that a disproportionate number of them are "problem" people?

## The Changing Racial Landscape

American society is becoming more racially and ethnically diverse. Recent immigration (both legal and illegal), especially by Latinos and Asians, accounts for most of this change. If current trends continue, Latinos will surpass African-Americans as the largest racial minority by the year 2020. In some areas of the country, most notably in California, the new immigration has created a patchwork of barrios, Koreatowns, Little Taipeis, and Little Saigons. These changes have also created competition and conflict over scarce resources and have led to battles over disputed turf among rival gangs and intense rivalries between members of the white working class and people of color. Moreover, communities, corporations, and schools have had difficulty providing the newcomers with the services they require because of the language and cultural barriers.

## The Changing Government Policy

One of the reasons that the disadvantaged are faring less well now than a generation ago is that government policies today are less helpful to them. At the very time that good jobs in manufacturing began disappearing, the government was reducing various forms of aid to those negatively affected by the changing economy. During the administrations of the last three presidents—Reagan, Bush, and Clinton—the funds for government programs designed for the economically disadvantaged have diminished by more than 25 percent. In 1996, for example, Congress passed legislation that: 1) ended the 61-year-old federal guarantee of cash assistance to people whose need makes them eligible; 2) reduced federal spending on food stamps by $23 billion over six years; 3) made legal immigrants ineligible for most federal benefits for their first five years in the

U.S.; and 4) demanded that each of the states require at least half of all single mothers on welfare be working by 2002 or lose some federal funds. The Urban Institute estimates that among the negative consequences of these policies, the number of children in poverty will increase by more than 10 percent, adding 1.1 million to the officially impoverished and worsening the conditions for millions already below the poverty line. The bitter irony is that these disadvantaged young people will end up, disproportionately, as society's losers, and most Americans will blame them for their failure.[2]

## The Changing Family

A number of recent trends regarding the family suggest a lessening of family influence on children. Let me note just a few. First, more and more families include two primary wage earners. This means, in effect, that more and more women are working outside the home. Over 50% of mothers with children under age 6 work outside the home, and about 70% of mothers with children between the ages of 6 and 17 are in the workplace. As a result, more and more children are being raised in families in which the parents have less and less time for them. This also means that more and more preschoolers are being cared for by adults who are not their parents—a situation that is not necessarily bad, though it can be.

Second, although the divorce rate has declined slightly since 1981, it remains at a historically high level. More than one million children each year experience the divorce of their parents, up from about 300,000 a year in 1950.

Third, it is estimated that 60% of today's 5-year-olds will live in a single-parent family before they reach the age of 18; 90% of them will

[2]This paragraph was updated by Professor Eitzen in January 1997.—Eds.

live with their mothers, which usually means that they will exist on a decidedly lower income than in a two-parent family. Research has shown that children from one-parent families differ significantly from the children of two-parent families with regard to school behaviors. Children from single-parent families are less likely to be high achievers; they are consistently more likely to be late, truant, and subject to disciplinary action; and they are more than twice as likely to drop out of school.

Fourth, about three million children between the ages of 5 and 13 have no adult supervision after school. One study has found that these latchkey children are twice as likely to use drugs as those who come home from school to find an adult waiting.

These trends indicate widespread family instability in American society—and that instability has increased dramatically in a single generation. Many of the children facing such unstable situations cope successfully. Others do not. Rejection from one or both parents may lead some children to act out in especially hostile ways. Low self-esteem can lead to sexual promiscuity or to alcohol or drug abuse. Whatever the negative response of the children, I believe that we can conclude that the victims of family instability are not completely to blame for their misbehaviors.

## The Cultural Milieu

The structural changes that I have noted occur within a cultural milieu. I will address only two aspects of that culture here: American values and the messages sent by the media. Let's begin with values. The highly valued individual in American society is the self-made person—that is, one who has achieved money, position, and privilege through his or her own efforts in a highly competitive system. Economic success, as evidenced by material possessions, is the most common indicator of who is and who is not successful. Moreover, economic success has come to be the common measure of self-worth.

Competition is pervasive in American society, and we glorify the winners. That is never truer than in economic competition. What about the losers in that competition? How do they respond to failure? How do we respond to them? How do they respond to ridicule? How do they react to the shame of being poor? How do the children of the poor respond to having less than their peers? How do they respond to social ostracism for "living on the other side of the tracks"? They may respond by working harder to succeed, which is the great American myth. Alternatively, they may become apathetic, drop out, tune out with drugs, join others who are also "failures" in a fight against the system that has rejected them, or engage in various forms of social deviance to obtain the material manifestations of success.

The other aspect of culture that has special relevance here is the influence of the media, particularly the messages purveyed by television, by the movies, and by advertising. These media outlets glamorize—among other things—materialism, violence, drug and alcohol use, hedonistic lifestyles, and easy sex. The messages children receive are consistent. They are bombarded with materialism and consumerism, with what it takes to be a success, with the legitimacy of violence, and with what it takes to be "cool."

Consider the following illustrations of the power of the media. Three-year-olds watch about 30 hours of television a week, and by the time an American child graduates from high school she or he will have spent more time in front of the television set than in class. Between the ages of 2 and 18 the average American child sees 100,000 beer commercials on television, and young people see on average some 12,000 acts of televised violence a year.

A study by the University of Pennsylvania's Annenberg School of Communications revealed that children watching Saturday morning cartoons in 1988 saw an average of 26.4 violent acts each hour, up from 18.6 per hour in 1980. Two of the conclusions by the authors of this study were that: 1) in these cartoons children see a mean and dangerous world in which people are not to be trusted and disputes are legitimately settled by violence, and 2) children who see so much violence become desensitized to it. The powerful and consistent messages from television are reinforced in the movies children watch and in the toys that are spun off from them.

Given these strong cultural messages that pervade society, is it any wonder that violence is widespread among the youth of this generation? Nor should we be surprised at children using alcohol, tobacco, and other drugs and experimenting with sex as ways to act "adult." Moreover, we should not be puzzled by those young people who decide to drop out of school to work so that they can buy the clothing and the cars that will bring them immediate status.

The current generation of young people is clearly different from earlier ones. Its members manifest problems that are structural in origin. Obviously, these social problems cannot be solved by the schools alone, although the community often blames the schools when these problems surface.

Since the problems of today's young people are largely structural, solving them requires structural changes. The government must create jobs and supply job training. There must be an adequate system for delivering health care, rather than our current system that rations care according to ability to pay. There must be massive expenditures on education to equalize opportunities from state to state and from community to community. There must be equity in pay scales for women. And finally, there must be an unwavering commitment to eradicating institutional sexism and racism. Among other benefits, such a strategy will strengthen families and give children both resources and hope.

The government must also exert more control over the private sector. In particular, corporations must pay decent wages and provide adequate benefits to their employees. In addition, corporations contemplating a plant shutdown or a dramatic layoff must go beyond the present 60-day notification, so that communities and families can plan appropriate coping strategies.

These proposals seem laughable in the current political climate, where politicians are timid and citizens seem interested only in reducing their tax burden. The political agenda for meeting our social problems requires political leadership that is innovative and capable of convincing the public that sacrifices to help the disadvantaged today will pay long-term benefits to all. Such leadership will emerge from a base of educated citizens who are willing to work to challenge others to meet societal goals.

At the community level, we must reorder our priorities so that human and humane considerations are paramount. This means that community leaders must make the difficult decisions required to help the disadvantaged secure decent jobs, job training, health care, housing, and education. Schools must be committed to the education of all children. This requires a special commitment to invest extra resources in the disadvantaged, by assigning the most creative and effective teachers to them and by providing a solid preschool foundation to children through such programs as Head Start. Most important, though, all children must be shown that the school and the community want them to succeed. Then the self-fulfilling prophecy we create will be a positive one.

**TERM TO NOTE**
Head Start

In 1990 Roger Wilkins presented a visual essay on the Public Broadcasting Service series "Frontline," titled "Throw-away People." This essay examined the structural reasons for the emergence in this past generation of a black underclass in Washington, D.C. His conclusion is appropriate for this discussion.

If [the children of the underclass] are to survive, America must come back to them with imagination and generosity. These are imperiled children who need sustained services to repair the injuries that were inflicted on them before they were born. Adults need jobs, jobs that pay more than the minimum wage, that keep families together, that make connections with the outside world, and [they need] the strength to grow. We can face the humanity of these people and begin to attack their problems, or we can continue to watch the downward rush of this generation, in the middle of our civilization, eroding the core of our conscience and destroying our claim to be an honorable people.

Every day teachers are confronted by the unacceptable behaviors of students. Obviously, they must be handled. I hope that this discussion will help teachers and administrators understand the complex sources of these objectionable and seemingly irrational behaviors. We must begin with an understanding of these problem children. From my point of view, such an understanding begins with underlying social factors. Most important, we must realize that social and economic factors have battered down certain children and increased the likelihood that they will fail and that they will behave in ways that we deplore.

Everyone needs a dream. Without a dream, we become apathetic. Without a dream, we become fatalistic. Without a dream and the hope of attaining it, society becomes our enemy. We educators must realize that some young people act in antisocial ways because they have lost their dreams. And we must realize that we as a society are partly responsible for that loss. Teaching is a noble profession whose goal is to increase the success rate for *all* children. We must do everything we can to achieve this goal. If not, we—society, schools, teachers, and students—will all fail.

## SOURCES AND RECOMMENDED READINGS

Eitzen, D. Stanley, and Maxine Baca Zinn, eds. *The Reshaping of America: Social Consequences of the Changing Economy.* Englewood Cliffs, N.J.: Prentice-Hall, 1989.

Ellwood, David T. *Poor Support: Poverty in the American Family.* New York: BasicBooks, 1988.

Levy, Frank. *Dollars and Dreams: The Changing American Income Distribution.* New York: Russell Sage Foundation, 1987.

MacLeod, Jay. *Ain't No Makin' It: Leveled Aspirations in a Low-Income Neighborhood.* Boulder, Colo.: Westview Press, 1987.

Mattera, Philip. *Prosperity Lost: How a Decade of Greed Has Eroded Our Standard of Living and Endangered Our Children's Future.* Reading, Mass.: Addison-Wesley, 1991.

Schorr, Lisbeth B., with Daniel Schorr. *Within Our Reach: Breaking the Cycle of Disadvantage.* New York: Doubleday, 1988.

## POSTNOTE

A century and a half ago, Alexis de Tocqueville (1805-1859), one of the most perceptive commentators on American politics and culture, wrote, "America is great because it is good. When it is no longer good, it will cease to be great."

The article you just read suggests two issues: First, adult Americans have turned away from their responsibilities as parents; and second, American children are growing up with values and behaviors that not only threaten their happiness but threaten the republic as well. All segments of society—homes, schools, churches, and communities—must devote more time and energy to our children. The stakes could not be higher.

## DISCUSSION QUESTIONS

1. Of the problems of youth identified by Eitzen, which is most serious? Why?

2. What strong and positive actions can schools take to help solve the problems of youth?

3. In what ways are schools limited in their efforts to help the young? What boundaries define schools' roles?

# Hostile Hallways

Jacqueline Woods

## 15

We all remember that high school classmate —the one whom all the other girls scorned. That girl had her phone number scrawled on every bathroom wall in the school. She endured heckles—and worse—as she walked down the halls. She suffered disapproving glances from students and teachers. In private, she wondered what she had done to deserve such treatment and if she could ever go anywhere or meet anyone without her reputation preceding her.

A 2001 American Association of University Women (AAUW) Educational Foundation report, *Hostile Hallways: Bullying, Teasing, and Sexual Harassment in School,* examines the results of a survey of public school students in grades 8–11. The survey sought to determine how physical and nonphysical harassment in school affects students' lives.[1] The report indicates that sexual harassment happens often, occurs right under teachers' noses, can begin in elementary school, and upsets both girls and boys.

## What Is Sexual Harassment?

In an employment context, courts generally recognize two types of sexual harassment: quid pro quo and hostile environment. These correspond to some aspects of the school environment as well. Quid pro quo harassment occurs when, for example, a teacher offers to raise a student's grade in exchange for a sexual act. By contrast,

**TERM TO NOTE**

Sexual harassment

Jacqueline Woods is executive director of the American Association of University Women, 1111 Sixteenth St., NW, Washington, DC 20036. From Jacqueline Woods, "Hostile Hallways," *Educational Leadership,* December 2001/January 2002, pp. 20–23. Reprinted with permission of the Association for Supervision and Curriculum Development. Copyright © 2002 by ASCD. All rights reserved.

hostile environment harassment in school includes continual sexual taunting.

The AAUW Educational Foundation survey defined sexual harassment as "unwanted and unwelcome sexual behavior that interferes with your life." Sexual harassment does not include behaviors that students like or want (for example, wanted kissing, touching, or flirting). Students responding to the survey reported hearing sexual comments or seeing graffiti, being called *gay* and *lesbian,* being touched or grabbed in a sexual way, being forced to kiss someone or perform other sexual acts, or being bullied or threatened because of their sexual orientation.

## How Pervasive and Damaging Is It?

The *Hostile Hallways* survey found that four out of five students (81 percent) experience some form of sexual harassment, and 18 percent of students fear being hurt by someone in their school. Girls and boys reported that harassment makes them feel embarrassed (53 and 32 percent respectively), self-conscious (44 and 19 percent), and less confident (32 and 16 percent). Harassed students said that they talk less in class and find it hard to pay attention. Not surprisingly, students change their behaviors to avoid harassers, including skipping school (16 percent), dropping out of a particular activity or sport (9 percent), and dropping courses (3 percent). Girls commented that being sexually harassed makes them feel "dirty—like a piece of trash," "terrible," "awkward," and "like a second-class citizen."

## Is Harassment Against the Law?

Title IX of the Education Amendments of 1972 prohibits sexual discrimination, including sexual

77

harassment, in federally funded schools, programs, and activities. States have also enacted statutes against sexual harassment in schools. The Illinois legislature, for example, passed a law requiring schools to create an anti-bullying policy.

The equal protection clause of the Fourteenth Amendment to the U.S. Constitution has been invoked by gay teens seeking relief from sexual harassment. In the case of *Nabozny v. Podlesny* (1996), Jamie Nabozny was constantly harassed, both verbally and physically, at school. Harassment included a mock rape in front of his classmates and a beating that left him with broken ribs. When he complained to a school official, Nabozny was told that he "had to expect that kind of stuff" because of his sexual orientation. Nabozny moved to another state to obtain a graduate equivalent degree, and, in 1995, he sued the school district in which he had been harassed. Judges for the 7th U.S. Circuit Court of Appeals ruled that they were "unable to garner any rational basis for permitting one student to assault another based on the victim's sexual orientation" (*Nabozny v. Podlesny*, 1996, at 458) and eventually awarded Nabozny $900,000 in damages.

In 1999, the U.S. Supreme Court ruled in *Davis v. Monroe County Board of Education* that a school district can be held liable in sexual harassment cases when the school knows about the harassment and fails to deal with it adequately. LaShonda Davis, a 5th grader, reported to her teacher that she had been harassed by a fellow 5th grader who attempted to fondle her breasts, said that he wanted to get in bed with her, and rubbed against her in a sexually suggestive way. Davis complained to three different teachers on several different occasions. One of the teachers told the principal, yet the harassment continued. Finally, Davis's mother pressed charges against the boy for sexual battery, to which he pled guilty. Throughout the ordeal, Davis's grades dropped, and she wrote a suicide note. Davis's mother sued the school district for deliberate indifference, alleging that the principal's inaction led to Davis's emotional distress.

## What Can Schools Do?

### Establish a Harassment Policy

As reported in *Hostile Hallways*, 70 percent of students know that their schools have a policy that prohibits sexual harassment, a significant increase from the 25 percent of students who knew about such policies when the first AAUW survey was conducted in 1993. One-third of students responded that their schools distribute booklets, handouts, and other literature on sexual harassment. The first step in stopping harassment must be to ensure that all schools have policies on how to handle sexual harassment and that all students understand those policies.

The U.S. Department of Education's Office of Civil Rights (1999) publishes guidelines for creating a school harassment policy. Guidelines include the following suggestions:

- Define the types of harassment—race, color, national origin, ethnicity, sex, disability, sexual orientation, and religion—covered by the policy.

- Identify the kinds of activities and sites where prohibited conduct could occur.

- Include standards for determining whether a hostile environment exists.

- Specify that the school will take remedial action to stop the harassment and prevent recurrence.

- Include specific procedures to address formal complaints of discrimination.

- Require staff to report harassment when they become aware of it.

- Prohibit retaliation against people who report harassment or participate in related proceedings.

The AAUW, in conjunction with the National Education Association, is forming a task force to develop an assessment tool that schools can use to evaluate the effectiveness of their sexual harassment policies.

A zero tolerance policy may indicate that the school does not accept sexual harassment. Such a policy may send mixed signals, however, about which behaviors are acceptable and which are prohibited. After all, sexual harassment does not include such behaviors as kissing or holding hands when these behaviors are welcomed. A zero tolerance policy may also create an adversarial relationship between students and faculty members that discourages students from reporting sexual harassment.

### Discuss Harassment with Students

Once an anti-harassment policy is in place, students need more than pamphlets to help them understand sexual harassment. Students need dialogue. They need an opportunity to ask questions about sexual harassment. They need an opportunity to talk to one another about how harassment makes them feel.

Students surveyed for *Hostile Hallways* described the inadequacy of many school programs to deal with harassment. One 8th grade girl suggested,

> Instead of popping in a video and expecting the problem to be solved, teachers need to take time out and talk to us. It's a problem that one video can't fix.

A 10th grade boy said, "They should help distinguish a little more the differences between sexual harassment and accidents."

Researcher Nan Stein (1999) emphasizes that schools have an obligation to be mindful of and vigilant about harassment and peer-on-peer interactions, but that they must also take advantage of "teachable moments"—incidents of inappropriate behavior that can spark students to discuss norms and behaviors in school.

### Enforce the Policy

Creating an anti-harassment policy and helping students understand harassment are not enough—the policy must be enforced. According to the AAUW survey, even though students know about school harassment policies, they report harassment in the hallways (71 percent of respondents had experienced physical harassment and 64 percent had experienced nonphysical harassment in the hallways), in the classroom (61 percent physical and 56 percent nonphysical), in the gym (45 percent physical and 43 percent nonphysical), and in the cafeteria (37 percent physical and 38 percent nonphysical). Teachers and administrators are present in all these public places and must be aware of harassment, yet victims—and harassers—know that, all too often, there will be no repercussions for harassing behavior.

All adults in schools, not just teachers, need training to identify sexual harassment and to enforce the school's sexual harassment policy. According to the Office of Civil Rights (1999),

> The lack of a strong, immediate response by a teacher or administrator who is aware of the harassment may be perceived by a student as approval of the activity or as an indication that the student deserves the harassment. (p. 25)

Several companies and individuals help schools train their staff to recognize and deal with sexual harassment.

### Create a Supportive Environment

An integral part of successfully preventing sexual harassment in schools includes providing an environment in which students feel comfortable talking to adults about harassment and in which students know that staff members will take their complaints seriously. Schools need to find a middle ground between a casual, laissez-faire attitude toward harassment that may be legally defined as neglectful and an intractable zero tolerance policy that causes staff members to overreact to questionable behaviors and that discourages conversation about the topic.

Some schools have created support groups as a forum for targeted students (gay and lesbian students, for example). Support groups send a message to everyone that such students are a respected part of the student body. Although support groups may cause an uproar in some communities, schools that encourage such groups will go a long way toward creating a supportive and safe environment for all students.

Everyone knows that sexual harassment takes place; in fact, many of us have felt its sting. Nevertheless, none of us should tolerate it. Our perceptions that "boys will be boys" and that "everyone gets teased" must change so that sexual harassment is seen as a serious issue—one that directly affects students' lives and learning.

## NOTE

1. From September through November 2000, Harris Interactive surveyed 2,064 public school students in grades 8–11; 1,559 students were surveyed during an English class, and 505 students were surveyed online. For more information about the survey, visit www.aauw.org.

## REFERENCES

*Davis v. Monroe County Board of Education,* 526 U.S. 629 (1999).

*Nabozny v. Podlesny,* 92 F.3d 446 (7th Cir. 1996).

Office of Civil Rights. (1999, January). *Protecting students from harassment and hate crime: A guide for schools.* Washington, DC: U.S. Department of Education. Available: www.ed.gov/PDFDocs/harassment.pdf

Stein, N. (1999). *Classrooms and courtrooms: Facing sexual harassment in K–12 schools.* New York: Teachers College Press.

Title IX of the Education Amendments, 20 U.S.C. § 1681 *et seq* (1972).

## POSTNOTE

The author ends her article urging educators to strike a middle ground between a casual, laissez-faire attitude and an intractable zero tolerance policy that might cause staff members to overreact and discourage conversation about the topic. "Striking a middle ground," while seeming reasonable, may be extremely difficult in the sex-saturated world of today's culture. Middle-school and high-school students in particular are extremely interested in sex, and most are coming into a time of peak sexual energy. Their sexual drives and curiosities are being catered to continually by much of their out-of-school life, such as popular music, TV sitcoms, movies, and Internet pornography. On the other hand, most educators and serious adults would agree that an active sex life or even a constant preoccupation with sex strongly interferes with being a successful student and preparing for adult responsibilities. Why not, then, a zero tolerance policy? Why not ban what used to be called "public displays of affection" in school? Why not ban crude language and sexual teasing? Why not have schools that run counter to the sexually toxic culture that has brought many students HIV and other STDs, unwanted pregnancies, and heartbreaking affairs? Why not?

## DISCUSSION QUESTIONS

1. Did you experience "hostile hallways" in your school experience?

2. Do you agree with the recommendations of the AAUW? Why or why not?

3. What sort of school policies vis-à-vis adolescent sexual behavior, language, and dress do you think educators should adopt?

# How to Create Discipline Problems

## M. Mark Wasicsko and Steven M. Ross

## 16

Creating classroom discipline problems is easy. By following the ten simple rules listed you should be able to substantially improve your skill at this popular teacher pastime.

1. *Expect the worst from kids.* This will keep you on guard at all times.

2. *Never tell students what is expected of them.* Kids need to learn to figure things out for themselves.

3. *Punish and criticize kids often.* This better prepares them for real life.

4. *Punish the whole class when one student misbehaves.* All the other students were probably doing the same thing or at least thinking about doing it.

5. *Never give students privileges.* It makes students soft and they will just abuse privileges anyway.

6. *Punish every misbehavior you see.* If you don't, the students will take over.

7. *Threaten and warn kids often.* "If you aren't good, I'll keep you after school for the rest of your life."

8. *Use the same punishment for every student.* If it works for one it will work for all.

9. *Use school work as punishment.* "Okay, smarty, answer all the questions in the book for homework!"

10. *Maintain personal distance from students.* Familiarity breeds contempt, you know.

We doubt that teachers would deliberately follow any of these rules, but punishments are frequently dealt out without much thought about their effects. In this article we suggest that many discipline problems are caused and sustained by teachers who inadvertently use self-defeating discipline strategies. There are, we believe, several simple, concrete methods to reduce classroom discipline problems.

## Expect the Best from Kids

That teachers' expectations play an important role in determining student behavior has long been known. One author remembers two teachers who, at first glance, appeared similar. Both were very strict, gave mountains of homework, and kept students busy from the first moment they entered the classroom. However, they differed in their expectations for students. One seemed to say, "I know I am hard on you, but it is because I know you can do the work." She was effective and was loved by students. The other conveyed her negative expectations, "If I don't keep these kids busy they will stab me in the back." Students did everything they could to live up to each teacher's expectations. Thus, by conveying negative attitudes toward students, many teachers create their own discipline problems.

A first step in reducing discipline problems is to demonstrate positive expectations toward

**TERMS TO NOTE**

Teachers' expectations

Discipline problems

M. Mark Wasicsko is currently dean of the College of Education at Eastern Kentucky University. Steven M. Ross is Executive Director at The Center for Research in Educational Policy (CREP) and is a professor of Educational Psychology and Research at The University of Memphis. From M. Mark Wasicsko and Steven M. Ross, "How to Create Discipline Problems," *The Clearing House*, May/June 1994, pp. 248–251. Reprinted with permission of the Helen Dwight Reid Educational Foundation. Published by Heldref Publications, 1319 Eighteenth Street, NW, Washington, DC, 20036-1802. Copyright © 1994.

students. This is relatively easy to do for "good" students but probably more necessary for the others. If you were lucky, you probably had a teacher or two who believed you were able and worthy, and expected you to be capable even when you presented evidence to the contrary. You probably looked up to these teachers and did whatever you could to please them (and possibly even became a teacher yourself as a result). Now is the time to return the favor. Expect the best from *each* of your students. Assume that *every* child, if given the chance, will act properly. And, most important, if students don't meet your expectations, *don't give up*! Some students will require much attention before they will begin to respond.

## Make the Implicit Explicit

Many teachers increase the likelihood of discipline problems by not making their expectations about proper behavior clear and explicit. For example, how many times have you heard yourself saying, "Now class, BEHAVE!"? You assume everyone knows what you mean by "behave." This assumption may not be reasonable. On the playground, for example, proper behavior means running, jumping, throwing things (preferably balls, not rocks), and cooperating with other students. Classroom teachers have different notions about proper behavior, but in few cases do teachers spell out their expectations carefully. Sad to say, most students must learn the meaning of "behave" by the process of elimination: "Don't look out the window. . . . Don't put hands on fellow students. . . . Don't put feet on the desk . . . don't . . . don't . . . don't. . . ."

A preferred approach would be to present rules for *proper* conduct on the front end (and try to phrase them positively: "Students should . . ."). The teacher (or the class) could prepare a poster on which rules are listed. In that way, rules are clear, explicit, and ever present in the classroom. If you want to increase the likelihood that rules will be followed, have students help make the rules. Research shows that when students feel responsible for rules, they make greater efforts to live by them.

## Rewards, Yes! Punishments, No!

A major factor in creating classroom discipline problems is the overuse of punishments as an answer to misbehavior. While most teachers would agree with this statement, recent research indicates that punishments outweigh rewards by at least 10 to 1 in the typical classroom. The types of punishments identified include such old favorites as The Trip to the Office and "Write a million times, 'I will not. . . .'" But punishments also include the almost unconscious (but frequent) responses made for minor infractions: the "evil eye" stare of disapproval and the countless pleas to "Face front," "Stop talking," "Sit down!" and so on.

Punishments (both major and minor) have at least four consequences that frequently lead to increased classroom disruption: 1) Punishment brings attention to those who misbehave. We all know the adage, "The squeaky wheel gets greased." Good behavior frequently leaves a student nameless and unnoticed, but bad behavior can bring the undivided attention of the teacher before an audience of classmates! 2) Punishment has negative side effects such as aggression, depression, anxiety, or embarrassment. At the least, when a child is punished he feels worse about himself, about you and your class, or about school in general. He may even try to reduce the negative side effects by taking it out on another child or on school equipment. 3) Punishment only temporarily suppresses bad behavior. The teacher who rules with an iron ruler can have students who never misbehave in her presence, but who misbehave the moment she leaves the room or turns her back. 4) Punishment disrupts the continuity of your lessons and reduces the time spent on productive learning. These facts, and because punishments are usually not premeditated (and frequently do not address the real problems of misbehavior such as boredom, frustration, or physical discomfort), usually work to increase classroom discipline problems rather than to reduce them.

In view of these factors, the preferred approach is to use rewards. Rewards bring attention to *good* behaviors: "Thank you for being prepared." Rewards provide an appropriate model for other students, and make students feel positive about themselves, about you, and about your class. Also, reinforcing positive behaviors reduces the inclination toward misbehavior and enhances the flow of your lesson. You stay on task, get more student participation, and accentuate the correct responses.

## Let the Punishment Fit the Crime

When rewards are inappropriate, many teachers create discipline problems by using short-sighted or ineffective punishments. The classic example is the "whole class punishment." "Okay, I said if anyone talked there would be no recess, so we stay in today!" This approach frustrates students (especially the ones who were behaving properly) and causes more misbehavior.

Research indicates that punishments are most effective when they are the natural consequences of the behavior. For example, if a child breaks a window, it makes sense to punish him with clean-up responsibilities and by making him pay for damage. Having him write 1,000 times, "I will not break the window," or having him do extra math problems (!) does little to help him see the relationship between actions and consequences.

In reality, this is one of the hardest suggestions to follow. In many cases, the "natural consequences" are obscure ("Okay, Steve, you hurt Carlton's feelings by calling him fat. For your punishment, you will make him feel better."). So, finding an appropriate punishment is often difficult. We suggest that after racking your brain, you consult with the offenders. They may be able to come up with a consequence that at least appears to them to be a fit punishment. In any case, nothing is lost for trying.

## If You Must Punish, Remove Privileges

In the event that there are no natural consequences that can serve as punishments, the next best approach is to withdraw privileges. This type of punishment fits in well with the actual conditions in our society. In "real life" (located somewhere outside the school walls) privileges and responsibilities go hand in hand. People who do not act responsibly quickly lose freedoms and privileges. Classrooms provide a great opportunity to teach this lesson, but there is one catch: *There must be privileges to withdraw!* Many privileges already exist in classrooms and many more should be created. For example, students who finish their work neatly and on time can play an educational game, do an extra credit math sheet, work on homework, or earn points toward fun activities and free time. The possibilities are limitless. The important point, however, is that those who break the rules lose out on the privileges.

## "Ignor"ance Is Bliss

One of the most effective ways to create troubles is to reward the very behaviors you want to eliminate. Many teachers do this inadvertently by giving attention to misbehaviors. For example, while one author was observing a kindergarten class, a child uttered an expletive after dropping a box of toys. The teachers quickly surrounded him and excitedly exclaimed, "That's nasty! Shame! Shame! Don't ever say that nasty word again!" All the while the other kids looked on with studied interest. So by lunch time, many of the other students were chanting, "... (expletive deleted) ..." and the teachers were in a frenzy!

Teachers create similar problems by bringing attention to note passing, gum chewing, and countless other minor transgressions. Such problems can usually be avoided by ignoring minor misbehaviors and, at a later time, talking to the student individually. Some minor misbehavior is probably being committed by at least one student during every second you teach! Your choice is to spend your time trying to correct (and bring attention to) each one *or* to go about the business of teaching.

## Consistency Is the Best Policy

Another good way to create discipline problems is to be inconsistent with rules, assignments, and punishments. For example, one author's daughter was given 750 math problems to complete over the Christmas holidays. She spent many hours (which she would rather have spent playing with friends) completing the task. As it turned out, no one else completed the assignment, so the teacher extended the deadline by another week. In this case, the teacher was teaching students that it is all right to skip assignments. When events like this recur, the teacher loses credibility and students are taught to procrastinate, which they may continue to do throughout their lives.

Inconsistent punishment has a similar effect. By warning and rewarning students, teachers actually cultivate misbehavior. "The next time you do that, you're going to the office!" Five minutes pass and then, "I'm warning you, one more time and you are gone!" And later, "This is your last warning!" And finally, "Okay, I have had it with you, go stand in the hall!" In this instance, a student has learned that a punishment buys him/her a number of chances to misbehave (she/he might as well use them all), and that the actual punishment will be less severe than the promised one (not a bad deal).

To avoid the pitfalls of inconsistency, mean what you say, and, when you say it, follow through.

## Know Each Student Well

Discipline problems can frequently be caused by punishing students we intended to reward and vice versa. When a student is told to clean up the classroom after school, is that a reward or punishment? It's hard to tell. As we all know, "One person's pleasure is another's poison."

One author remembers the difficulty he had with reading in the fourth grade. It made him so anxious that he would become sick just before reading period in the hope that he would be sent to the clinic, home, or anywhere other than to "the circle." One day, after helping the teacher straighten out the room before school, the teacher thanked him with, "Mark, you've been so helpful, you can be the first to read today." The author made sure he was never "helpful" enough to be so severely punished again.

The opposite happens just as often. For example, there are many class clowns who delight in such "punishments" as standing in the corner, leaving the room, or being called to the blackboard. The same author recalls having to stand in the school courtyard for punishment. He missed math, social studies, and English, and by the end of the day had entertained many classmates with tales of his escapades.

The key to reducing discipline problems is to know your students well; know what is rewarding and what is punishing for each.

## Use School Work as Rewards

One of the worst sins a teacher can commit is to use school work as punishments. There is something sadly humorous about the language arts teacher who punishes students with, "Write 1,000 times, I will not. . . ." or the math teacher who assigns 100 problems as punishment. In cases like these we are actually punishing students with that which we want them to use and enjoy! Teachers can actually reduce discipline problems (and increase learning) by using their subjects as rewards. This is done in subtle and sometimes indirect ways, through making lessons meaningful, practical, and fun. If you are teaching about fractions, bring in pies and cakes and see how fast those kids can learn the difference between ½, ¼, and ⅛. Reading teachers should allow free reading as a reward for good behavior. Math teachers can give extra credit math sheets (points to be added to the next test) when regular assignments are completed. The possibilities are endless and the results will be less misbehavior and a greater appreciation for both teacher and subject.

## Treat Students with Love and Respect

The final suggestion for reducing discipline problems is to treat students kindly. It is no secret that people tend to respond with the same kind of treatment that they are given. If students are treated in a cold or impersonal manner, they are less likely to care if they cause you grief. If they are treated with warmth and respect they will want to treat you well in return. One of the best ways to show you care (and thus reduce discipline problems) is to surprise kids. After they have worked particularly hard, give them a treat. "You kids have worked so hard you may have 30 minutes extra recess." Or have a party one day for no good reason at all. Kids will come to think, "This school stuff isn't so bad after all!" Be careful to keep the surprises unexpected. If kids come to expect them, surprises lose their effectiveness. Recently, one

author heard a student pay a teacher the highest tribute. He said, "She is more than just a teacher; she is our friend." Not surprisingly, this teacher is known for having few major discipline problems.

## Final Thoughts

When talking about reducing discipline problems, we need to be careful not to suggest that they can or should be totally eliminated. When children are enthusiastic about learning, involved in what they are doing, and allowed to express themselves creatively, "discipline problems" are apt to occur. Albert Einstein is one of numerous examples of highly successful people who were labeled discipline problems in school. It was said of Einstein that he was "the boy who knew not merely which monkey wrench to throw in the works, but also how best to throw it." This led to his expulsion from school because his "presence in the class is disruptive and affects the other students." For dictators and tyrants, robot-like obedience is a major goal. For teachers, however, a much more critical objective is to help a classroom full of students reach their maximum potential as individuals.

The theme of this article has been that many teachers create their own discipline problems. Just as we teach the way we were taught, we tend to discipline with the same ineffectual methods that were used on us. By becoming aware of this and by following the simple suggestions presented above, learning and teaching can become more rewarding for all involved.

## POSTNOTE

A friend of ours, Ernie Lundquist, claims that as a student he actually saw a sign on his principal's door that read, "The beatings will continue until the morale improves." While over the years Ernie has not proved to be a particularly reliable source in these matters, his reported sign-sighting underlines the point that student misbehavior often brings out the very worst in educators. In dealing with disruptive, misbehaving students, we who are supposed to stand for the use of intelligence, compassion, and imagination all too often demonstrate stupidity, insensitivity, and a complete lack of imagination.

The authors of this essay take the problem and turn it inside out, suggesting how we can create discipline problems for ourselves. But the real answer they offer us, and one the teacher frequently forgets in the heat of dealing with a discipline problem, is to *be creative!* We expect creativity from our students. Why not show a little in dealing with our discipline problems?

## DISCUSSION QUESTIONS

1. Which of the authors' "ten simple rules" have you seen demonstrated most frequently in our schools?

2. What do you believe is the central message of this article?

3. What, in your judgment, are the three most practical suggestions offered by the authors? Why?

# At Risk for Abuse: A Teacher's Guide for Recognizing and Reporting Child Neglect and Abuse

Dennis L. Cates, Marc A. Markell, and Sherrie Bettenhausen

In 1992, 2.9 million children were reported as suspected victims of abuse or neglect, an increase of 8% from 1991 (Children, Youth, & Families Department [CYFD], 1993). The exact number of children who are abused is, of course, difficult to determine because many cases of abuse go unreported and the definition of abuse varies from state to state (Winters Communication [WCI], 1988). Not only does the definition of abuse differ among states, but professionals also define abuse in different ways (Pagelow, 1984). Additional reasons for the difficulty in determining an accurate rate is that there may be a failure to recognize and report child abuse among professionals. Giovannoni (1989) stated that the failure to uncover child abuse and neglect is generally a result of three factors: a) failure to detect injury caused by abuse, particularly when parents use different medical treatment facilities each time or do not seek medical treatment; b) failure to recognize the indicators of abuse and neglect, especially for middle- and upper-income families; and c) failure to report

**TERM TO NOTE**
Child abuse

At the time this article was written, Dennis L. Cates was an assistant professor in Programs in Special Education at the University of South Carolina in Columbia and Marc A. Markell was an associate professor in the Department of Special Education at St. Cloud State University in St. Cloud, Minnesota. Sherrie Bettenhausen is a professor in the Special Education Department of the University of Charleston. Dennis L. Cates, Marc A. Markell, and Sherri Bettenhausen, "At Risk for Abuse: A Teacher's Guide for Recognizing and Reporting Child Neglect and Abuse," from *Preventing School Failure*, Vol. 39, No. 2, Winter 1995. Reprinted by permission of the authors.

the case to the appropriate agency when injury is detected and recognized as abuse or neglect.

Although exact numbers for children who are abused are not available, it is known that an alarming number of children are abused each year. These children are in our classrooms throughout the United States.

Child abuse can lead to the development of a full range of problems in children, from poor academic performance and socialization to a variety of physical and cognitive disabilities. Because children are required to attend school, teachers and other educators are faced with the responsibility of maintaining a protective and vigilant posture in relation to their students' well-being.

Studies have shown that children with disabilities are at greater risk for abuse and neglect than are nondisabled children (Ammerman, Lubetsky, Hersen, & Van Hasselt, 1988). Meier and Sloan (1984) suggested that "most certifiably abused children have been identified as suffering from various developmental handicaps" (p. 247). They further stated that "it is seldom clear whether or not the handicapping conditions are a result of inflicted trauma or, because of a misreading of the child's abilities by parents, such disappointing delays precipitate further abuse" (pp. 247–248). Blacher (1984) suggested that children with disabilities are more likely to supply the "trigger mechanism" for abuse or neglect. It has further been indicated that parents who abuse often describe their children as being backward, hyperactive, continually crying, or difficult to control.

The premise that a disability, developmental delay, or problem adjusting to the school environment may be directly linked to an abusive home environment requires that educators must be especially vigilant in dealing with those children who are at risk for the development of educational disabilities or poor school performance. Because many children will not report abuse directly, teachers need to be aware of specific behavioral and physical indicators that may indicate that abuse has occurred (Parent Advocacy for Educational Rights [PACER], 1989). The purpose of this article is to provide teachers with potential indicators of abuse, guidelines in dealing with child abuse in at-risk children, and information related to their legal responsibilities in reporting suspected child abuse.

## Definitions and Extent of the Problem

The Child Abuse Prevention and Treatment Act of 1974 defines child abuse and neglect as follows:

> the physical or mental injury, sexual abuse or exploitation, negligent treatment, or maltreatment of a child under the age of eighteen, or the age specified by the child protection law of the state in question, by a person who is responsible for the child's welfare under the circumstances which indicate that the child's health or welfare is harmed or threatened thereby (42 U.S.C. § 5102).

Maltreatment of a child can be further described in terms of neglect and physical, verbal, emotional, and sexual abuse.

Neglect typically involves a failure on the part of a parent, guardian, or other responsible party to provide for the child's basic needs, such as food, shelter, medical care, educational opportunities, or protection and supervision. Further, neglect is associated with abandonment and inadequate supervision (Campbell, 1992).

Verbal abuse may involve excessive acts of derision, taunting, teasing, and mocking. Verbal abuse also involves the frequent humiliation of the child as well as a heavy reliance on yelling to convey feelings. Physical abuse can involve shaking, beating, or burning.

Emotional abuse is a pattern of behavior that takes place over an extended period of time, characterized by intimidating, belittling, and otherwise damaging interactions that affect a child's emotional development (PACER, 1989). It may be related to an intent to withhold attention or a failure to provide adequate supervision, or relatively normal living experiences. Sensory deprivation and long periods of confinement are also related to emotional abuse. Emotional abuse is very difficult to define or categorize.

Sexual abuse of children is also referred to as child sexual abuse and child molesting. It is typically defined in terms of the criminal laws of a state and involves intent to commit sexual acts with minors or to sexually exploit children for personal gratification (Campbell, 1992). Sexual intercourse need not take place and, in fact, is rare in prepubertal children. Sexual abuse involves coercion, deceit, and manipulation to achieve power over the child (PACER, 1989).

In Table 1, we provide possible physical and behavioral indicators of neglect and physical, emotional, and sexual abuse. A child who persistently shows several of these characteristics *may* be experiencing the symptoms of abuse or neglect.

It is important to note that the physical and behavioral indicators of neglect and emotional, sexual, and physical abuse *suggest* or *indicate* that abuse *may* have taken place. They *do not prove* that abuse has occurred and may be indicators of other situations happening in the child's life. Additionally, educators need to be cognizant of the fact that children who are motorically delayed or impaired may be prone to accidents and as a result have bruises, scrapes, cuts, or other minor injuries. This may also be true of children with severely limited vision. Children with diagnosed medical conditions may develop symptoms that result in a change

**TERMS TO NOTE**

Physical indicators

Behavioral indicators

| PHYSICAL INDICATORS | BEHAVIORAL INDICATORS |
|---|---|
| *Emotional Abuse and Neglect* | |
| ■ Height and weight significantly below age level<br>■ Inappropriate clothing for weather, scaly skin<br>■ Poor hygiene, lice, body odor<br>■ Child left unsupervised or abandoned<br>■ Lack of a safe and sanitary shelter<br>■ Unattended medical or dental needs<br>■ Developmental lags<br>■ Habit disorders | ■ Begging or stealing food<br>■ Constant fatigue<br>■ Poor school attendance<br>■ Chronic hunger<br>■ Dull, apathetic appearance<br>■ Running away from home<br>■ Child reports that no one cares for/looks after him/her<br>■ Sudden onset of behavioral extremes (conduct problems, depression) |
| *Physical Abuse* | |
| ■ Frequent injuries such as cuts, bruises, or burns<br>■ Wearing long sleeves in warm weather<br>■ Pain despite lack of evident injury<br>■ Inability to perform fine motor skills because of injured hands<br>■ Difficulty walking or sitting | ■ Poor school attendance<br>■ Refusing to change clothes for physical education<br>■ Finding reasons to stay at school and not go home<br>■ Frequent complaints of harsh treatments by parents<br>■ Fear of adults |
| *Sexual Abuse* | |
| ■ Bedwetting or soiling<br>■ Stained or bloody underclothing<br>■ Venereal disease<br>■ Blood or purulent discharge from genital or anal area<br>■ Difficulty walking or sitting<br>■ Excessive fears, clinging | ■ Unusual, sophisticated sexual behavior/knowledge<br>■ Sudden onset of behavioral extremes<br>■ Poor school attendance<br>■ Finding reasons to stay at school and not go home |

**TABLE 1**
Physical and Behavioral Indicators of Possible Neglect and Abuse

of demeanor or physical appearance. It is important that teachers who serve these children become familiar with the child's condition and be well acquainted with the child's family. Frequent meetings, by telephone and in person, will assist the teacher in keeping up to date with changing medical conditions and aid in monitoring changes in family life patterns.

A teacher who is equipped with knowledge of the symptoms of child abuse and neglect and the characteristics of the child and the family will be able to better determine whether an at-risk learner or child with a disability is a victim of abuse.

## Legal Obligations

Children who are at risk for developmental delays are at greater risk for child abuse than children who are not. Teachers who work with these students should, therefore, be aware of their responsibilities relative to child abuse and neglect.

Child abuse cannot be legally ignored by school officials. Teachers and administrators are required by law in all 50 states to report suspected child abuse (Fossey, 1993; Trudell & Whatley, 1988). In most jurisdictions, it is a criminal offense for a person to fail to report abuse when he or she is required by law to do so (Fossey, 1993). Therefore, failure to act may result in the filing of criminal charges or civil suits. The courts have also ruled against teachers for delaying their actions (McCarthy & Cambron-McCabe, 1992). The possibility of criminal or civil proceedings may give many teachers pause and result in undue anxiety or overreaction to the problem. Educators must, therefore, become aware of their legal and administrative responsibilities.

The state laws governing the reporting of child abuse generally require teachers, doctors, school counselors, nurses, dentists, and police, to name a few, to report suspected child abuse to those human services agencies responsible for child welfare. Generally, teachers are required only to have a reasonable suspicion that child abuse has occurred before they are required to report it. Reasonable suspicion suggests that one is relieved of the responsibility of researching a case or of having specific facts related to the incidence of abuse. Given teachers' training in child behavior and their daily contact with children, they are in a position to recognize unusual circumstances. Exercising prudence in reporting suspected abuse will generally protect the teacher from criminal or civil action. Persons who report abuse and neglect *in good faith* to the

appropriate state agency are immune from civil liability (Fossey, 1993). Laws vary from state to state in this regard, however.

Reporting laws in all states give final authority to investigate abuse charges to agencies other than the schools (Fossey, 1993). The advantage of reporting suspected abuse to agencies other than the school lies in the fact that the burden of gathering facts does not rest with the school. These agencies can research each case objectively and determine the need for action. Teachers may report child abuse to law enforcement officials; however, most states require them to report to local service agencies such as children's protective services, child abuse hotlines, local welfare departments, local social service agencies, public health authorities, school social workers, nurses, or counselors. In extreme cases, teachers may be required to report cases to hospital emergency rooms. Questions often arise, however, about the procedures for reporting abuse.

Should teachers report suspected abuse directly to the appropriate human service agency or to their building principal or immediate supervisor? These questions may be difficult to answer if specific policies and procedures have not been outlined. If no policy exists, and a teacher reports suspected abuse to the principal, and the principal fails or refuses to report the case to the proper authorities, both teacher and principal may be subject to legal action. In such a case, a teacher may be held responsible depending upon specific circumstances involved.

A specific policy or procedure for reporting abuse should protect the teacher from legal liability if those procedures are followed. A policy requiring a teacher to report to the principal or school counselor relieves the teacher of the need to second-guess the system. Teachers are encouraged to familiarize themselves with existing law as well as district policies related to child abuse. If policies do not exist or are not clear, teachers should work through their professional organizations to help promote institutionalization of such policies.

McCarthy and Cambron-McCabe (1992) suggest that low levels of reporting by teachers may be related to the lack of clearly defined administrative policy. Additionally, they recommend the development of in-service programs to acquaint teachers with their legal responsibilities as well as the signs of abuse.

Even though specific laws may require the person suspecting abuse to report specific information, the following suggestions from PACER (1989), CYFD (1992), and WCI (1988) should answer many questions a teacher may have concerning the reporting of suspected abuse.

1. *To whom should I report suspected child abuse?* If the teacher suspects that a child has been abused, she or he must report the suspected abuse to the local social service agency, the local police, or the local county sheriff's department. Reporting the suspected abuse to another teacher or the school principal may not be enough to fulfill the requirements of mandatory reporting.

2. *Should I tell the parents or alleged abuser of my suspicion of child abuse?* The teacher should not disclose the suspicion of abuse or neglect of a child to either the parents, the caregiver, or the alleged perpetrators. The teacher should report the suspected abuse to the local social service agency, the local police, or the county sheriff's department.

3. *What should I report?* The teacher should report the following information (if known):

   ▶ identifying information about the child (name, age, grade, address, and names of parents)

   ▶ name of the person responsible for the abuse

   ▶ where the alleged abuse took place

   ▶ description of the child, any relevant statements made by the child, and any observations made

   ▶ how long ago the incident described took place

   ▶ the reporter's name, address, and phone number

   ▶ if the child has a disability, any information that may be helpful to the officials (i.e., if the child has difficulty with communication, uses a hearing aid, has mental retardation, emotional, or behavioral difficulties, or has a learning disability that indicates special needs)

## Summary

To ensure that accurate information is reported to the appropriate human service agency, teachers who serve children at risk for the development of educational problems must be prudent in their efforts to know their children and their families well. Parents who abuse or neglect their children often exhibit characteristics that may be heightened or triggered during family crises. This is of critical importance to teachers of children at risk for developing educational problems because of the additional stress that often results from the child's presence. Parents who abuse or neglect their child may exhibit low self-esteem or appear to be isolated from the community. They typically fail to appear for parent–teacher conferences and are often defensive when questioned about their child. Their child's injuries are often blamed on others or unsatisfactorily explained. The child may relate stories of abuse or unusual behavior by his or her parents. Limited parenting skills may be a result of lack of education, experience, or maturity. Parents may lack patience and be overly demanding of a child who, because of developmental difficulties, is unable to meet their demands in a timely manner. Often, parents who abuse their children were abused themselves.

In determining whether a child is subject to abuse or neglect, the teacher should make note of consistent behaviors or physical evidence, being aware that one incident may not be evidence of child abuse. An isolated incident should be recorded for future reference but should not necessarily be reported immediately. This will depend, of course, on the severity of the injury or the effect on the child's behavior. Knowing the parents well will certainly aid in making a decision relative to reporting of abuse and neglect.

Recognizing abuse and reporting it to the appropriate agency is expected of all teachers and administrators. The experienced teacher makes the extra effort to gather information about the family, to become well acquainted with the parents, and to monitor all of his or her students' physical and behavioral conditions. Teachers must know their students if they intend to effectively deal with child abuse and neglect.

In addition to understanding the procedures for reporting abuse and neglect, teachers may also contribute to improved parent–student relations by participating in the development of parenting education programs or in setting up a more flexible schedule for parent conferences. Efforts should be made to help parents see the advances and improvements made by their children. As parents develop a more realistic view of their child's abilities and potential, they may become more patient and understanding of their child's actions. Teachers should preface a note home with a friendly telephone call or an informal letter discussing the child's overall performance in school. Given a situation in which abuse is present, a teacher's first note home detailing a disciplinary action may precipitate undue punishment. One key to reduced child abuse is improved parent–teacher communication. Teachers cannot afford to wait for the parent to initiate contact. Open lines of communication must be established and supported by the school's administration.

Children at risk for the development of educational problems are at greater risk for abuse and neglect than those children who develop normally. Teachers who serve these children must be aware of this and be able to recognize the warning signs. They must also have a complete understanding of the legal and administrative procedures for reporting abuse. Most important, they must know their students and work to establish effective parent–teacher communication. To stem the tide of abuse and neglect among disabled and at-risk children, teachers must be vigilant, understanding, observant, prudent, and effective record keepers.

## Acknowledgment

We wish to thank Dr. J. David Smith and Dr. Mitchell L. Yell for their editorial assistance in the preparation of this manuscript.

### REFERENCES

Ammerman, R., Lubetsky, M., Hersen, M., & Van Hasselt, V. (1988). Maltreatment of children and adolescents with multiple handicaps: Five case examples. *Journal of the Multihandicapped Person, 1,* 129–139.

Blacher, J. (1984). A dynamic perspective on the impact of a severely handicapped child on the family. In J. Blacher (Ed.), *Severely handicapped young children and their families: Research in review* (pp. 3–50). New York: Academic Press.

Campbell, R. (1992). Child abuse and neglect. In L. Bullock (Ed.), *Exceptionalities in children and youth* (pp. 470–475). Boston: Allyn and Bacon.

Child Abuse Prevention and Treatment Act of 1974, 42 U.S.C. § 5101 et. seq.

Children, Youth, and Families Department (CYFD). (1993). *Stop child abuse/neglect: Prevention and reporting kit.* Available from Children, Youth and Families Department, Social Services Division, Child Abuse Prevention Unit, 300 San Mateo NE, Suite 802, Albuquerque, NM 87108-1516.

Fossey, R. (1993). Child abuse investigations in the public school: A practical guide for school administrators. *Education Law Reporter.* St. Paul, Minn.: West.

Giovannoni, J. (1989). Definitional issues in child maltreatment. In D. Cicchitti & V. Carlson (Eds.), *Child maltreatment: Theory and research on the causes and consequences of child abuse and neglect* (pp. 48–50). New York: Cambridge University Press.

McCarthy, M., & Cambron-McCabe, N. (1992). *Public school law: Teachers' and students' rights.* Boston: Allyn and Bacon.

Meier, J., & Sloan, M. (1984). The severely handicapped and child abuse. In J. Blacher (Ed.), *Severely handicapped young children and their families: Research in review* (pp. 247–272). New York: Academic Press.

Pagelow, M. D. (1984). *Family violence.* New York: Praeger Publishing.

Parent Advocacy for Educational Rights (PACER). (1989). *Let's prevent abuse: An informational guide for educators.* Available from PACER Center, Inc.,

4826 Chicago Avenue South, Minneapolis, Minnesota 55407-1055.

Trudell, B., & Whatley, M. H. (1988). School sexual abuse prevention: Unintended consequences and dilemmas. *Child Abuse and Neglect, 12,* 103–113.

Winters Communication, Inc. (WCI). (1988). *Child abuse and its prevention.* Available from Winters Communication, Inc., 1007 Samy Drive, Tampa, Florida 33613.

## POSTNOTE

The abuse (or, more accurately stated, the torture) of a helpless child by an adult is one of those crimes that truly cries out for attention. The effects of abuse usually spill over into a child's school life and can make him or her impervious to the best schooling. Recently, greater attention has been given to child abuse in the hope of alerting teachers and other youth workers to the problem and sensitizing adults to its long-term harm.

The National Clearinghouse on Child Abuse and Neglect Information (in the U.S. Department of Health and Human Services) distributes materials, collects data, and conducts research into this problem area. If you wish to obtain more information, one especially useful report from the Center is titled, "The Role of Educators in the Prevention and Treatment of Child Abuse and Neglect," which can be found at http://www.calib.com/nccanch/.

## DISCUSSION QUESTIONS

1. Describe a case of child abuse you know of personally or through media accounts. What was the outcome of the case for all parties involved?

2. What legal responsibilities do teachers have in your state for reporting child abuse? Do they have any legal protection (such as anonymity) once they have reported a case? How comfortable are you with the possibility of meeting these responsibilities?

3. What services are available in your area for children who have been abused? Consider child protection or welfare services as well as law enforcement agencies at the state, county, and city levels.

## 18

# What Do Students Want (and What Really Motivates Them)?

### Richard Strong, Harvey F. Silver, and Amy Robinson

Ten years ago, we began a research project by asking both teachers and students two simple questions: What kind of work do you find totally engaging? and What kind of work do you hate to do? Almost immediately, we noticed distinct patterns in their responses.

Engaging work, respondents said, was work that stimulated their curiosity, permitted them to express their creativity, and fostered positive relationships with others. It was also work at which they were *good*. As for activities they hated, both teachers and students cited work that was repetitive, that required little or no thought, and that was forced on them by others.

How, then, would we define engagement? Perhaps the best definition comes from the work of Phil Schlecty (1994), who says students who are engaged exhibit three characteristics: (1) they are attracted to their work, (2) they persist in their work despite challenges and obstacles, and (3) they take visible delight in accomplishing their work.

Most teachers have seen these signs of engagement during a project, presentation, or lively class discussion. They have caught glimpses of the inspired inner world of a child, and hoped to sustain this wonder, enthusiasm, and perseverance every day. At the same time, they may have felt stymied by traditions of reward and punishment. Our challenge is to transcend these very real difficulties and provide a practical model for understanding what our students want and need.

## Goals and Needs: The SCORE

TERMS TO NOTE
Engagement
SCORE

As the responses to our questions showed, people who are engaged in their work are driven by four essential goals, each of which satisfies a particular human need:

▶ *Success* (the need for mastery),

▶ *Curiosity* (the need for understanding),

▶ *Originality* (the need for self-expression),

▶ *Relationships* (the need for involvement with others).

These four goals form the acronym for our model of student engagement—*SCORE.* Under the right classroom conditions and at the right level for each student, they can build the motivation and *Energy* (to complete our acronym) that is essential for a complete and productive life. These goals can provide students with the energy to deal constructively with the complexity, confusion, repetition, and ambiguities of life (the drive toward *completion*).

## Rethinking Motivation

The concept of "score" is a metaphor about performance, but one that also suggests a work or art, as in a musical score. By aiming to combine achievement and artistry, the SCORE model can

At the time this article was written, Robert Strong was vice president and director of curriculm development, Harvey F. Silver was vice president and director of program development, and Amy Robinson was director of research and publishing for Silver Strong and Associates of 34 Washington Rd., Princeton, NJ 08550. From Richard Strong, Harvey F. Silver, and Amy Robinson, "What Do Students Want (and What Really Motivates Them)?" *Educational Leadership*, September 1995, pp. 8–12. Reprinted by permission of the Association for Supervision and Curriculum Development. Copyright © 1995 by ASCD. All rights reserved.

reach beyond strict dichotomies of right/wrong and pass/fail, and even bypass the controversy about intrinsic and extrinsic motivation, on which theories of educational motivation have long been based.

Extrinsic motivation—a motivator that is external to the student or the task at hand—has long been perceived as the bad boy of motivational theory. In *Punished by Rewards*, Alfie Kohn (1995) lays out the prevailing arguments against extrinsic rewards, such as grades and gold stars. He maintains that reliance on factors external to the task and to the individual consistently fails to produce any deep and long-lasting commitment to learning.

Intrinsic motivation, on the other hand, comes from within, and is generally considered more durable and self-enhancing (Kohn 1993). Still, although intrinsic motivation gets much better press, it, too, has its weaknesses. As Kohn argues, because intrinsic motivation "is a concept that exists only in the context of the individual," the prescriptions its proponents offer teachers are often too radically individualized, or too bland and abstract, to be applied in classroom settings. . . .

Perhaps it is the tradition of separating extrinsic and intrinsic motivation that is flawed. Robert Sternberg and Todd Lubart recently addressed this possibility in *Defying the Crowd* (1995). They assert that any in-depth examination of the work of highly creative people reveals a blend of both types of motivation.

## Knowing the SCORE

After taking into consideration the needs and drives we've mentioned, our model poses four important questions that teachers must ask themselves in order to score the level of engagement in their classrooms.

1. Under what conditions are students most likely to feel that they can be successful?

2. When are students most likely to become curious?

3. How can we help students satisfy their natural drive toward self-expression?

4. How can we motivate students to learn by using their natural desire to create and foster good peer relationships?

Much of what we will discuss is already taking place in classrooms across the country. The point of our SCORE model of engagement is first to help teachers discover what they are already doing right and then to encourage the cultivation of everyday classroom conditions that foster student motivation and success.

## Convincing Kids They Can Succeed

Students want and need work that enables them to demonstrate and improve their sense of themselves as competent and successful human beings. This is the drive toward mastery. But success, while highly valued in our society, can be more or less motivational. People who are highly creative, for example, actually experience failure far more often than success.

Before we can use success to motivate our students to produce high-quality work, we must meet three conditions:

1. We must clearly articulate the criteria for success and provide clear, immediate, and constructive feedback.

2. We must show students that the skills they need to be successful are within their grasp by clearly and systematically modeling these skills.

3. We must help them see success as a valuable aspect of their personalities.

All this seems obvious enough, but it is remarkable how often we fail to meet these conditions for our students. Take skills. Can you remember any crucial skills that you felt you did not successfully master because they were not clearly taught? Was it finding themes in literature? Reading and interpreting primary texts? Thinking through nonroutine math problems? Typically, skills like these are routinely assigned or assumed, rather than systematically modeled or practiced by teachers.

So how can we help students master such skills? When teaching your students to find themes, for example, deliberately model interpretation. Ask your students to give you a poem you have never seen, and then interpret it both for and with them. If they are reading primary texts, use what we call the "main idea" strategy. Teach them how to find the topic (usually a noun or noun phrase), the main idea (a sentence that states the text's position on the topic), and reasons or evidence to support the main idea. If students are concerned about writer's block, remember that perhaps the most difficult task of a teacher is to teach how to think creatively. Model the process of brainstorming, demonstrating that no idea is unworthy of consideration.

These are not revolutionary ideas. They simply illustrate how easily classroom practices can be improved, thus increasing the chance that your students will succeed.

But what of the *criteria* for success? Teachers define success in many ways. We must not only broaden our definition, but also make sure the definition is clear to everyone. In this way, students will *know* when they have done a good job, and they will *know* how to improve their work.

To achieve this clarity, we can present examples of work that illustrate high, average, and low levels of achievement. Such exemplars can significantly motivate students, as well as increase their understanding of their own ability to achieve.

## *Arousing* Curiosity

Students want and need work that stimulates their curiosity and awakens their desire for deep understanding. People are naturally curious about a variety of things. Einstein wondered his whole life about the relationships among gravity, space, and electromagnetic radiation. Deborah Tannen, the prominent linguistic psychologist, has spent years pondering the obstacles that prevent men and women from conversing meaningfully.

How can we ensure that our curriculum arouses intense curiosity? By making sure it features two defining characteristics: the information about a topic is fragmentary or contradictory, and the topic relates to students' personal lives.

It is precisely the *lack* of organization of a body of information that compels us to understand it further. This may explain why textbooks, which are highly organized, rarely arouse student interest. We have stimulated students' curiosity by using a strategy called "mystery." We confront the class with a problem—for example, "What killed off the dinosaurs?"—and with the actual clues that scientists or historians have used to try to answer that question and others. Clues might include:

▶ Mammals survived the changes that killed the dinosaurs.

▶ Chickens under stress lay eggs with thinner shells than do chickens not under stress.

▶ While flowering plants evolved, dinosaurs increased in population and in number of species.

▶ Some flowering plants contain alkaloids.

Students then work together in groups, retracing the steps scientists took in weighing the available evidence to arrive at an explanation. We have seen students work diligently for several days dealing with false hypotheses and red herrings, taking great delight when the solutions begin to emerge.

As for topics that relate to students' lives, the connection here cannot be superficial; it must involve an issue or idea that is both manageable and unresolved. We must ask, With what issues are adolescents wrestling? How can we connect them to our curriculum? Figure 1 illustrates some possibilities for adolescents.

| ADOLESCENT ISSUE | TOPIC | CONNECTION |
|---|---|---|
| Independence: How can I separate myself from parents and other adults? | American Revolution | When is rebellion justified? |
| The search for identity: Who do I want to be? What do I want to become? | Percentages | To determine your likes and dislikes, compute the percentage of your life spent in various activities. |
| Relationships and stature: How important are my opinions of my peers, my family? | Jane Austen's *Emma* | Discuss how stature and reputation affect Emma's decisions and your own. |
| Responsibility: For what do I want to take responsibility? What is expected of me? | Ecology | Investigate social organizations working to improve the environment. |

**FIGURE 1**

The Curiosity Connection: Relating Content to Students' Lives

Adapted from Beane, J. A., and R. P. Lipka. (1986). *Self-Concept, Self-Esteem, and the Curriculum.* New York: Teachers College Press.

## *Encouraging* Originality

Students want and need work that permits them to express their autonomy and originality, enabling them to discover who they are and who they want to be. Unfortunately, the ways schools traditionally focus on creativity actually thwart the drive toward self-expression. There are several reasons for this.

First, schools frequently design whole programs (art, for example) around projects that teach technique rather than self-expression. Second, very often only students who display the most talent have access to audiences, thus cutting off all other students from feedback and a sense of purpose. Finally, and perhaps most destructive, schools frequently view creativity as a form of play, and thus fail to maintain the high standards and sense of seriousness that make creative work meaningful.

How, then, should self-expression be encouraged? There are several ways.

▶ *Connect creative projects to students' personal ideas and concerns.* One of our favorite teachers begins her study of ceramics by having students examine objects found in the homes of a variety of ancient civilizations. She then asks the class to design a ceramic object that expresses their feeling about their home.

▶ *Expand what counts as an audience.* One of the most successful creative projects we have seen involved an audience of one. Each student in a middle school class was linked to an older member of the community and asked to write that person's "autobiography."

▶ *Consider giving students more choice.* The medium of expression, for example, is often as important to an artist as the expression itself. What would have happened to the great tradition of American blues if the early musicians were forced to adhere to traditions of European music? This is one more argument for instructional methods that emphasize learning styles, multiple intelligences, and cultural diversity.

▶ *Use the "abstracting" strategy to help students fully understand a genre and to maintain high standards* (Marzano et al. 1992). Too often, students prefer video art to a book because they perceive it as less demanding or requiring less commitment. Teaching students to abstract the essence of a genre will change their perceptions.

Begin by studying examples of high-quality work within a genre (the science-fiction story, poster art, sonnets, frontier diaries, television news programs, and so on). Examine the structure of the works and the standards by which they are judged. Then, ask students to produce their own work in that genre that expresses their own concerns, attempting to meet the high standards embodied in the original work. Finally, have the students ask themselves four questions about their work: How good is my technique? Does my work truly express my own concerns? Does it demonstrate my understanding of the genre in which I am working? Does it successfully relate to its audience?

Some people worry that the stringency of this model might actually block self-expression, but our experience is precisely the opposite. Students' drive toward self-expression is ultimately a drive to produce work that is of value to others. Lower standards work to repress, not to enhance, the creation of high-quality work.

## Fostering Peer Relations

Students want and need work that will enhance their relationships with people they care about.

This drive toward interpersonal involvement is pervasive in all our lives. Further, most of us work hardest on those relationships that are reciprocal—what you have to offer is of value to me, and what I have to offer is of some value to you. In general, unbalanced, nonreciprocal relationships prove transient and fail to generate much energy or interest.

How does this insight apply to life in the classroom? Consider a student's perception of homework. The only relationship that can be advanced through the typical homework assignment is the one between student and teacher. And this relationship is essentially unbalanced. Students do not feel that the teacher needs their knowledge, and the teacher, with possibly 145 students a day, probably isn't seeking a deep relationship either.

But suppose student work is complementary: one student's job is to learn about tortoises, another's is to learn about snakes, and a third student is boning up on lizards. After they do their research, they jointly develop a poster comparing and contrasting these three reptile types. The students actually need one another's knowledge.

Annemarie Palincsar Brown has applied this "jigsaw" strategy to inner-city students using in-classroom computer networks (Brown et al. 1993). She found that it significantly improved their motivation, reading, and writing. Elizabeth Cohen (1994) builds reciprocal groups by asking students with different talents and abilities to work on one project that requires all of their gifts.

## Orchestrating Classroom Performance

As teachers, the first thing we should try to "score" is our *own* performance. Different people value the four goals we have discussed to different degrees in different situations. Which ones are particularly important to you? How does this preference affect the way you run your classroom? By observing and understanding how classroom conditions can create or repress student engagement, we can gradually move toward a more successful, curious, creative, and reciprocal school system.

All students, to some extent, seek mastery, understanding, self-expression, and positive interpersonal relationships. But they are all different as well. Imagine what could happen if we engaged our students in a discussion of these four types of motivation. What might they tell us about themselves and their classrooms? Could we actually teach them to design their own work in ways that match their own unique potential for engagement?

Last, we can score the change process itself. What professional conditions block teachers' motivation? We can redesign staff development to promote understanding and respect among school staff members.

By seeking to break down boundaries between teacher and teacher, teacher and student, student and the learning process, we will learn what students want and need. As a result, more and more teachers may go to bed at night remembering the images of wonder, enthusiasm, and perseverance on the faces of their students.

## REFERENCES

Brown, A., D. Ash, M. Rutherford, K. Nakagawa, A. Gordon, and J. Campione. (1993). "Distributed Expertise in the Classroom." In *Distributed Cognitions: Psychological and Educational Considerations,* edited by G. Salomon. New York: Cambridge University Press.

Cohen, E. G. (1994). *Designing Groupwork: Strategies for the Heterogeneous Classroom.* 2nd Edition. New York: Teachers College Press

Kohn, A. (1993). *Punished by Rewards: The Trouble with Gold Stars, Incentive Plans, A's, Praise, and Other Bribes.* Boston: Houghton Mifflin.

Marzano, R., D. Pickering, D. Arredondo, G. Blackburn, R. Brandt, and C. Moffett. (1992). *Dimensions of Learning.* Alexandria, Va.: Association for Supervision and Curriculum Development.

Schlecty, P. (January 1994). "Increasing Student Engagement." Missouri Leadership Academy.

Sternberg, R. J., and T. I. Lubart. (1995). *Defying the Crowd: Cultivating Creativity in a Culture of Conformity.* New York: The Free Press.

## POSTNOTE

Student engagement is an important concept related to educational success. A recent book by Lawrence Steinberg, *Beyond the Classroom,* identifies the lack of student engagement in American high schools as an alarming problem in our educational system. According to Steinberg, the problem results from peer culture influence that devalues educational effort, from part-time employment that undermines students' commitment to school, and from reduced involvement by parents in school activities. No amount of school reform will succeed, Steinberg contends, unless we as a nation face and resolve this issue.

This article examines what schools can do to increase motivation among students. Selection 40 in this book addresses the same topic from the perspective of an individual teacher. Together, these articles offer plenty of good advice. But unless the underlying factors identified by Steinberg are also addressed, schools are not likely to be successful.

## DISCUSSION QUESTIONS

1. What reactions did you have to the SCORE model of student engagement?

2. In your opinion, what is the appropriate role of extrinsic motivation in school? What were your reactions to Kohn's proposition that extrinsic motivation is ineffective in producing long-lasting learning?

3. What steps would you encourage to decrease student apathy and increase student engagement in school?

## PART THREE

# Schools

Schools and schooling in the United States have been the object of careful scrutiny and considerable criticism in recent years. Disappointing test scores, disciplinary problems, violence, and a lack of clear direction are all points of tension. In the past few years, there has been a shift in what educators, legislators, and critics say schools must do to address these and other problems. There is a sense that schools have drifted away from their most important purpose—that is, to prepare students academically and intellectually. Schools have lost sight, they say, of a sense of excellence.

Some of the selections in this section consider this emphasis, whereas others pose alternative solutions. The topics include characteristics of good schools, school culture, the size of schools, schools that focus on teachers, and some of the new approaches to school improvement.

# 19

**CLASSIC** *The Culture Builder*

Roland S. Barth

Probably the most important—and the most difficult—job of an instructional leader is to change the prevailing culture of a school. The

**TERM TO NOTE**
School culture

school's culture dictates, in no uncertain terms, "the way we do things around here." A school's culture has far more influence on life and learning in the schoolhouse than the president of the country, the state department of education, the superintendent, the school board, or even the principal, teachers, and parents can ever have. One cannot, of course, change a school culture alone. But one can provide forms of leadership that invite others to join as observers of the old and architects of the new. The effect must be to transform what we did last September into what we would like to do next September.

The culture of a school is apparent to the newcomer. In one school, a beginning teacher stands up in a faculty meeting to express her views to the others on, say, pupil evaluation. Her contribution is received with mockery, cold stares, and put-downs. "Who does she think she is?" As the new teacher quickly learns, the culture at her school dictates that newcomers must not speak until they have experienced, for at least two or three years, the toil and tedium of the old-timers. "That's the way we do things around here." And she learns that cruel and unusual punishments await those who violate the cultural taboos of the school.

Roland S. Barth is a former teacher, principal, and member of the faculty of Harvard University, where he founded the Harvard Principals' Center and the International Network of Principals' Centers. From *Learning by Heart*, by Roland S. Barth. Copyright © 2001 by Jossey-Bass. This material is used by permission of John Wiley & Sons, Inc. Available at www.jbp.com or (800) 956-7739.

In another school, a high school student is tormented by his peers for studying on the day of the football game. And, indeed, the culture in many schools dictates that learning is not "cool" on Saturdays—or on any day of the week, for that matter.

In yet another school, a teacher encounters trouble managing a class full of difficult youngsters. Within a few days, every other teacher in the building knows of her problem—and volunteers to help. In the same school, when a student is experiencing difficulty with an assignment or a new concept, several fellow students step in to assist. "That's the way we do things around here."

A school's culture is a complex pattern of norms, attitudes, beliefs, behaviors, values, ceremonies, traditions, and myths that are deeply ingrained in the very core of the organization. It is the historically transmitted pattern of meaning that wields astonishing power in shaping what people think and how they act.

Every school has a culture. Some are hospitable, others toxic. A school's culture can work for or against improvement and reform. Some schools are populated by teachers and administrators who are reformers, others by educators who are gifted and talented at subverting reform. And many school cultures are indifferent to reform.

And all school cultures are incredibly resistant to change, which makes school improvement—from within or from without—usually futile. Unless teachers and administrators act to change the culture of a school, all innovations, high standards,and high-stakes tests will have to fit in and around existing elements of the culture. They will remain superficial window dressing, incapable of making much of a difference.

To change the culture requires that the instructional leader become aware of the culture, the way things are done here. What do you see, hear, and experience in the school? What *don't* you see and hear? What are the clues that reveal the school's culture? What behaviors get rewards and status? Which ones are greeted with reprimands? Do the adults model the behavior they expect of students? Who makes the decisions? Do parents experience welcome, suspicion, or rejection when they enter the school?

## Nondiscussables

An important part of awareness is attending to "nondiscussables." Nondiscussables are subjects sufficiently important that they are talked about frequently but are so laden with anxiety and fearfulness that these conversations take place only in the parking lot, the rest rooms, the playground, the car pool, or the dinner table at home. Fear abounds that open discussion of these incendiary issues—at a faculty meeting, for example—will cause a meltdown. The nondiscussable is the elephant in the living room. Everyone knows that this huge pachyderm is there, right between the sofa and the fireplace, but we go on mopping and dusting and vacuuming around it as if it did not exist.

Each school has its own nondiscussables. For one it is "the leadership of the principal." For another, it is "the way decisions are made here." For many it is "race" or "the underperforming teacher." Schools are full of these land mines from which trip wires emanate. We walk about carefully, trying not to detonate them. Yet by giving these nondiscussables this incredible power over us, by avoiding them at all cost, we issue the underperforming teacher a license to continue this year as he did last year, taking a heavy toll on countless students and other teachers. We deprive the principal of honest, timely feedback and thereby continue to suffer from poor leadership. We condemn ourselves to live with all the debilitating tensions that surround race.

The health of a school is inversely proportional to the number of nondiscussables: the fewer nondiscussables, the healthier the school; the more nondiscussables, the more pathology in the school culture. To change the culture of the school, the instructional leader must enable its residents to name, acknowledge, and address the nondiscussables—especially those that impede learning. No mean task, for as one principal put it, "These nondiscussables are the third rail of school leadership."

## Changing the Culture

It is said that a fish would be the last creature on earth to discover water, so totally and continuously immersed in it is he. The same might be said of those working within the school culture. By the time a beginning teacher waits the obligatory three years to speak in a faculty meeting, she, too, is likely to be so immersed in the culture that she will no longer be able to see with a beginner's clarity the school's cultural patterns of leadership, competition, fearfulness, self-interest, or lack of support.

To change the culture requires that more desirable qualities replace the existing unhealthy elements. Clear personal and collective visions are crucial for this enterprise. Educators Saphier and King identified a dozen healthy cultural norms: collegiality, experimentation, high expectations, trust and confidence, tangible support, reaching out to the knowledge bases, appreciation and recognition, caring celebration and humor, involvement in decision making, protection of what's important, traditions, and honest and open communication.[1] These qualities dramatically affect the capacity of a school to improve—and to promote learning.

To change a school's culture requires mustering the courage and skill to not remain victimized by the toxic elements of the school's culture and to address them instead. Culture building requires the will to transform the elements of school culture into forces that support rather than subvert the school's purposes. Of course, these acts violate the taboos of many school cultures, which is why culture changing is the most important, difficult, and perilous job of school-based reformers.

E. B. White observed, "A person must have something to cling to. Without that we are as a pea vine sprawling in search of a trellis." We educators need a trellis to keep us off the ground in the face of the cold rains and hot winds that buffet the schoolhouse. The trellis of our profession—and the most crucial element of school culture—is an ethos hospitable to the promotion of human learning.

## Learning Curves off the Chart

The ability to learn prodigiously from birth to death sets human beings apart from other forms of life. The greatest purpose of school is to unlock, release, and foster this wonderful capability.

Schools exist to promote learning in all their inhabitants. Whether we are teachers, principals, professors, or parents, our primary responsibility is to promote learning in others and in ourselves. That responsibility sets educators apart from insurance salespeople, engineers, and doctors. To the extent that our activities in school are dedicated to getting learning curves off the chart, what we do is a calling. To the extent that we spend most of our time doing something else in school, we are engaged in a job.

Recent school reforms are an invitation—nay, a demand—to examine every school policy, practice, and decision and ask, What, if anything, of importance is anyone learning as a consequence of doing *that*? Who learns what from ability grouping? Who learns what from letter grades of *A*, *B*, and *C*? Who learns what from having 26 students in a class? Who learns what from the annual practice of principals evaluating

teachers? We created the myriad school practices that now clutter a school's culture because at some time someone believed that this policy, practice, or procedure was capable of getting someone's learning curve off the chart.

The instructional leader must assist the faculty in taking continual, fresh inventory of these and other habituated practices encrusted in our schools' cultures and in categorizing them. Some—such as the practice of providing individual instruction or giving students immediate feedback on their work—seem undeniably associated with promoting learning. Keep those. Others—such as ability grouping or parent nights—we may need to study to determine just what effect, if any, they are having on people's learning. Still other practices—perhaps faculty meetings or intrusive announcements over the loudspeaker—appear to contribute to no one's learning—or may even impede learning—and need to be scrapped. A final category is for the activities that must continue but in a more successful way.

Residing in all the stakeholders in schools—parents, teachers, students, principals—are wonderful, fresh, imaginative ideas about a better way. Achieving that better way takes recognition of and moral outrage at ineffective practices, confidence that there *is* a better way, and the courage and invention to find that way and implement it. Whose learning curve goes off the chart by doing *that*? is a revolutionary question whose time has finally come.

## At-Risk Students

Unhealthy school cultures tend to beget at-risk students—students who leave school before or after graduation with little possibility of continuing learning.

I remember visiting a high school just after the last spring exams and before graduation. As I approached the school grounds, I saw a group of students standing around a roaring fire, to which they were heartily contributing. I went over and asked, "What's up?"

"We're burning our notes and our books," replied one. "We're outta here!"

On further conversation, I learned that these students were not from the bottom ability group, but rather *A*, *B*, and *C* students, many headed for college.

That fire continues to smolder within me. I wonder how many of our students not so labeled are in fact at risk, with little possibility of continuing learning. How many of them graduate from our schools and exult in the belief that they have learned all they ever need or intend to know?

One reason that those students were burning those books, literally, and that so many more students burn their books figuratively at the end of the school year is that lurking beneath the culture of most schools is a chilling message: *Learn or we will hurt you.* Educators have taken learning—a wonderful, spontaneous capacity of all human beings—and coupled it with punitive measures. We have developed an arsenal of sanctions and punishments that we inextricably link with learning experiences. "Johnny, if you don't learn your multiplication tables, you're going to have to repeat 4th grade." "Mary, if you don't improve your compositions, I'm not going to write a favorable recommendation for college." "Tom, if your standardized test scores don't improve, you don't graduate." And so it goes. What those students burning their books are really telling us is, "You can't hurt me anymore."

But so closely have we coupled learning and punishment that the students throw one into the fire with the other. School cultures in which students submit to learning, and to the threats of punishment for not learning, generate students who want to be finished with learning when they graduate. And, of course, this applies to adults as well. The state tells the teacher or principal, "Unless you complete 15 hours of continuing education credits this year, we will not renew your certification." Learn or we will hurt you.

An immense challenge to the instructional leader—and to our profession—is to find ways to *un*couple learning and punishment. We must change the message to students—and to their educators—from "Learn or we will hurt you" to "Learn or you will hurt yourself." Students who burn their books and their notes and celebrate the conclusion of their learning will be relegated to the periphery of the 21st century. Those who will thrive in the years ahead, in contrast, will be those who have become—during their school experience—active, voracious, independent, lifelong learners. The nature of the workplace, our society, and learning dictates that we need to learn as we go along, or we won't survive.

## Yearning for Learning

The most important requirement for graduation—whether from 4th, 9th, or 12th grade—is some evidence that this student is becoming or has become an independent, lifelong learner. We must look closely at what students choose to do with their own time. What evidence is there of enduring intellectual passion in this student? Is the student capable of posing questions, marshaling resources, and pursuing learning with dedication, independence, imagination, and courage?

If your school has succeeded in getting 95 percent of its students scoring at the 95th percentile on standardized tests, and if, at the same time, students are leaving a teacher, a grade, or the school "burning their books" and saying "I'm done with this stuff; I'm outta here," then you have won a battle but lost the war. The price of short-term success is long-term failure. Enhancement of performance has led to a curtailment of lifelong learning. The school has failed in its most important mission—to create and provide a culture hospitable to human learning and to make it likely that students and educators will become and remain life-long learners. This is what instructional leadership is all about.

"Our School Is a Community of Learners!" How many times do we see and hear this assertion? It is both an ambitious, welcome vision and an empty promissory note. The vision is, first, that the school will be a *community,* a place full of adults and students who care about, look after, and root for one another and who work together for the good of the whole, in times of need and in times of celebration. Every member of the community holds some responsibility for the welfare of every other and for the welfare of the community as a whole. Schools face tremendous difficulty in fulfilling this definition of a community. More are organizations, institutions, or bureaucracies.

As if community were not ambitious enough, the defining, underlying culture of this community is *learning.* The condition for membership in the community is that one learns, continues to learn, and supports the learning of others. Everyone. A tall order to fill, and one to which few schools aspire and even fewer attain.

When we come to believe that our schools should be providing a culture that creates and sustains a community of student and adult learning—that this is the trellis of our profession—then we will organize our schools, classrooms, and learning experiences differently. Show me a school where instructional leaders constantly examine the school's culture and work to transform it into one hospitable to sustained human learning, and I'll show you students who do just fine on those standardized tests.

## NOTE

1. Saphier, J., and King, M. (1985). Good seeds grow in strong cultures. *Educational Leadership, 42*(6), 67–74.

## POSTNOTE

We have selected this article as a Classic because it points out the rarely recognized and rarely addressed educative power of a school's culture. Only rarely do we step back and acknowledge that this or that is "the way we do things around here." Except for the very wise ones, old-timers are rarely aware of the dynamics (sometimes quite bizarre) of their culture. Newcomers, on the other hand, are often surprised and sometimes quite disoriented by their new culture. As Roland Barth makes clear in his article, schools have cultures and those cultures vary enormously. The experienced teachers in a school, the old hands, are quite accustomed to the school's culture, even if it is rather dysfunctional. A new teacher, however, sees the school and its culture with fresh eyes, particularly if it is different from the schools he or she has attended. Not a few first-year teachers get off on the wrong foot with veteran fellow teachers by disparaging what they find odd or foolish or wrong about their new surroundings. Prudence recommends that new teachers "hold their fire" until they are fully respected by their new peers and have been able to establish themselves. The author of this postnote was once-upon-a-time a rather brash first-year teacher. His department chairman, a former army sergeant, gave him a tip from his military years when he said, "Don't sound off until your barracks bag stops swinging." In other words, wait a while until you start making suggestions for improvement.

## DISCUSSION QUESTIONS

1. Have you ever been in a new culture and been confused by what was going on around you? Specifically, what was different and what did you do?

2. Reflecting on your own school experience, do you see aspects of school culture that differ significantly from what you believe would be good educational practice?

3. What would you suggest (for yourself and other teachers) to continually keep perspective on your school's culture?

# 20

# *The Cosmopolitan School*

David Elkind

When society changes, schools change. Tectonic shifts in society in the United States over the past 50 years have transformed our classrooms; the public school at the beginning of the 21st century is a far different social institution than it once was.

Our society has changed from modern to postmodern. Modern society in the United States was *provincial* in its conservative social values, its clearly articulated sexual and occupational roles, and its spatially and temporally defined activities. In contrast, our postmodern society is *cosmopolitan*—a worldly mixture of liberal cultural values, blended sexual and occupational roles, and spatially and temporally overlapping activities.

## Modern Provincialism

The prevalent belief in our modern, provincial society was that the United States had a common ethos, or set of values, different from, and superior to, all others (Carter, 1998) and that all immigrant groups would accept and incorporate these values. The metaphor for becoming assimilated was the cultural *melting pot*. Our educational system was the operative melting pot, instilling middle-class values in the newcomers whatever their ethnic, racial, or religious backgrounds. The Dick and Jane reading series pre-

**TERMS TO NOTE**

Melting pot

Modern

Postmodern

David Elkind is professor of child development in the Eliot Pearson Department of Child Development, Tufts University, 101 College St., Medford, MA 02155; delkind@emerald.tufts.edu. From David Elkind, "The Cosmopolitan School," *Educational Leadership*, December 2000/January 2001, pp. 12–17. Reprinted with permission of the Association for Supervision and Curriculum Development.

sented white, middle-class children as models for all children to emulate.

Clearly demarcated roles defined parents, principals, teachers, and children. Mothers were homemakers and fathers were good providers (Bernard, 1981). Likewise, teachers taught children, and parents reared them. During the early days of Head Start, much discussion centered on whether teachers should serve the children lunch; providing meals was considered a parental, not an educational, prerogative.

Expectations were that boys would be naughty and girls well behaved, that children would show respect for their teachers and other adults in positions of authority, that adolescents needed moral guidance, and that youth valued what they learned from adults. Many adults organized and led clubs to provide guidance and support for young people. There were exceptions and role reversals, but the expectations were clear.

Place, time, and activities were closely tied with one another in the modern school. Many modern elementary schools did not have lunchrooms because children ate lunch at home. Children did homework, but school was the venue for most educational activities. Time and function were also closely joined; the school day was a time for work, and after school, weekends, and summers were times for play. Meals had a regular schedule and were devoted to eating and to conversation.

## Postmodern Cosmopolitanism

The postmodern period has challenged our provincial notions of common values and defined roles. The civil rights movement revealed the prejudice embodied in society's ethos and the need for equal educational and occupational opportunities as well as for the recognition and valuation of minority achievements. In addition, the women's rights movement overturned the traditional differences between male and female roles. The acceptance and valuation of cultural diversity has generally replaced the white, middle-class ethos. We are rewriting our history books to acknowledge the contributions of minority men and women to science, literature, music, and sports. Contemporary reading primers depict children of different racial and ethnic groups and at different socioeconomic levels.

The clearly demarcated social roles of the modern era have given way to the more overlapping and less rigid roles of the postmodern era. Today, women are free to enter all occupations, and as many women as men are currently entering medical and law schools. Male roles have not changed as much, but society expects men to be sensitive and compassionate as well as competitive and high achieving.

Parents have transferred many of their traditional functions to the school, a change that has transformed the teacher's role. Teachers now engage in more socialization of their students than ever before. New technologies have also contributed to a change in the teacher's role. Many young people are now more proficient in these technologies than the teachers are, so teachers often learn about new technology from their pupils.

Children's roles have changed as well. The modern child was regarded as *innocent* and in need of adult guidance and protection. In contrast, the postmodern child is seen as *competent*, ready and able to deal with life's challenges. This new perception of competence helps explain why educators are pushing down the curriculum, expecting children to know their numbers and letters before entering 1st grade. Society also expects adolescents to be sophisticated in matters of technology, sex, and drugs. Middle and high schools provide fewer adult-organized activities for young people than in the past (Elkind, 1994).

Finally, many of the technological changes that contributed to the transition to postmodernism have helped sever the once tight connections among space, time, and activities. Thanks to the fast-food revolution, we now eat 25 percent of our meals in cars. Individuals and families eat meals in front of the television; professionals eat lunch in their offices; and travelers eat dinner on a plane while watching a movie. The eating place is now also the travel place, the recreation place, and the workplace.

The ties between time and activity have melted as well. Television has turned many forms of information into entertainment. When children watch *Sesame Street*, they are being entertained and are also, presumably, learning. This blurring results in the expectation that teachers be entertaining—half ham and half egghead. With cell phones, fax machines, and notebook computers, adults work during vacations, further dissolving the boundaries between time and activity.

## Postmodern Innovations

The public schools have mirrored these social transformations of the postmodern era. Problems arise when we treat the sociological imperatives for postmodern innovations in the schools as if each change had a curricular rationale. Such misreading often means that the new programs fail to achieve their intended goals and sometimes even have a regressive impact. Postmodern innovations—inclusion, multiculturalism, full-day kindergarten, and character education—are the offspring of our new, cosmopolitan society. Educators who understand the origins of these innovations will be able to implement changes more effectively.

### Inclusion

The inclusion of students with special needs into the regular classroom is a postmodern innovation. It stems directly from broadening our national social ethos to acknowledge and appreciate those who are physically and mentally challenged. Inclusion, however, does *not* arise from any new theories or research regarding the educational effectiveness or value of this practice (Elkind, 1998). The Individuals with Disabilities Education Act, federal legislation that mandates the mainstreaming of students with special needs, was passed in 1975 as a result of the lobbying efforts of parents, not of educators.

Nonetheless, inclusion is too often regarded as an educational, rather than a social, challenge (Agne, 1998). Educators focus on the curriculum and not on the social adjustment of the children. Developing a curriculum, however, is much less important than making each student feel welcome and accepted among his or her peers (Sapon-Shevin, 1996). Developing social acceptance is the real challenge of inclusion. Teachers have to model a respect both for the child as an individual and for his or her special needs. Discussions about the types and number of students with special needs to include in any particular classroom are really about social dynamics, not the curriculum. When we look at inclusion as primarily an effort to gain respect and appreciation for a particular group, then we have inclusion in the right perspective (Giangreco, 1996).

## Multiculturalism

Like inclusion, multiculturalism reflects the change in our national ethos, from the glorification of the melting pot to the valuation of the rainbow. At the heart of multiculturalism is the recognition of our common humanity and of the truth that our differences just make us different, not better or worse, than one another. This openness does not mean that anything goes. There is evil in the world, and every society has prohibitions against murder, incest, and violations of persons or property. Individuals can be right or wrong, good or evil, kind or cruel—but races, cultures, religions, and ethnic groups are not.

**TERMS TO NOTE**
Inclusion
Multiculturalism

Unfortunately, as in the case of inclusion, we too often treat multiculturalism as a curricular issue rather than as a matter of teaching tolerance (Banks, 1991). Certainly, it is important for children to learn about different cultures, races, and religions and to study different histories, languages, and modes of life. All too often, however, the curricular focus on difference undermines the real goal of multiculturalism. Emphasizing differences, without making a serious effort to help children value them, may have the wrong effect. Children may unwittingly associate being different with being bad or inferior (Elrich, 1994). True multiculturalism emphasizes our common humanity. It teaches children that whatever our religious preferences, whatever the color of our skin, whatever our cultural values, we all love our parents and children, take pride in achievements, and grieve for failures and disappointments.

Presenting multiculturalism in this way is not always easy. In teaching about other races and cultures, for example, teachers tend to look at, or away from, a minority student whose race or ethnicity is under discussion. Teachers also face the dilemma of recognizing a particular child's ethnicity but continuing to treat him or her as any other child. And there is always the temptation of asking a child to speak for his or her race or ethnic group when the child does not want to be acknowledged in this way. Respecting children as both unique and part of the group is one of the major adaptational problems posed to teachers by the new valuation of our common humanity. It is much more than a matter of curriculum or instruction.

## Full-Day Kindergarten

The development of full-day kindergarten is a good illustration of how a social problem gets misinterpreted and given an educational solution.

The changing roles of women in our society and the entrance of many mothers of young children into the workforce created an enormous need for child care. There were not enough affordable, accessible, and quality child care facilities to meet the needs of all the parents who required these services. Many working parents began looking to the schools for help. Parents trust schools. Schools are safe and clean, and the teachers are trained and certified. The need for child care, combined with the new view of children as competent, created a strong demand for full-day kindergarten.

Administrators, for their part, found that arguing for funding for full-day kindergarten required playing the education card. Full-day kindergarten, they argued, would better prepare children for 1st grade. Unfortunately, this argument has become a self-fulfilling prophecy. The widespread introduction of full-day kindergarten has led both administrators and 1st grade teachers to raise their expectations for the skills necessary to succeed in 1st grade.

In the past, children with and without academic skills entered 1st grade, but this open door is fast closing. Many 1st grade teachers expect that children coming into their classrooms will know numbers and letters, and if a child does not, the teachers recommend holding the child back in kindergarten. In fact, we retain 10 to 25 percent of kindergarten children each year in the United States in spite of considerable controversy over the efficacy of retention (Thomas et al., 1992). Full-day kindergarten was introduced to meet a child care need but has contributed to too many children being held back or put into transition kindergarten classes.

Likewise, the current movement toward universal preschool is another child care initiative, not an educational one. The distinction between child care and education is not always easy to draw because good child care is always educational. The issue, however, is not educational versus noneducational. The real concern is appropriateness. Full-day kindergarten or programs for 4-year-olds can be beneficial if the programs take into account the children's need to rest in the afternoon and to learn from

manipulatives rather than from symbols. The mischief starts when the 1st grade curriculum gets pushed down to kindergarten and 4-year-old preschool programs.

## Character Education

Like the full-day kindergarten, the introduction of character education into the public school curriculum has a social, rather than an educational, rationale.

The introduction of character education into our schools began around the turn of the last century and lasted for a few decades. Introduced as a response to the waves of immigrants arriving in the United States, character education was supposed to combat the lawlessness and immorality of the so-called ignorant hordes. After World War I and the decline in immigration, the demands for character education subsided. For example, psychologist Gordon Allport (1927) argued that measurable personality, as opposed to immeasurable character, should be the proper focus of psychological and educational concern. The coup de grace came with the studies of Hugh Hartshorne and Mark May (1928–1930), who found that moral education had little or no relation to moral behavior.

**TERMS TO NOTE**
Full-day kindergarten
Character education

The work of Lawrence Kohlberg (1975), who elaborated and extended the work of Jean Piaget (1948), brought about a revival of interest in moral education. Coming on the heels of the civil rights and women's rights movements and the concern for social, economic, and educational inequalities in our society, Kohlberg's work was timely. Moral development became a major topic in psychological textbooks and found its way into the school in many different guises, such as "value clarification" curriculums.

Although the impetus for moral education came first from the social justice movements, changes in the family and in gender roles fostered a new interest in moral education. Single parents and dual-career parents have, on the average, less time to parent. In addition, children and teenagers face influences from television, video games, and mass marketing. Parents are not able to monitor children's exposure to these new sources of information, entertainment, and sales promotion. As a result, parents share their role in character formation with outside influences over which they have little or no control.

This lack of control, together with the many cases of cruelty and violence in schools, has fueled the contemporary enthusiasm for character education. Indeed, the Internet has hundreds of sites devoted to character education, which has become a widely accepted curriculum topic in our schools. Yet the contemporary demand for character education, like that at the turn of the last century, is a response to a social problem and not a reflection of research supporting the effectiveness of these programs (Kohn, 1997).

Character education programs are almost sure to fail their intended aims. They are ineffectual because they attempt to use schools to solve social problems that originate elsewhere. Using schools in this way has not worked in the past and will not work now. School busing is a case in point. It solved neither the educational inequality of our schools nor the racism that gave rise to it. Busing did not work because most parents did not integrate with those of other races; they did not socialize even though their children did. At home, children still picked up vicious racist messages that smothered any positive sentiments they might acquire at school. Children learn racism from their parents and other significant adults, not from one another.

The same is true for character education. First, character is an ambiguous term. In education, the most common definition is that of the "good person," who is a paragon of such virtues as honesty, truthfulness, fairness, generosity, loyalty, and fidelity. Most character education programs, however, focus on two major traits, honesty and fairness, which are basic to main-

taining the school's sense of society. Even if we limit the discussion to these two moral attributes, there are still problems. One of these is developmental, the other situational.

With regard to the development of honesty and fairness, we need to remember that children understand these terms in different ways as they mature. Children who are 8 or 9 years old, for example, often invent hypotheses (that adults are tempted to call lies) to explain their dishonest actions (such as taking something from a store). Once they verbalize such hypotheses, the children often believe their stories and may even bend the facts to fit them. What an adult would call a lie is thus not a lie from the perspective of the child, who now believes in the reality he or she has created. We should not condone either stealing or lying, but we should approach the child's behavior from a developmental perspective. We might, for example, test out the child's hypothesis without judging it false in advance.

This example illustrates two points. One is that character education is better learned from real experiences than from fictional stories. Second, a teacher's modeling of fairness and honesty is the best way to teach honesty and fairness. A teacher who does not prejudge, but instead allows children to test out their hypotheses, provides a model of objectivity and fairness that children can emulate.

Moral behavior is situational as well as developmental. A child may behave morally in relation to his or her friends, for example, but not in relation to strangers. This tendency is not limited to children. Adults at a convention in a strange city where they are not known may behave in ways that they would never behave at home. And we all tend to be more moral when we are under public surveillance than when we are not. There is thus a clear difference between moral knowledge and moral behavior. Character is not absolute; it is relative to both development and situation.

Character education, then, like the full-day kindergarten, has its origin in social change, not in any newly demonstrated research as to its efficacy. In fact, character education can be counterproductive if it merely adds to the teacher's already heavy curricular load. Character education does take place in the classroom, but not by way of any curriculum. Educators who are competent, prepared, and responsive to their students' individual needs are the best teachers of moral values. Once we see that the demand for character education is a social and not an educational imperative, we can remove character education as a curricular subject and give teachers the time and freedom they need to be the best moral exemplars they can be.

## Technological Innovations

Technological innovations have played a dramatic role in creating our postmodern, cosmopolitan society. Computers, fax machines, the Internet, and cell phones have liberated activities from their usual spatial and temporal ties, and we can now reach anyone at any hour. Unlike the postmodern school innovations that have sociological rather than educational origins, technological innovations can benefit education directly, but their misuse for sociological or psychological purposes can compromise their educational value.

Internet research, for example, has broken the spatial tie between research and the library. Karl Marx camped out in the British Museum doing the background reading for his classic *Das Kapital*, but today's student can sit at home and conduct a more extensive library search than Marx ever could have. Unfortunately, prurient appeals linked even to the most neutral words and the relentless stream of sales pitches can compromise the educational value of Internet research.

As for e-mail communications, students and teachers can contact one another not only in the classroom and during school hours, but at any hour. This increases teacher-student communication, but the informal nature of email sometimes encourages inappropriate requests.

One of the most far-reaching educational advances to derive from the new technologies is distance learning. Attending a lecture was once limited to being in the same room as the lecturer, but that is no longer the case. For instance, with the help of a video camera and a telephone hookup, I recently gave a lecture and answered questions from students on several different campuses simultaneously. Distance learning also breaks the once close ties between time and activity. With electronically stored lectures. students no longer have to attend lectures at particular hours on particular days; they instead can listen to them whenever they choose.

**TERM TO NOTE**
Distance learning

We do not yet know the sociological and psychological consequences of distance learning, but it may pose a risk to teachers' job security. If students throughout the world can take a master teacher's course in economics, the need for tenured economics teachers may decrease. Another risk might be the lack of direct contact with teachers; distance learning does not provide for the personal contact, advice, and supervision that are important parts of the educational process.

## Understanding Innovations

Mirroring society's transformations, our schools have changed from provincial to cosmopolitan institutions. When we fail to see cosmopolitan innovations as social problems to be solved and misread them as subject to be taught, we force curricular changes that do not achieve their intended social aims. Instead, we should pay attention to how the potential misuse of technological innovations can compromise their educational value. Understanding the origins of postmodern innovations can help us place them in the proper perspective. We need to recognize that social change creates problems and that new curriculums are not always the solutions.

## REFERENCES

Agne, K. (1998, Spring). The dismantling of the great American public school. *Educational Horizons, 76*(3), 143–146.

Allport, G. (1927). Character and personality. *Psychological Bulletin, 24,* 284–293.

Banks, J. A. (1991). *Teaching strategies for ethnic studies* (5th ed.). Boston: Allyn and Bacon.

Bernard, J. (1981). The good provider role: Its rise and fall. *American Psychologist, 36,* 1–12.

Carter, S. P. (1998). *Civility.* New York: BasicBooks.

Elkind, D. (1994). *Ties that stress.* Cambridge, MA: Harvard University Press.

Elkind, D. (1998). Behavioral disorders: A postmodern perspective. *Behavioral Disorders, 23*(3), 153–159.

Elrich. M. (1994). The stereotype within. *Educational Leadership, 51*(8), 12–14.

Giangreco, M. F. (1996). What do I do now? A teacher's guide to including students with disabilities. *Educational Leadership, 53*(5), 56–59.

Hartshorne, H., and May, M. (1928–1930). *Studies in the nature of character* (Vols. 1–2). New York: Macmillan.

Kohlberg, L. (1975). The cognitive developmental approach to moral development. *Phi Delta Kappan, 56*(10), 670–677.

Kohn, A. (1997, February). How not to teach values: A critical look at character education. *Phi Delta Kappan, 78*(6), 429–437.

Piaget, J. (1948). *The moral judgment of the child.* Glencoe, IL: The Free Press.

Thomas, A. M., Armistead, L., Kempton, T., Lynch, S., Forehand, R., Nousinen, S., Neighbors, B., and Tannenbaum, L. (1992, October). Early retention: Are there long-term beneficial effects? *Psychology in the Schools, 29*(4), 342–347.

Sapon-Shevin, M. (1996). Full inclusion as a disclosing tablet. *Theory into Practice, 35*(1), 60–68.

## POSTNOTE

We respectfully take issue with one of the author's major points: that character education is a flawed sociological innovation of the postmodern era. He is correct that social forces, from parental work patterns to youth crime statistics, have awakened new interest in character education. He is correct, too, about the push for character education resulting from waves of immigrants in the nineteenth and twentieth centuries. On the other hand, he has ignored the fact that our great educational thinkers, from Plato to Aristotle, from Maria Montessori to John Dewey, have been clear that the education on a child's character is fundamental to the individual and to the society. Socrates claimed that the purpose of education is to make people both smart [knowledgeable] and good [possessing virtuous habits]. America's Founding Fathers were insistent about the need for schools to educate people in the civic virtues needed to maintain a democratic government. Many saw character education as the first priority of our nation's new schools.

The author appears to set up character education as something of a straw man. On the one hand, he asserts that character formation is developmental and situational. Further, he states, "a teacher's modeling of fairness and honesty is the best way to teach honesty and fairness." On the other hand, we have never encountered an advocate of character education who would disagree with these points. In fact, much of the teaching about how to conduct good character education stresses these issues. He is somewhat correct that "character" is an ambiguous term. But so is "education." And because we cannot define "the good person" shouldn't mean that we abandon efforts to help children become good people. Although it is difficult to define "good student" or "good teacher" or "good psychologist," that hardly ever stops our striving to do so. It hardly keeps us from teaching about what is a good person and what we need to do to form ourselves into people of strong character.

It is impossible to create a school that does not have an effect on a child's character. Schools are, by their nature, moral environments that place demands on students and that reward and punish certain behaviors. Character education is an intrinsic part of education and schooling. Whether we like It or not, whether we do it well or poorly, teachers are educators of character.

## DISCUSSION QUESTIONS

1. Specifically, what is the difference between a "provincial" society and a "postmodern" society?

2. What are the characteristics of a "cosmopolitan school?"

3. The author suggests that a number of postmodern social innovations have dictated changes in schooling. What are these changes, and do you agree that it is the role of the postmodern school to respond to these changes in the larger society?

# 21 CLASSIC *A Tale of Two Schools*

## Larry Cuban

For this entire century, there has been conflict among educators, public officials, researchers, and parents over whether traditionalist or progressive ways of teaching reading, math, science, and other subjects are best. Nowhere has this unrelenting search for the one best way of teaching a subject or skill been more obvious than in the search for "good" schools. Progressives and traditionalists each have scorn for those who argue that there are many versions of "good" schools. Partisan debates have consumed policymakers, parents, practitioners, and researchers, blocking consideration of the unadorned fact that there is more than one kind of "good" school.

What follows is a verbal collage of two elementary schools I know well. School A is a quiet, orderly school where the teacher's authority is openly honored by both students and parents. The principal and faculty seek out students' and parental advice when making schoolwide decisions. The professional staff sets high academic standards, establishes school rules that respect differences among students, and demands regular study habits from the culturally diverse population. Drill and practice are parts of each teacher's daily lesson. Report cards with letter grades are sent home every nine weeks. A banner in the school says: Free Monday through Friday: Knowledge—Bring Your Own Container." These snippets describe what many would call a "traditional" school.

School B prizes freedom for students and teachers to pursue their interests. Most classrooms are multiage (6- to 9-year-olds and 7- to 11-year-olds). Every teacher encourages student-initiated projects and trusts children to make the right choices. In this school, there are no spelling bees; no accelerated reading program; no letter or numerical grades. Instead, there is a year-end narrative in which a teacher describes the personal growth of each student. Students take only those standardized tests required by the state. A banner in the classroom reads: "Children need a place to run! explore! a world to discover." This brief description describes what many would call a "progressive" school.

**TERMS TO NOTE**
Traditional school
Progressive school
Good school

I will argue that both Schools A and B are "good" schools. What parents, teachers, and students at each school value about knowledge, teaching, learning, and freedom differs. Yet both public schools have been in existence for 25 years. Parents have chosen to send their children to the schools. Both schools have staffs that volunteered to work there. And both schools enjoy unalloyed support: Annual surveys of parent and student opinion have registered praise for each school; each school has had a waiting list of parents who wish to enroll their sons and daughters; teacher turnovers at each school have been virtually nil.

Moreover, by most student-outcome measures, both schools have compiled enviable records. In academic achievement, measured by standardized tests, School A was in the top 10 schools in the entire state. School B was in the upper quartile of the state's schools.

These schools differ dramatically from one another in how teachers organize their classrooms, view learning, and teach the curriculum. Can both of them be "good"? The answer is yes.

What makes these schools "good"? They have stable staffs committed to core beliefs about

Larry Cuban is an emeritus professor of education at Stanford University, Stanford, Calif. Reprinted with permission from *Education Week*, Vol. 17, No. 20, January 28, 1998, and from the author.

what is best for students and the community, parents with beliefs that mirror those of the staffs, competent people working together, and time to make it all happen. Whether one was traditional or progressive was irrelevant. The century-long war of words over traditional vs. progressive schooling is a cul-de-sac, a dead end argument that needs to be retired once and for all.

What partisans of each fail to recognize is that this pendulum-like swing between traditional and progressive schooling is really a deeper political conflict over what role schools should play in society. Should schools in a democracy primarily concentrate on making citizens who fulfill their civic duties? Should schools focus on efficiently preparing students with skills credentials to get jobs and maintain a healthy economy? Honor individual excellence yet treat everyone equally? Or should schools do everything they can to develop the personal and social capabilities of each and every child? For almost two centuries of tax-supported public schooling in the United States, all of these goals have been viewed as both important and achievable.

The war of words between progressives and traditionalists has been a proxy for this political struggle over goals. Progressive vs. traditionalist battles over discipline in schools, national tests, tracking students by their performance, and school uniforms mask a more fundamental tension in this country over which goals for public schools should have priority.

The problem lies not in knowing how to make schools better. Many parents and educators already know what they want and possess the requisite knowledge and skills to get it. Schools A and B are examples of that knowledge in action. The problem is determining what goals public schools should pursue, given the many goals that are desired and inescapable limits on time, money, and people.

Determining priorities among school goals is a political process of making choices that involves policymakers, school officials, taxpayers, and parents. Deciding what is important and how much should be allocated to it is at the heart of the process. Political parties, lobbies, and citizen groups vie for voters' attention. Both bickering and deliberation arise from the process. Making a school "good" is not a technical problem that can be solved by experts or scientific investigation into traditional or progressive approaches. It is a struggle over values that are worked out in elections for public office, tax referendums, and open debate in civic meetings, newspapers, and TV talk shows. Yet these simple distinctions between the political and the technical, between goals for schools and the crucial importance of the democratic process determining which goals should be primary, seem to have been lost in squabbles over whether progressive or traditional schools are better.

And that is why I began with my descriptions of the two schools. They represent a way out of this futile struggle over which kind of schooling is better than the other. I argue that both these schools are "good."

One is clearly traditional in its concentration on passing on to children the best knowledge, skills, and values in society. The other is progressive in its focus on students' personal and social development. Each serves different goals, each honors different values. Yet—and this is the important point that I wish to drive home— these seemingly different goals are not inconsistent. They derive from a deeply embedded, but seldom noticed, common framework of what parents and taxpayers want their public schools to achieve.

What is different, on the surface, are the relative weights that each "good" school gives to these goals, how they go about putting into practice what they seek, and the words that they use to describe what they do. The common framework I refer to is the core duty of tax-supported public schools in a democracy to pass on to the next generation democratic attitudes, values, and behaviors. Too often we take for granted the linkage between the schools that we have and the kind of civic life that we want for ourselves and our children. What do I mean by democratic attitudes, values, and behaviors? A few examples may help:

▶ Open-mindedness to different opinions and a willingness to listen to such opinions.

▶ Respect for values that differ from one's own.

▶ Treating individuals decently and fairly, regardless of background.

▶ A commitment to talk through problems, reason, deliberate, and struggle toward openly arrived-at compromises.

I doubt whether partisans for traditional and progressive schools, such as former U.S. Secretary of Education William J. Bennett, educator Deborah Meier, and academics like Howard Gardner and E. D. Hirsch, Jr., would find this list unimportant.

Tax-supported public schools in this country were not established 150 years ago to get jobs for graduates. They were not established to replace the family or church. They were established to make sure that children grew into literate adults who respected authority, could make reasoned judgments, accept differences of opinions, and fulfill their civic duties to participate in the political life of their communities. Over time, of course, as conditions changed, other responsibilities were added to the charter of public schools. But the core duty of schools, teachers, and administrators—past and present—has been to turn students into citizens who can independently reason through difficult decisions, defend what they have decided, and honor the rule of law. Our traditional and progressive schools each have been working on these paramount and essential tasks.

Consider such democratic values as individual freedom and respect for authority. In School A, students have freedom in many activities, as long as they stay within the clear boundaries established by teachers on what students can do and what content they must learn. Staff members set rules for behavior and academic performance, but students and parents are consulted; students accept the limits easily, even enjoying the bounded freedom that such rules give them. School A's teachers and parents believe that students' self-discipline grows best by setting limits on freedom and learning what knowledge previous generations counted as important. From these will evolve students' respect for the rule of law and their growth into active citizens.

In School B, more emphasis is placed on children's individual freedom to create, diverge from the group, and work at their own pace. Students work on individually designed projects over the year. They respect teachers' authority but often ask why certain things have to be done. The teacher gives reasons and, on occasion, negotiates over what will be done and how it will be done. School B's teachers and parents believe that students' self-discipline, regard for authority, and future civic responsibility evolve out of an extended, but not total, freedom.

Thus, I would argue, both of these schools prize individual freedom and respect for authority, but they define each value differently in how they organize the school, view the curriculum, and engage in teaching. Neither value is ignored. Parents, teachers, and students accept the differences in how their schools put these values into practice. Moreover, each school, in its individual way, cultivates the deeper democratic attitudes of open-mindedness, respect for others' values, treating others decently, and making deliberate decisions.

Because no researcher could ever prove that one way of schooling is better than the other, what matters to me in judging whether schools are "good" is whether they are discharging their primary duty to help students think and act democratically. What we need to talk about openly in debates about schooling is not whether a traditional school is better or worse than a progressive one, but whether that school concentrates on instilling within children the virtues that a democratic society must have in each generation. Current talk about national goals is *not* about this core goal of schooling. It is about being first in the world in science and math achievement; it is about preparing students to use technology to get better jobs. Very little is said about the basic purpose of schooling except in occasional one-liners or a paragraph here and there in speeches by top public officials.

What are other criteria for judging goodness? I have already suggested parent, student, and teacher satisfaction as reasonable standards to use in determining how "good" a school is. I would go further and add: To what degree has a school achieved its own explicit goals? By this criterion, School A is a clear success. Parents and teachers want children to become literate, respectful of authority, and responsible. Although School B scores well on standardized tests, parents and teachers are less interested in test results. What School B wants most are students who can think on their own and work together easily with those who are different from themselves; students who, when faced with a problem, can tackle it from different vantage points and come up with solutions that are creative. Parents and teachers have plenty of stories about students' reaching these goals, but there are few existing tests or quantitative measures that capture these behaviors.

So, another standard to judge "goodness" in a school is to produce graduates who possess these democratic behaviors, values, and attitudes. This is, and always has been, the common, but often ignored, framework for our public schools. It has been lost in the battle of words

and programs between public officials and educators who champion either traditional or progressive schools. A "good" school, I would argue, even in the face of the technological revolution and globalization of the U.S. economy in this century, is one that has students who display those virtues in different situations during their careers as students and afterwards as well.

My criteria, then, for determining good schools are as follows: Are parents, staff, and students satisfied with what occurs in the school? Is the school achieving the explicit goals it has set for itself? And, finally, are democratic behaviors, values, and attitudes evident in the students?

Why is it so hard to get past the idea that there is only one kind of "good" school? Varied notions of goodness have gotten mired in the endless and fruitless debate between traditionalists and progressives. The deeply buried but persistent impulse in the United States to create a "one best system," a solution for every problem, has kept progressives and traditionalists contesting which innovations are best for children, while ignoring that there are more ways than one to get "goodness" in schools.

Until Americans shed the view of a one best school for all, the squabbles over whether a traditional schooling is better than a progressive one will continue. Such a futile war of words ignores the fundamental purpose of public schooling as revitalizing democratic virtues in each generation and, most sadly, ignores the good schools that already exist.

## POSTNOTE

We select this article as a Classic because of the profound importance of its message: a call to educators to rise above ideological squabbles and get on with the serious business of educational excellence.

What one defines as a good school depends on what one values, says Larry Cuban, which makes perfectly good sense. A person's educational philosophy will determine how that person views schooling, teaching, and curriculum. Thus, many different types of good schools can and do exist.

Cuban's point argues for giving parents choices about the kind of school that their children attend. By offering different kinds of schools that represent different educational philosophies and by allowing parents to select the school of their choice, school boards can better satisfy parents' educational preferences. In this way, more parents will believe that their children attend good schools.

## DISCUSSION QUESTIONS

1. Of the two schools that Cuban describes in his article, would you prefer to teach in School A or School B? Why?

2. Describe the characteristics of the kind of school that you would consider to be "good."

3. Do you agree with Cuban's assertion that the common framework of public schools should be to "pass on to the next generation democratic attitudes, values, and behaviors"? Is there anything else that you would add to this common framework?

## 22

# Schools Our Teachers Deserve

Rosetta Marantz Cohen

It seems that a spate of recent books has appeared on the old, familiar subject of school reform. As always, some of these works have focused on the curriculum and call for more progressive approaches and an end to standardized testing.[1] Others have addressed the issues of low standards or parent involvement or the moral culture of the schools.[2] However, not one has focused its arguments on the one indispensable element in all successful schools—the one variable always given short shrift, it seems, whenever reformers think about school change—the teacher.

For more than five decades now, warehouses of writing on school reform have focused on the needs of the *students*, calling for the creation of "child-centered classrooms" and "learner-centered schools." Every administrator in America intones, "It's all about the kids!" And those words echo through every disaffected, demoralized student-centered high school building in the land. The whole failed history of modern education reform—from the prescriptive lesson-plan formats of the 1970s to the restructuring plans in the 1980s to the state testing and curriculum of the 1990s—has addressed the "needs of the child." It has paid hardly any attention to the work of the teacher, the one critical player in the school who makes the biggest difference.

"In this school, the teacher comes first." I would wager there isn't a public school in the land with such a motto. School reform efforts most frequently proceed *despite*, not because of, the teacher. When states impose new curricular mandates or introduce new statewide standard-

ized tests, teachers are often viewed as stumbling blocks to implementation. Administrators try to "get the teachers on board," as if they were prisoners diving seaward to escape the shackles and whip. Even "bottom-up" reform is rarely that. In most districts that tried site-based management, it came and went a decade ago with hardly a teacher mourning its passing. Frequently, such "teacher-centered" strategies simply burdened faculty members with the minutiae of daily governance without relieving them of any other responsibilities. The teacher's job was not redefined; rather, it was extended and expanded. Newly "empowered" teachers were burdened with clerical work and logistical concerns about building maintenance and scheduling—the very concerns that many teachers enter teaching to avoid. Indeed, such teacher-empowering reforms seemed calculated, in advance, to fail.

**TERM TO NOTE**
Site-based
management

Everyone knows that teachers resist change.[3] Why shouldn't they? Any teacher who has spent more than a decade in the profession has already intuited what school reformers haven't gleaned in a century of tinkering: lasting and meaningful change doesn't come from fiats, whether external or internal. It doesn't have anything to do with long blocks or short blocks, cooperative learning or direct instruction. It has to do with how an individual teacher feels about his or her work and how the school perceives that teacher. If the teacher is perceived as a hero, the school will flourish. If the teacher is perceived as a pain in the ass, the school is going downhill—long blocks, cooperative learning, and all. For a school to be an intellectual center, for it to have the ethos, the sense of community, and the "spirit" that so many parents

**TERMS TO NOTE**
Block scheduling
Cooperative
learning
Direct instruction

Rosetta Marantz Cohen is an associate professor in the Department of Education and Child Study, Smith College, Northampton, Mass. Rosetta Marantz Cohen, "Schools Our Teachers Deserve: A Proposal for Teacher-Centered Reform," *Phi Delta Kappan*, March 2002. Reprinted with permission of Rosetta Marantz Cohen.

and administrators seek, it must celebrate the work of its teachers in a way that is rarely seen in public schools. It must attend to the needs of teachers, it must accommodate their sensibilities, and it must treat the teachers' contributions with as much genuine concern as it does those of any other constituency—maybe more.

## Why Focus on the Teacher?

One good reason to focus on the teacher has to do with the nature of healthy institutions. Almost 20 years ago Sara Lawrence Lightfoot told us that successful high schools are those that possess powerful traditions and embedded norms. In the best schools (or hospitals or corporations), values are consistent and known; they are embodied in the experiences of everyday life.[4] How do those traditions get transferred to young people? Not by administrators. Principals have little direct contact with students and certainly not enough to transmit the subtleties of an institution's culture and beliefs. If a school is to have a powerful ethos, it is the *teachers* who must communicate it, embody it, transmit it. Indeed, teachers are the one stable influence on a culture that is, by definition, always in flux. Students seldom stay in a school longer than four years; many teachers remain in the system for 30 years or more. Because they are the fixed and tenured bearers of the school's values and ethos, it is critical that teachers feel good about the institution they are charged with representing.

This argument is even borne out in recent corporate management theory. Education policy makers have long been influenced by the models put forward by business and industry. In the 1980s, for example, corporate downsizing and bottom-line accountability certainly inspired education policy reforms in the areas of testing and teacher accountability. Cooperative learning and goals-based performance standards also have their roots in management theory.

What then is the most recent thinking about corporate competitiveness and productivity?

Many of the most influential books that have been published on this subject in the last five years have shifted their primary focus away from concerns with markets and economies of scale. Instead, employee morale has become a central priority. Jeffrey Pfeffer, a professor of organizational behavior at Stanford University, reflects the new thinking in his field when he argues that a loyal, intelligent work force is the key factor in corporate competitiveness—more critical than technology or protected and regulated markets.[5] When workers are disgruntled, distracted, or poorly trained, no brilliant strategy for expanding market share will compensate for that liability. Why should it be any different for schools?

A second reason for shifting the reformers' emphasis from the student to the teacher concerns the nature of the teaching force itself. Demographics within the profession have in recent years put schools in an unusual position. In general, the teacher population across the country is aging. In certain states, particularly in the Northeast, the average teacher's age is 40 or above. As teachers continue to age and then retire, schools will be faced with two very different challenges. First, they will have to attract excellent new people into the field. Second, they will have to figure out ways to help large numbers of older teachers stay invested in and committed to their work.

In the case of the hiring of new faculty members, schools will be confronted with the problem of incentives. What can a school offer a high-achieving college graduate to lure him or her away from business or law school? Obviously, schools will never be able to compete in terms of salary and other material benefits. But teaching holds a natural attraction for many idealistic, intelligent young people. Many students at competitive academic institutions are willing to consider teaching as a career.

Our introductory education classes at Smith College have some of the largest enrollments on campus. However, too many students are chased away from the field after their initial observations in local high schools that are part of their pre-practicum experiences. What they see when they visit schools is often demoralizing for them. Teachers work in isolation, and they work with too many students. They rarely interact with other faculty members, except over rushed lunches. They teach from books that they sometimes do not like themselves and that—to judge by their condition—seem to have been used by generations of students. By the time students at Smith become seniors, less than a handful each year are interested in becoming certified to teach high school. If schools are going to attract good new teachers, then they need to figure out ways to make the profession *look better* from the outside.

In terms of the burgeoning ranks of *veteran* teachers, the problem is even more complex. If good new teachers are hard to attract, it is even harder to reenergize those who have been victims of the system for decades. Some of these teachers, particularly those in their forties and fifties, have almost half a career ahead of them. With salaries frontloaded and no vertical advancement in the field, such teachers have little incentive to grow. As any high school student will tell you, the sullenness and exhaustion of these teachers and their cynicism and contempt for the system are the real root causes of bad schooling. Poorly written curricula, scheduling, and structural concerns are of so much lesser importance than teacher morale that they might as well not be factors at all.

Finally, the most obvious reason to focus on the teacher has to do with the nature of good teaching itself. Good teaching (as any good teacher will tell you) is not only about content and curriculum. It is also about the intersection of that content with the individual who is presenting it. For better or worse, teachers teach themselves, and any teacher who denies it is either lying or is out of touch with his or her effect on a class. School reformers almost always think in terms of *what* should be taught, how, when, and with what materials. And yet to a great extent teachers *are* the curriculum: affect, attitude, and persona have a much more

powerful impact on classes than do the books they use or the pedagogical techniques they employ. One need only recall one's own best high school teachers to know how true this is. We remember the human beings and their passion or energy. The texts and techniques are secondary.

## Teacher-Centered Reform

How then can a school nurture and promote the kind of teacher energy and enthusiasm that will "reform" schools? Forget the workshops on cooperative learning, the curriculum revision committees, the endless tinkering with the schedule. Focus instead on what can be done to make teachers feel better about their work. In other words, ask yourself, How can schools be made into adult-friendly places?

To answer that question, it seems logical to look to those schools that have succeeded in making teachers feel valuable: the best private schools and the best colleges. In both of these settings, money has little to do with job satisfaction. Private schools, as we all know, pay teachers less than public schools. And the salaries of assistant and even associate professors on many campuses fall below those of suburban public school teachers. Nor is workload necessarily the key. Some of the most competitive teaching jobs in the country can be found in private schools that require enormous service from their faculty members, including 24-hour, on-call availability in dormitories, extracurricular work, and lengthy written evaluations of students.

Why is it then that the best college graduates interested in teaching so often compete for the scarce jobs at Exeter and Andover, eschewing public schools even in the most affluent communities? I believe it is because these institutions hold out for bright graduates the promise of a truly intellectual life. Smart college students who choose to teach high school most frequently do so because they hope to continue to read and practice the subjects they love. Public schools, partly *because* of the very student-centered policies they persist in defending, fail to convey to these aspiring teachers the promise of such a life.

Similarly, many of the most passionately intellectual students at our college overlook the notion of high school teaching altogether. Their ambitions are set, from the start, on teaching at the college level. These students are not choosing college teaching because of a smaller workload or an easier life. Any freshman at Smith can see that introductory classes can be as large as 80 students and that the pressures to publish and the tensions associated with tenure complicate the lives of young professors. But in college teaching, these students do envision themselves respected as intellectuals, rewarded for using their minds in original ways, and capable of choosing and changing what they will teach. Good liberal arts colleges, like good private schools, really are "teacher-centered" institutions. Both seem to recognize that the way to foster excellence in students is to foster excellence in teachers. Good high schools need to prize young teachers who love their disciplines, and they need to celebrate book knowledge as an important, core value in the institutional culture.

Some may argue that a call to nurture "intellectual" teachers is a luxury in a public school system filled with so many students performing below grade level. Quite the contrary. Schools have for generations placed their least academically inclined teachers in classrooms with the lowest-ability students. No one would argue that such a strategy has raised levels of achievement among those students. If anything, a situation in which weak teachers teach weak students creates a self-fulfilling prophecy and helps perpetuate the very problems schools are trying to reverse. Teachers with intelligence, with passion and enthusiasm for their subjects, are every bit as important for at-risk students as they are for high-achieving students—and probably more so. For some low-achieving students, teachers are the one plausible role model for a life of literacy and reflection, a life in which intellect matters.

## A Teacher-Centered Reform Agenda

What would a teacher-centered public high school look like? How could it be created? What follow are suggested reforms that I contend would have a powerful effect on the morale of any public high school. Many of these reforms are commonsensical. Many of them cost nothing. None of them requires radical restructuring or retraining, expensive testing, or additional personnel.

### Offer Sabbaticals

The notion of a sabbatical, a paid period of leave in which a scholar can pursue scholarly ideas, stands as a key characteristic of intellectual teaching. Good colleges, of course, build periodic sabbaticals into the compensation packages for their faculty members. Many private schools also offer sabbatical leaves to faculty members on a competitive basis. Budgeting a single sabbatical leave (for which teachers would compete) into the yearly expenses of a public high school would not bankrupt any school system. Knowing that such a leave exists, however, would have an immensely salutary effect on the intellectual life of a staff. It would allow teachers to think in terms of ambitious scholarly projects; it would give them incentive to develop proposals for new classes or to outline for themselves lists of new readings they want to do—not only to enrich their curricula, but also for their own personal growth. For many years, the National Endowment for the Humanities has offered summer stipends for teachers to study literary or historical topics presented by college and university faculty. NEH studies show that teachers who take these seminars return to their classrooms energized and stimulated. The same good would emerge from the semester-long or yearlong sabbatical. It

**TERM TO NOTE**

Sabbatical

would reinforce the idea, too often ignored, that teaching is essentially an intellectual activity. Finally, the sabbatical would serve as another excellent lure for teacher candidates.

### Reallocate Budgets So That More Money Is Available for Books; Let Teachers Choose What They Teach

In many good private schools and in most colleges, teachers design their own classes and choose their own books. This is rarely true in public high schools, where teachers inherit curricula and use whatever books are available—regardless of their age or the teacher's interest in a particular work. Common sense suggests that one would teach better—with more passion and enthusiasm—a class that one has had a hand in designing. Clearly, teachers must work within certain inevitable constraints: states have curricular mandates, and certain texts are not appropriate for younger students. But within those obvious boundaries there could be a good deal more creative freedom than now exists in most public schools. Book ordering needs to be a high priority for school districts, and teachers need to have a much greater say in what books get bought, how many get bought, and when.

### Involve Teachers in the Evaluation Process

In no other profession do outsiders, individuals with no direct contact with the work of the professional, routinely evaluate and hire individuals within the profession. In law, for example, it would seem absurd for an outsider (one not even a practicing lawyer) to pass judgment on the work of a new lawyer in the firm. And yet this is precisely what happens in many schools and districts in which new teachers are hired without any input from faculty members in the departments in which they will teach. Teachers, too, are routinely evaluated by administrators who have not taught for decades, have never

taught the particular subject under scrutiny, or have no larger context (What did the class do yesterday? Last week?) for the brief evaluation. States like Texas hire supervisors who don't even work in the school itself; they arrive unannounced from a central office and then proceed, without any first-hand knowledge of the school's culture, to evaluate its teachers.

For teaching to gain real professional status, teachers need to control hiring and firing, they need to lay out their own criteria for acceptable practice, and they need to do their own evaluating. This is certainly not a new idea; unions have supported such practice for decades. But too few school systems go to the trouble of acting on the concept, either out of laziness or out of fear that, once so empowered, teachers will become less dependent on them and so less tractable.

### Change Hiring Practices

Several years ago, a gifted teacher I know, a 35-year veteran, an Advanced Placement history teacher, informed the school district in May that she was intending to retire. Then she waited to see advertisements for her position posted in professional journals or in newspapers in the two neighboring cities near her home. Nothing happened. It was not until the last week of August that the job was listed under the heading "Teacher, H.S. History" in the local newspaper, sandwiched between ads for "Tag Sale Coordinator" and "Truckdriver, Part Time."

Teaching will never be the most desirable profession in the land. In order to attract smart college graduates, districts have to work hard at it—devoting energy and ingenuity to the task. Hiring is by far the most important work of any school administrator, and it should be a high priority for the district superintendent as well. Administrators need to pound the pavement in search of top candidates; they need to visit college campuses, forge contacts with teacher education personnel in the best schools, track and follow potential teachers who have not yet graduated. Today, few districts do any of this. Hiring is perceived as a last minute catch-as-catch-can process in which having a credential is far more important than the quality of a transcript. Again, good colleges and private schools seem to understand the importance of hiring the best staff possible. They recruit actively and compete with one another for good teachers. Just knowing that you are pursued makes an enormous difference for a new teacher. It communicates the fact that the district values you. No last-minute hire—the product of an abstracted, impersonal interview—can begin his or her work with that same sense.

## Make Tenure Mean Something

As long as tenure exists, it is absurd not to use this mechanism to improve the quality of teaching. If the public school system is burdened by large numbers of uninspiring or incompetent teachers, it is partly because those individuals were not weeded out in the first years of their employment. While it is unfair to evaluate the long-term success of a teacher in the first year or two, it certainly becomes less difficult after three or four years. An insightful administrator (or better, a team of talented teachers) can certainly begin to see talent or its absence by then. It is critical that poor teachers not get re-hired, not slip through the cracks of an ineffectual system of supervision.

> **TERM TO NOTE**
> Tenure

For real substantive evaluation before tenure to work, the period of probation for teachers needs to be extended. Currently, teachers have a three-year probationary period, after which time—barring grievous malfeasance—they are automatically tenured. Colleges generally require seven years before tenure, and tenure itself becomes a critical rite of passage, like the formal initiation into an exclusive club. Tenure in colleges really means something. While I'm not proposing that the criteria for high school tenure should change (I don't think high school teachers

should be required to publish, for example), I do think that the quality of one's teaching should be much more carefully scrutinized—and by individuals who really *know* something about good teaching.

## Reallocate the Use of Time to Protect Teachers

Long blocks, short blocks, whatever. There are good arguments for all kinds of different scheduling formats, and the students themselves don't much care. The decision on how best to structure the day should be left to the teachers, who will weigh the merits of any scheduling system according to how they feel they can best present the material. Schools that move summarily to one scheduling system or another, without prioritizing the needs and preferences of teachers, do nothing more than alienate that critical constituency.

Teachers, like any other professionals, also need opportunities to work and reflect with one another. Again, many private schools seem to understand this fact. They build large chunks of time into the weekly schedule for teacher curriculum work and consulting. While public schools cannot afford to have half-day Wednesdays, as many private institutions do, they can at least prioritize the scheduling of teachers' free periods to benefit those within a given department. Or they can schedule longer, common lunch periods (duty-free) to allow teachers time to have leisurely discussions with one another.

## Administrators Should Teach

Of all the traits that characterize the very best schools, this one is perhaps the most important. Teachers have long noted a curious phenomenon: when teachers become full-time administrators, they quickly lose their capacity to empathize with their former colleagues. It is extraordinary how quickly one forgets the complex stresses and challenges of teaching once one is charged with implementing bureaucratic mandates or fielding parent complaints. The only way to avoid this sort of amnesia is for principals and assistant principals to continue to interact with students in a classroom. Even one class a day is enough to retain the flavor of the work and to maintain credibility with teachers—who often measure administrative effectiveness against what the principal seems to know about real teaching.

Finally, administrators who teach are far more likely to understand the importance of praising their teachers' best work. Teachers receive so little in the way of positive reinforcement. Unbelievable as it seems, a good teacher can spend years in the profession without hearing a single compliment about his or her work. Memos and reminders about tardy forms and report cards abound, but there is no mechanism in the profession for cataloguing and celebrating the good things that happen daily in the classroom. Teachers are just supposed to revel in the intrinsic rewards of their private successes. This lack of positive feedback from any adult peer can wear down even the most robust of spirits. And when the silence is compounded by other kinds of ego assaults (infantilizing inservice workshops or top-down mandates for reform), it is no wonder that so many teachers become cynical. When administrators teach, they remember to *think* about teaching; they remember how hard it is; they remember to value it.

Schools don't need large ranks of exceptional teachers, and it is unrealistic to expect they will ever attract so many. What they do need is a critical mass of impassioned, intellectual individuals—enough to influence the tone and character of the institution. By improving the morale of even a handful of a school's faculty, these "teacher-centered" reforms cannot help but benefit students. From any perspective, it just seems so obvious: if we can create the schools our *teachers* deserve, we will have created the schools our *children* deserve—and desperately need.

## NOTES

1. Alfie Kohn, *The Schools Our Children Deserve* (Boston: Houghton Mifflin, 1999).

2. Martin Gross, *The Conspiracy of Ignorance: The Failure of American Public Education* (New York: HarperCollins, 1999); and Theodore Sizer and Nancy Faust Sizer, *The Students Are Watching: Schools and the Moral Contract* (Boston: Beacon Press, 1999).

3. Dan Lortie, *Schoolteacher: A Sociological Study* (Chicago: University of Chicago Press, 1975).

4. Sara Lawrence Lightfoot, *The Good High School: Portraits of Character and Culture* (Boston: Basic Books, 1983).

5. Jeffrey Pfeffer, *Competitive Advantage Through People: Unleashing the Power of the Workforce* (Boston: Harvard Business School Press, 1994). See also Natalie J. Allen and John Meyer, *Commitment in the Workplace: Theory, Research, and Application* (Thousand Oaks, Calif.: Sage, 1997); and Oliver E. Williamson, *Organization Theory* (New York: Oxford University Press, 1995).

## POSTNOTE

A good general always keeps in touch with his troops. He realizes that his foot soldiers have more knowledge about what is going on in the trenches than he and his staff have back at headquarters. This may also be the case with educational "generals." The author makes a strong plea for giving greater attention to teachers and the wisdom they possess about the real world of schools.

One telling point is that teachers in private schools are honored to a greater degree than those in public schools. While they typically receive lower salaries, their role and position are given prominence. Private school boards and administrators, whose schools cater to the rich and powerful, appreciate that the quality of their schools is directly related to the quality of their teachers. Typically, private school teachers are respected. They are listened to. As more Americans make the connection that our nation's future is tied to the quality of a child's education, the author's ideas for enhancing the status of classroom teachers should take hold. Until this connection is made, real educational reform will be elusive.

## DISCUSSION QUESTIONS

1. In the schools you attended, were teachers respected? Specifically, how?

2. Do you agree with the author's view that schools need to become more "teacher-centered" rather than "student-centered"?

3. Which of the author's several reform suggestions do you think is more valuable? Why?

# Small Classes, Small Schools: The Time Is Now

**23**

Patricia A. Wasley

For many years, educators have debated the effects of class size and school size on student learning. The class size debate centers on the number of students a teacher can work with effectively in any given class period. The school size issue focuses on whether smaller schools encourage optimal student learning and development—and how small a "small school" must be to produce such effects.

This [article] examines the issues surrounding class size and school size to determine what the research says and what experts recommend. To frame these issues, I want to pose a series of questions:

▶ Why have issues of class and school size gained prominence?

▶ What does the research say?

▶ What does my experience lead me to believe about the impact of class and school size on teaching and learning?

## Why Are Class and School Size Important?

Issues of class size and school size have resurfaced as important school improvement ideas for a variety of reasons. First, the standards movement has encouraged the resurgence of the class size and school size

TERMS TO NOTE
Standards
High-stakes tests

Patricia A. Wasley is dean of the College of Education at the University of Washington, Seattle; pwasley@ u.washington.edu. From Patricia A. Wasley, "Small Classes, Small Schools," *Educational Leadership*, February 2002, pp. 6–10. Reprinted with permission of Patricia A. Wasley.

debates. All U.S. states but one have academic standards in place. Of those states with standards, 36 use or plan to use test results to make high-stakes decisions about students. Standards enable educators and the public to clarify what they believe students should know and be able to do before the students leave school.

The standards movement has highlighted the fact that schools are largely inequitable places. Students in schools with large populations of disadvantaged students perform least well on standardized assessments. Evidence also suggests that these schools often have the least-experienced teachers (NCTAF, 1996; Roza, 2001). In effect, having standards in place emphasizes that standards are necessary but insufficient in themselves to improve student performance. Unless we change students' learning opportunities, especially for students who are ill-served by their schools, standards alone are unlikely to influence student learning. Educators and policymakers are looking for strategies that will enable students to succeed on the new assessments (thereby supporting the standards movement) and, more important, that will enhance students' learning opportunities. Small classes and small schools may be two such strategies.

Second, class size and school size issues have resurfaced because of the increasing consensus among educators and the public that all students can learn. When I began teaching in the early 1970s, teachers generally accepted the notion that some students had an exceptional aptitude for learning and others did not. At that time, my colleagues and I believed that as long as one-fourth of the students in a class performed exceptionally well and another half of the class did reasonably well, we were fulfilling our responsibilities as educators—even if

**129**

one-fourth of the students in a class failed to learn at an acceptable level. We had been taught that the normal distribution of scores (the "bell curve") was what teachers should aim for and what we should accept as reasonable evidence of accomplishment. In the ensuing years, cognitive scientists, neurological biologists, and educators determined that all students have the capacity to learn. This new, convincing research means that no student should be left behind in the learning process. Educators need to examine all approaches to schooling to determine which strategies are most likely to return gains for students who typically have not done well in schools. Proponents of reduced class size and school size suggest that these factors contribute to the success of a broader swath of learners.

Third, following the events of September 11, educators have a renewed appreciation for the importance of the basic freedoms we enjoy and the advantages that a democracy provides its citizens. We know that a democratic citizenry must value differences among its participants. Schools should strive to develop in students the skills that they need to examine their differences productively and to coexist peacefully while protecting basic freedoms for all (Goodlad, Soder, & Sirotnik, 1990). Schools also have a central responsibility for helping students learn the basic skills of productive citizenry. Both class size and school size influence whether teachers are able to engage students in meaningful discussions of these issues and to help them build these crucial citizenship skills.

Renewed interest in class size and school size is broad-based and nationwide. The Bill & Melinda Gates Foundation has dedicated more than $250 million to reducing the size of U.S. high schools. The U.S. Department of Education has committed $125 million to fund small-school initiatives. In Boston, Chicago, and New York, small-school initiatives are under way. Small-school collaboratives, designed to support the change from comprehensive high schools to smaller learning communities, are springing up everywhere and include New Visions for Learning in New York, the Small Schools Workshop in Chicago (Illinois), the Small Schools Project in Seattle (Washington), and the Bay Area Coalition of Essential Schools in Oakland (California).

Lawmakers in Kentucky, California, Georgia, and Washington have passed legislation to reduce class sizes, believing that teachers will be better able to help all students meet the standards when the teacher-student ratio is substantially reduced.

## What Does Research Tell Us?

The United States has had large schools for a relatively short period of time. Until the middle of the 20th century, most U.S. schools were small. In 1930, 262,000 U.S. public schools served 26 million students; by 1999, approximately 90,000 U.S. public schools served about 47 million students (National Center for Education Statistics, 1999). Responding to the recommendations of the Committee of Ten in 1894 and the authors of the Conant Report in 1959, proponents of the school consolidation movement suggested that schools would be more efficient and effective if they were larger. Single plants housing 500–2,000 students presumably could offer greater variety in subject matter, would provide teachers with the opportunity to track their students according to ability, and might put less strain on community resources (Wasley & Fine, 2000).

Research conducted on the validity of the assertions favoring large schools has suggested that less-advantaged students end up in the largest classes, with the least-experienced teachers and the least-engaging curriculum and instructional strategies (Oakes, 1987; Wheelock, 1992). Further research suggests that schools are organized more for purposes of maintaining control than for promoting learning (McNeil, 1988).

Powell (1996) examined independent schools in the United States and learned that private preparatory schools value both small school and small class size as necessary conditions for student success. In 1998, the average private school class size was 16.6 at the elementary level and 11.6 at the high school level. By contrast, the average class size was 18.6 in public elementary schools and 14.2 in public high schools (National Center for Education Statistics, 1999).[1]

Powell also determined that independent elementary schools tend to be small and independent high schools tend to be even smaller—in contrast to public schools, which tend to increase in size as the students they serve get older. In *The Power of Their Ideas,* Meier (1995) suggests that we abandon adolescents just at the time when they most often need to be in the company of trusted adults. . . .

## What Has My Experience Taught Me?

Over the years, I have taught students at nearly every level, from 3rd grade through graduate school. As a researcher, I have spent time gathering data on students at every level from preschool through 12th grade.My teaching and research experiences have provided me with data that convince me that both small classes and small schools are crucial to a teacher's ability to succeed with students.

One of my earliest teaching experiences was in a large comprehensive high school in Australia that included grades 7–10. I had more than 40 students in each of seven classes each day. During my second year, I taught Ray Campano. He was a quiet 10th grader who wasn't doing well in English. His parents, aware of his academic weaknesses, came to see me early in the first term. They asked that I keep them informed of the homework required and let them know if Ray was in danger of failing. They wanted to help and were supportive of my efforts on their son's behalf. In the ensuing weeks, I kept track of

Ray's progress, but I gradually paid less attention to him. He was pleasant and quiet and well behaved, but there were other students in the class who were not. Other students demanded that I give them individual attention because they wanted to excel. These two groups of students—the rebellious and the demanding—absorbed most of my time, while Ray quietly slipped out of my attention. To be sure, I saw him each day and recorded whether his work was coming in, but I neglected to examine his performance in the midst of competing demands to plan, grade papers, and work with the needier or more demanding students.

When midterm reports came due, I was horrified to realize that I had neglected to keep my eye on Ray's performance, which was less than satisfactory. I met with his parents and explained that I had not kept my end of our bargain. They were angry—and rightly so—but they were fair. Ray's mother asked to come to class for a week to see what was going on. At the end of that week, she said that she thought the work I asked the students to do was appropriate and that I was relatively well organized and focused. Nevertheless, she couldn't imagine how a teacher could manage anything more than a cursory relationship with any given student in so large a classroom. Mrs. Campano confirmed my own experience, which suggested that really knowing all 40 students in each of seven classes was impossible. Despite parental involvement and teachers' good intentions, it is easy for students to get lost in large classes and in large schools.

As Dean of Bank Street College of Education in New York City several years ago, I team-taught 5th and 6th graders in the College's School for Children. We were looking for a course of study that would engage the students in making some contribution to the local community while simultaneously building their reading, computer, writing, and observation skills. After long deliberation and engagement in a number of exploratory activities, our 5th and 6th graders decided that they would tutor younger students in a neighborhood public school. One of the

[1]The low average class size of public high schools obscures the fact that upper division courses in math and science and Advanced Placement courses are typically smaller, whereas many lower-track courses have more than 30 students.

students cried, "How are we supposed to teach reading? We're only kids. We just learned to read ourselves a few years ago!" A heated discussion ensued, during which one of the girls ran up to the chalkboard and said, "I know. Let's map how each of us learned to read."

The students made a chart of how old they were, where they were (home or school), with whom they were engaged in a reading activity, and what activity they were engaged in at the precise moment that they understood that they could read. Seventeen students in the classroom generated 14 different approaches to learning to read. I suggested that the students pick several of the most commonly used approaches and organize a seminar on each approach so that they could learn several methods for working with their reading buddies. They looked at me as if either I had lost my mind or I hadn't been listening. "We can't learn just three approaches, or we'll never learn to help all these kids learn to read! If we needed a bunch of different approaches to learn to read, why wouldn't they?"

This experience reinforced my belief that different students learn differently and that teachers need to build a repertoire of instructional strategies to reach individual students. Small class size is integral to this individualization: Teachers should be responsible for a smaller number of students so that they can get to know each student and his or her learning preferences. It takes time to get to know one's students and to individualize the learning experience, and doing so requires concentration. In a classroom with a large number of students, such attention simply isn't an option.

Colleagues and I recently conducted a study of small schools in Chicago. Part of our time was spent in a small school-within-a-school with eight teachers. Because they were few, they could meet together every day for an hour, work toward common agreements and understandings, and accept shared responsibility for their students. They discussed the curriculum in all subjects, agreed on

**TERM TO NOTE**

School-within-a-school

instructional approaches, and tried to build as much coherence in the curriculum as they could manage. In the larger school, which had some 70 faculty members, a common agenda simply wasn't possible.

The school-within-a-school teachers spent an enormous amount of time talking about their 300 students. They argued about students, challenged one another to see individual students differently, and agreed to work together to communicate to students that math or English or science was important for everyone. By the end of the first year, students in the smaller school-within-a-school had outperformed their peers on a number of measures: More of the smaller-school students had stayed in school, completed their courses, and received higher grades than had students in the host school. For example, between September 1998 and September 1999, approximately 11.1 percent of school-within-a-school students dropped out of school. By contrast, about 19.8 percent of their host-school peers dropped out during the same period (Wasley et al., 2000).

When we asked the school-within-a-school students why they thought they had achieved such results, they said that their teachers "dog us every day. They're relentless. They call our parents. They really care whether we get our work done. There's no hiding in this school!"

The time is ripe for educators to make the case for what research suggests and what our own experience has been telling us for years: Students do best in places where they can't slip through the cracks, where they are known by their teachers, and where their improved learning becomes the collective mission of a number of trusted adults. We have the resources to ensure that every student gets a good education, and we know what conditions best support their success. It is time to do what is right.

## REFERENCES

Goodlad, J. I., Soder, R., & Sirotnik, K. A. (Eds.). (1990). *The moral dimensions of teaching.* San Francisco: Jossey-Bass.

McNeil, L. M. (1988). *Contradictions of control: School structure and school knowledge.* New York: Routledge.

Meier, D. (1995). *The power of their ideas: Lessons for America from a small school in Harlem.* Boston: Beacon Press.

Snyder, T. D. (2000). *Digest of education statistics, 1999.* Washington, DC: U.S. Department of Education, National Center for Education Statistics.

National Commission on Teaching and America's Future. (1996). *What matters most: Teaching for America's future.* New York: NCTAF.

Oakes, J. (1987). *Improving inner-city schools. Current directions in urban district reform.* Santa Monica, CA: RAND.

Powell, A. G. (1996). *Lessons from privilege: The American prep school tradition.* Cambridge, MA: Harvard University Press.

Roza, M. (2001). The challenge for Title I. *Education Week, 20*(29), 38, 56.

Wasley, P. A., & Fine, M. (2000). *Small schools and the issue of scale.* New York: Bank Street College of Education.

Wasley, P. A., Fine, M., Gladden, M., Holland, N. E., King, S. P., Mosak, E., & Powell, L. C. (2000). *Small schools: Great strides.* New York: Bank Street College of Education.

Wheelock, A. (1992). *Crossing the tracks: How untracking can save America's schools.* New York: The New Press.

## POSTNOTE

The focus of this article on the values of small classes and small schools is appropriately on students. The many benefits that accrue to students are persuasive, especially the effects of small classes in the early grades and small schools for high school students. Not fully articulated are the effects of small classes and schools on teachers, especially those in middle and high schools. While the many and varied courses, extracurricular clubs, sports, and other activities in large schools appeal to certain types of teachers, most people who select education as a life's work have chosen it because of their deep interest in young people. They want to help students make the transition into adulthood. They want to be a positive influence in their students' lives. For them, the impersonality that is a by-product of large schools is often a source of their frustration with teaching. It limits their opportunity to forge significant relationships with the students who quickly pass through their classes and go on to other teachers. And as the author concludes, "Students do best in places where they can't slip through the cracks, where they are known by their teachers, and where their improved learning becomes the collective mission of a number of trusted adults." These are the conditions that appeal to most teachers.

## DISCUSSION QUESTIONS

1. What do you see as the primary gains from large schools?

2. What do you see as the major gains from small schools?

3. If the positive effects of small class size for the early grades are so compelling, why do you suppose more states haven't reduced class size in grades K–3?

# 24

# *Why Some Parents Don't Come to School*

## Margaret Finders and Cynthia Lewis

In our roles as teachers and as parents, we have been privy to the conversations of both teachers and parents. Until recently, however, we did not acknowledge that our view of parental involvement conflicts with the views of many parents. It was not until we began talking with parents in different communities that we were forced to examine our own deeply seated assumptions about parental involvement.

**TERMS TO NOTE**

Parental involvement

Institutional perspective

From talking with Latino parents and parents in two low-income Anglo neighborhoods, we have gained insights about why they feel disenfranchised from school settings. In order to include such parents in the educational conversation, we need to understand the barriers to their involvement from their vantage point, as that of outsiders. When asked, these parents had many suggestions that may help educators re-envision family involvement in the schools.

## The Institutional Perspective

The institutional perspective holds that children who do not succeed in school have parents who do not get involved in school activities or support school goals at home. Recent research emphasizes the importance of parent involvement in

At the time this article was written, Margaret Finders was an assistant professor of English education at Purdue University, West Lafayette, Indiana. Cynthia Lewis was on the faculty at Grinnell College, Grinnell, Iowa. From Margaret Finders and Cynthia Lewis, "Why Some Parents Don't Come to School," *Educational Leadership*, May 1994, pp. 50-54. Reprinted with permission of the Association for Supervision and Curriculum Development. Copyright © 2001 by ASCD. All rights reserved.

promoting school success (Comer 1984, Lareau 1987). At the same time, lack of participation among parents of socially and culturally diverse students is also well documented (Clark 1983, Delgado-Gaitan 1991).

The model for family involvement, despite enormous changes in the reality of family structures, is that of a two-parent, economically self-sufficient nuclear family, with a working father and homemaker mother (David 1989). As educators, we talk about "the changing family," but the language we use has changed little. The institutional view of nonparticipating parents remains based on a deficit model. "Those who *need* to come, don't come," a teacher explains, revealing an assumption that one of the main reasons for involving parents is to remediate them. It is assumed that involved parents bring a body of knowledge about the purposes of schooling to match institutional knowledge. Unless they bring such knowledge to the school, they themselves are thought to need education in becoming legitimate participants.

Administrators, too, frustrated by lack of parental involvement, express their concern in terms of a deficit model. An administrator expresses his bewilderment:

> Our parent-teacher group is the foundation of our school programs. . . . This group (gestures to the all-Anglo, all-women group seated in the library) is the most important organization in the school. You know, I just don't understand why *those other parents* won't even show up.

Discussions about family involvement often center on what families lack and how educators can best teach parents to support instructional agendas at home (Mansbach 1993). To revise this limited model for interaction between home and school, we must look outside of the institutional perspective.

## The Voices of "Those Other Parents"

We asked some of "those other parents" what they think about building positive home/school relations. In what follows, parents whose voices are rarely heard at school explain how the diverse contexts of their lives create tensions that interfere with positive home/school relations. For them, school experiences, economic and time constraints, and linguistic and cultural practices have produced a body of knowledge about school settings that frequently goes unacknowledged.

### Diverse School Experiences Among Parents

Educators often don't take into account how a parent's own school experiences may influence school relationships. Listen in as one father describes his son's school progress:

> They expect me to go to school so they can tell me my kid is stupid or crazy. They've been telling me that for three years, so why should I go and hear it again? They don't do anything. They just tell me my kid is bad.
>
> See, I've been there. I know. And it scares me. They called me a boy in trouble but I was a troubled boy. Nobody helped me because they liked it when I didn't show up. If I was gone for the semester, fine with them. I dropped out nine times. They wanted me gone.

This father's experiences created mistrust and prevent him from participating more fully in his son's education. Yet, we cannot say that he doesn't care about his son. On the contrary, his message is urgent.

For many parents, their own personal school experiences create obstacles to involvement. Par-

ents who have dropped out of school do not feel confident in school settings. Needed to help support their families or care for siblings at home, these individuals' limited schooling makes it difficult for them to help their children with homework beyond the early primary level. For some, this situation is compounded by language barriers and lack of written literacy skills. One mother who attended school through 6th grade in Mexico, and whose first language is Spanish, comments about homework that "sometimes we can't help because it's too hard." Yet the norm in most schools is to send home schoolwork with little information for parents about how it should be completed.

### Diverse Economic and Time Constraints

Time constraints are a primary obstacle for parents whose work doesn't allow them the autonomy and flexibility characteristic of professional positions. Here, a mother expresses her frustrations:

> Teachers just don't understand that I can't come to school at just any old time. I think Judy told you that we don't have a car right now. . . . Andrew catches a different bus than Dawn. He gets here a half an hour before her, and then I have to make sure Judy is home because I got three kids in three different schools. And I feel like the teachers are under pressure, and they're turning it around and putting the pressure on me cause they want me to check up on Judy and I really can't.

Often, parents work at physically demanding jobs, with mothers expected to take care of child-care responsibilities as well as school-related issues. In one mother's words:

> What most people don't understand about the Hispanic community is that you come home and you take care of your husband and your family first. Then if there's time you can go out to your meetings.

Other parents work nights, making it impossible to attend evening programs and difficult to appear at daytime meetings that interfere with family obligations and sleep.

At times, parents' financial concerns present a major obstacle to participation in their child's school activities. One mother expresses frustration that she cannot send eight dollars to school so her daughter can have a yearbook to sign like the other girls.

> I do not understand why they assume that everybody has tons of money, and every time I turn around it's more money for this and more money for that. Where do they get the idea that we've got all this money?

This mother is torn between the pressures of stretching a tight budget and wanting her daughter to belong. As is the case for others, economic constraints prevent her child from full participation in the culture of the school. This lack of a sense of belonging creates many barriers for parents.

### Diverse Linguistic and Cultural Practices

Parents who don't speak fluent English often feel inadequate in school contexts. One parent explains that "an extreme language barrier" prevented her own mother from ever going to anything at the school. Cultural mismatches can occur as often as linguistic conflicts. One Latino educator explained that asking young children to translate for their parents during conferences grates against a cultural norm. Placing children in a position of equal status with adults creates dysfunction within the family hierarchy.

One mother poignantly expresses the cultural discomfort she feels when communicating with Anglo teachers and parents:

> [In] the Hispanic culture and the Anglo culture things are done different and you really don't know—am I doing the right thing? When they call me and say, "You bring the

plates" [for class parties], do they think I can't do the cookies, too? You really don't know.

Voicing a set of values that conflicts with institutional constructions of the parent's role, a mother gives this culturally-based explanation for not attending her 12-year-old's school functions:

> It's her education, not mine. I've had to teach her to take care of herself. I work nights, so she's had to get up and get herself ready for school. I'm not going to be there all the time. She's gotta do it. She's a tough cookie. . . . She's almost an adult, and I get the impression that they want me to walk her through her work. And it's not that I don't care either. I really do. I think it's important, but I don't think it's my place.

This mother does not lack concern for her child. In her view, independence is essential for her daughter's success.

Whether it is for social, cultural, linguistic, or economic reasons, these parents' voices are rarely heard at school. Perhaps, as educators, we too readily categorize them as "those other parents" and fail to hear the concern that permeates such conversations. Because the experiences of these families vary greatly from our own, we operate on assumptions that interfere with our best intentions. What can be done to address the widening gap between parents who participate and those who don't?

### Getting Involved: Suggestions from Parents

Parents have many suggestions for teachers and administrators about ways to promote active involvement. Their views, however, do not always match the role envisioned by educators. Possessing fewer economic resources and educational skills to participate in traditional ways (Lareau 1987), these parents operate at a disadvantage until they understand how schools are organized and how they can promote systemic change (Delgado-Gaitan 1991).

If we're truly interested in establishing a dialogue with the parents of all of our nation's students, however, we need to understand what parents think can be done. Here are some of their suggestions.

### Clarify How Parents Can Help

Parents need to know exactly how they can help. Some are active in church and other community groups, but lack information about how to become more involved in their children's schooling. One Latina mother explains that most of the parents she knows think that school involvement means attending school parties.

As Concha Delgado-Gaitan (1991) points out ". . . the difference between parents who participate and those who do not is that those who do have recognized that they are a critical part of their children's education." Many of the parents we spoke to don't see themselves in this capacity.

### Encourage Parents to Be Assertive

Parents who do see themselves as needed participants feel strongly that they must provide their children with a positive view of their history and culture not usually presented at school.

Some emphasize the importance of speaking up for their children. Several, for instance, have argued for or against special education placement or retention for their children; others have discussed with teachers what they saw as inappropriate disciplinary procedures. In one parent's words:

> Sometimes kids are taken advantage of because their parents don't fight for them. I say to parents, if you don't fight for your child, no one's going to fight for them.

Although it may sound as if these parents are advocating adversarial positions, they are simply pleading for inclusion. Having spent much time on the teacher side of these conversations, we realize that teachers might see such talk as challenging their positions as professional decision makers. Yet, it is crucial that we expand the dialogue to include parent knowledge about school settings, even when that knowledge conflicts with our own.

### Develop Trust

Parents affirm the importance of establishing trust. One mother attributes a particular teacher's good turnout for parent/teacher conferences to her ability to establish a "personal relationship" with parents. Another comments on her need to be reassured that the school is open, that it's OK to drop by "anytime you can."

In the opportunities we provide for involvement, we must regularly ask ourselves what messages we convey through our dress, gestures, and talk. In one study, for example, a teacher described her school's open house in a middle-class neighborhood as "a cocktail party without cocktails" (Lareau 1987). This is the sort of "party" that many parents wouldn't feel comfortable attending.

Fear was a recurrent theme among the parents we interviewed: fear of appearing foolish or being misunderstood, fear about their children's academic standing. One mother explained:

> Parents feel like the teachers are looking at you, and I know how they feel, because I feel like that here. There are certain things and places where I still feel uncomfortable, so I won't go, and I feel bad, and I think maybe it's just me.

This mother is relaying how it feels to be culturally, linguistically, and ethnically different. Her body of knowledge does not match the institutional knowledge of the school and she is therefore excluded from home/school conversations.

### Build on Home Experiences

Our assumptions about the home environments of our students can either build or serve as links between home and school. An assumption that "these kids don't live in good environments" can destroy the very network we are trying to create. Too often we tell parents what we want them to do at home with no understanding of the rich social interaction that already occurs there (Keenan et al. 1993). One mother expresses her frustrations:

> Whenever I go to school, they want to tell me what to do at home. They want to tell me how to raise my kid. They never ask me what I think. They never ask me anything.

When we asked parents general questions about their home activities and how these activities might build on what happens at school, most thought there was no connection. They claimed not to engage in much reading and writing at home, although their specific answers to questions contradicted this belief. One mother talks about her time at home with her teenage daughter:

> My husband works nights and sometimes she sleeps with me. . . . We would lay down in bed and discuss the books she reads.

Many of the parents we spoke to mentioned Bible reading as a regular family event, yet they did not see this reading in relation to schoolwork. In one mother's words:

> I read the Bible to the children in Spanish, but when I see they're not understanding me, I stop (laughing). Then they go and look in the English Bible to find out what I said.

Although the Bible is not a text read at public schools, we can build on the literacy practices and social interactions that surround it. For instance, we can draw upon a student's ability to compare multiple versions of a text. We also can include among the texts we read legends, folktales, and mythology—literature that, like the Bible, is meant to teach us about our strengths and weaknesses as we strive to make our lives meaningful.

As teachers, of course, we marvel at the way in which such home interactions do, indeed, support our goals for learning at school; but we won't know about these practices unless we begin to form relationships with parents that allow them to share such knowledge.

## Use Parent Expertise

Moll (1992) underscores the importance of empowering parents to contribute *"intellectually to the development of lessons."* He recommends assessing the "funds of knowledge" in the community, citing a teacher who discovered that many parents in the Latino community where she taught had expertise in the field of construction. Consequently, the class developed a unit on construction, which included reading, writing, speaking, and building, all with the help of responsive community experts—the children's parents.

Parents made similar suggestions—for example, cooking ethnic foods with students, sharing information about multicultural heritage, and bringing in role models from the community. Latino parents repeatedly emphasized that the presence of more teachers from their culture would benefit their children as role models and would help them in home/school interactions.

Parents also suggested extending literacy by writing pen pal letters with students or involving their older children in tutoring and letter writing with younger students. To help break down the barriers that language differences create, one parent suggested that bilingual and monolingual parents form partnerships to participate in school functions together.

## An Invitation for Involvement

Too often, the social, economic, linguistic, and cultural practices of parents are represented as serious problems rather than valued knowledge. When we reexamine our assumptions about parental absence, we may find that our interpretations of parents who care may simply be parents who are like us, parents who feel comfortable in the teacher's domain.

Instead of operating on the assumption that absence translates into noncaring, we need to focus on ways to draw parents into the schools. If we make explicit the multiple ways we value the language, culture, and knowledge of the parents in our communities, parents may more readily accept our invitations.

## REFERENCES

Clark, R. M. (1983). *Family Life and School Achievement: Why Poor Black Children Succeed or Fail.* Chicago: University of Chicago Press.

Comer, J. P. (1984). "Homeschool Relationships as They Affect the Academic Success of Children." *Education and Urban Society* 16: 323–337.

David, M. E. (1989). "Schooling and the Family." In *Critical Pedagogy, the State, and Cultural Struggle,* edited by H. Giroux and P. McLaren. Albany, N.Y.: State University of New York Press.

Delgado-Gaitan, C. (1991). "Involving Parents in the Schools: A Process of Empowerment." *American Journal of Education* 100: 20–46.

Keenan, J. W., J. Willett, and J. Solsken. (1993). "Constructing an Urban Village: School/Home Collaboration in a Multicultural Classroom." *Language Arts* 70: 204–214.

Lareau, A. (1987). "Social Class Differences in Family-School Relationships: The Importance of Cultural Capital." *Sociology of Education* 60: 73–85.

Mansbach, S. C. (February/March 1993). "We Must Put Family Literacy on the National Agenda." *Reading Today:* 37.

Moll, L. (1992). "Bilingual Classroom Studies and Community Analysis: Some Recent Trends." *Educational Researcher* 21: 20–24.

## POSTNOTE

Much research supports the principle that children whose parents are active in their schools are more likely to succeed in school, whereas children whose parents are not involved are more apt to do poorly. Some parents are eager to work as partners with schools to be certain that their children are well prepared for the life and career choices they will make. Other parents are almost never involved with the school.

This article is useful to educators working at schools where parental involvement is less than what they hoped for. By understanding why some parents never show up at schools, educators can take steps to help overcome the parents' reluctance. Remember, teachers need parents to help them succeed.

## DISCUSSION QUESTIONS

1. List some of the main reasons Finders and Lewis give for parents not coming to school. Which of these reasons do you find compelling? Do any of the reasons surprise you?

2. Can you identify any additional reasons for parents to stay away from school, besides those given by the authors?

3. What strategies for involving parents in school have you seen employed, and how successful were they?

# 25

# *Life After School*

## Sandra L. Hofferth and Zita Jankuniene

How students spend their nonschool hours is important to their social development and academic achievement. Today, about 30 percent of a student's week is discretionary or free time (Hofferth & Sandberg, 200lb). What students do during that time—whether they play, read, watch television, play video games, or hang out with friends—will affect their long-term achievement and social adjustment (Eccles & Barber, 1999).

We wanted to find out how preadolescent students spend their time from the end of the school day until they go to sleep at night. In particular, we wondered

▶ Where do students go after school?

▶ What do students do?

▶ Whom do students spend time with?

▶ How does location affect disadvantaged students' involvement in activities?

Although many researchers have studied students' use of time (Asmussen & Larson, 1991; Bianchi & Robinson, 1997; Hofferth & Sandberg, 2001a; Hofferth & Sandberg, 2001b; Timmer, Eccles, & O'Brien, 1985), few studies have focused on what students do after school (Eccles & Barber, 1999; Medrich, Roizen, Rubin, & Buckley, 1982; Miller, O'Connor, Sirignano, & Joshi, 1996). Fewer still have explored supervision after school among elementary school students. Our study attempted to fill that gap.

Sandra L. Hofferth is Senior Research Scientist, University of Michigan Institute for Social Research, P. O. Box 1248, Ann Arbor, MI 48106; hofferth@umich.edu. Zita Jankuniene is Database Marketing Analyst, Time Inc.
From Sandra L. Hofferth and Zita Jankuniene, "Life After School," *Educational Leadership*, April 2001, pp. 19–23. Reprinted with permission of the Association for Supervision and Curriculum Development.

## Background

Research suggests that what students do after school depends on where they go, what their own and their families' characteristics are, and with whom they spend time when they get there. When we began our study, we wanted to examine the following factors:

**Location** Physical context is an important determinant of what students do. One study (Medrich, Roizen, Rubin, & Buckley, 1982) found that nearly three-quarters of the students in the sample went straight home from school, regardless of whether an adult was home to greet them.

**Students' Characteristics** What students do and the amount of time they spend doing it are likely to be affected by the students' characteristics, such as age and gender. As students mature, the range of activities that they want and are allowed to do broadens. In addition, gender differences exist, particularly in such activities as household work, personal care, and participation in household conversations. Gender differences show up more clearly in older students.

**Family Economics** What students do also depends on their parents' education levels and income. Well-educated parents often encourage students to participate in educational activities, such as reading and studying. Higher-income families typically can afford more expensive sports clubs and lessons for their children than lower-income families can.

**Supervision and Companionship** The type of activity, the location, and the kind and amount of supervision are closely linked. In this study, we examined whether location is linked to supervision and the involvement of adults and peers.

## Our Study

For our study, we classified the primary activities of students grades K–7 into 20 major categories. We used 18 categories from another study (Timmer, Eccles, & O'Brien, 1985), such as personal care, eating, sleeping, household work, school, studying, and reading, plus participation in day care and youth organizations.

## Data

The data come from the 1997 Child Development Supplement to the Panel Study of Income Dynamics (Hofferth, Davis-Kean, Davis, & Finkelstein, 1999), an annual 30-year longitudinal survey of a representative sample of U.S. men, women, children, and the families with whom they reside. In spring and fall 1997, data were collected on randomly selected 0- to 12-year-olds, both from the primary caregivers and from the students themselves. We looked at a sample of 1,484 students grades K–7 who went to school on a sample day. Because we were interested in students' time during after-school waking hours, we studied only those activities that they participated in after the school day ended until they went to bed, a six-hour period.

We based the study on 24-hour time diaries during one weekday. An interviewer asked either the parent or the parent and the student questions about the student's flow of activities during the 24-hour period beginning at midnight. The interviewer asked about the primary activity that the child was doing, when the activity began and ended, and whether any other activity took place concurrently. The interviewer also asked where the child was during the activity, who participated with the child, and whether anyone else was with the child but was not directly involved in the activity.

**Student Characteristics** Because a major transition in child care occurs at about age 9 or 10 (Hofferth, Brayfield, Deich, & Holcomb, 1991), we divided the students into three age groups: kindergarten (age 5), grades 1–3 (ages 6–8), and grades 4–7 (ages 9–12). In our sample, 12 percent of the students were in kindergarten, 39 percent in grades 1–3, and 48 percent in grades 4–7. The sample contained an equal proportion of boys and girls.

**Family Characteristics** We categorized the mothers' education levels: 18 percent of the mothers had less than a high school education, 33 percent had a high school diploma, 27 percent had some college education, 14 percent had a college degree, and 8 percent had some graduate school experience. We also compared the income of students' families to the poverty line that was calculated by the U.S. Bureau of the Census and identified those families who were under 100 percent of the poverty line, between 100 and 200 percent, and 200 percent and over.

## Results

**Where Do Students Go First?** At the end of the school day, 73 percent of the students went directly home, 8 percent stayed at school, 11 percent went to a day-care center or a family day-care home, and 8 percent went somewhere else, such as a parent's workplace, indoor or outdoor recreation centers, stores or shopping centers, restaurants, nonretail businesses, or churches. Where students went varied, first of all, by their grade level. More students in grades 4–7 went directly home and fewer were in day care, which makes sense: Older students are more often able to care for themselves. The number of students who stayed at school did not vary by age.

**Participation in After-School Activities** All students spent some time at home, and most spent some time elsewhere. One-quarter spent time in day care or at someone else's home, and 13 percent spent some time at school during the after-school hours.

**Home**   At home, television viewing topped the list of activities. Seventy-six percent of students of all ages watched television. Playing and studying were also common; half the students played and half studied. A surprising one-third did household chores. One-quarter spent some time reading for pleasure. About 15 percent engaged in sports activities or household conversations. Ten percent engaged in "passive leisure," which involved such activities as listening to music or just sitting around.

**School**   Students who stayed at school participated in sports (24 percent) and art activities (11 percent). They also studied (8 percent), visited with others (8 percent), and played (9 percent). Eleven percent were involved in youth organizations. About 10 percent engaged in passive leisure, and about 1 percent watched television at school.

**Elsewhere**   Of students who went to other locations after school, half played sports and one-quarter went shopping. Fourteen percent visited other people and 12 percent played. Fifteen percent engaged in educational activities, such as religious education or tutoring. Twelve percent reported that they did nothing or they just "hung out." Again, about 1 percent reported watching television.

## Interpretation of Findings

### Location and Activity

Students played in all locations, most commonly at home (54 percent) and in day care (43 percent), and less frequently at school (9 percent) and in other locations (12 percent). Students played sports at school (24 percent) and elsewhere (46 percent). They read for pleasure primarily at home, where 25 percent of students read for about half an hour.

Students watched television mainly in the home, though a small proportion watched television in day-care centers or in a caregiver's home. They spent about 1 hour and 40 minutes watching television at home after school and about one hour watching in a child care setting.

About 20 percent of the students attended a youth organization meeting, mostly at school or elsewhere. Although this is a lower rate than the total number of students enrolled in those organizations, it gives an accurate picture of the involvement of youth in organizations on any given day. They spent between 30 minutes to 1 hour and 20 minutes at youth organizations.

Students did schoolwork in a variety of settings. Although some studied in child care and after-school programs, most studied at home. About half the students spent some time studying at home; however, they only studied for 45 minutes in the early primary grades and for one hour in grades 4–7.

### Gender Differences

Gender differences were reflected only in certain activities. At home, boys in grades 4–7 tended to do more studying, sports, and playing, and less visiting, art, reading, and other passive leisure activities than girls did. At school, twice as many boys played sports. Girls did more tidying up, visiting, art, and passive leisure activities. But girls studied more at school than boys did. In other locations, boys were twice as likely to play sports, and girls were more likely to do household work, visit, and participate in art activities.

### Supervision

Adult supervision varied by location. Although students were highly supervised for most of the time in all settings, adult supervision was greatest in day care and at school and was least available at home and in other settings. At school and day care, students were almost never unsupervised. At home, students spent more time unsupervised, but only a fraction—3 percent—were alone. Students spent the largest proportion of time (10 percent) with peers or siblings only in other locations and at home. The older the students, the less adult supervision they had and the more time they spent with peers or alone. Students in grades 4–7 spent almost 6 percent of their home time alone and 10 percent of home time with peers only, compared with kindergartners, who spent 1 percent alone and 6 percent with peers.

### Family Income and Education

As we might expect, family income and maternal education related to the amount of time that students spent in activities after school. One of the best examples of income differences was participation in sports activities. Better-educated parents and those with higher incomes were able to afford more opportunities for their children. Schools equalized many of these opportunities, however. Although students from low-income families were no more or less likely to be enrolled in sports activities outside of school, they were more likely to be enrolled in school settings.

### What Educators Need to Know

Although 73 percent of elementary school students go home right after school, the proportion increases—from two-thirds of kindergartners to three-fourths of students grades 4–7—as students become more responsible for their own care. Students' activities vary substantially, depending on where they go after school. At school and day-care programs after school, students watch little television and do little studying or reading. They participate in structured activities, such as sports and youth organizations. Students do the majority of studying, playing, television watching, and reading at home.

What are the implications? With both parents more likely to work outside the home in recent decades, students spend less time at home. Although students study and play in several contexts, our findings showed that their reading time takes place primarily at home. As their time at home declines, so too will their time spent reading for pleasure. Because reading is the activity most strongly and consistently associated with student achievement (Hofferth & Sandberg, 2001b), this finding is worrisome.

Our findings also suggest that schools can play an equalizing role in providing access to certain activities after school for less-privileged students. Low-income students and students whose mothers have little education are less likely to play sports in indoor or outdoor recreation centers than at school or home, but they are more likely to play sports at school. Program planners in schools must take this fact into account.

School-based programs provide supervision and a safe environment. As students mature, however, they often prefer to spend time after school at home, even if unsupervised, because they can relax, read, and watch television. To appeal to the 10- to 12-year-old group, after-school programs need to take into account the need for independence and self-determination as well as the need for supervision and help with homework. Serving this in-between age of students is a challenge for educators. Information on what students choose to do at home and in other locations may help educators plan attractive after-school activities for this group.

### REFERENCES

Asmussen, L., & Larson, R. (1991). The quality of family time among young adolescents in single-parent and married-parent families. *Journal of Marriage and the Family, 53*, 1021–1030.

Bianchi, S., & Robinson, J. (1997). What did you do today? Children's use of time, family composition, and the acquisition of social capital. *Journal of Marriage and the Family, 59*, 332–344.

Eccles, J., & Barber, B. (1999). Student council, volunteering, basketball, or marching band: What kind of extracurricular involvement matters? *Journal of Adolescent Research, 14*, 10–43.

Hofferth, S. L., Brayfield, A., Deich, S., & Holcomb, P. (1991). *National child care survey, 1990.* Washington, DC: The Urban Institute.

Hofferth, S. L., Davis-Kean, P., Davis, J., & Finkelstein, J. (1999). *1997 user guide: The child development supplement to the Panel Study of Income Dynamics.* Ann Arbor, MI: Institute for Social Research.

Hofferth, S. L., & Sandberg, J. F. (2001a). Changes in American children's time, 1981–1997. In T. Owens & S. L. Hofferth (Eds.), *Children at the millennium: Where have we come from, where are we going?* New York: Elsevier Science.

Hofferth, S. L., & Sandberg, J. F. (2001b, forthcoming). How American children use their time. *Journal of Marriage and the Family, 63*(3).

Medrich, E., Roizen, J., Rubin, V., & Buckley, S. (1982). *The serious business of growing up: A study of children's lives outside school.* Berkeley: University of California Press.

Miller, B., O'Connor, S., Sirignano, S., & Joshi, P. (1996). *I wish the kids didn't watch so much TV:*

*Out-of-school time in three low-income communities* [School-age child care project]. Wellesley, MA: Center for Research on Women.

Timmer, S. G., Eccles, J., & O'Brien, K. (1985). How children use time. In F. S. Juster (Ed.), *Time, goods, and well-being* (pp. 353–382). Ann Arbor, MI: Institute for Social Research.

*Author's note:* The National Institute of Child Health and Human Development funded this research under grant U01-HD37563, the Family and Child Well-Being Research Network.

## POSTNOTE

Once upon a time, American students left school at three o'clock, went home to Mom, had milk and cookies, went out to play with the neighborhood kids, had supper with the family at six, and spent the rest of the evening with a little television and a solid period of homework. For most American children that world is past. Most dramatically, with some 80 percent of mothers in the work force, there is no one home to serve up the milk and cookies. Plus, many of our neighborhoods are hardly as safe as they once were.

While many parents try to provide for their children's after-school supervision by rearranging their work schedules or providing after-school programs for them, many leave their children unsupervised. This "leaving children unsupervised" is part of a large social movement which has been described as the uncoupling or disengagement of the adult world from the close supervision of children. Many families today provide less guidance and have weaker authority over their children. Children fend for themselves at an earlier age and make their own choices, choices such as whether or not to do homework and how much and what television to watch. Of course, many young people rise to the challenge and take constructive control of their lives. But then there are the others who become addicted to television, Internet pornography, early sexuality, and that great American pastime: cruising the mall.

## DISCUSSION QUESTIONS

1. When you were in elementary and secondary schools, what kind of after-school experiences did you have?

2. Do you believe the school has the right and the responsibility to provide guidance to parents about what kinds of structured environment their children should have when they leave school for the day?

3. What do you think of our society's early disengagement of adults from children? What has been your own experience?

# Home Schooling Comes of Age

Patricia M. Lines

## 26

This fall, when school bells summoned school-aged children, some did not respond. These children turned, instead, to home schooling, learning primarily at home or in the nearby community. Not so long ago, the families of these children might have gone underground, hiding from public view. Now they feel that they are simply exercising a valid educational option.

Home schooling has come of age. On any given day, more than a half million children are home schooled—perhaps little more than 1 percent of all school-aged children and about 10 percent of those who are privately schooled. This rough estimate assumes modest growth since 1990–1991, when I collected data from three independent sources—state education agencies, distributors of popular curricular packages, and state and local home-school associations. Knowing that all these figures represented the tip of the iceberg, I also used surveys of home-schoolers to estimate how many remained submerged (Lines 1991).

**TERM TO NOTE**
Home schooling

My current estimate rests in part on evidence of growth since then together with a rough assessment of the Census Bureau's 1994 Current Population Survey. Assuming the average home-schooling experience lasts only two years, as many as 6 percent of all families with children could have some home-schooling experience.

Patricia M. Lines (JD, University of Minnesota; PhD, Catholic University of America) is Discovery Institute's senior fellow specializing in education issues. From Patricia M. Lines, "Home Schooling Comes of Age." *Educational Leadership*, October 1996, pp. 63–67. Reprinted with permission of the Association for Supervision and Curriculum Development. Copyright © 1996 by ASCD. All rights reserved.

## Making It Legal

A more favorable legal climate also signals the coming of age of home schooling. Twenty years ago, many states did not allow it. Constitutional protection for parents has always been ambiguous. The U.S. Supreme Court has never explicitly ruled on home schooling, although in 1972, in *Wisconsin v. Yoder*, the Court did restrict compulsory school requirements in a limited ruling involving the right of Amish students not to attend high school. Nearly a half century earlier, in a case involving a Catholic private school (*Pierce v. Society of Sisters*, 1925), the high court upheld, in more general terms, the right of parents to direct the education of their children.

Home-schoolers have argued that these cases protect them. But public officials have often disagreed, charging parents with violating compulsory education laws. In most cases, the courts have avoided the heart of the matter and—as is traditional in the American judicial system—ruled on narrow legal grounds. For example, some courts have struck down compulsory education laws as too vague, or found that restrictive school board regulations exceeded the board's statutory authority. Yet some courts have upheld states' legal requirements and found that parents met or did not meet them. A few parents have gone to jail for the cause.

State legislatures have responded more vigorously than the courts. Where many states once forbade home schooling, all states now allow it. At the same time, all states do expect the home-schooling family to file basic information with either the state or local education agency. And some states have additional requirements, such as the submission of a curriculum plan; the testing of students; or, in a few cases, education requirements or testing for parents.

## Bending Stereotypes

What do today's home-schoolers look like? The stereotypical view is that they are loners who do not care about the opinions of others. But in at least one survey of home-schooling parents, 95 percent of respondents said the single most important thing that they wanted was support and encouragement from family, friends, church, and community (Mayberry et al. 1995).

Certainly the image of the isolated family does not fit any home-schooling family that I have met. On the contrary, these families seem highly connected to other families and other institutions. Indeed, the most universal resource that home-schooling families draw upon are like-minded families. Wherever there is more than a handful of home-schooling families in an area, they tend to form at least one home-schooling association.

Though home-schoolers look to one another, they hardly look *like* one another. One family may start the day with prayer or a flag salute, followed by a traditional, scheduled curriculum. Another may throw out the schedule and opt for child-led learning, providing help as the child expresses interest in a topic. In either type of family, the children are likely to take increasing responsibility for choosing and carrying out projects as they mature. And either type of family is likely to collaborate with other families.

Some home-schooled children will spend part of their time—with or without parents—at a local public or private school or at a nearby college. Substantial numbers of home-schoolers have invaded the electronic world, using it heavily for educational materials and networking. Families also draw upon resources at libraries, museums, parks departments, churches, and local businesses and organizations, and take advantage of extension courses and various mentors. In addition, they use the curriculum packages, books, and other materials that many private schools offer for use in home schooling.

## Courting Public Opinion

Now that all states have adopted more flexible legislation, the most important factor contributing to the growth of home schooling may be the increased receptivity of the general public. In the 1980s, few Americans gave home-schoolers much support or encouragement. In 1985, for example, only 16 percent of respondents to the annual *Phi Delta Kappan* Gallup poll thought that home schooling was a "good thing." By 1988, 28 percent thought so. That same year, Gallup asked whether parents should or should not have the legal right to home-school. Fifty-three percent said "should" and 39 percent said "should not" (Gallup and Elam 1988; Gallup 1984).

Because the *Kappan* Gallup poll has not asked these questions again, one must turn to other sources to gauge changing attitudes. Increasingly favorable media reports are one indicator. Mayberry and her colleagues have observed that media in the 1970s reported "the most divisive and extreme home education court cases and their outcomes" and tended to show home-schooling parents "as neglectful and irresponsible" (Mayberry et al. 1995). They note that recent news stories not only portray home-schoolers in a more positive light, but sometimes as folk heroes.

In a similar vein, Pat Farenga, a home-schooling leader employed by Holt publishers, told me that 10 years ago, *Good Housekeeping* and *Publisher's Weekly* would never run stories suggesting home schooling as an option for their readers, but both now do. (Based in Cambridge, Massachusetts, Holt Associates Inc. publishes *Growing Without Schooling*, a bimonthly newsletter designed to give practical advice to home-schooling parents.)

Last April, participants in a Home-School Association online discussion group (AHAonline @aol.com) reported how dramatically things have changed over the last decade. One home-schooler recalled that 10 years ago, if she told someone what she was doing, the first response would be "Is that legal?" Often this would be followed by strong disapproval. Another participant, Ann Lahrson (author of *Home Schooling in Oregon: The Handbook*), told how some friends, neighbors, and family members "rejected us, ignored us, clucked at us." She added that "professionally, I was shunned by colleagues at the public school where I had previously taught." Today, these home-schoolers said, they mostly hear remarks like, "Oh, do you enjoy it?" or "Oh, yeah, my brother/neighbor/cousin/fellow employee does that!"

## Partnering Public Schools

Professional educators, on the other hand, remain wary. In 1988, the National Educational Association adopted a resolution calling for more rigorous regulation of home schooling. In March 1993, the National Association of Elementary School Principals adopted a resolution declaring that education is "most effectively done through cohesive organizations in formal settings" and specifically criticized home schooling. Even the national Parent-Teachers Association has passed a resolution opposing home schooling.

Other public educators have decided to work with home-schoolers. Most state education agencies have a home-schooling liaison, who at minimum will help a family understand state requirements. A small but growing number of school districts are offering home-schoolers access to schools on a part-time basis and, in some cases, special programs for home-schoolers.

**TERM TO NOTE**
Home-school liaison

In fact, the most exciting development in the home-schooling world is the emergence of partnerships between public schools and home schools, an arrangement that educators in Alaska pioneered. Teachers in Juneau work with students all over the state, staying in touch by mail and telephone and through occasional visits. Although the program was designed for students in remote areas, Alaska has never denied access to it because a child was near a school. The majority of the students now live in the Anchorage area.

Similar partnerships have emerged at the district level in other states. In California, for example, a child may enroll in an independent study program in a public school and base his or her studies in the home. Washington public schools must enroll children part-time if their families request it. The Des Moines (Iowa) School District, as well as several dozen in Washington, California, and other states, offer special programs for home-schooled children. Usually a child may enroll in such programs anywhere in the state. In a preview of education in the 21st century, these fledgling programs often rely heavily on electronic communications programs and software.

A few educators actually urge collaboration with home-schoolers, in the belief that they provide good models in exploring ways to involve parents and to individualize instruction and assessment (Weston 1996). For example, Dan Endsley, one of the founders of the Home Education League of Parents (HELP) in Toledo, Ohio, observes that

> As we helped more and more families learn about the home-school option, we found that school administrators also became more tolerant of home schooling. In several cases, public school administrators even recommended that families get in touch with HELP and gave them our address and phone numbers.

## Remaining Vigilant

Given the more favorable legal climate for home schooling, families are now freer to concentrate on access to public resources and scholastic and athletic competitions. Still, home-schoolers remain watchful. There are several national organizations and at least one statewide organization in every state. Some states also have a dozen or more regional associations. All these groups monitor issues that might affect home schoolers, and they can mobilize large numbers of constituents where their interests are at stake.

The Home-School Legal Defense Association, based in Paeonian Springs, Virginia, and headed by Michael P. Farris, maintains a staff of about seven lawyers specializing in home-schooling law. The organization routinely monitors developments in every state, and keeps its national membership informed of potential problems. The group is also ready to negotiate or sue where it believes a policy might threaten its members' interests. An affiliated organization, the National Center for Home Education, runs an aggressive congressional action program with a facsimile alert system (Mayberry et al. 1995). State associations provide the same services for their constituencies. So, too, do other organizations, such as Clonlara Home-Based Education, an Ann Arbor, Michigan–based group that offers support nationwide.

As a result of these interest groups, efforts to pass stricter home-schooling laws or to seek enforcement that exceeds statutory authorization are likely to face organized and informed opposition and legal challenges. Clonlara, for example, argued successfully that the Michigan Board of Education exceeded its statutory authority to regulate (*Clonlara v. State Board* 1993).

In an interview with me, an experienced staff member of the Congressional Research Service compared the activity of the home-schooling lobby to that of the lobby for the Individuals with Disabilities Education Act. He noted, though, that unlike disability law backers, home-schoolers are merely reactive, rarely taking the offensive.

**TERM TO NOTE**

Individuals with Disabilities Education Act (IDEA)

## Pointing the Way for Reform?

Does home schooling help children academically? There is considerable disagreement on this question. No one has undertaken research involving controls that indicates whether the *same* children would do better or worse in home schooling than in a public or private school classroom. States that require testing, however, have analyzed test scores, and home-schooling associations have a multitude of data from these states. Yet information from both these sources may reflect only a select group of home-schoolers, as not all families cooperate with state testing requirements, and private efforts rely on voluntary information. These caveats notwithstanding, virtually all the available data show that scores of the tested home-schooled children are above average, and comparable to the higher achievement pattern of private school students (Ray and Wartes 1991).

People also disagree on whether home schooling helps or hinders children's social development. Children engaged in home schooling spend less time with their peer group and more time with people of different ages. Most spend time with other children through support and networking groups, scouting, churches, and other associations. Many spend time with adults other than their parents through activities such as community volunteer work, home-based businesses, and tutoring or mentoring. No conclusive research suggests that time spent with same-aged peers is preferable to time spent with people of varying ages.

That said, limited testing of a self-selected group of home-schooled children suggests that these children are above average in their social and psychological development (Sheirs 1992, Delahooke 1986). At the very least, anyone who has observed home-schoolers will notice a high level of sharing, networking, collaboration, and cooperative learning.

Clearly, home schooling offers the potential for a very different educational environment for children. As such, it could be an important resource for studying how children learn, and whether and when formal or informal learning environments are superior. To the extent that home-schoolers are willing to cooperate, they could provide an opportunity to study the effects of one-on-one lay tutoring, child-led learning, and distance learning.

Although the percentage of children in home schooling on any one day is small, the number of adults in the home-schooling movement is much larger. Growth in numbers, increased acceptance by the public, and opportunities for engaging in the policy arena mean that home-schoolers could be an important part of a coalition seeking education reform at the state or national level.

## REFERENCES

Delahooke, M. M. (1986). "Home Educated Children's Social/Emotional Adjustment and Academic Achievement: A Comparison Study." Doctoral diss. Los Angeles: California School of Professional Psychology.

Gallup, A. M. (1984). "The Gallup Poll of the Public's Attitudes Toward the Public Schools." *Phi Delta Kappan* 66, 1: 23–28.

Gallup, A. M., and S. M. Elam. (September 1988). "The 20th Annual Gallup Poll of the Public's Attitudes Toward the Public Schools." *Phi Delta Kappan* 70, 1: 33–46.

Lines, P. (October 1991). "Estimating the Home-Schooled Population," U.S. Department of Education, Office of Research Working Paper.

Mayberry, M., J. G. Knowles, B. Ray, and S. Marlow. (1995). *Home Schooling: Parents as Educators.* Thousand Oaks, Calif.: Corwin Press.

*Pierce v. Society of Sisters.* (1925). 268 U.S. 510.

Ray, B. D., and J. Wartes. (1991). "The Academic Achievement and Affective Development of Home-Schooled Children." In *Home Schooling: Political, Historical and Pedagogical Perspectives,* edited by J. Van Galen and M. A. Pitman. Norwood, N.J.: Ablex Publishing Corporation.

Sheirs, L. E. (1992). "Comparison of Social Adjustment Between Home- and Traditionally-Schooled Students." Doctoral diss., University of Florida.

Weston, M. (April 3, 1996). "Reformers Should Take a Look at Home Schools." *Education Week:* 34.

*Wisconsin v. Yoder.* (1972). 406 U.S. 205.

*Author's note:* For an expanded version of this article, see P. Lines, (in press). "Home Schooling," In *Private Education and Educational Choice,* edited by J. G. Cibulka (Westport, Conn.: Greenwood Press).

## POSTNOTE

Widespread criticism of our schools, along with the growing realization of education's importance, has set off an educational growth phase in the United States. As a historically innovative and experimental country, the United States is responding true to form, by striking out in new directions. The home-schooling movement is one such effort, as are charter schools, voucher experiments, and educational networks like the Coalition of Essential Schools.

Educational critics used to complain that our schools were captured by the "one right way" mentality. No longer. Home schooling is a case in point. It appears to be the right way for some, but for others it can be a disaster. To home-school well takes a special set of resources, among them a parent (or two) with the willingness and ability to teach. As this article suggests, however, home schooling seems to be satisfying the educational needs of hundreds of thousands of children and parents.

## Discussion Questions

1. What do you believe are the greatest potential advantages and disadvantages of home schooling?

2. Why do you suppose there has been such strong opposition to home schooling in the United States?

3. List what you think are the resources needed by someone to be a successful home-school teacher.

# Curriculum and Standards

The bedrock question of education is: What knowledge is most worth knowing? This question goes right to the heart of individual and social priorities. As our world has become more and more drenched with information, information pouring out at us from many different media, the question of what is worth our limited time and attention has increased in importance. It is the quintessential curriculum question.

In recent years, however, policymakers and educators have attempted to improve our schools by establishing what should be learned through state-mandated curriculum standards and by enforcing those standards through regular testing. In very real ways, this effort has dramatically affected what is going on in today's classrooms. The "Leave No Child Behind" Act of 2001 requires states to test students each year in grades 3–8.

The question of what is most worth knowing, however, begets others. What is the purpose of knowledge? To make a great deal of money? To become a wise person? To prepare oneself for important work? To contribute to the general good of society?

This difficult question becomes more and more complex and swiftly takes us into the realm of values. Nevertheless, it is a question communities must regularly address in our decentralized education system. In struggling with curriculum issues, a community is really making a bet on the future needs of society and of the young people who will have to live in that society. Behind the choice of a new emphasis on foreign language instruction or on computer literacy is a social gamble, and the stakes are high. Offering students an inadequate curriculum is like sending troops into battle with popguns.

# 27 CLASSIC *The Saber-Tooth Curriculum*

## J. Abner Peddiwell

T he first great educational theorist and practitioner of whom my imagination has any
record (began Dr. Peddiwell in his best professional tone) was a man of Chellean times
whose full name was *New-Fist-Hammer-Maker*
but whom, for convenience, I shall hereafter
call *New-Fist*.

New-Fist was a doer, in spite of the fact that
there was little in his environment with which to
do anything very complex. You have undoubtedly heard of the pear-shaped, chipped-stone
tool which archaeologists call the *coup-de-poing*
or fist hammer. New-Fist gained his name and
a considerable local prestige by producing one
of these artifacts in less rough and more useful form than any previously known to his
tribe. His hunting clubs were generally superior
weapons, moreover, and his fire-using techniques were patterns of simplicity and precision. He knew how to do things his community
needed to have done, and he had the energy
and will to go ahead and do them. By virtue of
these characteristics he was an educated man.

New-Fist was also a thinker. Then, as now,
there were few lengths to which men would not
go to avoid the labor and pain of thought. More
readily than his fellows, New-Fist pushed himself
beyond those lengths to the point where cere-
bration was inevitable. The same quality of intelligence which led him into the socially approved
activity of producing a superior artifact also led
him to engage in the socially disapproved practice of thinking. When other men gorged themselves on the proceeds of a successful hunt and

vegetated in dull stupor for many hours thereafter, New-Fist ate a little less heartily, slept a
little less stupidly, and arose a little earlier than
his comrades to sit by the fire and think. He
would stare moodily at the flickering flames
and wonder about various parts of his environment until he finally got to the point where he
became strongly dissatisfied with the accustomed ways of his tribe. He began to catch
glimpses of ways in which life might be made
better for himself, his family, and his group. By
virtue of this development, he became a dangerous man.

This was the background that made this
doer and thinker hit upon the concept of a conscious, systematic education. The immediate
stimulus which put him directly into the practice of education came from watching his children at play. He saw these children at the cave
entrance before the fire engaged in activity with
bones and sticks and brightly colored pebbles.
He noted that they seemed to have no purpose
in their play beyond immediate pleasure in the
activity itself. He compared their activity with
that of the grown-up members of the tribe. The
children played for fun; the adults worked for
security and enrichment of their lives. The children dealt with bones, sticks, and pebbles; the
adults dealt with food, shelter, and clothing. The
children protected themselves from boredom;
the adults protected themselves from danger.

"If I could only get these children to do the
things that will give more and better food, shelter, clothing, and security," thought New-Fist,
"I would be helping this tribe to have a better
life. When the children became grown, they
would have more meat to eat, more skins to
keep them warm, better caves in which to sleep,
and less danger from the striped death with the
curving teeth that walks these trails at night."

---

J. Abner Peddiwell is the pseudonym for Harold W.
Benjamin, a professor of education who died in
1969. From *The Saber-Tooth Curriculum* by J. Abner
Peddiwell. Copyright © 1959 by McGraw-Hill, Inc.
Used with permission of The McGraw-Hill Companies.

Having set up an educational goal, New-Fist proceeded to construct a curriculum for reaching that goal. "What things must we tribesmen know how to do in order to live with full bellies, warm backs, and minds free from fear?" he asked himself.

To answer this question, he ran various activities over in his mind. "We have to catch fish with our bare hands in the pool far up the creek beyond that big bend," he said to himself. "We have to catch fish with our bare hands in the pool right at the bend. We have to catch them in the same way in the pool just this side of the bend. And so we catch them in the next pool and the next and the next. And we catch them with our bare hands."

Thus New-Fist discovered the first subject of the first curriculum—fish-grabbing-with-the-bare-hands.

"Also we club the little woolly horses," he continued with his analysis. "We club them along the bank of the creek where they come down to drink. We club them in the thickets where they lie down to sleep. We club them in the upland meadow where they graze. Wherever we find them we club them."

So woolly-horse-clubbing was seen to be the second main subject of the curriculum.

"And finally, we drive away the saber-tooth tigers with fire," New-Fist went on in his thinking. "We drive them from the mouth of our caves with fire. We drive them from our trail with burning branches. We wave firebrands to drive them from our drinking hole. Always we have to drive them away, and always we drive them with fire."

Thus was discovered the third subject—saber-tooth-tiger-scaring-with-fire.

Having developed a curriculum, New-Fist took his children with him as he went about his activities. He gave them an opportunity to practice these three subjects. The children liked to learn. It was more fun for them to engage in these purposeful activities than to play with colored stones just for the fun of it. They learned the new activities well, and so the educational system was a success.

As New-Fist's children grew older, it was plain to see that they had an advantage in good and safe living over other children who had never been educated systematically. Some of the more intelligent members of the tribe began to do as New-Fist had done, and the teaching of fish-grabbing, horse-clubbing, and tiger-scaring came more and more to be accepted as the heart of real education.

For a long time, however, there were certain more conservative members of the tribe who resisted the new, formal educational system on religious grounds. "The Great Mystery who speaks in thunder and moves in lightning," they announced impressively, "the Great Mystery who gives men life and takes it from them as he wills—if that Great Mystery had wanted children to practice fish-grabbing, horse-clubbing, and tiger-scaring before they were grown up, he would have taught them these activities himself by implanting in their natures instincts for fish-grabbing, horse-clubbing, and tiger-scaring. New-Fist is not only impious to attempt something the Great Mystery never intended to have done; he is also a damned fool for trying to change human nature."

Whereupon approximately half of these critics took up the solemn chant, "If you oppose the will of the Great Mystery, you must die," and the remainder sang derisively in unison, "You can't change human nature."

Being an educational statesman as well as an educational administrator and theorist, New-Fist replied politely to both arguments. To the more theologically minded, he said that, as a matter of fact, the Great Mystery had ordered this new work done, that he even did the work himself by causing children to want to learn, that children could not learn by themselves without divine aid, that they could not learn at all except through the power of the Great Mystery, and that nobody could really understand the will of the Great Mystery concerning fish, horses, and saber-tooth tigers unless he had been well grounded in three fundamental subjects of the New-Fist school. To the human-nature-cannot-be-changed shouters, New-Fist pointed out the fact that paleolithic culture had attained its high level by changes in human nature and that it seemed almost unpatriotic to deny the very process which had made the community great.

"I know you, my fellow tribesmen," the pioneer educator ended his argument gravely, "I know you as the humble and devoted servants of the Great Mystery. I know that you would not for one moment consciously oppose yourselves to his will. I know you as intelligent and loyal citizens of the great cave-realm, and I know that your pure and noble patriotism will not permit you to do anything which will block the development of that most cave-realmish of all our institutions—the paleolithic educational system. Now that you understand the true nature and purpose of this institution, I am serenely confident that there are no reasonable lengths to which you will not go in its defense and its support."

By this appeal the forces of conservatism were won over to the side of the new school, and in due time everybody who was anybody in the community knew that the heart of good education lay in the three subjects of fish-grabbing, horse-clubbing, and tiger-scaring. New-Fist and his contemporaries grew older and were gathered by the Great Mystery to the Land of the Sunset far down the creek. Other men followed their educational ways more and more, until at last all the children of the tribe were practiced systematically in the three fundamentals. Thus the tribe prospered and was happy in the possession of adequate meat, skins, and security.

It is to be supposed that all would have gone well forever with this good educational system if conditions of life in that community had remained forever the same. But conditions changed, and life which had once been so safe and happy in the cave-realm valley became insecure and disturbing.

A new ice age was approaching in that part of the world. A great glacier came down from the neighboring mountain range to the north. Year

after year it crept closer and closer to the headwaters of the creek which ran through the tribe's valley, until at length it reached the stream and began to melt into the water. Dirt and gravel which the glacier had collected on its long journey were dropped into the creek. The water grew muddy. What had once been a crystal-clear stream in which one could see easily to the bottom was now a milky stream into which one could not see at all.

At once the life of the community was changed in one very important respect. It was no longer possible to catch fish with the bare hands. The fish could not be seen in the muddy water. For some years, moreover, the fish in the creek had been getting more timid, agile, and intelligent. The stupid, clumsy, brave fish, of which originally there had been a great many, had been caught with the bare hands for fish generation after fish generation, until only fish of superior intelligence and agility were left. These smart fish, hiding in the muddy water under the newly deposited glacial boulders, eluded the hands of the most expertly trained fish-grabbers. Those tribesmen who had studied advanced fish-grabbing in the secondary school could do no better than their less well-educated fellows who had taken only an elementary course in the subject, and even the university graduates with majors in ichthyology were baffled by the problem. No matter how good a man's fish-grabbing education had been, he could not grab fish when he could not find fish to grab.

The melting waters of the approaching ice sheet also made the country wetter. The ground became marshy far back from the banks of the creek. The stupid woolly horses, standing only five or six hands high and running on four-toed front feet and three-toed hind feet, although admirable objects for clubbing, had one dangerous characteristic. They were ambitious. They all wanted to learn to run on their middle toes. They all had visions of becoming powerful and aggressive animals instead of little and timid ones. They dreamed of a far-distant day when some of their descendants would be sixteen hands high, weigh more than half a ton, and be able to pitch their would-be riders into the dirt. They knew they could never attain these goals in a wet, marshy country, so they all went east to the dry, open plains, far from the paleolithic hunting grounds. Their places were taken by little antelopes who came down with the ice sheet and were so shy and speedy and had so keen a scent for danger that no one could approach them closely enough to club them.

The best trained horse-clubbers of the tribe went out day after day and employed the most efficient techniques taught in the schools, but day after day they returned empty-handed. A horse-clubbing education of the highest type could get no results when there were no horses to club.

Finally, to complete the disruption of paleolithic life and education, the new dampness in the air gave the saber-tooth tigers pneumonia, a disease to which these animals were peculiarly susceptible and to which most of them succumbed. A few moth-eaten specimens crept south to the desert, it is true, but they were pitifully few and weak representatives of a once numerous and powerful race.

So there were no more tigers to scare in the paleolithic community, and the best tiger-scaring techniques became only academic exercises, good in themselves, perhaps, but not necessary for tribal security. Yet this danger to the people was lost only to be replaced by another and even greater danger, for with the advancing ice sheet came ferocious glacial bears which were not afraid of fire, which walked the trails by day as well as by night, and which could not be driven away by the most advanced methods developed in the tiger-scaring course of the schools.

The community was now in a very difficult situation. There was no fish or meat for food, no hides for clothing, and no security from the hairy death that walked the trails day and night. Adjustment to this difficulty had to be made at once if the tribe was not to become extinct.

Fortunately for the tribe, however, there were men in it of the old New-Fist breed, men who had the ability to do and the daring to think. One of them stood by the muddy stream, his stomach contracting with hunger pains, longing for some way to get a fish to eat. Again and again he had tried the old fish-grabbing technique that day, hoping desperately that at last it might work, but now in black despair he finally rejected all that he had learned in the schools and looked about him for some new way to get fish from that stream. There were stout but slender vines hanging from trees along the bank. He pulled them down and began to fasten them together more or less aimlessly. As he worked, the vision of what he might do to satisfy his hunger and that of his crying children back in the cave grew clearer. His black despair lightened a little. He worked more rapidly and intelligently. At last he had it—a net, a crude seine. He called a companion and explained the device. The two men took the net into the water, into pool after pool, and in one hour they caught more fish—intelligent fish in muddy water—than the whole tribe could have caught in a day under the best fish-grabbing conditions.

Another intelligent member of the tribe wandered hungrily through the woods where once the stupid little horses had abounded but where now only the elusive antelope could be seen. He had tried the horse-clubbing technique on the antelope until he was fully convinced of its futility. He knew that one would starve who relied on school learning to get him meat in those woods. Thus it was that he too, like the fish-net inventor, was finally impelled by hunger to new ways. He bent a strong, springy young tree over an antelope trail, hung a noosed vine therefrom, and fastened the whole device in so ingenious a fashion that the passing animal would release a trigger and be snared neatly when the tree jerked upright. By setting a line of these snares, he was able in one night to secure more meat and skins than a dozen horse-clubbers in the old days had secured in a week.

A third tribesman, determined to meet the problem of the ferocious bears, also forgot what he had been taught in school and began to think in direct and radical fashion. Finally, as a result of this thinking, he dug a deep pit in a bear trail, covered it with branches in such a way that a bear would walk on it unsuspectingly, fall through to the bottom, and remain trapped until the tribesmen could come up and despatch him with sticks and stones at their leisure. The inventor showed his friends how to dig and camouflage other pits until all the trails around the community were furnished with them. Thus the tribe had even more security than before and in addition had the great additional store of meat and skins which they secured from the captured bears.

As the knowledge of these new inventions spread, all the members of the tribe were engaged in familiarizing themselves with the new ways of living. Men worked hard at making fish nets, setting antelope snares, and digging bear pits. The tribe was busy and prosperous.

There were a few thoughtful men who asked questions as they worked. Some of them even criticized the schools.

"These new activities of net-making and operating, snare-setting, and pit-digging are indispensable to modern existence," they said. "Why can't they be taught in school?"

The safe and sober majority had a quick reply to this naive question. "School!" they snorted derisively. "You aren't in school now. You are out here in the dirt working to preserve the life and happiness of the tribe. What have these practical activities got to do with schools? You're not saying lessons now. You'd better forget your lessons and your academic ideals of fish-grabbing, horse-clubbing, and tiger-scaring if you want to eat, keep warm, and have some measure of security from sudden death."

The radicals persisted a little in their questioning. "Fishnet-making and using, antelope-snare construction and operation, and bear-catching and killing," they pointed out, "require intelligence and skills—things we claim to develop in schools. They are also activities we need to know. Why can't the schools teach them?"

But most of the tribe, and particularly the wise old men who controlled the school, smiled indulgently at this suggestion. "That wouldn't be *education*," they said gently.

"But why wouldn't it be?" asked the radicals.

"Because it would be mere training," explained the old men patiently. "With all the intricate details of fish-grabbing, horse-clubbing, and tiger-scaring—the standard cultural subjects—the school curriculum is too crowded now. We can't add these fads and frills of net-making, antelope-snaring, and—of all things—bear-killing. Why, at the very thought, the body of the great New-Fist, founder of our paleolithic educational system, would turn over in its burial cairn. What we need to do is to give our young people a more thorough grounding in the fundamentals. Even the graduates of the secondary schools don't know the art of fish-grabbing in any complete sense nowadays, they swing their horse clubs awkwardly too, and as for the old science of tiger-scaring—well, even the teachers seem to lack the real flair for the subject which we oldsters got in our teens and never forgot."

"But, damn it," exploded one of the radicals, "how can any person with good sense be interested in such useless activities? What is the point of trying to catch fish with the bare hands when it just can't be done any more? How can a boy learn to club horses when there are no horses left to club? And why in hell should children try to scare tigers with fire when the tigers are dead and gone?"

"Don't be foolish," said the wise old men, smiling most kindly smiles. "We don't teach fish-grabbing to grab fish; we teach it to develop a generalized agility which can never be developed by mere training. We don't teach horse-clubbing to club horses; we teach it to develop a generalized strength in the learner which he can never get from so prosaic and specialized a thing as antelope-snare-setting. We don't teach tiger-scaring to scare tigers; we teach it for the purpose of giving that noble courage which carries over into all the affairs of life and which can never come from so base an activity as bear-killing."

All the radicals were silenced by this statement, all except the one who was most radical of all. He felt abashed, it is true, but he was so radical that he made one last protest.

"But—but anyway," he suggested, "you will have to admit that times have changed. Couldn't you please *try* these other, more up-to-date activities? Maybe they have *some* educational value after all?"

Even the man's fellow radicals felt that this was going a little too far.

The wise old men were indignant. Their kindly smiles faded. "If you had any education yourself," they said severely, "you would know that the essence of true education is timelessness. It is something that endures through changing conditions like a solid rock standing squarely and firmly in the middle of a raging torrent. You must know that there are some eternal verities, and the saber-tooth curriculum is one of them!"

## POSTNOTE

The Saber-Tooth Curriculum is truly one of the greatest Classic curriculum articles ever written; its message is timeless. One might think that *The Saber-Tooth Curriculum* had been written by a modern-day critic of the public school curriculum instead of someone writing in 1939. It is virtually impossible to read this selection without drawing parallels to courses and curricula that we have experienced. Fish-grabbing-with-the-bare-hands has not disappeared. It still exists today in many American schools, but it is called by a different name. And the same arguments used by the elders to defend the saber-tooth curriculum are used today to defend subjects that have outlived their right to remain in the curriculum. Why do they remain?

## DISCUSSION QUESTIONS

1. What is the main message of this excerpt from *The Saber-Tooth Curriculum?*

2. What subjects, if any, in the current school curriculum would you equate with fish-grabbing-with-the-bare-hands? Why?

3. What new subjects would you suggest adding to the school curriculum to avoid creating our own saber-tooth curriculum? Why?

# 28 The Authentic Standards Movement and Its Evil Twin

Scott Thompson

One thing the standards movement will never be accused of is a lack of critical opposition. But for all the fiery rhetoric that critics direct against this powerful, nationwide movement, there is perhaps no greater threat to standards-based reform than much of what is being perpetrated in the name of standards-based reform. The so-called movement—so-called, because it is not truly a single movement but twin movements bearing the same name—has become its own worst enemy.

If giving twins the same name is a recipe for confusion, consider the havoc that gets unleashed when one of them proves to be an "evil twin."[1] In the case of the standards movement, the evil twin is the more visible and powerful of the siblings, and so its authentic namesake is in an increasingly perilous situation. In fact, the problem is even worse: the two are essentially joined at the hip.

So what are these twin movements? First, let's distinguish them by name. I would rename the evil twin "test-based reform" or more specifically "high-stakes, standardized, test-based reform." The sibling, then, is "authentic, standards-based reform." The defining distinction between them is their respective influence on the instructional core of schooling and on equity issues.

When academic progress is judged by a single indicator and when high stakes—such as whether a student is promoted from one grade to the next or is eligible for a diploma—are attached to that single indicator, the common effect is to narrow curriculum and reduce instruction to test "prepping." What gets lost when teachers and students are pressured to make students better test-takers is precisely the rich, high-level teaching and learning that authentic, standards-based reform aims to promote in all classrooms and for all students.

Authentic, standards-based reform is fundamentally concerned with equity. It departs radically from the tracking and sorting carried out by the factory-style school of yore. Instead, it aims to hold high expectations and *provide high levels of support* for all students, teachers, and educational leaders. Under the evil twin's (per)version of standards and accountability, we see students retained in grade because of a single test score, and we typically see a corresponding increase in dropout rates where such *worst* practice is in place.[2] Equity then becomes the casualty rather than the fruit of reform. And as Sandra Feldman, president of the American Federation of Teachers, recently observed, "When tests are allowed to become the be-all and end-all, they deform, not reform, education."[3]

In its influence on both the instructional core of schooling and on equity, the evil twin constitutes an inversion of the "real thing." It is a politically warped variation on what is arguably among this nation's most powerful and promising education reforms. Although the evil twin purports to be standards-based, it actually flies in the face of research-based standards on

Scott Thompson is assistant director of the Panasonic Foundation, Secaucus, N.J. Scott Thompson, "The Authentic Standards Movement and Its Evil Twin," January 2001 *Phi Delta Kappan*. Originally appeared in *Improving Schools for African American Students: A Reader for Educational Leaders*, edited by Sheryl Denbo and Lynson Moore Beaulieu, September 2002, Charles C. Thomas Publishers. Reprinted with permission of Charles C. Thomas and the author.

**TERMS TO NOTE**

Standards movement

Standards-based reform

High-stakes tests

Assessment

Tracking

the appropriate use of testing. Consider, for example, the conclusions of the National Research Council's Committee on Appropriate Test Use, which are being systematically, if not willfully, ignored by many education policy makers, especially at the state level: "An educational decision that will have a major impact on a test taker should not be made solely or automatically on the basis of a single test score."[4]

There are many reasons not to use any single assessment as the basis for assignment high-stakes consequences. Not only does such a practice tend to diminish curriculum and instruction, but most psychometricians will tell you that the assessment has yet to be created with a high enough level of validity and reliability to justify its use as the sole basis for making consequential decisions about the test-taker. This problem is not unique to education. Consider the words of Lt. Gen. Roland Kadish, director of the Ballistic Missile Defense Organization: "I don't think we should draw conclusions from any one test that are irrevocable. No one test tells you everything you need to know."[5]

Another problem is that tests are frequently misused. Standardized tests designed for na-

**TERM TO NOTE**
Standardized tests

tional comparisons between students, without reference to a particular school's curriculum or content standards, are, for example, too often used to evaluate teachers and schools. As I have noted elsewhere, that's a bit like trying to use a jigsaw and screw driver to eat a plate of angel hair pasta. The tools are not necessarily bad in themselves, but they are certainly ill-suited to the task.[6]

High-stakes, test-based reform is an approach that is most often driven by state-level mandate, and it suits the political appetite for rapid, quantifiable (hence readily digestible by the public) results.[7] Test-based reform represents a potentially lethal threat to its authentic twin. Whether by design or happenstance, it is effectively sabotaging the authentic standards movement. And not surprisingly, it is unleashing a swelling and intensifying backlash against

standards and testing that is taking form legally and politically, as well as through mobilized grassroots opposition.[8]

It is the combination of test-based reform, in the name of standards, and the wholesale backlash that such practice provokes that is placing the authentic standards movement in peril. Not only in the general media, but also in specialized education media, one can see that the war between proponents and opponents of high-stakes testing tends to define the entire standards movement in such a way that its actual nature and potential, which some school districts are beginning to demonstrate, gets buried under an avalanche of rhetoric.

## A Rationale for Authentic, Standards-Based Reform

Too few children in many of our public schools are receiving the quality of education needed for successful life and work in a rapidly changing world. The imperative to provide them with a high-quality education is not so much economic as moral. Given what we know of the lifelong consequences for individuals of educational deprivation—not to mention the broader consequences for society and democracy—providing a high-quality education for all children is quite simply the right thing to do.

We know that some good schools have succeeded in providing a high-quality education to students deemed least likely to succeed: students of color and students in poverty.[9] But in a nation of 50 million schoolchildren, we face an enormous, yet-to-be-met challenge: namely, taking such success to scale. There are various theories of change that aim to address this challenge. The theory of change behind authentic, standards-based reform (again, I'm not talking about test-based reform) is that, if you want to improve student learning across the board, then you need to improve the quality of instructional content and practice across the board. In order to do that, you must fundamentally transform schools and school systems so that their focus, energy, and resources are wholly aimed at the primary goal of improving instruction in order to improve learning and thus to improve student performance as measured by a variety of assessments. In short, it is all about quality.

We know that bureaucratic school systems that focus on monitoring mandated inputs for compliance hold little, if any, promise of creating and sustaining good schools for children across the socioeconomic spectrum. An authentic, standards-based system departs radically from this model. It shifts from a focus on inputs to a focus on outcomes or performance. It shifts from a focus on quantity to a focus on quality. It shifts from a concern with organizational doings to a singular, systemwide focus on improving the performance of every student. It shifts from what Richard Elmore calls the "loose coupling" approach to educational governance to a system of governance that is structured around public accountability for educational results.[10]

Loose coupling is an arrangement in which governing authorities in public schools—from school boards down to principals—essentially run political interference so that classroom teachers are shielded from public scrutiny and can pursue their idiosyncratic pedagogical approaches. Under this governing structure, which is pervasive in public schools at this time, you can easily find that second-grade teachers in neighboring classrooms are doing completely different things with their students—in terms of content, instructional practice, and even basic objectives.

A standards-based approach departs from this model in two ways. First, it breaks down teacher isolation and calls for collaboration around a common set of standards so that students, parents, and teachers have a widely shared understanding of common educational goals at various levels of schooling. Second, it responds to the demands for public accountability by assuming a results orientation and making those results public.

These shifts mean that structures, roles, responsibilities, and budgets must be rethought and redesigned to dramatically increase the system's investment in high-quality learning for teachers, for school leaders, and for those in the central office whose job it is to support teachers and school leaders. A school system that is not accountable for providing continuous, high-quality, standards-based professional development for teachers and leaders has no business holding students and their teachers accountable for performance against student learning standards.

The urgency of the need for systematic improvement of public education would be difficult to overstate. Any observer of public education whose eyes are even partially open has discerned various currents that represent a potential threat to our public schools. The number of parents who are home schooling their children is growing significantly, as are the number of states that are fostering charter schools, some of which are operated by for-profit firms. Meanwhile, efforts to secure vouchers—including both private and public schools—are not going away.

**TERMS TO NOTE**
Home schooling
Charter schools
Vouchers
Privatization
Professional development

Over the next decade or two, it is not difficult to imagine a scenario unfolding in which home-schoolers begin forming cooperatives and the number of students participating in them greatly expands.[11] In this scenario, publicly funded vouchers also take off, and the charter school movement increasingly caters to groups of families with specialized interests. We might then find textbook publishers customizing their wares for the narrow interests of parents whose children are being educated in cooperatives or in independent schools organized around parochial values. Meanwhile, the remaining public school systems would find themselves increasingly segregated and educationally crippled. The common school—as a meeting ground for students from diverse economic, cultural, and racial backgrounds—would be lost, as society itself became ever more fragmented. Such a scenario would represent a serious threat to the health of our democracy.

The real potential of authentic, standards-based reform can be seen most clearly against this disturbing backdrop. We live in a time when both politicians and the general public are demanding educational accountability. Public opinion research shows that, while the public favors public schools over publicly funded vouchers, patience is wearing thin.[12] Public schools must demonstrate their ability to help students across the socioeconomic spectrum achieve high-quality educational results. Majorities of the public and of teachers support the movement toward high standards. But, according to poll results recently released by the American Association of School Administrators, a majority of voters reject the idea that a single test can accurately measure students' educational growth.[13]

Authentic, standards-based reform holds the potential for improving the quality of student performance to meet systemwide standards. It is an approach that is designed to make schools accountable to the communities they are meant to serve and to do so by focusing on high-quality teaching and learning, not on test scores. It is an approach that could stand up to the threat of privatization. It is an approach that aspires to reach a goal this nation has never achieved through its systems of public education: a high-quality education for all students, regardless of socioeconomic background. But authentic, standards-based reform—and arguably public education itself—is seriously threatened when high standards get confused with high-stakes, standardized tests.

## A 180-Degree Inversion

Identical twins can be difficult to distinguish solely by surface characteristics. But if one is evil and the other virtuous, their character traits or essential natures will stand in stark contrast. So it is with test-based reform and standards-based reform. On the face of it, they are both about

moving from an approach to education that values inputs to an approach that values outputs or results. But a deeper look into the essential natures of these twins reveals that test-based reform is nothing less than a 180-degree inversion of its authentic counterpart. This, I believe, becomes readily apparent when their essential characteristics are considered side by side.

▶ Authentic, standards-based reform involves teachers, parents, and others as active participants in developing and refining common learning standards. Test-based reform uses high-stakes tests, written in secret by expert psychometricians, as single indicators for deciding whether students are promoted or graduate, thereby making the tests the *real* standards.

▶ Authentic standards describe what *all* students should be learning at each level (not necessarily at each grade level). Test-based reform makes the scores on standardized tests for students at specific grade levels, in effect, the only meaningful standards.

▶ Under a system of authentic standards, the school system invests heavily in high-quality professional development for teachers and administrators in an effort to support their work in teaching to the standards. Under a system of test-based reform, teachers and principals are pressured in a variety of ways to raise test scores, and students are drilled accordingly.

▶ Under a system of authentic reform, student assessments are aligned with the standards, and students have numerous opportunities to demonstrate that they have met the standards. No single test is used to determine whether a standard has been met. Under test-based reform, a single state or national test is used to determine whether students are promoted to the next grade or are allowed to receive a diploma.

▶ High-quality, individualized support for students is a hallmark of authentic, standards-based reform. Such support is rare in test-based reform efforts. When it is present, it tends to focus on test-taking techniques rather than on teaching and learning.

▶ Authentic, standards-based reform has implications for every person, policy, and practice in a school system because it involves a complete abandonment of the bureaucratic, "seat time" approach to education and replaces it with a system of learning communities dedicated to helping all students reach their intellectual, social, and personal potential. By contrast, test-based reform, through its focus on high-stakes tests, narrows the curriculum to what is included on the tests and reduces instructional practice to test preparation.

A still more profound point of contrast between the two movements emerges when we consider what educational *purpose* is implicit in each kind of reform. In the case of test-based reform, the purpose of education is raising test scores. In the case of authentic, standards-based reform, the purpose is enabling all students to achieve as much of their creative, intellectual, and social potential as possible. Thus the goal of authentic, standards-based reform is to prepare students to live successfully and contribute actively in their communities.

## The Wrong Question

As opposition to high-stakes testing mounts and as negative consequences pile up, observers and policy makers are beginning to ask, "Are we moving too quickly?"[14] But this is the wrong question, and it represents an extreme misreading of the problem at hand. The problem is not one of pacing, quantity, or timing. It is a problem of replacing a reform aimed at systematically enriching and deepening teaching and learning with a reform aimed at raising test scores, regardless of the impact on the quality of instruction or on the number of students being pushed out of schools and onto the streets. At *whatever* point a high-stakes, standardized test

is imposed as the sole basis for determining student success, that test will replace whatever content and performance standards were previously in place. It's something like a computer virus that erases and replaces everything that was stored on one's hard drive.

We could realize significant progress in public education if the proponents of standards-based reform joined hands with the critics of high-stakes testing and effectively outlawed the use of high-stakes tests as sole indicators of student success. Moreover, such a move need not lead to toothless standards. It is possible to require all students to meet a set of rigorous standards in order to graduate from high school without using a single test as the means of determining whether those standards have been met. We should be interested in students who can produce high-quality work rather than students who have mastered the ability to take standardized tests. It is the former who will be rewarded in their personal and professional lives after graduation, when test-taking skills will no longer be relevant.

## A Personal Note

I hope my use of the "evil twin" metaphor helps bring some clarity to this time of rampant educational confusion. But I want to be clear about what I don't mean, as well as what I do mean, in using this metaphor. I do not intend to call any individuals "evil." I believe that the tendency to demonize people who hold opposing points of view has a coarsening influence on civil discourse and so is bad for democracy itself. What I refer to as the "evil twin" is a set of actions and the consequences I believe these actions can have and are having on children and on schools. Determining whether such consequences are intended or unintended requires discerning what is at work in the hearts and minds of many people who are crafting and enacting such policies. The human hearts and minds of others, I believe, are simply too complex and too inaccessible to read as a book.

But I see the metaphor as useful in bringing out how sharp the contrast actually is between the two movements. At the same time, it's important to acknowledge the complexity of the relationship between the authentic, standards-based reform and test-based reform. As I noted above, these twins are often essentially joined at the hip. What I mean by that is that most of the districts that I would point to as exemplars of authentic, standards-based reform are operating within state systems that more or less exemplify test-based reform.

## The Theory in Action

The task of sorting through the complexities of conflicting policy contexts is daunting, but when it is done, what emerges is evidence of what the authentic twin is already beginning to accomplish in a number of school districts. I would point, for example, to District 2 in New York City, which has posted some exemplary early results in its efforts to institute best practices. This story has been extensively documented by Richard Elmore, Deanna Burney, and others, and I recommend that readers explore their work.[15] Anthony Alvarado, who was the chief architect of the reform effort in District 2, has since become the chancellor of instruction in San Diego. That district is now moving forward rapidly along the same lines and has developed a unique "blueprint" for intervention and for support of students who are failing to meet standards.

As uneven as some of the early results may be at this stage, I would point to a number of other districts whose experience suggests the potential of standards-based reform: Aurora, Colorado; Clovis, California; Edmonds, Washington; Minneapolis; and the three districts constituting the El Paso Collaborative for Academic Excellence, as well as the Houston In-

dependent School District.[16] And there are certainly others.[17]

For an example of a state accountability system that balances the public's need for individual student and school-level results against the school's need for support and for a genuine measure of autonomy in achieving those results, I would point readers to Rhode Island's SALT (School Accountability for Learning and Teaching), an accountability program that gathers extensive qualitative as well as quantitative data on school quality for the purpose of supporting continuous, standards-based school improvement.[18] Each school in the state engages in self-study and develops a school improvement plan. Periodically, a team of teachers, parents, and administrators from outside the district spends a full week in the school, reviewing the self-study and other data, shadowing students, visiting classes, and interviewing teachers, parents, and administrators. The results of this external review are written up as a report containing conclusions, recommendations, and commendations. The full report is read to the entire faculty by the chair of the visit on the Monday following the visit.

School districts that are working to fulfill the original promise of standards-based reform can play a vital role in the future of public education. They will be more likely to succeed in this critical task if increasing numbers of states adopt approaches to standards and accountability that look more like Rhode Island's SALT and less like a brawny and aggressive twin—wielding a high-stakes weapon.

## NOTES

1. Richard Elmore has observed, "We will get standards-based reform. But what kind is in doubt. Will it be the version that proponents envision or a corrupted and poorly-thought-out evil twin?" See Richard F. Elmore, "Building a New Structure for School Leadership," *American Educator*, Winter 1999–2000, p. 8.

2. See, for example, Maureen Kelleher, "Dropout Rate Climbs as Schools Dump Truants," *Catalyst*, June 1999;

and Walter M. Haney, *Supplementary Report on Texas Assessment of Academic Skills Exit Test (TAAS-X)* (Los Angeles: Mexican American Legal Defense and Education Fund, 30 July 1999).

3.  Sandra Feldman, "Where We Stand," *Education Week,* 12 July 2000, p. 17.

4.  Jay P. Heubert and Robert M. Hauser, eds., *High Stakes: Testing for Tracking, Promotion, and Graduation* (Washington, D.C.: National Academy Press, 1999), p. 15.

5.  Quoted in Elaine Sciolino, "Key Missile Parts Are Left Untested as Booster Fails," *New York Times,* 9 July 2000.

6.  Scott Thompson, "Shared Accountability—Shifting from Heavy-Handed to Helping Hands," *Strategies,* May 2000, p. 1.

7.  Donald B. Gratz, "High Standards for Whom?," *Phi Delta Kappan,* May 2000, p. 684.

8.  See, for example, Lynn Olson, "Worries of a Standards 'Backlash' Grow," *Education Week,* 5 April 2000, p. 1; and Drew Lindsay, "Contest," *Education Week,* 5 April 2000, p. 30. For more information on the growing opposition to test-based reform, see Alfie Kohn, "Fighting the Tests: A Practical Guide to Rescuing Our Schools," pp. 348–57, this *Kappan.*

9.  The evidence along these lines is enormous. One good example is a study conducted by the Center for Performance Assessment on what it calls the "90/90/90 Schools." These are schools in which more than 90% of students qualify for a subsidized lunch, more than 90% of students are ethnic minorities, and more than 90% of students still achieved "high academic standards, according to independently conducted tests of academic achievement." The results of this study appear in Douglas B. Reeves, *Accountability in Action* (Denver, Colo.: Advanced Learning Press, 1999), chap. 19. See also "Doing What Works: Improving Big City School Districts," AFT Educational Issues Policy Brief No. 12, Washington, D.C., October 2000, pp. 1–12; and Scott Justus et al., *Student Achievement and Reform Trends in 13 Urban Districts* (Washington, D.C.: The McKenzie Group, May 2000).

10.  Richard F. Elmore, "Building a New Structure for School Leadership," *American Educator,* Winter 1999–2000, p. 8.

11.  I credit the observations in this paragraph to Phillip Schlechty, who outlined a similar scenario in a keynote speech he delivered to the Panasonic Foundation's Leadership Associates Program in October 1999. He has since written up this scenario in the epilogue to his new book, *Shaking Up the Schoolhouse* (San Francisco: Jossey-Bass, 2001).

12.  Jean Johnson, *Assignment Incomplete: The Unfinished Business of Education Reform* (New York: Public Agenda, 1995).

13.  Lynn Olson, "Poll Shows Public Concern over Emphasis on Standardized Tests," *Education Week,* 12 July 2000, p. 9.

14.  "High-Stakes Testing: Too Much? Too Soon?," *State Education Leader,* Winter 2000, p. 1. See also Chris Pipho, "The Sting of High-Stakes Testing and Accountability," *Phi Delta Kappan,* May 2000, pp. 645–46.

15.  Richard F. Elmore with Deanna Burney, *Investing in Teacher Learning: Staff Development and Instructional Improvement in Community School District #2, New York City* (New York: National Commission on Teaching and America's Future and the Consortium for Policy Research in Education, 1997); Richard F. Elmore and Deanna Burney, "School Variation and Systemic Instructional Improvement in Community School District #2, New York City," unpublished paper prepared for High Performance Learning Communities Project, Learning Research and Development Center, University of Pittsburgh, October 1997; idem, "Continuous Improvement in Community District #2, New York City," unpublished paper prepared for High Performance Learning Communities Project, Learning Research and Development Center, University of Pittsburgh, December 1998; "District 2, NYC: Teacher Learning Comes First," *Strategies,* August 1998; pp. 11–13; and Liz Gewirtzman and Elaine Fink, *Realignment of Policies & Resources* (Chicago: Cross City Campaign for Urban School Reform, 2000).

16.  "Aurora, CO: A Long, Bumpy Road," *Strategies,* August 1998, pp. 4–10; "Clovis, CA: Thirty Years and Counting—Sustaining Continuous Improvement," *Strategies,* July 1999, pp. 4–7; "Minneapolis: Aligning Assessments," *Strategies,* August 1998, pp. 13–14; Stephen Fink and Scott Thompson, "Standards and Whole System Change," unpublished paper on standards-based reform in Edmonds, Washington, prepared for Panasonic Foundation, December 1998; M. Susanna Navarro and Diana S. Natalicio, "Closing the Achievement Gap in El Paso: A Collaboration for K–16 Renewal," *Phi Delta Kappan,* April 1999, pp. 597–601; "Houston, TX: Aiming High," *Strategies,* May 2000, pp. 3–6; and Rod Paige, "No Simple Answer," *Education Week,* 8 November 2000, p. 48. (*Strategies* can be accessed at http:www.aasa.org/publications/strategies/index.htm.)

17.  See, for example, "Doing What Works."

18.  "Rhode Island: Accountability = School Improvement," *Strategies,* May 2000, pp. 3–6; and "Coming to Judgment," *Strategies,* May 2000, pp. 7–8.

# POSTNOTE

Scott Thompson makes a very important distinction between content standards and how they are being assessed through high-stakes, standardized tests. He takes strong issue with the latter. The problem with high-stakes tests, as he points out, is that they narrow the curriculum and reduce instruction to test "prepping." In our conversations with teachers, they, too, echo this concern. Some teachers report to us that rather than spending time on enrichment topics, they feel pressure to cover over and over again the content on which the students will be tested. Furthermore, many of these teachers also report that considerable time is given to teaching students how to take the tests. The result is that the tail wags the dog, certainly an unintended consequence of the standards movement.

Many people point to elite private schools as the kind of schooling that public schools should emulate. However, elite private schools typically don't have a set of uniform standards to which all students are held accountable. Nor do they place such strong emphasis on a single standardized test to assess student learning. In these private schools, teachers are given much more freedom in curriculum choice than are public school teachers. If these elite private schools are to be emulated, why are states implementing policies for public schools that are so opposite to what is going on in the private schools?

# DISCUSSION QUESTIONS

1. For what reasons do you think many states use only one "high-stakes" test to assess student achievement on content standards?

2. Should teachers be held accountable for their students' mastery of course content to some expected standard? List reasons teachers should or should not be held accountable for their students' test results.

3. In what ways should teachers be held accountable? Parents?

# 29 CLASSIC The Paideia Proposal: Rediscovering the Essence of Education

Mortimer J. Adler

In the first 80 years of this century, we have met the obligation imposed on us by the principle of equal educational opportunity, but only in a quantitative sense. Now, as we approach the end of the century, we must achieve equality in qualitative terms.

This means a completely one-track system of schooling. It means, at the basic level, giving all the young the same kind of schooling, whether or not they are college bound.

We are aware that children, although equal in their common humanity and fundamental human rights, are unequal as individuals, differing in their capacity to learn. In addition, the homes and environments from which they come to school are unequal—either predisposing the child for schooling or doing the opposite.

Consequently, the Paideia Proposal, faithful to the principle of equal educational opportunity, includes the suggestion that inequalities due to environmental factors must be overcome by some form of preschool preparation—at least one year for all and two or even three for some. We know that to make such preschool tutelage compulsory at the public expense would be tantamount to increasing the duration of compulsory schooling from 12 years to 13, 14, or 15 years. Nevertheless, we think that

**TERM TO NOTE**
Paideia

At the time this article was written, Mortimer J. Adler was chairman of the board of editors of *Encyclopaedia Britannica* and director of the Institute of Philosophical Research in Chicago, Illinois. Adler died in 2001. From "The Paideia Proposal: Rediscovering the Essence of Education" by Mortimer J. Adler. Reprinted with permission, from *The American School Board Journal*, July 1982. Copyright © 1982, the National School Boards Association. All rights reserved.

this preschool adjunct to the 12 years of compulsory basic schooling is so important that some way must be found to make it available for all and to see that all use it to advantage.

## The Essentials of Basic Schooling

The objectives of basic schooling should be the same for the whole school population. In our current two-track or multitrack system, the learning objectives are not the same for all. And even when the objectives aimed at those on the upper track are correct, the course of study now provided does not adequately realize these correct objectives. On all tracks in our current system, we fail to cultivate proficiency in the common tasks of learning, and we especially fail to develop sufficiently the indispensable skills of learning.

The uniform objectives of basic schooling should be threefold. They should correspond to three aspects of the common future to which all the children are destined: (1) Our society provides all children ample opportunity for personal development. Given such opportunity, each individual is under a moral obligation to make the most of himself and his life. Basic schooling must facilitate this accomplishment. (2) All the children will become, when of age, full-fledged citizens with suffrage and other political responsibilities. Basic schooling must do everything it can to make them good citizens, able to perform the duties of citizenship with all the trained intelligence that each is able to achieve. (3) When they are grown, all (or certainly most) of the children will engage in some form of work to earn a living. Basic schooling must prepare them for earning a living, but not by training them for this or that specific job while they are still in school.

To achieve these three objectives, the character of basic schooling must be general and liberal. It should have a single, required, 12-year course of study for all, with no electives except one—an elective choice with regard to a second language, to be selected from such modern languages as French, German, Italian, Spanish, Russian, and Chinese. The elimination of all electives, with this one exception, excludes what *should* be excluded—all forms of specialization, including particularized job training.

In its final form, the Paideia Proposal will detail this required course of study, but I will summarize the curriculum here in its bare outline. It consists of three main columns of teaching and learning, running through the 12 years

and progressing, of course, from the simple to the more complex, from the less difficult to the more difficult, as the students grow older. Understand: The three columns (see table below) represent three distinct modes of teaching and learning. They do not represent a series of courses. A specific course or a class may employ more than one mode of teaching and learning, but all three modes are essential to the overall course of study.

*The first column* is devoted to acquiring knowledge in three subject areas: (A) language, literature, and the fine arts; (B) mathematics and natural science; (C) history, geography, and social studies.

*The second column* is devoted to developing the intellectual skills of learning. These include all the language skills necessary for thought

|  | *COLUMN ONE* | *COLUMN TWO* | *COLUMN THREE* |
|---|---|---|---|
| *Goals* | Acquisition of Organized Knowledge | Development of Intellectual Skills and Skills of Learning | Improved Understanding of Ideas and Values |
|  | by means of | by means of | by means of |
| *Means* | Didactic Instruction, Lecturing, and Textbooks | Coaching, Exercises, and Supervised Practice | Maieutic or Socratic Questioning and Active Participation |
|  | in these three subject areas | in these operations | in these activities |
| *Subject Areas, Operations, and Activities* | Language, Literature, and Fine Arts | Reading, Writing, Speaking, Listening, Calculating, Problem Solving, Observing, Measuring, Estimating, Exercising Critical Judgment | Discussion of Books (Not Textbooks) and Other Works of Art |
|  | Mathematics and Natural Science |  |  |
|  | History, Geography, and Social Studies |  | Involvement in Music, Drama, and Visual Arts |

The three columns do not correspond to separate courses, nor is one kind of teaching and learning necessarily confined to any one class.

The Paideia Curriculum

and communication—the skills of reading, writing, speaking, listening. They also include mathematical and scientific skills; the skills of observing, measuring, estimating, and calculating; and skills in the use of the computer and of other scientific instruments. Together, these skills make it possible to think clearly and critically. They once were called the liberal arts—the intellectual skills indispensable to being competent as a learner.

*The third column* is devoted to enlarging the understanding of ideas and values. The materials of the third column are books (*not* textbooks), and other products of human artistry. These materials include books of every variety —historical, scientific, and philosophical as well as poems, stories, and essays—and also individual pieces of music, visual art, dramatic productions, dance productions, film or television productions. Music and works of visual art can be used in seminars in which ideas are discussed; but as with poetry and fiction, they also are to be experienced aesthetically, to be enjoyed and admired for their excellence. In this connection, exercises in the composition of poetry, music, and visual works and in the production of dramatic works should be used to develop the appreciation of excellence.

The three columns represent three different kinds of learning on the part of the student and three different kinds of instruction on the part of teachers.

In the first column, the students are engaged in acquiring information and organized knowledge about nature, man, and human society. The method of instruction here, using textbooks and manuals, is didactic. The teacher lectures, invites responses from the students, monitors the acquisition of knowledge, and tests that acquisition in various ways.

In the second column, the students are engaged in developing habits of performance, which is all that is involved in the development of an art or skill. Art, skill, or technique is nothing more than a cultivated, habitual ability to do a certain kind of thing well, whether that is

swimming and dancing or reading and writing. Here, students are acquiring linguistic, mathematical, scientific, and historical *know-how* in contrast to what they acquire in the first column, which is *know-that* with respect to language, literature, and the fine arts, mathematics and science, history, geography, and social studies. Here, the method of instruction cannot be didactic or monitorial; it cannot be dependent on textbooks. It must be coaching, the same kind used in the gym to develop bodily skills; only here it is used by a different kind of coach in the classroom to develop intellectual skills.

In the third column, students are engaged in a process of enlightenment, the process whereby they develop their understanding of the basic and controlling ideas in all fields of subject matter and come to appreciate better all the human values embodied in works of art. Here, students move progressively from understanding less to understanding more—understanding better what they already know and appreciating more what they already have experienced. Here, the method of instruction cannot be either didactic or coaching. It must be the Socratic, or maieutic, method of questioning and discussing. It should not occur in an ordinary classroom with the students sitting in rows and the teacher in front of the class, but in a seminar room, with the students sitting around a table and the teacher sitting with them as an equal, even though a little older and wiser.

Of these three main elements in the required curriculum, the third column is completely innovative. Nothing like this is done in our schools, and because it is completely absent from the ordinary curriculum of basic schooling, the students never have the experience of having their minds addressed in a challenging way or of being asked to think about important ideas, to express their thoughts, to defend their opinions in a reasonable fashion.

The only thing that is innovative about the second column is the insistence that the method of instruction here must be coaching carried on either with one student at a time or with very small groups of students. Nothing else can be effective in the development of a skill, be it bodily or intellectual. The absence of such individualized coaching in our schools explains why most of the students cannot read well, write well, speak well, listen well, or perform well any of the other basic intellectual operations.

The three columns are closely interconnected and integrated, but the middle column—the one concerned with linguistic, mathematical, and scientific skills—is central. It both supports and is supported by the other two columns. All the intellectual skills with which it is concerned must be exercised in the study of the three basic subject-matters and in acquiring knowledge about them, and these intellectual skills must be exercised in the seminars devoted to the discussion of books and other things.

In addition to the three main columns in the curriculum, ascending through the 12 years of basic schooling, there are three adjuncts: One is 12 years of physical training, accompanied by instruction in bodily care and hygiene. The second, running through something less than 12 years, is the development of basic manual skills, such as cooking, sewing, carpentry, and the operation of all kinds of machines. The third, reserved for the last year or two, is an introduction to the whole world of work—the range of occupations in which human beings earn their livings. This is not particularized job training. It is the very opposite. It aims at a broad understanding of what is involved in working for a living and of the various ways in which that can be done. If, at the end of 12 years, students wish training for specific jobs, they should get that in two-year or in technical institutes of one sort or another.

Everything that has not been specifically mentioned as occupying the time of the school day should be reserved for after-hours and have the status of extracurricular activities.

Please note: The required course of study just described is as important for what it *displaces* as for what it introduces. It displaces a multitude of elective courses, especially those

offered in our secondary schools, most of which make little or no contribution to general, liberal education. It eliminates all narrowly specialized job training, which now abounds in our schools. It throws out of the curriculum and into the category of optional extracurricular activities a variety of things that have little or no educational value.

If it did not call for all these displacements, there would not be enough time in the school day or year to accomplish everything that is essential to the general, liberal learning that must be the content of basic schooling.

## The Quintessential Element

So far, I have set forth the bare essentials of the Paideia Proposal with regard to basic schooling. I have not yet mentioned the quintessential element—the *sine qua non*—without which nothing else can possibly come to fruition, no matter how sound it might be in principle. The heart of the matter is the quality of learning and the quality of teaching that occupies the school day, not to mention the quality of the homework after school.

First, the learning must be active. It must use the whole mind, not just the memory. It must be learning by discovery, in which the student, never the teacher, is the primary agent. Learning by discovery, which is the only genuine learning, may be either unaided or aided. It is unaided only for geniuses. For most students, discovery must be aided.

Here is where teachers come in—as aids in the process of learning by discovery, not as knowers who attempt to put the knowledge they have into the minds of their students. The quality of the teaching, in short, depends crucially upon how the teacher conceives his role in the process of learning, and that must be as an aid to the student's process of discovery.

I am prepared for the questions that must be agitating you by now: How and where will we get the teachers who can perform as teachers should? How will we be able to staff the program with teachers so trained that they will be competent to provide the quality of instruction required for the quality of learning desired?

The first part of our answer to these questions is negative: We *cannot* get the teachers we need for the Paideia program from schools of education *as they are now constituted*. As teachers are now trained for teaching, they simply will not do. The ideal—an impracticable ideal—would be to ask for teachers who are, themselves, truly educated human beings. But truly educated human beings are too rare. Even if we could draft all who are now alive, there still would be far too few to staff our schools.

Well, then, what can we look for? Look for teachers who are actively engaged in the process of *becoming* educated human beings, who are themselves deeply motivated to develop their own minds. Assuming this is not too much to ask for the present, how should teachers be schooled and trained in the future? First, they should have the same kind of basic schooling that is recommended in the Paideia Proposal. Second, they should have additional schooling, at the college and even the university level, in which the same kind of general, liberal learning is carried on at advanced levels—more deeply, broadly, and intensively than it can be done in the first 12 years of schooling. Third, they must be given something analogous to the clinical experience in the training of physicians. They must engage in practice-teaching under supervision, which is another way of saying that they must be *coached* in the arts of teaching, not just given didactic instruction in educational psychology and in pedagogy. Finally, and most important of all, they must learn how to teach well by being exposed to the performances of those who are masters of the arts involved in teaching.

It is by watching a good teacher at work that they will be able to perceive what is involved in the process of assisting others to learn by discovery. Perceiving it, they must then try to emulate what they observe, and through this process, they slowly will become good teachers themselves.

The Paideia Proposal recognizes the need for three different kinds of institutions at the collegiate level: The two-year community or junior college should offer a wide choice of electives that give students some training in one or another specialized field, mainly those fields of study that have something to do with earning a living. The four-year college also should offer a wide variety of electives, to be chosen by students who aim at the various professional or technical occupations that require advanced study. Those elective majors chosen by students should be accompanied, for all students, by one required minor, in which the kind of general and liberal learning that was begun at the level of basic schooling is continued at a higher level in the four years of college. And we should have still a third type of collegiate institution—a four-year college in which general, liberal learning at a higher level constitutes a required course of study that is to be taken by all students. *It is this third type of college, by the way, that should be attended by all who plan to become teachers in our basic schools.*

At the university level, there should be a continuation of general, liberal learning at a still higher level to accompany intensive specialization in this or that field of science or scholarship, this or that learned profession. Our insistence on the continuation of general, liberal learning at all the higher levels of schooling stems from our concern with the worst cultural disease that is rampant in our society—*the barbarism of specialization.*

There is no question that our technologically advanced industrial society needs specialists of all sorts. There is no question that the advancement of knowledge in all fields of science and scholarship, and in all the learned professions, needs intense specialization. But for the sake of preserving and enhancing our cultural traditions, as well as for the health of science and scholarship, we need specialists who also are generalists—generally cultivated human beings, not just good plumbers. We need truly educated human beings who can perform their special tasks better precisely because they have general cultivation as well as intensely specialized training.

Changes indeed are needed in higher education, but those improvements cannot reasonably be expected unless improvement in basic schooling makes that possible.

## The Future of Our Free Institutions

I already have declared as emphatically as I know how that the quality of human life in our society depends on the quality of the schooling we give our young people, both basic and advanced. But a marked elevation in the quality of human life is not the only reason improving the quality of schooling is so necessary—not the only reason we must move heaven and earth to stop the deterioration of our schools and turn them in the opposite direction. The other reason is to safeguard the future of our free institutions.

They cannot prosper, they may not even survive, unless we do something to rescue our schools from their current deplorable deterioration. Democracy, in the full sense of the term, came into existence only in this century and only in a few countries on earth, among which the United States is an outstanding example. But democracy came into existence in this century only in its initial conditions, all of which hold out promises for the future that remain to be fulfilled. Unless we do something about improving the quality of basic schooling for all and the quality of advanced schooling for some, there is little chance that those promises ever will be fulfilled. And if they are not, our free institutions are doomed to decay and wither away.

We face many insistently urgent problems. Our prosperity and even our survival depend on the solution of those problems—the threat of nuclear war, the exhaustion of essential resources and of supplies of energy, the pollution or spoilage of the environment, the spiraling of inflation accompanied by the spread of unemployment.

To solve these problems, we need resourceful and innovative leadership. For that to arise and be effective, an educated populace is needed. Trained intelligence—not only on the part of leaders, but also on the part of followers—holds the key to the solution of the problems our society faces. Achieving peace, prosperity, and plenty could put us on the threshold of an early paradise. But a much better educational system than now exists is needed, for that alone can carry us across the threshold. Without it, a poorly schooled population will not be able to put to good use the opportunities afforded by the achievement of the general welfare. Those who are not schooled to enjoy society can only despoil its institutions and corrupt themselves.

## POSTNOTE

This article by Mortimer J. Adler is representative of a *perennialist* philosophy. Perennialists believe that truth is best revealed in the enduring classics of Western culture and that the schools' curriculum should consist of the traditional subjects—history, language, mathematics, science, and the arts.

The late Mortimer Adler was an erudite, multifaceted scholar whose contributions to education through his work with the *Encyclopaedia Britannica*, the Great Books program, and the Paideia Program have earned him a spot among our Classic selections. Derived from the Greek word, *paideia* signifies the general level of personal excellence that should be the possession of all human beings.

By eliminating a differentiated curriculum from elementary and secondary schools and requiring all students to take a common curriculum, Adler believed that we can give all students the quality education currently available only to those on a high track. Adler and many of his supporters established a network of individuals who are implementing these ideas in a variety of public and private schools around the country.

## DISCUSSION QUESTIONS

1. What do you see as the merits of Adler's proposal? The drawbacks? Why?

2. What kinds of individuals or groups are likely to be supportive of a curriculum structured according to Adler's "three columns"? Who is apt to oppose this type of curriculum? Why?

3. Should vocational education be eliminated from K–12 schooling? Why or why not?

# CLASSIC *Seeking Breadth* and *Depth* in the *Curriculum*

E. D. Hirsch, Jr.

In the education field, we encounter a lot of what I call "premature polarities." This is a phrase that I have adapted from I. A. Richards, the Cambridge theorist of an earlier generation, who spoke of *premature ultimates*—those conversation stoppers that "bring investigation to a dead end too suddenly." (Richards, 1925, p. 87). I define premature polarities in education as the habitual, almost automatic taking of sides on educational issues on the basis of whether one considers oneself to be politically liberal or conservative.

Unfortunately, taking such ideological stands not only brings investigation to an end but also tends to replace thought. In the reading wars, for example, premature ideological polarization has caused some educators and the public to view phonics as an agency of right-wing suppression that deprives reading of naturalness and impairs love of literature. Whole language, on the other hand, is attacked as a left-wing abandonment of adult responsibility. Similarly, in the math debates, some people view memorizing the multiplication table as conservative, whereas others see the use of calculators as a pernicious liberal policy.

It is mysterious how these education theories came to be associated so mindlessly with politics. Ideological polarities are valuable spirit-raisers in a real war. Everyone understands that in war, the first casualty is truth. But in the

E. D. Hirsch, Jr. is an emeritus professor of English from the University of Virginia and chairman of the Board of the Core Knowledge Foundation, 801 East High Street, Charlottesville, VA 22902; www.coreknowledge.org. From E. D. Hirsch, Jr., "Seeking Breadth and Depth in the Curriculum, *Educational Leadership*, October 2001, pp. 22–25. Reprinted with permission of the Core Knowledge Foundation.

phony wars of education, slogans and polarizations are barriers to progress. And no barrier is greater than the sloganized polarity between deep understanding (or learning to learn) and the rote learning of mere facts.

## Four Principles

Some relevant and reliable research about how people learn has yielded a solid scientific consensus in the field of cognitive psychology. Yet, I do not find many references to that research consensus in education journals. We can summarize the research that is relevant to the premature polarization of "learning to learn" versus the "piling up of mere facts," in four principles (see Willingham, 2001).

▶ *The ability to learn something new is not primarily a general, formal skill.* It is chiefly a domain-specific skill. For instance, the ability to learn

**TERM TO NOTE**
Domain-specific knowledge

something new about math, music, or history depends on the knowledge that one already possesses about those subjects. This means that learning to learn always entails acquiring relevant knowledge about specific domains.

▶ *General ability to learn is highly correlated with general knowledge.* A stunning statistic illustrates this point. The positive correlation of learning ability with socioeconomic status is 0.422, whereas the correlation of learning ability with general knowledge is nearly twice as high—0.811 (Lubinski & Humphreys, 1997). We are so used to emphasizing the importance of socioeconomic status that this statistic comes as a surprise. Yet, the fact is just what we might have inferred from our knowledge that learning ability depends chiefly on having relevant prior knowledge.

▶ *The best way to learn a subject is to learn its general principles and to study an ample number of diverse examples that illustrate those principles.* In math, for example, students need to know what multiplication is in principle, but to gain real insight into multiplication, they also need to do different types of multiplication problems. This finding bears directly on the depth versus breadth issue in education. A broad range of examples should be studied, but studying too many is a waste of time.

▶ *Broad general knowledge is the best entree to deep knowledge.* I draw this conclusion from the field of psychology called discourse analysis. The most effective way to introduce the meaning of a discourse is to start with a summary such as an abstract found in learned journals. After students gain a broad context by developing a sense of the whole domain, they can mentally fit the various parts that follow into that whole, and make sense of them. For example, teachers could show 1st graders a globe that shows oceans and continents before teaching them about specific places.

What do these four principles imply for the question of what we should teach? They force us to abandon the sloganized polarity between deep understanding and the rote learning of mere facts. We cannot gain deep understanding without having broad factual knowledge. On the other hand, piling up more and more facts that don't really add much to our understanding or ability to learn wastes our time.

If we wish to educate students to become well-rounded citizens and life-long learners, these four principles give us a preliminary handle on an answer to the question of what we should teach. We should teach a diversity of subjects that will lead to broad general knowledge, and we should also teach in some depth a moderate number of specific examples. Neither the deep understanding pole nor the lots-of-facts pole is an optimal approach to teaching and learning. Because competence and ability to learn are correlated with broad knowledge, we can infer that we should teach a broad range of subjects—not just the formal skills of reading, writing, and arithmetic, but also science, history, ethics, literature, and the arts.

## Choosing Content

But within those fields, what shall we teach? Our four principles have already established that teaching either a single topic in depth or a great many topics superficially is not optimal. Yet we still have the problem of choosing a moderate number of topics in the different domains. How do we choose what the moderate number should be? Will any set of topics do?

One school of thought essentially says, yes—any set of topics will do. According to this view, studying any topic provides access to an entire domain. This view is not well based in theory or in fact (Hirsch, 1996). The theory that studying any topic provides access to an entire domain has left us with low achievement as a nation and has perpetuated the test score gap between socioeconomic groups. My colleagues and I at the Core Knowledge Foundation sponsor an alternative view. We maintain that schools need to develop a specific sequence of topics at each grade level that will prepare students to learn what the next grade has to offer.

**TERM TO NOTE**
Core knowledge

This curriculum structure is implied by the first principle, which states that new learning depends on relevant prior knowledge. Nations other than the United States that follow this principle by adopting a common core curriculum in the early grades—France and Japan are excellent examples—have significantly higher achievement and greater equity in achievement among students than nations that do not. Students in core-curriculum nations enter each new grade ready to learn the new lessons (Woessmann, 2001).

But that still leaves unanswered the question that we started with. Even if we argue in favor of a common core curriculum that covers several domains and provides a moderate number of specific topics, we still have not determined what those specific topics should be.

At the Core Knowledge Foundation, we have argued in favor of teaching topics that have the greatest potential for developing general competence and narrowing the test-score gap among student populations. We inventoried the knowledge that is characteristically shared by those at the top of the socioeconomic ladder in the United States. This knowledge is taken for granted as a common knowledge that people in the United States share and is part of the dialogue in college classrooms, in casual conversations, and in books and newspapers. For instance, 1st graders in Core Knowledge schools learn the meaning of "sour grapes" and "wolf in sheep's clothing." Because that knowledge is taken for granted and not explained, ignorance of that assumed knowledge seriously handicaps those who lack it. We argue, therefore, that every citizen in a democracy should possess this "elite" knowledge. The desire to change and improve the character of that assumed knowledge is admirable, but until we succeed in doing so, we should not withhold it and thereby handicap those who lack it through no fault of their own.

People who have called this approach a collection of mere facts or labeled it Eurocentric and elitist have not bothered to find out just what is in the Core Knowledge sequence, or to notice how carefully selected the topics are that it sets forth. The Core Knowledge sequence is the result of a long process of research and consensus building. The first draft (1990) was a distillation of guidelines from professional organizations and states and from principles in the core curriculums of such high-performing countries as France, Japan, and Sweden. We also included input from an advisory board on multiculturalism. We sent this initial draft to three groups of teachers in three parts of the United States who met to hammer out a practical sequence for 50 percent of the content in grades 1–6. As more schools have used the sequence, we have periodically updated and revised it. To get a sense of how carefully selected the topics are, let's look at two sections from the Core Knowledge sequence in the primary grades (Core Knowledge Foundation, 1999).

During 1st grade, students following our sequence focus on early civilizations. When teachers introduce the topic, they keep in mind the question, What is civilization? The teachers help students identify such recurring features of civilizations as settling down, practicing agriculture, building towns and cities, and learning how to write. For example, as they study Mesopotamia—the "cradle of civilization"—the students explore the importance of the Tigris and Euphrates rivers; the origins of writing and why writing is important to the development of civilization; and the Code of Hammurabi (an early code of laws) and why rules and laws are important to the development of civilization. When studying Ancient Egypt, the class learns about the geography of Africa, including the Sahara desert; explores the importance of the Nile River, with special focus on floods and farming; learns about the Pharaohs by studying Tutankhamen (the boy king) and Hatshepsut (a female pharaoh); and studies pyramids, mummies, animal gods, and the Sphinx. The students focus on writing when they learn about hieroglyphics.

When they reach 2nd grade, students build on and expand their knowledge of early civilizations by studying Asia. They look at the geography of Asia, learn that it is the largest continent and that it has the most populous countries in the world, and locate China, India, and Japan on maps and globes. Then students focus on India, learning about the Indus and Ganges rivers and studying Buddhism and Hinduism. While learning about Hinduism, students will learn about the gods and goddess—Brahma, Vishnu, and Shiva—and about several holy books, including the Rig-Veda.

Next, students turn their attention to China. They study the Yellow (Huang He) and Yangtze

(Chang Jiang) rivers, the teachings of Confucius, the Great Wall of China, the Chinese New Year, the invention of paper, and the importance of silk. The Core Knowledge sequence reminds the 2nd grade teachers that students will study China again in the 4th grade and encourages the teachers to examine the 4th grade guidelines to see how these topics build into the later grade.

Our experiences in classrooms suggest that these guidelines strike a reasonable balance between deep, large-scale generalizations and specific factual knowledge. We know from independent evaluations that teaching the Core Knowledge topics in a coherent and cumulative way enhances student achievement and narrows the test score gap between socioeconomic groups.

For schools that don't relish the idea of using a core sequence made by others, how can the four principles regarding the need for specific content be put into effect? The most important step that a school's faculty can take is to agree on the specific core topics that students will learn about in a particular grade. This will avoid big gaps in the students' knowledge and boring repetitions, such as studying rain forests

three years in a row. Not only will you notice a rise in the interest and competence of your students, but you will also notice an increase in the collegiality and morale of the faculty as you work together to fulfill a fundamental professional responsibility.

## REFERENCES

Hirsch, E. D., Jr. (1996). *The schools we need: And why we don't have them.* New York: Doubleday.

Hirsch, E. D., Jr. (1999). *Core knowledge sequence: Content guidelines for grades K–8* (Rev. ed.). Charlottesville, VA: Core Knowledge Foundation.

Lubinski, D., & Humphreys, L. G. (1997). Incorporating general intelligence into epidemiology and the social sciences. *Intelligence, 24*(1), 159–202.

Richards, I. A. (1925). *Principles of literary criticism.* London: Macmillan.

Willingham, D. C. (2001). *Cognition.* Upper Saddle River, NJ: Prentice Hall.

Woessmann, L. (2001, Summer). Why students in some countries do better. International evidence on the importance of education policy. *Education Matters, 1*(2), 67–74.

## POSTNOTE

Don Hirsch is so right when he accuses those in the education field of polarizing issues in education. We're either for phonics or whole language approaches to reading. We're either for a "fact-based" curriculum or one that emphasizes problem solving and "learning to learn." Forcing issues and educational approaches to one end of a continuum or the other seems to be how we tend to think of things. Finding good in each of two opposing positions doesn't seem to be in our way of thinking.

Don Hirsch is a major educational thinker and reformer whose work with the Core Knowledge sequence has earned him a place among our Classic selections. The four learning principles that Hirsch identifies make sense and are supported by cognitive psychology research. His conclusion that the school curriculum should teach a diversity of subjects that will lead to broad general knowledge and that a moderate number of specific examples should be taught in depth addresses the issue of breadth vs. depth in the curriculum. As he states, we should teach breadth and depth.

## DISCUSSION QUESTIONS

1.  Can you think of other examples of educational issues that have been polarized in addition to those Hirsch identifies?

2.  Would you like to teach in a school that has implemented the Core Knowledge curriculum? Why or why not?

3.  Do you think the United States should have a common national curriculum as many other countries do? Why or why not?

# 31 🏛 CLASSIC *The Quality School Curriculum*

## William Glasser

Recently I had a chance to talk to the staff members of a high school who had been hard at work for six months trying to change their school into a Quality School. They believed that they were much less coercive than in the past, but they complained that many of their students were still not working hard and that a few continued to be disruptive. They admitted that things were better but asked me if maybe they should reinject a little coercion back into their classroom management in order to "stimulate" the students to work harder.

I assured them that the answer to their complaints was to use less, not more, coercion. At the same time, I realized that in their teaching they had not yet addressed a vital component of the Quality School, the curriculum. To complete the move from coercive boss-managing to noncoercive lead-managing,[1] they had to change the curriculum they were teaching.

This was made ever clearer to me during the break when I talked to a few teachers individually. They told me that they had already made many of the changes that I suggest below and that they were not having the problems with students that most of the staff members were having. Until almost all the teachers change their curriculum, I strongly believe that they will be unable to rid their classrooms of the coercion that causes too many of their students to continue to be their adversaries.

William Glasser, M.D., is a board-certified psychiatrist and founder and president of the William Glasser Institute, an international training organization devoted to teaching his ideas in countries across the world. Glasser, William, "The Quality School Curriculum," *Phi Delta Kappan*, May 1992. Copyright © 1992 by Phi Delta Kappa. Reprinted by permission of author and publisher.

In Chapter 1 of *The Quality School*, I briefly cited the research of Linda McNeil of Rice University to support my claim that boss-management is destructive to the quality of the curriculum.[2] From feedback I have been receiving, it seems that the schools that are trying to become Quality Schools have not paid enough attention to this important point. I am partly at fault. When I wrote *The Quality School*, I did not realize how vital it is for teachers to make sure that they teach quality, and I did not explain sufficiently what this means. To correct this shortcoming, I want to expand on what I wrote in the book, and I strongly encourage staff members of all the schools that seek to move to quality to spend a great deal of time discussing this matter.

We must face the fact that a majority of students, even good ones, believe that much of the present academic curriculum is not worth the effort it takes to learn it. No matter how well the teachers manage them, if students do not find quality in what they are asked to do in their classes, they will not work hard enough to learn the material. The answer is not to try to make them work harder; the answer is to increase the quality of what we ask them to learn.

Faced with students who refuse to make much effort, even teachers who are trying to become lead-managers give a lot of low grades— a practice so traditional that they fail to perceive it as coercive. Then the students deal with their low grades by rebelling and working even less than before. The teachers, in turn, resent this attitude. They believe that, because they are making the effort to be less coercive, the students should be appreciative and work harder. The teachers fail to see that the students are not rebelling against them and their efforts to become lead-managers; they are rebelling against a curriculum that lacks quality. Therefore, if we want to create Quality Schools, we must stop *all* coercion, not just some, and one way to do this is to create a quality curriculum.

Before I describe a quality curriculum, let me use a simple nonschool example to try to explain what it is about the curriculum we have now that lacks quality. Suppose you get a job in a factory making both black shoes and brown shoes. You are well-managed and do quality work. But soon you become aware that all the brown shoes you make are sold for scrap; only the black shoes are going into retail stores. How long would you continue to work hard on the brown shoes? As you slack off, however, you are told that this is not acceptable and that you will lose pay or be fired if you don't buckle down and do just as good a job on the brown as on the black. You are told that what happens to the brown shoes is none of your business. Your job is to work hard. Wouldn't it be almost impossible to do as you are told?

As silly as the preceding example may seem, students in schools, even students in colleges and graduate schools, are asked to learn well enough to remember for important tests innumerable facts that both they and their teachers know are of no use except to pass the tests. I call this throwaway information because, after they do the work to learn it, that is just what students do with it. Dates and places in history, the names of parts of organisms and organs in biology, and formulas in mathematics and science are all examples of throwaway information.

Newspapers sometimes publish accounts of widespread cheating in schools and label it a symptom of the moral disintegration of our society. But what they call "cheating" turns out to be the ways that students have devised to avoid the work of memorizing throwaway knowledge. The honest students who are penalized are not pleased, but many students and faculty members and most of the informed public do not seem unduly upset about the "cheating." They are aware that there is no value to much of what

students are asked to remember. I certainly do not condone cheating, but I must stress that, as long as we have a curriculum that holds students responsible for throwaway information, there will be cheating—and few people will care.

Elsewhere I have suggested that this throwaway knowledge could also be called "nonsense."[3] While it is not nonsense to ask students to be aware of formulas, dates, and places and to know how to use them and where to find them if they need them, it becomes nonsense when we ask students to memorize this information and when we lower their grades if they fail to do so. Whether called throwaway knowledge or nonsense, this kind of memorized information can never be a part of the curriculum of a Quality School.

This means that in a Quality School there should never be test questions that call for the mere regurgitation of bare facts, such as those written in a book or stored in the memory of a computer. Students should never be asked to commit this portion of the curriculum to memory. All available information on what is being studied should always be on hand, not only during class but during all tests. No student should ever suffer academically because he or she forgot some fact or formula. The only useful way to test students' knowledge of facts, formulas, and other information is to ask not what the information is, but where, when, why, and how it is of use in the real world.

While a complete definition of quality is elusive, it certainly would include usefulness in the real world. And useful need not be restricted to practical or utilitarian. That which is useful can be aesthetically or spiritually useful or useful in some other way that is meaningful to the student—but it can never be nonsense.

In a Quality School, when questions of where, why, when, and how are asked on a test, they are never part of what is called an "objective" test, such as a multiple-choice, true/false, or short answer test. For example, if a multiple-choice test is used to ask where, why, when, and how, the student in a Quality School should not be restricted to a list of predetermined choices. There should always be a place for a student to write out a better answer if he or she believes that the available choices are less accurate than another alternative. For example, a multiple-choice test question in history might be: "George Washington is called 'the father of his country' for the following reasons: [four reasons would then be listed]. Which do you think is the best reason?" The student could choose one of the listed answers or write in another and explain why he or she thought it better than those listed.

In a Quality School questions as narrow as the preceding example would be rare, simply because of the constant effort to relate all that is taught to the lives of the students. Therefore, if a question asking where, when, why, and how certain information could be used were asked, it would always be followed by the further question: "How can you use this information in your life, now or in the future?"

However, such a follow-up question would never come out of the blue. The real-world value of the material to be learned would have been emphasized in lectures, in class discussions, in cooperative learning groups, and even in homework assignments that ask students to discuss with parents or other adults how what they learn in school might be useful outside of school. The purpose of such follow-up questions is to stress that the curriculum in a Quality School focuses on useful skills, not on information that has no use in the lives of those who are taught it. I define a *skill* as the ability to use knowledge. If we emphasized such skills in every academic subject, there would be no rebellion on the part of students. Students could earn equal credit on a test for explaining why what was taught was or was not of use to them. This would encourage them to think, not to parrot the ideas of others.

Continuing with the George Washington question, if a student in a Quality School said that Washington's refusal to be crowned king makes him a good candidate to be considered

father of this republic, a teacher could ask that student how he or she could use this information in life now or later. The student might respond that he or she prefers to live in a republic and would not like to live in a country where a king made all the laws. A student's answer could be more complicated than this brief example, but what the student would have thought over would be how Washington's decision affects his or her life today.

Without memorizing any facts, students taught in this way could learn more history in a few weeks than they now learn in years. More important, they would learn to *like* history. Too many students tell me that they hate history, and I find this to be an educational disaster. I hope that what they are really saying is that they hate the history curriculum, not history.

Another important element in the curriculum of a Quality School is that the students be able to *demonstrate* how what they have learned can be used in their lives now or later. Almost all students would have no difficulty accepting that reading, writing, and arithmetic are useful skills, but in a Quality School they would be asked to demonstrate that they can use them. For example, students would not be asked to learn the multiplication tables as if this knowledge were separate from being able to use the tables in their lives.

To demonstrate the usefulness of knowing how to multiply, students would be given problems to solve and asked to show how multiplication helped in solving them. These problems might require the use of several different mathematical processes, and students could show how each process was used. Students would learn not only how to multiply but also when, where, and why to do so. Once students have demonstrated that they know *how* to multiply, the actual multiplication could be done on a small calculator or by referring to tables.

In a Quality School, once students have mastered a mathematical process they would be encouraged to use a calculator. To do math processes involving large numbers over and over is boring and nonessential. Today, most students spend a lot of time memorizing the times tables. They learn how to multiply, but fail to demonstrate when, where, and why to multiply. I will admit that the tables and the calculators do not teach students *how* to multiply, but they are what people in the real world use to find answers—a fact finally recognized by the Educational Testing Service, which now allows the use of calculators on the Scholastic Aptitude Test.

Teachers in a Quality School would teach the "how" by asking students to demonstrate that they can do calculations without a calculator. Students would be told that, as soon as they can demonstrate this ability by hand, they will be allowed to use a calculator. For most students, knowing that they will never be stuck working one long, boring problem after another would be more than enough incentive to get them to learn to calculate.

In a Quality School there would be a great deal of emphasis on the skill of writing and much less on the skill of reading. The reason for this is that anyone who can write well can read well, but many people who can read well can hardly write at all. From grade 1 on, students would be asked to write: first, words; then, sentences and paragraphs; and finally, articles, stories, and letters. An extremely good project is to have each middle school student write a book or keep a journal. Students who do so will leave middle school with an education—even if that is all that they have done.

To write a great deal by hand can be onerous, but using a computer makes the same process highly enjoyable. In a Quality School, all teachers would be encouraged to learn word-processing skills and to teach them to their students. Moreover, these skills should be used in all classes. Computers are more readily available in schools today than would seem to be the case, judging from their actual use. If they are not readily available, funds can be raised to buy the few that would be needed. If students were encouraged to write, we would

see fewer students diagnosed as having language learning disabilities.

At Apollo High School,[4] where I consult, the seniors were asked if they would accept writing a good letter on a computer as a necessary requirement for graduation. They agreed, and almost all of them learned to do it. One way they demonstrated that their letters were good was by mailing them and receiving responses. They were thrilled by the answers, which we used as one criterion for satisfying the requirement. Clearly, demonstrating the use of what is learned in a real-life situation is one of the best ways to teach.

While demonstrating is the best way to show that something worthwhile has been learned, it is not always easy or even possible to do so. Thus there must be some tests. But, as I stated above, the tests in a Quality School would always show the acquisition of skills, never the acquisition of facts or information alone.

Let me use an example from science to explain what would be considered a good way to test in a Quality School. Science is mostly the discovery of how and why things work. But where and when they work can also be important. Too much science is taught as a simple listing of what works—e.g., these are the parts of a cell. Students all over America are busy memorizing the parts of a cell, usually by copying and then labeling a cell drawn in a textbook. The students are then tested to see if they can do this from memory—a wonderful example of throwaway information, taught by coercion. Teaching and testing in this way is worse than teaching no science at all, because many students learn to hate science as a result. Hating something as valuable as science is worse than simply not knowing it.

The students in a Quality School would be taught some basics about how a cell works, and they would be told that all living organisms are made up of cells. To show them that this is useful knowledge, the teacher might bring up the subject of cancer, explaining how a cancer cell fails to behave as normal cells do and so can kill the host in which it grows. All students know something about cancer, and all would consider this useful knowledge.

The subsequent test in a Quality School might ask students to describe the workings of a cell (or of some part of a cell) with their books open and available. They would then be asked how they could use this information in their lives and would be encouraged to describe the differences between a normal cell and a cancer cell. They would be taught that one way to use this information might be to avoid exposure to too much sunlight because excessive sunlight can turn normal skin cells into cancer cells. For most students, this information would be of use because all students have some fear of cancer.

Readers might feel some concern that what I am suggesting would not prepare students for standardized tests that mostly ask for throw-away information, such as the identification of the parts of a cell. My answer is that students would be better prepared—because, by learning to *explain* how and why something works, they are more likely to remember what they have learned. Even if less ground is covered, as is likely to be the case when we move from facts to skills, a little ground covered well is better preparation, even for nonsense tests, than a lot of ground covered poorly.

We should never forget that people, not curriculum, are the desired outcomes of schooling. What we want to develop are students who have the skills to become active contributors to society, who are enthusiastic about what they have learned, and who are aware of how learning can be of use to them in the future. The curriculum changes I have suggested above will certainly produce more students who fit this profile.

Will the students agree that these outcomes are desirable? If we accept control theory, the answer is obvious. When the outcomes the teachers want are in the quality worlds of their students, the students will accept them. In my

experience skills will be accepted as quality in almost all cases; facts and information will rarely be accepted.

Assuming that skills are taught, the teacher must still explain clearly what will be asked on tests. Sample questions should be given to the students, and the use of all books, notes, and materials should be permitted. Even if a student copies the workings of a cell from a book at the time of the test, the student will still have to explain how this information can be used in life. If students can answer such questions, they can be said to know the material—whether or not they copied some of it.

Tests—especially optional retests for students who wish to improve their grades—can be taken at home and can include such items as, "Explain the workings of a cell to an adult at home, write down at least one question that was asked by that person, and explain how you answered it." All the facts would be available in the test; it is the skill to use them that would be tested. The main thing to understand here is that, after a school stops testing for facts and begins to test for skills, it will not be long before it is clear to everyone that skills are the outcomes that have value; facts and information have none.

In most schools, the teacher covers a body of material, and the students must guess what is going to appear on the test. Some teachers even test for material that they have not covered. In a Quality School this would not happen. There would be no limitation on input, and the teacher would not ask students to figure out which parts of this input will be on the test. There would be no hands raised asking the age-old question, Is this going to be on the test?

Since it is always skills that are tested for in a Quality School, it is very likely that the teacher would make the test available to the students before teaching the unit so that, as they went through the material in class, they would know that these are the skills that need to be learned. Students could also be asked to describe any other skill that they have learned from the study of the material. This is an example of the open-endedness that is always a part of testing and discussion in a Quality School. A number of questions would be implicit in all tests: What can you contribute? What is your opinion? What might I (the teacher) have missed? Can you give a better use or explanation?

Keep in mind that, in a Quality School, students and teachers would evaluate tests. Students who are dissatisfied with either their own or the teacher's evaluation could continue to work on the test and improve. Building on the thinking of W. Edwards Deming, the idea is to constantly improve usable skills. In a Quality School, this opportunity is always open.

As I look over what I have written, I see nothing that requires any teacher to change anything that he or she does. If what I suggest appeals to you, implement it at your own pace. Those of us in the Quality School movement believe in lead-management, so there is no coercion—no pressure on you to hurry. You might wish to begin by discussing any of these ideas with your students. In a Quality School students should be aware of everything that the teachers are trying to do. If it makes sense to them, as I think it will, they will help you to put it into practice.

## NOTES

1. For a definition of boss-management and lead-management, see William Glasser, "The Quality School," *Phi Delta Kappan*, February 1990, p. 428.

2. William Glasser, The Quality School: Managing Students Without Coercion (New York: Harper & Row, 1990), Ch. 1.

3. See Supplementary Information Bulletin No. 5 of the Quality School Training Program. All of these bulletins are available from the Institute for Reality Therapy, 7301 Medical Center Dr., Suite 104, Canoga Park, CA 91307.

4. Apollo High School is a school for students who refuse to work in a regular high school. It enrolls about 240 students (9–12) and is part of the Simi Valley (Calif.) Unified School District.

## POSTNOTE

William Glasser's training as a psychiatrist has enabled him to examine schools and their effects on children in ways that are unique and important, earning his article a place among our Classic selections. His *choice theory* represents an attempt to base schooling on different principles that satisfy students' needs for friendship, freedom, fun, and power. Glasser's philosophy has been implemented by many educators for whom his humanistic approach has great appeal.

In this article, Glasser asserts that a majority of students believe that much of the present academic curriculum is not worth the effort needed to learn it. To overcome this problem, Glasser suggests that the quality of what we ask students to learn must be increased. Some guiding principles of this quality curriculum include reducing the quantity of what students are asked to memorize, emphasizing the usefulness of knowledge and the development of useful skills (including writing skills), covering less material, and assessing performance.

Many of Glasser's ideas are compatible with the curriculum reform movement occurring in such fields as mathematics, science, and history. Asking students to construct their own knowledge, rather than memorize packaged knowledge, is clearly the direction in which these curriculum efforts are headed. However, many of the content standards being implemented by states, along with their associated assessments, seem to be emphasizing memorization of facts.

## DISCUSSION QUESTIONS

1. Do Glasser's ideas appeal to you? Why or why not? What problems, if any, do you see in implementing them?

2. What do you think about Glasser's notion of allowing open-book tests? Explain your position.

3. Glasser states that in looking over his ideas, he sees nothing that requires teachers to change what they do. Do you agree or disagree with his statement? Why?

# The Relevance of Religion to the Curriculum

## 32

Warren A. Nord

For some time now, public school administrators have been on the front lines of our culture wars over religion and education—and I expect it would be music to their ears to hear that peace accords have been signed.

Unfortunately, the causes of war are deep-seated. Peace is not around the corner.

At the same time, however, it is also easy to overstate the extent of the hostilities. At least at the national level—but also in many communities across America—a large measure of common ground has been found. The leaders of most major national educational, religious and civil liberties organizations agree about the basic principles that should govern the role of religion and public schools. No doubt we don't agree about everything, but we agree about a lot.

For example, in 1988, a group of 17 major religious and educational organizations—the American Jewish Congress and the Islamic Society of North America, the National Association of Evangelicals and the National Council of Churches, the National Education Association and American Federation of Teachers, the National School Boards Association and AASA among them—endorsed a statement of principles that describes the importance of religion in the public school curriculum.

The statement, in part, says this: "Because religion plays significant roles in history and

Warren Nord is director of the Program in the Humanities and Human Values and teaches the philosophy of religion at the University of North Carolina. He is the author of *Religion and American Education: Rethinking a National Dilemma* and co-author with Charles Haynes of *Taking Religion Seriously Across the Curriculum*. Reprinted with permission from the January 1999 issue of *The School Administrator* magazine.

society, study about religion is essential to understanding both the nation and the world. Omission of facts about religion can give students the false impression that the religious life of humankind is insignificant or unimportant. Failure to understand even the basic symbols, practices and concepts of the various religions makes much of history, literature, art and contemporary life unintelligible."

## A Profound Problem

As a result of this (and other "common ground" statements) it is no longer controversial to assert that the study of religion has a legitimate and important place in the public school curriculum.

Where in the curriculum? In practice, the study of religion has been relegated almost entirely to history texts and courses, for it is widely assumed that religion is irrelevant to every other subject in the curriculum—that is, to understanding the world here and now.

This is a deeply controversial assumption, however. A profoundly important educational problem lingers here, one that is almost completely ignored by educators.

Let me put it this way. Several ways exist for making sense of the world here and now. Many Americans accept one or another religious interpretation of reality; others accept one or another secular interpretation. We don't agree—and the differences among us often cut deeply.

Yet public schools systematically teach students to think about the world in secular ways only. They don't even bother to inform them about religious alternatives—apart from distant history. That is, public schooling discriminates against religious ways of making sense of the world. This is no minor problem.

## An Economic Argument

To get some sense of what's at issue, let's consider economics.

One can think about the economic domain of life in various ways. Scriptural texts in all religious traditions address questions of justice and morality, poverty and wealth, work and stewardship, for example. A vast body of 20th century literature in moral theology deals with economic issues. Indeed most mainline denominations and ecumenical agencies have official statements on justice and economics. What's common to all of this literature is the claim that the economic domain of life cannot be understood apart from religion.

Needless to say, this claim is not to be found in economics textbooks. Indeed, if we put end to end all the references to religion in the 10 high school economics texts I've reviewed in the past few years, they would add up to about two pages—out of 4,400 pages combined (and all of the references are to premodern times). There is but a single reference to religion—a passing mention in a section on taxation and nonprofit organizations—in the 47 pages of the new national content standards in economics. Moreover, the textbooks and the standards say virtually nothing about the problems that are the major concern of theologians—problems relating to poverty, justice, our consumer culture, the Third World, human dignity and the meaningfulness of work.

The problem isn't just that the texts ignore religion and those economic problems of most concern to theologians. A part of the problem is what the texts do teach—that is, neoclassical economic theory. According to the texts, economics is a science, people are essentially self-interested utility-maximizers, the economic realm is one of competition for scarce resources, values are personal preferences and value judgments are matters of cost-benefit analysis. Of course, no

religious tradition accepts this understanding of human nature, society, economics and values.

That is, the texts and standards demoralize and secularize economics.

## An Appalling Claim

To be sure, they aren't explicitly hostile to religion; rather they ignore it. But in some ways this is worse than explicit hostility, for students remain unaware of the fact that there are tensions and conflicts between their religious traditions and what they are taught about economics.

In fact, the texts and the standards give students no sense that what they are learning is controversial. Indeed, the national economics standards make it a matter of principle that students be kept in the dark about alternatives to neoclassical theory. As the editors put it in their introduction, the standards were developed to convey a single conception of economics, the "majority paradigm" or neoclassical model of economic behavior. For, they argue, to include "strongly held minority views of economic processes [would only risk] confusing and frustrating teachers and students who are then left with the responsibility of sorting the qualifications and alternatives without a sufficient foundation to do so."

This is an appalling statement. It means, in effect, that students should be indoctrinated; they should be given no critical perspective on neoclassical economic theory.

The problem with the economics texts and standards is but one aspect of the much larger problem that cuts across the curriculum, for in every course students are taught to think in secular ways that often (though certainly not always) conflict with religious alternatives. And this is always done uncritically.

Even in history courses, students learn to think about historical meaning and causation in exclusively secular ways in spite of the fact that Judaism, Christianity and Islam all hold that God acts in history, that there is a religious meaning to history. True, they learn a few facts about religion, but they learn to think about history in secular categories.

## Nurturing Secularity

Outside of history courses and literature courses that use historical literature, religion is rarely even mentioned, but even on those rare occasions when it is, the intellectual context is secular. As a result, public education nurtures a secular mentality. This marginalizes religion from our cultural and intellectual life and contributes powerfully to the secularization of our culture.

Ignoring religious ways of thinking about the world is a problem for three important reasons.

▶ *It is profoundly illiberal.*

Here, of course, I'm not using the term "liberal" to refer to the left wing of the Democratic Party. A liberal education is a broad education, one that provides students with the perspective to think critically about the world and their lives. A good liberal education should introduce students—at least older students—to the major ways humankind has developed for making sense of the world and their lives. Some of those ways of thinking and living are religious and it is illiberal to leave them out of the discussion. Indeed, it may well constitute indoctrination—secular indoctrination.

We indoctrinate students when we uncritically initiate them into one way of thinking and systematically ignore the alternatives. Indeed, if students are to be able to think critically about the secular ways of understanding the world that pervade the curriculum, they must understand something about the religious alternatives.

▶ *It is politically unjust.*

Public schools must take the public seriously. But religious parents are now, in effect, educationally disenfranchised. Their ways of thinking and living aren't taken seriously.

Consider an analogy. A generation ago textbooks and curricula said virtually nothing about women, blacks and members of minority sub-

cultures. Hardly anyone would now say that that was fair or just. We now—most of us—realize this was a form of discrimination, of educational disenfranchisement. And so it is with religious subcultures (though, ironically, the multicultural movement has been almost entirely silent about religion).

▶ *It is unconstitutional.*

It is, of course, uncontroversial that it is constitutionally permissible to teach about religion in public schools when done properly. No Supreme Court justice has ever held otherwise. But I want to make a stronger argument.

The court has been clear that public schools must be neutral in matters of religion—in two senses. Schools must be neutral among religions (they can't favor Protestants over Catholics or Christians over Jews), and they must be neutral between religion and nonreligion. Schools can't promote religion. They can't proselytize. They can't conduct religious exercises.

Of course, neutrality is a two-edged sword. Just as schools can't favor religion over nonreligion, neither can they favor nonreligion over religion. As Justice Hugo Black put it in the seminal 1947 *Everson* ruling, "State power is no more to be used so as to handicap religions than it is to favor them."

Similarly, in his majority opinion in *Abington v. Schempp* in 1963, Justice Tom Clark wrote that schools can't favor "those who believe in no religion over those who do believe." And in a concurring opinion, Justice Arthur Goldberg warned that an "untutored devotion to the concept of neutrality [can lead to a] pervasive devotion to the secular and a passive, or even active, hostility to the religious."

Of course this is just what has happened. An untutored, naïve conception of neutrality has led educators to look for a smoking gun, an explicit hostility to religion, when the hostility has been philosophically rather more subtle—though no less substantial for that.

The only way to be neutral when all ground is contested ground is to be fair to the alternative. That is, given the Supreme Court's longstanding interpretation of the Establishment Clause, public schools must require the study of religion if they require the study of disciplines that cumulatively lead to a pervasive devotion to the secular—as they do.

## Classroom Practices

So how can we be fair? What would a good education look like? Here I can only skim the surface—and refer readers to *Taking Religion Seriously Across the Curriculum,* in which Charles Haynes and I chart what needs to be done in some detail.

Obviously a great deal depends on the age of students. In elementary schools students should learn something of the relatively uncontroversial aspects of different religions—their traditions, holidays, symbols and a little about religious histories, for example. As students mature, they should be initiated into the conversation about truth and goodness that constitutes a good liberal education. Here a two-prong approach is required.

First, students should learn something about religious ways of thinking about any subject that is religiously controversial in the relevant courses. So, for example, a biology text should include a chapter in which scientific ways of understanding nature are contrasted with religious alternatives. Students should learn that the relationship of religion and science is controversial, and that while they will learn what most biologists believe to be the truth about nature, not everyone agrees.

Indeed, every text and course should provide students with historical and philosophical perspective on the subject at hand, establishing connections and tensions with other disciplines and domains of the culture, including religion.

This is not a balanced-treatment or equal-time requirement. Biology courses should continue to be biology courses and economics courses should continue to be economics courses. In any case, given their competence and

training, biology and economics teachers are not likely to be prepared to deal with a variety of religious ways of approaching their subject. At most, they can provide a minimal fairness.

A robust fairness is possible only if students are required to study religious as well as secular ways of making sense of the world in some depth, in courses devoted to the study of religion.

A good liberal education should require at least one year-long high school course in religious studies (with other courses, I would hope, available as electives). The primary goal of such a course should be to provide students with a sufficiently intensive exposure to religious ways of thinking and living to enable them to actually understand religion (rather than simply know a few facts about religion). It should expose students to scriptural texts, but it also should use more recent primary sources that enable students to understand how contemporary theologians and writers within different traditions think about those subjects in the curriculum—morality, sexuality, history, nature, psychology and the economic world—that they will be taught to interpret in secular categories in their other courses.

Of course, if religion courses are to be offered, there must be teachers competent to teach them. Religious studies must become a certifiable field in public education, and new courses must not be offered or required until competent teachers are available.

Indeed, all teachers must have a much clearer sense of how religion relates to the curriculum and, more particularly, to their respective subjects. Major reforms in teacher education are necessary—as is a new generation of textbooks sensitive to religion.

Some educators will find it unrealistic to expect such reforms. Of course several decades ago textbooks and curricula said little about women and minority cultures. Several decades ago, few universities had departments of religious studies. Now multicultural education is commonplace and most universities have departments of religious studies. Things change.

## Stemming an Exodus

No doubt some educators will find these proposals controversial, but they will be shortsighted if they do. Leaving religion out of the curriculum is also controversial. Indeed, because public schools don't take religion seriously many religious parents have deserted them and, if the Supreme Court upholds the legality of vouchers, as they may well do, the exodus will be much greater.

In the long run, the least controversial position is the one that takes everyone seriously. If public schools are to survive our culture wars, they must be built on common ground. But there can be no common ground when religious voices are left out of the curricular conversation.

It is religious conservatives, of course, who are most critical of public schooling—and the most likely to leave. But my argument is that public schooling doesn't take any religion seriously. It marginalizes all religion—liberal as well as conservative, Catholic as well as Protestant, Jewish, Muslim and Buddhist as well as Christian. Indeed, it contributes a great deal to the secularization of American culture—and this should concern any religious person.

But, in the end, this shouldn't concern religious people only. Religion should be included in the curriculum for three very powerful secular reasons. The lack of serious study of religion in public education is illiberal, unjust and unconstitutional.

## POSTNOTE

Parents rightfully want to pass on to their children their most deeply held beliefs. Many of these beliefs about what constitutes a good life, and what is a person's true nature, are theological questions that are embedded in their religious convictions. For a variety of reasons, many of which are touched on in this article, the public schools have ignored and marginalized religion. Besides the educational implications of this policy, the impact on the public support of public schools is beginning to show. America is a religious nation, founded on religious principles ("In God we trust" and "All men are created equal"). Also, over 90 percent of Americans believe in God and close to 90 percent report membership in a particular church. It would seem, then, that the current condition of the two powerful educational influences on children, the media and the public school system, being areligious or antireligious is bound to have political consequences. Since parents can do little to punish Hollywood, the temptation to take out their resentments on the local, tax-supported schools is strong.

## DISCUSSION QUESTIONS

1. Professor Nord ends his essay with the words, "The lack of serious study of religion in public education is illiberal, unjust and unconstitutional." What is your reaction to this statement?

2. Has your previous school experience strengthened, undermined, or had no effect on your religious convictions?

3. What solutions to the problem he has outlined does Nord offer? Do you agree with them? Why? Why not?

# 33

# *Teaching Themes of Care*

## Nel Noddings

Some educators today—and I include myself among them—would like to see a complete reorganization of the school curriculum. We would like to give a central place to the questions and issues that lie at the core of human existence. One possibility would be to organize the curriculum around themes of care—caring for self, for intimate others, for strangers and global others, for the natural world and its non-human creatures, for the human-made world, and for ideas.[1]

A realistic assessment of schooling in the present political climate makes it clear that such a plan is not likely to be implemented. However, we can use the rich vocabulary of care in educational planning and introduce themes of care into regular subject-matter classes. In this article, I will first give a brief rationale for teaching themes of care; second, I will suggest ways of choosing and organizing such themes; and, finally, I'll say a bit about the structures required to support such teaching.

## Why Teach Caring?

In an age when violence among schoolchildren is at an unprecedented level, when children are bearing children with little knowledge of how to care for them, when the society and even the schools often concentrate on materialistic messages, it may be unnecessary to argue that we should care more genuinely for our children and teach them to care. However, many otherwise

reasonable people seem to believe that our educational problems consist largely of low scores on achievement tests. My contention is, first, that we should want more from our educational efforts than adequate academic achievement and, second, that we will not achieve even that meager success unless our children believe that they themselves are cared for and learn to care for others.

There is much to be gained, both academically and humanly, by including themes of care in our curriculum. First, such inclusion may well expand our students' cultural literacy. For example, as we discuss in math classes the attempts of great mathematicians to prove the existence of God or to reconcile a God who is all good with the reality of evil in the world, students will hear names, ideas, and words that are not part of the standard curriculum. Although such incidental learning cannot replace the systematic and sequential learning required by those who plan careers in mathematically oriented fields, it can be powerful in expanding students' cultural horizons and in inspiring further study.

Second, themes of care help us to connect the standard subjects. The use of literature in mathematics classes, of history in science classes, and of art and music in all classes can give students a feeling of the wholeness in their education. After all, why should they seriously study five different subjects if their teachers, who are educated people, only seem to know and appreciate one?

Third, themes of care connect our students and our subjects to great existential questions. What is the meaning of life? Are there gods? How should I live?

Fourth, sharing such themes can connect us person-to-person. When teachers discuss themes

Nel Noddings is a professor of education at Teachers College, Columbia University. Noddings, Nel, "Teaching Themes of Care," from *Phi Delta Kappan*, May 1995.

of care, they may become real persons to their students and so enable them to construct new knowledge. Martin Buber put it this way:

> Trust, trust in the world, because this human being exists—that is the most inward achievement of the relation in education. Because this human being exists, meaninglessness, however hard pressed you are by it, cannot be the real truth. Because this human being exists, in the darkness the light lies hidden, in fear salvation, and in the callousness of one's fellow-man the great love.[2]

Finally, I should emphasize that caring is not just a warm, fuzzy feeling that makes people kind and likable. Caring implies a continuous search for competence. When we care, we want to do our very best for the objects of our care. To have as our educational goal the production of caring, competent, loving, and lovable people is not anti-intellectual. Rather, it demonstrates respect for the full range of human talents. Not all human beings are good at or interested in mathematics, science, or British literature. But all humans can be helped to lead lives of deep concern for others, for the natural world and its creatures, and for the preservation of the human-made world. They can be led to develop the skills and knowledge necessary to make positive contributions, regardless of the occupation they may choose.

## Choosing and Organizing Themes of Care

Care is conveyed in many ways. At the institutional level, schools can be organized to provide continuity and support for relationships of care and trust.[3] At the individual level, parents and teachers show their caring through characteristic forms of attention: by cooperating in children's activities, by sharing their own dreams and doubts, and by providing carefully for the steady growth to the children in their charge. Personal manifestations of care are probably more important in children's lives than any particular curriculum or pattern of pedagogy.

However, curriculum can be selected with caring in mind. That is, educators can manifest their care in the choice of curriculum, and appropriately chosen curriculum can contribute to the growth of children as carers. Within each large domain of care, many topics are suitable for thematic units: in the domain of "caring for self," for example, we might consider life stages, spiritual growth, and what it means to develop an admirable character; in exploring the topic of caring for intimate others, we might include units on love, friendship, and parenting; under the theme of caring for strangers and global others, we might study war, poverty, and tolerance; in addressing the idea of caring for the human-made world, we might encourage competence with the machines that surround us and a real appreciation for the marvels of technology. Many other examples exist. Furthermore, there are at least two different ways to approach the development of such themes: units can be constructed by interdisciplinary teams, or themes can be identified by individual teachers and addressed periodically throughout a year's or semester's work.

The interdisciplinary approach is familiar in core programs, and such programs are becoming more and more popular at the middle school level. One key to a successful interdisciplinary unit is the degree of genuinely enthusiastic support it receives from the teachers involved. Too often, arbitrary or artificial groupings are formed, and teachers are forced to make contributions that they themselves do not value highly. For example, math and science teachers are sometimes automatically lumped together, and rich humanistic possibilities may be lost. If I, as a math teacher, want to include historical, biographical, and literary topics in my math lessons, I might prefer to work with English and social studies teachers. Thus it is important to involve teachers in the initial selection of broad areas for themes, as well as in their implementation.

Such interdisciplinary arrangements also work well at the college level. I recently received a copy of the syllabus for a college course titled "The Search for Meaning," which was co-taught by an economist, a university chaplain, and a psychiatrist.[4] The course is interdisciplinary, intellectually rich, and aimed squarely at the central questions of life.

At the high school level, where students desperately need to engage in the study and practice of caring, it is harder to form interdisciplinary teams. A conflict arises as teachers acknowledge the intensity of the subject-matter preparation their students need for further education. Good teachers often wish there were time in the day to co-teach unconventional topics of great importance, and they even admit that their students are not getting what they need for full personal development. But they feel constrained by the requirements of a highly competitive world and the structures of schooling established by that world.

Is there a way out of this conflict? Imaginative, like-minded teachers might agree to emphasize a particular theme in their separate classes. Such themes as war, poverty, crime, racism, or sexism can be addressed in almost every subject area. The teachers should agree on some core ideas related to caring that will be discussed in all classes, but beyond the central commitment to address themes of care, the topics can be handled in whatever way seems suitable in a given subject.

Consider, for example, what a mathematics class might contribute to a unit on crime. Statistical information might be gathered on the location and number of crimes, on rates for various kinds of crime, on the ages of offenders, and on the cost to society; graphs and charts could be constructed. Data on changes in crime rates could be assembled. Intriguing questions could be asked: Were property crime rates lower when penalties were more severe—when, for example, even children were hanged as thieves? What does an average criminal case cost by way of lawyers' fees, police investigation, and court

processing? Does it cost more to house a youth in a detention center or in an elite private school?

None of this would have to occupy a full period every day. The regular sequential work of the math class could go on at a slightly reduced rate (e.g., fewer textbook exercises as homework), and the work on crime could proceed in the form of interdisciplinary projects over a considerable period of time. Most important would be the continual reminder in all classes that the topic is part of a larger theme of caring for strangers and fellow citizens. It takes only a few minutes to talk about what it means to live in safety, to trust one's neighbors, to feel secure in greeting strangers. Students should be told that metal detectors and security guards were not part of their parents' school lives, and they should be encouraged to hope for a safer and more open future. Notice the words I've used in this paragraph: caring, trust, safety, strangers, hope. Each could be used as an organizing theme for another unit of study.

English and social studies teachers would obviously have much to contribute to a unit on crime. For example, students might read *Oliver Twist*, and they might also study and discuss the social conditions that seemed to promote crime in 19th-century England. Do similar conditions exist in our country today? The selection of materials could include both classic works and modern stories and films. Students might even be introduced to some of the mystery stories that adults read so avidly on airplanes and beaches, and teachers should be engaged in lively discussion about the comparative value of the various stories.

Science teachers might find that a unit on crime would enrich their teaching of evolution. They could bring up the topic of social Darwinism, which played such a strong role in social policy during the late 19th and early 20th centuries. To what degree are criminal tendencies inherited? Should children be tested for the genetic defects that are suspected of predisposing some people to crime? Are females less competent than males in moral reasoning? (Why did some scientists and philosophers think this was true?) Why do males commit so many more violent acts than females?

Teachers of the arts can also be involved. A unit on crime might provide a wonderful opportunity to critique "gangsta rap" and other currently popular forms of music. Students might profitably learn how the control of art contributed to national criminality during the Nazi era. These are ideas that pop into my mind. Far more various and far richer ideas will come from teachers who specialize in these subjects.

There are risks, of course, in undertaking any unit of study that focuses on matters of controversy or deep existential concern, and teachers should anticipate these risks. What if students want to compare the incomes of teachers and cocaine dealers? What if they point to contemporary personalities from politics, entertainment, business, or sports who seem to escape the law and profit from what seems to be criminal behavior? My own inclination would be to allow free discussion of these cases and to be prepared to counteract them with powerful stories of honesty, compassion, moderation, and charity.

An even more difficult problem may arise. Suppose a student discloses his or her own criminal activities? Fear of this sort of occurrence may send teachers scurrying for safer topics. But, in fact, any instructional method that uses narrative forms or encourages personal expression runs this risk. For example, students of English as a second language who write proudly about their own hard lives and new hopes may disclose that their parents are illegal immigrants. A girl may write passages that lead her teacher to suspect sexual abuse. A boy may brag about objects that he has "ripped off." Clearly, as we use these powerful methods that encourage students to initiate discussion and share their experiences, we must reflect on the ethical issues involved, consider appropriate responses to such issues, and prepare teachers to handle them responsibly.

Caring teachers must help students make wise decisions about what information they will share about themselves. On the one hand, teachers want their students to express themselves, and they want their students to trust in and consult them. On the other hand, teachers have an obligation to protect immature students from making disclosures that they might later regret. There is a deep ethical problem here. Too often educators assume that only religious fundamentalists and right-wing extremists object to the discussion of emotionally and morally charged issues. In reality, there is a real danger of intrusiveness and lack of respect in methods that fail to recognize the vulnerability of students. Therefore, as teachers plan units and lessons on moral issues, they should anticipate the tough problems that may arise. I am arguing here that it is morally irresponsible to simply ignore existential questions and themes of care; we must attend to them. But it is equally irresponsible to approach these deep concerns without caution and careful preparation.

So far I have discussed two ways of organizing interdisciplinary units on themes of care. In one, teachers actually teach together in teams; in the other, teachers agree on a theme and a central focus on care, but they do what they can, when they can, in their own classrooms. A variation on this second way—which is also open to teachers who have to work alone—is to choose several themes and weave them into regular course material over an entire semester or year. The particular themes will depend on the interests and preparation of each teacher.

For example, if I were teaching high school mathematics today, I would use religious/existential questions as a pervasive theme because the biographies of mathematicians are filled with accounts of their speculations on matters of God, other dimensions, and the infinite—and because these topics fascinate me. There are so many wonderful stories to be told: Descartes's proof of the existence of God, Pascal's famous wager, Plato's world of forms, Newton's attempt to verify Biblical chronology, Leibnitz' detailed theodicy, current attempts to describe a divine domain in terms of metasystems, and mystical speculations on the infinite.[5] Some of these stories can be told as rich "asides" in five minutes or less. Others might occupy the better part of several class periods.

Other mathematics teachers might use an interest in architecture and design, art, music, or machinery as continuing themes in the domain of "caring for the human-made world." Still others might introduce the mathematics of living things. The possibilities are endless. In choosing and pursuing these themes, teachers should be aware that they are both helping their students learn to care and demonstrating their own caring by sharing interests that go well beyond the demands of textbook pedagogy.

Still another way to introduce themes of care into regular classrooms is to be prepared to respond spontaneously to events that occur in the school or in the neighborhood. Older teachers have one advantage in this area: they probably have a greater store of experience and stories on which to draw. However, younger teachers have the advantage of being closer to their students' lives and experiences; they are more likely to be familiar with the music, films, and sports figures that interest their students.

All teachers should be prepared to respond to the needs of students who are suffering from the death of friends, conflicts between groups of students, pressure to use drugs or to engage in sex, and other troubles so rampant in the lives of today's children. Too often schools rely on experts—"grief counselors" and the like—when what children really need is the continuing compassion and presence of adults who represent constancy and care in their lives. Artificially separating the emotional, academic, and moral care of children into tasks for specially designated experts contributes to the fragmentation of life in schools.

Of course, I do not mean to imply that experts are unnecessary, nor do I mean to suggest that some matters should not be reserved for parents or psychologists. But our society has gone too far in compartmentalizing the care of its children. When we ask whose job it is to teach children how to care, an appropriate initial response is "Everyone's." Having accepted universal responsibility, we can then ask about the special contributions and limitations of various individuals and groups.

## Supporting Structures

What kinds of schools and teacher preparation are required, if themes of care are to be taught effectively? First, and most important, care must be taken seriously as a major purpose of our schools; that is, educators must recognize that caring for students is fundamental in teaching and that developing people with a strong capacity for care is a major objective of responsible education. Schools properly pursue many other objectives—developing artistic talent, promoting multicultural understanding, diversifying curriculum to meet the academic and vocational needs of all students, forging connections with community agencies and parents, and so on. Schools cannot be single-purpose institutions. Indeed, many of us would argue that it is logically and practically impossible to achieve that single academic purpose if other purposes are not recognized and accepted. This contention is confirmed in the success stories of several inner-city schools.[6]

Once it is recognized that school is a place in which students are cared for and learn to care, that recognition should be powerful in guiding policy. In the late 1950s, schools in the U.S., under the guidance of James Conant and others, placed the curriculum at the top of the educational priority list. Because the nation's leaders wanted schools to provide high-powered courses in mathematics and science, it was recommended that small high schools be replaced by efficient larger structures complete with sophisticated laboratories and specialist teachers. Economies of scale were anticipated, but the main argument for consolidation and regionalization centered on the curriculum. All over the country, small schools were closed, and students were herded into larger facilities with "more offerings." We did not think carefully about schools as communities and about what might be lost as we pursued a curriculum-driven ideal.

Today many educators are calling for smaller schools and more family-like groupings. These are good proposals, but teachers, parents, and students should be engaged in continuing discussion about what they are trying to achieve through the new arrangements. For example, if test scores do not immediately rise, participants should be courageous in explaining that test scores were not the main object of the changes. Most of us who argue for caring in schools are intuitively quite sure that children in such settings will in fact become more competent learners. But, if they cannot prove their academic competence in a prescribed period of time, should we give up on caring and on teaching them to care? That would be foolish. There is more to life and learning than the academic proficiency demonstrated by test scores.

In addition to steadfastness of purpose, schools must consider continuity of people and place. If we are concerned with caring and community, then we must make it possible for students and teachers to stay together for several years so that mutual trust can develop and students can feel a sense of belonging in their "school-home."[7]

More than one scheme of organization can satisfy the need for continuity. Elementary school children can stay with the same teacher for several years, or they can work with a stable team of specialist teachers for several years. In the latter arrangement, there may be program advantages; that is, children taught by subject-matter experts who get to know them well over an extended period of time may learn more about the particular subjects. At the high school level, the same specialist teaching might work with students throughout their years in high school. Or, as Theodore Sizer has suggested, one teacher might teach two subjects to a group of 30 students rather than one subject to 60 students, thereby reducing the number of different adults with whom students interact each day.[8] In all the suggested arrangements, placements should be made by mutual consent whenever possible. Teachers and students who hate or distrust one another should not be forced to stay together.

A policy of keeping students and teachers together for several years supports caring in two essential ways: it provides time for the development of caring relations, and it makes teaching themes of care more feasible. When trust has been established, teachers and students can discuss matters that would be hard for a group of strangers to approach, and classmates learn to support one another in sensitive situations.

The structural changes suggested here are not expensive. If a high school teacher must teach five classes a day, it costs no more for three of these classes to be composed of continuing students than for all five classes to comprise new students—i.e., strangers. The recommended changes come directly out of a clear-headed assessment of our major aims and purposes. We failed to suggest them earlier because we had other, too limited, goals in mind.

I have made one set of structural changes sound easy, and I do believe that they are easily made. But the curricular and pedagogical changes that are required may be more difficult. High school textbooks rarely contain the kinds of supplementary material I have described, and teachers are not formally prepared to incorporate such material. Too often, even the people we regard as strongly prepared in a liberal arts major are unprepared to discuss the history of their subject, its relation to other subjects, the biographies of its great figures, its connections to the great existential questions, and the ethical responsibilities of those who work in that discipline. To teach themes of care in an academically effective way, teachers will have to engage in projects of self-education.

At present, neither liberal arts departments nor schools of education pay much attention to connecting academic subjects with themes of care. For example, biology students may learn something of the anatomy and physiology of mammals but nothing at all about the care of living animals; they may never be asked to consider the moral issues involved in the annual euthanasia of millions of pets. Mathematics students may learn to solve quadratic equations but never study what it means to live in a mathematicized world. In enlightened history classes, students may learn something about the problems of racism and colonialism but never hear anything about the evolution of childhood, the contributions of women in both domestic and public caregiving, or the connection between the feminization of caregiving and public policy. A liberal education that neglects matters that are central to a fully human life hardly warrants the name,[9] and a professional education that confines itself to technique does nothing to close the gaps in liberal education.

The greatest structural obstacle, however, may simply be legitimizing the inclusion of themes of care in the curriculum. Teachers in the early grades have long included such themes as a regular part of their work, and middle school educators are becoming more sensitive to developmental needs involving care. But secondary schools—where violence, apathy, and alienation are most evident—do little to develop the capacity to care. Today, even elementary teachers complain that the pressure to produce high test scores inhibits the work they regard as central to their mission: the development of caring and competent people. Therefore, it would seem that the most fundamental change required is one of attitude. Teachers can be very special people in the lives of children, and it should be legitimate for them to spend time developing relations of trust, talking with students about problems that are central to their lives, and guiding them toward greater sensitivity and competence across all the domains of care.

## NOTES

1. For the theoretical argument, see Nel Noddings, *The Challenge to Care in Schools* (New York: Teachers College Press, 1992); for a practical example and rich documentation, see Sharon Quint, *Schooling Homeless Children* (New York: Teachers College Press, 1994).

2. Martin Buber, *Between Man and Man* (New York: Macmillan, 1965), p. 98.

3. Noddings, chap. 12.

4. See Thomas H. Naylor, William H. Willimon, and Magdalena R. Naylor, *The Search for Meaning* (Nashville, Tenn.: Abingdon Press, 1994).

5. For many more examples, see Nel Noddings, *Educating for Intelligent Belief and Unbelief* (New York: Teachers College Press, 1993).

6. See Deborah Meier, "How Our Schools Could Be," *Phi Delta Kappan*, January 1995, pp. 369–73; and Quint, op. cit.

7. See Jane Roland Martin, *The Schoolhome: Rethinking Schools for Changing Families* (Cambridge, Mass.: Harvard University Press, 1992).

8. Theodore Sizer, *Horace's Compromise: The Dilemma of the American High School* (Boston: Houghton Mifflin, 1984).

9. See Bruce Wilshire, *The Moral Collapse of the University* (Albany: State University of New York Press, 1990).

## POSTNOTE

Getting over selfishness and self-preoccupation is a major task of one's young years. Schools have a responsibility to help children develop the habit of caring for others, as Nel Noddings demonstrates in this article. She makes a strong case for giving this task a more prominent place in our educational planning.

As children get older, however, they need to develop some sterner virtues to complement caring. They need to acquire self-discipline and self-control. They need to acquire the habit of persistence at hard tasks. They need, too, to learn how to strive for individual excellence and to compete against others without hostility. We could argue that both a strong individual and a strong nation need a balance of strengths. To pursue one strength, such as caring, without developing the full spectrum of human virtues, leaves both the individual and the nation vulnerable.

## DISCUSSION QUESTIONS

1.  Do you agree with the primacy given to caring by the author? Why or why not?

2.  What are the "supporting structures" the article suggests are necessary to teach caring effectively?

3.  What practical classroom suggestions to advance caring have you gleaned from this article?

# 34   *Mining the Values in the Curriculum*

Kevin Ryan

While the development of a child's character is clearly not the sole responsibility of
the school, historically and legally schools have
been major players in this arena. Young people
spend much of their lives within school walls.
There they will learn, either by chance or design, moral lessons about how people behave.

In helping students develop good character
—the capacity to know the good, love the good,
and do the good—schools should above all be
contributing to a child's knowing what is good.
But what is most worth knowing? And for what
purpose? How do educators decide what to
teach? Pressing concerns for ancient philosophers, these questions are even more demanding today as we struggle to make order out of
our information-saturated lives. New dilemmas
brought on by such developments as computers, doomsday weaponry, and lethal viruses
challenge us daily.

## What Is a Good Person?

Before curriculum builders can answer "What's
most worth knowing?" we have to know "For
what?" To be well adjusted to the world around
us? To become wealthy and self-sufficient? To
be an artist? With a little reflection, most of us
would come to similar conclusions as our great

Kevin Ryan is founder and director emeritus of the
Center for the Advancement of Ethics and Character,
School of Education, Boston University, Massachu-
setts. From Kevin Ryan, "Mining the Values in the
Curriculum." *Educational Leadership*, November 1993,
pp. 16–18. Reprinted with permission of the Associa-
tion for Supervision and Curriculum Development.
Copyright © 1993 by ASCD. All rights reserved.

philosophers and spiritual leaders: education
should help us become wise and good people.

What constitutes a "good person" has paralyzed many sincere educators and noneduca-
tors. Because the United States is a multiracial,
multiethnic nation, many educators despair of
coming up with a shared vision of the good person to guide curriculum builders. Our founders
and early educational pioneers saw in the very
diverse, multicultural American scene of the
late 18th and early 19th centuries the clear need
for a school system that would teach the civic
virtues necessary to maintain our novel political and social experiment. They saw the school's
role not only as contributing to a person's understanding of what it is to be good, but also as
teaching the enduring habits required of a democratic citizen.

Yet the school's curriculum must educate
more than just the citizen. Conway Dorsett recently suggested that a good curriculum respects and balances the need "to educate the
'three people' in each individual: the worker, the
citizen, and the private person" (1993). Our
schools must provide opportunities for students
to discover what is most worth knowing, as they
prepare, not only to be citizens, but also good
workers and good private individuals.

The work of C. S. Lewis may provide us
with the multicultural model of a good person
that we are seeking. Lewis discovered that certain ideas about how one becomes a good person recur in the writing of ancient Egyptians,
Babylonians, Hebrews, Chinese, Norse, Indians,
and Greeks, and in Anglo-Saxon and American
writings as well. Common values included
kindness; honesty; loyalty to parents, spouses,
and family members; an obligation to help the
poor, the sick, and the less fortunate; and the
right to private property. Some evils, such as

treachery, torture, and murder, were considered worse than one's own death (1947).

**TERM TO NOTE**
Tao

Lewis called this universal path to becoming a good person by the Chinese name, "the Tao." Combining the wisdom of many cultures, this Tao could be our multicultural answer for how to live our lives, the basis for what is most worth knowing.

Over the years, teachers, curriculum specialists, and school officials have used the Tao, albeit unconsciously, to guide the work of schools. Translated into curriculum, the Tao guides schools to educate children to be concerned about the weak and those in need; to help others; to work hard and complete their tasks well and promptly, even when they do not want to; to control their tempers; to work cooperatively with others and practice good manners; to respect authority and other people's rights; to help resolve conflicts; to understand honesty, responsibility, and friendship; to balance pleasures with responsibilities; and to ask themselves and decide "What is the right thing to do?"

Most educators agree that our schools should teach these attitudes both in the formal and in the hidden curriculum.

## The Formal Curriculum

The formal curriculum is usually thought of as the school's planned educational experiences—the selection and organization of knowledge and skills from the universe of possible choices. Of course, not all knowledge nor every skill contributes directly to knowing the good, but much of the subject matter of English and social studies is intimately connected to the Tao. Stories, historical figures, and events are included in the formal curriculum to illuminate the human condition. From them we can learn how to be a positive force in the lives of others, and we can also see the effects of a poorly lived life.

The men and women, real or fictitious, who we learn about in school are instruments for understanding what it is to be (or not to be) a good person. One of the strengths and attractions of good literature is its complexity. As students read, they learn about themselves and the world. For example, students come face-to-face with raw courage in the exploits of Harriet Tubman and further understand the danger of hate and racism through *The Diary of Anne Frank*. They glimpse in Edward Arlington Robinson's poem "Miniver Cheevy" the folly of storing up earthly treasures. They see in Toni Cade Bambera's "Your Blues Ain't Like Mine" the intrinsic dignity of each human being. They gain insight into the heart of a truly noble man, Atticus Finch, in *To Kill a Mockingbird*. They perceive the thorny relationships between the leader and the led by following the well-intended but failed efforts of Brutus in Shakespeare's *Julius Caesar*.

Our formal curriculum is a vehicle to teach the Tao, to help young people to come to know the good. But simply selecting the curriculum is not enough; like a vein of precious metal, the teacher and students must mine it together. To engage students in the lessons in human character and ethics contained in our history and literature without resorting to empty preaching and crude didacticism is the great skill of teaching.

## The Hidden Curriculum

In addition to the formal curriculum, students learn from a hidden curriculum—all the personal and social instruction that they acquire from their day-to-day schooling. Much of what has been written about the hidden curriculum in recent decades has stressed that these school experiences often lead to students' loss of self-esteem, unswerving obedience to silly rules, and the suppression of their individuality. While true of some students and some schools, the hidden curriculum can lead either to negative or positive education.

Many of education's most profound and positive teachings can be conveyed in the hidden curriculum. If a spirit of fairness penetrates every corner of the school, children will learn to be fair. Through the service of teachers, administrators, and older students, students learn to be of service to others. By creating an atmosphere of high standards, the hidden curriculum can teach habits of accuracy and precision. Many aspects of school life, ranging from homework assignments to sporting events, can teach self-control and self-discipline.

While unseen, the hidden curriculum must be considered with the same seriousness as the written, formal curriculum. The everyday behavior of the faculty, staff, and other students cannot fail to have an impact on a student.

One school concerned with the hidden curriculum is Roxbury Latin, a fine academic high school in Boston. In the spring of 1992, an accredited team interviewed 27 students, ranging from 7th to 12th grade, asking them the same question, "What do you think is Roxbury Latin's philosophy of education?" Every one of the students came back with the same answer: "This school is most concerned about what kind of people we are becoming." What the review team did not know was that every September, the school's headmaster, Anthony Jarvis, assembles all the new students and delivers a short message:

> We want you to excel in academics and sports and the arts while you are here. But, remember this: we care much more about your characters, what kind of people you are becoming.

End of message. End of assembly. All indications are that the message is getting through.

## Policies and Practices

A school that makes a positive impact on the character of young people helps children to know the Tao and make it part of their lives. Such a school has in place the following policies and practices.

- The school has a mission statement widely known by students, teachers, administrators, parents, and the entire school community.

- The school has a comprehensive program of service activities, starting in the early grades and requiring more significant contributions of time and energy in the later years of high school.

- School life is characterized by a high level of school spirit and healthy intergroup competition.

- The school has an external charity or cause (a local home for the elderly or educational fundraising for a Third World community) to which all members of the community contribute.

- The school has a grading and award system that does more than give lip service to character formation and ethics, but recognizes academic effort, good discipline, contributions to the life of the classroom, service to the school and the community, respect for others, and good sportsmanship.

- The school expects not only teachers but also the older students to be exemplars of high ethical standards.

- The school's classrooms and public areas display mottoes and the pictures of exemplary historical figures.

- The school has regular ceremonies and rituals that bring the community together to celebrate achievements of excellence in all realms: academic, athletic, artistic and ethical.[1]

Our students have a major task in life: to become individuals of character. Character education, then, is the central curriculum issue confronting educators. Rather than the latest fad, it is a school's oldest mission. Nothing is better for the human soul than to discuss excellence every day. The curriculum of our elementary and secondary schools should be the delivery system for this encounter with excellence.

## NOTE

1. Several of these policies and procedures are elaborated in *Reclaiming Our Schools: A Handbook for Teaching Character, Academics, and Discipline*, by E. A. Wynne and K. Ryan (Columbus, Ohio: Merrill, 1992).

## REFERENCES

Dorsett, C. (March 1993). "Multicultural Education: Why We Need It and Why We Worry About It." *Network News and Views* 12, 3:31.

Lewis, C. S. (1947). *The Abolition of Man*. New York: MacMillan.

*Author's note:* I wish to acknowledge Catherine Kinsella Stutz of Boston University for her contributions to this article.

## POSTNOTE

C. S. Lewis, the late English scholar and writer of children's stories (e.g., *the Tales of Narnia* and others), used to tell a modern fable about a country that decided to abandon teaching mathematics because the curriculum was too crowded and no one was exactly sure of what to teach. Dropping mathematics from the school curriculum pleased students and teachers, as well as parents who were no longer embarrassed each night, struggling over their children's homework. All went well for several years, until shopkeepers began to complain that their clerks couldn't "do sums" and kept billing customers incorrectly. Passengers on trains and buses were furious because they were continually getting shortchanged by ticket collectors. And worst of all, politicians became frenzied because people could not fill out their taxes properly. But still, no one thought to consider that mathematics was no longer in the curriculum. Lewis intended the fable as a parable about the failure to teach religion. Today, we might see parallels between the imaginary country's abandonment of mathematics and America's recent failure to consciously and directly teach character and ethical values.

## DISCUSSION QUESTIONS

1. What is the Tao? Should it be taught in American public schools? Why or why not?

2. Review Headmaster Anthony Jarvis's message to new students. Do you agree or disagree with it as the major purpose of schooling?

3. What are the strongest cases for and against character education in U.S. schools? And where do you stand on this issue: for or against? Why?

# 35

# What Does the Research Say About Sexuality Education?

Douglas Kirby

Sexuality education in the United States is as American as apple pie—most adults support sexuality education in schools, especially middle and high schools. This support may stem from the broad recognition that teenage pregnancy and sexually transmitted diseases (STDs), including HIV, are major problems in this country and that schools can help reduce them.

If polls consistently document that adults overwhelmingly favor sexuality education, why is there so much controversy about sexuality education in schools? Although most adults agree that schools should teach sexuality education, the same adults disagree about which topics sexuality education should cover and which it should not.

A small but vocal number of adults insist that such programs should teach only abstinence, and sometimes abstinence until marriage. Proponents of *abstinence-only* sexuality education believe that any discussion of condoms or contraceptives should be brief and emphasize only the possibilities of their failure. Among school districts with a district-wide policy on sex education, about 35 percent only allow abstinence-only sexuality education (Landry, Kaeser, & Richards, 1999).

**TERMS TO NOTE**

Sexually transmitted diseases (STDs)

HIV

Abstinence-only

Abstinence-plus

Most adults believe that schools should teach abstinence as the only completely effective method of protection against pregnancy and STDs, including HIV, but that schools should also discuss condoms and other contraceptives in a balanced and medically accurate manner. Such programs are often called *abstinence-plus* programs. In terms of policy, about two-thirds of the school districts that have districtwide policies allow abstinence-plus sexuality education, but a significant percentage has no districtwide policy at all. Therefore, it is difficult to know exactly how many schools implement abstinence-plus or HIV sexuality education (Landry, Kaeser, & Richards, 1999).

Religious and ethical beliefs sometimes divide the proponents of these two types of programs, but these proponents also have different answers to several important questions of fact.

▶ Do abstinence-only programs effectively delay the onset of intercourse or cause youth to stop having sex?

▶ By emphasizing the ineffectiveness of condoms and contraception, do abstinence-only programs discourage condom or contraceptive use and thereby increase adolescent sexual risk-taking behavior?

▶ Do abstinence-plus programs decrease sexual activity because they emphasize abstinence, or do they increase sexual activity because they describe how to have sex more safely by using condoms and contraception?

▶ Do abstinence-plus programs actually increase the use of condoms and contraception and thereby reduce sexual risk-taking behavior?

These are reasonable and important questions. Fortunately, two decades of research can answer some, although not all, of these questions.

Douglas Kirby is director of research at ETR Associates, P.O. Box 1830, Santa Cruz, CA 95061-1830; DougK@etr.org. From Douglas Kirby, "What Does the Research Say About Sexuality Education?" *Educational Leadership*, October 2000, pp. 72–76. Reprinted with permission of the author.

## The Effects of Abstinence-Only Programs

Before examining studies that have measured the impact of abstinence-only programs, I must emphasize that abstinence-only programs are very diverse and defined by just one common quality—their emphasis on abstinence as the only appropriate choice for young people. Thus, some abstinence-only programs are curriculum-based courses, whereas others are components of much broader youth-development programs. Some last for 15 to 20 sessions, and others last only 1 or 2 sessions. Some emphasize that it is immoral to have sex before marriage, and others encourage youth to postpone sex until a later age. Some are religious and begin with a prayer for God's guidance, and others are far more secular. Some rely primarily on didactic instruction, whereas others engage the participants in group activities and use role playing and other active-learning strategies to change group norms and to teach assertiveness skills. In other words, abstinence-only programs are a heterogenous group of programs.

Measuring the short-term impact of some abstinence-only programs on knowledge, attitudes, and values is relatively easy. Several studies (Olsen, Weed, Daly, & Jensen, 1992) have documented that abstinence-only programs can increase knowledge and change attitudes and values to favor abstinence. Some of these studies measure short-term effects, whereas others measure effects up to 18 months or longer (Kirby, 1997, 1999).

However, these results should be viewed somewhat cautiously for several reasons. First, response biases may have substantially inflated the findings and reduced their validity. For example, when a teacher emphasizes that it is wrong to have sex before marriage and then promptly asks students to complete a questionnaire that asks them whether premarital sex is wrong, some students may select the "correct"

answer even though their own attitudes may not have changed. Second, although attitudes and values are somewhat related to the actual initiation of sex, small changes in attitudes and values may not translate into a significant delay in the initiation of sex. Finally, some studies (Kirby, Korpi, Barth, & Cagampang, 1997) indicate that the impact of abstinence programs on attitudes and values does diminish with time.

Measuring the effect of abstinence-only programs on behavior—specifically, on delaying the onset of sexual intercourse—is much more challenging, for a variety of methodological and statistical reasons. To date, only five studies have measured the impact of abstinence-only programs on the initiation of sex. None of them has found a consistent or significant impact of such programs on delaying the onset of intercourse, and at least one study provided strong evidence that the program did not delay the onset of intercourse.

Although discouraging, these studies are misleading because all but one of these evaluations had significant methodological limitations that could have obscured the actual impact of the program. For example, two of the studies measured the impact of the program for only six weeks after the end of the program, which was too short to assess whether the abstinence lesson has any impact on sexual behavior. Another study included only 91 study participants. Only one study has successfully measured the impact of abstinence-only programs on contraceptive use, and it found that the program neither decreased nor increased condom or other contraceptive use (Kirby, Korpi, Barth, & Cagampang, 1997). Thus, at the present time, we do not know whether abstinence-only programs delay sexual activity, nor do we know which particular programs are effective.

We can't be certain about the behavioral impact of abstinence-only programs until researchers conduct rigorous studies with sufficiently large sample sizes, long-term measurements of behavior, and the random assignment of youth to intervention and control groups. Such studies are currently underway.

## The Effects of Abstinence-Plus Programs

Abstinence-plus programs also include a wide variety of programs, including sexuality education or AIDS education taught during regular school classes, on school campuses after school, or in homeless shelters and detention centers for high-risk youth. Abstinence-plus programs reflect the considerable creativity and diversity of the agencies implementing them.

In contrast to the studies of abstinence-only programs, a large number of studies during the past two decades have focused on abstinence-plus programs for sexuality and HIV education. Some of these studies have been very rigorous and provide solid evidence for the success of their respective programs.

Evaluations of almost 30 programs strongly support the conclusion that abstinence-plus programs for sexuality and HIV education do not increase adolescent sexual intercourse. They do not hasten the onset of intercourse, increase the frequency of intercourse, or increase the number of sexual partners (Kirby, forthcoming). These results are consistent with reviews of programs evaluated in other countries as well (Grunseit, Kippax, Aggleton, Baldo, & Slutkin, 1997).

In fact, several studies found that some abstinence-plus sexuality education or HIV education programs decreased one or more measures of sexual activity; they either significantly delayed the onset of intercourse, reduced the frequency of intercourse, or decreased the number of sexual partners. In addition, studies have demonstrated that some programs have increased condom or other contraceptive use and thereby reduced sexual risk-taking behavior for lengthy periods of time (Kirby, forthcoming).

Four abstinence-plus programs present particularly strong evidence that they positively changed behavior.

*Reducing the Risk* (Barth, 1996) is a 16-session curriculum for preventing pregnancy and STDs/HIV. Its central message is that youth should avoid unprotected sex—abstinence is the safest approach, but if young people have sex, they should always use condoms or other forms of contraception. The curriculum has been taught and evaluated independently in different parts of the country and found to either delay the onset of intercourse, increase the use of condoms or other contraception, or reduce the frequency of unprotected sex for 18 months (Hubbard, Geise, & Rainey, 1998; Kirby, Barth, Leland, & Fetro, 1991).

*Safer Choices* is a 20-session curriculum designed for two successive years (Coyle & Fetro, 1998; Fetro, Barth, & Coyle, 1998). It emphasizes that abstinence is the safest method for avoiding pregnancy and STDs/HIV and that the use of condoms is safer than unprotected sex. Research data from the schools in two states where the curriculum was implemented show that the program both increased condom use and reduced unprotected sex over a 31-month period (Coyle et al., forthcoming).

Finally, both *Be Proud! Be Responsible!* (Jemmott, Jemmott, & McCaffree, 1994) and *Becoming a Responsible Teen* (St. Lawrence, 1994) are HIV-prevention curriculums designed for higher-risk youth. Both emphasize abstinence and condom use, and studies show that both have succeeded in delaying the onset of intercourse, decreasing the frequency of sex, increasing condom use, or decreasing the frequency of unprotected sex over 12-month periods (Jemmott, Jemmott, & Fong, 1998; St. Lawrence, Jefferson, Alleyne, & Brasfield, 1995).

The data from several studies suggest that abstinence-plus sexuality and AIDS-education programs may be more effective with high-risk youth than with low-risk youth. This success stems in part from the program and in part from the statistical characteristics of the groups studied. When large percentages of the youth studied usually initiate sex within short periods of time or fail to use condoms consistently, the intervention group (the group in the program) is more likely to undergo statistically significant improvement over the control group.

## Common Characteristics of Effective Curriculums

Curriculums successful at changing behavior share several key characteristics that ineffective curriculums lack. Successful programs use effective pedagogical strategies and are similar to the educational programs that reduce substance abuse (Dusenbury & Falco, 1995). Effective programs share 10 key characteristics.

▶ Effective programs focus narrowly on reducing one or more sexual behaviors that lead to unintended pregnancy or STDs/HIV infection. They are not broad, comprehensive programs.

▶ Effective programs are based on theoretical approaches that have been successful in influencing other health-related risky behaviors.

▶ Effective programs give a clear message by continually reinforcing a clear stance on particular behaviors. They do not simply lay out the pros and cons of different sexual choices and implicitly let the students decide which is right for them; rather, most of the curriculum activities are directed at convincing the students that abstaining from sex or using condoms or other forms of contraception is the right choice.

▶ Effective programs provide basic, accurate information about the risks of unprotected intercourse and methods for avoiding unprotected intercourse. Although increasing knowledge is not the primary goal of these programs, they provide basic information that students need to assess risks and to avoid unprotected sex.

▶ Effective programs include activities that address social pressures associated with sexual behavior. For example, several curriculums discuss situations that might lead to sex and "lines" that are typically used to get someone to have sex.

▶ Effective programs provide modeling and the practice of communication, negotiation, and refusal skills. Some curriculums teach different ways to say no to sex or unprotected sex and how to insist on the use of condoms.

▶ Effective programs involve the participants and have them personalize the information. Instructors reach students through active learning, not through didactic instruction.

▶ Effective programs incorporate behavioral goals, teaching methods, and materials that are appropriate to the age, sexual experience, and culture of the students. For example, programs for younger youth, few of whom have engaged in intercourse, focus on delaying the onset of intercourse. Programs designed for high school students, some of whom have engaged in intercourse, emphasize that students should avoid unprotected intercourse, either by not having sex or by using contraception if they do have sex.

▶ Effective programs last a sufficient length of time to complete important activities adequately. Considerable time and multiple activities are necessary. Thus, short programs that last only a couple of hours do not appear to be effective, whereas longer programs that implement multiple activities have a greater effect.

▶ Effective programs select teachers or peers who believe in the program they are implementing and then provide training for those individuals. The training ranges from approximately six hours to three days.

## Choose Abstinence-Plus

Given both the great diversity of abstinence-only programs and the many limitations of previous studies, there is currently too little evidence to determine whether different types of abstinence-only programs actually delay the onset of intercourse or have other positive effects on sexual and contraceptive behavior.

Until such studies are completed, the educators and policymakers who want to implement programs with strong evidence for delaying sex or reducing unprotected sex should implement effective abstinence-plus programs that emphasize both abstinence and condoms or other contraceptives. Fortunately, a large number of studies demonstrate that abstinence-plus programs do not increase sexual activity as some people fear, but, to the contrary, can delay the onset of sex, reduce its frequency, reduce the number of sexual partners, increase condom use, and increase contraceptive use—thereby reducing sexual behavior that places youth at risk of pregnancy and STDs.

To reduce the tragic rates of unintended pregnancy and STDs, including HIV, U.S. schools should implement these effective programs more widely and with fidelity.

## REFERENCES

Barth, R. P. (1996). *Reducing the risk: Building the skills to prevent pregnancy* (3rd ed.). Santa Cruz, CA: Education Training Research (ETR) Associates.

Coyle, K. K., Basen-Engquist, K. M., Kirby, D., Parcel, G. S., Bauspach, S. W., Collins, J. L., Baumler, E. R., Carvagal, S., & Harrist, S. B. (forthcoming). Safer choices: Long-term impact of a multicomponent school-based HIV, STD, and pregnancy prevention program. *Public Health Reports.*

Coyle, K. K., & Fetro, J. V. (1998). *Safer choices: Preventing HIV, other STDs, and pregnancy: Level 2.* Santa Cruz, CA: ETR Associates.

Dusenbury, L., & Falco, M. (1995). Eleven components of effective drug abuse prevention curricula. *Journal of School Health, 65*(10), 420–425.

Fetro, J. V., Barth, R. B., & Coyle, K. K. (1998). *Safer choices: Preventing HIV, other STDs, and pregnancy: Level 1.* Santa Cruz, CA: ETR Associates.

Grunseit, A., Kippax, S., Aggleton, P., Baldo, M., & Slutkin, G. (1997, October). Sexuality education and young people's sexual behavior: A review of studies. *Journal of Adolescent Research, 12*(4), 421–453.

Hubbard, B. M., Giese, M. L., & Rainey, J. (1998). A replication of *Reducing the Risk,* a theory-based sexuality curriculum for adolescents. *Journal of School Health, 68*(6), 243–247.

Jemmott, J. B., Jemmott, L. S., & Fong, G. T. (1998, May). Abstinence and safer sex: A randomized trial of HIV sexual risk-reduction interventions for young African-American adolescents. *Journal of the American Medical Association, 279*(19), 1529–1536.

Jemmott, L. S., Jemmott, J. B., III, & McCaffree, K. A. (1994). *Be proud! Be responsible!* New York: Select Media.

Kirby, D. (2001). *Emerging answers: Research findings on programs to reduce teen pregnancy.* Washington, DC: National Campaign to Prevent Teen Pregnancy.

Kirby, D. (1999). The impact of abstinence-only programs. *PPFY (Pregnancy Prevention for Youth) Network, 2*(2), 2–3.

Kirby, D. (1997). *No easy answers: Research findings on programs to reduce teen pregnancy.* Washington, DC: National Campaign to Prevent Teen Pregnancy.

Kirby, D., Barth, R., Leland, N., & Fetro, J. (1991). Reducing the risk: A new curriculum to prevent sexual risk-taking. *Family Planning Perspectives, 23*(6), 253–263.

Kirby, D., Korpi, M., Barth, R. P., & Cagampang, H. H. (1997, May/June). The impact of postponing the sexual involvement curriculum among youths in California. *Family Planning Perspectives, 29*(3), 100–108.

Landry, D. J., Kaeser, L., & Richards, C. L. (1999). Abstinence promotion and the provision of information about contraception in public school district sexuality education policies. *Family Planning Perspectives, 31*(6), 280–286.

Olsen, J., Weed, S., Daly, D., & Jensen, L. (1992). The effects of abstinence sex education programs on virgin versus nonvirgin students. *Journal of Research and Development in Education, 25*(2), 69–75.

St. Lawrence, J. S. (1994). *Becoming a responsible teen: An HIV risk reduction intervention for African-American adolescents.* Jackson, MS: Jackson State University.

St. Lawrence, J. S., Jefferson, K. W., Alleyne, E., & Brasfield, T. L. (1995). Comparison of education versus behavioral skills training interventions in lowering sexual HIV risk behavior of substance dependent adolescents. *Journal of Consulting and Clinical Psychology, 63*(2), 221–237.

# POSTNOTE

In education, hot button issues come and go, but sexuality education just keeps rolling on. Part of the problem lies In the uncertainty many people share that the school, rather than parents or the church or the medical profession, should be engaging in sexuality education. By and large, though, most states and school boards assign responsibility for sexuality education to the schools. It is a part of the curriculum of nearly all school districts. The rub, however, is what "it" is. What is the content of what we tell young people about the birds and the bees? The wrong answer can split a school community wide open.

The author of this article, after having reviewed the current state of the research, believes that curricula based on an abstinence-plus position would be the most sensible approach available today for sexuality education. This raises two questions, though. The first has to do with the state of our research. While abstinence-plus programs are well developed, have been available for some time, and are supported by much research and development funding, abstinence-only programs are new, with little research and development support. In fairness and, perhaps, wisdom, we ought to call for more and better research on this important topic. Currently, we are spending vast amounts of social resources on unwanted pregnancies, single parent [or no visible parent] children, and sexually-related diseases. The second question has to do with the "plus" in abstinence-plus. Many believe that abstinence-plus sends adolescents a confused message. "Don't have sex, but if you are going to have sex, use a condom," is not unlike, "You shouldn't smoke, but if you do, try Marlboros!" or, "Don't eat sugar, but if you do, try peppermint chip ice cream." There are, of course, many studies suggesting the ineffectiveness of condom use, but the most convincing comes from a high school teacher who reports, "How can they expect my students to properly use a condom when most of them can't remember to bring a pencil with them to school?"

# DISCUSSION QUESTIONS

1. How would you evaluate the overall success of the sexuality education you received in school? Was it effective? Why or why not?

2. Do you believe some parents have a legitimate objection to abstinence-plus sexuality programs? Why or why not?

3. What, in your view, should be the limits to the content [if any] of a high school sexuality education program?

# Instruction

## PART FIVE

What should we teach? is the fundamental question. But next in importance is: How do we teach it? Instructional questions range from the very nature of students as learners to how to organize a third-grade classroom.

In this section, we present a palette of new and old ideas about how to organize classrooms and schools to meet the needs of new students and a new society. A number of the most high-profile topics in education—such as cooperative learning, assessment, constructivism, and differentiated instruction are presented. It is important to realize, however, as you read about an instructional methodology or set of procedures, that each represents a view of what the teaching-learning process is and what students are like. So, as you read these articles, we urge you to probe for their foundational ideas.

# 36

# *Closing the Achievement Gap*

## Kati Haycock

There's been a lot of talk lately about the achievement gap that separates low-income and minority youngsters from other young Americans. For more than a generation, we focused on improving the education of poor and minority students. Not surprisingly, we made real gains. Between 1970 and 1988, the achievement gap between African American and white students was cut in half, and the gap separating Latinos and whites declined by one-third. That progress came to a halt around 1988, however, and since that time, the gaps have widened.

Although everybody wanted to take credit for narrowing the gap, nobody wanted to take responsibility for widening it. So, for a while, there was mostly silence.

But that is changing. Good. Because if we don't get the numbers out on the table and talk about them, we're never going to close the gap once and for all. I worry, though, about how many people head into discussions without accurate data. And I worry even more about how many education leaders have antiquated—and downright wrong—notions about the whys beneath the achievement gap.

I want to respond to both these worries by putting some crucial data on the table and by sharing what both research and experience teach us about how schools can close the gaps between groups of students. Most of the data are from

**TERMS TO NOTE**
Achievement gap
National Assessment of Education Progress (NAEP)

Kati Haycock is director, The Education Trust, 1725 K St. NW, Ste. 200, Washington, DC 20006. From Kati Haycock, "Closing the Achievement Gap," *Educational Leadership,* March 2001. Reprinted with permission of the Association for Supervision and Curriculum Development. Copyright © 2001 by ASCD. All rights reserved.

standard national sources, including the National Center for Education Statistics (NCES) and the National Assessment of Education Progress (NAEP), as well as from states and local school districts that have been unusually successful at educating poor and minority students.[1]

## *Understanding Achievement Patterns*

The performance of African American and Latino youngsters improved dramatically during the 1970s and 1980s. The 1990s, however, were another matter. In some subjects and at some grade levels, the gaps started growing; in others, they were stagnant (National Center for Education Statistics, 2001).

▶ Reading achievement among 17-year-old African Americans and Latinos climbed substantially through the 1970s and 1980s, but gaps separating them from other students widened somewhat during the 1990s.

▶ The patterns in mathematics achievement look similar for 13-year-olds, with the African American and white gap reaching its narrowest in 1990 and the Latino and white gap narrowing until 1992, and the gaps widening thereafter.

In 1999, by the end of high school

▶ Only 1 in 50 Latinos and 1 in 100 African American 17-year-olds can read and gain information from specialized text—such as the science section in the newspaper (compared to about 1 in 12 whites), and

▶ Fewer than one-quarter of Latinos and one-fifth of African Americans can read the complicated but less specialized text that more than half of white students can read.

The same patterns hold in math.

▶ About 1 in 30 Latinos and 1 in 100 African Americans can comfortably do multistep problem solving and elementary algebra, compared to about 1 in 10 white students.

▶ Only 3 in 10 African American and 4 in 10 Latino 17-year-olds have mastered the usage and computation of fractions, commonly used percents, and averages, compared to 7 in 10 white students.

By the end of high school, in fact, African American and Latino students have skills in both reading and mathematics that are the same as those of white students in 8th grade. Significant differences also persist in the rates at which different groups of students complete high school and in their postsecondary education experiences.

▶ In the 18- to 24-year-old group, about 90 percent of whites and 94 percent of Asians have either completed high school or earned a GED. Among African Americans, the rate drops to 81 percent; among Latinos, 63 percent.

▶ Approximately 76 percent of white graduates and 86 percent of Asian graduates go directly to college, compared to 71 percent of African American and 71 percent of Latino graduates.

▶ Young African Americans are only about half as likely as white students to earn a bachelor's degree by age 29; young Latinos are only one-third as likely as whites to earn a college degree (see Table 1).

## What's Going On?

Over the past five years, staff members at the Education Trust have shared these and related data on the achievement gap with hundreds of audiences all over the United States. During that time, we've learned a lot about what people think is going on.

When we speak with adults, no matter where we are in the country, they make the same comments. "They're too poor." "Their parents don't care." "They come to school without an adequate breakfast." "They don't have enough books in the home." "Indeed, there aren't enough parents in the home." Their reasons, in other words, are always about the children and their families.

Young people, however, have different answers. They talk about teachers who often do not know the subjects that they are teaching. They talk about counselors who consistently underestimate their potential and place them in lower-level courses. They talk about principals who dismiss their concerns. And they talk about a curriculum and a set of expectations that feel so miserably low-level that they literally bore the students right out the school door.

| AGES 15 TO 29 | AFRICAN AMERICANS | ASIANS | LATINOS | WHITES |
|---|---|---|---|---|
| Graduate from high school | 88 | 90 | 63 | 88 |
| Complete at least some college | 50 | 74 | 33 | 59 |
| Obtain at least a bachelor's degree | 16 | 51 | 10 | 28 |

**TABLE 1**
Highest Educational Attainment for Every 100 Kindergartners
*Source:* U.S. Census Bureau. (1998). Educational Attainment Detailed Tables, October CPS

When we ask, "What about the things that the adults are always talking about—neighborhood violence, single-parent homes, and so on?"—the young people's responses are fascinating. "Sure, those things matter," they say. "But what hurts us more is that you teach us less."

The truth is that the data bear out what the young people are saying. It's not that issues like poverty and parental education don't matter. Clearly they do. But we take the students who have less to begin with and then systematically give them less in school. In fact, we give these students less of everything that we believe makes a difference. We do this in hundreds of different ways.

Let me be clear. It would help if changes were made outside of schools, too: if parents spent more time with their children, if poverty didn't crush so many spirits, and if the broader culture didn't bombard young people with so many destructive messages. But because both research and experience show that what schools do matters greatly, I'll concentrate on what works in education.

### Lesson 1: Standards Are Key

Historically, we have not agreed on what U.S. students should learn at each grade level—or on what kind of work is good enough. These decisions have been left to individual schools and teachers. The result is a system that, by and large, doesn't ask much of most of its students. And we don't have to go far to find that out: Ask the nearest teenager. In survey after survey, young people tell us that they are not challenged in school.

The situation is worse in high-poverty and high-minority schools. For the past six years, our staff at the Education Trust has worked with teachers who are trying to improve the achievement levels of their students. But while we've been observing these high-poverty classrooms, we've also looked carefully at what happens there—what kinds of assignments teachers give, for example—compared to what happens in other classrooms.

We have come away stunned. Stunned, first, by how little is expected of students in high-poverty schools—how few assignments they get in a given school week or month. Stunned, second, by the low level of the few assignments that they do get. In high-poverty urban middle schools, for example, we see a lot of coloring assignments, rather than writing or mathematics assignments. Even at the high school level, we found coloring assignments. "Read *To Kill a Mockingbird*," says the 11th grade English teacher, "and when you're finished, color a poster about it." Indeed, national data make it clear that we expect so little of students in high-poverty schools that we give them *A*s for work that would earn a *C* or *D* anywhere else.

Clear and public standards for what students should learn at benchmark grade levels are a crucial part of solving the problem. They are a guide—for teachers, administrators, parents, and students themselves—to what knowledge and skills students must master.

Kentucky was the first state to embrace standards-based reform. Ten years ago, the Kentucky legislature put out an ambitious set of learning goals and had the audacity to declare that all of its children—even the poorest—would meet those goals. Leaders in Kentucky are the first to acknowledge that they are not there yet. But their progress is clear and compelling. And poor children are, in fact, learning in all subjects. For example, in reading, 7 of the 20 top-performing elementary schools are high-poverty; in math, 8 of the top 20 are high-poverty; in writing, 13 of the top 20 are high-poverty.

### Lesson 2: All Students Must Have a Challenging Curriculum

Standards won't make much of a difference, though, if they are not accompanied by a rigorous curriculum that is aligned with those standards. Yet in too many schools, some students are taught a high-level curriculum, whereas other students continue to be taught a low-level curriculum that is aligned with jobs that no longer exist.

Current patterns are clearest in high schools, where students who take more-rigorous coursework learn more and perform better on tests. Indeed, the more-rigorous courses they take, the better they do.

▶ In mathematics, students who complete the full college preparatory sequence perform much higher on the National Assessment of Educational Progress (NAEP) than those who complete only one or two courses.

▶ The reverse is true of watered-down, traditional "vocational" courses. The more vocational education courses students take, the lower their performance on the NAEP.

▶ Although some of these differences are clearly attributable to the fact that higher-scoring students are often assigned to tougher classes, careful research shows the positive impact of more-rigorous coursework even on formerly low-achieving students.

Since 1983, we've made progress in increasing the number of students who take a rigorous, college-preparatory curriculum. But the pace is not fast enough.

▶ Almost three-quarters of high school graduates go on to higher education, but only about half of them complete even a mid-level college-preparatory curriculum (four years of English and three years each of math, science, and social studies). If we also include two years of a foreign language and a semester of computer science, the numbers drop to about 12 percent. The numbers are worse for African Americans, Latinos, and low-income students.

These patterns are disturbing because the quality and intensity of high school coursework are the most important determinants of success in college—more important than class rank or scores on college admissions tests (Adelman, 1998). Curriculum rigor is also important for work-bound students (Bottoms, 1998).

A few years ago, the chancellor of the New York City schools required all 9th graders to take the Regents math and science exams. Though many people were worried that failure rates would be astronomical, in one year the number of Latinos in New York City who passed the Regents science exam tripled, and the number of African Americans who passed doubled. Other groups also had gains in science and mathematics. Did they *all* pass? No, they didn't. But as a principal friend of mine used to say, "At least they failed something worthwhile." And remember, these youngsters previously would never even have been given a chance to learn higher-order content.

### Lesson 3: Students Need Extra Help

Ample evidence shows that almost all students can achieve at high levels if they are taught at high levels. But equally clear is that some students require more time and more instruction. It won't do, in other words, just to throw students into a high-level course if they can't even read the textbook.

One of the most frequent questions we are asked by stressed-out middle and high school teachers is "How am I supposed to get my students ready to pass the (fill-in-the-blank) grade test when they enter with 3rd grade reading skills and I have only my 35-minute period each day?"

The answer, of course, is "You can't." Especially when students are behind in foundational skills like reading and mathematics, we need to double or even triple the amount and quality of instruction that they get.

Around the United States, states and communities are wrestling with how best to provide those extras. Kentucky gives high-poverty schools extra funds every year to extend instruction in whatever way works best for their community: before school, after school, weekends, or summers. Maryland provides a wide range of assistance to students who are not on track to pass its new high school graduation test. And San Diego created more time, mostly within the regular school day, by doubling—even tripling—the amount of instructional time devoted to literacy and mathematics for low-performing students and by training *all* of its teachers.

## Lesson 4: Teachers Matter a Lot

If students are going to be held to high standards, they need teachers who know the subjects and know how to teach the subjects. Yet large numbers of students, especially those who are poor or are members of minority groups, are taught by teachers who do not have strong backgrounds in the subjects they teach.

▶ In every subject area, students in high-poverty schools are more likely than other students to be taught by teachers without even a minor in the subjects they teach (see Figure 1).

▶ The differences are often greater in predominantly minority high schools. In math and science, for example, only about half the teachers in schools with 90 percent or greater minority enrollments meet even their states' minimum requirements to teach those subjects—far fewer than in predominantly white schools.

▶ The patterns are similar regardless of the measure of teacher qualifications—experience, certification, academic preparation, or performance on licensure tests. We take the students who

most depend on their teachers for subject-matter learning and assign them teachers with the weakest academic foundations.

A decade ago, we might have said that we didn't know how much this mattered. We believed that what students learned was largely a factor of their family income or parental education, not of what schools did. But recent research has turned these assumptions upside down. What schools do matters enormously. And what matters most is good teaching.

▶ Results from a recent Boston study of the effects teachers have on learning are fairly typical (Boston Public Schools, 1998). In just one academic year, the top third of teachers produced as much as six times the learning growth as the bottom third of teachers. In fact, 10th graders taught by the least effective teachers made nearly no gains in reading and even lost ground in math.

▶ Groundbreaking research in Tennessee and Texas shows that these effects are cumulative and hold up regardless of race, class, or prior achievement levels. Some of the classrooms showing the greatest gains are filled with low-income students, some with well-to-do students. And the same is true with the small-gain classrooms. It's not the kids after all: Something very different is going on with the teaching (Sanders & Rivers, 1996).

Findings like these make us wonder what would happen if, instead of getting far fewer than their fair share of good teachers, underachieving students actually got more. In a study of Texas school districts, Harvard economist Ronald Ferguson (1998) found a handful of districts that reversed the normal pattern: Districts with initially high-performing (presumably relatively affluent) 1st graders hired from the bottom of the teacher pool, and districts with initially low-performing (presumably low-income) 1st graders hired from the upper tiers of the teacher pool. By the time their students reached high school, these districts swapped places in student achievement.

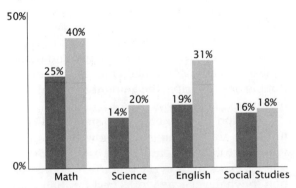

**FIGURE 1**

Percentage of Underqualified* Teachers in High School Classrooms

*Source:* National Commission on Teaching and America's Future, (1996). *What matters most: Teaching for America's future.* New York: Author, p. 16.

El Paso, Texas, is a community that has taken such research seriously. Eight years ago, despite the extraordinarily high poverty of their city, local education leaders set some very high standards for what their students should know and be able to do. Unlike other communities, though, they didn't stop there. At the University of Texas, El Paso, the faculty revamped how it prepared teachers. New elementary teachers, for example, take more than twice as much math and science as their predecessors. More to the point, though, the teachers of these courses are math and science professors who themselves participated in the standard-setting process and who know, at a much deeper level, what kinds of mathematical understanding the teachers need.

The community also organized a structure—the El Paso Collaborative—to provide support to existing teachers and to help them teach to the new standards. The collaborative sponsored intensive summer workshops, monthly meetings for teachers within content areas, and work sessions in schools to analyze student assignments against the standards. The three school districts also released 60 teachers to coach their peers.

The results are clear: no more low performing schools and increased achievement for *all groups of students,* with bigger increases among the groups that have historically been behind.

## An Academic Core

El Paso and the other successful communities and states have a lot to teach us about how to raise overall achievement and close gaps. Each community, of course, does things a little bit differently. What we learn is the value of a relentless focus on the academic core. Clear and high standards. Assessments aligned with those standards. Accountability systems that demand results for all kinds of students. Intensive efforts to assist teachers in improving their practice. And extra instruction for students who need it.

### NOTE

1. For state and national data on student achievement, visit the Education Trust Web site at **www.edtrust.org** and click the data icon.

### REFERENCES

Adelman, C. (1998). *Answers in the toolbox.* Washington, DC: U.S. Department of Education.

Boston Public Schools. (1998, March 9). High school restructuring. Boston: Author.

Bottoms, G. (1998). *High schools that work.* Atlanta, GA: Southern Regional Education Board.

Ferguson, R. (1998). Can schools narrow the black-white test score gap? In C. Jencks & M. Phillips (Eds.), *The black-white test score gap* (pp. 318–374). Washington, DC: The Brookings Institute.

National Center for Education Statistics. (2001). *NAEP summary data tables* [Online]. Washington, DC: U.S. Department of Education. Available: **http://nces.ed.gov/nationsreportcard**

Sanders, W., & Rivers, J. (1996). *Cumulative and residual effects of teachers on future student academic achievement.* Knoxville, TN: University of Tennessee Value-Added Research and Assessment Center.

## POSTNOTE

As Kati Haycock points out in her article, many people see the academic achievement problem of students from urban poverty schools as being intractable. Poverty is too great . . . parents don't care . . . drugs and violence take a toll. What Haycock shows us is that with high standards, a challenging curriculum, and good teachers, children from poverty schools can learn, and at surprisingly high levels. As Jaime Escalante demonstrated at Garfield High School in East Los Angeles, poor Latino youths could learn calculus well enough to score at high levels on

AP exams. He set high standards and made serious demands on students. His success is celebrated in the Academy Award–nominated movie, *Stand and Deliver*. Marva Collins, in Chicago, also demonstrated that poor African-American children could learn a classical curriculum at high levels.

Unfortunately, there are too few stories of this kind of successful teaching in urban poverty schools. What they show us, however, is that success with poor children is possible with high standards, a challenging curriculum, and good teachers.

## Discussion Questions

1. Was there anything in this article that surprised you? If so, what?

2. What does the author believe can be done to ensure that children in poverty have schools with highly-qualified teachers?

3. In addition to the author's suggestions, what do you believe can be done to improve the quality of schools serving the urban poor?

## 37

# Engaging Students: What I Learned Along the Way

Anne Wescott Dodd

When I was a first-year teacher, I was concerned with survival. My attempts to control students led to many power struggles from which both the students and I emerged discouraged or defeated. These feelings were not conducive to teaching or learning.

I wish someone had told me then that knowing my students was as important as knowing my subject. I didn't realize until much later that to motivate and engage students, teachers must create a classroom environment in which every student comes to believe, "I count, I care, and I can."

The best advice I could give to beginning teachers now is the secret of the fox in Antoine de Saint-Exupéry's *The Little Prince* (1943): "What is essential is invisible to the eye." What teachers need most to know about students is hidden; unless they develop a trusting relationship with their students, teachers will not have access to the knowledge they need either to solve classroom problems or to motivate students.

## I Wish I Had Known . . .

As a novice teacher, I didn't realize that a seemingly logical response to tardiness—detention—did not take into account students' reasons for being late, some of which were valid. If I had allowed students to explain why they were late before telling them to stay after school, I might

A former secondary school teacher and principal, Anne Westcott Dodd is a senior visiting lecturer at Bates College, Lewiston, Maine. From Anne Wescott Dodd, "Engaging Students: What I Learned Along the Way." *Educational Leadership*, September 1995, pp. 65–67. Reprinted with permission of the Association for Supervision and Curriculum Development. Copyright © 1995 by ASCD. All rights reserved.

have prevented hurt feelings and hostility. A 6th grader who hides from an 8th grade bully in the bathroom until the coast is clear shouldn't be treated the same as someone who chats too long with a friend in the hall.

I wish I had found out sooner that simply asking students to tell me their side of the story could make such a positive difference in their attitudes. When I tried to understand situations from their points of view, students were willing to consider them from my vantage point. These conversations opened the way for us to jointly resolve problems and did a great deal to build trust.

But, most of all, I wish someone had told me that understanding students' perspectives was the best way to foster engagement and learning. Like other novice teachers, I wasted a great deal of time searching for recipes to make learning more fun. Only much later did I find out that the most effective veteran teachers reflect on their classroom experience (Dodd 1994). Instead of thinking in terms of making learning *fun* (extrinsic motivation), they look for ways to make assignments and activities *engaging* (intrinsic motivation). Although they may express these ideas differently, effective teachers know that to become engaged, students must have some feelings of *ownership*—of the class or the task—and *personal power*—a belief that what they do will make a difference.

**TERMS TO NOTE**

Extrinsic motivation

Intrinsic motivation

## From the Student's Perspective

Because beginning teachers often focus on what they will do or require students to do, they often overlook some important principles about learning.

First, learning is personal and idiosyncratic. Thus, it helps to view students as individuals (Marina, Hector, and Scott) rather than as groups (Period 1 Class, Sophomore English). Consider that even when there is only *one* right answer, there are *many* ways students can misunderstand. Thus, teachers need to find out how students individually make sense of any lesson or explanation.

Second, every student behavior—from the most outrageous classroom outburst to the more common failure to do homework—is a way of trying to communicate something the student cannot express any other way or doesn't consciously understand. Punishing the behavior without learning its possible cause does nothing to solve a problem and, in fact, may intensify it. Because the student may interpret detention or a zero in the gradebook as additional evidence that the teacher is uncaring, he or she may become less inclined to do future assignments.

Third, teachers should never assume, because too often they can be wrong. Low grades on tests do not necessarily mean that students haven't studied. Some students may have been confused when the material was covered in class. Incomplete homework isn't always a sign that students don't care. A student may be too busy helping care for younger siblings to finish assignments. The student who sleeps in class or responds angrily to a teacher's question may be exhausted, ill, or unable to cope with personal difficulties.

By inviting students to share their feelings and perceptions, teachers can establish positive relationships with them and thus minimize classroom problems. But even more important, they will discover how to modify their teaching methods and personalize assignments in ways that engage students in learning.

## Getting Students to Open Up

There are many ways that teachers can get to know their students. Here are a few useful strategies.

▶ *On the first day of class, give students a questionnaire to complete, or invite them to write you a letter about themselves.* The sooner you learn something about your students, the better equipped you will be to build personal relationships and address their concerns. By knowing which students consider themselves math phobics, poor writers, or reluctant readers, you can find ways to make sure they have a chance to feel good about a small success right away.

▶ *Ask students who have not done the homework or who have come late to class to write a note explaining why.* Establish this requirement on the first day of class, but don't present it as a punishment. Students should see these notes as an opportunity to communicate privately with the teacher. As trust is established, students will feel freer about sharing personal concerns that affect their classroom performance. Even if you can do nothing to solve a problem a student has at home, you may be able to suggest better ways to deal with it.

▶ *Ask students to write learning logs from time to time. Logs are especially useful at the end of a class in which new material has been introduced.* For example, "Briefly summarize what you learned today, and note any questions you have." Don't grade the logs; just read them quickly to note common problems to address in the next class, and list names of students who may need extra help. Taking the time to write a short comment or just draw a smiley face on each student's log before returning them also shows students that you care about them as people and want them to learn.

The same kind of assignment can be added to a homework paper or as the last question on a test: "What did you find confusing about this assignment?" or "How do you feel you did on this test? What would have helped you do even better?"

▶ *Invite students to help you solve classroom problems, such as a lack of classroom participation or students' constantly interrupting one another.* Even if you wish to discuss the issue with the students, having them write their ideas down first will make the discussion more productive. Although students may not suggest any workable solutions to the problem, their comments can often lead to a strategy for solving the problem. Perhaps even more important, students will feel empowered.

Writing works because every student gets to share what he or she thinks, misunderstands, or needs to know. Teachers who depend on students to say aloud what they don't understand may be fooled into thinking that everything is okay when there are no questions. Many students, however, are reluctant to speak up in front of their peers for fear of looking foolish. Unfortunately, teachers don't have time for individual conversations with each student, but writing can be an invaluable substitute.

## How to Personalize Assignments

All of the information teachers gather from students will be of little use if students do not have any opportunity to personalize their learning. While the idea of having students doing a variety of things at the same time may appear chaotic, there are some easy ways to try out this approach to see how it works.

▶ Give students some choice of topics for research, books for reading, and planning methods for projects or papers (outlining, webbing, or focused free writing).

▶ Let students prepare a lesson and teach their classmates. (If teachers want students to be exposed to several aspects of the Civil War or three different novels, small groups of students learn about one aspect of the war or one of the novels in depth and the others in less detail. This approach is one way of solving the depth versus coverage dilemma all teachers wrestle with.)

▶ Encourage students who understand a concept to help those who don't understand. This is a productive way of channeling students' desire to be social.

▶ Allow students to choose how to demonstrate their understanding. (One student might draw the solution to a math problem or the plot in a novel; another might write about it; someone else might videotape a real-life connection for it.)

▶ Give students permission occasionally to work on homework or routine assignments together. They can learn from one another, and a test will show what each has learned.

## Reflection Is the Key

Trying out a practice offers fertile ground for reflection even if the trial fails. As teachers look for new ways to engage students in learning, they are likely to find that the search itself will re-energize their teaching.

Recipes are useful for beginners who haven't yet had time to analyze how and why students engage in learning, but reflection is the key to understanding why some recipes work better than others. That understanding depends on knowing more about students' perceptions. As teachers learn more about how students think and feel, they will be able to create classes where students have fun *because* they are engaged in learning in diverse, purposeful, and meaningful ways.

## REFERENCES

de Saint-Exupéry, A. (1943). *The Little Prince*. New York: Harcourt Brace.

Dodd, A. W. (1994). "Learning to Read the Classroom: The Stages Leading to Teacher Self-Actualization." *Northwords* 4: 13–26.

## POSTNOTE

This article is based on a fundamental principle of good teaching: engaging the student in his or her own learning. Along with the principle, the author offers several practical suggestions and thus adds to our large literature on the subject of good teaching—a literature that has been evolving for centuries. But why, if the principle is so fundamental, do so few teachers follow it?

One possible explanation is that beginning teachers quite naturally lack confidence. They are on the defensive and, as a result, are "self-focused": "Will I survive?" "Will they accept me as a teacher, or are they seeing through this teacher-act I am performing?" "Will they like me?" "Can they tell how little I really know about what I'm doing?" The great majority of teachers pass out of this phase, but some survive by imposing their will, their lesson plans, their expectations (or some downsized version of their original expectations) on the class. And that habit of mind, focusing on *their* plans, takes over and becomes for them "teaching." To put it another way, "engaging" students involves risks, and many new teachers are not ready to take risks.

## DISCUSSION QUESTIONS

1. Can you recall teachers who engaged you in your own learning? How did they do it?

2. The article's author, Anne Wescott Dodd, offers four suggestions for "getting students to open up." What are they, and are there any suggestions you can add?

3. What are some of the potential problems and risks in this approach?

# Students Need Challenge, Not Easy Success

## Margaret M. Clifford

**38**

Hundreds of thousands of apathetic students abandon their schools each year to begin lives of unemployment, poverty, crime, and psychological distress. According to Hahn (1987), "Dropout rates ranging from 40 to 60 percent in Boston, Chicago, Los Angeles, Detroit, and other major cities point to a situation of crisis proportions." The term *dropout* may not be adequate to convey the disastrous consequences of the abandonment of school by children and adolescents; *educational suicide* may be a far more appropriate label.

School abandonment is not confined to a small percentage of minority students, or low ability children, or mentally lazy kids. It is a systemic failure affecting the most gifted and knowledgeable as well as the disadvantaged, and it is threatening the social, economic, intellectual, industrial, cultural, moral, and psychological well-being of our country. Equally disturbing are students who sever themselves from the flow of knowledge while they occupy desks, like mummies.

Student apathy, indifference, and underachievement are typical precursors of school abandonment. But what causes these symptoms? Is there a remedy? What will it take to stop the waste of our intellectual and creative resources?

To address these questions, we must acknowledge that educational suicide is primarily

a motivational problem—not a physical, intellectual, financial, technological, cultural, or staffing problem. Thus, we must turn to motivational theories and research as a foundation for examining this problem and for identifying solutions.

Curiously enough, modern theoretical principles of motivation do not support certain widespread practices in education. I will discuss four such discrepancies and offer suggestions for resolving them.

## Moderate Success Probability Is Essential to Motivation

The maxim, "Nothing succeeds like success," has driven educational practice for several decades. Absolute success for students has become the means *and* the end of education: It has been given higher priority than learning, and it has obstructed learning.

A major principle of current motivation theory is that tasks associated with a moderate probability of success (50 percent) provide maximum satisfaction (Atkinson 1964). Moderate probability of success is also an essential ingredient of intrinsic motivation (Lepper and Greene 1978, Csikszentmihalyi 1975, 1978). We attribute the success we experience on easy tasks to task ease; we attribute the success we experience on extremely difficult tasks to luck. Neither type of success does much to enhance self-image. It is only success at moderately difficult or truly challenging tasks that we explain in terms of personal effort, well-chosen strategies, and ability; and these explanations give rise to feelings of pride, competence, determination, satisfaction, persistence, and personal

**TERM TO NOTE**
Intrinsic motivation

At the time this article was written, Margaret M. Clifford was professor emeritus of educational psychology, College of Education, University of Iowa, Iowa City. "Students Need Challenge, Not Easy Success" by Margaret M. Clifford, *Educational Leadership*, 48, 1:32–36. Reprinted with permission of the Association for Supervision and Curriculum Development and the author. Copyright © 1990 by ASCD. All rights reserved.

221

control. Even very young children show a preference for tasks that are just a bit beyond their ability (Danner and Lonky 1981).

Consistent with these motivational findings, learning theorists have repeatedly demonstrated that moderately difficult tasks are a prerequisite for maximizing intellectual development (Fischer 1980). But despite the fact that moderate challenge (implying considerable error-making) is essential for maximizing learning and optimizing motivation, many educators attempt to create error-proof learning environments. They set minimum criteria and standards in hopes of ensuring success for all students. They often reduce task difficulty, overlook errors, de-emphasize failed attempts, ignore faulty performances, display "perfect papers," minimize testing, and reward error-free performance.

It is time for educators to replace easy success with challenge. We must encourage students to reach beyond their intellectual grasp and allow them the privilege of learning from mistakes. There must be a tolerance for error-making in every classroom, and gradual success rather than continual success must become the yardstick by which learning is judged. Such transformations in educational practices will not guarantee the elimination of educational suicide, but they are sure to be one giant step in that direction.

### External Constraints Erode Motivation and Performance

Intrinsic motivation and performance deteriorate when external constraints such as surveillance, evaluation by others, deadlines, threats, bribes, and rewards are accentuated. Yes, even rewards are a form of constraint! The reward giver is the General who dictates rules and issues orders; rewards are used to keep the troops in line.

Means-end contingencies, as exemplified in the statement, "If you complete your homework,

you may watch TV" (with homework being the means and TV the end), are another form of external constraint. Such contingencies decrease interest in the first task (homework, the means) and increase interest in the second task (TV, the end) (Boggiano and Main 1986).

Externally imposed constraints, including material rewards, decrease task interest, reduce creativity, hinder performance, and encourage passivity on the part of students—even preschoolers (Lepper and Hodell 1989)! Imposed constraints also prompt individuals to use the "minimax strategy"—to exert the minimum amount of effort needed to obtain the maximum amount of reward (Kruglanski et al. 1977). Supportive of these findings are studies showing that autonomous behavior—that which is self-determined, freely chosen, and personally controlled—elicits high task interest, creativity, cognitive flexibility, positive emotion, and persistence (Deci and Ryan 1987).

Unfortunately, constraint and lack of student autonomy are trademarks of most schools. Federal and local governments, as well as teachers, legislate academic requirements; impose guidelines; create rewards systems; mandate behavioral contracts; serve warnings of expulsion; and use rules, threats, and punishments as routine problem-solving strategies. We can legislate school attendance and the conditions for obtaining a diploma, but we cannot legislate the development of intelligence, talent, creativity, and intrinsic motivation—resources this country desperately needs.

It is time for educators to replace coercive, constraint-laden techniques with autonomy-supportive techniques. We must redesign instructional and evaluation materials and procedures so that every assignment, quiz, text, project, and discussion activity not only allows for, but routinely *requires*, carefully calculated decision making on the part of students. Instead of minimum criteria, we must define multiple criteria (levels of minimum, marginal, average, good, superior, and excellent achievement), and we must free students to choose criteria that provide optimum challenge. Constraint gives a person the desire to escape; freedom gives a person the desire to explore, expand, and create.

## Prompt, Specific Feedback Enhances Learning

A third psychological principle is that specific and prompt feedback enhances learning, performance, and motivation (Ilgen et al. 1979, Larson 1984). Informational feedback (that which reveals correct responses) increases learning (Ilgen and Moore 1987) and also promotes a feeling of increased competency (Sansone 1986). Feedback that can be used to improve future performance has powerful motivational value.

Sadly, however, the proportion of student assignments or activities that are promptly returned with informational feedback tends to be low. Students typically complete an assignment and then wait one, two, or three days (sometimes weeks) for its return. The feedback they do get often consists of a number or letter grade accompanied by ambiguous comments such as "Is this your best?" or "Keep up the good work." Precisely what is good or what needs improving is seldom communicated.

But, even if we could convince teachers of the value of giving students immediate, specific, informational feedback, our feedback problem would still be far from solved. How can one teacher provide 25 or more students immediate feedback on their tasks? Some educators argue that the solution to the feedback problem lies in having a tutor or teacher aide for every couple of students. Others argue that adequate student feedback will require an increased use of computer technology. However, there are less expensive alternatives. First, answer keys for students should be more plentiful. Resource books containing review and study activities should be available in every subject area, and

each should be accompanied by a key that is available to students.

Second, quizzes and other instructional activities, especially those that supplement basic textbooks, should be prepared with "latent image" processing. With latent image paper and pens, a student who marks a response to an item can watch a hidden symbol emerge. The symbol signals either a correct or incorrect response, and in some instances a clue or explanation for the response is revealed. Trivia and puzzle books equipped with this latent image, immediate feedback process are currently being marketed at the price of comic books.

Of course, immediate informational feedback is more difficult to provide for composition work, long-term projects, and field assignments. But this does not justify the absence of immediate feedback on the learning activities and practice exercises that are aimed at teaching concepts, relationships, and basic skills. The mere availability of answer keys and latent image materials would probably elicit an amazing amount of self-regulated learning on the part of many students.

## Moderate Risk Taking Is a Tonic for Achievement

A fourth motivational research finding is that moderate risk taking increases performance, persistence, perceived competence, self-knowledge, pride, and satisfaction (Deci and Porac 1978, Harter 1978, Trope 1979). Moderate risk taking implies a well-considered choice of an optimally challenging task, willingness to accept a moderate probability of success, and the anticipation of an outcome. It is this combination of events (which includes moderate success, self-regulated learning, and feedback) that captivates the attention, interest, and energy of card players, athletes, financial investors, lottery players, and even juvenile video arcade addicts.

Risk takers continually and freely face the probability of failing to attain the pleasure of succeeding under specified odds. From every risk-taking endeavor—whether it ends in failure or success—risk takers learn something about their skill and choice of strategy, and what they learn usually prompts them to seek another risk-taking opportunity. Risk taking—especially moderate risk taking—is a mind-engaging activity that simultaneously consumes and generates energy. It is a habit that feeds itself and thus requires an unlimited supply of risk-taking opportunities.

Moderate risk taking is likely to occur under the following conditions.

▶ The success probability for each alternative is clear and unambiguous.

▶ Imposed external constraints are minimized.

▶ Variable payoff (the value of success increases as risk increases) in contrast to fixed payoff is available.

▶ The benefits of risk taking can be anticipated.

My own recent research on academic risk taking with grade school, high school, and college students generally supports these conclusions. Students do, in fact, freely choose more difficult problems (a) when the number of points offered increases with the difficulty level of problems, (b) when the risk-taking task is presented within a game or practice situation (i.e., imposed constraint or threat is minimized), and (c) when additional opportunities for risk taking are anticipated (relatively high risk taking will occur on a practice exercise when students know they will be able to apply the information learned to an upcoming test). In the absence of these conditions we have seen students choose tasks that are as much as one-and-a-half years below their achievement level (Clifford 1988). Finally, students who take moderately high risks express high task interest even though they experience considerable error making.

In summary, risk-taking opportunities for students should be (a) plentiful, (b) readily available, (c) accompanied by explicit information about success probabilities, (d) accompanied by immediate feedback that communicates competency and error information, (e) associated with payoffs that vary with task difficulty, (f) relatively free from externally imposed evaluation, and (g) presented in relaxing and nonthreatening environments.

In today's educational world, however, there are few opportunities for students to engage in academic risk taking and no incentives to do so. Choices are seldom provided within tests or assignments, and rarely are variable payoffs made available. Once again, motivational theory, which identifies risk taking as a powerful source of knowledge, motivation, and skill development, conflicts with educational practice, which seeks to minimize academic risk at all costs.

We must restructure materials and procedures to encourage moderate academic risk taking on the part of students. I predict that if we fill our classrooms with optional academic risk-taking materials and opportunities so that all students have access to moderate risks, we will not only lower our educational suicide rate, but we will raise our level of academic achievement. If we give students the license to take risks and make errors, they will likely experience genuine success and the satisfaction that accompanies it.

## Using Risk Can Ensure Success

Both theory and research evidence lead to the prediction that academic risk-taking activities are a powerful means of increasing the success of our educational efforts. But how do we get students to take risks on school-related activities? Students will choose risk over certainty when the consequences of the former are more satisfying and informative. Three basic conditions are needed to ensure such outcomes.

▶ First, students must be allowed to freely select from materials and activities that vary in difficulty and probability of success.

▶ Second, as task difficulty increases, so too must the payoffs for success.

▶ Third, an environment tolerant of error making and supportive of error correction must be guaranteed.

The first two conditions can be met rather easily. For example, on a 10-point quiz, composed of six 1-point items and four 2-point items, students might be asked to select and work only 6 items. The highest possible score for such quizzes is 10 and can be obtained only by correctly answering the four 2-point items and any two 1-point items. Choice and variable payoff are easily built into quizzes and many instructional and evaluation activities.

The third condition, creating an environment tolerant of error making and supportive of error correction, is more difficult to ensure. But here are six specific suggestions.

First, teachers must make a clear distinction between formative evaluation activities (tasks that guide instruction during the learning process) and summative evaluation activities (tasks used to judge one's level of achievement and to determine one's grade at the completion of the learning activity). Practice exercises, quizzes, and skill-building activities aimed at acquiring and strengthening knowledge and skills exemplify formative evaluation. These activities promote learning and skill development. They should be scored in a manner that excludes ability judgments, emphasizes error detection and correction, and encourages a search for better learning strategies. Formative evaluation activities should generally provide immediate feedback and be scored by students. It is on these activities that moderate risk taking is to be encouraged and is likely to prove beneficial.

**TERMS TO NOTE**
Formative evaluation
Summative evaluation

Major examinations (unit exams and comprehensive final exams) exemplify summative evaluation; these activities are used to determine course grades. Relatively low risk taking is to be expected on such tasks, and immediate feedback may or may not be desirable.

Second, formative evaluation activities should be far more plentiful than summative. If, in fact, learning rather than grading is the primary object of the school, the percentage of time spent on summative evaluation should be small in comparison to that spent on formative evaluation (perhaps about 1:4). There should be enough formative evaluation activities presented as risk-taking opportunities to satisfy the most enthusiastic and adventuresome learner. The more plentiful these activities are, the less anxiety-producing and aversive summative activities are likely to be.

Third, formative evaluation activities should be presented as optional; students should be enticed, not mandated, to complete these activities. Enticement might be achieved by (a) ensuring that these activities are course-relevant and varied (e.g., scrambled outlines, incomplete matrices and graphs, exercises that require error detection and correction, quizzes); (b) giving students the option of working together; (c) presenting risk-taking activities in the context of games to be played individually, with competitors, or with partners; (d) providing immediate, informational, nonthreatening feedback; and (e) defining success primarily in terms of improvement over previous performance or the amount of learning that occurs during the risk-taking activity.

Fourth, for every instructional and evaluation activity there should be at least a modest percentage of content (10 percent to 20 percent) that poses a challenge to even the best students completing the activity. Maximum development of a country's talent requires that *all* individuals (a) find challenge in tasks they attempt, (b) develop tolerance for error making, and (c) learn to adjust strategies when faced with failure.

To deprive the most talented students of these opportunities is perhaps the greatest resource-development crime a country can commit.

Fifth, summative evaluation procedures should include "retake exams." Second chances will not only encourage risk taking but will provide good reasons for students to study their incorrect responses made on previous risk-taking tasks. Every error made on an initial exam and subsequently corrected on a second chance represents real learning.

Sixth, we must reinforce moderate academic risk taking instead of error-free performance or excessively high or low risk taking. Improvement scores, voluntary correction of errors, completion of optional risk-taking activities—these are behaviors that teachers should recognize and encourage.

## Toward a New Definition of Success

We face the grim reality that our extraordinary efforts to produce "schools without failure" have not yielded the well-adjusted, enthusiastic, self-confident scholars we anticipated. Our efforts to mass-produce success for every individual in every educational situation have left us with cheap reproductions of success that do not even faintly represent the real thing. This overdose of synthetic success is a primary cause of the student apathy and school abandonment plaguing our country.

To turn the trend around, we must emphasize error tolerance, not error-free learning; reward error correction, not error avoidance; ensure challenge, not easy success. Eventual success on challenging tasks, tolerance for error making, and constructive responses to failure are motivational fare that school systems should be serving up to all students. I suggest that we engage the skills of researchers, textbook authors, publishers, and educators across the country to ensure the development and marketing of attractive and effective academic risk-taking materials

and procedures. If we convince these experts of the need to employ their creative efforts toward this end, we will not only stem the tide of educational suicide, but we will enhance the quality of educational success. We will witness self-regulated student success and satisfaction that will ensure the intellectual, creative, and motivational well-being of our country.

## REFERENCES

Atkinson, J. W. (1964). *An Introduction to Motivation.* Princeton, N.J.: Van Nostrand.

Boggiano, A. K., and D. S. Main. (1986). "Enhancing Children's Interest in Activities Used as Rewards: The Bonus Effect." *Journal of Personality and Social Psychology* 51: 1116–1126.

Clifford, M. M. (1988). "Failure Tolerance and Academic Risk Taking in Ten- to Twelve-Year-Old Students." *British Journal of Educational Psychology* 58: 15–27.

Csikszentmihalyi, M. (1975). *Beyond Boredom and Anxiety.* San Francisco: Jossey-Bass.

Csikszentmihalyi, M. (1978). "Intrinsic Rewards and Emergent Motivation." In *The Hidden Costs of Reward,* edited by M. R. Lepper and D. Greene,. N.J.: Lawrence Erlbaum Associates.

Danner, F. W., and D. Lonky. (1981). "A Cognitive-Developmental Approach to the Effects of Rewards on Intrinsic Motivation." *Child Development* 52: 1043–1052.

Deci, E. L., and J. Porac. (1978). "Cognitive Evaluation Theory and the Study of Human Motivation." In *The Hidden Costs of Reward,* edited by M. R. Lepper and D. Greene. Hillsdale, N.J.: Lawrence Erlbaum Associates.

Deci, E. L., and R. M. Ryan. (1987). "The Support of Autonomy and the Control of Behavior." *Journal of Personality and Social Psychology* 53: 1024–1037.

Fischer, K. W. (1980). "Learning as the Development of Organized Behavior." *Journal of Structural Learning* 3: 253–267.

Hahn, A. (1987). "Reaching Out to America's Dropouts: What to Do?" *Phi Delta Kappan* 69: 256–263.

Harter, S. (1978). "Effective Motivation Reconsidered: Toward a Developmental Model." *Human Development* 1: 34–64.

Ilgen, D. R., and C. F. Moore. (1987). "Types and Choices of Performance Feedback." *Journal of Applied Psychology* 72: 401–406.

Ilgen, D. R., C. D. Fischer, and M. S. Taylor. (1979). "Consequences of Individual Feedback on Behavior in Organizations." *Journal of Applied Psychology* 64: 349–371.

Kruglanski, A., C. Stein, and A. Riter. (1977). "Contingencies of Exogenous Reward and Task Performance: On the 'Minimax' Strategy in Instrumental Behavior." *Journal of Applied Social Psychology* 2: 141–148.

Larson, J. R., Jr. (1984). "The Performance Feedback Process: A Preliminary Model." *Organizational Behavior and Human Performance* 33: 42–76.

Lepper, M. R., and D. Greene. (1978). *The Hidden Costs of Reward.* Hillsdale, N.J.: Lawrence Erlbaum Associates.

Lepper, M. R., and M. Hodell. (1989). "Intrinsic Motivation in the Classroom." In *Motivation in Education, Vol. 3,* edited by C. Ames and R. Ames. New York: Academic Press.

Sansone, C. (1986). "A Question of Competence: The Effects of Competence and Task Feedback on Intrinsic Motivation." *Journal of Personality and Social Psychology* 51: 918–931.

Trope, Y. (1979). "Uncertainty Reducing Properties of Achievement Tasks." *Journal of Personality and Social Psychology* 37: 1505–1518.

## POSTNOTE

In the 1980s, educators and their many critics recognized that our schools were failing many of our students and that our students were failing many of our schools. An avalanche of reports, books, television specials, and columns lambasted the schools' performance. In response, standards have been raised, graduation requirements increased, and more rigorous courses of study implemented.

However, as an old adage says, "You can lead a horse to water, but you can't make it drink." Vast numbers of students still continue to commit "educational suicide," and student apathy, indifference, and underachievement are widespread. Margaret Clifford's remedy first takes a realistic look at the mismatch between the student and the school and then suggests quite tangible modifications to match the student's motivational system with the goals of schooling.

## DISCUSSION QUESTIONS

1. This article pinpoints student motivation as a major source of school problems. Do you agree with this assessment? Why or why not?

2. What are the most important remedies for our schools' ills offered by Clifford? In your review, will these remedies solve the problem?

3. What is the author's new definition of *success*? Do you agree with it? Why or why not?

# 39 · CLASSIC · *The Many Faces of Constructivism*

## David Perkins

Betty Fable's first day as a student at Constructivist High School was interesting but puzzling. In European history, the teacher challenged each student to write a letter from a French aristocrat to an Italian one, describing a key event of the French Revolution. In physics, the teacher asked students to predict whether heavy objects would fall faster than light ones, how much faster, and why. Then small groups of students designed their own experiments to test their theories. In algebra, where the class was learning the basic skill of simplifying algebraic expressions, the teacher insisted on conducting a discussion about what it means to simplify. Were simplified expressions the same as simplified equations? In English, after the class read Robert Frost's "Acquainted with the Night," the teacher asked students to relate the poem to an episode in their own lives.

**TERM TO NOTE**
Constructivism

Betty Fable expected all the teachers at Constructivist High to teach in a constructivist way—whatever that was. But what was it? Role playing, experimenting, analyzing, making connections to one's life? To her, each teacher seemed to be doing something different.

Many talented, dedicated, and experienced teachers find constructivist ideologies and practices just as bewildering, and for reasons not unlike Betty's. Constructivism does not seem to be one thing. And whatever constructivism is, its advocates sometimes have championed it to the point of overkill. Here and there, mentioning the C word is almost bad manners.

David Perkins is codirector of Project Zero at Harvard Graduate School of Education, 315 Longfellow Hall, Appian Way, Cambridge, MA 02138. From David Perkins, "The Many Faces of Constructivism," *Educational Leadership*, November 1999, pp. 6–11. Reprinted with permission of the author.

Perhaps it's possible to make better sense of the vexed and messy landscape of constructivism by asking appropriate questions.

## What is Constructivism in Its Variety?

No one can live in the world of education long without becoming aware that constructivism is more than one thing. But what accounts for the variety? Philosopher D. C. Phillips (1995) identifies three distinct roles in constructivism. We'll call them the *active learner*, the *social learner*, and the *creative learner*.

*The active learner: Knowledge and understanding as actively acquired.* Constructivism generally casts learners in an active role. Instead of just listening, reading, and working through routine exercises, they discuss, debate, hypothesize, investigate, and take viewpoints—a common thread in Betty Fable's first day at Constructivist High.

*The social learner: Knowledge and understanding as socially constructed.* Constructivists often emphasize that knowledge and understanding are highly social. We do not construct them individually; we coconstruct them in dialogue with others. The teaching of history should make students aware of how historical "truth" varies with the interest groups—hence in Betty's history class, the letters from the aristocratic perspective. The teaching of science should lead students to recognize that scientific truths are arrived at by a social critical process that shapes their supposedly objective reality—thus, the group work in Betty's science class.

*The creative learner: Knowledge and understanding as created or recreated.* Often, constructivists hold that learners need to create or recreate knowledge for themselves. It is not enough that they assume an active stance. Teachers should guide them to rediscover scientific theories, historical perspectives, and so on. Betty's history teacher hopes that the letter exercise will help students reconstruct the aristocratic perspective, and her science teacher hopes that the students' theories and experiments will build a strong understanding of why objects fall as they do.

It is natural to ask how the three constructivist roles relate to one another. An active role for the learner is basic; in practice, social and creative aspects often accompany this role. However, an active learner does not logically require the other two. Teachers can organize learning experiences in active ways that do not require learners to engage in testing and building knowledge in a social manner or to invent or reinvent theories or viewpoints.

## Why—and Why Not— Constructivism?

Why has constructivism enjoyed such advocacy for several decades? One reason is simply the search for better ways to teach and learn. With traditional methods, researchers and teachers have noted persistent shortfalls in students' understanding and a great deal of passive knowledge across all ages and grades, including the university (Gardner, 1991).

A philosophical argument also supports constructivist educational practices. The stimuli that we encounter, including messages from others, are never logically sufficient to convey meaning. To some extent, the individual always has to construct or reconstruct what things mean. It thus makes sense to organize learning to reflect this reality.

Another kind of argument looks to psychological sources (Perkins, 1992a; Duffy & Jonassen, 1992; Reigeluth, 1999; Wilson, 1996; Wiske, 1998). Considerable research shows that active engagement in learning may lead to better retention,

understanding, and active use of knowledge. A social dimension to learning—what is sometimes called *collaborative* or *cooperative learning*—often, although not always, fosters learning. Sometimes, engaging students in discovery or rediscovery processes energizes them and yields deeper understanding.

Such arguments certainly encourage constructivist teaching practices. However, complications arise. Constructivist techniques often require more time than do traditional educational practices—a cost worth paying, enthusiasts say, but many teachers feel the pressures and conclude that they need to make compromises. Asking learners to discover or rediscover principles can foster understanding, but learners sometimes persist in discovering the wrong principles—for instance, an idiosyncratic scientific theory. Although ardent constructivists may argue that process is all, others believe that one way or another, students need to arrive at an understanding of the best theories propounded by the disciplines.

Also, constructivist learning experiences can exert high cognitive demands on learners, and not all learners respond well to the challenge (Perkins, 1992b). Constructivist techniques can even seem deceptive and manipulative. "Why don't you just tell me what you want me to know instead of making a big secret of it?" is not always an unreasonable question.

## What Kind of Constructivism Makes Sense When?

The complications make it important to deploy constructivist techniques wisely, in the right place for the right purpose. How can a teacher create appropriate, targeted constructivist responses to learners' difficulties? One approach to the challenge recognizes that different kinds of knowledge—inert, ritual, conceptually difficult, and foreign—are likely to prove troublesome for learners in different ways.

## Inert Knowledge

Inert knowledge sits in the mind's attic, unpacked only when specifically called for by a quiz or a direct prompt but otherwise gathering dust (Bransford, Franks, Vye, & Sherwood, 1989; Bereiter & Scardamalia, 1985). A familiar and relatively benign example is passive vocabulary—words that we understand but do not use actively. Unfortunately, considerable knowledge that we would like to see used actively proves to be inert. Students commonly learn ideas about society and self in history and social studies but make no connections to today's events or family life. Students learn concepts in science but make little connection to the world around them. Students learn techniques in math but fail to connect them to everyday applications or to their science studies.

What is the constructivist response when teaching knowledge that is likely to become inert? One strategy is to engage learners in active problem solving with knowledge that makes connections to their world. Betty Fable's English teacher asked her students to make connections between Frost's "Acquainted with the Night" and episodes in their own lives. For another example, science students studying basic machines (levers, pulleys, and so on) might find and analyze examples around their homes.

Another approach is to engage students in problem-based learning, where they acquire the target concepts while addressing some medium-scale problem or project (Boud & Feletti, 1991; Savery & Duffy, 1996). The English students might search out varied poems for a project on the theme "poems of the nights of our lives." The science students might build a Rube Goldberg apparatus or construct useful gadgets that use basic machines.

## Ritual Knowledge

Ritual knowledge has a routine and rather meaningless character. It feels like part of a social or an individual ritual: how we answer when asked such-and-such, the routine that we execute to get a particular result. Names and dates often are little more than ritual knowledge. So are routines in arithmetic—an analogue of misconceptions in science (Gardner, 1991)—such as the notorious "invert and multiply" to divide fractions. Whereas inert knowledge needs more active use, ritual knowledge needs more meaningfulness (of course, knowledge can be both inert and ritualized).

A constructivist response to knowledge likely to become ritualized strives to make it more meaningful. For example, a teacher can wrap such knowledge in authentic problem-solving activities, another opportunity for problem-based learning. Students can explore its rationale and utility through discussion, as in the discussion of simplification in Betty Fable's algebra class. A teacher can sometimes involve students in surveying a large-scale story or historical episode or controversy that lends meaning to a piece of ritual knowledge. If Columbus "discovered" America in 1492, what else was going on in the world at about that time? How did Columbus's activities interact in the following decades with those other circumstances?

## Conceptually Difficult Knowledge

Before students reach the university level, they meet conceptually difficult knowledge most commonly in mathematics and science, although it can occur in any discipline.

Understanding objects in motion is a good example (McCloskey, 1983). Learners find it hard to accept that objects in motion will continue at the same rate in the same direction unless some force, such as friction or gravity, impedes them. They find it hard to believe that heavier objects fall at the same rate as lighter ones, air resistance aside.

A mix of misimpressions from everyday experience (objects slow down automatically), reasonable but mistaken expectations (heavier objects fall faster), and the strangeness and complexity of scientists' views of matter (Newton's laws; such concepts as velocity as a vector, momentum, and so on) stand in the way. The result is often a mix of misunderstandings and ritual knowledge: Students learn the ritual responses to definitional questions and quantitative problems, but their intuitive beliefs and interpretations resurface on qualitative problems and in outside-of-classroom contexts.

What are reasonable constructivist responses to conceptually difficult knowledge? Perhaps the most common is to arrange inquiry processes that confront students with discrepancies in their initial theories—either discrepancies between theory and observations (as in Betty Fable's experiments with falling objects) or logical discrepancies.

For example, students commonly believe that a fly on a table pushes down but that the table does not push up on the fly. But they believe that the same table *does* push up on a bowling ball sitting on it. Imagine the bowling ball shrinking down to fly size. Where, all of a sudden, does the table stop pushing? Discussing such cases provides "anchoring intuitions" that make the principle clear and provoke students to extend it (Clement, 1993).

As with the bowling ball example, it often helps to introduce learners to imagistic mental models or to invite them to invent their own (Gentner & Stevens, 1983). It also often helps to engage learners with qualitative problems rather than with the solely quantitative ones that dominate some textbooks. Qualitative problems lead students to confront the character of the phenomenon rather than just to master computational routines. Such strategies may involve asking learners to "rediscover" the principle in some sense. But not necessarily. The teacher can instead introduce the principles directly and ask learners to test them and to use them to interpret phenomena in an active, exploratory way.

### Foreign Knowledge

Foreign knowledge comes from a perspective that conflicts with our own. Sometimes the learner does not even recognize the knowledge as foreign. An example is "presentism" in historical understanding: Students tend to view past events through present knowledge and values (Carretero & Voss, 1994). Harry Truman's decision to drop the atomic bomb on Hiroshima may seem foolish to today's students. Perhaps it was vexed, but viewed through the knowledge and cultural mindsets of the era, it was hardly foolish.

Other examples include value systems carried by different nationalities, faiths, and ethnic groups. How indeed did the French aristocracy view the Revolution, the question that Betty Fable encountered in her history class? To pose such a puzzle is not, of course, to recommend the aristocratic view. But it *is* to recognize that many situations in history, contemporary society, literature, and current science and technology allow multiple serious, sincere, and well-elaborated perspectives that deserve understanding.

What then are constructivist responses to foreign knowledge? We can engage learners in recognizing that there *are* alternative perspectives by asking them to identify and elaborate on them. We can provoke compare-and-contrast discussions that map the perspectives in relation to one another. This method may sometimes involve extensive investigation as students set out to research what other perspectives have to say. Still another approach is to foster role-playing activities that ask students to get inside mindsets different from their own.

Of course, these are neither the only ways that knowledge can be troublesome nor the only constructivist responses possible. For instance, knowledge can be hard to remember—complex, with many pieces of information. Surprisingly, even this difficulty invites a constructivist response. Research shows that the best way to remember a body of information is to organize it actively, looking for internal patterns and relating it to what you already know. Simple repetition is much less effective. Or knowledge can be full of seeming inconsistencies and paradoxes, as when art critics or scientists disagree.

Or knowledge can be full of subtle distinctions, such as that between weight and mass. Add your own categories and your own constructivist responses, by all means.

## Pragmatic Constructivism

Often, the case made for constructivism seems resoundingly ideological. If learners do not rediscover Greek philosophy or Newton's laws for themselves, they will never truly understand them. To arrive at meaningful knowledge, they must learn through deep inquiry. As the unexamined life is not worth living, so the unexamined fact is not worth believing. And so on.

But the constructivist ideas assembled here are anything but ideological. They make up what we might call pragmatic constructivism. Their message asks us to view constructivism as a toolbox for problems of learning. Troublesome knowledge of various kinds invites constructivist responses to fit the difficulties—not one standard constructivist fix. If a particular approach does not solve the problem, try another—more structured, less structured, more discovery oriented, less discovery oriented, whatever works. And when knowledge is not particularly troublesome for the learners in question, well, forget about active, social, creative learners. Teaching by telling may serve just fine.

In keeping with this flexibility, active, social, and creative learning can play out in rather different ways, depending on the circumstances. Active learning is the common denominator. However, some examples more than others tapped the social dimension of constructivism. For instance, foreign knowledge intrinsically demands that we recognize differently constructed social perspectives. In contrast, inert or ritual knowledge may not call much upon the social dimension of constructivism, unless it happens to concern the social domain. Some constructivist responses to conceptually difficult knowledge ask learners to create and investigate their own theories. But responses to potentially inert and ritual knowledge may well simply foreground the wide and meaningful application of knowledge.

We began with Betty Fable's bewilderment about Constructivist High. In part, her confusion reflected the disparate constructivist moves in different classes. However, we see now that it also reflected a tension between ideological constructivism and pragmatic constructivism. The term *constructivism*, with its ideological overtones, suggests a single philosophy and a uniquely potent method—like one of those miracle knives advertised on late-night TV that will cut anything, even tin cans. But we could look at constructivism in another way, more like a Swiss army knife with various blades for various needs. Indeed, the miracle-knife version of constructivism has become as tired over the years as those TV commercials. At Constructivist High and elsewhere, it's high time we got pragmatic about constructivism.

## References

Bereiter, C., & Scardamalia, M. (1985). Cognitive coping strategies and the problem of inert knowledge. In S. S. Chipman, J. W. Segal, & R. Glaser (Eds.), *Thinking and learning skills, Vol. 2: Current research and open questions* (pp. 65–80). Hillsdale, NJ: Erlbaum.

Boud, D., & Feletti, G. (Eds.). (1991). *The challenge of problem-based learning.* New York: St. Martin's Press.

Bransford, J. D., Franks, J. J., Vye, N. J., & Sherwood, R. D. (1989). New approaches to instruction: Because wisdom can't be told. In S. Vosniadou & A. Ortony (Eds.), *Similarity and analogical reasoning* (pp. 470–497). New York: Cambridge University Press.

Carretero, M., & Voss., J. F. (Eds.). (1994). *Cognitive and instructional processes in history and the social sciences.* Hillsdale, NJ: Erlbaum.

Clement, J. (1993). Using bridging analogies and anchoring intuitions to deal with students' preconceptions in physics. *Journal of Research in Science Teaching, 30*(10), 1241–1257.

Duffy, T. M., & Jonassen, D. H. (Eds.). (1992). *Constructivism and the technology of instruction: A conversation.* Hillsdale, NJ: Erlbaum.

Gardner, H. (1991). *The unschooled mind: How children think and how schools should teach.* New York: Basic Books.

Gentner, D., & Stevens, A. L. (Eds.) (1983). *Mental models.* Hillsdale, NJ: Erlbaum.

McCloskey, M. (1983). Naive theories of motion. In D. Gentner & A. L. Stevens (Eds.), *Mental models* (pp. 299–324). Hillsdale, NJ: Erlbaum.

Perkins, D. N. (1992a). *Smart schools: From training memories to educating minds.* New York: Free Press.

Perkins, D. N. (1992b). What constructivism demands of the learner. In T. M. Duffy & D. H. Jonassen (Eds.), *Constructivism and the technology of instruction: A conversation* (pp. 161–165). Hillsdale, NJ: Erlbaum.

Phillips, D. C. (1995). The good, the bad, and the ugly: The many faces of constructivism. *Educational Researcher, 24*(7), 5–12.

Reigeluth, C. (Ed.). (1999). *Instructional design theories and models: Vol. II.* Mahwah, NJ: Erlbaum.

Savery, J. R., & Duffy, T. M. (1996). Problem-based learning: An instructional model and its constructivist framework. In B. G. Wilson (Ed.), *Constructivist learning environments: Case studies in instructional design* (pp. 130–143). Englewood Cliffs, NJ: Educational Technology Publications.

Wilson, B. G. (Ed.). (1996). *Constructivist learning environments: Case studies in instructional design.* Englewood Cliffs, NJ: Educational Technology Publications.

Wiske, M. S. (Ed.). (1998). *Teaching for understanding: Linking research with practice.* San Francisco: Jossey-Bass.

*Author's note:* Some of the ideas presented here were developed as part of the Understandings of Consequence Project, which is supported by the National Science Foundation, Grant No. REC-9725502 to Tina Grotzer and David Perkins, coprincipal investigators. Any opinions, conclusions, or recommendations expressed here are those of the author and do not necessarily reflect the views of the National Science Foundation.

## POSTNOTE

This article was chosen as a Classic because the topic of constructivism has become such a dominant instructional philosophy in American education. Research from cognitive scientists has taught us that when confronted with new learning, human beings "construct" new understandings of relationships and phenomena, rather than simply receiving others' understandings. Learners are always fitting new information into the schemas they carry in their heads, or else they adjust or change the schema to fit the new information. As the author of this article states, knowledge is not passively received, but actively constructed by learners on a base of prior knowledge, attitudes, and values.

The implications for teachers are enormous. Constructivism suggests that educators should invite students to explore the world's complexity, proposing situations for students to think about and observing how the students use their prior knowledge to confront the problems. When students make errors, teachers can analyze the errors to understand better just how the students are approaching the matter. Throughout the process, teachers must accept that there is no single "right" way to solve a problem.

## DISCUSSION QUESTIONS

1. In what ways does constructivism challenge your ideas about how people learn?

2. How do you think constructivism will affect what goes on in classrooms? Describe a scenario in which a teacher uses constructivist principles, similar to those the author presents at the beginning of the article, to conduct a lesson. Choose any subject or grade level you wish.

3. How does constructivism dispute the notion of a fixed world that students need to understand?

# Making the Grade: What Benefits Students?

Thomas R. Guskey

**40**

Charged with leading a committee that would revise his school's grading and reporting system Warren Middleton described his work this way:

> The Committee on Grading was called upon to study grading procedures. At first, the task of investigating the literature seemed to be a rather hopeless one. What a mass and a mess it all was! Could order be brought out of such chaos? Could points of agreement among American educators concerning the perplexing grading problem actually be discovered? It was with considerable misgiving and trepidation that the work was finally begun.

Few educators today would consider the difficulties encountered by Middleton and his colleagues to be particularly surprising. In fact, most probably would sympathize with his lament. What they might find surprising, however, is that this report from the Committee on Grading was published in 1933!

The issues of grading and reporting on student learning have perplexed educators for the better part of this century. Yet despite all the debate and the multitude of studies, coming up with prescriptions for best practice seems as challenging today as it was for Middleton and his colleagues more than 60 years ago.

Thomas R. Guskey is professor of education policy studies and evaluation, College of Education, University of Kentucky, Lexington, Kentucky. From Thomas R. Guskey, "Making the Grade: What Benefits Students?", *Educational Leadership*, October 1994, pp. 14–20. Reprinted with permission of the Association for Supervision and Curriculum Development.

## Points of Agreement

Although the debate over grading and reporting continues, today we know better which practices benefit students and encourage learning. Given the multitude of studies—and their often incongruous results—researchers do appear to agree on the following points:

**1.** *Grading and reporting aren't essential to instruction.* Teachers don't need grades or reporting forms to teach well. Further, students don't need them to learn (Frisbie and Waltman 1992).

Teachers do need to check regularly on how students are doing, what they've learned, and what problems or difficulties they've experienced. But grading and reporting are different from checking; they involve judging the adequacy of students' performance at a specific time. Typically, teachers use checking to diagnose and prescribe and use grading to evaluate and describe (Bloom et al. 1981).

When teachers do both checking and grading, they become advocates as well as judges—roles that aren't necessarily compatible (Bishop 1992). Finding a meaningful compromise between these dual roles makes many teachers uncomfortable, especially those with a child-centered orientation (Barnes 1985).

**2.** *No one method of grading and reporting serves all purposes well.* Grading enables teachers to communicate the achievements of students to parents and others, provides incentives to learn, and provides information that students can use for self-evaluation. In addition, schools use grades to identify or group students for particular educational paths or programs and to evaluate a

235

program's effectiveness (Feldmesser 1971, Frisbie and Waltman 1992). Unfortunately, many schools attempt to address all of these purposes with a single method and end up achieving none very well (Austin and McCann 1992).

Letter grades, for example, briefly describe learning progress and give some idea of its adequacy (Payne 1974). Their use, however, requires abstracting a great deal of information into a single symbol (Stiggins 1994). In addition, the cut-off between grade categories is always arbitrary and difficult to justify. If scores for a grade of *B* range from 80 to 89, students at both ends of that range receive the same grade, even though their scores differ by nine points. But the student with a score of 79—a one-point difference—receives a grade of *C*.

The more detailed methods also have their drawbacks. Narratives and checklists of learning outcomes offer specific information for documenting progress, but good narratives take time to prepare, and—not surprisingly—as teachers complete more narratives, their comments become increasingly standardized. From the parents' standpoint, checklists of learning outcomes often appear too complicated to understand. In addition, checklists seldom communicate the appropriateness of students' progress in relation to expectations for their level (Afflerbach and Sammons 1991).

Because one method won't adequately serve all purposes, schools must identify their primary purpose for grading and select or develop the most appropriate approach (Cangelosi 1990). This process often involves the difficult task of seeking consensus among several constituencies.

**3.** *Regardless of the method used, grading and reporting remain inherently subjective.*   In fact, the more detailed the reporting method and the more analytic the process, the more likely subjectivity will influence results (Ornstein 1994). That's why, for example, holistic scoring procedures tend to have greater reliability than analytic procedures.

Subjectivity in this process, however, isn't always bad. Because teachers know their students, understand various dimensions of students'

work, and have clear notions of the progress made, their subjective perceptions may yield very accurate descriptions of what students have learned (Brookhart 1993, O'Donnell and Woolfolk 1991).

When subjectivity translates into bias, however, negative consequences can result. Teachers' perceptions of students' behavior can significantly influence their judgments of scholastic performance (Hills 1991). Students with behavior problems often have no chance to receive a high grade because their infractions overshadow their performance. These effects are especially pronounced in judgments of boys (Bennett et al. 1993). Even the neatness of students' handwriting can significantly affect a teacher's judgment (Sweedler-Brown 1992).

Training programs can help teachers identify and reduce these negative effects and lead to greater consistency in judgments (Afflerbach and Sammons 1991). Unfortunately, few teachers receive adequate training in grading or reporting as part of their preservice experiences (Boothroyd and McMorris 1992). Also, few school districts provide adequate guidance to ensure consistency in teachers' grading or reporting practices (Austin and McCann 1992).

**4.** *Grades have some value as rewards, but no value as punishments.*   Although educators would undoubtedly prefer that motivation to learn be entirely intrinsic, the existence of grades and other reporting methods are important factors in determining how much effort students put forth (Chastain 1990, Ebel 1979). Most students view high grades as positive recognition of their success, and some work hard to avoid the consequences of low grades (Feldmesser 1971).

At the same time, no studies support the use of low grades as punishments. Instead of prompting greater effort, low grades usually cause students to withdraw from learning. To protect their self-image, many students regard the low grade as irrelevant and meaningless. Other students may blame themselves for the low mark, but feel helpless to improve (Selby and Murphy 1992).

Sadly, some teachers consider grades or reporting forms their "weapon of last resort." In their view, students who don't comply with requests suffer the consequences of the greatest punishment a teacher can bestow: a failing grade. Such practices have no educational value and, in the long run, adversely affect students, teachers, and the relationship they share. Rather than attempting to punish students with a low mark, teachers can better motivate students by regarding their work as incomplete and requiring additional effort.

**5.** *Grading and reporting should always be done in reference to learning criteria, never on the curve.* Using the normal probability curve as a basis for assigning grades typically yields greater consistency in grade distributions from one teacher to the next. The practice, however, is detrimental to teaching and learning.

Grading on the curve pits students against one another in a competition for the few rewards (high grades) distributed by the teacher. Under these conditions, students readily see that helping others will threaten their own chances for success (Johnson et al. 1979, Johnson et al. 1980). Learning becomes a game of winners and losers—with the most students falling into the latter category (Johnson and Johnson 1989). In addition, modern research has shown that the seemingly direct relationship between aptitude or intelligence and school achievement depends upon instructional conditions, not a probability curve.

When the instructional quality is high and well matched to students' learning needs, the magnitude of this relationship diminishes drastically and approaches zero (Bloom 1976). Moreover, the fairness and equity of grading on the curve is a myth.

### Learning Criteria

When grading and reporting relate to learning criteria, teachers have a clearer picture of what students have learned. Students and teachers alike generally prefer this approach because it seems fairer (Kovas 1993). The types of learning criteria usually used for grading and reporting fall into three categories:

▶ *Product criteria* are favored by advocates of performance-based approaches to teaching and learning. These educators believe grading and reporting should communicate a summative evaluation of student achievement (Cangelosi 1990). In other words, they focus on what students know and are able to do at that time. Teachers who use product criteria often base their grades or reports exclusively on final examination scores, overall assessments, or other culminating demonstrations of learning.

▶ *Process criteria* are emphasized by educators who believe product criteria don't provide a complete picture of student learning. From their perspective, grading and reporting should reflect not just the final results but also *how* students got there. Teachers who consider effort or work habits when reporting on student learning are using process criteria. So are teachers who take into consideration classroom quizzes, homework, class participation, or attendance.

**TERMS TO NOTE**
Product criteria
Process criteria
Progress criteria

▶ *Progress criteria*, often referred to as "improvement scoring" and "learning gain," consider how much students have gained from their learning experiences. Teachers who use progress criteria look at *how far* students have come rather than where they are. As a result, scoring criteria may become highly individualized.

Teachers who base their grading and reporting procedures on learning criteria typically use some combination of the three types (Frary et al. 1993; Nava and Loyd 1992; Stiggins et al. 1989). Most researchers and measurement specialists, on the other hand, recommend using product criteria exclusively. They point out that the more process and progress criteria come into play, the more subjective and biased grades become (Ornstein 1994). How can a teacher know, for example, how difficult a task was for students or how hard they worked to complete it? If these criteria are included at all, most experts recommend they be reported separately (Stiggins 1994).

## Practical Guidelines

Despite years of research, there's no evidence to indicate that one grading or reporting method works best under all conditions, in all circumstances. But in developing practices that seek to be fair, equitable, and useful to students, parents, and teachers, educators can rely on two guidelines:

▶ *Provide accurate and understandable descriptions of learning.* Regardless of the method or form used, grading and reporting should communicate effectively what students have learned, what they can do, and whether their learning status is in line with expectations for that level. More than an exercise in quantifying achievement, grading and reporting must be seen as a challenge in clear thinking and effective communication (Stiggins 1994).

▶ *Use grading and reporting methods to enhance, not hinder, teaching and learning.* A clear, easily understood reporting form facilitates communication between teachers and parents. When both parties speak the same language, joint efforts to help students are likely to succeed. But developing such an equitable and understandable system will require the elimination of long-time practices such as averaging and assigning a zero to work that's late, missed, or neglected.

▶ *Averaging* falls far short of providing an accurate description of what students have learned. For example, students often say, "I have to get a *B* on the final to pass this course." Such a comment illustrates the inappropriateness of averaging. If a final examination is truly comprehensive and students' scores accurately reflect what they've learned, why should a *B*

level of performance translate to a *D* for the course grade?

Any single measure of learning can be unreliable. Consequently, most researchers recommend using several indicators in determining students' grades or marks—and most teachers concur (Natriello 1987). Nevertheless, the key question remains, "What information provides the most accurate depiction of students' learning at this time?" In nearly all cases, the answer is "the most current information." If students demonstrate that past assessment information doesn't accurately reflect their learning, new information must take its place. By continuing to rely on past assessment data, the grades can be misleading about a student's learning (Stiggins 1994).

Similarly, assigning a score of zero to work that is late, missed, or neglected doesn't accurately depict learning. Is the teacher certain the student has learned absolutely nothing, or is the zero assigned to punish students for not displaying appropriate responsibility (Canady and Hotchkiss 1989, Stiggins and Duke 1991)?

Further, a zero has a profound effect when combined with the practice of averaging. Students who receive a single zero have little chance of success because such an extreme score skews the average. That is why, for example, Olympic events such as gymnastics and ice skating eliminate the highest and lowest scores; otherwise, one judge could control the entire competition

**TERM TO NOTE**

Median

simply by giving extreme scores. An alternative is to use the median score rather than the average (Wright 1994) but use of the most current information remains the most defensible option.

## Meeting the Challenge

The issues of grading and reporting on student learning continue to challenge educators today, just as they challenged Middleton and his colleagues in 1933. But today we know more than ever before about the complexities involved and how certain practices can influence teaching and learning.

What do educators need to develop grading and reporting practices that provide quality information about student learning? Nothing less than clear thinking, careful planning, excellent communication skills, and an overriding concern for the well-being of students. Combining these skills with our current knowledge on effective practice will surely result in more efficient and more effective reporting.

## A Look Back at Grading Practices

Although student assessment has been a part of teaching and learning for centuries, grading is a relatively recent phenomenon. The ancient Greeks used assessments as formative, not evaluative, tools. Students demonstrated, usually orally, what they had learned, giving teachers a clear indication of which topics required more work or instruction.

In the United States, grading and reporting were virtually unknown before 1850. Back then, most schools grouped students of all ages and backgrounds together with one teacher. Few students went beyond the elementary education offered in these one-room schoolhouses. As the country grew—and as legislators passed compulsory attendance laws—the number and diversity of students increased. Schools began to group students in grades according to their age, and to try new ideas about curriculum and teaching methods. Here's a brief timeline of significant dates in the history of grading:

**Late 1800s:** Schools begin to issue progress evaluations. Teachers simply write down the skills that students have mastered; once students complete the requirements for one level, they can move to the next level.

**Early 1900s:** The number of public high schools in the United States increases dramatically. While elementary teachers continue using written descriptions to document student learning, high school teachers introduce percentages as a way to certify students' accomplishments in specific subject areas. Few educators question the gradual shift to percentage grading, which seems a natural by-product of the increased demands on high school teachers.

**1912:** Starch and Elliott publish a study that challenges percentage grades as reliable measures of student achievement. They base their findings on grades assigned to two papers written for a first-year English class in high school. Of the 142 teachers grading on a 0 to 100 scale, 15 percent give one paper a failing mark; 12 percent give the same paper a score of 90 or more. The other paper receives scores ranging from 50 to 97. Neatness, spelling, and punctuation influenced the scoring of many teachers, while others considered how well the paper communicated its message.

**1913:** Responding to critics—who argue that good writing is, by nature, a highly subjective judgment—Starch and Elliott repeat their study but use geometry papers. Even greater variations occur, with scores on one paper ranging from 28 to 95. Some teachers deducted points only for wrong answers, but others took neatness, form, and spelling into account.

**1918:** Teachers turn to grading scales with fewer and larger categories. One three-point scale, for example, uses the categories of Excellent, Average, and Poor. Another has five categories (Excellent, Good, Average, Poor, and Failing) with the corresponding letters of *A, B, C, D,* and *F* (Johnson 1918, Rugg 1918).

**1930s:** Grading on the curve becomes increasingly popular as educators seek to minimize the subjective nature of scoring. This method ranks students according to some measure of their performance or proficiency. The top percentage receives an *A,* the next percentage receives a *B,* and so on (Corey 1930). Some advocates (Davis 1930) even specify the precise percentage of students to be assigned each grade, such as 6–22–44–22–6.

Grading on the curve seems fair and equitable, given research suggesting that students' scores on tests of innate intelligence approximate a normal probability curve (Middleton 1933).

As the debate over grading and reporting intensifies, a number of schools abolish formal grades altogether (Chapman and Ashbaugh 1925) and return to using verbal descriptions of student achievement. Others advocate pass-fail systems that distinguish only between acceptable and failing work (Good 1937). Still others advocate a "mastery approach": Once students have mastered a skill or content, they move to other areas of study (Heck 1938, Hill 1935).

**1958:** Ellis Page investigates how student learning is affected by grades and teachers' comments. In a now classic study, 74 secondary school teachers administer a test, and assign a numerical score and letter grade of *A, B, C, D,* or *F* to each student's paper. Next, teachers randomly divide the tests into three groups. Papers in the first group receive only the numerical score and letter grade. The second group, in addition to the score and grade, receive these standard comments: *A—Excellent! B—Good work. Keep at it. C—Perhaps try to do still better? D—Let's bring this up. F—Let's raise this grade!* For the third group, teachers mark the score and letter grade, and write individualized comments.

Page evaluates the effects of the comments by considering students' scores on the next test they take. Results show that students in the second group achieved significantly higher scores than those who received only a score and grade. The students who received individualized comments did even better. Page concludes that grades can have a beneficial effect on student learning, but only when accompanied by specific or individualized comments from the teacher.

*Source:* H. Kirschenbaum, S. B. Simon, and R. W. Napier (1971), *Wad-ja-get? The Grading Game in American Education,* (New York: Hart).

## REFERENCES

Afflerbach, P., and R. B. Sammons. (1991). "Report Cards in Literacy Evaluation: Teachers' Training, Practices, and Values." Paper presented at the annual meeting of the National Reading Conference, Palm Springs, Calif.

Austin, S., and R. McCann. (1992). "'Here's Another Arbitrary Grade for Your Collection': A Statewide Study of Grading Policies." Paper presented at the annual meeting of the American Educational Research Association, San Francisco.

Barnes, S. (1985). "A Study of Classroom Pupil Evaluation: The Missing Link in Teacher Education." *Journal of Teacher Education* 36, 4: 46–49.

Bennett, R. E., R. L. Gottesman, D. A. Rock, and F. Cerullo. (1993). "Influence of Behavior Perceptions and Gender on Teachers' Judgments of Students' Academic Skill." *Journal of Educational Psychology,* 85: 347–356.

Bishop, J. H. (1992). "Why U.S. Students Need Incentives to Learn." *Educational Leadership* 49, 6: 15–18.

Bloom, B. S. (1976). *Human Characteristics and School Learning.* New York: McGraw-Hill.

Bloom, B. S., G. F. Madaus, and J. T. Hastings (1981). *Evaluation to Improve Learning.* New York: McGraw-Hill.

Boothroyd, R. A., and R. F. McMorris. (1992). "What Do Teachers Know About Testing and How Did They Find Out?" Paper presented at the annual meeting of the National Council on Measurements in Education, San Francisco.

Brookhart, S. M. (1993). "Teachers' Grading Practices: Meaning and Values." *Journal of Educational Measurement* 30, 2: 123–142.

Canady, R. L., and P. R. Hotchkiss. (1989). "It's a Good Score! Just a Bad Grade." *Phi Delta Kappan* 71: 68–71.

Cangelosi, J. S. (1990). "Grading and Reporting Student Achievement." In *Designing Tests for Evaluating Student Achievement,* pp. 196–213. New York: Longman.

Chapman, H. B., and E. J. Ashbaugh. (October 7, 1925). "Report Cards in American Cities." *Educational Research Bulletin* 4: 289–310.

Chastain, K. (1990). Characteristics of Graded and Ungraded Compositions." *Modern Language Journal,* 74, 1: 10–14.

Corey, S. M. (1930). "Use of the Normal Curve as a Basis for Assigning Grades in Small Classes." *School and Society* 31: 514–516.

Davis, J. D. W. (1930). "Effect of the 6–22–44–22–6 Normal Curve System on Failures and Grade Values." *Journal of Educational Psychology* 22: 636–640.

Ebel, R. L. (1979). *Essentials of Educational Measurement* (3rd ed.). Englewood Cliffs, N.J.: Prentice-Hall.

Feldmesser, R. A. (1971). "The Positive Functions of Grades." Paper presented at the annual meeting of the American Educational Research Association, New York.

Frary, R. B., L. H. Cross, and L. J. Weber. (1993). "Testing and Grading Practices and Opinions of Secondary Teachers of Academic Subjects: Implications for Instruction in Measurement." *Educational Measurement: Issues and Practices* 12, 3: 23–30.

Frisbie, D. A., and K. K. Waltman. (1992). "Developing a Personal Grading Plan." *Educational Measurement: Issues and Practices* 11, 3: 35–42.

Good, W. (1937). "Should Grades Be Abolished?" *Education Digest* 2, 4: 7–9.

Heck, A. O. (1938). "Contributions of Research to Classification, Promotion, Marking and Certification." Reported in *The Science Movement in Education (Part II), Twenty-Seventh Yearbook of the National Society for the Study of Education.* Chicago: University of Chicago Press.

Hill, G. E. (1935). "The Report Card in Present Practice." *Education Methods* 15, 3: 115–131.

Hills, J. R. (1991). "Apathy Concerning Grading and Testing." *Phi Delta Kappan* 72, 2: 540–545.

Johnson, D. W., and R. T. Johnson. (1989). *Cooperation and Competition: Theory and Research.* Endina, Minn.: Interaction.

Johnson, D. W., L. Skon, and R. T. Johnson. (1980). "Effects of Cooperative, Competitive, and Individualistic Conditions on Children's Problem-Solving Performance." *American Educational Research Journal* 17, 1: 83–93.

Johnson, R. H. (1918). "Educational Research and Statistics: The Coefficient Marking System" *School and Society* 7, 181: 714–716.

Johnson, R. T., D. W. Johnson, and M. Tauer. (1979). "The Effects of Cooperative, Competitive, and Individualistic Goal Structures on Students' Attitudes and Achievement." *Journal of Psychology* 102: 191–198.

Kovas, M. A. (1993). "Making Your Grading Motivating: Keys to Performance-Based Evaluation." *Quill and Scroll* 68, 1: 10–11.

Middleton, W. (1933). "Some General Trends in Grading Procedure." *Education* 54, 1: 5–10.

Natriello, G. (1987). "The Impact of Evaluation Processes On Students." *Educational Psychologists* 22: 155–175.

Nava, F. J. G., and B. H. Loyd. (1992). "An Investigation of Achievement and Nonachievement Criteria in Elementary and Secondary School Grading." Paper presented at the annual meeting of the American Educational Research Association, San Francisco.

O'Donnell, A., and A. E. Woolfolk. (1991). "Elementary and Secondary Teachers' Beliefs About Testing and Grading." Paper presented at the annual meeting of the American Psychological Association, San Francisco.

Ornstein, A. C. (1994). "Grading Practices and Policies: An Overview and Some Suggestions." *NASSP Bulletin* 78, 559: 55–64.

Page, E. B. (1958). "Teacher Comments and Student Performance: A Seventy-Four Classroom Experiment in School Motivation." *Journal of Educational Psychology* 49: 173–181.

Payne, D. A. (1974). *The Assessment of Learning.* Lexington, Mass.: Heath.

Rugg, H. O. (1918). "Teachers' Marks and the Reconstruction of the Marking System." *Elementary School Journal* 18, 9: 701–719.

Selby, D., and S. Murphy. (1992). "Graded or Degraded: Perceptions of Letter-Grading for

Mainstreamed Learning-Disabled Students." *British Columbia Journal of Special Education* 16, 1: 92–104.

Starch, D., and E. C. Elliott. (1912). "Reliability of the Grading of High School Work in English." *School Review* 20: 442–457.

Starch, D., and E. C. Elliott. (1913). "Reliability of the Grading of High School Work in Mathematics." *School Review* 21: 254–259.

Stewart, L. G., and M. A. White. (1976). "Teacher Comments, Letter Grades, and Student Performance." *Journal of Educational Psychology* 68, 4: 488–500.

Stiggins, R. J. (1994). "Communicating with Report Card Grades." In *Student-Centered Classroom Assessment*, pp. 363–396. New York: Macmillan.

Stiggins, R. J., and D. L. Duke. (1991). "District Grading Policies and Their Potential Impact on At-risk Students." Paper presented at the annual meeting of the American Educational Research Association, Chicago.

Stiggins, R. J., D. A. Frisbie, and P. A. Griswold. (1989). "Inside High School Grading Practices: Building a Research Agenda." *Educational Measurement: Issues and Practice* 8, 2: 5–14.

Sweedler-Brown, C. O. (1992). "The Effect of Training on the Appearance Bias of Holistic Essay Graders." *Journal of Research and Development in Education* 26, 1: 24–29.

Wright, R. G. (1994). "Success for All: The Median Is the Key." *Phi Delta Kappan* 75, 9: 723–725.

## POSTNOTE

Grading students is one of the most troubling tasks that beginning teachers face. While working with students to help them learn and develop is a source of great pleasure for teachers, grading students provokes anxiety and avoidance. Unfortunately, grading is a part of almost all schooling and is not likely to go away anytime soon. Therefore, teachers need to learn how to grade in the fairest way possible.

To do this may require you to unlearn many aspects of grading that you have experienced as a student. For example, consider using the median instead of the mean when averaging a student's grades. Statistically, it is a more fair measure. In general, take time to learn effective and fair evaluation procedures.

## DISCUSSION QUESTIONS

1. Did any of the author's recommendations surprise you? If so, which ones and why?

2. Can you think of any time when you thought you didn't get the grade you deserved? What were the circumstances? In what way do you think you were treated unfairly?

3. How would a zero score count differently in averaging scores if you used the median instead of the mean as the measure of central tendency?

*Making Cooperative Learning Work*

David W. Johnson and Roger T. Johnson

S andy Koufax was one of the greatest pitchers in the history of baseball. Although he was naturally talented, he was also unusually well trained and disciplined. He was perhaps the only major-league pitcher whose fastball could be heard to hum. Opposing batters, instead of talking and joking around in the dugout, would sit quietly and listen for Koufax's fastball to hum. When it was their turn to bat, they were already intimidated.

There was, however, a simple way for Koufax's genius to have been negated: by making the first author of this article his catcher. To be great, a pitcher needs an outstanding catcher (his great partner was Johnny Roseboro). David is such an unskilled catcher that Koufax would have had to throw the ball much slower in order for David to catch it. This would have deprived Koufax of his greatest weapon.

Placing Roger at key defensive positions in the infield or outfield, furthermore, would have seriously affected Koufax's success. Sandy Koufax was not a great pitcher on his own. Only as part of a team could Koufax achieve greatness. In baseball and in the classroom, it takes a cooperative effort. Extraordinary achievement comes from a cooperative group, not from the individualistic or competitive efforts of an isolated individual.

In 1966 David began training teachers at the University of Minnesota in how to use small groups for instructional purposes. In 1969 Roger joined David at Minnesota, and the training of

David W. Johnson and Roger T. Johnson are professors of education and codirectors of the Cooperative Learning Center at the University of Minnesota. "Making Cooperative Learning Work" by David W. Johnson and Roger T. Johnson, *Theory into Practice*, Volume 38, Number 2 (Spring 1999) is reprinted by permission. Copyright 1999 by the College of Education, The Ohio State University. All rights reserved.

teachers in how to use cooperative learning groups was extended into teaching methods courses in science education. The formation of the Cooperative Learning Center soon followed to focus on five areas:

1. Summarizing and extending the theory on cooperation and competition.

2. Reviewing the existing research in order to validate or disconfirm the theory and establish what is known and unknown.

3. Conducting a long-term program of research to validate and extend the theory and to identify (a) the conditions under which cooperative, competitive, and individualistic efforts are effective and (b) the basic elements that make cooperation work.

4. Operationalizing the validated theory into a set of procedures for teachers and administrators to use.

5. Implementing the procedures in classes, schools, school districts, colleges, and training programs.

These five activities result in an understanding of what is and is not a cooperative effort, the different types of cooperative learning, the five basic elements that make cooperation work, and the outcomes that result when cooperation is carefully structured.

## What Is and Is Not a Cooperative Effort

Not all groups are cooperative. There is nothing magical about working in a group. Some kinds of learning groups facilitate student learning and increase the quality of life in the classroom. Other types of learning groups hinder student learning and create disharmony and dissatisfaction. To use cooperative learning effectively, one must know what is and is not a cooperative group (Johnson, Johnson, & Holubec, 1998b).

1. *Pseudo learning group:* Students are assigned to work together but they have no interest in doing so and believe they will be evaluated by being ranked from the highest to the lowest performer. Students hide information from each other, attempt to mislead and confuse each other, and distrust each other. The result is that the sum of the whole is less than the potential of the individual members. Students would achieve more if they were working alone.

2. *Traditional classroom learning group:* Students are assigned to work together and accept that they have to do so. Assignments are structured so that students are evaluated and rewarded as individuals, not as members of the group. They seek each other's information but have no motivation to teach what they know to group-mates. Some students seek a free ride on the efforts of group-mates, who feel exploited and do less. The result is that the sum of the whole is more than the potential of some of the members, but the more hard working and conscientious students would perform higher if they worked alone.

3. *Cooperative learning group:* Students work together to accomplish shared goals. Students seek outcomes that are beneficial to all. Students discuss material with each other, help one another understand it, and encourage each other to work hard. Individual performance is checked regularly to ensure that all students are contributing and learning. The result is that the group is more than a sum of its parts, and all students perform higher academically than they would if they worked alone.

4. *High-performance cooperative learning group:* This is a group that meets all the criteria for being a cooperative learning group and outperforms all reasonable expectations, given its membership. The level of commitment members have to each other and the group's success is beyond that of most cooperative groups. Few groups ever achieve this level of development.

How well any small group performs depends on how it is structured. Seating people together and calling them a cooperative group does not make them one. Study groups, project groups, lab groups, homerooms, and reading groups are groups, but they are not necessarily cooperative. Even with the best of intentions, teachers may be using traditional classroom learning groups rather than cooperative learning groups. To ensure that a group is cooperative, educators must understand the different ways cooperative learning may be used and the basic elements that need to be carefully structured within every cooperative activity.

## Types of Cooperative Learning

Two are better than one, because they have a good reward for toil. For if they fall, one will lift up his fellow; but woe to him who is alone when he falls and has not another to lift him up. . . . And though a man might prevail against one who is alone, two will withstand him. A threefold cord is not quickly broken. (Ecclesiastics 4:9-12)

Cooperative learning is a versatile procedure and can be used for a variety of purposes. Cooperative learning groups may be used to teach specific content (formal cooperative learning groups), to ensure active cognitive processing of information during a lecture or demonstration (informal cooperative learning groups), and to provide long-term support and assistance for academic progress (cooperative base groups) (Johnson, Johnson, & Holubec, 1998a, 1998b).

*Formal cooperative learning* consists of students working together, for one class period or several weeks, to achieve shared learning goals and complete specific tasks and assignments (e.g., problem solving, writing a report, conducting a survey or experiment, learning vocabulary, or answering questions at the end of the chapter) (Johnson, Johnson, & Holubec, 1998b). Any course requirement or assignment may be structured cooperatively. In formal cooperative learning groups, teachers:

1. Make a number of *preinstructional decisions.* Teachers specify the objectives for the lesson (both academic and social skills) and decide on the size of groups, the method of assigning students to groups, the roles students will be assigned, the materials needed to conduct the lesson, and the way the room will be arranged.

2. *Explain* the task and the positive interdependence. A teacher clearly defines the assignment, teaches the required concepts and strategies, specifies the positive interdependence and individual accountability, gives the criteria for success, and explains the social skills to be used.

3. *Monitor* students' learning and *intervene* within the groups to provide task assistance or to increase students' interpersonal and group skills. A teacher systematically observes and collects data on each group as it works. When needed, the teacher intervenes to assist students in completing the task accurately and in working together effectively.

4. *Assess* students' learning and help students process how well their groups functioned. Students' learning is carefully assessed and their performances evaluated. Members of the learning groups then discuss how effectively they worked together and how they can improve in the future.

*Informal cooperative learning* consists of having students work together to achieve a joint learning goal in temporary, ad-hoc groups that last from a few minutes to one class period (Johnson,

Johnson, & Holubec, 1998a; Johnson, Johnson, & Smith, 1998). During a lecture, demonstration, or film, informal cooperative learning can be used to (a) focus student attention on the material to be learned, (b) set a mood conducive to learning, (c) help set expectations as to what will be covered in a class session, (d) ensure that students cognitively process the material being taught, and (e) provide closure to an instructional session.

During direct teaching the instructional challenge for the teacher is to ensure that students do the intellectual work of organizing material, explaining it, summarizing it, and integrating it into existing conceptual structures. Informal cooperative learning groups are often organized so that students engage in 3–5 minute focused discussions before and after a lecture and 2–3 minute turn-to-your-partner discussions interspersed throughout a lecture.

*Cooperative base groups* are long-term, heterogeneous cooperative learning groups of 3–4 members with stable membership (Johnson, Johnson, & Holubec, 1998a; Johnson, Johnson, & Smith, 1998). Base groups give the support, help, encouragement, and assistance each member needs to make academic progress (attend class, complete all assignments, learn) and develop cognitively and socially in healthy ways. Base groups meet daily in elementary school and twice a week in secondary school (or whenever the class meets). They are permanent (lasting from one to several years) and provide the long-term caring peer relationships necessary to influence members consistently to work hard in school.

The use of base groups tends to improve attendance, personalize the work required and the school experience, and improve the quality and quantity of learning. School and classroom management is enhanced when base groups are given the responsibility for conducting a year-long service project to improve the school. The larger the class or school and the more complex and difficult the subject matter, the more important it is to have base groups. Base groups are also helpful in structuring homerooms and when a teacher meets with a number of advisees.

## Example of Integrated Use of Cooperative Learning

An example of the integrated use of the cooperative learning procedures is as follows. Students arrive at class and meet in their base groups to welcome each other, check each student's homework to make sure all members understand the academic material and are prepared for the class session, and tell each other to have a great day.

The teacher then begins a lesson on the limitations of being human (Billion-Dollar Being, 1974). To help students cognitively organize in advance what they know about the advantages and disadvantages of being human, the teacher uses informal cooperative learning. The teacher asks students to form a triad and ponder, "What are five things you cannot do with your human limitations that a billion-dollar being might be designed to do?" Students have 4 minutes to do so. In the next 10 minutes, the teacher explains that while the human body is a marvelous system, we (like other organisms) have very specific limitations. We cannot see bacteria in a drop of water or the rings of Saturn unaided. We cannot hear as well as a deer or fly like an eagle. Humans have never been satisfied being so limited and, therefore, we have invented microscopes, telescopes, and our own wings. The teacher then instructs students to turn to the person next to them and answer the questions, "What are three limitations of humans, what have we invented to overcome them, and what other human limitations might we be able to overcome?"

Formal cooperative learning is now used in the lesson. The teacher has the 32 students count off from 1 to 8 to form groups of four randomly. Group members sit in a semicircle so they can face each other and still be facing the teacher. Each member is assigned a role: researcher/runner, summarizer/timekeeper, collector/recorder, and technical adviser (role interdependence). Every group gets one large (2×3-feet) piece of

paper, a marking pen, a rough draft sheet for designing the being, an assignment sheet explaining the task and cooperative goal structure, and four student self-evaluation checklists (resource interdependence). The task is to design a billion-dollar being that overcomes the human limitations thought of by the class and the group. The group members are to draw a diagram of the being on the scratch paper and, when they have something they like, transfer it to the larger paper.

The teacher establishes positive goal interdependence by asking for one drawing from the group that all group members contribute to and can explain. The criterion for success is to complete the diagram in the 30-minute time limit. The teacher observes each group to ensure that members are fulfilling their roles and that any one member can explain any part of the being at any time. The teacher informs students that the expected social skills to be used by all students are encouraging each other's participation, contributing ideas, and summarizing. She defines the skill of encouraging participation and has each student practice it twice before the lesson begins.

While students work in their groups, the teacher monitors by systematically observing each group and intervening to provide academic assistance and help in using the interpersonal and small group skills required to work together effectively. At the end of the lesson, the groups hand in their diagrams of the billion-dollar being to be assessed and evaluated. Group members then process how well they worked together by identifying actions each member engaged in that helped the group succeed and one thing that could be added to improve their group next time.

The teacher uses informal cooperative learning to provide closure to the lesson by asking students to meet in new triads and write out six conclusions about the limitations of human beings and what we have done to overcome them. At the end of the class session, the cooperative base groups meet to review what students believe is the most important thing they have learned during the day, what homework has been assigned, what help each member needs to complete the homework, and to tell each other to have a fun afternoon and evening.

## The Cooperative School

Teachers are not the only ones who need to carefully structure cooperation. Administrators need to create a learning community by structuring cooperation at the school level (Johnson & Johnson, 1994, 1999). In addition, they have to attend to the cooperation among faculty, between the school and parents, and between the school and the community.

Administrators, for example, may structure three types of cooperative faculty teams. Collegial teaching teams are formed to increase teachers' instructional expertise and success. They consist of 2–5 teachers who meet weekly and discuss how to better implement cooperative learning within their classrooms. Teachers are assigned to task forces to plan and implement solutions to school-wide issues and problems such as curriculum adoptions and lunchroom behavior. Ad hoc decision-making groups are used during faculty meetings to involve all staff members in important school decisions.

The use of cooperative teams at the building level ensures that there is a congruent cooperative team-based organizational structure within both classrooms and the school. Finally, the superintendent uses the same types of cooperative teams to maximize the productivity of district administrators.

## Basic Elements of Cooperation

In order for an activity to be cooperative, five basic elements are essential and need to be included (Johnson & Johnson, 1989; Johnson, Johnson, & Holubec, 1998a). The five essential elements are as follows.

1. *Positive interdependence:* Positive interdependence is the perception that we are linked with others in a way so that we cannot succeed unless they do. Their work benefits us and our work benefits them. Within every cooperative lesson, positive goal interdependence must be established through mutual learning goals (learn the assigned material and make sure that all members of your group learn the assigned material). In order to strengthen positive interdependence, joint rewards (if all members of your group score 90 percent correct or better on the test, each will receive 5 bonus points), divided resources (giving each group member a part of the total information required to complete an assignment), and complementary roles (reader, checker, encourager, elaborator) may also be used.

2. *Individual accountability:* Individual accountability exists when the performance of each individual student is assessed and the results are given back to the group and the individual. The purpose of cooperative learning groups is to make each member a stronger individual. Students learn together so that they can subsequently perform higher as individuals. To ensure that each member is strengthened, students are held individually accountable to do their share of the work. Common ways to structure individual accountability include (a) giving an individual test to each student, (b) randomly selecting one student's product to represent the entire group, or (c) having each student explain what they have learned to a classmate.

3. *Face-to-face promotive interaction:* Individuals promote each other's success by helping, assisting, supporting, encouraging, and praising each other's efforts to achieve. Certain cognitive activities and interpersonal dynamics only occur when students get involved in promoting each other's learning. These include orally explaining how to solve problems, discussing the nature of the concepts being learned, teaching one's knowledge to classmates, and connecting present with past learning. Accountability to peers, ability to influence each other's reasoning and

conclusions, social modeling, social support, and interpersonal rewards all increase as the face-to-face interactions among group members increase.

In addition, the verbal and nonverbal responses of other group members provide important information concerning a student's performance. Silent students are uninvolved students who are not contributing to the learning of others as well as themselves. To obtain meaningful face-to-face interaction, the size of groups needs to be small (2–4 members).

4. *Social skills:* Contributing to the success of a cooperative effort requires interpersonal and small group skills. Placing socially unskilled individuals in a group and telling them to cooperate does not guarantee that they will be able to do so effectively. Persons must be taught the leadership, decision-making, trust-building, communication, and conflict-management skills just as purposefully and precisely as academic skills. Procedures and strategies for teaching students social skills may be found in Johnson (1997) and Johnson and F. Johnson (1997).

5. *Group processing:* Group processing exists when group members discuss how well they are achieving their goals and maintaining effective working relationships. Groups need to describe what member actions are helpful and unhelpful and make decisions about what behaviors to continue or change. When difficulties in relating to each other arise, students must engage in group processing and identify, define, and solve the problems they are having working together effectively.

Understanding these five basic elements and developing skills in structuring them allows teachers to (a) adapt cooperative learning to their unique circumstances, needs, and students, (b) fine tune their use of cooperative learning, and (c) prevent and solve problems students have in working together.

## What Do We Know About Cooperative Efforts?

Everyone has to work together; if we can't get everybody working toward common goals, nothing is going to happen. (Harold K. Sperlich, president, Chrysler Corporation)

A great deal of research has been conducted comparing the relative effects of cooperative, competitive, and individualistic efforts on instructional outcomes. During the past 100 years, over 550 experimental and 100 correlational studies have been conducted by a wide variety of researchers in different decades with different age subjects, in different subject areas, and in different settings (see Johnson & Johnson, 1989, for a complete listing and review of these studies).

The type of interdependence structured among students determines how they interact with each other, which, in turn, largely determines instructional outcomes. Structuring situations cooperatively results in students interacting in ways that promote each other's success, structuring situations competitively results in students interacting in ways that oppose each other's success, and structuring situations individualistically results in no interaction among students. These interaction patterns affect numerous instructional outcomes, which may be subsumed within the three broad and interrelated categories of effort exerted to achieve, quality of relationships among participants, and participants' psychological adjustment and social competence (see Figure 1) (Johnson & Johnson, 1989).

### Achievement

Achievement is a we thing, not a me thing, always the product of many hands and heads. (John Atkinson)

Regarding the question of how successful competitive, individualistic, and cooperative efforts are in promoting productivity and achievement, over 375 studies have been conducted in

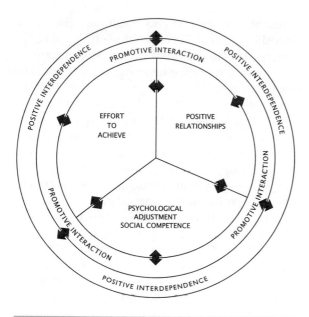

**FIGURE 1**

Outcomes of cooperative learning

*Source:* (Johnson & Johnson, 1989).

Cooperative learning ensures that all students are meaningfully and actively involved in learning. Active, involved students do not tend to engage in disruptive, off-task behavior. Cooperative learning also ensures that students are achieving up to their potential and are experiencing psychological success, so they are motivated to continue to invest energy and effort in learning. Those who experience academic failure are at risk for tuning out and acting up, which often leads to physical or verbal aggression.

## Interpersonal Relationships

A faithful friend is a strong defense, and he that hath found him, hath found a treasure. (Ecclesiastics 6:14)

Over 180 studies have been conducted since the 1940s on the relative impact of cooperative, competitive, and individualistic experiences on interpersonal attraction (Johnson & Johnson, 1989). The data indicate that cooperative experiences promote greater interpersonal attraction than do competitive or individualistic ones. Cooperative learning promotes the development of caring and committed relationships for every student. Even when individuals initially dislike each other or are obviously different from each other, cooperative experiences have been found to promote greater liking than is found in competitive and individualistic situations.

the past 100 years (Johnson & Johnson, 1989). Working together to achieve a common goal produces higher achievement and greater productivity than does working alone. This is so well confirmed by so much research that it stands as one of the strongest principles of social and organizational psychology.

Cooperative learning, furthermore, results in process gain (i.e., more higher-level reasoning, more frequent generation of new ideas and solutions), greater transfer of what is learned within one situation to another (i.e., group to individual transfer), and more time on task than does competitive or individualistic learning. The more conceptual the task, the more problem solving required; the more higher-level reasoning and critical thinking, the more creativity required; and the greater the application required of what is being learned to the real world, the greater the superiority of cooperative over competitive and individualistic efforts.

Cooperative groups help students establish and maintain friendships with peers. As relationships become more positive, there are corresponding improvements in productivity, morale, feelings of personal commitment and responsibility to do the assigned work, willingness to take on and persist in completing difficult tasks, and commitment to peers' success and growth. Absenteeism and turnover of membership decreases. Students who are isolated or alienated from their peers and who do not have friends are more likely to be at risk for violent and destructive behavior than students who experience social support and a sense of belonging.

## Psychological Health and Social Competence

Working cooperatively with peers, and valuing cooperation, results in greater psychological health, higher self-esteem, and greater social competencies than does competing with peers or working independently. When individuals work together to complete assignments, they interact (improving social skills and competencies), promote each other's success (gaining self-worth), and form personal as well as professional relationships (creating the basis for healthy social development).

Cooperative efforts with caring people tend to increase personal ego-strength, self-confidence, independence, and autonomy. They provide the opportunity to share and solve personal problems, which increases an individual's resilience and ability to cope with adversity and stress. The more individuals work cooperatively, the more they see themselves as worthwhile and as having value and the more autonomous and independent they tend to be.

Cooperative groups provide an arena in which individuals develop the interpersonal and small group skills needed to work effectively with diverse schoolmates. Students learn how to communicate effectively, provide leadership, help the group make good decisions, build trust, repair hurt feelings, and understand others' perspectives. Even kindergartners can practice social skills each day in cooperative activities. Cooperative experiences are not a luxury. They are a necessity for the healthy social and psychological development of individuals who can function independently.

## Conclusion

Cooperative learning is the instructional use of small groups in which students work together to maximize their own and each other's learning. Cooperative learning may be differentiated from pseudo groups and traditional classroom learning groups. There are three types of cooperative learning: formal cooperative learning, informal cooperative learning, and cooperative base groups. The basic elements that make cooperation work are positive interdependence, individual accountability, promotive interaction, appropriate use of social skills, and periodic processing of how to improve the effectiveness of the group.

When efforts are structured cooperatively, there is considerable evidence that students will exert more effort to achieve (learn more, use higher-level reasoning strategies more frequently, build more complete and complex conceptual structures, and retain information learned more accurately), build more positive and supportive relationships (including relationships with diverse individuals), and develop in more healthy ways (psychological health, self-esteem, ability to manage stress and adversity).

## REFERENCES

Billion-Dollar Being. (1974). *Topics in applied science.* Golden, CO: Jefferson County Schools.

Johnson, D. W. (1997). *Reaching out: Interpersonal effectiveness and self-actualization* (6th ed.). Boston: Allyn & Bacon.

Johnson, D. W., & Johnson, F. (1997). *Joining together: Group theory and group skills* (6th ed.). Boston: Allyn & Bacon.

Johnson, D. W., & Johnson, R. (1989). *Cooperation and competition: Theory and research.* Edina, MN: Interaction Book Co.

Johnson, D. W., & Johnson, R. (1994). *Leading the cooperative school* (2nd ed.). Edina, MN: Interaction Book Co.

Johnson, D. W., & Johnson, R. (1999). The three Cs of classroom and school management. In H. Freiberg (Ed.), *Beyond behaviorism: Changing the classroom management paradigm.* Boston: Allyn & Bacon.

Johnson, D. W., Johnson, R., & Holubec, E. (1998a). *Advanced cooperative learning* (3rd ed.). Edina, MN: Interaction Book Co.

Johnson, D. W., Johnson, R., & Holubec, E. (1998b). *Cooperation in the classroom* (7th ed.). Edina, MN: Interaction Book Co.

Johnson, D. W., Johnson, R., & Smith, K. (1998). *Active learning: Cooperation in the college classroom* (2nd ed.). Edina, MN: Interaction Book Co.

## POSTNOTE

The authors have been researching and championing cooperative learning for many years, and their efforts have made a major contribution to American education. Cooperative learning has become a staple in both preservice and inservice teacher education. Roger and David Johnson's contributions in developing and researching cooperative learning strategies have placed them among our Classic selections.

Although most educators applaud the idea of cooperative learning, few use it on a regular basis. Many young teachers read about cooperative learning, become advocates, try it a few times with few of the positive results discussed in this article, then put it away in a mental closet (labeled "Great Ideas from the Ivory Tower that don't work in the Trenches") and go on to more traditional "sage on the stage" instructional approaches. The key to a more widespread use of cooperative learning may be captured by the well-known story of the tourist in New York City who stops a native and asks: "Sir, how do I get to Carnegie Hall?" The New Yorker doesn't stop, but yells over his shoulder, "Practice! Practice! Practice!" From personal experiences, we know that becoming skillful at cooperative learning takes more than just knowledge of it. Like Sandy Koufax, knowing the mechanics of throwing a fastball is hardly enough. Our advice: Practice! Practice! Practice!

## DISCUSSION QUESTIONS

1. As a student, what experiences have you had with cooperative learning?

2. Do you agree or disagree with the common criticism that cooperative learning is unfair because it slows down the progress of the academically gifted?

3. Which aspects of cooperative learning are most appealing? Which are least appealing?

# 42  *Homework for All—in Moderation*

## Harris Cooper

Almost like clockwork, the controversy regarding the value of homework has begun again. Homework controversies follow a 30-year cycle, with outcries for more homework or less homework occurring about 15 years apart.

At the start of the 20th century, scientists viewed the mind as a muscle that could be strengthened through mental exercise. People viewed homework favorably as an exercise that could be done at home. During the 1940s, the emphasis in education shifted from drill to problem solving. In the 1950 edition of the *Encyclopedia of Educational Research*, Professor H. J. Otto wrote, "Compulsory homework does not result in sufficiently improved academic accomplishments" (p. 380). The launch of Sputnik by the Russians in the mid-1950s, however, reversed this thinking. The public worried that education in the United States lacked rigor and that it left students unprepared for complex technologies. Homework might accelerate knowledge acquisition.

The 1960s witnessed yet another reversal, with homework perceived as a symptom of needless pressure on students. Educator P. R. Wildman (1968) wrote,

> Whenever homework crowds out social experience, outdoor recreation, and creative activities, and whenever it usurps time devoted to sleep, it is not meeting the basic needs of children and adolescents. (p. 203)

Harris Cooper is chair, Department of Psychological Sciences, University of Missouri–Columbia, Columbia, MO.
From Harris Cooper, "Homework for All—In Moderation," *Educational Leadership*, April 2001, pp. 34–38. Reprinted with permission of the Association for Supervision and Curriculum Development.

In the 1980s, homework again leapt back into favor. A primary stimulus was the report *A Nation at Risk* (National Commission on Excellence in Education, 1983), which cited homework as a defense against the rising tide of mediocrity in U.S. education. The push for more homework continued into the 1990s, fueled by educators who used it to meet increasingly rigorous state-mandated academic standards.

As the century turned, a predictable backlash set in, led by beleaguered parents concerned about their stressed-out children (Winerip, 1999). There is evidence, however, that the outcry results not from a widely held distress, but rather from a vocal minority. A recent national survey of 803 parents of public school students revealed that 64 percent of parents believed that their child was getting "about the right amount" of homework, 25 percent believed that their child was getting "too little" homework, and only 10 percent believed that their child was getting "too much homework" (Public Agenda, 2000, p. 6).

## Research on the Effects of Homework

Policymakers have used research to muster a case for every possible position on homework. Advocates and opponents may refer to small portions of the literature or imprecisely weigh the accumulated evidence. When I received a grant from the National Science Foundation to examine the research on the effects of homework, I had no predisposition about whether homework was good or bad. I attempted to uncover the past evidence, both positive and negative (Cooper, 1989). After reviewing nearly 120 studies of homework's effects, I synthesized the information and discovered factors in the school and home environment that influence homework's impact (Cooper, 1998).

My task began with cataloging homework's positive and negative effects. Among the suggested positive effects of homework, the most obvious is that it will have an immediate impact on the retention and understanding of the material it covers. More indirectly, homework will improve students' study skills, improve their attitudes toward school, and teach them that learning can take place anywhere, not just in school buildings.

Homework has many potential nonacademic benefits as well, most of which relate to fostering independent and responsible character traits. Finally, homework can involve parents in the schooling process, enhancing their appreciation of education and allowing them to express positive attitudes toward their children's achievements and accomplishments.

The suggested negative effects of homework make more interesting reading. Some educators and parents worry that homework could lead to students feeling satiated with academic information. They suggest that any activity can remain rewarding for only so long. If students are required to spend too much time on academic material, they are bound to grow bored with it. Others say that homework denies access to leisure time and community activities. Children learn important lessons, both academic and nonacademic, from soccer and scouts. Another problem is that parental involvement can often turn into parental interference. For example, parents can confuse students if the instructional techniques they use differ from those used by teachers. Homework can also lead to the acquisition of undesirable character traits by promoting cheating, through either the direct copying of assignments or help with homework that goes beyond tutoring.

Finally, homework could accentuate existing social inequities. Students from low-income homes will have more difficulty completing assignments than their middle-class counterparts. Low-income students are more likely to work

after school or may not have quiet, well-lighted places in which to complete their assignments. Homework, opponents argue, is not the great equalizer.

## Does Homework Work?

Three kinds of studies focused on whether homework improves students' achievement (Cooper, 1989).

In the first set of studies, researchers simply compared the achievement of students given homework assignments with students not given homework or any other activity to compensate for their lack of home study. Of these 20 studies, 14 produced effects favoring homework and 6 favored no homework.

The most interesting result from these studies was the dramatic association between grade level and homework's effectiveness. Let us assume that a fictional teacher has two classes of 25 students, and, through some remarkable accident of nature, each student in one class has an exact counterpart in the other. Assume further that the teacher uses the same instructional methods in both classes, except that one class gets homework and the other class does not.

The studies revealed that if the teacher were teaching high school students, the average student in the homework class (50th percentile) would outperform 69 percent of the students in the no-homework class. Put differently, the student who ranked 13th in achievement in the homework class would rank 8th if he or she were shifted into the no-homework class just before the final exam. If the teacher teaches in junior high school, the 13th-ranked homework-doer would rank 10th in the no-homework class. In elementary school, however, homework would not help the student surpass other schoolmates.

The second set of evidence compared homework to in-class supervised study. In these investigations, students not receiving homework were required to engage in some other kind of activity. Most often, students did homework-like assignments while in school.

These studies were not as favorable toward homework as the first set. Overall, the positive effect of homework was about half of what it was when compared to no assignment for home study. This should not surprise us. There is no reason to believe that homework would be more effective than in-class study for improving test scores. Most important in these studies was the emergence once again of a strong grade-level effect. When homework and in-class study were compared in elementary schools, in-class study proved superior. In junior high, homework was superior, and in high school the superiority of homework was most impressive.

The third set of studies correlated the amount of time students reported spending on homework with their achievement levels. Many of the correlations in these 50 studies came from statewide surveys or national assessments. Of course, correlation does not mean causation; it is just as likely that high achievement causes students to do more homework as vice versa.

In all, 43 correlations indicated that students who did more homework had better achievement

## What Are the Effects of Homework?

**Positive Effects**

*Immediate achievement and learning*

- better retention of factual knowledge
- increased understanding
- better critical thinking, concept formation, information processing
- curriculum enrichment

*Long-term academic benefits*

- learning during leisure time
- improved attitude toward school
- better study habits and skills

*Nonacademic benefits*

- greater self-direction
- greater self-discipline
- better time organization
- more inquisitiveness
- more independent problem solving

*Greater parental appreciation of and involvement in schooling*

**Negative Effects**

*Satiation*

- loss of interest in academic material
- physical and emotional fatigue
- denial of access to leisure time and community activities

*Parental interference*

- pressure to complete assignments and perform well
- conflicting instructional techniques

*Cheating*

- copying from other students
- help beyond tutoring

*Increased differences between students from low-income and affluent homes* scores, whereas only 7 indicated that those who did more homework had lower achievement scores. Again, a strong grade-level qualifier appeared. For students in grades 3–5, the correlation between the amount of homework and achievement was nearly zero; for students in grade 6–9, the correlation was somewhat higher (+0.07); and for high school students, the correlation was highest (+0.25). The new evidence that has accumulated since my original review of the research more than a decade ago lends even more support to these findings (Cooper, Lindsay, Nye, & Greathouse, 1998).

In sum, homework has substantial positive effects on the achievement of high school students, and junior high students benefit about half as much. For elementary school students, the effect of homework on achievement is trivial, if it exists at all.

Cognitive and developmental psychology sheds light on the grade-level effect (Muhlenbruck, Cooper, Nye, & Lindsay, 2000). Studies indicate that younger students have limited attention spans, or more specifically, limited abilities to tune out distractions. Thus, the distractions at home more easily entice them away from the books spread out on the kitchen table. Also, younger students haven't yet learned proper study skills. They don't know how to apportion their time between easy and hard tasks or how to engage in effective self-testing. Each of these cognitive limitations suggests that homework should not be expected to impressively improve test scores and that expectations for homework assigned in primary grades should be aligned with other goals.

## An Optimum Amount

Nine studies correlate time on homework with achievement, looking at how performance levels are a function of the amount of time spent on homework (Cooper, 1989). As we might expect, the line of progress is flat for younger students.

For junior high school students, achievement continues to improve with more homework until assignments last between one and two hours a night, at which point achievement levels do not improve. For high school students, however, progress continues to go up to the largest number of hours spent on homework each night. Although common sense dictates that there is a point of diminishing returns, the more homework that high school students do, the higher their achievement levels.

## Guidelines for Homework Policies

The following homework policy guidelines (Cooper, 2001) can make homework an effective teaching tool. The guidelines are general and should serve only as a starting point for discussions about homework.

### Coordinate Policies

Districts, schools, and classrooms should coordinate their policies. Some of the issues addressed at each level are unique, but others overlap.

### State the Rationale

Districts need to state clearly the broad rationale for homework, why it is often mandatory, and what the general time requirements ought to be. Schools need to further specify time requirements, coordinate assignments among classes (if desired), and set out the role of teachers and principals. Teachers need to adopt classroom policies that outline what is expected of students and why.

### Assign Homework

The amount and type of homework that students do should depend on their developmental level and the quality of their support at home. In a guide for parents, the National Parent Teacher

Association and the National Education Association (2000) state,

> Most educators agree that for children in grades K–2, homework is most effective when it does not exceed 10–20 minutes each day; older children, in grades 3–6, can handle 30–60 minutes a day.

Educators often refer to this as the Ten Minute Rule, or 10 minutes multiplied by the student's grade level per night. My combined analyses of dozens of studies support these recommendations. If educators and parents expect homework far out of line with these recommendations to result in big gains in test scores, they are likely to be disappointed.

If homework for younger students bears no relation to achievement, why assign it at all? As I noted earlier, homework can have beneficial effects other than knowledge acquisition. In the primary grades, homework can help younger students develop good study habits and grow as their cognitive capacities mature. Homework can help students recognize that they can learn at home as well as at school. It can foster independent learning and responsible character traits. Homework can give parents an opportunity to see what's going on at school and express positive attitudes toward achievement. To obtain these outcomes, however, homework assignments in elementary grades should be short, employ materials commonly found in the home, and lead to successful experiences.

## Use Other Approaches, Too

Homework can be an effective instructional device, but it must serve different purposes at different grade levels. Our expectations for its effects, especially in the short term and in earlier grades, must be modest. Homework should be one of several approaches we use, along with soccer and scouts, to show our children that learning takes place everywhere.

The question for educators and parents is not whether homework has positive or negative effects. Either of these effects can occur. To avoid the negative effects, flexible homework policies should let individual schools and teachers take into account the unique needs and circumstances of their students. School districts, teachers, and parents should avoid the extremes.

## REFERENCES

Cooper, H. (1989). *Homework.* New York: Longman.

Cooper, H. (1998). *Synthesizing research: A guide for literature reviews* (3rd ed.). Thousand Oaks, CA: Sage.

Cooper, H. (2001). *The battle over homework: Common ground for administrators, teachers, and parents.* Newbury Park, CA: Corwin Press.

Cooper, H., Lindsay, J. J., Nye, B., & Greathouse, S. (1998). Relationships between attitudes about homework, the amount of homework assigned and completed, and student achievement. *Journal of Educational Psychology, 90,* 70–83.

Muhlenbruck, L., Cooper, H., Nye, B., & Lindsay, J. J. (2000). Homework and achievement: Explaining the different relations at the elementary and secondary school levels. *Social Psychology of Education, 4,* 295–317.

National Commission on Excellence in Education. (1983). *A nation at risk: The imperative for educational reform.* Washington. DC: U.S. Department of Education.

National Parent Teacher Association and National Education Association (2000). *Helping your student get the most out of homework* [Online]. Available: www. pta.org/programs/edulibr/homework.htm

Otto, H. J. (1950). Elementary education. In W. S. Monroe (Ed.), *Encyclopedia of Educational Research* (pp. 380–381). New York: Macmillan.

Public Agenda. (2000). *Survey finds little sign of backlash against academic standards or standardized tests* [Online]. New York: Author. Available: www.publicagenda.org/aboutpa/pdf/standards-backlash.pdf

Wildman, P. R. (1968). Homework pressures. *Peabody Journal of Education, 45,* 202–204.

Winerip. M. (1999, January 3). Homework bound. *New York Times: Education Life,* pp. 28–31.

## POSTNOTE

School homework—how much, when, what kind? Educators and parents alike have debated questions like these for decades. The author of this article, Harris Cooper, clearly reveals the benefits and drawbacks of homework. He suggests a moderate approach based on the unique needs and circumstances of students. We strongly agree with this position.

One of the often ignored benefits of homework is helping children to develop a solid work ethic. The habit of independently sitting down to work and carefully completing assignments is an important contributor to academic success and an invaluable life-skill. In the abstract, homework is neither good nor bad, but depending on the circumstances of each school and each child, it can help to further unlock a student's potential. Like many things in life, however, when overused or poorly used, negative consequences can occur.

## DISCUSSION QUESTIONS

1. Did any of the research findings on homework surprise you? If so, which ones?

2. Do you think homework should be graded? Why or why not?

3. One of the strongest arguments against grading homework is that grading usually reflects socioeconomic status and parental involvement. That is, more affluent families pitch in to either help or ensure that the children do their homework. What is your response to this argument?

# 43

# *Assessment Crisis: The Absence of Assessment* FOR *Learning*

## Richard J. Stiggins

If we are finally to connect assessment to school improvement in meaningful ways, we must come to see assessment through new eyes. Our failure to find a potent connection has resulted in a deep and intensifying crisis in assessment in American education. Few elected officials are aware of this crisis, and almost no school officials know how to address it. Our current assessment systems are harming huge numbers of students for reasons that few understand.

**TERMS TO NOTE**

Standardized tests

Assessment

And that harm arises directly from our failure to balance our use of standardized tests and classroom assessments in the service of school improvement. When it comes to assessment, we have been trying to find answers to the wrong questions.

Politicians routinely ask. How can we use assessment as the basis for doling our rewards and punishments to increase teacher and student effort? They want to know how we can intensify the intimidation associated with annual testing so as to force greater achievement. How we answer these questions will certainly affect schools. But that impact will not always be positive. Moreover, politicians who ask such questions typically look past a far more important pair of prior questions: How can we use assessment to help all our students *want* to learn? How can we help them feel *able* to learn? Without answers to these questions, there will be no school improvement. I explain why below.

School administrators in federal, state, and local education agencies contribute to our increasingly damaging assessment crisis when they merely bow to politicians' beliefs and focus unwaveringly on the question of how to make our test scores go up. To be sure, accountability for student learning is important. I am not opposed to high-stakes testing to verify school quality—as long as the tests are of sound quality.[1] However, our concern for test scores must be preceded by a consideration of more fundamental questions: Are our current approaches to assessment improving student learning? Might other approaches to assessment have a greater impact? Can we design state and district assessment systems that have the effect of helping our students want to learn and feel able to learn?

Furthermore, the measurement community, of which I am a member, also has missed an essential point. For decades. our priorities have manifested the belief that our job is to discover ever more sophisticated and efficient ways of generating valid and reliable test scores. Again, to be sure, accurate scores are essential. But there remains an unasked prior question: How can we maximize the positive impact of our scores on learners? Put another way, How can we be sure that our assessment instruments, procedures, and scores serve to help learners want to learn and feel able to learn?

We are a nation obsessed with the belief that the path to school improvement is paved with better, more frequent, and more intense standardized testing. The problem is that such tests, ostensibly developed to "leave no student behind," are in fact causing major segments of our student population to be left behind because the tests cause many to give up in hopelessness—just the opposite effect from that which politicians intended.

Student achievement suffers because these once-a-year tests are incapable of providing teachers with the moment-to-moment and day-to-day information about student achievement that they need to make crucial instructional decisions. Teachers must rely on classroom assessment to do this. The problem is that teachers are unable to gather or effectively use dependable information on student achievement each day because of the drain of resources for excessive standardized testing. There are no resources left to train teachers to create and conduct appropriate classroom assessments. For the same reasons, district and building administrators have not been trained to build assessment systems that balance standardized tests and classroom assessments. As a direct result of these chronic, long-standing problems, our classroom, building, district, state, and national assessment systems remain in constant crisis, and students suffer the consequences. All school practitioners know this, yet almost no politicians do.

We know how to build healthy assessment environments that can meet the information needs of all instructional decision makers, help students want to learn and feel able to learn, and thus support unprecedented increases in student achievement. But to achieve this goal, we must put in place the mechanisms that will make healthy assessment possible. Creating those mechanisms will require that we begin to see assessment through new eyes. The well-being of our students depends on our willingness to do so.

### The Evolution of Our Vision of Excellence in Assessment

The evolution of assessment in the United States over the past five decades has led to the strongly held view that school improvement requires:

▶ the articulation of higher achievement *standards,*

▶ the transformation of those expectations into rigorous *assessments,* and

▶ the expectation of *accountability* on the part of educators for student achievement, as reflected in test scores.

Standards frame accepted or valued definitions of academic success. Accountability compels attention to these standards as educators plan and deliver instruction in the classroom. Assessment provides the evidence of success on the part of students, teachers, and the system.

To maximize the energy devoted to school improvement, we have "raised the bar" by setting world-class standards for student achievement, as opposed to minimum competencies. To further intensify the impact of our standards and assessments, policy makers often attach the promise of rewards for schools that produce high scores and sanctions for schools that do not.

In this context, we rely on high-stakes assessments *of learning* to inform our decisions about accountability. These tests tell us how much students have learned, whether standards are being met, and whether educators have done the job they were hired to do.

**TERM TO NOTE**
High-stakes tests

Such assessments of learning have been the norm throughout the U.S. for decades. We began with standardized college admissions tests in the early decades of the last century, and this use of testing continues essentially unchanged today. But these tests are not used merely for college admission. For decades, we have ranked states according to average SAT scores.

Meanwhile, in response to demands for accountability in public schools in the 1960s, we launched districtwide standardized testing programs that also remain in place today. In the 1970s, we began the broad implementation of statewide testing programs, and these programs have spread throughout the land. Also in the 1970s and extending into the 1980s, we added a national assessment program that continues to this day. During the 1990s, we became deeply involved and invested in international assessment programs. Across the nation, across the various levels of schooling, and over the decades, we have invested billions of dollars to ensure the accuracy of the scores on these assessments of learning. Now in 2002, President Bush has signed a school reform measure that requires standardized testing of every pupil in the U.S. in mathematics and reading every year in grades 3 through 8, once again revealing our faith in assessment as a tool for school improvement.

In the context of school improvement, we have seen assessment merely as an index of the success of our efforts. It is testimony to our societal belief in the power of standardized tests that we would permit so many levels of testing to remain in place, all at the same time and at very high cost. Clearly, over the decades, we have believed that by checking achievement status and reporting the results to the public we can apply the pressure needed to intensify—and thus speed—school improvement. At the same time, we have believed that providing policy makers and practicing educators with test results can inform the critically important school improvement decisions that are made at district, state, and federal levels.

## The Flaw in the Vision

The assessment environment described above is a direct manifestation of a set of societal beliefs about what role assessment ought to play in American schools. Over the decades, we have succeeded in carrying these beliefs to unfortunate extremes.

For example, we have believed that assessment should serve two purposes: inform decisions and motivate learning. With respect to the former, we have built our assessment systems around the belief that the most important decisions are made by those program planners and policy makers whose actions affect the broadest range of classrooms and students. The broader the reach of the decision makers (across an entire school district or state), the more weight we have given to meeting their information needs first. This is the foundation of our strong belief in the power of standardized tests. These are the tests that provide comparable data that can be aggregated across schools, districts, and states to inform far-reaching programmatic decisions.

With respect to the use of assessment to motivate, we all grew up in classrooms in which our teachers believed that the way to maximize learning was to maximize anxiety, and assessment has always been the great intimidator. Because of their own very successful experiences in ascending to positions of leadership and authority, most policy makers and school leaders share the world view that, "when the going gets tough, the tough get going." They learned that the way to succeed when confronted with a tougher challenge is to redouble your efforts—work harder and work smarter. If you do so, you win. And so, they contend, the way to cause students to learn more—and thus the way to improve schools—is to confront them with a tougher challenge. This will cause them to redouble their efforts, they will learn more, their test scores will go up, and the schools will become more effective. We can motivate students to greater effort, they believe, by "setting higher academic standards," "raising the bar," and implementing more high-stakes testing. This is the foundation of our belief in the power of accountability-oriented standardized tests to drive school improvement.

In point of fact, when some students are confronted with the tougher challenge of high-stakes testing, they do redouble their efforts, and they do learn more than they would have without the added incentive. Please note, however, that I said this is true for "some students."

Another huge segment of our student population, when confronted with an even tougher challenge than the one that it has already been failing at, will not redouble its efforts—a point that most people are missing. These students will see both the new high standards and the demand for higher test scores as unattainable for them, and they will *give up in hopelessness*.

Many political and school leaders have never experienced the painful, embarrassing, and discouraging trauma of chronic and public academic failure. As a result, they have no way of anticipating or understanding how their high-stakes testing program, whether local or statewide, could lead to even greater failure for large numbers of students. But tapping the intimidation power of standardized tests for public accountability has an effect on the success of this segment of the student population that is exactly the opposite of what we intend.

Thus it is folly to build our assessment environments on the assumption that standardized testing will have the same effect on all students. It will not. Some students approach the tests with a strong personal academic history and an expectation of success. Others approach them with a personal history and expectation of very painful failure. Some come to slay the dragon, while others expect to be devoured by it. As a result, high-stakes assessment will enhance the learning of some while discouraging others and causing them to give up. Yet, as they attempt to weave assessment into the school improvement equation, federal, state, and local policy makers seem unable to understand or to accommodate this difference.

## A More Powerful Vision

There is another way in which assessment can contribute to the development of effective schools that has been largely ignored in the evolution of the standards, assessment, and accountability movement described above. We can also use assessments *for learning*.[2] If assessments *of learning* provide evidence of achievement for public reporting, then assessments *for learning* serve to help students learn more. The crucial distinction is between assessment to determine the status of learning and assessment to promote greater learning.

Assessments *of* and *for* learning are both important. Since we in the U.S. already have many assessments *of* learning in place, if we are to balance the two, we must make a much stronger investment in assessment *for* learning. We can realize unprecedented gains in achievement if we turn the current day-to-day classroom assessment process into a more powerful tool for learning. We know that schools will be held

accountable for raising test scores. Now we must provide teachers with the assessment tools needed to do the job.

It is tempting to equate the idea of assessment *for learning* with our more common term, "formative assessment." But they are not the same. Assessment *for learning* is about far more then testing more frequently or providing teachers with evidence so that they can revise instruction, although these steps are part of it. In addition, we now understand that assessment *for learning* must involve students in the process.

**TERMS TO NOTE**
Formative assessment
Summative assessment

When they assess *for learning,* teachers use the classroom assessment process and the continuous flow of information about student achievement that it provides in order to advance, not merely check on, student learning. They do this by:

▶ understanding and articulating *in advance of teaching* the achievement targets that their students are to hit;

▶ informing their students about those learning goals, *in terms that students understand,* from the very beginning of the teaching and learning process;

▶ becoming assessment literate and thus able to transform their expectations into assessment exercises and scoring procedures that *accurately reflect student achievement;*

▶ using classroom assessments to *build students' confidence* in themselves as learners and help them take responsibility for their own learning, so as to lay a foundation for lifelong learning;

▶ translating classroom assessment results into frequent *descriptive feedback* (versus judgmental feedback) for students, providing them with specific insights as to how to improve;

▶ continuously *adjusting instruction* based on the results of classroom assessments;

▶ engaging students in *regular self-assessment,* with standards held constant so that students can watch themselves grow over time and thus feel in charge of their own success; and

▶ actively involving students in *communicating* with their teacher and their families about their achievement status and improvement.

In short, the effect of assessment *for learning*, as it plays out in the classroom, is that students keep learning and remain confident that they can continue to learn at productive levels if they keep trying to learn. In other words, students don't give up in frustration or hopelessness.

## Are Teachers Ready?

Few teachers are prepared to face the challenges of classroom assessment because they have not been given the opportunity to learn to do so. It is currently the case that only about a dozen states explicitly require competence in assessment as a condition to be licensed to teach. Moreover, there is no licensing examination in place at the state or federal level in the U.S. that verifies competence in assessment. Thus teacher preparation programs have taken little note of competence in assessment, and the vast majority of programs fail to provide the assessment literacy required to enable teachers to engage in assessment *for learning*. It has been so for decades.

Furthermore, lest we believe that teachers can turn to their principals for help, it is currently the case that almost no states require competence in assessment as a condition to be licensed as a principal or school administrator at any level. Consequently, assessment training is almost nonexistent in administrator training programs. It has been so for decades.

Thus we remain a national faculty that is unschooled in the principles of sound assessment—whether assessment *of* or *for* learning. This fact has been a matter of record for decades. To date, as a nation, we have invested almost nothing in assessment *for learning*. Teachers rarely have the opportunity to learn how to use assessment as a teaching and learning tool. And our vigorous

efforts to assess learning through our various layers of standardized tests cannot overcome the effects of this reality.

As a result of this state of affairs, we face the danger that student progress may be mismeasured, day to day, in classrooms across the nation. That means that all the critically important day-to-day instructional decisions made by students, teachers, and parents may be based on misinformation about student success. The result is the misdiagnosis of student needs, students' misunderstanding of their own ability to learn, miscommunication to parents and others about student progress, and virtually no effective assessment *for learning* in classrooms. The extremely harmful consequences for student learning are obvious.

## Relevant Position Statements

The dire consequences of this assessment crisis and the urgent need for action have not gone unnoticed. For example, during the 1990s, virtually every professional association that had anything to do with teaching adopted standards of professional competence for teachers that include an assessment component.[3] This group included the American Federation of Teachers (AFT), the National Education Association (NEA), the Council of Chief State School Officers, the National Board for Professional Teaching Standards, and the National Council on Measurement in Education (NCME).

The documents that were issued included a collaborative statement of assessment competencies for teachers developed by a joint committee representing AFT, NEA, and NCME.[4] In addition to other standards, this joint statement expects teachers to be trained to choose and develop proper assessment methods; to administer, score, and interpret assessment results; to connect those results to specific decisions; to assign grades appropriately; and to communicate effectively about student achievement. It is troubling to realize that these standards are more than a decade old and still have had little impact on the preparation of teachers and administrators.

In its 2001 report, the Committee on the Foundations of Assessment of the National Research Council advanced recommendations for the development of assessment in American schools that included the following:

> *Recommendation 9: Instruction in how students learn and how learning can be assessed should be a major component of teacher preservice and professional development programs.* This training should be linked to actual experience in classrooms in assessing and interpreting the development of student competence. To ensure that this occurs, state and national standards for teacher licensure and program accreditation should include specific requirements focused on the proper integration of learning and assessment in teachers' educational experience.[5]

\* \* \*

> *Recommendation 11: The balance of mandates and resources should be shifted from an emphasis on external forms of assessment to an increased emphasis on classroom formative assessment designed to assist learning.*[6]

Similarly, the Commission on Instructionally Supportive Assessment convened by the American Association of School Administrators, the National Association of Elementary School Principals, the National Association of Secondary School Principals, the NEA, and the National Middle School Association included the following in its list of nine requirements for state-mandated accountability tests:

> *Requirement 8: A state must ensure that educators receive professional development focused on how to optimize children's learning based on the results of instructionally supportive assessment.*[7]

We understand what teachers need to know and the proficiencies that they need to develop in order to be able to establish and maintain productive assessment environments. The challenge we face is to provide the opportunity for teachers to master those essential classroom assessment competencies. The depth of this challenge becomes clear when we realize that we must provide opportunities both for new teachers to gain these competencies before they enter the classroom and for experienced teachers who had no chance to master them during their training to gain them as well.

## Balancing Assessments of and for Learning

Therefore, our national assessment priority should be to make certain that assessments both *of* and *for* learning are accurate in their depiction of student achievement and are used to benefit students. Since our standardized assessments *of learning* have been developed by professionals and are currently in place, they are poised to detect any improvements in the level or rate of student achievement.

But these tests provide information only once a year, and we must not delude ourselves into believing that they can serve all assessment purposes. They can reflect large-group increases or decreases in learning on an annual basis, and they can serve as gatekeepers for high-stakes decisions. They cannot inform the moment-to-moment, day-to-day, and week-to-week instructional decisions faced by students and teachers seeking to manage the learning process as it unfolds. They cannot diagnose student needs during learning, tell students what study tactics are or are not working, or keep parents informed about how to support the work of their children. These kinds of uses require assessments *for learning*. The critical question for school improvement is, What would happen to standardized test scores if we brought assessments *for learning* online as a full partner in support of student learning? Several published reviews of research reveal the startling and very encouraging answer.

In 1984 Benjamin Bloom provided a summary of research comparing standard whole-class instruction (the control condition) with two experimental interventions, a mastery learning environment and one-on-one tutoring of individual students. One hallmark of both experimental conditions was the extensive use of classroom assessment *for learning* as a key part of the instructional process. The analyses revealed differences ranging from one to two standard deviations in student achievement attributable to differences between experimental and control conditions.[8]

In their 1998 research review, Paul Black and Dylan Wiliam examined the research literature on assessment worldwide, asking if improved formative (i.e., classroom) assessments yield higher student achievement as reflected in summative assessments. If so, they asked, what kinds of improvements in classroom assessment practice are likely to yield the greatest gains in achievement?

Black and Wiliam uncovered and then synthesized more than 250 articles that addressed these issues. Of these, several dozen directly addressed the question of the impact on student learning with sufficient scientific rigor and experimental control to permit firm conclusions. Upon pooling the information on the estimated effects of improved formative assessment on summative test scores, they reported unprecedented positive effects on student achievement. They reported effect sizes of one-half to a full standard deviation. Furthermore, Black and Wiliam reported that "improved formative assessment helps low achievers more than other students and so reduces the range of achievement while raising achievement overall."[9] This result has direct implications for districts seeking to reduce achievement gaps between minorities and other students. Hypothetically, if assessment *for learning*, as described above, became standard practice only in classrooms of low-achieving, low-socioeconomic-status students, the achievement gaps that trouble us so deeply today would be erased. I know of no other school improvement innovation that can claim effects of this nature or size.

To fully appreciate the magnitude of the effect sizes cited above, readers need to understand that a gain of one standard deviation, applied to the middle of the test score distribution on commonly used standardized achievement tests, can yield average gains of more than 30 percentile points, two grade-equivalents, or 100 points on the SAT scale. Black and Wiliam report that gains of this magnitude, if applied to the most recent results of the Third International Mathematics and Science Study, would have raised a nation in the middle of the pack among the 42 participating countries (where the U.S. is ranked) to the top five.

This research reveals that these achievement gains are maximized in contexts where educators increase the accuracy of classroom assessments, provide students with frequent informative feedback (versus infrequent judgmental feedback), and involve students deeply in the classroom assessment, record keeping, and communication processes. In short, these gains are maximized where teachers apply the principles of assessment *for learning*.

Black and Wiliam conclude their summary of self-assessment by students as follows:

> Thus self-assessment by pupils, far from being a luxury, is in fact *an essential component of formative assessment*. When anyone is trying to learn, feedback about the effort has three elements: redefinition of the *desired goal*, evidence about *present position*, and some understanding of a *way to close the gap between the two*. All three must be understood to some degree by anyone before he or she can take action to improve learning.[10] (Emphasis in original.)

## Anticipating the Benefits of Balance

Students benefit from assessment *for learning* in several critical ways. First, they become more confident learners because they get to watch themselves succeeding. Thus success permits them to take the risk of continuing to try to learn. The result is greater achievement for all students—especially low achievers, which helps reduce the achievement gap between middle-class and low-socioeconomic-status students. Furthermore, students come to understand what it means to be in charge of their own learning—to monitor their own success and make decisions that bring greater success. This is the foundation of lifelong learning.

Teachers benefit because their students become more motivated to learn. Furthermore, their instructional decisions are informed by more accurate information about student achievement. Teachers also benefit from the savings in time that result from their ability to develop and use classroom assessments more efficiently.

Parents benefit as well in seeing higher achievement and greater enthusiasm for learning in their children. They also come to understand that their children are learning to manage their own lifelong learning.

School administrators and instructional leaders benefit from the reality of meeting accountability standards and from the public recognition of doing so. Political officials benefit in the same way. When schools work more effectively, both political leaders and school leaders are recognized as contributing to that outcome.

In short, everyone wins. There are no losers. But the price that we must pay to achieve such benefits is an investment in teachers and their classroom assessment practices. We must initiate a program of professional development specifically designed to give teachers the expertise they need to assess *for learning.*

### An Action Plan

If we wish to maximize student achievement in the U.S., we must pay far greater attention to the improvement of classroom assessment. Both assessment *of learning* and assessment *for learning* are essential. One is in place; the other is not. Therefore, we must:

▶ match every dollar invested in instruments and procedures intended for assessment *of learning* at national, state, and local levels with another dollar devoted to the development of assessment *for learning;*

▶ launch a comprehensive, long-term professional development program at the national, state, and local levels to foster literacy in classroom assessment for teachers, allocating sufficient resources to provide them with the opportunity to learn and grow professionally;

▶ launch a similar professional development program in effective large-scale and classroom assessment for state, district, and building administrators, teaching them how to provide leadership in this area of professional practice;

▶ change teacher and administrator licensing standards in every state and in all national certification contexts to reflect an expectation of competence in assessment both *of* and *for* learning; and

▶ require all teacher and administrator preparation programs to ensure that graduates are assessment literate—in terms both of promoting and of documenting student learning.

Federal education officials, state policy makers, and local school leaders must allocate resources in equal proportions to ensure the accuracy and effective use of assessments both *of* and *for* learning. Only then can we reassure families that their children are free from the harm that results from the mismeasurement of their achievement in schools. Only then can we maximize students' confidence in themselves as learners. Only then can we raise achievement levels for all students and "leave no child behind."

### NOTES

1. For specific standards of quality, refer to Commission on Instructionally Supportive Assessment, *Building Tests to Support Instruction and Accountability* (Washington, D.C.: AASA, NAESP, NASSP, NEA, and NMSA, 2001).

2. This term was coined by Assessment Reform Group, *Assessment for Learning: Beyond the Black Box* (Cambridge: School of Education, Cambridge University, 1999).

3. See the special section on Quality Teaching for the 21st Century in the November 1996 *Phi Delta Kappan*, pp. 190–227.

4. American Federation of Teachers, National Council on Measurement in Education, and National Education Association, "Standards for Teacher Competence in Educational Assessment of Students," *Educational Measurement: Issues and Practice,* vol. 9, no. 4, 1990, pp. 30–32.

5. James W. Pellegrino, Naomi Chudowsky, and Robert Glaser, eds., *Knowing What Students Know: The Science and Design of Educational Assessment* (Washington, D.C.: National Academy Press, 2001), p. 14.

6. Ibid.

7. Commission on Instructionally Supportive Assessment, p. 25.

8. Benjamin Bloom, "The Search for Methods of Group Instruction as Effective as One-on-One Tutoring," *Educational Leadership,* May 1984, pp. 4–17.

9. Paul Black and Dylan Wiliam, "Inside the Black Box: Raising Standards Through Classroom Assessment," *Phi Delta Kappan,* October 1998, p. 141. Their work is reported in more detail in idem, "Assessment and Classroom Learning," *Assessment in Education,* March 1998, pp. 7–74.

10. Black and Wiliam, "Inside the Black Box," p. 143.

## POSTNOTE

Rick Stiggins asks a very important question, one that is rarely asked: "How can we be sure that our assessment instruments, procedures, and scores serve to help learners want to learn and feel able to learn?" Policymakers seem much more interested in assessment for accountability purposes, that is, holding educators and students accountable for student learning by offering rewards to those who succeed and punishments for those who don't. The high-stakes testing that accompanies most states' standards of learning are usually worthless as guides to teachers for adjusting instructional decisions to help particular students. The results come months after the students have taken the tests and don't provide enough information to guide students in self-assessments to improve their learning. Stiggins's call for more assessment *for* learning to balance the current overemphasis of assessment *of* learning makes great sense to us.

## DISCUSSION QUESTIONS

1. Stiggins asserts that most teachers don't receive enough training in the use and interpretation of assessment instruments. Do you agree with him? Why or why not?

2. Thinking back on your own educational experiences, have you ever experienced assessments (e.g., test, paper, project) that motivated you to want to learn more? If so, were they rare or frequent occurrences?

3. Describe the most creative assessment you ever completed as a student. What made it creative?

## 44

# Mapping a Route Toward Differentiated Instruction

## Carol Ann Tomlinson

Developing academically responsive class-rooms is important for a country built on the twin values of equality and excellence. Our schools can achieve both of these competing values only to the degree that they can establish heterogeneous communities of learning (attending to issues of equity) built solidly on high-quality curriculum and instruction that strive to maximize the capacity of each learner (attending to issues of excellence).

A serious pursuit of differentiation, or personalized instruction, causes us to grapple with many of our traditional—if questionable—ways of "doing school." Is it reasonable to expect all 2nd graders to learn the same thing, in the same ways, over the same time span? Do single-textbook adoptions send inaccurate messages about the sameness of all learners? Can students learn to take more responsibility for their own learning? Do report cards drive our instruction? Should the classroom teacher be a solitary specialist on all learner needs, or could we support genuinely effective generalist-specialist teams? Can we reconcile learning standards with learner variance?

**TERM TO NOTE**
Differentiation

The questions resist comfortable answers—and are powerfully important. En route to answering them, we try various roads to differentiation. The concreteness of having something ready to do Monday morning is satisfying—and inescapable. After all, the students will arrive and the day must be planned. So we talk about using reading buddies in varied ways to support a range of readers or perhaps developing a learning contract with several options for practicing math skills. Maybe we could try a tiered lesson or interest centers. Three students who clearly understand the chapter need an independent study project. Perhaps we should begin with a differentiated project assignment, allowing students to choose a project about the Middle Ages. That's often how our journey toward differentiation begins.

The nature of teaching requires doing. There's not much time to sit and ponder the imponderables. To a point, that's fine—and, in any case, inevitable. A reflective teacher can test many principles from everyday interactions in the classroom. In other words, philosophy can derive from action.

We can't skip one step, however. The first step in making differentiation work is the hardest. In fact, the same first step is required to make all teaching and learning effective: We have to know where we want to end up before we start out—and plan to get there. That is, we must have solid curriculum and instruction in place before we differentiate them. That's harder than it seems.

Carol Ann Tomlinson is professor of educational leadership, foundations and policy at the Curry School of Education, University of Virginia, Charlottesville, VA. She is the author of *The Differentiated Classroom: Responding to the Needs of All Learners* (ASCD, 1999). From Carol Ann Tomlinson, "Mapping a Route Toward Differentiated Instruction," *Educational Leadership*, September 1999, pp. 12–16. Reprinted with permission of the Association for Supervision and Curriculum Development. Copyright © 1999 by ASCD. All rights reserved.

## Looking Inside Two Classrooms

Mr. Appleton is teaching about ancient Rome. His students are reading the textbook in class today. He suggests that they take notes of important details as they read. When they finish, they answer the questions at the end of the chapter. Students who don't finish must do so at home. Tomorrow, they will answer the questions together in class. Mr. Appleton likes to lecture and works hard to prepare his lectures. He expects students to take notes. Later, he will give a quiz on both the notes and the text. He will give students a study sheet before the test, clearly spelling out what will be on the test.

Mrs. Baker is also teaching about ancient Rome. She gives her students graphic organizers to use as they read the textbook chapter and goes over the organizers with the class so that anyone who missed details can fill them in. She brings in pictures of the art and the architecture of the period and tells how important the Romans were in shaping our architecture, language, and laws. When she invites some students to dress in togas for a future class, someone suggests bringing in food so that they can have a Roman banquet—and they do. One day, students do a word-search puzzle of vocabulary words about Rome. On another day, they watch a movie clip that shows gladiators and the Colosseum and talk about the favored "entertainment" of the period. Later, Mrs. Baker reads aloud several myths, and students talk about the myths that they remember from 6th grade. When it's time to study for the test, the teacher lets students go over the chapter together, which they like much better than working at home alone, she says.

She also wants students to like studying about Rome, so she offers a choice of 10 projects. Among the options are creating a poster listing important Roman gods and goddesses, their roles, and their symbols; developing a travel brochure for ancient Rome that a Roman of the day might have used; writing a poem about life in Rome; dressing dolls like citizens of Rome or drawing the fashions of the time; building a model of an important ancient Roman building or a Roman villa; and making a map of the Holy Roman Empire. Students can also propose their own topic.

## Thinking About the Two Classrooms

Mr. Appleton's class is not differentiated. He does not appear to notice or respond to student differences. Mrs. Baker's is differentiated—at least

by some definitions. Each class has serious flaws in its foundations, however, and for that reason, Mrs. Baker's class may not be any more successful than Mr. Appleton's—and perhaps less so.

Successful teaching requires two elements: student understanding and student engagement. In other words, students must really understand, or make sense of, what they have studied. They should also feel engaged in or "hooked by" the ways that they have learned. The latter can greatly enhance the former and can help young people realize that learning is satisfying.

Mr. Appleton's class appears to lack engagement. There's nothing much to make learning appealing. He may be satisfied by his lecture, but it's doubtful that many of the students are impressed. It is also doubtful that much real student understanding will come from the teaching-learning scenario. Rather, the goal seems to be memorizing data for a test.

Memorizing and understanding are very different. The first has a short life span and little potential to transfer into a broader world. However, at least Mr. Appleton appears clear about what the students should memorize for the test. Mrs. Baker's class lacks even that clarity.

Students in Mrs. Baker's classroom are likely engaged. It is a lively, learner-friendly place with opportunity for student movement, student choice, and peer work. Further, Mrs. Baker's list of project options draws on different student interests or talents—and she is even open to their suggestions.

Although Mrs. Baker succeeds to some degree with engagement, a clear sense of what students should understand as a result of their study is almost totally missing. Thus her careful work to provide choice and to build a comfortable environment for her learners may not net meaningful, long-term learning. Her students are studying "something about ancient Rome." Nothing focuses or ties together the ideas and information that they encounter. Activities are more about being happy than about making meaning. No set of common information, ideas, or skills will stem from completing the various projects. In essence, she has accomplished little for the long haul. Her "differentiation" provides varied avenues to "mush"—multiple versions of fog. Her students work with different tasks, not differentiated ones.

Mr. Appleton's class provides little engagement, little understanding, and scant opportunity for attending to student differences. Mrs. Baker's class provides some engagement, little understanding, and no meaningful differentiation.

## An Alternative Approach

To make differentiation work—in fact, to make teaching and learning work—teachers must develop an alternative approach to instructional planning beyond "covering the text" or "creating activities that students will like."

Ms. Cassell has planned her year around a few key concepts that will help students relate to, organize, and retain what they study in history. She has also developed principles or generalizations that govern or uncover how the concepts work. Further, for each unit, she has established a defined set of facts and terms that are essential for students to know to be literate and informed about the topic. She has listed skills for which she and the students are responsible as the year progresses. Finally, she has developed essential questions to intrigue her students and to cause them to engage with her in a quest for understanding.

Ms. Cassell's master list of facts, terms, concepts, principles, and skills stems from her understanding of the discipline of history as well as from the district's learning standards. As the year evolves, Ms. Cassell continually assesses the readiness, interests, and learning profiles of her students and involves them in goal setting and decision making about their learning. As she comes to understand her students and their needs more fully, she modifies her instructional framework and her instruction.

**TERM TO NOTE**
Readiness

Ms. Cassell is also teaching about ancient Rome. Among the key concepts in this unit, as in many others throughout the year, are culture, change, and interdependence. Students will be responsible for important terms, such as *republic, patrician, plebeian, veto, villa,* and *Romance language;* names of key individuals, for example, Julius Caesar, Cicero, and Virgil; and names of important places, for instance, the Pantheon and the Colosseum.

For this unit, students explore key generalizations or principles: Varied cultures share common elements. Cultures are shaped by beliefs and values, customs, geography, and resources. People are shaped by and shape their cultures. Societies and cultures change for both internal and external reasons. Elements of a society and its cultures are interdependent.

Among important skills that students apply are using resources on history effectively, interpreting information from resources, blending data from several resources, and organizing effective paragraphs. The essential question that Ms. Cassell often poses to her students is, How would your life and culture be different if you lived in a different time and place?

## Looking Inside the Third Classroom

Early in the unit, Ms. Cassell's students begin work, both at home and in class, on two sequential tasks that will extend throughout the unit as part of their larger study of ancient Rome. Both tasks are differentiated.

For the first task, students assume the role of someone from ancient Rome, such as a soldier, a teacher, a healer, a farmer, a slave, or a farmer's wife. Students base their choice solely on their own interests. They work both alone and with others who select the same topic and use a wide variety of print, video, computer, and human resources to understand what their life in ancient Rome would have been like.

Ultimately, students create a first-person data sheet that their classmates can use as a resource for their second task. The data sheet calls for the person in the role to provide accurate, interesting, and detailed information about what his or her daily schedule would be like, what he or she would eat and wear, where he or she would live, how he or she would be treated by the law, what sorts of problems or challenges he or she would face, the current events of the time, and so on.

Ms. Cassell works with both the whole class and small groups on evaluating the availability and appropriate use of data sources, writing effective paragraphs, and blending information from several sources into a coherent whole. Students use these skills as they develop the first-person data sheets. The teacher's goal is for each student to increase his or her skill level in each area.

The second task calls on students to compare and contrast their own lives with the lives of children of similar age in ancient Rome. Unlike the first task, which was based on student interest, this one is differentiated primarily on the basis of student readiness. The teacher assigns each student a scenario establishing his or her family context for the task: "You are the eldest son of a lawmaker living during the later years of the period known as Pax Romana," for example. Ms. Cassell bases the complexity of the scenario on the student's skill with researching and thinking about history. Most students work with families unlike those in their first task. Students who need continuity between the tasks, however, can continue in a role familiar from their first investigation.

All students use the previously developed first-person data sheets as well as a range of other resources to gather background information. They must address a common set of specified questions: How is what you eat shaped by the economics of your family and by your location? What is your level of education and how is that affected by your status in society? How is your life interdependent with the lives of others in ancient Rome? How will Rome change during your lifetime? How will those changes affect your life? All students must also meet certain research and writing criteria.

Despite the common elements, the task is differentiated in several ways. It is differentiated by interest because each student adds questions that are directed by personal interests: What games did children play? What was the practice of science like then? What was the purpose and style of art?

Readiness differentiation occurs because each student adds personal research and writing goals, often with the teacher's help, to his or her criteria for success. A wide range of research resources is available, including books with varied readability levels, video and audiotapes, models, and access to informed people. The teacher also addresses readiness through small-group sessions in which she provides different sorts of teacher and peer support, different kinds of modeling, and different kinds of coaching for success, depending on the readiness levels of students.

Finally, the teacher adds to each student's investigation one specific question whose degree of difficulty is based on her most recent assessments of student knowledge, facility with research, and thinking about history. An example of a more complex question is, How will your life differ from that of the previous generation in your family, and how will your grandchildren's lives compare with yours? A less complex, but still challenging question is, How will language change from the generation before you to two generations after you, and why will those changes take place?

Learning-profile differentiation is reflected in the different media that students use to express their findings: journal entries, an oral monologue, or a videotape presentation. Guidelines for each type of product ensure quality and focus on essential understandings and skills established for the unit. Students may work alone or with a "parallel partner" who is working with the same role, although each student must ultimately produce his or her own product.

At other points in the study of ancient Rome, Ms. Cassell differentiates instruction. Sometimes she varies the sorts of graphic organizers that students use when they read, do research, or take notes in class. She may use review groups of mixed readiness and then conduct review games with students of like readiness working together. She works hard to ask a range of questions that move from concrete and familiar to abstract and unfamiliar in all class discussions. She sometimes provides homework options in which students select the tasks that they believe will help them understand important ideas or use important skills best. Of course, the class also plans, works, reviews, and debates as a whole group.

Students find Ms. Cassell's class engaging—and not just because it's fun. It's engaging because it shows the connection between their own lives and life long ago. It helps them see the interconnectedness among times in history and make links with other subjects. It tickles their curiosity. And it provides a challenge that pushes each learner a bit further than is comfortable—and then supports success. Sometimes those things are fun. Often they are knotty and hard. Always they dignify the learner and the subject.

Mr. Cassell's class is highly likely to be effective for her varied learners, in part because she continually attempts to reach her students where they are and move them on—she differentiates instruction. The success of the differentiation, however, is not a stand-alone matter. It is successful because it is squarely rooted in student engagement plus student understanding.

This teacher knows where she wants her students to arrive at the end of their shared learning journey and where her students are along that journey at a given time. Because she is clear about the destination and the path of the travelers, she can effectively guide them, and she varies or differentiates her instruction to accomplish this goal. Further, her destination is not merely the amassing of data but rather the constructing of understanding. Her class provides a good example of the close and necessary relationship between effective curriculum and instruction and effective differentiation.

## The First Step Is the Compass

Mr. Appleton may have a sense of what he wants his students to know at the end of the road, but not about what his students should understand and be able to do. He teaches facts, but no key concepts, guiding principles, or essential questions. With a fact-based curriculum, differentiating instruction is difficult. Perhaps some students could learn more facts and some, fewer. Perhaps some students could have more time to drill the facts, and some, less. It's difficult to envision a defensible way to differentiate a fact-driven curriculum, probably because the curriculum itself is difficult to defend.

Mrs. Baker also appears to lack a clear vision of the meaning of her subject, of the nature of her discipline and what it adds to human understanding, and of why it should matter to a young learner to study old times. There is little clarity about facts—let alone concepts, guiding principles, or essential questions. Further, she confuses folly with engagement. She thinks that she is differentiating instruction, but without instructional clarity, her activities and projects are merely different—not differentiated. Because there is no instructional clarity, there is no basis for defensible differentiation.

Ms. Cassell plans for what students should know, understand, and be able to do at the end of a sequence of learning. She dignifies each learner by planning tasks that are interesting, relevant, and powerful. She invites each student to wonder. She determines where each student is in knowledge, skill, and understanding and where he or she needs to move. She differentiates instruction to facilitate that goal. For her, differentiation is one piece of the mosaic of professional expertise. It is not a strategy to be plugged in occasionally or often, but is a way of thinking about the classroom. In her class, there is a platform for differentiation.

Ms. Cassell helps us see that differentiated instruction must dignify each learner with learning that is "whole," important, and meaning making. The core of *what* the students learn remains relatively steady. *How* the student learns—including degree of difficulty, working arrangements, modes of expression, and sorts of scaffolding—may vary considerably. Differentiation is not so much the "stuff" as the "how." If the "stuff" is ill conceived, the "how" is doomed.

The old saw is correct: Every journey *does* begin with a single step. The journey to successfully differentiated or personalized classrooms will succeed only if we carefully take the first step—ensuring a foundation of best-practice curriculum and instruction.

## POSTNOTE

The term *differentiated instruction* is relatively new in education circles, but its practice is as old as teachers and classrooms. Teachers know that their classrooms contain students with tremendous diversity—ethnic, cultural, racial, academic, learning styles, to name but a few of the diverse characteristics. How can teachers plan and deliver instruction and assessment that will respond to these forms of diversity to help students learn better? Differentiated instruction is teaching with student variance in mind and using practical ways to respond to learner needs. Instead of presuming that all of your students are essentially alike, differentiated instruction means starting where the students are and planning varied approaches to what individual students need to learn, how they will learn it, and how they can express what they have learned. The idea of differentiated or personalized instruction has great appeal to teachers and teacher educators, but its implementation may seem overwhelming, particularly for new teachers. In other writings, Carol Tomlinson advises that teachers start the process slowly and gradually expand differentiation as they feel comfortable and have the time. Most important is making a commitment to the process of responding to student differences.

## DISCUSSION QUESTIONS

1. As you read the three vignettes involving Mr. Appleton, Mrs. Baker, and Ms. Cassell, which approach was more indicative of your elementary and secondary schooling? Which approach did you find more appealing? Why?

2. What concerns or questions do you have regarding differentiated instruction?

3. Did you have a teacher who used differentiated instruction particularly successfully? Describe what he/she did that made their instruction successful.

# Connecting Brain Research with Dimensions of Learning

## 45

Mariale M. Hardiman

In the past 10 years, teachers have been bombarded by education reform initiatives, including standards-based instruction, teaching to students' learning styles, performance-based instruction, multiple intelligences, and, most recently, brain-based learning. In addition, during the 1990s, the Individuals with Disabilities Education Act (IDEA) mandated that students with disabilities have access to the general education curriculum. This mandate has resulted in more students with special needs being taught in general education classrooms (Lombardi & Butera, 1998).

**TERM TO NOTE**
Individuals with Disabilities Education Act (IDEA)

Meeting the needs of diverse learners can be challenging enough for teachers without the charge of determining how to incorporate reform initiatives into practice. Merely superimposing reforms upon existing practices and requirements is generally ineffective. Education initiatives that link current practice with promising new research in neurological and cognitive sciences, however, offer real possibilities for improving teaching and learning, especially for students with diverse learning needs.

Scientists and researchers are making exciting new discoveries related to how the brain processes and stores information (Sousa, 1998). This research has the potential to unlock the mysteries of learning itself. For example, recent research highlights the differences in brain anatomy of students with learning disabilities and attention deficits that can shed light on their performance in the classroom (Semrud-Clikeman et al., 2000). Yet, despite the enormous implications of such research, it is not being effectively disseminated to education practitioners, who, among all professionals, need it most (Sousa, 1998).

How can we familiarize teachers with brain-based learning so that they can apply this latest research to meet the needs of all students, including those with disabilities, in the general education classroom? A basic precept of brain-based research states that learning is best achieved when linked with the learner's previous knowledge, experience, or understanding of a given subject or concept (Perry, 2000). Therefore, we can assume that the use of brain-based research would be most effective when combined with previously established frameworks for teaching and learning (Brandt, 1999).

One such framework that Roland Park Elementary/Middle School has used since 1994 is the Dimensions of Learning model (Marzano, 1992). Roland Park, a Blue Ribbon School of Excellence in Baltimore, Maryland, has steadily improved the achievement of its 1,350 students during the past six years. Our progress, in part, may be attributed to our use of Dimensions of Learning, which addresses the development of higher-order thinking skills. Robert Marzano describes the five dimensions as "loose metaphors for how the mind works during learning" (1992, p. 2). Linking the five dimensions with the latest brain research suggests a number of best practices for teaching all children—especially students with learning disabilities.

**TERMS TO NOTE**
Dimensions of learning model
Higher-order thinking skills

Mariale M. Hardiman is principal of Roland Park Elementary/Middle School, 5207 Roland Ave., Baltimore, MD. From Mariale M. Hardiman, "Connecting Brain Research with Dimensions of Learning," *Educational Leadership*, November 2001, pp. 52–55. Reprinted with permission of the Association for Supervision and Curriculum Development. Copyright © 2001 by ASCD. All rights reserved.

## Dimension One: Positive Attitudes

Dimension One explains that a student's attitudes and perceptions serve as filters that enhance or inhibit natural learning. Although educators may have long suspected that attitudes affect learning, brain research clearly supports the link between emotions and cognition. Robert Leamnson (2000) explains that neural pathways connect the limbic system, the brain's emotional center, to the frontal lobes, which play a major role in learning. In addition, hormones alter the chemical makeup of the brain of a person under stress. When the person is threatened, chemicals are released that can impair memory and learning (Jensen, 1998).

### Best Practices

▶ Provide a challenging yet supportive classroom environment by reducing the stress that may come from embarrassment because of academic difficulties or peer rejection. At Roland Park, we make students feel more comfortable by assigning a "peer buddy" as a homework helper, arranging for tutoring in study skills and test-taking strategies, and providing special meetings outside of class time to encourage a trusting teacher-student relationship.

▶ Teach peer acceptance and social behaviors explicitly. Students with learning disabilities may experience an added fear of rejection from the stigma of special education. Our teachers hold class meetings to encourage social acceptance and interaction, use literature and history to provide instructional materials that demonstrate acceptance of diversity, and model an attitude of acceptance and appreciation for those with different learning styles and needs.

▶ To cement long-term memory, connect emotions to learning. Techniques such as dramatizations, humor, movement, or arts integration can arouse the emotional systems of the brain and stimulate peak performance. For example, teachers may tell a funny instructional story at the beginning of class to foster a relaxed yet supportive atmosphere.

## Dimension Two: Acquiring and Integrating Knowledge

Dimension Two pertains to the acquisition and integration of knowledge. Marzano (1992) proposes that learning new information must occur within the context of what the learner already knows and must be adequately assimilated so that the information can be used easily in new situations.

Much of brain-based research has focused on how the brain acquires, stores, and uses information (Valiant, 1998). Learning occurs through the growth of neural connections, stimulated by the passage of electrical current along nerve cells and enhanced by chemicals discharged into the synapse between neighboring cells. The more often the "trail is blazed," the more automatic a task or memory becomes (Buchel, Coull, & Friston, 1999). Therefore, the more a student repeats a learning task, the greater the connectivity. Researchers also point out that different parts of the brain store particular parts of a memory (Fishback, 1999). For example, one part of the brain might store the lyrics of a song and another part, the melody. Further, Leamnson (2000) explains that the brain must reconstruct a memory each time the person recalls the memory. Learning thus requires both the acquisition of information and the ability to retrieve and reconstruct that information whenever necessary. Evidence from brain-mapping technology indicates that individual differences in learning styles affect this retrieval process. In a study that investigated the differences between normal and disabled readers in visual-perceptual tasks, Richard S. Kruk and Dale M. Willows (2001) found significant processing differences that affected the rate of visual processing for students with reading disabilities. Jean Robertson (2000) suggests that the inability to shift control from the right to the left hemisphere of the brain may cause early reading disorders.

### Best Practices

▶ Present new information within the context of prior knowledge and previously learned content (Perry, 2000). For example, students may better understand the bicameral system of U.S. government by comparing it with their own student government.

▶ Allow students to repeat learning tasks to cement them in memory (Sprenger, 1998). This is especially important for activities that require an automatic response, such as blending phonemes into words (Shaywitz, 1998) or mastering math facts.

▶ Use mnemonics, which can significantly increase the memory of content (Carney & Levin, 2000), especially for students with special needs (Lombardi & Butera, 1998). For example, telling students to "write with their FEAT" can remind them to use the transition words "for example" or "according to" to introduce supportive text in their writing.

**TERM TO NOTE**
Mnemonics

▶ Use visually stimulating material and manipulatives to activate the right hemisphere of the brain and text presentation to activate the left hemisphere (Robertson, 2000). The right brain's visual-spatial skills can be activated with features such as a balance scale to help visualize algebraic equations or pictures and graphs to enhance the meaning of text.

▶ Integrate art, music, and movement into learning activities to activate multiple parts of the brain and enhance learning (Rauscher et al., 1997; Vogel, 2000). For example, students can learn how the earth's tilt and rotation create seasons through body movements—tilting the body toward the center of a circle to simulate late spring; turning and tilting away from the center to simulate fall.

## Dimension Three: Extending and Refining Knowledge

Extending and refining knowledge requires examining it in a deeper, more analytical way by doing such things as comparing, classifying, inducing, deducing, analyzing errors, constructing support, abstracting, and analyzing perspective (Marzano, 1992). The thinking skills involved in Dimension Three require that the brain use multiple and complex systems of retrieval and integration (Lowery, 1998). Ron Brandt (2000) states that brain research supports thinking-skills programs that have students compare and classify familiar concepts. He explains that neurons that often fire at the same time as certain other neurons become more likely to fire whenever those other neurons fire. . . . We use less brain energy when performing familiar functions than when learning new skills. (p. 75)

### Best Practices

▶ Design tasks that allow students to use prior knowledge to learn new information. For example, students use their prior understanding of photosynthesis to explain the differences between plant and animal cells.

▶ Offer students an opportunity to compare their performances with model responses and to analyze their error patterns. For example, when asking students to write an essay, provide a model paper that clearly identifies the main idea, supporting details, transition words, and conclusion. Let students use the model to organize their own writing.

▶ Teach students to identify general patterns that underlie concepts. For example, compare the leadership characteristics of current leaders with those of successful leaders of the past.

## Dimension Four: Using Knowledge Meaningfully

Marzano (1992) states that we learn best when we need information to accomplish a goal. Using Dimension Four thinking strategies, students apply information in activities that require them to make decisions, investigate, conduct experiments, and solve real-world problems. Brain research confirms that this type of experiential learning activates the area of the brain responsible for higher-order thinking (Sousa, 1998). Moreover, enriched instruction has been shown to produce significant chemical changes in the brains of students with learning disabilities—changes that indicate less exertion of effort in learning (Richards et al., 2000). A similar study (Bower, 1999) indicated that reinforcement of active learning tasks improves brain efficiency.

Leamnson (2000) warns, however, that merely providing students with hands-on activities does not guarantee learning. Teachers must pair physical activities with problem-solving tasks to connect the "acting modules" of the brain—the motor cortex—with the "thinking modules"—the frontal lobes. Such experiences increase memory and learning, thereby modifying brain structures (Kandel & Squire, 2000).

### Best Practices

▶ Assign students active, hands-on tasks that require them to investigate, analyze, and solve problems using real-world applications (Green, 1999). For example, students can apply the formula for the area of a rectangle by determining how much paint it would take to paint a room given the dimensions of walls, doors, and windows.

▶ Allow students to use multiple ways to demonstrate learning, such as inventions, experiments, dramatizations, visual displays, music, and oral presentations. For instance, assigning groups of students to write scripts and perform skits to represent each of the 12 labors of Hercules makes this myth come alive.

## Dimension Five: Habits of Mind

Dimension Five describes the mental habits that enable students to facilitate their own learning. These habits include monitoring one's own thinking (*metacognitive thinking*), goal setting, maintaining one's own standards of evaluation, self-regulating, and applying one's unique learning style to future learning situations. Understanding and facilitating one's own learning style is especially important for students with learning disabilities. According to Martin Languis (1998), brain-mapping tests reveal individual differences in brain organization and structure that relate to specific differences in learning style. Studies showed that students who were more skilled in spatial-visualization tasks such as visualizing three-dimensional objects demonstrated different brain-processing patterns compared with less-skilled students. Students, however, significantly improved their scores in spatial-visualization assessments after taking courses that taught them specific learning strategies such as the use of imagery, graphic organizers, and puzzles.

**TERM TO NOTE**
Metacognitive thinking

### Best Practices

▶ Provide ways for students to engage in metacognitive reflection. Students benefit from the use of think logs, reflective journals, and group discussions within a cooperative learning setting.

▶ Include reflective discussions of lessons to foster the habit of reflection on learning. Ask students to record one important concept that they learned from the lesson and several important facts.

## Putting the Research to Use

Although most researchers agree that our understanding of the human brain is in its infancy, the explosion of research in the field of neurology and cognitive sciences in the past 10 years can and should play an important role in education reform, especially for students who demonstrate differences in their thinking and learning patterns. If teachers combine brain research with a thinking skills framework such as Dimensions of Learning as we have at Roland Park Elementary/Middle School, the research will translate more effectively into practice. Our use of this model has resulted in exciting learning experiences for students as well as increased scores on our state performance assessment every year since 1994. Moreover, the potential of brain research to provide new approaches to teaching students with information-processing difficulties makes its use all the more vital in classrooms today. Students with learning differences, including those with learning disabilities who are in general education classrooms, deserve to have available to them a program of research-based instruction to nurture and enhance both thinking and learning.

### REFERENCES

Bower, B. (1999, March 6). Learning may unify distant brain regions. *Science News* [Online]. Available: www.findarticles.com/cf_01/m1200/mag.jhmtl

Brandt. R. (1999). Educators need to know about the human brain. *Phi Delta Kappan, 81,* 235–238.

Brandt, R. (2000). On teaching brains to think: A conversation with Robert Sylwester. *Educational Leadership, 57*(7), 72–75.

Buchel, C., Coull, J. T., & Friston, K. J. (1999). The predictive value of changes in effective connectivity for human learning. *Science, 283,* 1538–1541.

Carney, R. N., & Levin, J. R. (2000). Mnemonic instruction, with a focus on transfer. *Journal of Educational Psychology, 92,* 783–790.

Fishback, S. J. (1999). Learning and the brain. *Adult Learning, 10*(2), 18–22.

Green, F. E. (1999). Brain and learning research: Implications for meeting the needs of diverse learners. *Education, 119,* 682–687.

Jensen, E. (1998). How Julie's brain learns. *Educational Leadership, 56*(3), 41–45.

Kandel, E. R., & Squire, L. R. (2000). Neuroscience: Breaking down scientific barriers to the study of brain and mind. *Science, 290,* 1113–1120.

Kruk, R. S., & Willows, D. M. (2001). Backward pattern masking of familiar and unfamiliar materials in disabled and normal readers. *Cognitive Neuropsychology, 18*(1), 19–37.

Languis, M. (1998). Using knowledge of the brain in educational practice. *NASSP Bulletin, 82*(598), 38–47.

Leamnson, R. (2000). Learning as biological brain change. *Change, 32*(6), 34–40. Available: www.findarticles.com/cf_01/m1254/mag.jhtml

Lombardi, T., & Butera, G. (1998, May). Mnemonics: Strengthening thinking skills of students with special needs. *The Clearing House, 71*(5), 284–286.

Lowery, L. (1998). How new science curriculums reflect brain research. *Educational Leadership, 56*(3), 26–30.

Marzano, R. J. (1992). *A different kind of classroom: Teaching with Dimensions of Learning.* Alexandria, VA: ASCD.

Perry, B. (2000). How the brain learns best. *Instructor, 11*(4), 34–35.

Rauscher, F., Shaw, G., Levine, L., Wright, E., Dennis, W., & Newcomb, R. (1997). Music training causes long-term enhancement of preschool children's spatial-temporal reasoning. *Neurological Research, 19*(1), 2–8.

Richards, T., Corina, D., Serafini, S., Steury, K., Echelard, D. R., Dager, S. R., Marro, K., Abbott, R. D., Maravilla, K. R., & Berninger, V. W. (2000). Effects of a phonologically driven treatment for dyslexia on lactate levels measured by Proton MR spectroscopic imaging. *American Journal of Neuroradiology, 21,* 916–922.

Robertson, J. (2000). Neuropsychological intervention in dyslexia: Two studies on British pupils. *Journal of Learning Disabilities, 33*(2), 137–148.

Semrud-Clikeman, M., Steingard, R. J., Filipeck, P., Biederman, J., Bekken, K., & Renshaw, P. F. (2000). Using MRI to examine brain-behavior relationships in males with attention deficit disorder with hyperactivity. *Journal of the American Academy of Child & Adolescent Psychiatry, 39*(4), 477–484.

Shaywitz, S. E. (1998). Dyslexia. *The New England Journal of Medicine, 338,* 307–312.

Sousa, D. (1998). Brain research can help principals reform secondary schools. *NASSP Bulletin, 82*(598), 21–28.

Sprenger, M. (1998). Memory lane is a two-way street. *Educational Leadership, 56*(3), 65–67.

Valiant, R. (1998). Growing brain connections: A modest proposal. *Schools in the Middle, 7*(4), 24–26.

Vogel, G. (2000). Neuroscience: New brain cells prompt new theory of depression. *Science, 290*(5490), 258–259.

## POSTNOTE

American society seems to give little attention or funding to the study of the development of the brain in children, despite much evidence about the importance of a child's earliest years. Instead, we all too often place children in front of television sets to absorb cartoons and commercials in a passive manner. And while there are, admittedly, many fine daycare centers, there are huge numbers of daycare facilities that are stunting children. At this critical period in their children's development, parents leave them with untrained personnel to languish for hour after precious hour with only minimal human attention. Current child-care arrangements may be squandering our most precious natural resource, the healthy development of our young.

Like the general public, many American educators are also unaware of the recent brain research findings reported in this article. Strong professional development programs are needed to make educators aware of these findings and to show them how this research can be used in their classrooms to enhance student learning.

## DISCUSSION QUESTIONS

1. Which of the findings reported in this article do you think is the most important? Why?

2. Which of the findings was the greatest surprise to you? Why?

3. Describe ways in which your former or current teachers structured classes or lessons that were consistent with some of the findings reported in this article.

# Foundations

## PART SIX

As a career, education is a practical field like medicine or criminal justice. It is not a discipline or content area, such as anthropology, physics, or English literature. However, education draws on these various disciplines and fields of knowledge to guide teachers in their work.

The term *foundations* refers to the particular group of academic disciplines that the practice of education draws on quite heavily, including philosophy, history, psychology, and sociology. It is often said that a house is as good as the foundation upon which it rests. In our view, likewise, the most effective teaching is firmly grounded on these educational foundations.

# 46 CLASSIC *My Pedagogic Creed*

### John Dewey

## Article I—What Education Is

*I believe that*

▶ all education proceeds by the participation of the individual in the social consciousness of the race. This process begins unconsciously almost at birth, and is continually shaping the individual's powers, saturating his consciousness, forming his habits, training his ideas, and arousing his feelings and emotions. Through this unconscious education the individual gradually comes to share in the intellectual and moral resources which humanity has succeeded in getting together. He becomes an inheritor of the funded capital of civilization. The most formal and technical education in the world cannot safely depart from this general process. It can only organize it or differentiate it in some particular direction.

▶ the only true education comes through the stimulation of the child's powers by the demands of the social situations in which he finds himself. Through these demands he is stimulated to act as a member of a unity, to emerge from his original narrowness of action and feeling, and to conceive of himself from the standpoint of the welfare of the group to which he belongs. Through the responses which others make to his own activities he comes to know what these mean in social terms. The value which they have is reflected back into them. For instance, through the response which is made to the child's instinctive babblings the child comes to know what those babblings

mean; they are transformed into articulate language, and thus the child is introduced into the consolidated wealth of ideas and emotions which are now summed up in language.

▶ this educational process has two sides—one psychological and one sociological—and that neither can be subordinated to the other, or neglected, without evil results following. Of these two sides, the psychological is the basis. The child's own instincts and powers furnish the material and give the starting-point for all education. Save as the efforts of the educator connect with some activity which the child is carrying on of his own initiative independent of the educator, education becomes reduced to a pressure from without. It may, indeed, give certain external results, but cannot truly be called educative. Without insight into the psychological structure and activities of the individual the educative process will, therefore, be haphazard and arbitrary. If it chances to coincide with the child's activity it will get a leverage; if it does not, it will result in friction, or disintegration, or arrest of the child-nature.

▶ knowledge of social conditions, of the present state of civilization, is necessary in order properly to interpret the child's powers. The child has his own instincts and tendencies, but we do not know what these mean until we can translate them into their social equivalents. We must be able to carry them back into a social past and see them as the inheritance of previous race activities. We must also be able to project them into the future to see what their outcome and end will be. In the illustration just used, it is the ability to see in the child's babblings the promise and potency of a future social intercourse and conversation which enables one to deal in the proper way with that instinct.

John Dewey was a philosopher and educator; he founded the progressive education movement. This article was published originally as a pamphlet by E. L. Kellogg and Co., 1897.

▶ the psychological and social sides are organically related, and that education cannot be regarded as a compromise between the two, or a superimposition of one upon the other. We are told that the psychological definition of education is barren and formal—that it gives us only the idea of a development of all the mental powers without giving us any idea of the use to which these powers are put. On the other hand, it is urged that the social definition of education, as getting adjusted to civilization, makes of it a forced and external process, and results in subordinating the freedom of the individual to a preconceived social and political status.

▶ each of these objections is true when urged against one side isolated from the other. In order to know what a power really is we must know what its end, use, or function is, and this we cannot know save as we conceive of the individual as active in social relationships. But, on the other hand, the only possible adjustment which we can give to the child under existing conditions is that which arises through putting him in complete possession of all his powers. With the advent of democracy and modern industrial conditions, it is impossible to foretell definitely just what civilization will be twenty years from now. Hence it is impossible to prepare the child for any precise set of conditions. To prepare him for the future life means to give him command of himself; it means so to train him that he will have the full and ready use of all his capacities; that his eye and ear and hand may be tools ready to command, that his judgment may be capable of grasping the conditions under which it has to work, and the executive forces be trained to act economically and efficiently. It is impossible to reach this sort of adjustment save as constant regard is had to the individual's own powers, tastes, and interests—that is, as education is continually converted into psychological terms.

In sum, I believe that the individual who is to be educated is a social individual, and that society is an organic union of individuals. If we eliminate the social factor from the child we are left only with an abstraction; if we eliminate the individual factor from society, we are left only with an inert and lifeless mass. Education, therefore, must begin with a psychological insight into the child's capacities, interests, and habits. It must be controlled at every point by reference to these same considerations. These powers, interests, and habits must be continually interpreted—we must know what they mean. They must be translated into terms of their social equivalents—into terms of what they are capable of in the way of social service.

## Article II—What the School Is

*I believe that*

▶ the school is primarily a social institution. Education being a social process, the school is simply that form of community life in which all those agencies are concentrated that will be most effective in bringing the child to share in the inherited resources of the race, and to use his own powers for social ends.

▶ education, therefore, is a process of living and not a preparation for future living.

▶ the school must represent present life—life as real and vital to the child as that which he carries on in the home, in the neighborhood, or on the playground.

▶ that education which does not occur through forms of life, forms that are worth living for their own sake, is always a poor substitute for the genuine reality, and tends to cramp and to deaden.

▶ the school, as an institution, should simplify existing social life; should reduce it, as it were, to an embryonic form. Existing life is so complex that the child cannot be brought into contact with it without either confusion or distraction; he is either overwhelmed by the multiplicity of activities which are going on, so that he loses his own power of orderly reaction, or he is so stimulated by these various activities that his powers are prematurely called into play and he becomes either unduly specialized or else disintegrated.

▶ as such simplified social life, the school life should grow gradually out of the home life; that it should take up and continue the activities with which the child is already familiar in the home.

▶ it should exhibit these activities to the child, and reproduce them in such ways that the child will gradually learn the meaning of them, and be capable of playing his own part in relation to them.

▶ this is a psychological necessity, because it is the only way of securing continuity in the child's growth, the only way of giving a background of past experience to the new ideas given in school.

▶ it is also a social necessity because the home is the form of social life in which the child has been nurtured and in connection with which he has had his moral training. It is the business of the school to deepen and extend his sense of the values bound up in his home life.

▶ much of the present education fails because it neglects this fundamental principle of the school as a form of community life. It conceives the school as a place where certain information is to be given, where certain lessons are to be learned, or where certain habits are to be formed. The value of these is conceived as lying largely in the remote future; the child must do these things for the sake of something else he is to do; they are mere preparations. As a result they do not become a part of the life experience of the child and so are not truly educative.

▶ the moral education centers upon this conception of the school as a mode of social life,

**TERM TO NOTE**

Moral education

that the best and deepest moral training is precisely that which one gets through having to enter into proper relations with others in a unity of work and thought. The present

educational systems, so far as they destroy or neglect this unity, render it difficult or impossible to get any genuine, regular moral training.

▶ the child should be stimulated and controlled in his work through the life of the community.

▶ under existing conditions far too much of the stimulus and control proceeds from the teacher, because of neglect of the idea of the school as a form of social life.

▶ the teacher's place and work in the school is to be interpreted from this same basis. The teacher is not in the school to impose certain ideas or to form certain habits in the child, but is there as a member of the community to select the influences which shall affect the child and to assist him in properly responding to these influences.

▶ the discipline of the school should proceed from the life of the school as a whole and not directly from the teacher.

▶ the teacher's business is simply to determine, on the basis of larger experience and riper wisdom, how the discipline of life shall come to the child.

▶ all questions of the grading of the child and his promotion should be determined by reference to the same standard. Examinations are of use only so far as they test the child's fitness for social life and reveal the place in which he can be of the most service and where he can receive the most help.

## Article III—The Subject-Matter of Education

*I believe that*

▶ the social life of the child is the basis of concentration, or correlation, in all his training or growth. The social life gives the unconscious the unity and the background of all his efforts and of all his attainments.

▶ the subject-matter of the school curriculum should mark a gradual differentiation out of the primitive unconscious unity of social life.

▶ we violate the child's nature and render difficult the best ethical results by introducing the child too abruptly to a number of special studies, of reading, writing, geography, etc., out of relation to this social life.

▶ the true center of correlation on the school subjects is not science, nor literature, nor history, nor geography, but the child's own social activities.

▶ education cannot be unified in the study of science, or so-called nature study, because apart from human activity, nature itself is not a unity; nature in itself is a number of diverse objects in space and time, and to attempt to make it the center of work by itself is to introduce a principle of radiation rather than one of concentration.

▶ literature is the reflex expression and interpretation of social experience; that hence it must follow upon and not precede such experience. It, therefore, cannot be made the basis, although it may be made the summary of unification.

▶ history is of educative value in so far as it presents phases of social life and growth. It must be controlled by reference to social life. When taken simply as history it is thrown into the distant past and becomes dead and inert. Taken as the record of man's social life and progress it becomes full of meaning. I believe, however, that it cannot be so taken excepting as the child is also introduced directly into social life.

▶ the primary basis of education is in the child's powers at work along the same general constructive lines as those which have brought civilization into being.

▶ the only way to make the child conscious of his social heritage is to enable him to perform those fundamental types of activity which make civilization what it is.

▶ the so-called expressive or constructive activities are the center of correlation.

▶ this gives the standard for the place of cooking, sewing, manual training, etc., in the school.

▶ they are not special studies which are to be introduced over and above a lot of others in the way of relaxation or relief, or as additional accomplishments. I believe rather that they represent, as types, fundamental forms of social activity, and that it is possible and desirable that the child's introduction into the more formal subjects of the curriculum be through the medium of these activities.

▶ the study of science is educational in so far as it brings out the materials and processes which make social life what it is.

▶ one of the greatest difficulties in the present teaching of science is that the material is presented in purely objective form, or is treated as a new peculiar kind of experience which the child can add to that which he has already had. In reality, science is of value because it gives the ability to interpret and control the experience already had. It should be introduced, not as so much new subject-matter, but as showing the factors already involved in previous experience and as furnishing tools by which that experience can be more easily and effectively regulated.

▶ at present we lose much of the value of literature and language studies because of our elimination of the social element. Language is almost always treated in the books of pedagogy simply as the expression of thought. It is true that language is a logical instrument, but it is fundamentally and primarily a social instrument. Language is the device for communication; it is the tool through which one individual comes to share the ideas and feelings of others. When treated simply as a way of getting individual information, or as a means of showing off what one had learned, it loses its social motive and end.

▶ there is, therefore, no succession of studies in the ideal school curriculum. If education is life, all life has, from the outset, a scientific aspect, an aspect of art and culture, and an aspect of communication. It cannot, therefore, be true that the proper studies for one grade are mere reading and writing, and that at a later grade, reading, or literature, or science, may be introduced. The progress is not in the succession of studies, but in the development of new attitudes towards, and new interests in, experience.

▶ education must be conceived as a continuing reconstruction of experience; that the process and the goal of education are one and the same thing.

▶ to set up any end outside of education, as furnishing its goal and standard, is to deprive the educational process of much of its meaning, and tends to make us rely upon false and external stimuli in dealing with the child.

## Article IV—The Nature of Method

*I believe that*

▶ the question of method is ultimately reducible to the question of the order of development of the child's powers and interests. The law for presenting and treating material is the law implicit within the child's own nature. Because this is so I believe the following statements are of supreme importance as determining the spirit in which education is carried on:

▶ the active side precedes the passive in the development of the child-nature; that expression comes before conscious impression; that the muscular development precedes the sensory; that movements come before conscious sensation; I believe that consciousness is essentially motor or impulsive; that conscious states tend to project themselves in action.

▶ the neglect of this principle is the cause of a large part of the waste of time and strength in school work. The child is thrown into a passive, receptive, or absorbing attitude. The conditions are such that he is not permitted to follow the law of nature; the result is friction and waste.

▶ ideas (intellectual and rational processes) also result from action and devolve for the sake of the better control of action. What we term reason is primarily the law of orderly and effective action. To attempt to develop the reasoning powers, the powers of judgment, without reference to the selection and arrangement of means in action, is the fundamental fallacy in our present methods of dealing with this matter. As a result we present the child with arbitrary symbols. Symbols are a necessity in mental development, but they have their place as tools for economizing effort; presented by themselves they are a mass of meaningless and arbitrary ideas imposed from without.

▶ the image is the great instrument of instruction. What a child gets out of any subject presented to him is simply the images which he himself forms with regard to it.

▶ if nine-tenths of the energy at present directed towards making the child learn certain things were spent in seeing to it that the child was forming proper images, the work of instruction would be indefinitely facilitated.

▶ much of the time and attention now given to the preparation and presentation of lessons might be more wisely and profitably expended in training the child's power of imagery and in seeing to it that he was continually forming definite, vivid, and growing images of the various subjects with which he comes in contact in his experience.

▶ interests are the signs and symptoms of growing power. I believe that they represent dawning capacities. Accordingly the constant and careful observation of interests is of the utmost importance for the educator.

▶ these interests are to be observed as showing the state of development which the child has reached.

▶ they prophesy the stage upon which he is about to enter.

▶ only through the continual and sympathetic observation of childhood's interests can the adult enter into the child's life and see what it is ready for, and upon what material it could work most readily and fruitfully.

▶ these interests are neither to be humored nor repressed. To repress interest is to substitute the adult for the child, and so to weaken intellectual curiosity and alertness, to suppress initiative, and to deaden interest. To humor the interests is to substitute the transient for the permanent. The interest is always the sign of some power below; the important thing is to discover this power. To humor the interest is to fail to penetrate below the surface, and its sure result is to substitute caprice and whim for genuine interest.

▶ the emotions are the reflex of actions.

▶ to endeavor to stimulate or arouse the emotions apart from their corresponding activities is to introduce an unhealthy and morbid state of mind.

▶ if we can only secure right habits of action and thought, with reference to the good, the true, and the beautiful, the emotions will for the most part take care of themselves.

▶ next to deadness and dullness, formalism and routine, our education is threatened with no greater evil than sentimentalism.

▶ this sentimentalism is the necessary result of the attempt to divorce feeling from action.

## Article V—The School and Social Progress

*I believe that*

▶ education is the fundamental method of social progress and reform.

▶ all reforms which rest simply upon enactment of law, or the threatening of certain penalties, or upon changes in mechanical or outward arrangements, are transitory and futile.

▶ education is a regulation of the process of coming to share in the social consciousness; and that the adjustment of individual activity on the basis of this social consciousness is the only sure method of social reconstruction.

▶ this conception has due regard for both the individualistic and socialistic ideals. It is duly individual because it recognizes the formation of a certain character as the only genuine basis of right living. It is socialistic because it recognizes that this right character is not to be formed by merely individual precept, example, or exhortation, but rather by the influence of a certain form of institutional or community life upon the individual, and that the social organism through the school, as its organ, may determine ethical results.

▶ in the ideal school we have the reconciliation of the individualistic and the institutional ideals.

▶ the community's duty to education is, therefore, its paramount moral duty. By law and punishment, by social agitation and discussion, society can regulate and form itself in a more or less haphazard and chance way. But through education society can formulate its own purposes, can organize its own means and resources, and thus shape itself with definiteness and economy in the direction in which it wishes to move.

▶ when society once recognizes the possibilities in this direction, and the obligations which these possibilities impose, it is impossible to conceive of the resources of time, attention, and money which will be put at the disposal of the educator.

▶ it is the business of every one interested in education to insist upon the school as the primary and most effective interest of social progress and reform in order that society may be awakened to realize what the school stands for, and aroused to the necessity of endowing the educator with sufficient equipment properly to perform his task.

▶ education thus conceived marks the most perfect and intimate union of science and art conceivable in human experience.

▶ the art of thus giving shape to human powers and adapting them to social service is the supreme art; one calling into its service the best of artists; that no insight, sympathy, tact, executive power, is too great for such service.

▶ with the growth of psychological service, giving added insight into individual structure and laws of growth; and with growth of social science, adding to our knowledge of the right organization of individuals, all scientific resources can be utilized for the purpose of education.

▶ when science and art thus join hands the most commanding motive for human action will be reached, the most genuine springs of human conduct aroused, and the best service that human nature is capable of guaranteed.

▶ the teacher is engaged, not simply in the training of individuals, but in the formation of the proper social life.

▶ every teacher should realize the dignity of his calling; that he is a social servant set apart for the maintenance of proper social order and the securing of the right social growth.

▶ in this way the teacher always is the prophet of the true God and the usherer in of the true kingdom of God.

## POSTNOTE

This article is deemed a classic because it outlines the core beliefs of the American who has had the most powerful impact on our schools—John Dewey. Dewey, the father of progressivism, was the most influential educational thinker of the last 100-plus years. Many of the beliefs expressed in this article (originally published in 1897) have greatly affected educational practice in America. What we find most curious is how current some of these statements still are. On the other hand, many seem dated and clearly from another era. Those that appeal to altruism and idealism have a particularly old-fashioned ring to them. The question remains, however: Which is "out of sync"—the times or the appeals to idealism and altruism?

## DISCUSSION QUESTIONS

1. How relevant do you believe Dewey's statements are today? Why?

2. Which of Dewey's beliefs do you personally agree or disagree with? Why?

3. How does Dewey's famous statement that "education . . . is a process of living and not a preparation for future living" square with what your parents, guidance counselors, and teachers have told you over the years? If different, how do you explain this?

# *The Basis of Education*
## Robert Maynard Hutchins

The obvious failures of the doctrines of adaptation, immediate needs, social reform, and of the doctrine that we need no doctrine at all may suggest to us that we require a better definition of education. Let us concede that every society must have some system that attempts to adapt the young to their social and political environment. If the society is bad, in the sense, for example, in which the Nazi state was bad, the system will aim at the same bad ends. To the extent that it makes men bad in order that they may be tractable subjects of a bad state, the system may help achieve the social ideals of the society. It may be what the society wants; it may even be what the society needs, if it is to perpetuate its form and accomplish its aims. In pragmatic terms, in terms of success in the society, it may be a "good" system.

But it seems to me clearer to say that, though it may be a system of training, or instruction, or adaptation, or meeting immediate needs, it is not a system of education. It seems clearer to say that the purpose of education is to improve men. Any system that tries to make them bad is not education, but something else. If, for example, democracy is the best form of society, a system that adapts the young to it will be an educational system. If despotism is a bad form of society, a system that adapts the young to it will not be an educational system, and the better it succeeds in adapting them the less educational it will be.

Every man has a function as a man. The function of a citizen or a subject may vary from society to society, and the system of training, or adaptation, or instruction, or meeting immediate needs may vary with it. But the function of a man as man is the same in every age and in every society, since it results from his nature as a man. The aim of an educational system is the same in every age and in every society where such a system can exist: it is to improve man as man.

If we are going to talk about improving men and societies, we have to believe that there is some difference between good and bad. This difference must not be, as the **TERM TO NOTE** positivists think it is, merely Positivism conventional. We cannot tell this difference by any examination of the effectiveness of a given program as the pragmatists propose; the time required to estimate these effects is usually too long and the complexity of society is always too great for us to say that the consequences of a given program are altogether clear. We cannot discover the difference between good and bad by going to the laboratory, for men and societies are not laboratory animals. If we believe that there is no truth, there is no knowledge, and there are no values except those which are validated by laboratory experiment, we cannot talk about the improvement of men and societies, for we can have no standard of judging anything that takes place among men or in societies.

Society is to be improved, not by forcing a program of social reform down its throat, through the schools or otherwise, but by the improvement of the individuals who compose it. As Plato said, "Governments reflect human

Robert Maynard Hutchins (1899–1977) was a major figure in American education during the middle third of the twentieth century. A leading spokesperson for perennialist education, he was the long-time president of the University of Chicago. "The Basis of Education," from *The Conflict in Education in a Democratic Society* by Robert M. Hutchins. Copyright 1953 by Harper & Row, Publishers, Inc. Renewed © 1981 by Vesta S. Hutchins. Reprinted by permission of HarperCollins Publishers, Inc.

nature. States are not made out of stone or wood, but out of the characters of their citizens: these turn the scale and draw everything after them." The individual is the heart of society.

To talk about making men better we must have some idea of what men are, because if we have none, we can have no idea of what is good or bad for them. If men are brutes like other animals, then there is no reason why they should not be treated like brutes by anybody who can gain power over them. And there is no reason why they should not be trained as brutes are trained. A sound philosophy in general suggests that men are rational, moral, and spiritual beings and that the improvement of men means the fullest development of their rational, moral, and spiritual powers. All men have these powers, and all men should develop them to the fullest extent.

Man is by nature free, and he is by nature social. To use his freedom rightly he needs discipline. To live in society he needs the moral virtues. Good moral and intellectual habits are required for the fullest development of the nature of man.

To develop fully as a social, political animal man needs participation in his own government. A benevolent despotism will not do. You cannot expect the slave to show the virtues of the free man unless you first set him free. Only democracy, in which all men rule and are ruled in turn for the good life of the whole community, can be an absolutely good form of government.

The community rests on the social nature of men. It requires communication among its members. They do not have to agree with one another; but they must be able to understand one another. And their philosophy in general must supply them with a common purpose and a common concept of man and society adequate to hold the community together. Civilization is the deliberate pursuit of a common ideal. The good society is not just a society we happen to like or to be used to. It is a community of good men.

Education deals with the development of the intellectual powers of men. Their moral and spiritual powers are the sphere of the family and the church. All three agencies must work in harmony; for, though a man has three aspects, he is still one man. But the schools cannot take over the role of the family and the church without promoting the atrophy of those institutions and failing in the task that is proper to the schools.

We cannot talk about the intellectual powers of men, though we can talk about training them, or amusing them, or adapting them, and meeting their immediate needs, unless our philosophy in general tell us that there is knowledge and that there is a difference between true and false. We must believe, too, that there are other means of obtaining knowledge than scientific experimentation. If knowledge can be sought only in the laboratory, many fields in which we thought we had knowledge will offer us nothing but opinion or superstition, and we shall be forced to conclude that we cannot know anything about the most important aspects of man and society. If we are to set about developing the intellectual powers of men through having them acquire knowledge of the most important subjects, we have to begin with the proposition that experimentation and empirical data will be of only limited use to us, contrary to the convictions of many American social scientists, and that philosophy, history, literature, and art give us knowledge, and significant knowledge, on the most significant issues.

If the object of education is the improvement of men, then any system of education that is without values is a contradiction in terms. A system that seeks bad values is bad. A system that denies the existence of values denies the possibility of education. Relativism, scientism, skepticism, and anti-intellectualism, the four horsemen of the philosophical apocalypse, have produced that chaos in education which will end in the disintegration of the West.

**TERMS TO NOTE**
Relativism
Scientism
Skepticism

The prime object of education is to know what is good for man. It is to know the goods in their order. There is a hierarchy of values. The task of education is to help us understand it, establish it, and live by it. This Aristotle had in mind when he said: "It is not the possessions but the desires of men that must be equalized, and this is impossible unless they have a sufficient education according to the nature of things."

Such an education is far removed from the triviality of that produced by the doctrines of adaptation, of immediate needs, of social reform, or of the doctrine of no doctrine at all. Such an education will not adapt the young to a bad environment, but it will encourage them to make it good. It will not overlook immediate needs, but it will place these needs in their proper relationship to more distant, less tangible, and more important goods. It will be the only effective means of reforming society.

This is the education appropriate to free men. It is liberal education. If all men are to be free, all men must have this education. It makes no difference how they are to earn their living or what their special interests or aptitudes may be. They can learn to make a living, and they can develop their special interests and aptitudes, after they have laid the foundation of free and responsible manhood through liberal education. It will not do to say that they are incapable of such education. This claim is made by those who are too indolent or unconvinced to make the effort to give such education to the masses.

**TERM TO NOTE**
Liberal education

Nor will it do to say that there is not enough time to give everybody a liberal education before he becomes a specialist. In America, at least, the waste and frivolity of the educational system are so great that it would be possible through getting rid of them to give every citizen a liberal education and make him a qualified specialist, too, in less time than is now consumed in turning out uneducated specialists.

A liberal education aims to develop the powers of understanding and judgment. It is impossible that too many people can be educated in this sense, because there cannot be too many people with understanding and judgment. We hear a great deal today about the dangers that will come upon us through the frustration of educated people who have got educated in the expectation that education will get them a better job, and who then fail to get it. But surely this depends on the representations that are made to the young about what education is. If we allow them to believe that education will get them better jobs and encourage them to get educated with this end in view, they are entitled to a sense of frustration if, when they have got the education, they do not get the jobs. But, if we say that they should be educated in order to be men, and that everybody, whether he is a ditch-digger or a bank president, should have this education because he is a man, then the ditch-digger may still feel frustrated, but not because of his education.

Nor is it possible for a person to have too much liberal education, because it is impossible to have too much understanding and judgment. But it is possible to undertake too much in the name of liberal education in youth. The object of liberal education in youth is not to teach the young all they will ever need to know. It is to give them the habits, ideas, and techniques that they need to continue to educate themselves. Thus the object of formal institutional liberal education in youth is to prepare the young to educate themselves throughout their lives.

I would remind you of the impossibility of learning to understand and judge many of the most important things in youth. The judgment and understanding of practical affairs can amount to little in the absence of experience with practical affairs. Subjects that cannot be understood without experience should not be taught to those who are without experience. Or, if these subjects are taught to those who are without experience, it should be clear that these subjects can be taught only by way of introduction and that their value to the student depends on his continuing to study them as he acquires experience. The tragedy in America is that economics, ethics, politics, history, and literature are studied in youth, and seldom studied again.

Therefore the graduates of American universities seldom understand them.

This pedagogical principle, that subjects requiring experience can be learned only by the experienced, leads to the conclusion that the most important branch of education is the education of adults. We sometimes seem to think of education as something like the mumps, measles, whooping-cough, or chicken-pox. If a person has had the education in childhood, he need not, in fact he cannot, have it again. But the pedagogical principle that the most important things can be learned only in mature life is supported by a sound philosophy in general. Men are rational animals. They achieve their terrestrial felicity by the use of reason. And this means that they have to use it for their entire lives. To say that they should learn only in childhood would mean that they were human only in childhood.

And it would mean that they were unfit to be citizens of a republic.[1] A republic, a true *res publica*, can maintain justice, peace, freedom, and order only by the exercise of intelligence. When we speak of the consent of the governed, we mean, since men are not angels who seek the truth intuitively and do not have to learn it, that every act of assent on the part of the governed is a product of learning. A republic is really a common educational life in process. So Montesquieu said that, whereas the principle of a monarchy was honor, and the principle of tyranny was fear, the principle of a republic was education.

Hence the ideal republic is the republic of learning. It is the utopia by which all actual political republics are measured. The goal toward which we started with the Athenians twenty-five centuries ago is an unlimited republic of learning and a world-wide political republic mutually supporting each other.

All men are capable of learning. Learning does not stop as long as a man lives, unless his learning power atrophies because he does not use it. Political freedom cannot endure unless it is accompanied by provision for the unlimited acquisition of knowledge. Truth is not long retained in human affairs without continual learning and relearning. Peace is unlikely unless there are continuous, unlimited opportunities for learning and unless men continuously avail themselves of them. The world of law and justice for which we yearn, the world-wide political republic, cannot be realized without the world-wide republic of learning. The civilization we seek will be achieved when all men are citizens of the world republic of law and justice and of the republic of learning all their lives long.

### NOTE

1. I owe this discussion to the suggestions of Scott Buchanan.

## POSTNOTE

Much of the energy behind the current school reform movement grows out of concern that our young may be unable to meet the demands of the twenty-first century. Our global economic competitors, the argument goes, and possibly our military competitors as well, are more hard-working and disciplined than we are. Grown soft, we have created a soft educational system, at least by the standards of the nations with which we are in competition. Therefore, the public schools must do a better job of preparing our students, as future workers and citizens, to take over the reins of our economy and preserve the nation.

Robert Hutchins, one of the great educational thinkers and innovators of the twentieth century, took a different view. This article is a Classic because it is one of the clearest statements of conservative educational thought. Education is for individual people first and foremost, Hutchins believed. Developing a person with the powers of understanding and judgment (as opposed to salable skills) is the true purpose of education. During his lifetime, Hutchins often reminded us that the state is designed to serve the ends of humans, not vice versa. Since Hutchins wrote this piece half a century ago, the state has become bigger and bigger and more and more of a presence in our daily lives. In the face of this growth, educators need to wrestle continually with his question, "What is good for man?"

## DISCUSSION QUESTIONS

1. How would you describe Hutchins's philosophy of education?

2. Do you agree with the idea that schools have become the state's training ground? Why or why not?

3. If Hutchins is correct, and "the prime object of education is to know what is good for man," how should this be reflected in the school curriculum?

# 48

**CLASSIC** *Personal Thoughts on Teaching and Learning*

Carl Rogers

I wish to present some very brief remarks, in the hope that if they bring forth any reaction from you, I may get some new light on my own ideas.

I find it a very troubling thing to *think*, particularly when I think about my own experiences and try to extract from those experiences the meaning that seems genuinely inherent in them. At first such thinking is very satisfying, because it seems to discover sense and pattern in a whole host of discrete events. But then it very often becomes dismaying, because I realize how ridiculous these thoughts, which have much value to me, would seem to most people. My impression is that if I try to find the meaning of my own experience it leads me, nearly always, in directions regarded as absurd.

So in the next three or four minutes, I will try to digest some of the meanings which have come to me from my classroom experience and the experience I have had in individual and group therapy. They are in no way intended as conclusions for someone else, or a guide to what others should do or be. They are the very tentative meanings, as of April 1952, which my experience has had for me, and some of the

bothersome questions which their absurdity raises. I will put each idea or meaning in a separate lettered paragraph, not because they are in any particular logical order, but because each meaning is separately important to me.

a. I may as well start with this one in view of the purposes of this conference. *My experience has been that I cannot teach another person how to teach.* To attempt it is for me, in the long run, futile.

b. *It seems to me that anything that can be taught to another is relatively inconsequential, and has little or no significant influence on behavior.* That sounds so ridiculous I can't help but question it at the same time that I present it.

c. *I realize increasingly that I am only interested in learnings which significantly influence behavior.* Quite possibly this is simply a personal idiosyncrasy.

d. *I have come to feel that the only learning which significantly influences behavior is self-discovered, self-appropriated learning.*

e. *Such self-discovered learning, truth that has been personally appropriated and assimilated in experience, cannot be directly communicated to another.* As soon as an individual tries to communicate such experience directly, often with a quite natural enthusiasm, it becomes teaching, and its results are inconsequential. It was some relief recently to discover that Søren Kierkegaard, the Danish philosopher, had found this too, in his own experience, and stated it very clearly a century ago. It made it seem less absurd.

**TERMS TO NOTE**

Self-discovered learning

Inconsequential learning

**f.** As a consequence of the above, *I realize that I have lost interest in being a teacher.*

**g.** When I try to teach, as I do sometimes, I am appalled by the results, which seem a little more than inconsequential, because sometimes the teaching appears to succeed. When this happens I find that the results are damaging. It seems to cause the individual to distrust his own experience, and to stifle significant learning. *Hence I have come to feel that the outcomes of teaching are either unimportant or hurtful.*

**h.** When I look back at the results of my past teaching, the real results seem the same—either damage was done, or nothing significant occurred. This is frankly troubling.

**i.** As a consequence, *I realize that I am only interested in being a learner, preferably learning things that matter, that have some significant influence on my own behavior.*

**j.** *I find it very rewarding to learn,* in groups, in relationship with one person as in therapy, or by myself.

**k.** *I find that one of the best, but most difficult ways for me to learn is to drop my own defensiveness, at least temporarily, and try to understand the way in which his experience seems and feels to the other person.*

**l.** *I find that another way of learning for me is to state my own uncertainties, to try to clarify my puzzlements, and thus get closer to the meaning that my experience actually seems to have.*

**m.** This whole train of experiencing, and the meanings that I have thus far discovered in it, seem to have launched me on a process which is both fascinating and at times a little frightening. *It seems to mean letting my experience carry me on, in a direction which appears to be forward, toward goals that I can but dimly define, as I try to understand at least the current meaning of that experience.* The sensation is that of floating with a complex stream of experience, with the fascinating possibility of trying to comprehend its ever changing complexity.

I am almost afraid I may seem to have gotten away from any discussion of learning, as well as teaching. Let me again introduce a practical note by saying that by themselves these interpretations of my own experience may sound queer and aberrant, but not particularly shocking. It is when I realize the *implications* that I shudder a bit at the distance I have come from the commonsense world that everyone knows is right. I can best illustrate that by saying that if the experiences of others had been the same as mine, and if they had discovered similar meanings in it, many consequences would be implied.

**a.** Such experience would imply that we would do away with teaching. People would get together if they wished to learn.

**b.** We would do away with examinations. They measure only the inconsequential type of learning.

**c.** The implication would be that we would do away with grades and credits for the same reason.

**d.** We would do away with degrees as a measure of competence partly for the same reason. Another reason is that a degree marks an end or a conclusion of something, and a learner is only interested in the continuing process of learning.

**e.** It would imply doing away with the exposition of conclusions, for we would realize that no one learns significantly from conclusions.

I think I had better stop there. I do not want to become too fantastic. I want to know primarily whether anything in my inward thinking as I have tried to describe it, speaks to anything in your experience of the classroom as you have lived it, and if so, what the meanings are that exist for you in *your* experience.

## POSTNOTE

This article is selected for Classic designation because it had a significant influence on educational practice during the 1960s and 70s, some of the effects of which are still with us. Rogers's personal philosophy of teaching and learning, so well expressed in this selection, is of course quite controversial. Give it a little test for yourself. Think of a couple of the most significant things you have learned as a human being. Now think of how you learned them. Did someone teach them to you, or did you discover them yourself through experience? Try it from a different approach and ask yourself what of significance you have ever been taught. Be specific. How do you feel about Rogers's statements now?

## DISCUSSION QUESTIONS

1. Do you agree or disagree with Rogers's ideas on teaching and learning? Why?

2. Do Rogers's statements have any implications for you as a teacher? Explain your answer.

3. Compare the messages that Rogers presents with those of E. D. Hirsch, Jr. in selection 49, "Romancing the Child." How are they similar or different?

# Romancing the Child

## E. D. Hirsch, Jr.

## 49

The Disney Corporation's Celebration School sounded like yet another fairy tale from the creators of the *Little Mermaid* and the *Lion King*. It was supposed to be the ideal school, set in Disney's newly created Florida community, Celebration. According to the *New York Times*, the school was to follow the "most advanced" progressive educational methods. In fact these "new" methods were rebottled versions of earlier progressive schemes going back at least 100 years—as Diane Ravitch has documented in her recent book *Left Back*—schemes such as multi-aged groups in which each child goes at his or her own pace; individualized assessments instead of objective tests; teachers as coaches rather than sages; projects instead of textbooks.

Such methods, although they have been in use for decades, have rarely worked well. The Celebration School was no exception. As the *Times* headline put it, there was "Trouble at the Happiest School on Earth." The *Times* article began, "The start of the school year here is just a few days away, so it was no surprise that there was a line of parents at the Celebration School office the other day. But the reason for the line was: they were queuing up to withdraw their children." Parents said they were dissatisfied with the lack of clear academic goals and measures of achievement, as well as with the lack of order and structure that accompanied the progressive methods.

The Celebration School's failure was wholly predictable. In the 1980s, the distinguished sociologist James Coleman conducted carefully controlled, large-sample research that demonstrated the ineffectiveness of progressive methods in raising general academic achievement and in closing the achievement gap between advantaged and disadvantaged students. Coleman found that Catholic schools achieve more educational equity than public schools because they follow a rich and demanding curriculum; provide a structured, orderly environment; offer lots of explicit instruction, including drill and practice; and expect every child to reach minimal goals in each subject by the end of the year. All of this stands in stark contrast to the progressive ideals of unstructured, implicit teaching and "individually tailored" instruction that now predominate in public schools. As a result, disadvantaged children prosper academically in Catholic schools, and the schools narrow the gaps among races and social classes. When criticized for condemning public schools, Coleman pointed out that the very same democratic results were being achieved by the few public schools that were also defying progressivist doctrine. Along with large-scale international comparisons, Coleman's work is the most reliable observational data that we have regarding the validity of progressive ideas, and it has never been refuted.

**TERM TO NOTE**
Progressivism

The evidence against progressive educational theories mounts still higher if you combine Coleman's data with the research on so-called "effective schools." Effective schools are characterized by explicit, agreed-upon academic goals for all children; a strong focus on academics; order and discipline in the classroom; maximum time on learning tasks; and frequent evaluations of student performance—all principles repudiated by the Disney school

**TERM TO NOTE**
Effective schools

E. D. Hirsch, Jr. is a professor emeritus of education and humanities at the University of Virginia and author of *The Schools We Need and Why We Don't Have Them*. This article was adapted from a speech given at Harvard University in October 1999. From E. D. Hirsch, Jr., "Romancing the Child," *Education Matters*, Spring 2001. Reprinted with permission of The Hoover Institution.

and also by many "new" education reforms. In fact, the progressive way of running a school is essentially the opposite of what the effective-schools research has taught us. A recent review of this research by the late, great scholar Jeanne Chall may be found in *The Academic Achievement Challenge: What Really Works in the Classroom*? (2000).

One would think that the failures of progressivism might induce more skepticism among both its adherents and the public. Yet the unempirical theories of progressive educators—generally dressed up with empirical claims—remain highly influential among teachers, administrators, and distinguished professors. Their unspoken assumptions work a hidden sway over the American public as well. For example, test-bashing wouldn't be so popular if progressive theories about education didn't resonate somehow with widespread American beliefs about children and learning. One can understand why progressives should want to bash tests, when their methods consistently fail to improve test scores. But why should others accept the disparagement of, say, reading tests, which are among the most valid and reliable of existing instruments?

In my mind, progressive educational ideas have proved so seductive because their appeal lies not in their practical effects but in their links to romanticism, the 19th-century philosophical movement, so influential in American culture, that elevated all that is natural and disparaged all that is artificial. The progressives applied this romantic principle to education by positing that education should be a natural process of growth that flows from the child's natural instincts and interests. The word "nature" in the romantic tradition connotes the sense of a direct connection with the holy, lending the tenets of progressivism all the weight of religious conviction. We know in advance, in our bones, that what is natural must be better than what is artificial. This revelation is the absolute truth against which experience itself must be measured, and

**TERM TO NOTE**
Romanticism

any failure of educational practice must be due to faulty implementation of progressive principles or faulty interpretation of educational results. Thus the results of mere reading tests must not be taken at face value, because such blunt instruments cannot hope to measure the true effects of education. The fundamental beliefs of progressivism are impervious to unfavorable data because its philosophical parent, romanticism, is a kind of secular theology that, like all religions, is inherently resistant to data. A religious believer scorns mere "evidences."

## The Chasm Between

There are many disputes within the education field, but none so vituperative as the reading and math wars—the battles over how best to teach children to read and to solve arithmetic problems. These aren't just disputes over instructional techniques; they are expressions of two distinct and opposing understandings of children's nature and how children learn. The two sides are best viewed as expressions of romantic versus classical orientations to education. For instance, the "whole language," progressive approach to teaching children how to read is romantic in impulse. It equates the natural process of learning an oral first language with the very unnatural process of learning alphabetic writing. The emotive weight in progressivist ideas is on naturalness. The natural is spiritually nourishing; the artificial, deadening. In the 1920s, William Kilpatrick and other romantic progressivists were already advocating the "whole language" method for many of the same reasons advanced today.

The classical approach, by contrast, declines to assume that the natural method is always the best method. In teaching reading, the classicist is quite willing to accept linguistic scholarship that discloses that the alphabet is an artificial device for encoding the sounds of language. Learn the 40-odd sounds

**TERMS TO NOTE**
Whole language
Classicism

of the English language and their corresponding letter combinations, and you can sound out almost any word. Yet adherents of "whole language" regard phonics as an unnatural approach that, by divorcing sounds and letters from meaning and context, fails to give children a real appreciation for reading.

The progressivist believes that it is better to study math and science through real-world, hands-on, *natural* methods than through the deadening modes of conceptual and verbal learning, or the repetitive practicing of math algorithms, even if those "old fashioned" methods are successful. The classicist is willing to accept the verdict of scholars that the artificial symbols and algorithms of mathematics are the very sources of its power. Math is a powerful instrument precisely because it is unnatural. It enables the mind to manipulate symbols in ways that transcend the direct natural reckoning abilities of the mind. Natural, real-world intuitions are helpful in math, but there should be no facile opposition between terms like "understanding," "hands-on," and "real-world applications" and terms like "rote learning" and "drill and kill." What is being killed in memorizing the multiplication table? The progressivist says: children's joy in learning, their intrinsic interest, and their deep understanding.

The romantic poet William Wordsworth said, "We murder to dissect"; the progressivist says that phonemics and place value should not be dissected in isolation from their natural use, nor imposed before the child is naturally ready. Instead of explicit, analytical instruction, the romantic wants implicit, natural instruction through projects and discovery. This explains the romantic preference for "integrated learning" and "developmental appropriateness." Education that places subject matter in its natural setting and presents it in a natural way is superior to the artificial analysis and abstractions of language. Hands-on learning is superior to verbal learning. Real-world applications of mathematics provide a truer understanding of math than empty mastery of formal relationships.

## Natural Supernaturalism

The religious character of progressivism is rarely noted because it is not an overtly religious system of belief. Romanticism is a *secularized* expression of religious faith. In a justly famous essay, T. E. Hulme defined romanticism as "spilt religion." Romanticism, he said, redirects religious emotions from a transcendent God to the natural divinity of this world. Transcendent feelings are transferred to everyday experience—like treacle spilt all over the table, as Hulme put it. M. H. Abrams offered a more sympathetic definition of this tendency to fuse the secular and religious by entitling his fine book on romanticism *Natural Supernaturalism*. The natural is supernatural. Logically speaking, it's a contradiction, but it captures the romantic's faith that a divine breath infuses natural human beings and the natural world.

> **TERM TO NOTE**
> Secularism

In emotional terms, romanticism is an affirmation of this world—a refusal to deprecate this life in favor of pie in the sky. In theological terms, this sentiment is called "pantheism"—the faith that God inhabits all reality. Transcendent religions like Christianity, Islam, and Hinduism see this world as defective, and consider the romantic divinizing of nature to be a heresy. But for the romantic, the words "nature" and "natural" take the place of the word "God" and give nature the emotional ultimacy that attaches to divinity. As Wordsworth said,

> One impulse from a vernal wood
> May teach you more of man,
> Of moral evil and of good,
> Than all the sages can

—*The Tables Turned* (1798)

The romantic conceives of education as a process of natural growth. Botanical metaphors are so pervasive in American educational literature that we take them for granted. The teacher, like a gardener, should be a watchful guide on the side, not a sage on the stage. (The word "kindergarten"—literally "children-garden"—was invented by the romantics.) It was the romantics who began mistranslating the Latin word *educare* (ee-duh-kar'e), the Latin root word for education, as "to lead out" or "to unfold," confusing it with *educere* (eh-diu'ke-re), which *does* mean "to lead out." It was a convenient mistake that fit in nicely with the theme of natural development, since the word "development" itself means "unfolding." But *educare* actually means "to bring up" and "instruct." It implies deliberate training according to social and cultural norms, in contrast to words like "growth" and "development," which imply that education is the unfolding of human nature, analogous to a seed growing into a plant.

The same religious sentiment that animates the romantics' fondness for nature underlies their celebration of individuality and diversity. According to the romantics, the individual soul partakes of God's nature. Praise for diversity as being superior to uniformity originates in the pantheist's sense of the plenitude of God's creation. "Nature's holy plan," as Wordsworth put it, unfolds itself with the greatest possible variety. To impose uniform standards on the individuality of children is to thwart their fulfillment and to pervert the design of Providence. Education should be child-centered; motivation to learn should be stimulated through the child's inherent interest in a subject, not through artificial rewards and punishments.

Whether these educational tenets can withstand empirical examination is irrelevant. Their validation comes from knowing in advance, with certainty, that the natural is superior to the artificial.

## A More Complicated Nature

Plato and Aristotle based their ideas about education, ethics, and politics on the concept of nature, just as the romantics did. A classicist knows that any attempt to thwart human nature is bound to fail. But the classicist does not assume that a providential design guarantees that relying on our individual natural impulses will always yield positive outcomes. On the contrary, Aristotle argued that human nature is a battleground of contradictory impulses and appetites. Selfishness is in conflict with altruism; the fulfillment of one appetite is in conflict with the fulfillment of others. Follow nature, yes, but which nature and to what degree?

Aristotle's famous solution to this problem was to optimize human fulfillment by balancing the satisfactions of all the human appetites—from food and sex to the disinterested contemplation of truth—keeping society's need for civility and security in mind as well. This optimizing of conflicting impulses required the principle of moderation, the golden mean, not because moderation was a good in itself, but because, in a secular view of conflicted human nature, this was the most likely route to social peace and individual happiness. The romantic poet William Blake countered, "The road of excess leads to the palace of wisdom." But again, that would be true only if a providential nature guaranteed a happy outcome. Absent such faith in the hidden design of natural providence, the mode of human life most in accord with nature must be, according to Aristotle, a *via media* that is artficially constructed. By this classical logic, the optimally natural must be self-consciously artificial.

Renewed interest in evolutionary psychology has given the classic-romantic debate new currency. Darwinian moral philosophers such as George Williams reject the notion that evolution should be a direct guide to ethics or to education. On the contrary, evolutionary psychology reintroduces in its own way the classical idea that there are inherent conflicts in human nature—both selfishness and altruism, both a desire to possess one's neighbor's spouse and a desire to get along with one's neighbor. The adjudication of these contradictory impulses requires an anti-natural construct like the Ten Commandments. Similarly, from the standpoint of evolution, most of the learning required by modern schooling is not natural at all. Industrial and postindustrial life, very recent phenomena in evolutionary terms, require kinds of learning that are constructed artificially and sometimes arduously on the natural learning capacities of the mind—a point that has been made very effectively and in detail by David Geary, a research psychologist specializing in children's learning of mathematics at the University of Missouri. Geary makes a useful distinction between primary and secondary learnings, with most school learnings, such as the base-ten system and the alphabetic principle, being the "unnatural," secondary type.

The very idea that skills as artificial and difficult as reading, writing, and arithmetic can be made natural for everyone is an illusion that has flourished in the peaceful, prosperous United States. The old codger Max Rafferty, an outspoken state superintendent of education in California, once denounced the progressive school Summerhill, saying:

> Rousseau spawned a frenetic theory of education which after two centuries of spasmodic laboring brought forth . . . Summerhill. . . . The child is a Nobel Savage, needing only to be let alone in order to insure his intellectual salvation. . . . Twaddle. Schooling is not a natural process at all. It's highly artificial. No boy in his right mind ever wanted to study multiplication tables and historical dates when he could be out hunting rabbits or climbing trees. In the days when hunting and climbing contributed to the survival of Homo sapiens, there was some sense in letting the kids do what comes naturally, but when man's future began to hang upon the systematic mastery of orderly subject matter, the primordial, happy-go-lucky, laissez faire kind of learning had to go.

The romantic versus classic debate extends beyond the reading and math wars to the domain of moral education. The romantic tradition holds that morality (like everything else) comes naturally. The child, by being immersed in real-life situations and being exposed to good role models, comes to understand the need for sharing, kindness, honesty, diligence, loyalty, courage, and other virtues. Wordsworth's account of his own education, which he called "Growth of a Poet's Mind," contained a section entitled, "Love of Nature Leading to Love of Mankind."

The romantic wishes to encourage the basic goodness of the natural soul, unspoiled by habit, custom, and convention. The principal means for such encouragement is to develop the child's creativity and imagination—two words that gained currency in the romantic movement. Before the romantics, using the term "creativity" for human productions was considered impious. But that ended when the human soul was conceived as inherently godly. Moral education and the development of creativity and imagination went hand in hand. In the 19th and early 20th centuries, textbooks like the McGuffey Readers strongly emphasized moral instruction and factual knowledge. With the rise of progressive ideas, however, the subject matter of language arts in the early grades began to focus on fairy tales and poetry. The imparting of explicit moral instruction gave way to the development of creativity and imagination. Imagination, the romantic poet and essayist Samuel Taylor Coleridge said, "brings the whole soul of man into activity." When we exercise our imaginations, we connect with our divine nature, develop our moral sensibilities.

## Romance or Justice?

One cannot hope to argue against a religious faith that is impervious to refutation. But there *can* be hope for change when that religious faith is secular and pertains to the world itself. When the early romantics lived long enough to experience the disappointments of life, they abandoned their romanticism. This happened to Blake, Wordsworth, and Coleridge. One of Wordsworth's most moving works was the late poem, "Elegiac Stanzas," which bade farewell to his faith in nature. Similar farewells to illusion were penned by the other romantics. There is a potential instability in *natural* supernaturalism. Romantic religion is vulnerable because it is a religion of this world. If one's hopes and faith are pinned on the here and now, on the faith that reading, arithmetic, and morals will develop naturally out of human nature, then that faith may gradually decline when this world continually drips its disappointments.

So far, progressivism has proved somewhat invulnerable to its failures. But its walls are beginning to crumble, and none too soon. Only when widespread doubt is cast on public education's endemic romanticism will we begin to see widespread improvements in achievement. Everyone grants that schooling must start from what is natural. But schooling cannot effectively stay mired there. With as much certainty as these things can be known, we know that analytical and explicit instruction works better than inductive, implicit instruction for most school learning. To be analytical and explicit in instruction is to be artificial. Also, it is to be skeptical that children will naturally construct for themselves either knowledge or goodness.

The romantic thinks nature has a holy plan. The classicist, the modernist, and the pragmatist do not. And neither does the scientist. In the end, the most pressing questions in the education wars are not just empirical, scientific questions, but also ethical ones regarding the unfortunate social consequences of the progressive faith, especially the perpetuation of the test-score gaps among racial and economic groups. Are we to value the aesthetics of diversity and the theology of spilt religion above social justice? That is the unasked question that needs to be asked ever more insistently. Economic and political justice are strenuous goals. They cannot be achieved by doing what comes naturally.

## POSTNOTE

Who can be against romance! Romance makes the world go round. It's the butter on the toast of life. It's the syrup on the pancakes! It's also, according to E. D. Hirsch, the sand in the gears of American education. Hirsch is the author of the influential *Cultural Literacy: What Every American Needs to Know* and the developer of the Core Knowledge curriculum.

Romanticism is thought by many to be the secular theology of American educational thought, running just below the surface, but affecting all of our major movements. Romanticism rejects the conceptual teachings of most theologies and classical philosophies that state that humans are conceived in sin or are capable of great evil. It is somewhat surprising that romanticism survived the twentieth century, the bloodiest of them all, with its two world wars, the Holocaust, the dropping of atomic weapons on civilians, the gulags where millions perished, and all the rest of the long litany of humankind's most recent inhumanity to humankind. It is particularly surprising that it has survived in schools where teachers daily see the various cruelties that students inflict on one another—"She's a slut!", "Let's get Larry in the bathroom!", or "Let's tell everyone that Ms. Pennywickle is pregnant." It is most surprising, given the daily resistance of so many students to taking an interest in academic work and to staying on task, that our romantic view of the self-directed, intrinsically motivated learner has survived.

# DISCUSSION QUESTIONS

1. What do you believe is E. D. Hirsch's essential critique of romanticism?

2. What is the connection between progressive education and philosophical romanticism?

3. What is the case in support of progressive education that Hirsch has Ignored?

# 50  CLASSIC *The Educated Person*

## Ernest L. Boyer

As we anticipate a new century, I am drawn back to questions that have, for generations, perplexed educators and philosophers and parents. What *is* an educated person? What *should* schools be teaching to students?

In searching for answers to these questions, we must consider first not the curriculum, but the human condition. And we must reflect especially on two essential realities of life. First, each person is unique. In defining goals, it is crucial for educators to affirm the special characteristics of each student. We must create in schools a climate in which students are empowered, and we must find ways in the nation's classrooms to celebrate the potential of each child. But beyond the diversity of individuals, educators also must acknowledge a second reality: the deeply rooted characteristics that bind together the human community. We must show students that people around the world share a great many experiences. Attention to both these aspects of our existence is critical to any discussion of what all children should learn.

What, then, does it mean to be an educated person? It means developing one's own aptitudes and interests and discovering the diversity that makes us each unique. And it means becoming permanently

**TERMS TO NOTE**

Educated person

Carnegie unit

empowered with language proficiency, general knowledge, social confidence, and moral awareness in order to be economically and civically successful. But becoming well educated also means discovering the connectedness of things. Educators must help students see relationships across the disciplines and learn that education is a communal act, one that affirms not only individualism, but community. And for these goals to be accomplished, we need a new curriculum framework that is both comprehensive and coherent, one that can encompass existing subjects and integrate fragmented content while relating the curriculum to the realities of life. This curriculum must address the uniqueness of students' histories and experiences, but it also must guide them to understand the many ways that humans are connected.

Some schools and teachers are aiming to fully educate students, but most of us have a very long way to go in reaching this goal. Today, almost all students in U.S. schools still complete Carnegie units in exchange for a diploma. The time has come to bury the old Carnegie unit; since the Foundation I now head created this unit of academic measure nearly a century ago, I feel authorized to declare it obsolete. Why? Because it has helped turn schooling into an exercise in trivial pursuit. Students get academic "credit," but they fail to gain a coherent view of what they study. Education is measured by seat time, not time for learning. While curious young children still ask why things are, many older children ask only, "Will this be on the test?" All students should be encouraged to ask "Why?" because "Why?" is the question that leads students to connections.

In abandoning the Carnegie unit, I do not endorse the immediate adoption of national assessment programs; indeed, I think we must postpone such programs until we are much clearer about what students should be learning. The goal, again, is not only to help students become well informed and prepared for lifelong learning, but also to help them put learning into the larger context of discovering the connectedness of things. Barbara McClintock, the 1983 winner of the Nobel Prize for Physiology–Medicine, asserts: "Everything is one. There is no way to draw a line between things." Contrary to McClintock's vision, the average school or college catalog dramatizes the separate academic boxes.

Frank Press, president of the National Academy of Sciences, compares scientists to artists, evoking the magnificent double helix, which broke the genetic code. He said the double helix is not only rational, but beautiful. Similarly, when scientists and technicians watch the countdown to a space launch, they don't say, "Our formulas worked again." They respond, "Beautiful!" instinctively reaching for the aesthetic term to praise a technological achievement. When physicist Victor Weisskopf was asked, "What gives you hope in troubled times?" he replied, "Mozart and quantum mechanics." Most schools, however, separate science and art, discouraging students from seeing the connections between them.

How, then, can we help students see relationships and patterns and gain understanding beyond the separate academic subjects? How can we rethink the curriculum and use the disciplines to illuminate larger, more integrated ends?

## Human Commonalities

In the 1981 book *A Quest for Common Learning*, I suggested that we might organize the curriculum not on the basis of disciplines or departments, but on the basis of "core commonalities." By core commonalities, I mean universal experiences that make us human, experiences shared by all cultures on the planet. During the past decade and a half, my thinking abut this thematic structure has continued to evolve. I now envision eight commonalities that bind us to one another:

## I. The Life Cycle

As life's most fundamental truth, we share, first, the experience that connects birth, growth, and death. This life cycle binds each of us to others, and I find it sad that so many students go through life without reflecting on the mystery of their own existence. Many complete twelve or sixteen years of formal schooling not considering the sacredness of their own bodies, not learning to sustain wellness, not pondering the imperative of death.

In reshaping the curriculum to help students see connections, I would position study of "The Life Cycle" at the core of common learning. Attention would go to nutrition, health, and all aspects of wellness. For a project, each student would undertake the care of some life form.

My wife is a certified nurse-midwife who delivers babies, including seven grandchildren of our own. Kay feels special pain when delivering the baby of a teenage girl because she knows that she is delivering one child into the arms of another, and that both have all too often lived for nine months on soda and potato chips. Some young mothers first learn about the birth process between the sharp pains of labor.

Too many young women and young men pass through our process of education without learning about their own bodies. Out of ignorance, they suffer poor nutrition, addiction, and violence. "Maintaining children's good health is a shared responsibility of parents, schools, and the community at large," according to former Secretary of Education William Bennett (1986, p. 37). He urges elementary schools "to provide children with the knowledge, habits, and attitudes that will equip them for a fit and healthy life."

Study of the Life Cycle would encourage students to reflect sensitively on the mystery of birth and growth and death, to learn about body functions and thus understand the role of choice in wellness, to carry some of their emotional and intellectual learning into their relations with others, and to observe, understand, and respect a variety of life forms.

## II. Language

Each life on the planet turns to symbols to express feelings and ideas. After a first breath, we make sounds as a way of reaching out to others, connecting with them. We develop a variety of languages: the language of words (written and spoken), the language of symbols (mathematics, codes, sign systems), and the language of the arts (aesthetic expressions in language, music, painting, sculpture, dance, theater, craft, and so on). A quality education develops proficiency in the written and the spoken word, as well as a useful knowledge of mathematical symbol systems and an understanding that the arts provide countless ways to express ourselves.

Our sophisticated use of language sets human beings apart from all other forms of life. Through the created words and symbols and arts, we connect to one another. Consider the miracle of any moment. One person vibrates his or her vocal cords. Molecules shoot in the direction of listeners. They hit the tympanic membrane; signals go scurrying up the eighth cranial nerve. From that series of events, the listener feels a response deep in the cerebrum that approximates the images in the mind of the speaker. Because of its power and scope, language is the means by which all other subjects are pursued.

The responsible use of language demands both *accuracy* and *honesty*, so students studying "Language" must also learn to consider the ethics of communication. Students live in a world where obscenities abound. They live in a world where politicians use sixty-second sound bites to destroy integrity. They live in a world where clichés substitute for reason. To make their way in this world, students must learn to distinguish between deceit and authenticity in language.

Writers and mathematicians have left a long and distinguished legacy for students to learn from. Through words, each child can express something personal. Through symbols, each child can increase the capacity to calculate and reason. Through the arts, each child can express a thought or a feeling. People need to write with clarity, read with comprehension, speak effectively, listen with understanding, compute accurately, and understand the communicative capabilities of the arts. Education for the next century means helping students understand that language in all its forms is a powerful and sacred trust.

## III. The Arts

All people on the planet respond to the aesthetic. Dance, music, painting, sculpture, and architecture are languages understood around the world. "Art represents a social necessity that no nation can neglect without endangering its intellectual existence," said John Ruskin (Rand 1993). We all know how art can affect us. Salvador Dali's painting *The Persistence of Memory* communicates its meaning to anyone ever haunted by time passing. The gospel song "Amazing Grace" stirs people from both Appalachia and Manhattan. "We Shall Overcome," sung in slow and solemn cadence, invokes powerful feelings regardless of the race or economic status of singer or audience.

Archaeologists examine the artifacts of ancient civilization—pottery, cave paintings, and musical instruments—to determine the attainments and quality of a culture. As J. Carter Brown (1986) observes, "The texts of man's achievements are not written exclusively in words. They are written, as well, in architecture, paintings, sculpture, drawing, photography, and in urban, graphic, landscape, and industrial design."

Young children understand that the arts are language. Before they learn to speak, they respond intuitively to dance, music, and color. The arts also help children who are disabled. I once taught deaf children, who couldn't speak because they couldn't hear. But through painting, sculpture, and rhythm, they found new ways to communicate.

Every child has the urge and capacity to be expressive. It is tragic that for most children the universal language of the arts is suppressed, then destroyed, in the early years of learning, because traditional teaching does not favor self-expression and school boards consider art a frill. This is an ironic deprivation when the role of art in developing critical thinking is becoming more widely recognized.

Jacques d'Amboise, former principal dancer with the New York City Ballet, movie star, and founder of the National Dance Institute, offers his view on how art fits into education: "I would take the arts, science and sports, or play, and make all education involve all of them. It would be similar to what kindergarten does, only more sophisticated, right through life. All of the disciplines would be interrelated. You dance to a poem: poetry is meter, meter is time, time is science" (Ames and Peyser 1990).

For our most moving experiences, we turn to the arts to express feelings and ideas that words cannot convey. The arts are, as one poet has put it, "the language of the angels." To be truly educated means being sensitively responsive to the universal language of art.

## IV. Time and Space

While we are all nonuniform and often seem dramatically different from one another, all of us have the capacity to place ourselves in time and space. We explore our place through geography and astronomy. We explore our sense of time through history.

And yet, how often we squander this truly awesome capacity for exploration, neglecting even our personal roots. Looking back in my own life, my most important mentor was Grandpa Boyer, who lived to be one hundred. Sixty years before that, Grandpa moved his little family into the slums of Dayton, Ohio. He then spent the next forty years running a city mission, working for the poor, teaching me more by deed than by word that to be truly human, one must serve. For far too many children, the influence of such intergenerational models has diminished or totally disappeared.

Margaret Mead said that the health of any culture is sustained when three generations are vitally interacting with one another—a "vertical culture" in which the different age groups are connected. Yet in America today we've created a "horizontal culture," with each generation living alone. Infants are in nurseries, toddlers are in day care, older children are in schools organized by age. College students are isolated on campuses. Adults are in the workplace. And older citizens are in retirement villages, living and dying all alone.

For several years, my own parents chose to live in a retirement village where the average age was eighty. But this village had a day-care center, too, and all the three- and four-year-olds had adopted grandparents to meet with every day. The two generations quickly became friends. When I called my father, he didn't talk about his aches and pains, he talked about his little friend. And when I visited, I saw that my father, like any proud grandparent, had the child's drawings taped to the wall. As I watched the two of them together, I was struck by the idea that there is something really special about a four-year-old seeing the difficulty and courage of growing old. And I was struck, too, by watching an eighty-year-old being informed and inspired by the energy and innocence of a child. Exposure to such an age difference surely increases the understanding of time and personal history.

The time has come to break up the age ghettos. It is time to build intergenerational institutions that bring together the old and young. I'm impressed by the "grandteacher" programs in the schools, for example. In the new core curriculum, with a strand called "Time and Space," students should discover their own roots and complete an oral history. But beyond their own extended family, all students should also become well informed about the influence of the culture that surrounds them and learn about the traditions of other cultures.

A truly educated person will see connections by placing his or her life in time and space. In the days ahead, students should study *Western* civilization to understand our past, but they should study *non-Western* cultures to understand our present and our future.

## V. Groups and Institutions

All people on the planet belong to groups and institutions that shape their lives. Nearly 150 years ago, Ralph Waldo Emerson observed, "We do not make a world of our own, but rather fall into institutions already made and have to accommodate ourselves to them." Every society organizes itself and carries on its work through social interaction that varies from one culture to another.

Students must be asked to think about the groups of which they are members, how they are shaped by those groups, and how they help to shape them. Students need to learn about the social web of our existence, about family life, about how governments function, about the informal social structures that surround us. They also must discover how life in groups varies from one culture to another.

Civic responsibility also must be taught. The school itself can be the starting point for this education, serving as a "working model" of a healthy society in microcosm that bears witness to the ideals of community. Within the school, students should feel "enfranchised." Teachers, administrators, and staff should meet often to find their *own* relationship to the institution of the school. And students should study groups in their own community, finding out about local government.

One of my sons lives in a Mayan village in the jungle of Belize. When my wife and I visit Craig each year, I'm impressed that Mayans and Americans live and work in very similar ways. The jungle of Manhattan and the one of Belize are separated by a thousand miles and a thousand years, and yet the Mayans, just like us, have their family units. They have elected leaders, village councils, law enforcement officers, jails, schools, and places to worship. Life there is both different and very much the same. Students in the United States should be introduced to institutions in our own culture and in other cultures, so they might study, for example, both Santa Cruz, California, and Santa Cruz, Belize.

We all belong to many groups. Exploring their history and functions helps students understand the privileges and the responsibilities that belong to each of us.

## VI. Work

We all participate, for much of our lives, in the commonality of work. As Thoreau reminds us, we both "live" and "get a living." Regardless of differences, all people on the planet produce and consume. A quality education will help students understand and prepare for the world of work. Unfortunately, our own culture has become too preoccupied with *consuming*, too little with the tools for *producing*. Children may see their parents leave the house carrying briefcases or lunch pails in the morning and see them come home again in the evening, but do they know what parents actually do during the day?

Jerome Bruner (1971) asks: "Could it be that in our stratified and segmented society, our students simply do not know about local grocers and their styles, local doctors and their styles, local taxi drivers and theirs, local political activists and theirs? . . . I would urge that we find some way of connecting the diversity of the society to the phenomenon of school" (p. 7). A new, integrative curriculum for the schools needs to give attention to "Producing and Consuming," with each student studying simple economics, different money systems, vocational studies, career planning, how work varies from one culture to another, and with each completing a work project to gain a respect for craftsmanship.

Several years ago when Kay and I were in China, we were told about a student who had defaced the surface of his desk. As punishment, he spent three days in the factory where desks were made, helping the woodworkers, observing the effort involved. Not surprisingly, the student never defaced another desk.

When I was Chancellor of the State University of New York, I took my youngest son, then eight, to a cabin in the Berkshires for the weekend. My goal: to build a dock. All day, instead of playing, Stephen sat by the lake, watching me work. As we drove home, he looked pensive. After several miles, he said, "Daddy, I wish you'd grown up to be a carpenter—instead of you-know-what!"

## VII. Natural World

Though all people are different, we are all connected to the earth in many ways. David, my grandson in Belize, lives these connections as he chases birds, bathes in the river, and watches corn being picked, pounded into tortillas, and heated outdoors. But David's cousins in Boston and Princeton spend more time with appliances, asphalt roadways, and precooked food. For them, discovering connectedness to nature does not come so naturally.

When I was United States Commissioner of Education, Joan Cooney, the brilliant creator of *Sesame Street*, told me that she and her colleagues at Children's Television Workshop wanted to start a new program on science and technology for junior high school kids. They wanted young people to learn a little more about their world and what they must understand as part of living. Funds were raised, and *3–2–1 Contact* went on the air. To prepare scripts, staff surveyed junior high school kids in New York City, asking questions such as "Where does water come from?"—which brought from some students the disturbing reply, "The faucet." They asked, "Where does light come from?" and heard, "The switch." And they asked, "Where does garbage go?" "Down the chute." These students' sense of connectedness stopped at the VCR or refrigerator door.

Canadian geneticist David Suzuki, host of *The Nature of Things*, says: "We ought to be greening the school yard, breaking up the asphalt and concrete. . . . We have to give children hand-held lenses, classroom aquariums and terrariums, lots of field trips, organic garden plots on the school grounds, butterfly gardens, trees. Then insects, squirrels—maybe even raccoons and rabbits—will show up, even in the city. We've got to reconnect those kids, and we've got to do it very early. . . . Our challenge is to reconnect children to their natural curiosity" (Baron Estes 1993).

With all our differences, each of us is inextricably connected to the natural world. During their days of formal learning, students should explore this commonality by studying the principles of science, by discovering the shaping power of technology, and, above all, by learning that survival on this planet means respecting and preserving the earth we share.

## VIII. Search for Meaning

Regardless of heritage or tradition, each person searches for some larger purpose. We all seek to give special meaning to our lives. Reinhold Neibuhr said, "Man cannot be whole unless he be committed, he cannot find himself, unless he find a purpose beyond himself." We all need to examine values and beliefs, and develop convictions.

During my study of the American high school, I became convinced ours is less a school problem and more a youth problem. Far too many teenagers feel unwanted, unneeded, and unconnected. Without guidance and direction, they soon lose their sense of purpose—even their sense of wanting purpose.

Great teachers allow their lives to express their values. They are matchless guides as they give the gift of opening truths about themselves to their students. I often think of three or four teachers, out of the many I have worked with, who changed my life. What made them truly great? They were well informed. They could relate their knowledge to students. They created an active, not passive, climate for learning. More than that, they were authentic human beings who taught their subjects and were open enough to teach about themselves.

Service projects instill values. All students should complete a community service project, working in day-care centers and retirement villages or tutoring other students at school. The North Carolina School of Science and Math develops an ethos of responsible citizenship. To be admitted, a child must commit to sixty hours of community service per summer and three hours per week during the school year (Beach 1992, p. 56).

Martin Luther King, Jr., preached: "Everyone can be great because everyone can serve." I'm convinced the young people of this country want inspiration from this kind of larger vision, whether they come across it in a book or in person, or whether they find it inside themselves.

## Values, Beliefs, and Connections

What, then, does it mean to be an educated person? It means respecting the miracle of life, being empowered in the use of language, and responding sensitively to the aesthetic. Being truly educated means putting learning in historical perspective, understanding groups and institutions, having reverence for the natural world, and affirming the dignity of work. And, above all, being an educated person means being guided by values and beliefs and connecting the lessons of the classroom to the realities of life. These are the core competencies that I believe replace the old Carnegie units.

And all of this can be accomplished as schools focus not on seat time, but on students involved in true communities of learning. I realize that remarkable changes must occur for this shift in goals to take place, but I hope deeply that in the century ahead students will be judged not by their performance on a single test but by the quality of their lives. It is my hope

that students in the classrooms of tomorrow will be encouraged to create more than conform, and to cooperate more than compete. Each student deserves to see the world clearly and in its entirety and to be inspired by both the beauty and the challenges that surround us all.

Above all, I pray that Julie and David, my granddaughter in Princeton and my grandson in Belize, along with all other children on the planet, will grow to understand that they belong to the same human family, the family that connects us all.

Fifty years ago, Mark Van Doren wrote, "The connectedness of things is what the educator contemplates to the limit of his capacity." The student, he says, who can begin early in life to see things as connected has begun the life of learning. This, it seems to me, is what it means to be an educated person.

## REFERENCES

Ames, Katrine, and Marc Peyser. (Fall/Winter 1990). "Why Jane Can't Draw (or Sing, or Dance . . . )." *Newsweek* Special Edition: 40–49.

Baron Estes, Yvonne. (May 1993). "Environmental Education: Bringing Children and Nature Together." *Phi Delta Kappan* 74, 9: K2.

Beach, Waldo. (1992). *Ethical Education in American Public Schools*. Washington, D.C.: National Education Association.

Bennett, William J. (1986). *First Lessons*. Washington, D.C.: U.S. Department of Education.

Boyer, Ernest L. (1981). *A Quest for Common Learning: The Aims of General Education*. Washington, D.C.: Carnegie Foundation for the Advancement of Teaching.

Brown, J. Carter. (November/December 1983). "Excellence and the Problem of Visual Literacy." *Design for Arts in Education* 84, 3.

Bruner, Jerome. (November 1971). "Process of Education Reconsidered." An address presented before the 16th Annual Conference of the Association for Supervision and Curriculum Development.

Rand, Paul. (May 2, 1993). "Failure by Design," *The New York Times*, p. E19.

## POSTNOTE

This article is selected as a Classic because its author, the late Ernest Boyer, demonstrates his power as a profound educational thinker. Boyer was widely acknowledged during the last two decades of the twentieth century as America's leading practitioner of education. There is no more important or fundamental question in education than "What is most worth knowing?" Schools have a mission, derived from the society at large, to prepare children to be fully developed people, to prepare them for the demands of adult life in an unknown future. As educators, our mission is to identify what our students need today and will need in the future. But the universe of knowledge, which once inched along at a snail's pace, is currently racing ahead like a sprinter. The child's future, which once we could say would be much like his or her parents' life, now is impossible to predict.

In this essay, Ernest Boyer lays out his answer to the question of what an educated person most needs to know. Though there is great merit in his educational vision, a question arises: How many of us as teachers have a clear sense of goals, guided by a similar vision of what a person really is and what a person ought to become?

## DISCUSSION QUESTIONS

1. What feature of Boyer's "educated person" do you believe currently receives the greatest attention in our schools?

2. What feature of his vision do you believe receives the least attention today? Why?

3. Why do you think there is so little discussion of the question, "What is most worth knowing?"

# 51

# The Changing Landscape of U.S. Education

## James C. Carper

Since the 1960s, the educational landscape of the United States has been swept by the winds of change. Old educational forms have been reformed and new ones created. For example, the public sector now includes magnet and charter schools, while the private sector has further diversified the development of various kinds of independent Christian schools. Muslim schools, and a revival of the virtually extinct practice of home schooling. Despite standardizing pressures driven largely by recent accountability reforms, alternative forms of schooling are increasing in number and popularity. Other innovations, such as experimental voucher programs in Milwaukee and Cleveland and various kinds of tax credits for educational expenses and donations, suggest that the trend toward institutional diversity is being paralleled by a blurring of the line between the state and private sectors. If these two trends continue, the educational landscape of the future may bear a resemblance to that of the distant past.

## Colonial Educational Pluralism

Prior to the advent of modern public education in the mid-19th century, institutional diversity dominated U.S. education, and the line

James C. Carper is an associate professor of social foundations of education at the University of South Carolina-Columbia. From James C. Carper, "The Changing Landscape of U.S. Education," *Kappa Delta Pi Record*, Spring 2001. Copyright © 2001 Kappa Delta Pi, International Honor Society in Education. Reprinted with permission.

between "public" and "private" schools was often blurred. Colonial education consisted of an incredible variety of institutions, including a significant amount of home education. From the town schools of various types, dame schools—where women taught reading skills in their homes for a small fee—and private-venture

schools of New England; to the various denominational, charity, and pay schools of the Middle Colonies; to the old-field schools and Society for the Propagation of the Gospel in Foreign Parts missionary efforts in the South; to academies that appeared throughout the provinces in the 1700s, the colonial educational landscape was dotted with many kinds of institutions. Classifying schools as purely public or private is problematic from a historical perspective. To most colonials, a school was public if it served a public purpose, such as promoting civic responsibility. Public education, therefore, did not necessarily require public support and control (Bailyn 1960; Carper 2000).

Indeed, colonial institutions were supported from various sources, including taxation, land grants by the colony to a town for school purposes, private subscriptions, bequests and donations, endowments, tuition, lotteries, rents, and income from public utilities, such as fisheries. It was not unusual for educational institutions to depend on support from a variety of public and private sources. Often, schools administered by public officials charged tuition to students able to pay, while institutions under the control of boards of trustees or religious bodies received public funds or land grants, frequently for providing charity education for the poor, and were often perceived as public schools.

For example, "public" town schools in Massachusetts, mandated by the famous 1647 "Old Deluder" school law, were often funded by tuition charges to parents of school children as well as by taxes. Entrance fees and firewood charges were also levied occasionally. On the other hand, schools not under town control and heavily dependent on tuition charges received local and colonial land grants and appropriations as well as a share of town taxes. In 1660, for example, the privately endowed Roxbury Grammar School received 500 acres of land from the General Court. Dame schools likewise often received public aid. This pattern of mixed support of schools was common in New Hampshire, Connecticut, Rhode Island, and Massachusetts. Although schooling opportunities in Virginia, the Carolinas, and Georgia were fewer than in New England, patterns of school finance were similar. In Virginia, for instance, schools considered orthodox (Anglican) could obtain public funds to defray the costs of educating children too poor to pay tuition charges (Carper 1991; Gabel 1937).

**TERM TO NOTE**
Old Deluder Act

Reflecting the religious diversity of the region, denominational schooling was prevalent in the Middle Colonies. Dutch Reformed, Lutherans, Mennonites, Amish, Moravians, Quakers, Baptists, Episcopalians, Presbyterians, and Catholics established schools throughout the region for members of their respective congregations and occasionally opened them to all children in a given locality. For instance, the Quakers opened the William Penn Charter School in 1689; the school was chartered in 1697 as a *public* grammar school to instruct the rich at "reasonable rates, and the poor . . . for nothing." With the exception of the Dutch Reformed schools in New Netherlands, these denominational institutions apparently received little tax support during the colonial period (Carper 1991).

This broad concept of education persisted without major modification throughout the Early National Period (circa 1780s to 1820s). Almost every state provided land grants or financial aid to academies. Primary religious and private schools also received public support in many states, including Pennsylvania, Georgia, Connecticut, Ohio, Tennessee, Virginia, South Carolina, Indiana, New York, Illinois, and Maryland. Usually tax support was conditional upon providing charity education for poor students. Even privately organized Sunday schools received public funds from at least three states—Delaware, Virginia, and Maryland (Carper 1991; Gabel 1937).

By the 1820s, private and quasi-public schooling was widely available to children of European-American citizens in most settled parts of the country, though less so in the South. This was due primarily to the efforts of parents, churches, voluntary associations, entrepreneurs, and local communities rather than state mandates. In some areas, school attendance was nearly universal, though often irregular. Despite some references to common pay schools as private and charity school systems as public, these terms still lacked their modern connotations. Public funding of privately controlled institutions was a common practice. During the next three decades, however, this multifaceted educational arrangement inherited from the Colonial Era would be significantly altered (Cremin 1977; Kaestle 1983; Reese 1995).

## Common School Reform

The middle decades of the 19th century marked a period of intense debate and reform focusing on issues of control, finance, and curriculum that led to major changes in educational beliefs and practices. The modern concept and practice of public schooling was gradually emerging in the United States. Distressed by the social and cultural tensions wrought by mid-19th-century urbanization, industrialization, and immigration—that included many Roman Catholics—and energized by the values and beliefs of republicanism, Protestantism, and capitalism, educational reformers like Horace Mann touted the messianic power of tax-supported, universal common schooling. Common schools, proponents argued, would create a moral, disciplined, and unified population prepared to participate in U.S. political, social, and economic life. Private schools, which reformers believed would sabotage the goals of common schooling, were often cast as divisive, undemocratic, and inimical to the public interest (Glenn 1988; Kaestle 1983; Reese 1995).

With the exception of a few groups, such as Lutheran and Calvinist bodies that designed schools to preserve cultural or confessional purity, Protestants generally supported the common school movement. Indeed, many were in the vanguard of the reform effort. Rather than sharing public funds with Roman Catholic schools, as Bishop John Hughes proposed in the early 1840s in New York City, they united behind the "nonsectarian" (in reality, pan-Protestant) common school as the sole recipient of government funds for education. Catholic schools and those of other dissenters from the common school movement were thus denied tax dollars as well as legitimacy (Carper 2000; Curran 1954; Jorgenson 1987).

Reformers' efforts in the antebellum North were generally successful. By 1860, state legislatures had created common school systems. Common school reform led to a clear line of demarcation between private education and public schooling as states eliminated tax support for private schools, increased expenditures for public schools, and experienced a marked expansion of enrollment in the public sector.

As noted earlier, the distinction between public and private was still fuzzy in the early 19th century. By the 1860s, however, the label "public" became increasingly associated with free, tax-supported schools under government control. Driven to some degree by anti-Catholicism, Michigan (1835), New Hampshire (1848), Ohio (1851), Massachusetts (1855), Illinois (1855), California (1855), and New Jersey (1866) eliminated government funding of private schools by either statute or constitutional provision. Though these restrictions were neither ironclad

nor consistently enforced, particularly as applied to secondary schools, tax subsidies for private schools dropped precipitously after the Civil War as expenditures for public education increased markedly. In 1850, for example, only 47 percent of the $16.1 million spent on schools and colleges came from the public purse. By 1870, however, expenditures for schooling at all levels surged to $95.4 million, with 65 percent coming from public sources and more than 90 percent of the public school funds derived from public sources (Carper 1991, 1998; Cremin 1980).

Paralleling the sharpening distinction between public and private education, and a growing commitment to public funding, was a shift in enrollment from more or less private schools to public schools as free common schooling became more accessible and acceptable and charity schools came under the public aegis. This trend accelerated in the late 1800s as the modern definition of public was extended to secondary education and many academies were incorporated into expanding public systems. Academies that were not transformed into public high schools or state normal schools either went defunct or redefined themselves as colleges or elite boarding schools (Cremin 1980; Kaestle 1983; Reese 1995).

By 1890, then, there was far less institutional diversity in U.S. education than 100 years earlier. Ninety-two percent of school children in the country were enrolled in state school systems; 65 percent of the remainder attended the burgeoning Roman Catholic schools, with most of the rest in Lutheran, Reformed, Episcopal, or independent institutions (Carper 1991).

As had been the case with the common school movement, protean educational reform in the Progressive Era impacted private as well as public schools. Although pedagogical progressives stimulated the creation of independent schools devoted to active, child-centered learning, such as Marietta Johnson's School of Organic Education (1907) and Carolina Pratt's Play School (1914), administrative progressives influenced efforts to regulate alternatives to the public schools or simply to abolish them. Roman Catholic and Lutheran schools bore the brunt of these initiatives during the late 19th and the first quarter of the 20th centuries. Restrictions on foreign-language instruction were the most common form of state regulation of nonpublic schools, but several states attempted to go much further. In 1922, for example, Oregon required that, with few exceptions, all children between the ages of eight and 16 attend public schools. Drawing upon *Meyer v. Nebraska* (1923), which overturned restrictions on foreign-language instruction in nonpublic schools, the U.S. Supreme Court in *Pierce v. Society of Sisters* (1925) declared Oregon's law unconstitutional. In this case, the court asserted the right of private schools to exist, affirmed the fundamental right of parents to direct the "education and upbringing" of their children, and maintained that the state could "reasonably" regulate nonpublic schools (Cremin 1988; Randall 1994; Ross 1994).

After the passions of World War I and the "Red Scare" subsided and immigration rates fell precipitously, major private school groups became more accepting of the public school model and associated accreditation and certification standards. As a consequence, disputes between the state and private schools in general and religious schools in particular declined markedly after 1930. For nearly four decades, guidelines for state regulation of private schools laid down in *Meyer* and *Pierce* were widely accepted, and, at least in the realm of state regulation, peaceful coexistence was the rule.

## Diversity Redivivus

Private as well as public institutions have been affected by both the tumultuous, two-decade-long period of reform that commenced in the late 1950s and the era of reform that began in the mid-1980s (Tyack and Cuban 1995). Equality concerns of the earlier period certainly have impacted alternatives to the state system. While the federal government provided funds for services for disadvantaged students in private schools, it also threatened some of them. In particular, the "segregation academies" founded in the South between the mid-1960s and early '70s—in response to court-ordered integration of public schools—lost their tax-exempt status for failure to abide by civil rights regulations (Nevin and Bills 1976; Skerry 1980). At the same time, however, many private schools voluntarily opened their doors to minorities who sought alternatives to public schools. As early as 1982, James Coleman (1982) had asserted that the private sector was more racially integrated than the public sector.

Besides the increase in minority enrollments, the nonpublic sector has been shaped by three additional trends since the 1960s. First, though enrollment in the private sector has fallen from about 15 percent of the elementary and secondary student population in the mid-1960s to around 11 percent currently, enrollment patterns within the sector have shifted markedly. Although Catholic school enrollment has increased slightly since the mid-1990s to approximately 2.5 million, it is down considerably from the high watermark of 5.6 million students in 1965. On the other hand, enrollment in other religious and nonreligious school groups has increased significantly, to 35 and 15 percent, respectively, in 1995. (Carper 1991; National Center for Education Statistics 1998, 2000).

Second, since the mid-1960s, many evangelical Protestants and their churches have forsaken their longstanding commitment to public education and founded at least 10,000 independent Christian day schools, including a small growing number established by and for African Americans. In the 1970s and '80s, these Christian schools were occasionally embroiled in legal battles over the extent to which religious educational institutions must abide by rules and regulations applied to public schools (Carper 1983, 1985, 1997). In the mid-1990s, enrollment in these schools had topped one million.

Finally, adding further to the diversity of educational institutions in the United States, a growing number of middle-class parents, a majority of whom would be classified as conservative Christians, have chosen to teach their children at home since the 1970s. Their decision to revert to a practice common 300 years ago has been influenced by the same factors that contributed to the growth of the 1960s and '70s alternative school movement—objections to the rigidity of public school pedagogy and structure—and the aforementioned Christian day school movement—objections to the religious, moral, and academic climate of public education. Like other patrons of private schools, home school parents have often clashed with government officials regarding regulation of home education. Such conflict has not slowed the growth of this alternative to public and private schooling that now embraces more than 1 million children as compared to a mere 10,000–15,000 in the late 1970s (Carper 2000; Ray 1997).

Counting children taught by their parents, enrollment in the private sector, including at least 30 different groups of religious and non-affiliated schools, now exceeds the 1965 level. Alternatives to the traditional school are also thriving in the public sector. For example, since the first charter school was founded in 1991, the number of these quasi-independent public schools has increased to more than 1,700, with an enrollment of about 400,000 students (Center for Education Reform 2000).

Accompanying the increasing diversity in both public and private sectors, experimental voucher programs and tax credits for educational expenses and donations suggest the line between the two sectors is becoming more blurred. With its 2000 decision in *Mitchell v. Helms* upholding government provision of computer resources to students in nonpublic schools, the U.S. Supreme Court appears to have adopted a strong position that government aid may be directed toward the education of children regardless of their enrollment status. Some

observers of the court believe that this decision suggests that it would uphold a carefully crafted voucher program. Such a reform would certainly further blur the line between the non-government and public sectors (Bork, Smolin, Kmiec, George, Uhlmann, and McConnell 2000).

Often, the future is merely the past in different garb. If the aforementioned trends continue, perhaps the educational landscape of the United States will come to resemble that of the Colonial Era, with a variety of educational institutions sharing equally in public resources and contributing in different ways to the accomplishment of public purposes. Education of the public, rather than public education, might become the primary concern of the state. The winds of change continue to blow.

## REFERENCES

Bailyn, B. 1960. *Education in the forming of American society.* New York: Norton.

Bork, R. H., D. M. Smolin, D. W. Kmiec, R. P. George, M. M. Uhlmann, and M. W. McConnell, 2000. The Supreme Court: A symposium. *First Things: A Journal of Religion and Public Life* 106 (October): 25–38.

Carper, J. C. 1982. The *Whisner* decision: A case study in state regulation of Christian day schools. *Journal of Church and State* 24(2): 281–302.

Carper, J. C. 1983. The Christian day school movement. *Educational Forum* 47(2): 135–49.

Carper, J. C. 1991. An historical view of private schooling in the United States. Paper presented at the Dollars and Cents of Private Schools Conference, 9–10 May, Washington, D.C.

Carper, J. C. 1998a. History, religion, and schooling: A context for conversation. In *Curriculum, religion, and public education: Conversations for an enlarging public square,* ed. J. T. Sears with J. C. Carper, 11–24. New York: Teachers College Press.

Carper, J. C. 1998b. William Morgan Beckner: The Horace Mann of Kentucky. *Register of the Kentucky Historical Society* 96(1): 29–60.

Carper, J. C. 2000. Pluralism to establishment to dissent. The religious and educational context of home schooling. *Peabody Journal of Education* 75(1/2): 8–19.

Carper, J. C., and N. E. Devins. 1985. The state and the Christian day school. In *Religion and the state: Essays in honor of Leo Pfeffer,* ed. J. E. Wood Jr., 211–32. Waco, Tex.: Baylor University Press.

Carper, J. C., and J. Layman. 1995. Independent Christian day schools: Past, present, and prognosis. *Journal of Research on Christian Education* 4(1): 7–19.

Carper, J. C., and J. Layman. 1997. Blackflight academies: The new Christian day schools. *The Educational Forum* 61(2): 114–21.

Center for Education Reform. 2000. *National charter school directory 2000.* Washington, D.C.: CER.

Coleman, J. S., T. Hoffer, and S. Kilgore. 1982. *High school achievement: Public, Catholic, and private schools compared.* New York: Basic Books.

Cremin, L. A. 1980. *American education: The democratic experience, 1783–1876.* New York: Harper & Row.

Cremin, L. A. 1988. *American education: The metropolitan experience, 1876–1980.* New York: Harper & Row.

Cremin, L. A. 1997. *Traditions of American education.* New York: Basic Books.

Curran, F. X. 1954. *The churches and the schools: American Protestantism and popular elementary education.* Chicago: Loyola University Press.

Gabel, R. J. 1937. Public funds for church and private schools. Ph.D. diss., The Catholic University of America.

Glenn, C. L. 1988. *The myth of the common school.* Amherst: University of Massachusetts Press.

Jorgenson, L. P. 1987. *The state and the nonpublic school, 1825–1925.* Columbia: University of Missouri Press.

Kaestle, C. F. 1983. *Pillars of the republic: Common schools in American society, 1780–1860.* New York: Hill & Wang.

Nevin, D., and R. E. Bills. 1976. *The schools that fear built: Segregation academies in the South.* Washington, D.C.: Acropolis Books.

National Center for Education Statistics. 1998. Private school universe survey, 1995–96. Washington, D.C.: U.S. Department of Education.

National Center for Education Statistics. 2000. *Minidigest of education statistics. 1999.* Washington, D.C.: U.S. Department of Education.

Randall, E. V. 1994. *Private schools and public power. A case for pluralism.* New York: Teachers College Press.

Ray, B. D. 1997. *Strengths of their own—Home schoolers across America: Academic achievement, family characteristics, and longitudinal traits.* Salem, Ore.: National Home Education Research Institute.

Reese, W. F. 1995. *Origins of the American high school.* New Haven, Conn.: Yale University Press.

Ross, W. G. 1994. *Forging new freedoms: Nativism, education, and the constitution, 1917–1927.* Lincoln: University of Nebraska Press.

Skerry, P. 1980. Christian schools versus the I.R.S. *Public Interest* 61 (October): 18–41.

Tyack, D. and L. Cuban. 1995. *Tinkering toward utopia: A century of public school reform.* Cambridge, Mass.: Harvard University Press.

## POSTNOTE

This article shows that American schools have not been static institutions. They have evolved to meet the needs and values of society as our country has developed. During the course of our history, schools have been the battleground for competing groups, interests, and philosophies.

Writing in the spring of 2001, Carper accurately predicted the 2002 Supreme Court decision upholding the use of "carefully crafted" vouchers which enable parents in certain circumstances to use public tax money to purchase private, even religious, education for their children. Whether vouchers will be limited to students in failing public schools or will be offered to all parents, independent of income, appears to be the next educational policy battle.

## DISCUSSION QUESTIONS

1. Which of the many revealing facts about the history of our schools was most surprising to you?

2. What does Carper's second-to-last sentence mean—"Education of the public, rather than public education, might become the primary concern of the state."?

3. Are you in favor of choice within the public schools or a more radical choice plan, such as giving parents an educational check or voucher that allows them to buy the schooling they desire for their children? What are your reasons?

# Dichotomizing Education: Why No One Wins and America Loses

## 52

Carl D. Glickman

I did not lightly take pen in hand (yes, I still use a pen) in writing this article. I have devoted my entire professional life to working with colleagues to create, establish, and sustain public schools that are driven by collaboration, personalization, and active and participatory student learning.[1] And I will continue to do so, as I personally believe such is the best way to prepare all students for the intellectual, social, and aesthetic life of a democracy.

Yet, even in the fervor of my beliefs, I still see other concepts of education that generate degrees of uncertainty in me. My memories of my own best teachers are revealing. Most taught in highly interactive ways, but one grand elder taught from behind a podium in a huge auditorium and engaged in little interaction with students. He was perhaps my greatest teacher. Such discrepancies don't change the strength of my own beliefs; they simply remind me that the viable possibilities of educating students well are broad indeed.

Ultimately, an American education must stand on a foundation that is wider than the beliefs of any one individual or any one group. It should encourage, respect, and support any conceptions—no matter how diametrically opposed to one's own—that are willing to be tested openly and freely. Furthermore, it should involve the willing and nondiscriminatory participation of *all* students, parents, and educators. That is what should be at the core of an American education. But with the "winner take all" wars being fought today, I am seriously concerned about the future of our students and of our public schools and about the vitality of a better democracy.

## Ideological Absolutes

The either/or debates about standards versus no standards, intrinsic versus extrinsic motivation, core versus multicultural knowledge, direct instruction versus constructivist learning, and phonics versus whole language are symptomatic of ideologies that attempt to crush one another and leave only one solution standing. Whether the ideology is education anchored in traditional, behaviorist authority or progressive, inquiry-based learning, the stance toward the final outcome is the same. One group possesses the truth, and the other side is demonized as a pack of extremists: scary, evil persons. Articles and books present educators and the public with a forced choice that unfortunately disregards reality and endangers the very concept of an American education.[2]

Let me illustrate the incompleteness of ideological absolutes with one of today's most emotional issues, the relationship of race to socioeconomic achievement. One side of this debate argues that America is the land of opportunity,

**TERMS TO NOTE**
Standards
Extrinsic motivation
Intrinsic motivation
Direct instruction
Constructivism
Phonics
Whole language
Behaviorist
Progressivism
Inquiry

From Carl D. Glickman, "Dichotomizing Education: Why No One Wins and America Loses," *Phi Delta Kappan*, October 2001. Carl Glickman is the Roy F. and Joann Cole Mitte Endowed Chair in School Improvement at Southwest Texas State University, San Marcos and University Professor Emeritus of Education, University of Georgia, Athens. He wishes to thank Donna Alvermann, Gene Hall, Alice Sampson, Bobby Starnes, and Margaret Wilder, who graciously provided feedback on this article.

where freedom rings, where anyone—regardless of race, religion, gender, or class—can work hard and rise to a position of authority, success, and accomplishment. The other side argues that America is a hegemonic system, protecting the ruling class and extant privilege while keeping the poor, the dispossessed, and people of color stifled, oppressed, and marginalized. Well, which side of this debate is correct? The answer to that question has important implications for what our society needs to change in terms of practices, programs, and the targeting of resources. But the truth is that both contradictory realities have compelling evidence and must be used together to figure out what needs to be done next.

Consider the economic component of this debate. Seymour Martin Lipset compares the United States with other Western industrialized nations.[3] Since the post-Civil War era, America has been the wealthiest country, with a steady rise in living standards and unparalleled social and economic advances for the poor and working class. Yet the income of the poorest fifth of this nation continues to *decline* relative to that of other Americans.

The African American scholar Henry Louis Gates, Jr., takes on this same dichotomy in reference to race. He observes that, since 1967, the number of middle-class African American families has quadrupled. Since 1973 the top 100 African American businesses have moved from sales of $473 million to $11.7 billion. In 1970 "only one in ten blacks had attended college; today one in three has." He then goes on to discuss the continuous wrenching poverty of a third of African Americans today and concludes: "We need something we don't have: a way of speaking about black poverty that doesn't falsify the reality of black advancement, a way of speaking about black advancement that doesn't distort the enduring realities of black poverty. I'd venture that a lot depends on whether we get it."[4]

In truth, America has been one of the leading countries of opportunity for disenfranchised

persons and, at the same time, a country of the greatest economic stratification between the luxury of the wealthiest and the wretched conditions of the poorest.[5] In essence, the beliefs of Ayn Rand and Pete Seeger are both correct. To speak only of one side and ignore the other is to create disbelief in most ordinary citizens, who know firsthand of counterexamples to any single view. And this is what I believe to be the danger of ideological truth in education. Many educators in classrooms and schools feel that they have become pawns in the reformers' and policy makers' propaganda game that insists there is a single best way to change the system of American schools.

## Ideology in Education

The attacks by E. D. Hirsch, Jr., against progressive education and the equally strident attacks by others such as Alfie Kohn against traditional education are wonderful examples of this either/or ideological stance. Hirsch argues that a common core of knowledge is essential for all students, if they are to succeed in mainstream society. Without a common framework of spoken and written English, historical and cultural references, and direct instruction, marginalized and poor children are deprived of the education that wealthier children pick up automatically from their parents and peers. Thus there is the need to rid our schools of the overwhelming "permissive" practices of activity-based education and to use tests of common knowledge to ensure that all children are acquiring the "cultural capital" needed for success in later life. Kohn in turn speaks against standards, core knowledge, and tests and says that children, regardless of their circumstances, are innately curious and that teachers should explore the topics that intrigue them to open up new freedoms and possibilities. Each proponent has his version of "truth." Each sees little validity in any research supporting the methods that oppose his ideology. Again, the reality is that education is composed of many complexities that defeat any singular truth of how the world can and should work.

For example, might it be that both Hirsch and Kohn have valid perspectives? Focusing on core knowledge that students themselves might not choose but that gives them access to a society in which they might possibly change the current balance of power, wealth, and control seems quite reasonable. Using the curiosity of students to learn multiple histories and cultures and to explore a variety of intelligences in an intensely involving way also seems quite reasonable. It is important that schools be joyful and engaging places. Yet is all learning intrinsically or extrinsically motivated? Most would say it's both—we learn for the joy of it, but some of the most useful learning has taken place because others, not we ourselves, demanded that we do it, do it well, and do it until we got it right.

The polemics surrounding standards versus no standards do not account for complex realities. Are external standards bad or good? Might they be both? Might we have state standards and assessments for most (but not all) public schools in the same state? Some states have standards and assessments that have been well received by educators and the public—not seen as heavy-handed, intrusive, or unfair. Many states have standards and assessments that are volatile in makeup, format, pressure, and consequences.

The standards polarization—again, only one side can win—has come about because people have applied the term "standards" to all systems as if they were identical. However, Maine's standards are quite different from Virginia's. Elements of standards systems can be quite good, such as using disaggregated data to focus on the progress of all students, equalizing funding for poor students and communities, and targeting additional resources. Some states grant variances

**TERM TO NOTE**
Disaggregated data

allowing schools and districts to develop their own assessments. And yes, there are cases in which it is good that standards can be used to close and reorganize schools that have done a disservice to students and parents. Standards systems can be demeaning and harmful—when they equate education with narrowly derived assessments and tests. They can also be tremendously positive in challenging schools and communities to leave no student behind.[6] We need to acknowledge simultaneous realities if we are to educate all students better than before.

## Pedagogical Pain

The "single-truth" wars have created much pain among teachers and school leaders who are swept into the battles. When whole language gained currency as "the" way to teach reading, teachers using phonics were lambasted, swept aside, and made to feel that they were evil, archaic, fascist practitioners of an indefensible method. Recently, the opposing force has "won" in states led by California and Texas. They have blamed whole language and invented spelling for declining literacy in America. Now teachers of whole language are made to feel abandoned and rejected as "feel-good," self-esteem-promoting contributors to the demise of basic skills.

These periodic surges and countersurges occur because one set of believers ignores any possible merits of the other side. Isn't it possible that many highly literate and culturally diverse people—people that you and I both know—were taught how to read mainly by decoding, phonics, and grammatical rules? Isn't it equally obvious that many highly literate and culturally diverse people have learned to read through literacy immersion, writing workshops, and experiential learning? Why is it so difficult to accept that an open mind about possibilities in education should be seen as a virtue rather than a liability?

Cooperative versus competitive learning is another such brawl. Cooperation is a key aspect

| | of how one learns with and |
|---|---|
| **TERM TO NOTE** | |
| Cooperative | from others, and it undergirds |
| learning | much of community, civic, |

and business life. Research exists that demonstrates the power of structured team activities for academic and social development. Yet humans, as part of the animal kingdom, are also moved to learn by traits that have helped them to survive: dominance, power, and the need to test oneself against others. Cooperation and competition are not different versions of humanity; they are different dimensions of the same humanity. And thus there is evidence that both cooperation and competition bring out high performance in individuals.

The overarching debate about progressive, learner-centered schools versus teacher-centered, direct-instruction schools will be my last venture into the foolishness of single truths. This debate simplifies and silences the cultural and family values that Lisa Delpit so eloquently writes about in *Other People's Children*.[7] Asking students to conform to certain manners, expecting them to learn what adults determine is important for them, being didactic in instruction, and using "call and response" methods have resulted in great success for teachers and leaders such as Marva Collins, Jaime Escalante, and Lorraine Monroe and for a number of school programs.[8] Regardless of what one personally believes about the atmosphere of such classrooms and schools, students and parents in these settings see such didactic methods as expressions of teachers' love, care, and cultural solidarity.[9] The teachers are proud to demand that their students learn, and they go to almost any length to see that their students can compete with other students.

Yet progressive classrooms and schools that are activity- or project-centered and that cultivate imagination, problem solving, responsibility, and a variety of intellectual pursuits have, in the hands of the most dedicated teachers, also attained incredible success for students. Educators such as Eliot Wigginton, Deborah Meier,

George Wood, Gloria Ladson-Billings, Sonia Nieto, and Jabari Mahiri have shown the power of inquiry-centered, progressive learning.

My point is *not* that all methods, techniques, curricula, and structures are of equal worth or that the attitude "anything goes" is acceptable. My point is that, when a group of students and parents choose to be with a group of educators dedicated to a particular philosophy and way of learning, the results for students can be awesome. No one group should have the presumption or power to tell another group that only its way is the right way. Instead, in accordance with publicly determined purposes and criteria, we should be seeking, testing, and developing research-based alternative conceptions and practices of successful education. Kenneth Wilson, a Nobel laureate in physics, remarked about the need to test a multitude of educational approaches through longitudinal research and self-correction to find out what works well, what can be adapted, and what should be discarded.[10] The idea is not to prove that one way is the only way but instead to allow for different conceptions of education to flourish in the marketplace of public education.

## Religion in America and an Educated American

Of all Western nations, America is the country with the highest percentage of citizens actively involved in religious and spiritual practices.[11] Why? Because it has no official state religion and no divine story behind its creation. Those countries that do have histories of such official state religion—a one way to believe for all—tend to have lower percentages of citizen involvement in religious practice. This example suggests why we must avoid a single governmental (local, state, or national) conception of education. The analogy with religion ends at a certain point, as the U.S. government needs to remain neutral and not use public funds to promote any particular set of religious beliefs. But government must use public funds to support a public education consistent with democratic ideals.[12] And the best way for doing so is to create a system of state schools that promote various publicly determined conceptions of an educated American.

Public education can be defined in several overlapping ways. Public education is funded by taxpayers, it is an education for the public, it is open and without cost to students and parents, it is compulsory, it is governed by public authority, it is nonprofit, and it always *should be* nondiscriminatory and nonrepressive of students and parents.[13] It is public because it serves a common good: the education of students to have choice of "life, liberty, and the pursuit of happiness" and to acknowledge those choices for others.

Within these definitions of public, American education is always an experiment—one hopes a thoughtful one—that must constantly test ways to further realize the hopes and aspirations of all the nation's people. Whenever one truth stamps out all others—whether it be through one system of tests, one approach to curriculum, one conception of knowledge, a single method of instruction, or a uniform structure for all public schools—democracy itself and education for a democracy are subverted.

In first proposing the need for common schools, Horace Mann wrote in the 1840s that

**TERM TO NOTE**
Common school

public schools would be the great equalizers of human conditions, the balance wheel of the social machinery. Poverty would disappear and with it the discord between the haves and the have-nots; life for all men would be longer, better, and happier. The common school would be free, for poor and rich alike, as good as any private school, and nonsectarian. (The common school was not to be a school for common people but rather a school common to all people.) And the pedagogy of the common or free school would stress the "self-discipline of individuals, self-control, and self-governance." The issue for Mann was that the educated person was to have a free, deliberate choice between obedience and anarchy.[14]

Another view of the educated person in a democracy was shaped by the Lockean sympathies of early American thought. The educated person would be the one who renounced self-indulgence, practiced restraint, and saw the virtue of frugality and labor. In this view, one would work not for what one could accumulate but in order to focus the human mind and body.

Jefferson's concept of the educated person was the farmer—a person who lived apart from others; pursued his own curiosity about science, philosophy, and art after a long day of self-sustaining chores; and then determined those times that he should participate in neighborhood and community affairs. The farmer's life was a combination of aloneness, individuality, and self-learning with minimal but significant civic responsibility.

W. E. B. Du Bois, referring to the need for African American children to learn, saw public education as giving "our children the fairness of a start which will equip them with such an array of facts and such an attitude toward truth that they can have a real chance to judge what the world is and what its greater minds have thought it might be."[15]

Education might also be defined as making a good neighbor—one who cares for and respects others, who takes care of his or her own family needs, and who contributes to the welfare of others.[16] Such a person would possess a respect for other people and an understanding of life conditions locally, nationally, and internationally; the ability to communicate with diverse others; analytic and problem-solving skills; and the competence to choose what to do with one's own life in economic, social, recreational, and aesthetic pursuits. Does one need three years of high school or college-level preparatory mathematics to develop these attributes? Does one need to learn French? How about Chinese? What level of mastery does one need in the various disciplines? Is it better to study discrete subjects or an integrated curriculum with applications to the world outside of school? The question here is, What knowledge, skills, and understandings are needed to be a good neighbor and citizen?

In a high school curriculum controlled by college admission requirements, there are expected core courses, and good scores on the SAT or ACT have become essential measures of an educated American. Whether going to college or not, most students will not use most of what they are required to learn, whether mathematics or history or language or science. Is it still essential? Again, says who? Dare I ask the unspeakable: Can one be a good neighbor and a wise and productive citizen without going to college?

Is the purpose of public education to train a highly skilled work force to support American corporations? If so, the definition of a well-educated American as a good worker will place a great deal of emphasis on technology. But again, who should determine what is a well-educated person? For example, the Waldorf schools in America have children work with natural materials for the first three to five years of schooling.[17] Children work only with wood, clay, water, and paint, in long, painstaking projects for several years before the manmade world becomes a source of their learning—no televisions, no phones, no computers in early childhood and primary classrooms. The prime emphasis is on imagination and work in an all-natural environment. Are these students educated less well than others? According to what criteria?

To be blunt, any single truth or concept of an educated American will be fraught with contradictions. The real danger of any one reform effort, such as a standards movement that relies on a single test, is the promotion of a single definition of the well-educated citizen as a college graduate who is technologically prepared to lead a successful economic life. The idea that an educated citizen might not want to make vast sums of money or work in a corporation but instead might seek success in quietness, resistance, or even detachment from corporate/college-controlled work, has eroded in America. Even to mention the idea that education is not mostly about jobs or money but about choosing how to live one's life among others is to be seen as a romantic, a throwback to another time.

My point is not to convince others of any one definition of a well-educated person but to share the need for varied conceptions of education, conceptions that must be in conformance with "public" criteria and equally based on data about student accomplishments and successes.

## What Do We Do?

As a reformer who advocates the progressive tradition and assists schools in keeping it alive, I do not seek a common ground for public education—an eclectic "all things of equal merit" ground—but instead wish to move beyond that to a higher ground that incorporates complexity and competing conceptions. A higher ground where contradictory truths must be part and parcel of American democracy. We need an education system that supports multiple conceptions of an educated American, that subjects all such conceptions to the scrutiny of research and public accountability, and that fixes all actions of classrooms and schools within the boundaries of equity. American students and schools lose each time one "truth" gains currency and suppresses competing notions of public education.

So let me end by stating that, in my experience with schools, education reformers, policy makers, legislators, corporate persons, community activists, and citizens at large, I have found people of astonishingly good will and passionate intent who labor in the light of controversy about what our schools need or deserve. They are accused by their opponents of being self-indulgent conspirators with sinister motives, but most of them, or at least those that I know, are not. However, many of those who are most influential or powerful are singularly convinced that theirs is the true way to improve education and that all other ways are false, bad, and corrupt.

We need to realize that, most often, life does not contain single truths but instead is about predicaments, competing views, and apparent conflicts. The public school system must value and allow multiple conceptions of education that students, parents, and faculty members can choose from—some purebreds, some hybrids, and some yet to be known, but all devoted to students and their pursuit of the American Dream.

We must fight against any single model, structure, method, or system of education. We must expand the freedom of schools to test new concepts of standards, assessments, and accountability. Ultimately, we must hold every school and district responsible for whether it has provided an education for all children that can be documented to increase choices of "life, liberty, and the pursuit of happiness." *That* is an American education.

## NOTES

1. Carl D. Glickman, *Revolutionizing America's Schools* (San Francisco: Jossey-Bass, 1998).

2. See E. D. Hirsch, Jr., *The Schools We Need and Why We Don't Have Them* (New York: Doubleday,1996); Alfie Kohn, *The Schools Our Children Deserve* (Boston: Houghton Mifflin, 1999); Susan Ohanian, *One Size Fits Few: The Folly of Educational Standards* (Portsmouth, N.H.: Heinemann, 1999); and I. de Pommereau, "Tougher High School Standards Signal Greater Demands on Students," *Christian Science Monitor,* 16 June 1996, p. 12, 1–C.

3. Seymour Martin Lipset, *American Exceptionalism: A Double-Edged Sword* (New York: Norton, 1996).

4. Henry Louis Gates, Jr., and Cornel West, *The Future of the Race* (New York: Vintage Books, 1996), pp. 19, 38.

5. Jim Myers, "Notes on the Murder of Thirty of My Neighbors," *Atlantic,* March 2000, pp. 72–88.

6. Chris Gallagher, "A Seat at the Table: Teachers Reclaiming Assessment Through Rethinking Accountability," *Phi Delta Kappan,* March 2000, pp. 502–7.

7. Lisa Delpit, *Other People's Children: Cultural Conflict in the Classroom* (New York: New Press, 1995).

8. See, for example, such schools as P.S. 161 in New York, KIPP Academics in Texas and New York, and the Frederick Douglass Middle School in New York.

9. Samuel Casey Carter, *No Excuses: Seven Principals of Low-Income Schools Who Set the Standards for High Achievement* (Washington, D.C.: Heritage Foundation, 1999); and Jacqueline Jordan Irvine, "Seeing with the Cultural Eye: Different Perspectives of African American Teachers and Researchers," DeWitt Wallace-Reader's Digest Distinguished Lecture presented at the annual meeting of the American Educational Research Association, New Orleans, April 2000.

10. Kenneth Wilson and Bennett Daviss, *Redesigning Education* (New York: Teachers College Press, 1994).

11. Lipset, op. cit.; and Warren A. Nord, *Religion and American Education: Rethinking a National Dilemma* (Chapel Hill: University of North Carolina Press, 1995).

12. John Dayton and Carl D. Glickman, "Curriculum Change and Implementation: Democratic Imperatives," *Peabody Journal of Education,* vol. 9, no. 4, 1994, pp. 62–86; Benjamin R. Barber, *An Aristocracy of Everyone: The Politics of Education and the Future of America* (New York: Ballantine, 1992); and Amy Gutmann, *Democratic Education* (Princeton, N.J.: Princeton University Press, 1987).

13. Gutmann, op. cit.

14. Lawrence A. Cremin, *The Transformation of the School: Progressivism in American Education 1876–1957* (New York: Vintage Books, 1964), pp. 3–11.

15. W. E. B. Du Bois, "The Freedom to Learn," in Philip S. Foner, ed., *W. E. B. Du Bois Speaks* (New York: Pathfinder, 1970), pp. 230–31.

16. George H. Wood, *A Time to Learn* (New York: Dutton, 1998).

17. Todd Oppenheimer, "Schooling the Imagination," *Atlantic,* September 1999, pp. 71–83.

## POSTNOTE

One of the most enduring characteristics of American education is its "constant change." Americans are a restless, energetic, and inventive people. We also place a very high value on the education of our children. We tend to lurch from one educational panacea to the next in a search for "the one right way." Carl Glickman calls for a truce among these competing solutions. He urges that we acknowledge the complexity of the teaching-learning situation and that we begin to honor the diversity of learning styles and capacities and the different conceptions of education. And educators are beginning to respond. There is more recognition of alternative teaching and learning strategies today than even a decade ago. However, one significant problem persists. Unless we adopt real educational choice plans that match individual learning styles with instructional environments, we are placing a huge burden on classroom teachers. And if we persist without such choices, we must make a much greater commitment to providing teachers with the training they need to master the complexity of learning styles that exists in a single classroom.

## DISCUSSION QUESTIONS

1. Are you committed to one of the educational "truths" discussed by Glickman? Which one? Why?

2. Which of the truths and the teaching-learning approaches that flow from it do you feel least capable of putting into action?

3. Do you believe that Glickman's critique is accurate and his solution feasible? Why or why not?

# The Ethics of Teaching

Kenneth A. Strike

## 53

M rs. Porter and Mr. Kennedy have divided their third-grade classes into reading groups. In her class, Mrs. Porter tends to spend the most time with students in the slowest reading group because they need the most help. Mr. Kennedy claims that such behavior is unethical. He maintains that each reading group should receive equal time.

Miss Andrews has had several thefts of lunch money in her class. She has been unable to catch the thief, although she is certain that some students in the class know who the culprit is. She decides to keep the entire class inside for recess, until someone tells her who stole the money. Is it unethical to punish the entire class for the acts of a few?

Ms. Phillips grades her fifth-grade students largely on the basis of effort. As a result, less able students who try hard often get better grades than students who are abler but less industrious. Several parents have accused Ms. Phillips of unethical behavior, claiming that their children are not getting what they deserve. These parents also fear that teachers in the middle school won't understand Ms. Phillips' grading practices and will place their children in inappropriate tracks.

## The Nature of Ethical Issues

The cases described above are typical of the ethical issues that teachers face. What makes these issues ethical?

Kenneth A. Strike is a professor of philosophy of education at Cornell University, Ithaca, N.Y. Strike, Kenneth A., "The Ethics of Teaching," *Phi Delta Kappan*, October 1988. Copyright © 1988 by Phi Delta Kappa. Reprinted by permission of author and publisher.

First, ethical issues concern questions of right and wrong—our duties and obligations, our rights and responsibilities. Ethical discourse is characterized by a unique vocabulary that commonly includes such words as *ought* and *should*, *fair* and *unfair*.

**TERM TO NOTE**
Ethics

Second, ethical questions cannot be settled by an appeal to facts alone. In each of the preceding cases, knowing the consequences of our actions is not sufficient for determining the right thing to do. Perhaps, because Mrs. Porter spends more time with the slow reading group, the reading scores in her class will be more evenly distributed than the scores in Mr. Kennedy's class. But even knowing this does not tell us if it is fair to spend a disproportionate amount of time with the slow readers. Likewise, if Miss Andrews punishes her entire class, she may catch the thief, but this does not tell us whether punishing the entire group was the right thing to do. In ethical reasoning, facts are relevant in deciding what to do. But by themselves they are not enough. We also require ethical principles by which to judge the facts.

Third, ethical questions should be distinguished from values. Our values concern what we like or what we believe to be good. If one enjoys Bach or likes skiing, that says something about one's values. Often there is nothing right or wrong about values, and our values are a matter of our free choice. For example, it would be difficult to argue that someone who preferred canoeing to skiing had done something wrong or had made a mistake. Even if we believe that Bach is better than rock, that is not a reason to make people who prefer rock listen to Bach. Generally, questions of values turn on our choices: what we like, what we deem worth liking. But there is nothing obligatory about values.

On the other hand, because ethics concern what we ought to do, our ethical obligations are often independent of what we want or choose. The fact that we want something that belongs to someone else does not entitle us to take it. Nor does a choice to steal make stealing right or even "right for us." Our ethical obligations continue to be obligations, regardless of what we want or choose.

## Ethical Reasoning

The cases sketched above involve ethical dilemmas: situations in which it seems possible to give a reasonable argument for more than one course of action. We must think about our choices, and we must engage in moral reasoning. Teaching is full of such dilemmas. Thus teachers need to know something about ethical reasoning.

Ethical reasoning involves two stages: applying principles to cases and judging the adequacy or applicability of the principles. In the first stage, we are usually called upon to determine the relevant ethical principle or principles that apply to a case, to ascertain the relevant facts of the case, and to judge the facts by the principles.

Consider, for example, the case of Miss Andrews and the stolen lunch money. Some ethical principles concerning punishment seem to apply directly to the case. Generally, we believe that we should punish the guilty, not the innocent; that people should be presumed innocent until proven guilty; and that the punishment should fit the crime. If Miss Andrews punishes her entire class for the behavior of an unknown few, she will violate these common ethical principles about punishment.

Ethical principles are also involved in the other two cases. The first case involves principles of equity and fairness. We need to know what counts as fair or equal treatment for students of different abilities. The third case requires some principles of due process. We need to know what are fair procedures for assigning grades to students.

However, merely identifying applicable principles isn't enough. Since the cases described above involve ethical dilemmas, it should be possible to argue plausibly for more than one course of action.

For example, suppose Miss Andrews decides to punish the entire class. It could be argued that she had behaved unethically because she has punished innocent people. She might defend herself, however, by holding that she had reasons for violating ethical principles that we normally apply to punishment. She might argue that it was important to catch the thief or that it was even more important to impress on her entire class that stealing is wrong. She could not make these points by ignoring the matter. By keeping the entire class inside for recess, Miss Andrews could maintain, she was able to catch the thief and to teach her class a lesson about the importance of honesty. Even if she had to punish some innocent people, everyone was better off as a result. Can't she justify her action by the fact that everyone benefits?

## Two General Principles

When we confront genuine ethical dilemmas such as this, we need some general ethical concepts in order to think our way through them. I suggest two: the principle of benefit maximization and the principle of equal respect for persons.

The principle of benefit maximization holds that we should take that course of actions which will maximize the benefit sought. More generally, it requires us to do that which will make everyone, on the average, as well off as possible. One of the traditional formulations of this principle is the social philosophy known as utilitarianism, which holds that our most general moral obligation is to act in a manner that produces the greatest happiness for the greatest number.

We might use the principle of benefit maximization to think about each of these cases. The

**TERMS TO NOTE**

Benefit maximization

Equal respect

principle requires that in each case we ask which of the possible courses of action makes people generally better off. Miss Andrews has appealed to the principle of benefit maximization in justifying her punishment of the entire class. Ms. Phillips might likewise appeal to it in justifying her grading system. Perhaps by using grades to reward effort rather than successful performance, the overall achievement of the class will be enhanced. Is that not what is important?

It is particularly interesting to see how the principle of benefit maximization might be applied to the question of apportioning teacher time between groups with different levels of ability. Assuming for the moment that we wish to maximize the overall achievement of the class, the principle of benefit maximization dictates that we allocate time in a manner that will produce the greatest overall learning.

Suppose, however, we discover that the way to produce the greatest overall learning in a given class is for a teacher to spend the most time with the *brightest* children. These are the children who provide the greatest return on our investment of time. Even though the least able children learn less than they would with an equal division of time, the overall learning that takes place in the class is maximized when we concentrate on the ablest.

Here the principle of benefit maximization seems to lead to an undesirable result. Perhaps we should consider other principles as well.

The principle of equal respect requires that our actions respect the equal worth of moral agents. We must regard human beings as intrinsically worthwhile and treat them accordingly. The essence of this idea is perhaps best expressed in the Golden Rule. We have a duty to accord others the same kind of treatment that we expect them to accord us.

The principle of equal respect can be seen as involving three subsidiary ideas. First, it requires us to treat people as ends in themselves, rather than as means to further our own goals. We must respect their goals as well.

Second, when we are considering what it means to treat people as ends rather than as means, we must regard as central the fact that people are free and rational moral agents. This means that, above all, we must respect their freedom of choice. And we must respect the choices that people make even when we do not agree.

Third, no matter how people differ, they are of equal value as moral agents. This does not mean that we must see people as equal in abilities or capacities. Nor does it mean that we cannot take relevant differences between people into account when deciding how to treat them. It is not, for example, a violation of equal respect to give one student a higher grade than another because that student works harder and does better.

That people are of equal value as moral agents does mean, however, that they are entitled to the same basic rights and that their interests are of equal value. Everyone, regardless of native ability, is entitled to equal opportunity. No one is entitled to act as though his or her happiness counted for more than the happiness of others. As persons, everyone has equal worth.

Notice three things about these two moral principles. First, both principles (in some form) are part of the moral concepts of almost everyone who is reading this article. These are the sorts of moral principles that everyone cites in making moral arguments. Even if my formulation is new, the ideas themselves should be familiar. They are part of our common ethical understandings.

Second, both principles seem necessary for moral reflection. Neither is sufficient by itself.

**TERM TO NOTE**

Values

For example, the principle of equal respect requires us to value the well-being of others as we value our own well-being. But to value the welfare of ourselves *and* others is to be concerned with maximizing benefits; we want all people to be as well-off as possible.

Conversely, the principle of benefit maximization seems to presuppose the principle of equal respect. Why, after all, must we value the welfare of others? Why not insist that only our own happiness counts or that our happiness is more important than the happiness of others? Answering these questions will quickly lead us to affirm that people are of equal worth and that, as a consequence, everyone's happiness is to be valued equally. Thus our two principles are intertwined.

Third, the principles may nevertheless conflict with one another. One difference between the principle of benefit maximization and the principle of equal respect is their regard for consequences. For the principle of benefit maximization, only consequences matter. The sole relevant factor in choosing between courses of action is which action has the best overall results. But consequences are not decisive in the principle of equal respect; our actions must respect the dignity and worth of the individuals involved, even if we choose a course of action that produces less benefit than some other possible action.

The crucial question that characterizes a conflict between the principle of benefit maximization and the principle of equal respect is this:

When is it permissible to violate a person's rights in order to produce a better outcome? For example, this seems the best way to describe the issue that arises when a teacher decides to punish an entire class for the acts of a few. Students' rights are violated when they are punished for something they haven't done, but the overall consequence of the teacher's action may be desirable. Is it morally permissible, then, to punish everyone?

We can think about the issue of fair allocation of teacher time in the same way. Spending more time with the brightest students may enhance the average learning of the class. But we have, in effect, traded the welfare of the least able students for the welfare of the ablest. Is that not failing to respect the equal worth of the least able students? Is that not treating them as though they were means, not ends?

The principle of equal respect suggests that we should give the least able students at least an equal share of time, even if the average achievement of the class declines. Indeed, we might use the principle of equal respect to argue that we should allocate our time in a manner that produces more equal results—or a more equal share of the benefits of education.

I cannot take the discussion of these issues any further in this short space. But I do want to suggest some conclusions about ethics and teaching.

First, teaching is full of ethical issues. It is the responsibility of teachers, individually and collectively, to consider these issues and to have informed and intelligent opinions about them.

Second, despite the fact that ethical issues are sometimes thorny, they can be thought about. Ethical reflection can help us to understand what is at stake in our choices, to make more responsible choices, and sometimes to make the right choices.

Finally, to a surprising extent, many ethical dilemmas, including those that are common to teaching, can be illuminated by the principles of benefit maximization and equal respect for persons. Understanding these general ethical principles and their implications is crucial for thinking about ethical issues.

## POSTNOTE

Ethics seems to be making a comeback. We may not be behaving better, but we are talking about it more. Street crime and white-collar crime, drugs and violence, our inability to keep promises in our personal and professional lives—all these suggest a renewed need for ethics.

Kenneth Strike points out that teaching is full of ethical issues, and it is true that teachers make promises to perform certain duties and that they have real power over the lives of children. This article, however, speaks to only one end of the spectrum of ethical issues faced by the teacher: what we call "hard case" ethics, complex problems, often dilemmas. Certainly these are important, but there are also everyday teaching ethics—the issues that fill a teacher's day: Should I correct this stack of papers or watch *The Simpsons?* Should I "hear" that vulgar comment or stroll right by? Should I read this story again this year before I teach it tomorrow or spend some time with my colleagues in the teachers' lounge? Should I bend down and pick up yet another piece of paper in the hall or figure I've done my share for the day?

Like hard-case ethical issues, these questions, in essence, ask, What's the right thing to do? Our answers to these everyday questions often become our habits, good and bad. These, in turn, define much of our ethical behavior as teachers.

## DISCUSSION QUESTIONS

1. What three factors or qualities make an issue an ethical one?

2. What two ethical principles are mentioned in the article? Give your own examples of classroom situations that reflect these principles.

3. Why is there a greater interest in the ethics of teaching today than thirty years ago?

# 54

# The Teacher's Ten Commandments:
# School Law in the Classroom

Thomas R. McDaniel

I n recent years public school teachers have been made painfully aware that the law defines, limits, and prescribes many aspects of a teacher's daily life. Schools are no longer protected domains where teachers rule with impunity; ours is an age of litigation. Not only are parents and students ready to use the courts for all manner of grievances against school and teacher, the growing legislation itself regulates more and more of school life. In addition to an unprecedented number of laws at all levels of government, the mind-boggling array of complex case law principles (often vague and contradictory) adds to the confusion for the educator.

The Ten Commandments of School Law described below are designed to provide the concerned and bewildered teacher with some significant general guidelines in the classroom. While statutes and case law principles may vary from state to state or judicial circuit to judicial circuit, these school law principles have wide applicability in the United States today.

## Commandment I: Thou Shalt Not Worship in the Classroom

This may seem something of a parody of the Biblical First Commandment—and many teachers hold that indeed their religious freedom and that of the majority of students has been limited

Thomas R. McDaniel is provost of Converse College. "The Teacher's Ten Commandments: School Law in the Classroom" by Thomas R. McDaniel. Revised and updated from *Phi Delta Kappan*, June 1979. Reprinted by permission from Thomas R. McDaniel.

by the court cases prohibiting prayer and Bible reading—but the case law principles here have been designed to keep public schools *neutral* in religious matters. The First Amendment to the Constitution, made applicable by the Fourteenth Amendment to state government (and hence to public schools, which are agencies of state government), requires that there be no law "respecting the establishment of religion or prohibiting the free exercise thereof." As the Supreme Court declared in the *Everson* decision of 1947, "Neither [a state nor the federal government] can pass laws that aid one religion, aid all religions, or prefer one religion over another." Such rules, said the Court, would violate the separation of church and state principle of the First Amendment.

In 1971 the Supreme Court ruled in *Lemon v. Kurtzman* that separation of church and state required that government action or legislation in education must clear a three-pronged test. It must: 1) not have a religious purpose, 2) not have the primary effect of either enhancing or inhibiting religion, and 3) not create "excessive entanglement" between church and state. This Lemon Test has been attacked by Justice Anton Scalia and others in recent years but continues to be used (at least as a guideline) in court rulings. In a 1992 case, *Lee v. Wiseman*, the Supreme Court ruled that an invocation and benediction at commencement by a clergyman was unconstitutional—perhaps because the school principal chose the clergyman and gave him directions for the content of the prayer. In another 1992 case a circuit court of appeals upheld a policy that permitted high school seniors to choose student volunteers to deliver nonsectarian, nonproselytizing invocations at graduation ceremonies. Courts continue to wrestle with questions about "establishment" and "freedom" of religion. However, acts of worship in public schools usually violate the neutrality principle—especially when they appear to be planned and promoted by school officials.

On the other hand, public schools may offer courses in comparative religion, history of religion, or the Bible as literature, because these would be academic experiences rather than religious ones. "Released-time" programs during school hours for outside-of-school religious instruction have been held to be constitutional by the Supreme Court (*Zorach v. Clauson*, 1952). Other religious practices that have been struck down by the Supreme Court include a Kentucky statute requiring that the Ten Commandments be posted in every public school classroom, a Michigan high school's 30-year practice of displaying a 2-foot by 3-foot portrait of Jesus in the hallways, laws in Arkansas and Louisiana requiring that "scientific creationism" (based on Genesis) be taught in science classes to "balance" the teaching of evolution, the Gideons' distribution of Bibles in the public schools of Indiana. Other courts have questioned (or struck down) certain practices such as invocations at football games, nativity scenes and other religious displays, and laws requiring a "moment of silence" when the purpose is to promote prayer. Finding the line that separates church and state has not been easy. The "wall of separation" has often seemed more like a semi-permeable membrane.

In 1984, Congress passed the Equal Access Act. This statute made it unlawful for any public secondary school receiving federal funds to discriminate against any students who wanted to conduct a meeting on school premises during "non-instructional time" (before and after regular school hours) if other student groups (such as clubs) were allowed to use school facilities during these times. Religious groups that are voluntary and student initiated (not officially sponsored or led by school personnel) may, under the EAA, meet on school premises. Such

meetings may not be conducted or controlled by others not associated with the school nor may they interfere with educational activities of the school. In a 1990 case (*Westside Community Schools v. Mergens*) the Supreme Court upheld the constitutionality of the EAA and declared this federal statute did not violate the First Amendment or any of the three prongs of the Lemon Test. However, a 1993 case (*Sease v. School District of Philadelphia*) in Pennsylvania disallowed a gospel choir that advertised itself as sponsored by the school district, was directed by the school secretary, had another school employee attending all practices, and had non-school persons regularly attending meetings of the choir. There were several violations of the EAA in this case.

The application of the neutrality principle to education has resulted in some of the following guidelines for public schools:

1. Students may not be required to salute the flag nor to stand for the flag salute, if this conflicts with their religious beliefs.

2. Bible reading, even without comment, may not be practiced in a public school when the intent is to promote worship.

3. Prayer is an act of worship and as such cannot be a regular part of opening exercises or other aspects of the regular school day (including grace at lunch).

4. Worship services (e.g., prayer and Bible reading) are not constitutional even if voluntary rather than compulsory. Not consensus, not majority vote, nor excusing objectors from class or participation makes these practices legal.

5. Prayer and other acts of worship (benedictions, hymns, invocations, etc.) at school-related or school-sponsored events are increasingly under scrutiny by courts and may be disallowed when found to be initiated or controlled by school officials.

## Commandment II: Thou Shalt Not Abuse Academic Freedom

Under First Amendment protection, teachers are given the necessary freedom and security to use the classroom as a forum for the examination and discussion of ideas. Freedom of expression is a prerequisite for education in a democracy—and the schools, among other responsibilities, are agents of democracy. Students are citizens too, and they are also entitled to freedom of speech. As Justice Abe Fortas, who delivered the Supreme Court's majority opinion in the famous *Tinker* decision (1969), put it:

**TERM TO NOTE**
Academic freedom

> It can hardly be argued that either students or teachers shed their constitutional rights at the schoolhouse gate. . . . In our system state-operated schools may not be enclaves of totalitarianism . . . [and] students may not be regarded as closed-circuit recipients of only that which the state chooses to communicate.

Case law has developed over the years to define the parameters of free expression for both teachers and students:

1. Teachers may discuss controversial issues in the classroom if they are relevant to the curriculum, although good judgment is required. Issues that disrupt the educational process, are demonstrably inappropriate to the legitimate objectives of the curriculum, or are unreasonable for the age and maturity of the students may be prohibited by school officials. The routine use of profanity by teachers is not a protected First Amendment right (*Martin v. Parrish*, 1986, Fifth Circuit Court).

2. Teachers may discuss current events, political issues, and candidates so long as neutrality and balanced consideration prevail. When teachers become advocates and partisans, supporters of a single position rather than examiners of all positions, they run the risk of censure.

3. A teacher may use controversial literature containing "rough" language but must "take care not to transcend his legitimate professional purpose" (*Mailoux v. Kiley*, 1971, U.S. District Court, Massachusetts). Again, courts will attempt to determine curriculum relevance, disruption of the educational process, and appropriateness to the age and maturity of the students.

4. Teachers and students are increasingly (but not yet universally) guaranteed symbolic free speech, including hair length and beards, armbands, and buttons. Courts generally determine such issues in terms of the "substantial disruption" that occurs or is clearly threatened. Dress codes for students are generally allowable when they are intended to provide for health, safety, and "decency." When they exist merely to promote the "tastes" of the teacher or administration, they have usually been struck down by the courts.

5. Teachers have some control over school-sponsored publications and plays. In *Hazelwood School District v. Kuhlmeier* (1988) the Supreme Court held that "educators do not offend the First Amendment by exercising editorial control over the style and content of student speech in school-sponsored expressive activities so long as their actions are reasonably related to legitimate pedagogical concerns." This authority, however, does not extend to censorship of student expression. It does not appear to extend to a school board's banning and regulating textbooks and other "learning materials" (*Virgil v. School Board of Columbia County*, 1989, Eleventh Circuit).

6. Teachers do not have a constitutional right to use any teaching method they want. School district officials and boards may establish course content and teaching methods as matters of policy. Courts will support such policies but will examine the reasonableness of sanctions against teachers. For example, a California court ruled that firing a teacher

for unwittingly permitting students to read obscene poetry was too severe (*De Groat v. Newark*, 1976) while a nine-month suspension of a West Virginia teacher showing cartoons of "Fritz the Cat" undressing was judged appropriate (*DeVito v. Board of Education*, 1984).

Teachers in short are free to deal with controversial issues (including politics and sex) and to use controversial methods and materials if these are educationally defensible, appropriate to the students, and not "materially and substantially" disruptive. But school boards also have authority to maintain curricular policies governing what (and even how) teachers should teach. Courts use a balancing test to determine when students' and teachers' rights to academic freedom must give way to the competing need of society to have reasonable school discipline.

## Commandment III: Thou Shalt Not Engage in Private Activities That Impair Teaching Effectiveness

Of all the principles of school law, this commandment is probably the most difficult to delineate with precision. The private and professional areas of a teacher's life have been, for the most part, separated by recent court decisions. A mere 75 years ago teachers signed contracts with provisions prohibiting marriage, falling in love, leaving town without permission of the school board, smoking cigarettes, loitering in ice-cream stores, and wearing lipstick. But now a teacher's private life is considered his or her own business. Thus, for example, many court cases have established that teachers have the same citizenship rights outside the classroom that any other person has.

Teachers, however, have always been expected by society to abide by high standards of personal conduct. Whenever a teacher's private life undermines effective instruction in the class, there is a possibility that the courts will uphold his or her dismissal. To guard against this possibility, the teacher should consider some of the following principles:

1. Teachers may belong to any organization or association—but if they participate in illegal activities of that organization they may be dismissed from their job.

2. A teacher may write letters to newspapers criticizing school policies—unless it can be shown that such criticism impairs morale or working relationships. In the landmark *Pickering* decision (1968), the Supreme Court upheld a teacher who had written such a letter but pointed out that there was in this case "no question of maintaining either discipline by immediate supervisors or harmony among co-workers. . . ."

3. Teachers do not have a right to air private grievances or personnel judgments publicly. Free speech on public issues should not lead teachers to criticize superiors or other school employees in public settings. In a 1983 case, *Connick v. Myers*, the Supreme Court ruled against a discharged public employee, saying that he spoke out "not as a citizen upon matters of public concern but instead as an employee on matters of personal interest." A judge in Florida, applying *Connick* to a history teacher discharged for outspoken criticism of his administrators, ruled that the teacher's speech was "nothing more than a set of grievances with school administrators over internal school policies" (*Ferrara v. Mills*, 1984). Teachers should distinguish between *public* citizenship issues and *private* personnel issues before making controversial and critical public comments about their schools.

4. A teacher's private affairs do not normally disqualify him or her from teaching except to the extent that it can be shown that such affairs undermine teaching effectiveness. Teachers who are immoral in public, or who voluntarily (or through indiscretion) make known in public private acts of immorality,

may indeed be dismissed. Courts are still debating the rights of homosexual teachers, with decisions falling on both sides of this issue.

5. Laws which say that teachers may be dismissed for "unprofessional conduct" or "moral turpitude" are interpreted narrowly, with the burden of proof on the employer to show that the particular circumstances in a case constitute "unfitness to teach." Dismissal must be based on fact, not mere rumor.

6. Whenever a teacher's private affairs include sexual involvement with students, it may be presumed that courts will declare that such conduct constitutes immorality indicating unfitness to teach.

## Commandment IV: Thou Shalt Not Deny Students Due Process

The Fourteenth Amendment guarantees citizens "due process of law" whenever the loss of a right is at stake. Because education has come to be considered such a right (a "property" right), and because students are considered to be citizens, case law in recent years has defined certain procedures to be necessary in providing due process in particular situations:

**TERM TO NOTE**
Due process

1. A rule that is patently or demonstrably unfair or a punishment that is excessive may be found by a court to violate the "substantive" due process of a student (see, for example, the Supreme Court's 1969 *Tinker* decision). At the heart of due process is the concept of fair play, and teachers should examine the substance of their rules and the procedures for enforcing them to see if both are reasonable, nonarbitrary, and equitable.

2. The extent to which due process rights should be observed depends on the gravity of the offense and the severity of punishment that follows. The Supreme Court's *Goss v. Lopez* decision (1975) established minimal due process for suspensions of 10 days or less, including oral or written notice of charges and an opportunity for the student to present his or her side of the story.

3. When students are expelled from school, they should be given a statement of the specific charges and the grounds for expulsion, a formal hearing, names of witnesses, and a report of the facts to which each witness testifies (see the leading case, *Dixon v. Alabama State Board of Education*, 1961). Furthermore, it is probable that procedural due process for expelled students gives them the right to challenge the evidence, cross-examine witnesses, and be represented by counsel. (See, for example, the New York Supreme Court's 1967 *Goldwyn v. Allen* decision.) Finally, such students may appeal the decision to an impartial body for review.

4. Special education students have an added measure of due process protection. In 1990 Congress consolidated earlier special education federal statutes—including the 1975 Education of All Handicapped Children Act (Public Law 94-142) and section 504 of the Rehabilitation Act of 1973—into the Individuals with Disabilities Education Act (IDEA). These laws stipulate extensive due process rights for *all* children with disabilities (whether or not they have "the ability to benefit") to ensure a free, "appropriate" education. These provisions include prior written notice before any proposed change in a child's educational program; testing that is non-discriminatory in language, race, or culture; parental access to records; fair and impartial hearing by the State Education Agency or local district; and a student's right to remain in a current placement until due process proceedings are completed. These due process guarantees supersede district level policies relating to placement, suspension, or expulsion of students. As the Supreme Court ruled in *Honig v. Doe* (1988), the IDEA does not allow even for a "dangerous exception" to the "stay put" provision.

It is advisable for schools to develop written regulations governing procedures for such areas as suspension, expulsion, discipline, publications, and placement of the disabled. The teacher should be aware of these regulations and should provide his or her administration with specific, factual evidence whenever a student faces a serious disciplinary decision. The teacher is also advised to be guided by the spirit of due process—fairness and evenhanded justice—when dealing with less serious incidents in the classroom.

## Commandment V: Thou Shalt Not Punish Behavior Through Academic Penalties

It is easy for teachers to lose sight of the distinction between punishing and rewarding academic performance, on the one hand, and disciplinary conduct on the other. Grades, for example, are frequently employed as motivation for both study behavior and paying-attention behavior. There is a great temptation for teachers to use one of the few weapons still in their arsenal (i.e., grades) as an instrument of justice for social infractions in the classroom. While it may indeed be the case that students who misbehave will not perform well academically because of their conduct, courts are requiring schools and teachers to keep those two domains separate.

In particular, teachers are advised to heed the following general applications of this principle:

1. Denial of a diploma to a student who has met all the academic requirements for it but who has broken a rule of discipline is not permitted. Several cases (going back at least as far as the 1921 Iowa *Valentine* case) are on record to support this guideline. It is also probable that exclusion from a graduation ceremony as a punishment for behavior will not be allowed by the courts.

2. Grades should not be reduced to serve disciplinary purposes. In the *Wermuth* case (1965)

in New Jersey, the ruling against such practice included this observation by the state's commissioner of education: "Whatever system of marks and grades a school may devise will have serious inherent limitations at best, and it must not be further handicapped by attempting to serve disciplinary purposes too." In a 1984 case in Pennsylvania (*Katzman v. Cumberland Valley School District*) the court struck down a policy requiring a reduction in grades by two percentage points for each day of suspension.

3. Lowering grades—or awarding zeros—for absences is a questionable legal practice. In the Kentucky case of *Dorsey v. Bale* (1975), a student had his grades reduced for unexcused absences, and under the school's regulation, was not allowed to make up the work; five points were deducted from his nine-weeks' grade for each unexcused absence. A state circuit court and the Kentucky Court of Appeals declared the regulation to be invalid. The courts are particularly likely to invalidate regulations that constitute "double jeopardy"—e.g., suspending students for disciplinary reasons and giving them zeros while suspended.

In general, teachers who base academic evaluation on academic performance have little to fear in this area. Courts do not presume to challenge a teacher's grades *per se* when the consideration rests only on the teacher's right or ability to make valid academic judgments.

## Commandment VI: Thou Shalt Not Misuse Corporal Punishment

Corporal punishment is a controversial method of establishing discipline. The Supreme Court refused to disqualify the practice under a suit (*Ingraham v. Wright*, 1977) in which it was argued that corporal punishment was "cruel and unusual punishment" and thus a violation of the Constitution's Eighth Amendment. An increasing number of states—up from only two in

1979 to 27 in 1996—ban corporal punishment in public schools.

In those states not prohibiting corporal punishment, teachers may—as an extension of their *in loco parentis* authority—use "moderate" corporal punishment to establish discipline. There are, however, many potential legal dangers in the practice. *In loco parentis* is a limited, perhaps even a vanishing, concept, and teachers must be careful to avoid these misuses of corporal punishment if they want to stay out of the courtroom:

1. The punishment must never lead to permanent injury. No court will support as "reasonable" or "moderate" that physical punishment which permanently disables or disfigures a student. Many an assault and battery judgment has been handed down in such cases. Unfortunately for teachers, "accidents" that occur during corporal punishment and ignorance of a child's health problems (brittle bones, hemophilia, etc.) do not always excuse a teacher from liability.

2. The punishment must not be unreasonable in terms of the offense, nor may it be used to enforce an unreasonable rule. The court examines all the circumstances in a given case to determine what was or was not "reasonable" or "excessive." In 1980 the Fourth Circuit Court of Appeals ruled that "excessive" corporal punishment might well violate Fourteenth Amendment rights. In 1987 the Tenth Circuit Court of Appeals reached a similar conclusion.

3. The punishment must not be motivated by spite, malice, or revenge. Whenever teachers administer corporal punishment in a state of anger, they run a high risk of losing an assault and battery suit in court. Since corporal punishment is practiced as a method of correcting student behavior, any evidence that physical force resulted from a teacher's bad temper or quest for revenge is damning. On the other hand, in an explosive situation (e.g., a fight) teachers may protect themselves and use

that force necessary to restrain a student from harming the teacher, others, or himself.

4. The punishment must not ignore such variables as the student's age, sex, size, and physical condition.

5. The punishment must not be administered with inappropriate instruments or to parts of the body where risk of injury is great. For example, a Texas case ruled that it is not reasonable for a teacher to use his fists in administering punishment. Another teacher lost a suit when he struck a child on the ear, breaking an eardrum. The judge noted, "Nature has provided a part of the anatomy for chastisement, and tradition holds that such chastisement should there be applied." It should be noted that creating mental anguish and emotional stress by demeaning, harassing, or humiliating a child may be construed as illegal punishment too.

6. Teachers must not only take care not to harm children by way of corporal punishment; they also have a responsibility to report suspected child abuse by parents or others. Congress passed the National Child Abuse Prevention and Treatment Act in 1974 and followed with stronger laws in 1988 and 1992. Child abuse is a state (not federal) crime with many variations in definition and reporting procedure. But *all* states require reporting if the neglect or abuse results in physical injury. Teachers need not be absolutely certain of abuse but must act "in good faith" if they have "reason to believe" a child is being subjected to abuse or neglect. Every state also provides legal protection from suit for such reporting. In most states, failure to report is a misdemeanor.

Courts must exercise a good deal of judgment in corporal punishment cases to determine what is "moderate," "excessive," "reasonable," "cruel," "unusual," "malicious," or "capricious." Suffice it to say that educators should exercise great care in the use of corporal punishment.

## Commandment VII: Thou Shalt Not Neglect Students' Safety

One of the major responsibilities of teachers is to keep their students safe from unreasonable risk of harm or danger. The major cases involving teachers grow out of negligence charges relating to the teacher's failure to supervise properly in accordance with *in loco parentis* obligations (to act "in place of the parents"), contractual obligations, and professional responsibility. While the courts do not expect teachers to protect children from "unforeseeable accidents" and "acts of God," they do require teachers to act as a reasonably prudent teacher should in protecting students from possible harm or injury.

Negligence is a tort ("wrong") that exists only when the elements of *duty, violation, cause,* and *injury* are present. Teachers are generally responsible for using good judgment in determining what steps are necessary to provide for adequate supervision of the particular students in their charge, and the given circumstances dictate what is reasonably prudent in each case. A teacher who has a duty to his or her students but who fails to fulfill this duty because of carelessness, lack of discretion, or lack of diligence may violate this duty with a resultant injury to a student. In this instance the teacher may be held liable for negligence as the cause of the injury to the student.

Several guidelines can help teachers avoid this all-too-common and serious lawsuit:

1. Establish and enforce rules of safety in school activities. This is particularly important for the elementary teacher, since many injuries to elementary students occur on playgrounds, in hallways, and in classroom activity sessions. The prudent teacher anticipates such problems and establishes rules to protect students from such injuries. Generally, rules should be written, posted, and taught.

2. Be aware of school, district, and state rules and regulations as they pertain to student safety. One teacher was held negligent when a child was injured because the teacher did not know that there was a state law requiring safety glasses in a shop activity. It is also important that a teacher's own rules not conflict with regulations at higher levels. *Warn* students of any hazard in a room or in an instructional activity.

3. Enforce safety rules when violations are observed. In countless cases teachers have been found negligent when students repeatedly broke important safety rules, eventually injuring themselves or others, or when a teacher should have foreseen danger but did not act as a "reasonably prudent" teacher would have in the same situation to correct the behavior. One teacher observing a mumblety-peg game at recess was held negligent for not stopping it before the knife bounced up and put out an eye of one of the players.

4. Provide a higher standard of supervision when students are younger, disabled, and/or in a potentially dangerous activity. Playgrounds, physical education classes, science labs, and shop classes require particular care and supervision. Instruction must be provided to insure safety in accordance with the children's maturity, competence, and skill.

5. Learn first aid, because teachers may be liable for negligence if they do not get or give prompt, appropriate medical assistance when necessary. While teachers should not give children medicine, even aspirin, they should, of course, allow any legitimate prescriptions to be taken as prescribed. There should be school policy governing such procedures.

6. Advise substitute teachers (and student teachers) about any unusual medical, psychological, handicapping, or behavioral problem in your class. If there are physical hazards in your class—bare light cords,

sharp edges, loose boards, insecure window frames, etc.—warn everyone about these too. Be sure to report such hazards to your administration and janitorial staff—as a "prudent" teacher would do.

7. Be where you are assigned to be. If you have playground, hall, cafeteria, or bus duty, be there. An accident that occurs when you are someplace other than your assigned station may be blamed on your negligence, whereas if you had been there it would not be so charged. Your responsibility for safety is the same for extracurricular activities you are monitoring as it is for classes.

8. If you have to leave a classroom (particularly a rowdy one), stipulate the kind of conduct you expect and make appropriate arrangements—such as asking another teacher to check in. Even this may not be adequate precaution in terms of your duty to supervise if the students are known to be troublemakers, are quite immature, or are mentally retarded or emotionally disabled. You run a greater risk leaving a science class or a gym class than you do a social studies class.

9. Plan field trips with great care and provide for adequate supervision. Many teachers fail to realize that permission notes from home—no matter how much they disclaim teacher liability for injury—do not excuse a teacher from providing proper supervision. A parent cannot sign away this right of his or her child. Warn children of dangers on the trip and instruct them in rules of conduct and safety.

10. Do not send students on errands off school grounds, because they then become your agents. If they are injured or if they injure someone else, you may well be held liable. Again, the younger and less responsible the child, the greater the danger of a teacher negligence charge. To state the obvious, some children require more supervision than others.

Much of the advice is common sense, but the "reasonably prudent" teacher needs to be alert to the many requirements of "due care" and "proper supervision." The teacher who anticipates potentially dangerous conditions and actions and takes reasonable precautions—through rules, instruction, warnings, communications to superiors, and presence in assigned stations—will do a great deal in minimizing the chances of pupil injury and teacher negligence.

### Commandment VIII: Thou Shalt Not Slander or Libel Your Students

This tort is much less common than negligence, but it is an area of school law that can be troublesome. One of the primary reasons for the Family Educational Rights and Privacy Act (1974) was that school records contain so much misinformation and hearsay and so many untrue (or, at least, questionable) statements about children's character, conduct, and morality that access to these records by students or their parents, in order to correct false information, seemed warranted. A teacher's right to write anything about a student under the protection of confidential files no longer exists. Defamation of character through written communication is "libel" while such defamation in oral communication is "slander." There are ample opportunities for teachers to commit both offenses.

Teachers are advised to be careful about what they say about students (let alone other teachers!) to employers, colleges, parents, and other personnel at the school. Adhere to the following guidelines:

1. Avoid vague, derogatory terms on permanent records and recommendations. Even if you do not intend to be derogatory, value judgments about a student's character, lifestyle, or home life may be found defamatory in court. In one case, a North Carolina teacher was found guilty of libel when she said on a

permanent record card that a student was "ruined by tobacco and whiskey." Avoid characterizing students as "crazy," "immoral," or "delinquent."

2. Say or write only what you know to be true about a student. It is safer to be an objective describer of what you have observed than to draw possibly unwarranted and untrue conclusions and judgments. The truth of a statement is strong evidence that character has not been defamed, but in some cases where the intent has been to malign and destroy the person, truth is not an adequate defense.

3. Communicate judgments of character only to those who have a right to the information. Teachers have "qualified privileged communication," which means that so long as they communicate in good faith information that they believe to be true to a person who has reason to have this information, they are protected. However, the slandering of pupils in a teachers' lounge bull session is another thing altogether.

4. If a student confides a problem to you in confidence, keep that communication confidential. A student who is on drugs, let us say, may bring you to court for defamation of character and/or invasion of privacy if you spread such information about indiscriminately. On the other hand, if a student confides that he or she has participated in a felonious crime or gives you information that makes you aware of a "clear and present" danger, you are obligated to bring such information to the appropriate authorities. Find out the proper limits of communication and the authorized channels in your school and state.

5. As a related issue, be careful about "search and seizure" procedures too. Generally, school lockers are school property and may be searched by school officials if they have reasonable grounds to suspect that the locker has something dangerous or illegal in it. In its landmark 1985 decision in *New Jersey v. T.L.O.*, the Supreme Court rejected the notion that school officials had to have the police standard of "probable cause" before conducting a search; the court approved the lower standard of "reasonable suspicion." So long as both the grounds (i.e., reason) and scope are reasonable, school personnel can search student suspects. The growing concern in society about drugs and weapons in school has led courts to support school officials conducting searches for dangerous or illegal items. Strip searches, however, are often deemed to be too intrusive.

Teachers need to remember that students are citizens and as such enjoy at least a limited degree of the constitutional rights that adult citizens enjoy. Not only "due process," "equal protection," and "freedom of religion" but also protection from teacher torts such as "negligence" and "defamation of character" is provided to students through our system of law. These concepts apply to all students, including those in elementary grades.

## Commandment IX: Thou Shalt Not Photocopy in Violation of Copyright Law

In January, 1978, the revised copyright law went into effect and with it strict limitations on what may be photocopied by teachers for their own or classroom use under the broad concept of "fair use." The "fair use" of copyrighted material means that the use should not impair the value of the owner's copyright by diminishing the demand for that work, thereby reducing potential income for the owner.

In general, educators are given greater latitude than most other users. "Spontaneous" copying is more permissible than "systematic" copying. Students have greater latitude than teachers in copying materials.

Teachers may:

1. Make a single copy for their own research or class preparation of a chapter from a book; an

article from a periodical or newspaper; a short story, poem, or essay; a chart, graph, diagram, cartoon, or picture from a book, periodical, or newspaper.

2. Make multiple copies for classroom use only (but not to exceed one copy per student) of a complete poem, if it is fewer than 250 words and printed on not more than two pages; an excerpt from a longer poem, if it is fewer than 250 words; a complete article, story, or essay, if it is fewer than 2,500 words; an excerpt from a prose work, if it is fewer than 1,000 words or 10% of the work, whichever is less; one chart, graph, diagram, drawing, cartoon, or picture per book or periodical.

However, teachers may not:

1. Make multiple copies of work for classroom use if another teacher has already copied the work for use in another class in the same school.

2. Make copies of a short poem, article, story, or essay from the same author more than once in the same term.

3. Make multiple copies from the same collective work or periodical issue more than three times a term. (The limitation in Items 1–3 do not apply to current news periodicals or newspapers.)

4. Make a copy of works to take the place of anthologies.

5. Make copies of "consumable" materials such as workbooks, exercises, answer sheets to standardized tests, and the like.

More recent technologies have led to extended applications of the "fair use" doctrine:

1. The "fair use" doctrine does not apply to copyrighted computer software programs; however, teachers may load a copyrighted program onto a classroom terminal or make a "backup" copy for archival purposes. Teachers may not make copies of such programs for

student use. In 1991 the Department of Justice and Department of Education called on schools to teach the ethical use of computers to counteract illegal copying of software.

2. Schools may videotape copyrighted television programs but may keep the tape no longer than 45 days without a license. Teachers may use the tapes for instruction during the first 10 consecutive days after taping but may repeat such use only once. Commercial videotapes may not be rented to be played for instruction (or entertainment) in classrooms.

3. Scanning copyrighted material into a computer and distributing it via the Internet is a violation of copyright law. The Internet should be viewed as a giant photocopying machine. Bills are now in Congress to restrict and punish those who misuse the Internet. We may expect to see other legal complications from this emerging technology: defamation, obscenity, threats of violence, disruption of the academic environment, and sexual harassment—to list but a few.

When teachers make brief, spontaneous, and limited copies of copyrighted materials other than consumables, they are likely to be operating within the bounds of fair use. Whenever multiple copies of copyrighted materials are made (within the guidelines above), each copy should include a notice of the copyright. Teachers should consult media specialists and others in their school about questions relating to "fair use"—whether for print, videotape, or computer materials.

## Commandment X: Thou Shalt Not Be Ignorant of the Law

The axiom, "Ignorance of the law is no excuse," holds as true for teachers as anyone else. Indeed, courts are increasingly holding teachers to higher standards of competence and knowledge commensurate with their higher status as professionals. Since education is now considered a right—guaranteed to black and white, rich and poor, "normal" and disabled—the legal parameters have become ever more important to teachers in this litigious era.

How, then, can the teacher become aware of the law and its implications for the classroom? Consider the following possibilities:

1. Sign up for a course in school law. If the local college or university does not offer such a course, attempt to have one developed.

2. Ask your school system administration to focus on this topic in inservice programs.

3. Tap the resources of the local, state, and national professional organizations for pertinent speakers, programs, and materials.

4. Explore state department of education sources, since most states will have personnel and publications that deal with educational statutes and case law in your particular state.

5. Establish school (if not personal) subscriptions to professional journals. *Phi Delta Kappan*, *Journal of Law and Education*, and *Mental Disability Law Reporter* are only a few of the journals that regularly have columns and/or articles to keep the teacher aware of new developments in school law.

6. Make sure that your school or personal library includes such books as *Teachers and the Law* (Louis Fischer et al., 4th edition, Longman, 1995); *The Law of Schools, Students, and Teachers* (Kern and David Alexander, 2nd edition, West, 1995); *Special Education Law* (Laura Rothstein, 2nd edition, Longman, 1995); and *Deskbook Encyclopedia of American School Law* (Data Research, Rosemount, Minnesota, 1996). Monthly newsletters can keep schools up-to-date in the school law area. Consider a subscription to *School Law Bulletin* (Quinlan Publishing Company, Boston) or *Legal Notes for Educators* (Data Research, Rosemount, Minnesota).

The better informed teachers are about their legal rights and responsibilities, the more likely they are to avoid the courtroom—and there are many ways to keep informed.

My Teacher's Ten Commandments are not exhaustive, nor are they etched in stone. School law, like all other law, is constantly evolving and changing so as to reflect the thinking of the times; and decisions by courts are made in the context of particular events and circumstances that are never exactly the same. But prudent professionals will be well served by these commandments if they internalize the spirit of the law as a guide to actions as teachers—in the classroom, the school, and the community.

## POSTNOTE

The United States is an increasingly litigious society. Rather than settle disagreements and disputes face to face, we quickly turn over our problems to lawyers. In recent years, business owners and managers, doctors, and even lawyers have been held liable for various consequences of their work. Such situations were almost unknown to their colleagues in an earlier age.

Although relatively few teachers have been prosecuted successfully in the courts, the number of cases has dramatically increased. Therefore, it is important for teachers—both in training and in service—to be aware of areas of legal vulnerability. McDaniel, himself a former teacher, has presented an outstanding summary of the law as it affects teachers.

## DISCUSSION QUESTIONS

1. Before reading this article, were you aware that school law governed teachers' behavior as much as it does? In which of the areas described by McDaniel do you, personally, feel most vulnerable? Why?

2. What steps can you take to protect yourself as a teacher from legal liability?

3. Which of these "commandments" has the most negative impact on the effectiveness of the average teacher? Why?

CLASSIC # The Return of Character Education

Thomas Lickona

*To educate a person in mind and not in morals is to educate a menace to society.*

—Theodore Roosevelt

Increasing numbers of people across the ideological spectrum believe that our society is in deep moral trouble. The disheartening signs are everywhere: the breakdown of the family; the deterioration of civility in everyday life; rampant greed at a time when one in five children is poor; an omnipresent sexual culture that fills our television and movie screens with sleaze, beckoning the young toward sexual activity at ever earlier ages; the enormous betrayal of children through sexual abuse; and the 1992 report of the National Research Council that says the United States is now *the* most violent of all industrialized nations.

As we become more aware of this societal crisis, the feeling grows that schools cannot be ethical bystanders. As a result, character education is making a comeback in American schools.

> **TERM TO NOTE**
> Character education

## Early Character Education

Character education is as old as education itself. Down through history, education has had two great goals: to help people become smart and to help them become good.

Thomas Lickona is a developmental psychologist at the State University of New York at Cortland and one of the leading experts in character education. From Thomas R. Lickona, "The Return of Character Education." *Educational Leadership*, November 1993, pp. 6–11. Reprinted with permission of the Association for Supervision and Curriculum Development. Copyright © 1993 by ASCD. All rights reserved.

Acting on that belief, schools in the earliest days of our republic tackled character education head on—through discipline, the teacher's example, and the daily school curriculum. The Bible was the public school's sourcebook for both moral and religious instruction. When struggles eventually arose over whose Bible to use and which doctrines to teach, William McGuffey stepped onto the stage in 1836 to offer his McGuffey Readers, ultimately to sell more than 100 million copies.

McGuffey retained many favorite Biblical stories but added poems, exhortations, and heroic tales. While children practiced their reading or arithmetic, they also learned lessons about honesty, love of neighbor, kindness to animals, hard work, thriftiness, patriotism, and courage.

## Why Character Education Declined

In the 20th century, the consensus supporting character education began to crumble under the blows of several powerful forces.

Darwinism introduced a new metaphor—evolution—that led people to see all things, including morality, as being in flux.

The philosophy of logical positivism, arriving at American universities from Europe, asserted a radical distinction between *facts* (which could be scientifically proven) and *values* (which positivism held were mere expressions of feeling, not objective truth). As a result of positivism, morality was relativized and privatized—made to seem a matter of personal "value judgment," not a subject for public debate and transmission through the schools.

> **TERMS TO NOTE**
> Positivism
> Values
> Personalism

In the 1960s, a worldwide rise in personalism celebrated the worth, autonomy, and subjectivity of the person, emphasizing individual rights and freedom over responsibility. Personalism rightly protested societal oppression and injustice, but it also delegitimized moral authority, eroded belief in objective moral norms, turned people inward toward self-fulfillment, weakened social commitments (for example, to marriage and parenting), and fueled the socially destabilizing sexual revolution.

Finally, the rapidly intensifying pluralism of American society (Whose values should we teach?) and the increasing secularization of the public arena (Won't moral education violate the separation of church and state?) became two more barriers to achieving the moral consensus indispensable for character education in the public schools. Public schools retreated from their once central role as moral and character educators.

**TERMS TO NOTE**
Secularism
Values clarification

The 1970s saw a return of values education, but in new forms: values clarification and Kohlberg's moral dilemma discussions. In different ways, both expressed the individualist spirit of the age. Values clarification said, don't impose values; help students choose their values freely. Kohlberg said, develop students' powers of moral reasoning so they can judge which values are better than others.

Each approach made contributions, but each had problems. Values clarification, though rich in methodology, failed to distinguish between personal preferences (truly a matter of free choice) and moral values (a matter of obligation). Kohlberg focused on moral reasoning, which is necessary but not sufficient for good character, and underestimated the school's role as a moral socializer.

## The New Character Education

In the 1990s we are seeing the beginnings of a new character education movement, one which restores "good character" to its historical place as the central desirable outcome of the school's moral enterprise. No one knows yet how broad or deep this movement is; we have no studies to tell us what percentage of schools are making what kind of effort. But something significant is afoot.

In July 1992, the Josephson Institute of Ethics called together more than 30 educational leaders representing state school boards, teachers' unions, universities, ethics centers, youth organizations, and religious groups. This diverse assemblage drafted the Aspen Declaration on Character Education, setting forth eight principles of character education.[1]

The Character Education Partnership was launched in March 1993, as a national coalition committed to putting character development at the top of the nation's educational agenda. Members include representatives from business, labor, government, youth, parents, faith communities, and the media.

The last two years have seen the publication of a spate of books—such as *Moral, Character, and Civic Education in the Elementary School, Why Johnny Can't Tell Right from Wrong*, and *Reclaiming Our Schools: A Handbook on Teaching Character, Academics, and Discipline*—that make the case for character education and describe promising programs around the country. A new periodical, the *Journal of Character Education*, is devoted entirely to covering the field.[2]

## Why Character Education Now?

Why this groundswell of interest in character education? There are at least three causes:

**1.** *The decline of the family.* The family, traditionally a child's primary moral teacher, is for vast numbers of children today failing to perform that role, thus creating a moral vacuum. In her recent book *When the Bough Breaks: The Cost of Neglecting Our Children*, economist Sylvia Hewlett documents that American children, rich and poor, suffer a level of neglect unique among developed nations (1991). Overall, child well-being has declined despite a decrease in the number of children per family, an increase in the educational level of parents, and historically high levels of public spending in education.

In "Dan Quayle Was Right" (April 1993) Barbara Dafoe Whitehead synthesizes the social science research on the decline of the two biological-parent family in America:

> If current trends continue, less than half of children born today will live continuously with their own mother and father throughout childhood. . . . An increasing number of children will experience family break-up two or even three times during childhood.

Children of marriages that end in divorce and children of single mothers are more likely to be poor, have emotional and behavioral problems, fail to achieve academically, get pregnant, abuse drugs and alcohol, get in trouble with the law, and be sexually and physically abused. Children in stepfamilies are generally worse off (more likely to be sexually abused, for example) than children in single-parent homes.

No one has felt the impact of family disruption more than schools. Whitehead writes:

> Across the nation, principals report a dramatic rise in the aggressive, acting-out behavior characteristic of children, especially boys, who are living in single-parent families. Moreover, teachers find that many children are so upset and preoccupied by the explosive drama of their own family lives that they are unable to concentrate on such mundane matters as multiplication tables.

Family disintegration, then, drives the character education movement in two ways: schools have to teach the values kids aren't learning at home; and schools, in order to conduct teaching and learning, must become caring moral communities that help children from unhappy homes focus on their work, control their anger, feel cared about, and become responsible students.

**2.** *Troubling trends in youth character.* A second impetus for renewed character education is the sense that young people in general, not just those from fractured families, have been adversely affected by poor parenting (in intact as well as broken families); the wrong kind of adult role models; the sex, violence, and materialism portrayed in the mass media; and the pressures of the peer group. Evidence that this hostile moral environment is taking a toll on youth character can be found in 10 troubling trends: rising youth violence; increasing dishonesty (lying, cheating, and stealing); growing disrespect for authority; peer cruelty; a resurgence of bigotry on school campuses, from preschool through higher education; a decline in the work ethic; sexual precocity; a growing self-centeredness and declining civil responsibility; an increase in self-destructive behavior; and ethical illiteracy.

The statistics supporting these trends are overwhelming.[3] For example, the U.S. homicide rate for 15- to 24-year-old males is 7 times higher than Canada's and 40 times higher than Japan's. The U.S. has one of the highest teenage pregnancy rates, the highest teen abortion rate, and the highest level of drug use among young people in the developed world. Youth suicide has tripled in the past 25 years, and a survey of more than 2,000 Rhode Island students, grades six through nine, found that two out of three boys and one of two girls thought it "acceptable for a man to force sex on a woman" if they had been dating for six months or more (Kikuchi 1988).

**3.** *A recovery of shared, objectively important ethical values.* Moral decline in society has gotten bad enough to jolt us out of the privatism and relativism dominant in recent decades. We are recovering the wisdom that we do share a basic morality, essential for our survival; that adults must promote this morality by teaching the young, directly and indirectly, such values as respect, responsibility, trustworthiness, fairness, caring, and civil virtue; and that these values are not merely subjective preferences but that they have objective worth and a claim on our collective conscience.

Such values affirm our human dignity, promote the good of the individual and the common good, and protect our human rights. They meet the classic ethical tests of reversibility (Would you want to be treated this way?) and universalizability (Would you want all persons to act this way in a similar situation?). They define our responsibilities in a democracy, and they are recognized by all civilized people and taught by all enlightened creeds. *Not* to teach children these core ethical values is grave moral failure.

## What Character Education Must Do

In the face of a deteriorating social fabric, what must character education do to develop good character in the young?

First, it must have an adequate theory of what good character is, one which gives schools a clear idea of their goals. Character must be broadly conceived to encompass cognitive, affective, and behavioral aspects of morality. Good character consists of knowing the good, desiring the good, and doing the good. Schools must help children *understand* the core values, *adopt* or commit to them, and then *act upon* them in their own lives.

The cognitive side of character includes at least six specific moral qualities: awareness of the moral dimensions of the situation at hand, knowing moral values and what they require of us in concrete cases, perspective-taking, moral reasoning, thoughtful decision making, and moral self-knowledge. All these powers of rational moral thought are required for full moral maturity and citizenship in a democratic society.

People can be very smart about matters of right and wrong, however, and still choose the wrong. Moral education that is merely intellectual misses the crucial emotional side of character, which serves as the bridge between judgment and action. The emotional side includes at least the following qualities: conscience (the felt obligation to do what one judges to be right), self-respect, empathy, loving the good, self-control, and humility (a willingness to both recognize and correct our moral failings).

At times, we know what we should do, feel strongly that we should do it, yet still fail to translate moral judgment and feeling into effective moral behavior. Moral action, the third part of character, draws upon three additional moral qualities: competence (skills such as listening, communicating, and cooperating), will (which mobilizes our judgment and energy), and moral habit (a reliable inner disposition to respond to situations in a morally good way).

## Developing Character

Once we have a comprehensive concept of character, we need a comprehensive approach to developing it. This approach tells schools to look at themselves through a moral lens and consider how virtually everything that goes on there affects the values and character of students. Then, plan how to use all phases of classroom and school life as deliberate tools of character development.

If schools wish to maximize their moral clout, make a lasting difference in students' character, and engage and develop all three parts of character (knowing, feeling, and behavior), they need a comprehensive, holistic approach. Having a comprehensive approach includes asking, Do present school practices support, neglect, or contradict the school's professed values and character education aims?

In classroom practice, a comprehensive approach to character education calls upon the individual teacher to:

▶ *Act as caregiver, model, and mentor,* treating students with love and respect, setting a good example, supporting positive social behavior, and correcting hurtful actions through one-on-one guidance and whole-class discussions;

▶ *Create a moral community,* helping students know one another as persons, respect and care about one another, and feel valued membership in, and responsibility to, the group;

▶ *Practice moral discipline,* using the creation and enforcement of rules as opportunities to foster moral reasoning, voluntary compliance with rules, and respect for others;

▶ *Create a democratic classroom environment,* involving students in decision making and the responsibility for making the classroom a good place to be and learn;

▶ *Teach values through the curriculum,* using the ethically rich content of academic subjects (such as literature, history, and science), as well as outstanding programs (such as *Facing History and Ourselves*[4] and *The Heartwood Ethics Curriculum for Children*[5]), as vehicles for teaching values and examining moral questions;

▶ *Use cooperative learning* to develop students' appreciation of others, perspective taking, and ability to work with others toward common goals;

▶ *Develop the "conscience of craft"* by fostering students' appreciation of learning, capacity for hard work, commitment to excellence, and sense of work as affecting the lives of others;

▶ *Encourage moral reflection* through reading, research, essay writing, journal keeping, discussion, and debate;

▶ *Teach conflict resolution,* so that students acquire the essential moral skills of solving conflicts fairly and without force.

Besides making full use of the moral life of classrooms, a comprehensive approach calls upon the school *as a whole* to:

▶ *Foster caring beyond the classroom,* using positive role models to inspire altruistic behavior and providing opportunities at every grade level to perform school and community service;

▶ *Create a positive moral culture in the school,* developing a schoolwide ethos (through the leadership of the principal, discipline, a schoolwide

sense of community, meaningful student government, a moral community among adults, and making time for moral concerns) that supports and amplifies the values taught in the classrooms;

▶ *Recruit parents and the community as partners in character education,* letting parents know that the school considers them their child's first and most important moral teacher, giving parents specific ways they can reinforce the values the school is trying to teach, and seeking the help of the community, churches, businesses, local government, and the media in promoting the core ethical values.

## The Challenges Ahead

Whether character education will take hold in American schools remains to be seen. Among the factors that will determine the movement's long-range success are:

▶ *Support for schools.* Can schools recruit the help they need from the other key formative institutions that shape the values of the young—including families, faith communities, and the media? Will public policy act to strengthen and support families, and will parents make the stability of their families and the needs of their children their highest priority?

▶ *The role of religion.* Both liberal and conservative groups are asking, How can students be sensitively engaged in considering the role of religion in the origins and moral development of our nation? How can students be encouraged to use their intellectual and moral resources, including their faith traditions, when confronting social issues (for example, what is my obligation to the poor?) and making personal moral decisions (for example, should I have sex before marriage?)?

▶ *Moral leadership.* Many schools lack a positive, cohesive moral culture. Especially at the building level, it is absolutely essential to have moral

TERM TO NOTE
Moral leadership

leadership that sets, models, and consistently enforces high standards of respect and responsibility. Without a positive school-wide ethos, teachers will feel demoralized in their individual efforts to teach good values.

▶ *Teacher education.* Character education is far more complex than teaching math or reading; it requires personal growth as well as skills development. Yet teachers typically receive almost no preservice or inservice training in the moral aspects of their craft. Many teachers do not feel comfortable or competent in the values domain. How will teacher education colleges and school staff development programs meet this need?

"Character is destiny," wrote the ancient Greek philosopher Heraclitus. As we confront the causes of our deepest societal problems, whether in our intimate relationships or public institutions, questions of character loom large. As we close out a turbulent century and ready our schools for the next, educating for character is a moral imperative if we care about the future of our society and our children.

## NOTES

1. For a copy of the Aspen Declaration and the issue of *Ethics* magazine reporting on the conference, write the Josephson Institute of Ethics, 310 Washington Blvd., Suite 104, Marina del Rey, CA 90292.

2. For information write Mark Kann, Editor, *The Journal of Character Education*, Jefferson Center for Character Education, 202 S. Lake Ave., Suite 240, Pasadena, CA 91101.

3. For documentation of these youth trends, see T. Lickona, (1991), *Educating for Character: How Our Schools Can Teach Respect and Responsibility* (New York: Bantam Books).

4. *Facing History and Ourselves* is an 8-week Holocaust curriculum for 8th graders. Write Facing History and Ourselves National Foundation, 25 Kennard Rd., Brookline, MA 02146.

5. *The Heartwood Ethics Curriculum for Children* uses multicultural children's literature to teach universal values. Write The Heartwood Institute, 12300 Perry Highway, Wexford, PA 15090.

## REFERENCES

Benninga, J. S., ed. (1991). *Moral, Character, and Civic Education in the Elementary School*. New York: Teachers College Press.

Hewlett, S. (1991). *When the Bough Breaks: The Cost of Neglecting Our Children*. New York: Basic Books.

Kikuchi, J. (Fall 1988). "Rhode Island Develops Successful Intervention Program for Adolescents." *National Coalition Against Sexual Assault Newsletter*.

National Research Council. (1992). *Understanding and Preventing Violence*. Washington D.C.: National Research Council.

Whitehead, B. D. (April 1993). "Dan Quayle Was Right." *The Atlantic* 271: 47–84.

Wynne, E. A., and K. Ryan. (1992). *Reclaiming Our Schools: A Handbook on Teaching Character, Academics, and Discipline*. New York: Merrill.

## POSTNOTE

The force and clarity of this article in calling educators to recapture the school's moral mission earn it a place among our Classics. Education for good character is one of our schools' latest fads—and also one of their oldest missions. This article by the nation's leading proponent of character education lays out the case for our schools' involvement in teaching core moral values and helping children acquire good habits, such as respect and responsibility.

But despite the call for character education from our parents, pulpits, and politicians, schools and teachers are often unsure of what to do. Because character education has been absent from the great majority of our schools for fully three decades, few educators know how to translate their good intentions into practice. Many schools are having one or two inservice days, buying boxes of character-oriented banners to put up on their walls, and purchasing "Character Counts!" coffee cups for the teachers' lounge.

Developing in our young the strong moral habits that constitute good character needs to be a central priority for a school community. What Lickona calls a "comprehensive approach" will take time, energy, and deep commitment to achieve. But, curiously, schools that take on this mission wholeheartedly find that many of their other goals—academic, athletic, and social—are achieved in the process.

## DISCUSSION QUESTIONS

1. What is your personal experience with character education in the schools?

2. Do you agree with the thrust of this article, that schools have a major role in the fostering of good character?

3. From your perspective, what are the hard questions that schools must grapple with if they are to engage in character education responsibly?

# Educational Reform

S ince the publication of *A Nation at Risk* in 1983 (a report of President Reagan's National Commission on Excellence in Education), American schools have been in what is referred to as an "era of school reform." Both educators and private citizens are worried about our schools' ability to supply an adequately educated workforce. New jobs in the information age require a worker to solve problems, often as a member of a team, write and speak proficiently, and carry out higher levels of mathematical computations. Dismal research reports on the academic achievement of American students, particularly when compared with students from other countries, have sent a clear message: Something must be done.

The primary response has been at the state level, where governors and legislatures across the country have passed laws requiring higher standards for students and teachers alike. Ways of more effectively and efficiently organizing schools have surfaced—some borrowed from industry, some from schools in other nations. Increasingly, too, parents, politicians and policymakers are examining and experimenting with ways to offer students greater educational choice. This section presents an overview of some of the most important developments in reforming education.

# 56

**CLASSIC** *What Matters Most: A Competent Teacher for Every Child*

Linda Darling-Hammond

We propose an audacious goal . . . by the year 2006, America will provide all students with what should be their educational birthright: access to competent, caring, and qualified teachers.[1]

With these words, the National Commission on Teaching and America's Future summarized its challenge to the American public. After two years of intense study and discussion, the commission—a 26-member bipartisan blue-ribbon panel supported by the Rockefeller Foundation and the Carnegie Corporation of New York—concluded that the reform of elementary and secondary education depends first and foremost on restructuring its foundation, the teaching profession. The restructuring, the commission made clear, must go in two directions: toward increasing teachers' knowledge to meet the demands they face and toward redesigning schools to support high-quality teaching and learning.

**TERM TO NOTE**

National Commission on Teaching and America's Future

The commission found a profession that has suffered from decades of neglect. By the standards of other professions and other countries, U.S. teacher education has historically been thin, uneven, and poorly financed. Teacher recruitment is distressingly ad hoc, and teacher salaries lag significantly behind those of other professions. This produces chronic shortages of qualified teachers in fields like mathematics and science and the continual hiring of large numbers of "teachers" who are unprepared for their jobs.

Furthermore, in contrast to other countries that invest most of their education dollars in well-prepared and well-supported teachers, half of the education dollars in the United States are spent on personnel and activities outside the classroom. A lack of standards for students and teachers, coupled with schools that are organized for 19th-century learning, leaves educators without an adequate foundation for constructing good teaching. Under these conditions, excellence is hard to achieve.

The commission is clear about what needs to change. No more hiring unqualified teachers on the sly. No more nods and winks at teacher education programs that fail to prepare teachers properly. No more tolerance for incompetence in the classroom. Children are compelled to attend school. Every state guarantees them equal protection under the law, and most promise them a sound education. In the face of these obligations, students have a right to competent, caring teachers who work in schools organized for success.

The commission is also clear about what needs to be done. Like the Flexner report that led to the transformation of the medical profession in 1910, this report, *What Matters Most: Teaching for America's Future*, examines successful practices within and outside the United States to describe what works. The commission concludes that children can reap the benefits of current knowledge about teaching and learning only if schools and schools of education are dramatically redesigned.

The report offers a blueprint for recruiting, preparing, supporting, and rewarding excellent educators in all of America's schools. The plan is

Linda Darling-Hammond is professor of education at Stanford University. Darling-Hammond, Linda, "What Matters Most: A Competent Teacher for Every Child," *Phi Delta Kappan*, November 1996. Copyright © 1996 by Linda Darling-Hammond. Reprinted by permission of the author.

aimed at ensuring that all schools have teachers with the knowledge and skills they need to enable all children to learn. If a caring, qualified teacher for every child is the most important ingredient in education reform, then it should no longer be the factor most frequently overlooked.

At the same time, such teachers must have available to them schools and school systems that are well designed to achieve their key academic mission: they must be focused on clear, high standards for students; organized to provide a coherent, high-quality curriculum across the grades; and designed to support teachers' collective work and learning.

We note that this challenge is accompanied by an equally great opportunity: over the next decade we will recruit and hire more than two million teachers for America's schools. More than half of the teachers who will be teaching 10 years from now will be hired during the next decade. If we can focus our energies on providing this generation of teachers with the kinds of knowledge and skills they need to help students succeed, we will have made an enormous contribution to America's future.

## The Nature of the Problem

The education challenge facing the U.S. is not that its schools are not as good as they once were. It is that schools must help the vast majority of young people reach levels of skill and competence that were once thought to be within the reach of only a few.

After more than a decade of school reform, America is still a very long way from achieving its educational goals. Instead of all children coming to school ready to learn, more are living in poverty and without health care than a decade ago.[2] Graduation rates and student achievement in most subjects have remained flat or have increased only slightly.[3] Fewer than 10% of high school students can read, write, compute, and manage scientific material at the high levels required for today's "knowledge work" jobs.[4]

This distance between our stated goals and current realities is not due to lack of effort. Many initiatives have been launched in local communities with positive effects. Nonetheless, we have reached an impasse in spreading these promising efforts to the system as a whole. It is now clear that most schools and teachers cannot produce the kind of learning demanded by the new reforms—not because they do not want to, but because they do not know how, and the systems they work in do not support their efforts to do so.

## The Challenge for Teaching

A more complex, knowledge-based, and multicultural society creates new expectations for teaching. To help diverse learners master more challenging content, teachers must go far beyond dispensing information, giving a test, and giving a grade. They must themselves know their subject areas deeply, and they must understand how students think, if they are to create experiences that actually work to produce learning.

Developing the kind of teaching that is needed will require much greater clarity about what students need to learn in order to succeed in the world that awaits them and what teachers need to know and do in order to help students learn it. Standards that reflect these imperatives for student learning and for teaching are largely absent in our nation today. States are just now beginning to establish standards for student learning.

**TERM TO NOTE**

Standard

Standards for teaching are equally haphazard. Although most parents might assume that teachers, like other professionals, are educated in similar ways so that they acquire common knowledge before they are admitted to practice, this is not the case. Unlike doctors, lawyers, accountants, or architects, all teachers do not have the same training. Some teachers have very high levels of skills—particularly in states that require a bachelor's degree in the discipline to be taught—along with coursework in teaching, learning, curriculum, and child development; extensive practice teaching; and a master's degree in education. Others learn little about their subject matter or about teaching, learning, and child development—particularly in states that have low requirements for licensing.

And while states have recently begun to require some form of testing for a teaching license, most licensing exams are little more than multiple-choice tests of basic skills and general knowledge, widely criticized by educators and experts as woefully inadequate to measure teaching skill.[5] Furthermore, in many states the cutoff scores are so low that there is no effective standard for entry.

These difficulties are barely known to the public. The schools' most closely held secret amounts to a great national shame: roughly one-quarter of newly hired American teachers lack the qualifications for their jobs. More than 12% of new hires enter the classroom without any formal training at all, and another 14% arrive without fully meeting state standards.

Although no state will permit a person to write wills, practice medicine, fix plumbing, or style hair without completing training and passing an examination, more than 40 states allow districts to hire teachers who have not met basic requirements. States pay more attention to the qualifications of the veterinarians treating America's pets than to those of the people educating the nation's youngsters. Consider the following facts:

▶ In recent years, more than 50,000 people who lack the training required for their jobs have entered teaching annually on emergency or substandard licenses.[6]

▶ Nearly one-fourth (23%) of all secondary teachers do not have even a minor in their main teaching field. This is true for more than 30% of mathematics teachers.[7]

▶ Among teachers who teach a second subject, 36% are unlicensed in that field, and 50% lack a minor in it.[8]

▶ Fifty-six percent of high school students taking physical science are taught by out-of-field teachers, as are 27% of those taking mathematics and 21% of those taking English.[9] The proportions are much greater in high-poverty schools and lower-track classes.

▶ In schools with the highest minority enrollments, students have less than a 50% chance of getting a science or mathematics teacher who holds a license and a degree in the field in which he or she teaches.[10]

In the nation's poorest schools, where hiring is most lax and teacher turnover is constant, the results are disastrous. Thousands of children are taught throughout their school careers by a parade of teachers without preparation in the fields in which they teach, inexperienced beginners with little training and no mentoring, and short-term substitutes trying to cope with constant staff disruptions.[11] It is more surprising that some of these children manage to learn than that so many fail to do so.

## Current Barriers

Unequal resources and inadequate investments in teacher recruitment are major problems. Other industrialized countries fund their schools equally and make sure there are qualified teachers for all of them by underwriting teacher preparation and salaries. However, teachers in the U.S. must go into substantial debt to become prepared for a field that in most states pays less than any other occupation requiring a college degree.

This situation is not necessary or inevitable. The hiring of unprepared teachers was almost eliminated during the 1970s with scholarships and loans for college students preparing to teach, Urban Teacher Corps initiatives, and master of arts in teaching (MAT) programs, coupled with wage increases. However, the cancellation of most of these recruitment incentives in the 1980s led to renewed shortages when student enrollments started to climb once again, especially in cities. Between 1987 and 1991, the proportion of well-qualified new teachers—those entering teaching with a college major or minor and a license in their fields—actually declined from about 74% to 67%.[12]

There is no real system for recruiting, preparing, and developing America's teachers. Major problems include:

***Inadequate Teacher Education*** Because accreditation is not required of teacher education programs, their quality varies widely, with excellent programs standing alongside shoddy ones that are allowed to operate even when they do an utterly inadequate job. Too many American universities still treat their schools of education as "cash cows" whose excess revenues are spent on the training of doctors, lawyers, accountants, and almost any students other than prospective teachers themselves.

***Slipshod Recruitment*** Although the share of academically able young people entering teaching has been increasing, there are still too few in some parts of the country and in critical subjects like mathematics and science. Federal incentives that once existed to induce talented people into high-need fields and locations have largely been eliminated.

***Haphazard Hiring and Induction*** School districts often lose the best candidates because of inefficient and cumbersome hiring practices, barriers to teacher mobility, and inattention to teacher qualifications. Those who do get hired are typically given the most difficult assignments and left to sink or swim, without the kind of help provided by internships and residencies in other professions. Isolated behind classroom doors with little feedback or help, as many as 30% leave in the first few years, while others learn merely to cope rather than to teach well.

***Lack of Professional Development and Rewards for Knowledge and Skill*** In addition to the lack of support for beginning teachers, most school districts invest little in ongoing professional development for experienced teachers and spend much of these limited resources on unproductive "hit-and-run" workshops. Furthermore, most U.S. teachers have only three to five hours each week for planning. This leaves them with almost no regular time to consult together or to learn about new teaching strategies, unlike their peers in many European and Asian countries who spend between 15 and 20 hours per week working jointly on refining lessons and learning about new methods.

The teaching career does not encourage teachers to develop or use growing expertise. Evaluation and tenure decisions often lack a tangible connection to a clear vision of high-quality teaching, important skills are rarely rewarded, and—when budgets must be cut—professional development is often the first item sacrificed. Historically, the only route to advancement in teaching has been to leave the classroom for administration.

In contrast, many European and Asian countries hire a greater number of better-paid teachers, provide them with more extensive preparation, give them time to work together, and structure schools so that teachers can focus on teaching and can come to know their students well. Teachers share decision making and take on a range of professional responsibilities without leaving teaching. This is possible because these other countries invest their resources in many more classroom teachers—typically constituting 60% to 80% of staff, as compared to only 43% in the United States—and many fewer nonteaching employees.[13]

***Schools Structured for Failure*** Today's schools are organized in ways that support neither student learning nor teacher learning well. Teachers are isolated from one another so that they cannot share knowledge or take responsibility for overall student learning. Technologies that could enable alternative uses of personnel and time are not yet readily available in schools, and few staff members are prepared

to use them. Moreover, too many people and resources are allocated to jobs and activities outside of classrooms, on the sidelines rather than
at the front lines of teaching and learning.

High-performance businesses are abandoning the organizational assumptions that led to
this way of managing work. They are flattening
hierarchies, creating teams, and training employees to take on wider responsibilities using
technologies that allow them to perform their
work more efficiently. Schools that have restructured their work in these ways have been able to
provide more time for teachers to work together
and more time for students to work closely with
teachers around more clearly defined standards
for learning.[14]

## Goals for the Nation

To address these problems, the commission challenges the nation to embrace a set of goals that
will put us on the path to serious, long-term improvements in teaching and learning for America.
The commission has six goals for the year 2006.

▶ All children will be taught by teachers who
have the knowledge, skills, and commitment to
teach children well.

▶ All teacher education programs will meet professional standards, or they will be closed.

▶ All teachers will have access to high-quality
professional development, and they will have
regularly scheduled time for collegial work
and planning.

▶ Both teachers and principals will be hired and
retained based on their ability to meet professional standards of practice.

▶ Teachers' salaries will be based on their knowledge and skills.

▶ High-quality teaching will be the central investment of schools. Most education dollars will be
spent on classroom teaching.

## The Commission's Recommendations

The commission's proposals provide a vision and
a blueprint for the development of a 21st-century
teaching profession that can make good on the
nation's educational goals. The recommendations are systemic in scope—not a recipe for more
short-lived pilot and demonstration projects.
They describe a new infrastructure for professional learning and an accountability system that
ensures attention to standards for educators as
well as for students at every level: national, state,
district, school, and classroom.

The commission urges a complete overhaul
in the systems of teacher preparation and professional development to ensure that they reflect
current knowledge and practice. This redesign
should create a continuum of teacher learning
based on compatible standards that operate from
recruitment and preservice education through
licensing, hiring, and induction into the profession, to advanced certification and ongoing professional development.

The commission also proposes a comprehensive set of changes in school organization
and management. And finally, it recommends a
set of measures for ensuring that only those who
are competent to teach or to lead schools are
allowed to enter or to continue in the profession—a starting point for creating professional
accountability. The specific recommendations
are enumerated below.

### 1. Get Serious About Standards for Both Students and Teachers

"The Commission recommends that we renew
the national promise to bring every American
child up to world-class standards in core academic areas and to develop and enforce rigorous
standards for teacher preparation, initial licensing, and continuing development."

With respect to student standards, the commission believes that every state should work on

incorporating challenging standards for learning—such as those developed by professional bodies like the National Council of Teachers of Mathematics—into curriculum frameworks and new assessments of student performance. Implementation must go beyond the tautology that "all children can learn" to examine what they should learn and how much they need to know.

Standards should be accompanied by benchmarks of performance—from "acceptable" to "highly accomplished"—so that students and teachers know how to direct their efforts toward greater excellence.

Clearly, if students are to achieve high standards, we can expect no less from teachers and other educators. Our highest priority must be to reach agreement on what teachers should know and be able to do in order to help students succeed. Unaddressed for decades, this task has recently been completed by three professional bodies: the National Council for Accreditation of Teacher Education (NCATE), the Interstate New Teacher Assessment and Support Consortium (INTASC), and the National Board for Professional Teaching Standards (the National Board). Their combined efforts to set standards for teacher education, beginning teacher licensing, and advanced certification outline a continuum of teacher development throughout the career and offer the most powerful tools we have for reaching and rejuvenating the soul of the profession.

These standards and the assessments that grow out of them identify what it takes to be an effective teacher: subject-matter expertise coupled with an understanding of how children learn and develop; skill in using a range of teaching strategies and technologies; sensitivity and effectiveness in working with students from diverse backgrounds; the ability to work well with parents and other teachers; and assessment expertise capable of discerning how well children are doing, what they are learning, and what needs to be done next to move them along.

The standards reflect a teaching role in which the teacher is an instructional leader who orchestrates learning experiences in response to curriculum goals and student needs and who coaches students to high levels of independent performance. To advance standards, the commission recommends that states:

▸ establish their own professional standards boards;

▸ insist on professional accreditation for all schools of education;

▸ close inadequate schools of education;

▸ license teachers based on demonstrated performance, including tests of subject-matter knowledge, teaching knowledge, and teaching skill; and

▸ use National Board standards as the benchmark for accomplished teaching.

## 2. Reinvent Teacher Preparation and Professional Development

"The Commission recommends that colleges and schools work with states to redesign teacher education so that the two million teachers to be hired in the next decade are adequately prepared and so that all teachers have access to high-quality learning opportunities."

For this to occur, states, school districts, and education schools should:

▸ organize teacher education and professional development around standards for students and teachers;

▸ institute extended, graduate-level teacher preparation programs that provide yearlong internships in a professional development school;

▶ create and fund mentoring programs for beginning teachers, along with evaluation of teaching skills;

▶ create stable, high-quality sources of professional development—and then allocate 1% of state and local spending to support them, along with additional matching funds to school districts;

▶ organize new sources of professional development, such as teacher academies, school/university partnerships, and learning networks that transcend school boundaries; and

▶ make professional development an ongoing part of teachers' daily work.

If teachers are to be ready to help their students meet the new standards that are now being set for them, teacher preparation and professional development programs must consciously examine the expectations embodied in new curriculum frameworks and assessments and understand what they imply for teaching and for learning to teach. Then they must develop effective strategies for preparing teachers to teach in these much more demanding ways.

Over the past decade, many schools of education have changed their programs to incorporate new knowledge. More than 300 have developed extended programs that add a fifth (and occasionally a sixth) year to undergraduate training. These programs allow beginning teachers to complete a degree in their subject area as well as to acquire a firmer ground in teaching skills. They allow coursework to be connected to extended practice teaching in schools—ideally, in professional development schools that, like teaching hospitals in medicine, have a special mission to support research and training. Recent studies show that graduates of extended programs are rated as better-prepared and more effective teachers and are far more likely to enter and remain in teaching than are their peers from traditional four-year programs.[15]

New teachers should have support from an expert mentor during the first year of teaching.

Research shows that such support improves both teacher effectiveness and retention.[16] In the system we propose, teachers will have completed initial tests of subject-matter and basic teaching knowledge before entry and will be ready to undertake the second stage—a performance assessment of teaching skills—during this first year.

Throughout their careers, teachers should have ongoing opportunities to update their skills. In addition to time for joint planning and problem solving with in-school colleagues, teachers should have access to networks, school/university partnerships, and academies where they can connect with other educators to study subject-matter teaching, new pedagogies, and school change. The benefit of these opportunities is that they offer sustained work on problems of practice that are directly connected to teachers' work and student learning.

### 3. Overhaul Teacher Recruitment and Put Qualified Teachers in Every Classroom

"The Commission recommends that states and school districts pursue aggressive policies to put qualified teachers in every classroom by providing financial incentives to correct shortages, streamlining hiring procedures, and reducing barriers to teacher mobility."

Although each year the U.S. produces more new teachers than it needs, shortages of qualified candidates in particular fields (e.g., mathematics and science) and particular locations (primarily inner city and rural) are chronic.

In large districts, logistics can overwhelm everything else. It is sometimes the case that central offices cannot find out about classroom vacancies, principals are left in the dark about applicants, and candidates cannot get any information at all.

Finally, it should be stressed that large pools of potential mid-career teacher entrants—former employees of downsizing corporations, military and government retirees, and teacher aides already in the schools—are for the most part untapped.

To remedy these situations, the commission suggests the following actions:

- increase the ability of financially disadvantaged districts to pay for qualified teachers and insist that school districts hire only qualified teachers;

- redesign and streamline hiring at the district level—principally by creating a central "electronic hiring hall" for all qualified candidates and establishing cooperative relationships with universities to encourage early hiring of teachers;

- eliminate barriers to teacher mobility by promoting reciprocal interstate licensing and by working across states to develop portable pensions;

- provide incentives (including scholarships and premium pay) to recruit teachers for high-need subjects and locations; and

- develop high-quality pathways to teaching for recent graduates, mid-career changers, paraprofessionals already in the classroom, and military and government retirees.

## 4. Encourage and Reward Knowledge and Skill

"The Commission recommends that school districts, states, and professional associations cooperate to make teaching a true profession, with a career continuum that places teaching at the top and rewards teachers for their knowledge and skills."

Schools have few ways of encouraging outstanding teaching, supporting teachers who take on the most challenging work, or rewarding increases in knowledge and skill. Newcomers who enter teaching without adequate preparation are paid at the same levels as those who enter with highly developed skills. Novices take on exactly the same kind of work as 30-year veterans, with little differentiation based on expertise.

Mediocre teachers receive the same rewards as outstanding ones. And unlicensed "teachers" are placed on the same salary schedule as licensed teachers in high-demand fields such as mathematics and science or as teachers licensed in two or more subjects.

One testament to the inability of the existing system to understand what it is doing is that it rewards experience with easier work instead of encouraging senior teachers to deal with difficult learning problems and tough learning situations. As teachers gain experience, they can look forward to teaching in more affluent schools, working with easier schedules, dealing with "better" classes, or moving out of the classroom into administration. Teachers are rarely rewarded for applying their expertise to the most challenging learning problems or major needs of the system.

To address these issues, the commission recommends that state and local education agencies:

- develop a career continuum linked to assessments and compensation systems that reward knowledge and skill (e.g., the ability to teach expertly in two or more subjects, as demonstrated by additional licenses, or the ability to pass examinations of teaching skill, such as those offered by INTASC and the National Board);

- remove incompetent teachers through peer review programs that provide necessary assistance and due process; and

- set goals and enact incentives for National Board certification in every district, with the aim of certifying 105,000 teachers during the next 10 years.

If teaching is organized as are other professions that have set consistent licensing requirements, standards of practice, and assessment methods, then advancement can be tied to professional growth and development. A career continuum that places teaching at the top and supports growing expertise should 1) recognize accomplishment, 2) anticipate that teachers will continue to teach while taking on other roles that allow them to share their knowledge, and 3) promote continued skill development related to clear standards.

Some districts, such as Cincinnati and Rochester, New York, have already begun to develop career pathways that tie evaluations to salary increments at key stages as teachers move from their *initial license* to *resident teacher* (under the supervision of a mentor) to the designation of *professional teacher*. The major decision to grant *tenure* is made after rigorous evaluation of performance (including both administrator and peer review) in the first several years of teaching. Advanced certification from the National Board for Professional Teaching Standards may qualify teachers for another salary step and/or for the position of lead teacher—a role that is awarded to those who have demonstrated high levels of competence and want to serve as mentors or consulting teachers.

One other feature of a new compensation system is key. The central importance of teaching to the mission of schools should be acknowledged by having the highest-paid professional in a school system be an experienced, National Board–certified teacher. As in other professions, roles should become less distinct. The jobs of teacher, consultant, supervisor, principal, curriculum developer, researcher, mentor, and professor should be hyphenated roles, allowing many ways for individuals to use their talents and expertise without abandoning the core work of the profession.

## 5. Create Schools That Are Organized for Student and Teacher Success

"The Commission recommends that schools be restructured to become genuine learning organizations for both students and teachers: organizations that respect learning, honor teaching, and teach for understanding."

Many experts have observed that the demands of serious teaching and learning bear little relationship to the organization of the typical American school. Nothing more clearly reveals this problem than how we allocate the principal resources of school—time, money, and people. Far too many people sit in offices on the sidelines of the school's core work, managing routines rather than improving learning. Our schools are bureaucratic inheritances from the 19th century, not the kinds of learning organizations required of the 21st century.

Across the United States, the ratio of school staff to students is 1 to 9 (with "staff" including district employees, school administrators, teachers, instructional aides, guidance counselors, librarians, and support staff). However, actual class size averages about 24 and reaches 35 or more in some cities. Teaching loads for high school teachers generally exceed 100 students per day. Yet many schools have proved that it is possible to restructure adults' use of time so that more teachers and administrators actually work in the classroom, face-to-face with students on a daily basis, thus reducing class sizes while creating more time for teacher collaboration. They do this by creating teams of teachers who share students; engaging almost all adults in the school in these teaching teams, where they can share expertise directly with one another; and reducing pullouts and nonteaching jobs.

Schools must be freed from the tyrannies of time and tradition to permit more powerful student and teacher learning. To accomplish this the commission recommends that state and local boards work to:

▶ flatten hierarchies and reallocate resources to invest more in teachers and technology and less in nonteaching personnel;

▶ provide venture capital in the form of challenge grants that will promote learning linked to school improvement and will reward effective team efforts; and

▶ select, prepare, and retain principals who understand teaching and learning and who can lead high-performing schools.

If students have an inalienable right to be taught by a qualified teacher, teachers have a right to be supervised by a highly qualified principal. The job began as that of a "principal teacher," and this conception is ever more relevant as the focus of the school recenters on academic achievement for students. Principals should teach at least part of the time (as do most European, Asian, and private school directors), and they should be well prepared as instructional leaders, with a solid understanding of teaching and learning.

## Next Steps

Developing recommendations is easy. Implementing them is hard work. The first step is to recognize that these ideas must be pursued together—as an entire tapestry that is tightly interwoven.

The second step is to build on the substantial work of education reform undertaken in the last decade. All across the country, successful programs for recruiting, educating, and mentoring new teachers have sprung up. Professional networks and teacher academies have been launched, many teacher preparation programs have been redesigned, higher standards for licensing teachers and accrediting education schools have been developed, and, of course, the National Board for Professional Teaching Standards is now fully established and beginning to define and reward accomplished teaching.

While much of what the commission proposes can and should be accomplished by reallocating resources that are currently used unproductively, there will be new costs. The estimated additional annual costs of the commission's key recommendations are as follows: scholarships for teaching recruits, $500 million; teacher education reforms, $875 million; mentoring supports and new licensing assessments, $750 million; and state funds for professional development, $2.75 billion. The total is just under $5 billion annually—less than 1% of the amount spent on the federal savings-and-loan bailout. This is not too much, we believe, to bail out our schools and to secure our future.

## A Call to Action

Setting the commission's agenda in motion and carrying it to completion will demand the best of us all. The commission calls on governors and legislators to create state professional boards to govern teacher licensing standards and to issue annual report cards on the status of teaching. It asks state legislators and governors to set aside at least 1% of funds for standards-based teacher training. It urges Congress to put money behind the professional development programs it has already approved but never funded.

Moreover, the commission asks the profession to take seriously its responsibilities to children and the American future. Among other measures, the commission insists that state educators close the loopholes that permit administrators to put unqualified "teachers" in the classroom. It calls on university officials to take up the hard work of improving the preparation and skills of new and practicing teachers. It asks administrators and teachers to take on the difficult task of guaranteeing teaching competence in the classroom. And it asks local school boards and superintendents to play their vital role by streamlining hiring procedures, upgrading quality, and putting more staff and resources into the front lines of teaching.

If all of these things are accomplished, the teaching profession of the 21st century will look much different from the one we have today. Indeed, someone entering the profession might expect to advance along a continuum that unfolds much like this:

> For as long as she could remember, Elena had wanted to teach. As a peer tutor in middle school, she loved the feeling she got whenever her partner learned something new. In high school, she served as a teacher's aide for her community service project. She linked up with other students through an Internet group started by Future Educators of America.
>
> When she arrived at college she knew she wanted to prepare to teach, so she began

taking courses in developmental and cognitive psychology early in her sophomore year. She chose mathematics as a major and applied in her junior year for the university's five-year course of study leading to a master of arts in teaching. After a round of interviews and a review of her record thus far, Elena was admitted into the highly selective teacher education program.

The theories Elena studied in her courses came to life before her eyes as she conducted a case study of John, a 7-year-old whom she tutored in a nearby school. She was struck by John's amazing ability to build things, in contrast with his struggles to learn to read. She carried these puzzles back to her seminar and on into her other courses as she tried to understand learning.

Over time, she examined other cases, some of them available on a multimedia computer system that allowed her to see videotapes of children, samples of their work, and documentation from their teachers about their learning strategies, problems, and progress. From these data, Elena and her classmates developed a concrete sense of different learning approaches. She began to think about how she could use John's strengths to create productive pathways into other areas of learning.

Elena's teachers modeled the kinds of strategies she herself would be using as a teacher. Instead of lecturing from texts, they enabled students to develop and apply knowledge in the context of real teaching situations. These frequently occurred in the professional development school (PDS) where Elena was engaged in a yearlong internship, guided by a faculty of university- and school-based teacher educators.

**TERM TO NOTE**

Professional development school

In the PDS, Elena was placed with a team of student teachers who worked with a team of expert veteran teachers. Her team included teachers of art, language arts, and science, as well as mathematics. They discussed learning within and across these domains in many of their assignments and constructed interdisciplinary curricula together.

Most of the school- and university-based teacher educators who made up the PDS faculty had been certified as accomplished practitioners by the National Board for Professional Teaching Standards, having completed a portfolio of evidence about their teaching along with a set of rigorous performance assessments. The faculty members created courses, internship experiences, and seminars that allowed them to integrate theory and practice, pose fundamental dilemmas of teaching, and address specific aspects of learning to teach.

Elena's classroom work included observing and documenting the learning and behavior of specific children, evaluating lessons that illustrated important concepts and strategies, tutoring and working with small groups, sitting in on family conferences, engaging in school and team planning meetings, visiting homes and community agencies to learn about their resources, planning field trips and curriculum segments, teaching lessons and short units, and ultimately taking major responsibility for the class for a month at the end of the year. This work was supplemented by readings and discussions grounded in case studies of teaching.

A team of PDS teachers videotaped all their classes over the course of the year to serve as the basis for discussions of teaching decisions and outcomes. These teachers' lesson plans, student work, audiotaped planning journals, and reflections on lessons were also available in a multimedia database. This allowed student teachers to look at practice from many angles, examine how classroom situations arose from things that had happened in the past, see how various strategies turned out, and understand a teacher's thinking about students, subjects, and curriculum goals as he or she made decisions. Because the PDS was also wired for video and computer communication with the school of education, master teachers could hold conversations with student teachers by teleconference or e-mail when on-site visits were impossible.

When Elena finished her rich, exhausting internship year, she was ready to try her hand at what she knew would be a demanding first year of teaching. She submitted her portfolio for review by the state professional standards board and sat for the examination of subject-matter and teaching knowledge that was required for an initial teaching license. She was both exhilarated and anxious when she received a job offer, but she felt she was ready to try her hand at teaching.

Elena spent that summer eagerly developing curriculum ideas for her new class. She had the benefit of advice from the district mentor teacher already assigned to work with her in her first year of teaching, and she had access to an on-line database of teaching materials developed by teachers across the country and organized around the curriculum standards of the National Council of Teachers of Mathematics, of which she had become a member.

Elena's mentor teacher worked with her and several other new middle school mathematics and science teachers throughout the year, meeting with them individually and in groups to examine their teaching and provide support. The mentors and their first-year colleagues also met in groups once a month at the PDS to discuss specific problems of practice.

Elena met weekly with the other math and science teachers in the school to discuss curriculum plans and share demonstration lessons. This extended lunch meeting occurred while her students were in a Project Adventure/physical education course that taught them teamwork and cooperation skills. She also met with the four other members of her teaching team for three hours each week while their students were at community-service placements. The team used this time to discuss cross-disciplinary teaching plans and the progress of the 80 students they shared.

In addition to these built-in opportunities for daily learning, Elena and her colleagues benefited from the study groups they had developed at their school and the professional development offerings at the local university and the Teachers Academy.

At the Teachers Academy, school- and university-based faculty members taught extended courses in areas ranging from advances in learning theory to all kinds of teaching methods, from elementary science to advanced calculus. These courses usually featured case studies and teaching demonstrations as well as follow-up work in teachers' own classrooms. The academy provided the technologies needed for multimedia conferencing, which allowed teachers to "meet" with one another across their schools and to see one another's classroom work. They could also connect to courses and study groups at the university, including a popular master's degree program that helped teachers prepare for National Board certification.

With the strength of a preparation that had helped her put theory and practice together and with the support of so many colleagues, Elena felt confident that she could succeed at her life's goal: becoming—and, as she now understood, *always* becoming—a teacher.

## NOTES

1. *What Matters Most: Teaching for America's Future* (New York: National Commission on Teaching and America's Future, 1996). Copies of this report can be obtained from the National Commission on Teaching and America's Future, P.O. Box 5239, Woodbridge, VA 22194-5239. Prices, including postage and handling, are $18 for the full report, $5 for the summary report, and $20 for both reports. Orders must be prepaid.

2. *Income, Poverty, and Valuation of Non-Cash Benefits: 1993* (Washington, D.C.: U.S. Bureau of the Census,

Current Population Reports, Series P-60, No. 188, 1995), Table D-5, p. D-17. See also *Current Population Survey: March 1988/March 1995* (Washington, D.C.: U.S. Bureau of the Census, 1995).

3.  *National Education Goals Report: Executive Summary* (Washington, D.C.: National Education Goals Panel, 1995).

4.  National Center for Education Statistics, *Report in Brief: National Assessment of Educational Progress (NAEP) 1992 Trends in Academic Progress* (Washington, D.C.: U.S. Department of Education, 1994).

5.  For reviews of teacher licensing tests, see Linda Darling-Hammond, "Teaching Knowledge: How Do We Test It?," *American Educator*, Fall 1986, pp. 18–21, 46; Lee Shulman, "Knowledge and Teaching: Foundations of the New Reform," *Harvard Educational Review*, January 1987, pp. 1–22; C. J. MacMillan and Shirley Pendlebury, "The Florida Performance Measurement System: A Consideration," *Teachers College Record*, Fall 1985, pp. 67–78; Walter Haney, George Madaus, and Amelia Kreitzer, "Charms Talismanic: Testing Teachers for the Improvement of American Education," in Ernest Z. Rothkopf, ed., *Review of Research in Education, Vol. 14* (Washington, D.C.: American Educational Research Association, 1987), pp. 169–238; and Edward H. Haertel, "New Forms of Teacher Assessment," in Gerald Grant, ed., *Review of Research in Education, Vol. 17* (Washington D.C.: American Educational Research Association, 1991), pp. 3–29.

6.  C. Emily Feistritzer and David T. Chester, *Alternative Teacher Certification: A State-by-State Analysis* (Washington, D.C.: National Center for Education Information, 1996).

7.  Marilyn M. McMillen, Sharon A. Bobbitt, and Hilda F. Lynch, "Teacher Training, Certification, and Assignment in Public Schools: 1990–91," paper presented at the annual meeting of the American Educational Research Association, New Orleans, April 1994.

8.  National Center for Education Statistics, *The Condition of Education 1995* (Washington, D.C.: U.S. Department of Education, 1995), p. x.

9.  Richard M. Ingersoll, *Schools and Staffing Survey: Teacher Supply, Teacher Qualifications, and Teacher Turnover, 1990–1991* (Washington, D.C.: National Center for Education Statistics, 1995), p. 28.

10. Jeannie Oakes, *Multiplying Inequalities: The Effects of Race, Social Class, and Tracking on Opportunities to Learn Mathematics and Science* (Santa Monica, Calif.: RAND Corporation, 1990).

11. *Who Will Teach Our Children?* (Sacramento: California Commission on Teaching, 1985); and Linda Darling-Hammond, "Inequality and Access to Knowledge," in James Banks, ed., *Handbook of Research on Multicultural Education* (New York: Macmillan, 1995), pp. 465–83.

12. Mary Rollefson, *Teacher Supply in the United States: Sources of Newly Hired Teachers in Public and Private Schools* (Washington, D.C.: National Center for Education Statistics, 1993).

13. *Education Indicators at a Glance* (Paris: Organisation for Economic Cooperation and Development, 1995).

14. Linda Darling-Hammond, "Beyond Bureaucracy: Restructuring Schools for High Performance," in Susan Fuhrman and Jennifer O'Day, eds., *Rewards and Reform* (San Francisco: Jossey-Bass, 1996), pp. 144–94; Linda Darling-Hammond, Jacqueline Ancess, and Beverly Falk, *Authentic Assessment in Action: Studies of Schools and Students at Work* (New York: Teachers College Press, 1995); Fred Newman and Gary Wehlage, *Successful School Restructuring: A Report to the Public and Educators by the Center on Organization and Restructuring of Schools* (Madison: Board of Regents of the University of Wisconsin System, 1995); and Ann Lieberman, ed., *The Work of Restructuring Schools: Building from the Ground Up* (New York: Teachers College Press, 1995).

15. For data on effectiveness and retention, see Michael Andrew, "The Differences Between Graduates of Four-Year and Five-Year Teacher Preparation Programs," *Journal of Teacher Education*, vol. 41, 1990, pp. 45–51; Thomas Baker, "A Survey of Four-Year and Five-Year Program Graduates and Their Principals," *Southeastern Regional Association of Teacher Educators (SRATE) Journal*, Summer 1993, pp. 28–33; Michael Andrew and Richard L. Schwab, "Has Reform in Teacher Education Influenced Teacher Performance? An Outcome Assessment of Graduates of Eleven Teacher Education Programs," *Action in Teacher Education*, Fall 1995, pp. 43–53; Jon J. Denton and William H. Peters, "Program Assessment Report: Curriculum Evaluation of a Nontraditional Program for Certifying Teachers," unpublished report, Texas A & M University, College Station, 1988; and Hyun-Seok Shin, "Estimating Future Teacher Supply: An Application of Survival Analysis," paper presented at the annual meeting of the American Educational Research Association, New Orleans, April 1994.

16. Leslie Huling-Austin, ed., *Assisting the Beginning Teacher* (Reston, Va.: Association of Teacher Educators, 1989); Mark A. Smylie, "Redesigning Teachers' Work: Connections to the Classroom," in Linda Darling-Hammond, ed., *Review of Research in Education, Vol. 20* (Washington, D.C.: American Educational Research Association, 1994); and Linda Darling-Hammond, ed., *Professional Development Schools: Schools for Developing a Profession* (New York: Teachers College Press, 1994).

## POSTNOTE

The education of teachers has been a long-standing concern both inside and outside the profession. As Linda Darling-Hammond points out, many school reform efforts have been stymied because the teaching force was ill-equipped to put the reforms into effect. Two issues in particular have threatened efforts to reform teacher education. One is an on-the-cheap approach to the preparation of teachers. As a society, we spend few social resources on training teachers. While the preparation of most other professions has evolved out of the undergraduate years into concentrated graduate study and practical experience, most teachers still must skimp on their basic liberal education. Until we are ready to support the education of teachers at a much higher level, we will be sending teachers into schools with too much to learn on the job.

The second issue is related to the first: the underestimation of what it takes to be a teacher. If teaching is simply a matter of standing in front of students and transferring information, then perhaps limited teacher education programs are adequate. However, if we want our teachers to help children engage in their own discoveries and become self-starting inquirers, we need a larger vision of the teacher to guide teacher education. The report described by Darling-Hammond offers such a vision

Linda Darling-Hammond has become the foremost spokesperson for teacher education and the professionalization of teaching in the United States. Her work with the National Commission on Teaching and America's Future places her article among our Classic selections.

## DISCUSSION QUESTIONS

1. What are some of the developments leading to the call for reform of teacher education?

2. According to Darling-Hammond, what workplace factors are currently affecting the education of teachers?

3. In your own view, what aspect of teacher education is most in need of reform? Why?

# CLASSIC *The Kind of Schools We Need*

### Elliot W. Eisner

As everyone knows, there is both great interest in and great concern about the quality of education in American schools. Solutions to our perceived educational ills are often not very deep. They include mandating uniforms for students to improve their behavior; using vouchers to create a competitive climate to motivate educators to try harder; testing students each year for purposes of accountability; retaining students whose test scores have not reached specified levels; paying teachers and school administrators bonuses in relation to the measured performance of their students; and defining standards for aims, for content, for evaluation practices, and, most important, for student and teacher performance.

**TERMS TO NOTE**

Vouchers

Accountability

Standards

Ironically, what seldom gets addressed in our efforts to reform schools is the vision of education that serves as the ideal for both the practice of schooling and its outcomes. We are not clear about what we are after. Aside from literacy and numeracy, what do we want to achieve? What are our aims? What is important? What kind of educational culture do we want our children to experience? In short, what kind of schools do we need?

What we do seem to care a great deal about are standards and monitoring procedures. We want a collection of so-called best methods that will guarantee success. We want a testing program that will display the results of our efforts,

often in rank-ordered league standings. We want an assessment program that allows little space for personal judgment, at least when it comes to evaluation. Personal judgment is equated with subjectivity, and we want none of that. We want to boil down teaching and evaluation practices to a scientifically grounded technology.

Whether we can ever have a scientific technology of teaching practice, given the diversity of the students we teach, is problematic. Artistry and professional judgment will, in my opinion, always be required to teach well, to make intelligent education policy, to establish personal relationships with our students, and to appraise their growth. Those of us who work in the field of education are neither bank tellers who have little discretion nor assembly line workers whose actions are largely repetitive. Each child we teach is wonderfully unique, and each requires us to use in our work that most exquisite of human capacities, the ability to make judgments in the absence of rules. Although good teaching uses routines, it is seldom routine. Good teaching depends on sensibility and imagination. It courts surprise. It profits from caring. In short, good teaching is an artistic affair.

But even artistry can profit from a vision of the kind of education we want to provide. The reason I believe it is important to have a vision of education is because without one we have no compass, no way of knowing which way we are headed. As a result, we succumb to the pet ideas that capture the attention of policy makers and those with pseudo-solutions to supposed problems. Is it really the case that more testing will improve teaching and learning or that uniforms will improve student behavior and build character? I have my doubts. We need a conception of what good schools provide and what students and teachers do in them.

Elliot W. Eisner is Lee Jacks Professor of Education and Art, Stanford University, Stanford, Calif. His forthcoming book, *The Arts and the Creation of Mind*, will be published in the fall by Yale University Press. From Elliot W. Eisner, "The Kind of Schools We Need," *Phi Delta Kappan*, April 2002. Published with the permission of Elliot W. Eisner, Lee Jacks Professor of Education and Professor of Art, Stanford University.

So let me share with you one man's vision of the kind of schools we need.

*The kind of schools we need* would provide time during the school day at least once a week for teachers to meet to discuss and share their work, their hopes, and their problems with their colleagues. It is the school, not the university, that is the real center of teacher education.

The idea that the school is the center of teacher education is built on the realization that whatever teachers become professionally, the process is not finished when they complete their teacher education program at age 21. Learning to teach well is a lifetime endeavor. The growth of understanding and skill in teaching terminates only when we do.

This fact means that we need to rethink whom the school serves. The school serves the teachers who work there as well as the students who learn there. The school needs to be designed in a way that affords opportunities to teachers to learn from one another. Such learning is so important that it should not be an addendum, relegated to an after-school time slot. Teachers, like others who do arduous work, are tired at the end of the day. Learning from our colleagues certainly deserves space and attention, and, even more important, it requires a reconceptualization of the sources of teacher development. One thing we can be sure of is that the school will be no better for the students who attend than it is for the teachers who teach there. What we do typically to improve teaching is to send teachers somewhere else to be "inserviced"—every 6,000 miles or so—usually by someone who has never seen them teach. The expectation is that what teachers are exposed to will somehow translate more or less automatically into their classrooms. Again, I have my doubts.

Teaching from a cognitive perspective requires a change in paradigm, what Thomas Kuhn once described as a "paradigm shift." Such shifts are changes in conception. From a behavioral perspective, change requires the development of those sensibilities and pedagogical techniques that make it possible to realize the conceptions and values that one defines for oneself education-ally. Of course, the cognitive and the behavioral cannot truly be separated; I make the distinction here for purposes of clarity. What one conceptualizes as appropriate gives direction and guidance to what one does. And what one is able to do culminates in what one achieves. Schools ought to be places in which teachers have access to other teachers so that they have an opportunity to create the kind of supportive and educative community that culminates in higher-quality education than is currently provided.

*The kind of schools we need* would make teaching a professionally public process. By "professionally public" I mean that teachers would have opportunities to observe other teachers and provide feedback. No longer would isolated teachers be left to themselves to figure out what went on when they were teaching; secondary ignorance is too prevalent and too consequential to depend on one's personal reflection alone. I used the term "secondary ignorance," and I used it intentionally. I like to make a distinction between what I refer to as *primary* ignorance and *secondary* ignorance.

Primary ignorance refers to a condition in which an individual recognizes that he does not know something but also recognizes that, if he wanted to know it, he could find out. He could inquire of others, he could use the library, he could go to school. Primary ignorance is a condition that in some sense is correctable and often easily correctable.

Secondary ignorance, however, is another matter. When an individual suffers from secondary ignorance, not only does she not know something, but she does not know that she does not know. In such a situation, correcting the problem may not be possible. Secondary ignorance is as consequential for the process of parenting and for the sustenance of friendships as it is for the conduct of teaching. The way in which one remedies secondary ignorance is not through self-reflection, but through the assistance of others. Really good friends can help you understand aspects of your behavior that you might not have noticed. These observations need not be negative.

It is as important to appreciate one's virtues as to become cognizant of one's weaknesses.

For this process to occur professionally, teachers need access to other teachers' classrooms. Teaching needs to be made a professionally public endeavor. The image of the teacher isolated in a classroom from 8 a.m. to 3 p.m. for five days a week, 44 weeks per year, is not the model of professional teaching practice that we need. If even world-class artists and athletes profit from feedback on their performance from those who know, so too do the rest of us. We need a conception of schooling that makes possible teachers' access to one another in helpful and constructive ways. This will require redefining what the job of teaching entails.

For most individuals who select teaching as a career, the expectation is that they will be with children exclusively, virtually all day long. But teachers also need to interact with other adults so that the secondary ignorance that I described can be ameliorated.

The model of professional life that I am suggesting will not be easy to attain. We are often quite sensitive about what we do in our own classrooms, and many of us value our privacy. Yet privacy ought not to be our highest priority. We ought to hold as our highest priority our students' well-being. And their well-being, in turn, depends on the quality of our pedagogical work. This work, I am arguing, can be enhanced with the assistance of other caring adults.

*The kind of schools we need* would provide opportunities for members of subject-matter departments to meet to share their work. It would recognize that different fields have different needs and that sharing within fields is a way to promote coherence for students.

Departmentalization in our schools has been a long-standing way of life. It usually begins at the middle school level and proceeds through secondary school. Teachers of mathematics have a field and a body of content that they want to help students understand; so too do teachers of the arts. These commonalities within subject-matter fields can promote a wonderful sense of esprit, a sense built on a common language to describe shared work. The strength of the educational programs in these fields can be promoted when teachers in departmentalized systems have opportunities to meet and share their work, to describe the problems they have encountered, and to discuss the achievements they have made. In short, different fields often have different needs, and these different needs can be met within the school through the colleagueship that teachers within a discipline share. The department in the middle school and in the high school provides a substantial structure for promoting the sense of community I have described.

*The kind of schools we need* would have principals who spend about a third of their time in classrooms, so that they know firsthand what is going on. We often conceive of the role of the school principal not only as that of a skilled administrator but also as that of an educational leader. At least one of the meanings of educational leadership is to work with a staff in a way that will make leadership unnecessary. The aim of leadership in an educational institution is to work itself out of a job.

What this approach requires, at a minimum, is an understanding of the conditions of the school and the characteristics of the classrooms in which teachers work. To understand the school and the classroom requires that school administrators leave their offices and spend at least a third of their time in teachers' classrooms. In the business community this is called "supervision by walking around."

The term supervision is a bit too supervisory for my taste. I am not sure that school administrators have "super" vision. But they should have a grasp of what happens in their schools—substantively, as well as administratively. Administrators can be in a position to recognize different kinds of talents among faculty members; they can help initiate activities and support the initiatives of teachers. They can develop an intimacy that will enable them to promote and develop the leadership potential of teachers. Thus, paradoxically, the principal as leader is most successful when he or she no longer leads but promotes the initiative and leadership of others.

*The kind of schools we need* would use video-taped teaching episodes to refine teachers' ability to take the practice of teaching apart—not in the negative sense, but as a way of enlarging our understanding of a complex and subtle process. No one denies that teaching is a subtle and complex art. At least it is an art when it is done well. To teach really well, it is necessary to reflect on the processes of one's own teaching and on the teaching practices of others. Our ability to perform is related, as I suggested above, to our understanding of the relationship between teaching and learning. This relationship can be illuminated through the analysis of videotaped episodes of teaching practices. Just what is a teacher up to when he or she teaches? What are the consequences? What are the compromises and trade-offs that exist in virtually any context? What institutional or organizational pressures in a school must teachers contend with? How does a teacher insert herself into her teaching? What does his body language express?

Questions such as these can be profitably addressed through the analysis of videotapes. Indeed, the collaborative analysis of a teaching episode can provide a very rich resource that can illuminate differences in perspective, in educational values, and in the meanings being conveyed. This is all to the good. Teaching is not reducible to a single frame. From my perspective, the use of such tapes not only can make our understanding of teaching more appropriately complex, but it can also refine our ability to see and interpret the process of teaching. And the more subtle perspective on teaching that such analysis creates can only enhance the quality of what we have to say to one another about the kind of work we do.

*The kind of schools we need* would be staffed by teachers who are interested in the questions students ask after a unit of study as they are in the answers students give. On the whole, schools are highly answer-oriented. Teachers have the questions, and students are to have the answers. Even with a problem-solving approach, the focus of attention is on the student's ability to solve a problem that someone else has posed. Yet the most intellectually demanding tasks lie not so much in solving problems as in posing questions. The framing of what we might oxymoronically call the "telling question" is what we ought to care much more about.

Once students come to deal with real situations in life, they will find that few of them provide defined problems. On the contrary, the primary task is often to define a problem so that one can get on with its solution. And to define a problem, one needs to be able to raise a question.

What would it mean to students if they were asked to raise questions coming out of a unit of study? What kinds of questions would they raise? How incisive and imaginative would these questions be? Would the students who do well in formulating questions be the same ones who do well when asked to converge upon a correct answer?

What I am getting at is the importance of developing an intellectual context designed to promote student growth. That context must surely give students an opportunity to pose questions and to entertain alternative perspectives on what they study. The last thing we want in an intellectually liberating environment is a closed set of attitudes and fealty to a single set of correct answers.

*The kind of schools we need* would not hold as an ideal that all students get to the same destinations at the same time. They would embrace the idea that good schools increase the variance in student performance and at the same time escalate the mean.

To talk about the idea that schools should increase individual differences rather than reduce them may at first seem counterintuitive and perhaps even antidemocratic. Don't we want all students to do the same? If we have a set of goals, don't we want all students to achieve them? To both of those questions I would give a qualified yes and no.

Individuals come into the world with different aptitudes, and, over the course of their lives, they develop different interests and proclivities. In an ideal approach to educational practice—say, one in which teaching practices were ideally designed to suit each youngster— each youngster would learn at an ideal rate. Students whose aptitudes were in math would travel farther and faster in that subject than students who had neither interest not aptitude in math but who, for example, might have greater aptitude in language or in the visual arts. In those two fields, students would travel faster and farther than those with math aptitudes but with low interests or proclivities in language or the arts. Over time, the cumulative gap between students would grow. Students would travel at their own optimal rates, and some would go faster than others in different areas of work.

What one would have at the end of the school year is wide differences in students' performance. At the same time, since each program is ideally suited to each youngster, the mean for all students in all of the areas in which they worked would be higher than it would be in a more typical program of instruction.

Such a conception of the aims of education would actually be instrumental to the creation of a rich culture. It is through our realized aptitudes that we can contribute to the lives of others and realize our own potential. It is in the symbiotic relationships among us that we come to nurture one another, to provide for others what they cannot provide—at least, not as well—for themselves, and to secure from others the gifts they have to offer that we cannot create—at least, not as well—for ourselves.

The idea that getting everyone to the same place is a virtue really represents a limitation on our aspirations. It does not serve democratic purposes to treat everybody identically or to expect everyone to arrive at the same destination at the same time. Some students need to go farther in one direction and others need to go farther in a different direction because that's where their aptitudes lie, that's where their interests are, and that's where their proclivities lead them.

The British philosopher and humanist Sir Herbert Read once said that there were two principles to guide education.[1] One was to help children become who they are not; the other was to help children become who they are. The former dominates in fascist countries, he believed, where the image defined by the state becomes the model to which children must adapt. The fascist view is to help children become who they are not. Read believed that education was a process of self-actualization and that in a truly educational environment children would come to realize their latent potentials. In this age of high technology and highly monitored systems and standards, I believe that Read's views bear reflection.

*The kind of schools we need* would take seriously the idea that a child's personal signature, his or her distinctive way of learning and creating, is something to be preserved and developed. We are not in the shoe manufacturing business. By saying that we are not in the shoe manufacturing business, I mean that we are not in the business of producing identical products. On an assembly line, one seeks predictability, even certainty, in the outcomes. What one wants on both assembly lines and airlines flights are uneventful events. No surprises.

In education, surprise ought to be seen not as a limitation but as the mark of creative work. Surprise breeds freshness and discovery. We ought to be creating conditions in school that enable students to pursue what is distinctive about themselves; we ought to want them to retain their personal signatures, their particular ways of seeing things.

Of course, their ways of seeing things need to be enhanced and enriched, and the task of teaching is, in part, to transmit the culture while simultaneously cultivating those forms of seeing, thinking, and feeling that make it possible for personal idiosyncrasies to be developed. In the process, we will discover both who children are and what their capabilities are.

*The kind of schools we need* would recognize that different forms of representation develop different forms of thinking, convey different kinds of meaning, and make possible different qualities of life. Literacy should not be restricted to decoding text and number.

Normally the term literacy refers to the ability to read, and numeracy, the ability to compute. However, I want to recast the meaning of literacy so that it refers to the process of encoding or decoding meaning in whatever forms are used in the culture to express or convey meaning. With this conception in mind and with the realization that humans throughout history have employed a variety of forms to express meaning, literacy becomes a process through which meanings are made. Meanings, of course, are made in the visual arts, in music, in dance, in poetry, in literature, as well as in physics, in mathematics, and in history. The best way to ensure that we will graduate semiliterate students from our schools is to make sure that they have few (or ineffective) opportunities to acquire the multiple forms of literacy that make multiple forms of meaning possible.

That meanings vary with the forms in which they are cast is apparent in the fact that, when we bury and when we marry, we appeal to poetry and music to express what we often cannot express literally. Humans have invented an array of means through which meaning is construed. I use the word *construe* because meaning making is a construal, both with respect to the perception of forms made by others and with respect to the forms that we make ourselves.

We tend to think that the act of reading a story or reading a poem is a process of decoding. And it is. But it is also a process of encoding. The individual reading a story must *make* sense of the story; he or she must produce meanings from the marks on the page. The mind must be constructive, it must be active, and the task of teaching is to facilitate effective mental action so that the work encountered becomes meaningful.

*The kind of schools we need* would recognize that the most important forms of learning are those that students know how to use outside of school, not just inside school. And the teachers in such schools would consistently try to help students see the connections between the two. The transfer of learning cannot be assumed; it needs to be taught.

The idea that transfer needs to be taught is not a new one. I reiterate an old idea here because it is absolutely fundamental to effective education. If all that students get out

**TERM TO NOTE**
Transfer of learning

of what they learn in history or math or science are ideas they rapidly forget and cannot employ outside of the context of a classroom, then education is a casualty. The point of learning anything in school is not primarily to enable one to do well in school—although most parents and students believe this to be the case—it is to enable one to do well in life. The point of learning something in school is to enrich life outside of school and to acquire the skills and ideas that will enable one to produce the questions and perform the activities that one's outside life will require.

In the field of education, we have yet to begin to conceive of educational evaluation in these terms. But these are precisely the terms that we need to employ if what we do in school is to be more than mere jumping through hoops.

*The kind of schools we need* would take seriously the idea that, with regard to learning, the joy is in the journey. Intrinsic motivation counts the most because what students do when they

**TERM TO NOTE**
Intrinsic motivation

can do what they want to do is what really matters. It is here that the educational process most closely exemplifies the lived experience found in the arts. We ought to stop reinforcing our students' lust for "point accumulation."

Point accumulation is *not* an educational aim. Educational aims have to do with matters of enlightenment, matters of developing abilities, matters of aesthetic experience. What we ought to be focusing our attention on is the creation of conditions in our classrooms and in our schools that make the process of education a process that students wish to pursue. The joy must be in the journey. It is the quality of the chase that matters most.

Alfred North Whitehead once commented that most people believe that a scientist inquires in order to know. Just the opposite is true, he said. Scientists know in order to inquire. What Whitehead was getting at was the idea that the vitality, challenge, and engagement that scientists find in their work is what matters most to them. At its best, this kind of satisfaction is an aesthetic experience.

We don't talk much about the aesthetic satisfactions of teaching and learning, but those of us who have taught for more than a few years know full well the feeling we experience when things go really well in our teaching. When things go really well for students, they experience similar feelings.

We ought not to marginalize the aesthetic in our understanding of what learning is about because, in the end, it is the only form of satisfaction that is likely to predict the uses of the knowledge, skills, and perspectives that students acquire in school. There is a huge difference between what a child *can* do and what a child *will* do. A child who learns to read but has no appetite for reading is not really succeeding in school. We want to promote that appetite for learning, and it ought to be built on the satisfactions that students receive in our classrooms. It is the aesthetic that represents the highest forms of intellectual achievement, and it is the aesthetic that provides the natural high and contributes the energy we need to want to pursue an activity again and again and again.

*The kind of schools we need* would encourage deep conversation in classrooms. They would help students learn how to participate in that complex and subtle art, an art that requires learning how to listen as well as how to speak. Good conversation is an activity for which our voyeuristic interest in talk shows offers no substitute.

It may seem odd recommending that deep conversation be promoted in our classrooms. Conversation has a kind of shallow ring, as if it were something you do when you don't have anything really important to do. Yet conversation, when it goes well, when the participants really listen to each other, is like an acquired taste, an acquired skill. It does not take much in the way of resources, but, ironically, it is among the rarest features of classroom life. It

is also, I believe, among the rare features of our personal life, and that is why we often tune in to Oprah Winfrey, Larry King, and other talk show hosts to participate vicariously in conversation. Even when the conversations are not all that deep, they remain interesting.

How do we help students learn to become listeners? How do we enable them to understand that comments and questions need to flow from what preceded and not simply express whatever happens to be on one's mind at the time? How do we enable students to become more like the members of a jazz quartet, whose interplay good conversation sometimes seems to emulate? Conversation is akin to deliberation, a process that searches for possible answers and explores blind alleys as well as open freeways. How do we create in our classrooms a practice that, when done well, can be a model of intellectual activity?

Of course, all of us need to learn to engage in deep conversation. In many ways, we need to model what we expect our students to learn. But I am convinced that conversation about ideas that matter to students and teachers and that occupy a central place in our curriculum can be a powerful means of converting the academic institutions we call schools into intellectual institutions. Such a transformation would represent a paradigmatic shift in the culture of schooling.

*The kind of schools we need* would help students gradually assume increased responsibility for framing their own goals and learning how to achieve them. We want students eventually to become the architects of their own education. The long-term aim of teaching is to make itself unnecessary.

Saying that the long-term aim of teaching is to render itself unnecessary is simply to make explicit what I hope readers have gleaned from my arguments here. Helping students learn how to formulate their own goals is a way to enable them to secure their freedom. Helping them learn how to plan and execute their lives in relation to those goals is a way of developing their autonomy. Plato once defined a slave as someone who executes the purposes of another. Over the grade levels, we have conceived of teaching as setting problems that students solve. Only rarely have we created the conditions through which students set the problems that they wish to pursue. Yet this is precisely what they will need to be able to do once they leave the protected sphere of the school.

It is interesting to me that, in discourse about school reform and the relation of goals and standards to curriculum reform, the teacher is given the freedom to formulate means but not to decide upon ends. The prevailing view is that professional judgment pertains to matters of technique, rather than to matters of goals.

I believe this conception of school reform is shortsighted. If our students were simply inert entities, something like copper or plastic, it would be possible in principle to formulate methods of acting on them that would yield uniform responses. A thousand pounds of pressure by a punch press on a steel plate has a given effect. But our students are not uniform, they are not steel, and they do not respond in the same way to pressures of various kinds. Thus teachers will always need the discretionary space to determine not only matters of means but also matters of ends. And we want students, gradually to be sure, to have the opportunity to formulate ends as well. Withholding such opportunities is a form of de-skilling for both teachers and students.

*The kind of schools we need* would make it possible for students who have particular interests to pursue those interests in depth and, at the same time, to work on public service projects that contribute to something larger than their own immediate interests. This twofold aim—the ability to serve the self through intensive study and the desire and ability to provide a public service—is like the head and tail of a coin. Both elements need to be a part of our educational agenda.

The long-term aim of education may be said to be to learn how to engage in personally satisfying activities that are at the same time socially constructive. Students need to learn that there are people who need services and that they, the students themselves, can contribute to meeting

these people's needs. Service learning is a move in the right direction. It affords adolescents an opportunity to do something whose scope is beyond themselves. The result, at least potentially, is the development of an attitude that schools would do well to foster. That, too, should be a part of our curricular agenda.

*The kind of schools we need* would treat the idea of "public education" as meaning not only the education of the public inside schools, but also the education of the public outside schools. The school's faculty will find it difficult to proceed farther or faster than the community will allow. Our task, in part, is to nurture public conversation in order to create a collective vision of education.

Realistically speaking, our responsibilities as educators extend beyond the confines of our classrooms and even beyond the walls of our schools. We also have responsibilities to our communities. We need desperately to create educational forums for members of the community in which the purposes and processes of education can be discussed, debated, and deliberated and from which consensus can be arrived at with regard to our broad mission as an educational institution. Parents need to know why, for example, inquiry-oriented methods matter, why rote learning may not be in the best long-term interest of their children, why problem-centered activities are important, and why the ability to frame telling questions is crucial.

Most parents and even many teachers have a yellow-school-bus image when it comes to conceiving what teaching, learning, and schooling should look like. The yellow school bus is a metaphor for the model of education that they encountered and that, all too often, they wish to replicate in the 21st century. Our schools, as they are now designed, often tacitly encourage the re-creation of such a model. Yet we know there is a better way. That better way ought to be a part of the agenda the community discusses with teachers and school administrators. Principals and school superintendents ought to perform a leadership role in deepening that community conversation. Without having such a conversation, it will be very difficult to create the kind of schools we need.

I acknowledge that the features of schooling that I have described will not be easy to attain, but they are important. We get so caught up in debating whether or not we should extend the school year that we seem to forget to consider what should go into that year. We seem to forget about our vision of education and the kind of educational practices that will move the school in the direction we value. Too often we find ourselves implementing policies that we do not value. Those of us in education need to take a stand and to serve as public advocates for our students. Who speaks for our students? We need to.

Some of the features I have described—perhaps all of them—may not be ones that you yourself cherish. Fine. That makes conversation possible. And so I invite you to begin that conversation in your school, so that out of the collective wisdom of each of our communities can come a vision of education that our children deserve and, through that vision, the creation of the kind of schools that our children need.

## NOTE

1. Herbert Read, Education Through Art (New York: Pantheon Books, 1944).

## POSTNOTE

Elliot Eisner's contributions to education span many areas, including art education, curriculum development, quantitative research, and educational connoisseurship. His Renaissance qualities earn him a place among our Classic selections.

As young graduate students, both editors of *Kaleidoscope* were privileged to have Elliot Eisner (at the time, a young professor) as a teacher. It was at the height of interest in B. F. Skinner's behaviorism and the applications of programmed instruction and behavioral objectives to American classrooms. There was a heady belief throughout the educational community that this new movement would soon transform our schools. Professor Eisner would have little of it. His was one of the few voices at that time to raise questions and urge caution.

Today we are in the midst of a new national movement that many believe will revolutionize our schools and lead to much higher levels of academic achievement among our students. As he has throughout his career, Eisner is again asking the hard questions, this time about standards and the effects of the tests we use to gauge our successes and failures to reach those standards. Here, he asks us to step back and think hard about what we really desire. "What kind of schools do we *really* need?"

## DISCUSSION QUESTIONS

1. In what specific ways has Eisner's article challenged you? Or do you agree with everything he seems to suggest?

2. How do you as a potential teacher feel about his opening his question to the community, "What kind of schools do we need?"

3. What are the most positive suggestions for school improvement that the author makes?

## 58

# Accountability: What's Worth Measuring?

Mary Anne Raywid

I wish the accountability movement that is now so strong had been launched for different reasons. It emerged, of course, from a growing mistrust of public schools and just how well they are serving us. Because that sentiment continues strong and is likely to be with us for some time to come, the press for accountability is likely to remain with us as well.

We can't beat the accountability movement, so we had better join it and try to shape it. Actually, there are things we can do that could turn it into a very positive force. After all, at root, accountability demands an openness on the part of the education system that we've not always seen and are all entitled to expect: information on just how well or how poorly each public school is doing. And what accountability then demands is that something be done about those schools that are failing.

I am very sympathetic to both these demands. Regarding the first, surely the public is entitled to know how the schools it pays for are faring. If they are *public* schools, surely information about them should be accessible to all. And regarding the second, there are schools in some places that have been failing for years, with little or nothing being done about it. In what was a new and very different kind of move in 1983,

Mary Anne Raywid is professor emerita of educational administration and policy studies, Hofstra University, Hempstead, N.Y., and a member of the affiliate graduate faculty at the University of Hawaii, Manoa. This article is adapted from a speech to a conference on assessment, sponsored by the Hawaii Charter School Resources Center, May 2001. Raywid, Mary Anne, "Accountability: What's Worth Measuring?," *Phi Delta Kappan*, February 2002. Copyright © 2002 by Phi Delta Kappa. Reprinted by permission of author and publisher.

the chancellor of New York City's schools simply closed down a high school that was failing. Its numbers had been steadily worsening each year until finally it was failing, expelling, or otherwise pushing out 93% of its students. Only 7% of those enrolled were graduating. It is unforgivable to let things deteriorate to such a point.

Thus I am receptive to the idea of holding schools accountable and of forcing the failing ones to change. To my mind, accountability is a good thing. But the word is often used interchangeably with standards-based education, and they are not quite the same thing. For reasons that I hope will become clear, I think we ought to talk in terms of—and insist on—*accountability* rather than *standards-based education*. Doing so is by no means an abandonment of standards, but rather a broadening of concern.

**TERMS TO NOTE**
Accountability
Standards-based education

The hard questions begin with "Accountable for what?" It seems reasonable to expect schools to do what they set out to do and thus to hold them accountable for fulfilling their own goals. This means that some school-to-school differences in accountability make sense, given the differences among us as to the goals to be sought in our schools. But there is also a great deal of commonality as to what we want schools to accomplish with our children. It is this that concerns me here: the goals and expectations for schools that I believe we share.

I've put the matter in the form of the question "What's worth measuring?" Of course, what's worth measuring depends on what's worth learning and acquiring and, hence, what's worth teaching and cultivating. What's worth measuring also depends on our expectations about the conditions and circumstances under which this teaching and cultivating ought to occur.

## *Our Goals for Children*

There are really an awful lot of things we want our children to learn and our schools to teach them. We also have a number of different *kinds* of goals that we want to see fulfilled with and for our children, and we have some surrounding expectations that we want to see met. I'm going to present six rather different kinds of things that are worth learning—and thus worth measuring. I don't agree with the psychologist who launched the measurement movement in education by declaring that "whatever exists, exists in some amount and can be measured." He thought everything could be quantified, and I don't. But we can assess without quantifying, and, for me, if we have goals for children and expectations for schools, it's reasonable to try to find out whether they are being met. The short answer to my own question, then, is that whatever we're committed to accomplishing is worth measuring.

First, of course, are the things we call "basic skills"—the ability to read and report accurately on what one has read, to write, and to do elementary calculations. So important are these fundamental skills that they fill a lot of the time for the first three grades of a child's schooling. Much of the teaching that takes place in schools after the first three years calls for the application of these skills, so they really are essential groundwork. Thus it is important that we measure how well a child has learned them.

Second, there are all those pieces of information we want students to pick up: number facts, spelling facts, grammar facts, history facts, biology facts, geography facts, cultural facts, etc. There are lists and lists of these facts, without which you can't be an educated person. You can't even function very well in our society without many of them—like the number facts necessary to determine whether you are being given the right change. Teaching these facts is a perfectly reasonable expectation for schools, it

seems to me, even though in some respects facts are really the lowest level of what we want youngsters to learn. They are necessary. But they are only a beginning.

Third, we want learners to be able to do something with all the facts they've learned. There's not much point in having learned the rules of grammar if you can't put together a grammatical sentence. Other applications are even more involved. We want learners to be able to select and retrieve from the information stored in their heads those facts relevant to a given situation, to be able to assemble them, and then to apply them so as to appropriately respond to a challenge or solve a problem.

Fourth, something else that's well worth measuring because it's so very much worth learning is the set of skills involved in using one's mind. We're not born knowing how to do that. And ironically, schools tend to give the most exercise—and hence developmental assistance—along these lines to the ablest students. The youngsters who need the most help in developing such intellectual skills and inclinations as weighing evidence, judging sources, making legitimate inferences, and distinguishing observations from assumptions are the very ones we tend not to bother with such matters. Instead, we focus on getting them to concentrate on those things that can be acquired by rote and drill—the fact-type learnings. But unless all youngsters are helped to acquire the habits of mind involved in sound judgment and good decision-making, they can never be aware of themselves as creatures of intellect, as beings with the ability to take control of their lives and to alter their circumstance if need be. They can thus never be the citizens we want them to be, with the power to realize their own goals while helping to shape society.

Then there's a whole different kind of learning, the fifth type I find to be important, that we want very much for children to acquire. One principal summed it up recently: "Schools are about all those things that make individuals good and bad." We want our children to grow up as caring, empathetic, compassionate human beings with a sense of stewardship for the land and for one another. We also want them to grow up with integrity, initiative, a sense of responsibility, and a sense of humor. Schools really are in the person-shaping business: they can operate in ways that encourage and reinforce the traits and dispositions just mentioned, or they can operate so as to discourage and squelch them. Since these are the attitudes and inclinations that distinguish a good citizen and a good neighbor from a parasite or an assassin, we certainly want schools to instill them and children to acquire them. So this is yet another sort of goal, and we ought to measure progress toward it.

The sixth goal covers a lot of territory: we expect a school to contribute to a child's individual development. It means, for instance, that we want to see school make a difference in a child's cognitive development. Learning those facts and learning what to do with them are important, but we want school to do more than that. We want school to stimulate young minds to grow and expand their capacity. A school that doesn't lead to such growth isn't fulfilling reasonable expectations, and we need a way to find out whether this is the case. In other words, a school loaded with high achievers has got to make them still better learners. If not, there's been no value added, and that's what individual development is about. It's also about helping youngsters to develop whatever may be their particular talents. Whether it's music or writing or leading others or gymnastics, school ought to be a place that helps young people develop their talents.

These, then, are six different goals for learners that I think most of us can agree are important for schools to work toward: learning basic skills, learning facts, learning how to use information, acquiring desirable habits of mind, developing character and other desirable traits, and developing individual talents. But this isn't all. In addition to these goals and expectations for learners, we have certain expectations that apply specifically to schools.

## Reasonable Expectations of Schools

First, given that children are required to attend them, it seems reasonable to expect schools to be *effective* in teaching our children. This means we expect them to be successful with their students. We wouldn't accept a doctor's diagnosis of "incurable" without going elsewhere for another opinion, and we shouldn't settle for the diagnosis "uneducable" from a school. In other words, we don't expect schools to say, "Well, if you've got success in mind, you really should be sending us a different batch of kids."

On the contrary, we expect schools to be welcoming, user-friendly places, where all six of those different kinds of goals I named are pursued with all youngsters, where all are treated with respect and compassion, and where all can meet with some degree of success. This is a tall order.

But, as if this weren't enough, we also expect schools to carry out their functions in particular ways. For instance, we don't want any of those goals of ours to be pursued lackadaisically or perfunctorily. It's not enough merely to take a class to a concert; the teacher must demonstrate genuine engagement with the music. If instead, the teachers are grading papers or chatting together while the music plays, that's not modeling much by way of music appreciation.

Similarly in a classroom, if the teacher isn't fully engaged in listening and attending when children speak but is demonstrating what it is to half listen to another person, then it's anybody's guess whether children can take from these experiences the lessons we want them to learn. So just going through the motions in classrooms isn't enough. Activities must be conducted with a quality—an emotional tone—that can be as important as the content. Just how serious are teachers about what they are doing? We don't want them to appear to be in dead earnest all the time—in fact, that would be awful—but we do want them to be focused and trying all the time. This is certainly a central enough dimension of what we want school to be that it is worth measuring.

Another thing we expect from schools is that they teach in such a way that youngsters acquire positive attitudes toward what they are learning. If a teacher manages to convey the essentials of reading but strips all pleasure and delight from doing so, it's a questionable success. If a youngster manages to stumble his way through geometry but acquires a hatred for math in the process, that is also a questionable success. As a famous educational thinker put it many years ago, "It's not that children should do what they want, but it's important that they want what they do." And being able to generate this kind of positive receptivity with respect to learning is a legitimate expectation of schools and teachers. If learning new things is drudgery to be undergone only under duress, we haven't done much toward creating a lifelong learner. And since this is so widely voiced a concern, we surely ought to be making regular checks on how well teachers and schools are dealing with it.

These last several lessons are a part of the school's culture and hence of its "hidden curriculum." This curriculum con-

**TERMS TO NOTE**
School culture
Hidden curriculum

sists of the messages typically delivered otherwise than directly in words and usually only as an accompaniment to announced purposes and content. Sometimes it is conveyed in the arrangements. For instance, one famous principal insists that sending children to schools that are too large for teachers and administrators to learn their names teaches students that who they are as individuals, what they are experiencing, and how they feel about it are things that don't matter. Sending them to schools where the toilets are broken or the doors to the stalls have been removed also conveys a message about what doesn't matter. In this case, their need for privacy has no importance. It seems reasonable to expect schools to treat both

the children required to attend them and the teachers who teach in them with respect. And since this expectation is as reasonable as it is important, it's worth measuring.

So to our six goals we've added five expectations of schools: that they be successful, that they be welcoming and user-friendly places, that teachers be fully engaged in their teaching, that schools cultivate a receptivity to learning, and that the school's unspoken messages—its hidden curriculum—be positive and desirable ones.

## Some Notes About Measuring

Just how do we measure success with these goals and expectations? That is a matter that must be left to another time. But I can underscore some things to be kept in mind in seeking an answer to the question. Several things need to be said about the six goals for learners and five expectations of schools stated here. First, all appear reasonable, widely shared, and well worth seeking. This means that all are worth measuring in order to determine whether students and schools are living up to what we want from them.

It is also worth noting that holding schools accountable for meeting our list of school expectations directly implicates a number of people beyond teachers: principals, in particular, and their office staffs, but also librarians and counselors and coaches and cafeteria workers and security guards and custodians. Moreover, another thing our two lists make clear is that the answer to how well students and schools are faring is not going to be accessible simply through a single observation of a school; it takes a lot more than that. This is why ongoing evaluation is absolutely necessary to school accountability. The public can't determine whether its goals and expectations are being met without real evaluation—which must rely not only on what is directly observable but also on a great deal of indirect observation.

Another thing that merits emphasis is that, of our 11 goals and expectations, the standards-based education that many states have embarked on addresses only the first two goals for learners that we identified as widely shared (basic skills and information). The best tests perhaps address a bit of the third goal (ability to use information). That's why I think we ought to talk about "accountability" in preference to "standards-based education." Many people talk as if the standards we've set are sufficient to render the schools accountable, but they certainly won't render them accountable for all our goals and expectations. It's going to take a lot more than a series of tests to do that.

It seems clear that paper-and-pencil tests aren't going to suffice. For half of our goals for students (the fourth through the sixth), we'll need some other measure, just as we will for all five of the expectations for schools. I have several suggestions in this regard. At the outset, we must recognize that there's not going to be any single test for any one of them. We can't afford the bad judgments that reductionist measures are sure to support. Many of us find it absurd to think you can determine how much a youngster knows from a single test score, and the same is true for each of these other goals and expectations. We'll need to have a lot of other data to consider, and we'll have to construct an answer to how well students and schools are faring from weighing a variety of evidence that must first be gathered and then assembled. So don't look for a single measure that will reveal all, and don't settle for any measure that purports to do so. There aren't any. But here are several things you might put together.

First, you might look to what are called "unobtrusive measures" for evidence that can be revealing about both goals and expectations. Such measures don't involve any special test or assignment or activity, but rather the devising of telling questions that can be answered from observations. Actually, a lot of the data we need to gather with respect to our school expectations will provide unobtrusive measures for every-

body but the data collector. These measures make no demands on class time. They include such data as the attendance rates in schools and classrooms, the school dropout rate, the number of suspensions and expulsions, retention rates, the extent of teacher turnover. Each of these offers powerful testimony on whether schools are meeting our expectations.

But these are not what school evaluators usually have in mind when they speak of "unobtrusive measures." Here are a couple of the sorts of things they might be more likely to cite. John Goodlad used to say that one measure of how user-friendly first-grade classrooms are is the number of children who vomit before leaving home on school days. Another measure might be how quickly, and with what sorts of facial expressions, children *and* teachers leave school at the end of the day. Or we might look at the incidence of graffiti in and around the building. You can put together a set of such observations that should yield partial answers on some of the school expectations.

Student performance and behavior are other unobtrusive evaluation measures. Our fifth goal for learners, for instance—the development of character and other personal traits—could be measured by how youngsters carry out service-learning activities: how responsible they are, how sincere their efforts are, the degree of integrity and commitment and stewardship they display. The sixth goal for learners—individual development—may best be displayed through exhibitions in which the community is invited at intervals to observe students' artwork, dancing, singing, storytelling, or debating. In judging such performances, we need a set of carefully devised criteria for judging that are to be applied by a review panel consisting of parents and community members, some relevant experts, some teachers, and some fellow students.

Figuring out the measurements and doing the measuring will not be a simple task. But it is one that real accountability requires. If you agree that the goals and expectations I've stated here are both important and desirable, then we must try, despite the difficulty, to arrive at reliable and credible ways to check how well schools are succeeding at them. In this era of extreme accountability, it just might be our only way to keep test scores from deciding everything.

## POSTNOTE

The author's ideas of what schools should be about are certainly broader and more inclusive than simple standards-based reform. Besides learning content and how to use the content, she includes such learning goals as acquiring habits of mind—problem solving, making good decisions, judging sources; character development and good citizenship; and individual development of talent. She also expects schools to have certain characteristics, such as offering a welcoming atmosphere and effective teaching, modeling appropriate behavior, and sending good "hidden" messages.

The hidden curriculum mentioned by the author is an important concept. The hidden curriculum usually deals with attitudes, values, beliefs, and behavior—messages the school sends to students and teachers about what is valued. If a teacher consistently interrupts students when they are speaking, that teacher sends a message that students' ideas are not valued. If certain types of students receive favored treatment by teachers, other students receive the message that they are less valued. If a school building is always dirty, those who work and study in it receive the message that they are not valued. If athletes are feted, but scholars are not, messages are sent about what activities are valued. If you teach in or observe in a school, see if you pick up any aspects of its hidden curriculum.

## DISCUSSION QUESTIONS

1. Do you agree with the author's list of the six kinds of learning that are worth measuring and her five expectations of schools? Would you add any others to her list?

2. Can you identify any hidden curriculum messages that your high school consistently sent? If so, what were they?

3. Which of the six learning goals mentioned by the author do you think would be the most difficult to measure? Which would be the easiest?

## 59

# Putting Money Where It Matters

Karen Hawley Miles

The focus in the United States on creating accountable, standards-based education is pushing districts and schools to more clearly define their goals and priorities for student learning. Districts and states make headlines with bold proclamations about the importance of academic achievement for all students. But the gap between rhetoric and reality threatens hopes for improvement. While teachers scramble to help students meet more ambitious academic targets, school and district spending patterns and organization structures have changed little in the past three decades (Miles, 1997a). No matter what school leaders and communities say is important, the way schools and districts use their dollars, organize their staff, and structure their time dictates the results.

**TERMS TO NOTE**

Accountability

Standards-based education

As public institutions, schools and districts try to do everything for everyone—and do it all without making enemies. New dollars come to schools in small increments over time, usually tied to specific purposes. We add new priorities and programs on top of the old. Instead of restructuring and integrating school and district organizations, we create specialities and departments to meet newly defined needs. Schools and districts now spend significantly more to educate each pupil than ever before (Snyder & Hoffman, 1999). Taking advantage of these resources to meet higher academic standards requires a political will and singleness of purpose that is

difficult to sustain in public schools. Such action also demands an attention to organizational and budget details that does not come naturally to many educators and policymakers.

If we hope to meet our seemingly unreachable goals, districts and schools must define priorities for student performance, make choices about how to organize to meet them, and then move the dollars and people to match those commitments. If school leaders give priority to improving academic achievement, for example, then the district staff and budget should shift to support that goal. If the district declares that all students will read by 3rd grade, then staff, dollars, and time should support more effective literacy teaching. Districts and schools should expect to give up some long-standing and useful programs to support these choices.

## Matching Dollars to Priorities

For the past 10 years, I have helped districts and schools rethink their use of resources to support their reform efforts. In partnership with New American Schools and with support from Pew Charitable Trusts, I have worked with four large urban districts to analyze their district and school spending and then consider ways to reallocate dollars. My colleagues and I have discovered that, in many cases, the dollars needed for reform efforts are there, but they are tied up in existing staff, programs, and practices. We have found that schools need help shifting their use of resources to take advantage of what they already have and that districts often lag behind schools in changing their own spending and organization structures. To support schools in raising student performance, most districts need to realign spending and staffing in at least five ways.

***Restructure Salaries to Attract and Retain High-Quality Teachers***   It is no secret that U.S. teaching salaries lag behind those of other professions. The discrepancy is especially great for two types of teachers needed in schools: high-performing students from top colleges who have many other career options and teachers trained in math and science (Mohrman, Mohrman, & Odden, 1995). The earnings gap grows wider over a teaching career (Conley & Odden, 1995). Maximum teaching salaries fall well below those in other professions, meaning that the most talented individuals sacrifice much higher potential earnings if they remain in teaching. Districts need to reconsider their practice of paying all teachers the same regardless of subject area. In addition, they must find ways to restructure teacher salaries and responsibilities to provide the most talented, productive teachers with the opportunity to earn more competitive salaries during their careers.

Increasing salaries significantly without bankrupting districts means taking a hard look at the way salary dollars are spent. Since the 1920s, virtually all districts have used a salary structure that applies to every teacher regardless of grade or subject. Teachers can move up the salary ladder either by logging more years of teaching or accumulating education credits. Most districts increase salaries far more for experience than they do for education (Miles, 1997b). Boston Public Schools, for example, spent 36 percent of its 1998–99 salary budget to buy years of experience (29 percent) and education credits (7 percent).

For this investment to make sense for students, both teaching experience and accumulated credits would have to be clearly linked to student achievement. But research shows that after the first five years, the quality of teaching does not automatically improve with either course credits or years of teaching (Hanushek, 1994; Murnane, 1996). Experience and coursework have value, but neither is a fail-safe investment without coaching, hard work, and systems that reward and encourage good teaching. Many districts are currently experimenting with in-

creasing teacher salaries on the basis of more direct measures of teaching quality. Most of these plans give bonuses to teachers who meet certain criteria or student performance targets. These extra dollars are nice symbols, but the plans that have the most promise for significantly raising teacher salary levels redirect existing salary dollars even as they seek to add more.

***Redirect District Staff and Spending from Compliance Efforts to Provide Schools with Integrated Support and Accountability***   Using standards to measure school performance changes the role of the district office. If schools do not have to report student performance, schools and districts are only held accountable for whether they do as they are told and keep children safe. As a result, curriculum offices issue guidebooks and sometimes check whether they are used, and districts create departments to monitor whether dollars from each funding source are spent as stipulated.

When schools become accountable for student learning, the district role must shift to helping schools measure student learning and supporting the changes in teaching and organization that best support improvement. Most districts need to focus more on four purposes: defining standards and targets, supporting schools and teachers, creating accountability, and restructuring school organizations.

Supporting these four goals is often possible by reallocating existing resources. In many large districts, the traditional compliance focus has resulted in a structure that spreads resources thinly across many schools and priorities. For example, one district was surprised to find that it devoted nine experts to supervising services across 30 schools. Each expert was responsible for making sure that schools met program requirements in one specific area, such as special education, Title I, bilingual education, literacy, or technology. Because these nine individuals focused on only one issue in multiple schools, they could conduct only superficial reviews of effectiveness, and they certainly couldn't provide support to

**TERM TO NOTE**

Title I

underperforming schools. Even though the district devoted $24,000 in salaries and benefits to each school, the schools barely felt an impact. Instead, the schools needed deeper, integrated school support in specific areas where improvement was most needed.

### Shift More Resources to Teaching Literacy in Grades K-3
Research consistently shows that smaller group sizes matter most in early grades when students learn to read (Wenglinsky, 2001). It also shows that when students don't learn to read by 3rd grade, they continue to fall farther behind in school and are more likely to be assigned to costly special education programs and to drop out of school. Research suggests concrete ways to improve reading achievement:

▶ Class size reduction in grades pre-K–2 can make an important, lasting difference in student achievement.

▶ Small reductions in class size make little difference; only when class sizes get down to 15–17 students does achievement increase predictably.

▶ Even smaller group sizes, including one-on-one instruction, are critical for developing readers, especially those from disadvantaged homes.

▶ If teachers don't change their classroom practice to take advantage of class size reductions, they can't expect improved student performance.

To incorporate these lessons, both districts and schools need to shift their use of existing resources. U.S. school districts average one teacher for every 17 students—with the ratio much higher in many urban districts—and one adult for every nine students. Yet, elementary school class size averages in the mid-20s (Miles, 1997a; Snyder & Hoffman, 1999). Most districts allocate more staff and dollars per pupil to high schools than to elementary schools.

To focus resources where they matter most, districts need to look first at how much they spend at the elementary school level compared to the high school level. Next, they need to invest to ensure that teachers have access to powerful professional development in teaching literacy. Third, they must actively support school-level changes that shift resources toward literacy instruction.

This active support of school-level changes in the use of resources creates special challenges for districts. For example, many schools have found ways to create small reading groups for part of the day by making group sizes larger at other times of the day. Others have reconsidered the role of each teacher, support person, and instructional aide to ensure that they support the focus on literacy. In some schools, this may mean changing the role of physical education, art, and music teachers or making these class sizes larger. It may mean hiring a highly trained literacy specialist instead of a traditional librarian. And redirecting resources toward literacy will mean integrating bilingual, Title I, and special education teachers more fully into a schoolwide literacy strategy. Schools need help making these shifts, which require changes in district policy, contract language, and staff allocation practices. Districts also need to be prepared to defend school leaders who abandon popular, but outmoded or less important, programs and staff positions to support literacy efforts.

### Invest Strategically in Professional Development for Teachers
To take advantage of smaller class sizes and to improve literacy instruction, districts need to offer teachers high-quality professional development. The assertion that districts invest only a small percentage of their budgets in professional development has become a cliché among education reformers. Although some districts may need to invest more money, the priority, for many, will be to refocus existing efforts to create more effective professional development and more useful teacher time. Research shows that professional development that responds to school-level student performance priorities, focuses on instruction, and provides coaching for individual teachers and teams over time can have a powerful impact on teacher practice. But professional development doesn't follow this model in

**TERM TO NOTE**
Professional development

most districts. And providing teachers with more professional time and intensive coaching support can seem expensive to districts that use a few traditional workshops as their "training."

In a detailed analysis of four large urban district budgets, we found that districts spend more than they think on professional development (Miles & Hornbeck, 2000). In these four districts, spending on professional development from all sources ranged 2–4 percent of the district budget. These figures are much larger than those districts traditionally report and manage. For example, one district reported $460,000 spent on strategic professional development, but the district actually spent nearly 20 times this amount when professional development efforts by all departments and sources were included. Worse, our analysis showed that professional development spending is often divided among many fragmented, sometimes conflicting, programs managed by different departments. Spending to support improved academic instruction represented only a fraction of total dollars in these districts, and the amount aimed at literacy instruction was even smaller. Harnessing these dollars requires district and school leaders to challenge the status quo and to abandon worthwhile initiatives in order to support more integrated models of professional development.

### Reduce Spending on Nonacademic Teaching Staff in Secondary Schools

The traditional comprehensive high school often employs more teaching staff in nonacademic subjects than it does in English, math, science, and history. Traditional high schools devote only about half of each student's school day to courses covering academic skills, resulting in more than half the high school resources being aimed at goals that are not measured by the state and district standards. This allocation of resources also means that class sizes for the core subjects are usually 30 students or more, with teachers responsible for a total of more than 125 students.

But changing the balance of staff to make a meaningful difference in student loads and aca-demic time would require some high schools to double the number of academic staff. And shifting more resources toward academic subjects means reducing staff in other areas and challenging the structure—or even the existence—of such cherished programs as band and athletics. Given the number of the changes and their sometimes painful nature, it is unreasonable and impractical to expect principals or school-based decision-making groups to make them on their own. Until districts take steps to change the mix of staff, many high schools will make marginal improvements at best.

## Making Choices

Organizing resources to act on urgent priorities, such as teaching all students to read in urban schools, requires leaders to take politically difficult stands. Union, district, and school board leaders need courage and strong community support to say:

▶ Even though all subjects are important, literacy is most important.

▶ Even though all teachers are important, those who bring deep subject knowledge and can integrate across disciplines or programs are worth more.

▶ Even though band, sports, and other electives can be a crucial part of a balanced education, the community must find new ways to pay for and provide them.

▶ Even though student readiness and social health provide a base for student learning, schools cannot be held accountable for providing all services to students, and they aren't staffed to do so.

▶ Even though investments in teacher professional development and technology may mean an extra student in your class, we can't build and sustain excellent schools without more of such investments.

## Ensuring Adequate Funding

Regardless of overall spending levels, district and community leaders need to articulate priorities and direct spending to support them. But they must also ensure that schools have enough money to begin these tasks. There is no one way to define how much money is enough, but a few test questions can help put district spending in perspective: How does spending per pupil in your district compare to spending in other districts with similar student populations? How do teacher salary levels compare? How does the community's tax rate compare to the tax rates in similar districts?

If the community is underinvesting in education, leaders need to make the case for increased spending. But a community may be more likely to support increases in spending if citizens see that leaders have clear priorities and are willing to make difficult choices to ensure that new dollars get to the heart of improving student achievement.

## REFERENCES

Conley, S., & Odden, A. (1995). Linking teacher compensation to teacher career development: A strategic examination. *Educational Evaluation and Policy Analysis, 17*, 253–269.

Hanushek, E. A. (1994). *Making schools work: Improving performance and controlling costs.* Washington, DC: Brookings Institute.

Miles, K. H. (1997a). Finding the dollars to pay for 21st century schools: Taking advantage of the times. *School Business Affairs, 63*(6), 38–42.

Miles, K. H. (1997b). *Spending more on the edges: Public school spending from 1967 to 1991.* Ann Arbor, MI: UMI Press.

Miles, K. H., & Hornbeck, M. J. (2000). *Reinvesting in teaching: District spending on professional development.* Arlington, VA: New American Schools.

Mohrman, A., Mohrman, S. A., & Odden, A. (1995). Aligning teacher compensation with systemic school reform: Skill-based pay and group-based performance rewards. *Educational Evaluation and Policy Analysis, 18*, 51–71.

Murnane, R. J. (1996). Staffing the nation's schools with skilled teachers. In E. A. Hanushek & D. W. Jorgenson (Eds.), *Improving America's schools: The role of incentives* (pp. 243–260). Washington, DC: National Academy Press.

Snyder, T. D., & Hoffman, C. M. (1999). *Digest of education statistics 1999.* Washington, DC: National Center for Education Statistics, Office of Educational Research and Improvement, U.S. Department of Education.

Wenglinsky, H. (2001, June). The effect of class size on achievement [Memorandum]. Available: www.ets.org/search97cgi/s97_cgi

## POSTNOTE

Advocates of school choice, including school vouchers and charter schools, often point fingers at the educational bureaucracies in large school districts as a major culprit for student academic failures. These critics argue that these bureaucracies waste money, respond to problems too slowly, and lack accountability.

Rather than just criticizing large school districts, the author works actively with large school systems on how to get "more bang for the buck." The thrust of her recommendations is to invest money in good teachers and their continued professional development. More and more policymakers are coming to the conclusion that high-quality teachers are the essential key to successful educational reform, and school systems must be redesigned to provide the conditions and support that allow teachers to succeed. If school districts make student learning their top priority, then they must surely conclude that teachers need and deserve good working conditions to bring about student academic achievement. Only by investing in good teachers will we achieve the results with students that we seek.

## DISCUSSION QUESTIONS

1. The author recommends that school districts need to reconsider the practice of paying all teachers the same regardless of subject matter. Do you agree with her argument that because highly qualified teachers in certain subject fields (mathematics, special education, for example) are in short supply, their salaries need to be increased in order to attract people to the positions? Why or why not?

2. Do you agree with the author's suggestion that school districts might have to reduce staff or even abandon programs such as band and athletics to focus more on academics? Why or why not?

3. What additional recommendations would you make to ensure that educational dollars are spent wisely by school districts on the most important programs?

## 60

# Coming Around on School Choice

## Joseph P. Viteritti

**W**ant to stir things up at your next meeting of professional educators? Just mention "school choice." Better yet, bring up the topic of vouchers, now referred to as the "V word" even among the most ardent advocates. It is difficult to have a reasoned discussion about vouchers (or choice) without setting off loud voices, angry accusations, and dreadful predictions from both sides. Opponents argue that vouchers will bring about an end to public schools; supporters contend that a lack of adequate choice might well do the same. Surely much is at stake—if not the end of public education, then at least a redefinition of what public education means to parents, students, and educators.

**TERMS TO NOTE**
Vouchers
School choice

I first heard about vouchers 24 years ago. Fresh out of graduate school, I had taken a job as an aide to the incoming chancellor of the New York City public school system. The idea didn't pack much of a punch then. Our collective response at the time was one of suspicion and wonder. We knew that most of those who supported vouchers were down on public education and committed to an agenda that would divert resources from the public schools. We treated the voucher issue as a distraction from the more immediate problems we had to handle, like balancing a budget in the face of retrenchment, teaching basic skills to 1.1 million students, and dodging the political arrows that inevitably get aimed at school chiefs in large urban centers.

In 1978, the New York City school budget topped $3 billion, the state had just launched a new program of competency-based testing, and political minefields preceded every step the new school chief dared to take. Not much has changed since then except for the budget, which now, with the same number of students, exceeds $12 billion. The State Education Department is implementing a new competency-based testing program designed to raise academic standards, complemented by local initiatives. Student performance still lags abysmally. Only 22.8 percent of all 8th graders achieved passing grades on the most recent state test in math; in reading the pass rate was 33.1 percent (Goodnough, 2001).

**TERM TO NOTE**
Competency-based testing

Trying to make sense of the situation after several years of service in the chancellor's office, I wrote in 1983 that the fundamental political dilemma in urban education is a dichotomy between constituents and clients, each with different interests (Viteritti, 1983). On one side of the divide are those influential groups to whom school leaders are politically accountable; on the other are the parents of children whom schools are supposed to serve, who lack the clout to make the system respond to their needs. My initial observation was confirmed in later experiences that I had while working closely with school superintendents in Boston and San Francisco. It remains valid today in big-city school systems across the country. Proponents of school choice believe that it can alter the balance of power between those who govern public schools and those whose children attend them.

Joseph P. Viteritti is research professor of public policy at New York University's Wagner School of Public Service, where he is director of the program on education and civil society. He is the author of *Choosing Equality: School Choice, the Constitution, and Civil Society* (Brookings Institution Press, 1999). From Joseph Viteritti, "Coming Around on School Choice" *Educational Leadership*, April 2002, pp. 44–47. Reprinted with permission of the Association for Supervision and Curriculum Development. Copyright © 2002 by ACSD. All rights reserved.

## A Changing Dialogue

The conversation about choice is evolving. When economist Milton Friedman first proposed vouchers 50 years ago, he condemned public education in the United States as a failure. He argued that competition created by vouchers would force failing schools to close. He predicted that better-run private schools would replace public schools in a marketplace that would have little tolerance for academic failure.

Voucher opponents contended that vouchers would prompt an exodus from public schools, basing their thesis on several incriminating assumptions: that most parents are dissatisfied with public schools, that parents would prefer to send their children to private schools, and that parents send their children to public schools only for lack of a better choice.

Many opponents also predicted that a program of universal vouchers would have a disparate outcome, benefitting more aggressive and better-informed middle-class families who would take advantage of the opportunity, while leaving poor children behind in the worst public schools.

There is some evidence to support such claims, dating back to choice and magnet programs that were created to promote racial integration in the 1980s and 1990s (Fuller & Elmore, 1996). There is also a legal question as to whether providing students with public funding to attend religious schools violates the establishment clause of the First Amendment to the U.S. Constitution. This question should be resolved this spring when the U.S. Supreme Court rules on the constitutionality of the Ohio voucher program. Previous rulings by the Court suggest that it will approve the program, but whether it will do so remains to be seen (Viteritti, 1999).

The Ohio program, which began in 1995, and a similar initiative adopted in Wisconsin in 1990 signal how much the voucher debate has evolved. Rather than provide vouchers for all students, they target low-income students—serving 4,000 in Cleveland and 10,000 in Milwaukee. Another program in Florida targets students who attend chronically failing schools, but only a few dozen students are affected. Broad political coalitions composed of African American parents, white liberals, urban Democrats, and business leaders, as well as market-oriented conservatives and Republicans, supported the laws that brought about these programs.

For such advocates, a voucher is less an instrument for market discipline and more a means for enhancing education opportunity and equity (Viteritti, 1999). They see choice as a way for poor students to escape low-performing, inner-city schools. As they understand it, most middle-class parents in the United States already enjoy choice. Better-off families exercise choice by moving to high-priced communities that have good public schools or by using their own money to pay for tuition at private schools. Public voucher programs designed to aid economically and educationally disadvantaged students help level the playing field.

The Black Alliance for Educational Options, whose chairman of the board is former Milwaukee Superintendent of Schools Howard Fuller, demands choice in the name of social justice. Its logic is hard to refute. National test scores indicate that the average African American 12th grader is four years behind his or her white peer in academic achievement (National Center for Education Statistics, 2001). It is this stubborn learning gap—not public schools—that most contemporary choice advocates want to eliminate.

Most support charter schools—public schools that operate outside the legal jurisdiction of the local school district. Since 1991, 37 states and the District of Columbia have passed charter school laws. With 2,100 such schools in operation, public charter schools represent the bulk of opportunities advanced under the choice banner. When properly designed, charter laws grant school-based personnel the

**TERM TO NOTE**
Magnet schools

**TERM TO NOTE**
Charter schools

autonomy that they need to operate effectively, free from the usual bureaucratic constraints that hamper professional judgment. In a recent Public Agenda survey, 9 of 10 public school administrators reported that they lacked the managerial discretion to do their jobs properly. By devolving power to the school, charter laws enhance local authority (2001).

Beyond the public voucher and charter school initiatives now in existence, approximately 60,000 poor students around the country receive private tuition scholarships to attend nonpublic schools. Conceived as an abstract idea 50 years ago, choice is now a growing reality. The various programs implemented have provided researchers with a rich empirical base for assessing its merits. The evidence on these programs, although plentiful, remains inconclusive, however (Gill, Timpane, Ross, & Brewer, 2001; Peterson & Campbell, 2001).

## Preliminary Evidence

So far, the harrowing predictions of mass evacuations and disparate impact have not materialized. Polls consistently show that parents across the United States have confidence in public schools, evidently much more than choice opponents surmise (Moe, 2001). The exception is found among minority parents living in urban communities, who consistently support choice and vouchers. This perspective puts a different face on the overall condition of U.S. education. Academic failure is not endemic to public education. It can be defined more specifically as an inadequate number of effective urban schools.

Even in urban settings, however, choice has not depleted public school enrollments. With 10,739 students receiving vouchers and 1,559 attending charter schools, Milwaukee offers a wide range of choices to parents; yet, because of a bulging school-age population, enrollment in regular public schools remains stable at 103,500 (Borsuk, 2001). Since 1997, private philanthro-

pists have offered a full tuition scholarship to any student in the Edgewood, Texas, school district who wants to attend a private or parochial school. Yet only 11 percent of the students in this mostly Hispanic, low-performing district outside of San Antonio have taken advantage of the opportunity (McLemore, 2001).

By targeting disadvantaged students, public and private voucher programs have come a long way in assuring that choice is made available to those who need it most. Although charter schools enroll applicants on a first-come, first-served basis or by lottery, considerable evidence indicates that the profile of students attending charter schools is similar to those in nearby public schools (U.S. Department of Education, 2000). Many charter schools have a slight oversubscription of poor and minority students who are highly motivated to seek alternative providers of education services. Some evidence also shows that the poor students who take advantage of vouchers and charter schools have parents who are slightly better educated. But this is a far cry from the kind of middle-class "creaming" (a racially offensive term) predicted by choice opponents. The fact is that choice programs offer opportunities to disadvantaged students that were once available only to the middle class.

Most parents of students in public voucher, private scholarship, and charter school programs indicate that their students are better off for it. When asked, they point to more rigorous academic standards, higher expectations, safer environments, and a sense of community within their new schools as reasons for their satisfaction.

The evidence on academic performance is more mixed. Encouraging evidence suggests that African American students in voucher programs are registering higher gains than their public school peers. For example, research on inner-city Catholic high schools consistently shows that the low-income African American boys who attend them are more likely to graduate and attend college (Evans & Schwab, 1995). The data on Hispanic students are less positive, though.

Evidence on the academic performance of charter schools is also mixed, with some showing impressive results and others not doing as well as neighboring public schools. Some jurisdictions need to impose greater accountability standards on charter schools—and on many of their public schools as well. But if charter schools are to succeed as a viable alternative for under-served students, they must be adequately supported. The average charter school gets approximately 80 percent of the per-pupil funding received by regular public schools. Because of bargains struck between proponents and opponents in the legislative process, charter schools must function at a financial disadvantage.

In Cleveland, for example, per-pupil spending for regular public school students in $7,746, compared with $4,519 for students in charter schools. Each student who participates in the Cleveland voucher program receives $2,250 in public funding. In such cases, the home district of the student exercising choice gets to keep the portion of the funds that would have gone toward the student's education. Defenders of such practices claim that they protect school districts from financial hardship. If students are educated outside the district, however, the district has no justification for retaining the funds. The net result is to penalize the students. These are "opportunity costs" imposed on poor parents who seek to exercise education options similar to those enjoyed by their middle-class counterparts.

Proponents of the market model insist that the competition created by choice will provide underperforming public schools with an incentive to improve. That sounds reasonable enough, but again the evidence is inconclusive. Last year, after a decade of experimentation with choice, the Milwaukee school district failed to meet 14 of the 15 goals that it had set for itself. It is difficult to assess market effects when laws are written to curb competition. When the Wisconsin voucher plan was first enacted, participation was limited by statute to 1 percent of the student population. Most charter school laws impose strict caps on the number of schools allowed, re-

gardless of demand. I believe that if unencumbered choice were allowed, inner-city schools would rise to the occasion and improve, which would be a good reason to support choice. But I could be wrong. Some urban school districts might still resist change and continue to fail. And that would be an even more compelling reason to support choice.

## Plan for Success

School choice is not a panacea for the problems of urban schools. But to succeed on any level, school choice must be designed to succeed. It must be targeted to benefit those students with the greatest needs. Vouchers should be restricted to economically disadvantaged students who attend chronically failing schools. As long as the demand for seats in charter schools exceeds the supply, a certain percentage ought to be reserved for students from failing schools. No arbitrary cap should limit the number of students allowed to participate, and funding must be equitable.

Private schools that accept public vouchers should be held accountable to a public authority, just as charter schools are supposed to be. To

**TERM TO NOTE**
Accountability

qualify for public funding, private schools that accept students with vouchers should be required to demonstrate a level of academic proficiency comparable to those set by the states for regular public schools. Likewise, public schools that do not meet such standards should be reconstituted or closed. The real answer to the so-called "creaming" problem is a public policy that enforces a low tolerance for failing schools. That way no child gets left behind.

The fundamental injustice of urban education is that it consigns poor children to schools that most middle-class parents would not consider for their own children. The point was driven home in New York City last year during a hotly contested mayoral election between six major candidates. Despite their differences on issues, the candidates shared two things in common. All but one rejected school vouchers as a way to provide poor students with access to private schools, and all had sent their own children to private schools. This sounds incredible until you discover that the chancellor of schools and all but one member of the city's board of education also had sent their children to private schools. And one could add to the list of private school parents the mayor and the former mayor, the governor and the former governor, and the newly elected U.S. senator. Nearly every member of the political establishment in New York opposes private school vouchers for poor children while refusing to send their own children to public schools. As in other cities, the political and economic elite of New York views public schools as places for other people's children. The establishment provides the public school system with just enough support to keep it going but does not provide the commitment or determination to make it succeed.

Parents whose children get stuck in failing schools are told to be patient. Patience is an easy virtue when you do not need to live with the consequences of an inadequate education. But why is the public school system good enough for some kids and not for others? That position is no longer morally defensible. Indeed, it never was. That is why I have come around on school choice.

## REFERENCES

Borsuk, A. J. (2001, October 24). Choice program tops 10,000. *Milwaukee Sentinal Journal*, p. B1.

Evans, W. N., & Schwab, R. M. (1995). Finishing high school and starting college: Do Catholic schools make a difference? *Quarterly Journal of Economics, 110,* 941–974.

Fuller, B., & Elmore, R. F. (1996). *Who chooses? Who loses?* New York: Teachers College Press.

Gill, B. P., Timpane, P. M., Ross, K. E., & Brewer, D. J. (2001). *Rhetoric versus reality: What we know and what we need to know about vouchers and charter schools.* Santa Monica, CA: RAND.

Goodnough, A. (2001, October 24). Majority of eighth graders again fail statewide tests. *New York Times,* p. D5.

McLemore, D. (2001, November 11). Voucher program in its 4th year; school choice reviews mixed in San Antonio. *Dallas Morning News,* p. A45.

Moe, T. (2001). *Vouchers and the American public.* Washington, DC: Brookings Institution Press.

National Center for Education Statistics. (2001). *NAEP summary data tables.* Washington, DC: U.S. Department of Education.

Peterson, P. E., & Campbell, D. E. (2001). *Charters, vouchers, and public education.* Washington, DC: Brookings Institution Press.

Public Agenda. (2001). *Trying to stay ahead of the game: Superintendents and principals talk about school leadership.* Washington, DC: Author.

U.S. Department of Education. (2000, January). *The state of charter schools 2000: Fourth-year report.* Washington, DC: Author.

Viteritti, J. P. (1983). *Across the river: Politics and education in the city.* New York: Holmes & Meier.

Viteritti, J. P. (1999). *Choosing equality: School choice, the constitution, and civil society.* Washington, DC: Brookings Institution Press.

## *POSTNOTE*

This thoughtful article examines various forms of school choice, and the arguments for and against them. Few people object to choice within the public schools through such programs as magnet schools and intradistrict enrollment plans. Charter schools, though more controversial, are generally supported by both Democrats and Republicans as a way to encourage school reform, respond to parental demand, and still stay within the public school domain. It is school voucher plans that generate the greatest controversy, primarily by allowing public money to be spent sending children to private and religious schools.

In summer 2002, shortly after this article was published, the U.S. Supreme Court ruled in a 5–4 decision that Cleveland's voucher plan, which empowers parents to redeem tuition vouchers at religious as well as nonreligious private schools, does not violate the constitutional prohibition of "establishment" of religion because government aid goes directly to parents who use it at their discretion. This decision is interpreted as giving a green light to states to implement school voucher plans to assist students attending "failing schools," and we are likely to see more school voucher plans being implemented.

## DISCUSSION QUESTIONS

1. Considering the various forms of school choice discussed in this article, and others that you may know of, which would you support? Why?

2. What concerns, if any, do you have regarding the issue of school choice?

3. Many other countries (Chile, Netherlands, France, Australia, for example) already provide public money to send students to religious and private schools. Why do you think the issue is so controversial in the U.S.?

# The False Promise of Vouchers

Timothy McDonald

**61**

The book of Exodus tells the story of the Israelites who, losing hope as they waited for Moses to return from the mountaintop, began to worship the golden calf. For African Americans, this story provides an important context for one of our greatest challenges—the education of our children.

Too many African Americans live in communities where public schools have been struggling for a long time. Like the Israelites waiting for Moses's return, they fear that they have been abandoned. Now they are being asked to turn their backs on public schools and replace them with a golden calf called vouchers.

So far, the nationwide voucher movement has had little success. Voucher programs and tuition tax credit programs have been defeated in many states, including Maryland, California, Colorado, Washington, and Michigan (Walsh, 2000).

Both white Americans and people of color oppose vouchers. Election exit polls in Michigan and California, the two states that put voucher initiatives to a vote in 2000, found that African Americans and Hispanics had overwhelmingly voted no (People For the American Way Foundation, 2001). Results of a national poll released last fall found that when offered five options for improving education, only 5 percent of African Americans picked vouchers as the best approach. African Americans were much more likely to favor reducing class size (36 percent), improving teacher quality (23 percent),

**TERMS TO NOTE**

Voucher

Class size

and increasing training for teachers and principals (26 percent) (Zogby International, 2001).

## Vouchers Don't Improve Student Achievement

More than a decade after the first publicly funded voucher program began, we have no good evidence that vouchers do a better job of educating students than do public schools. The U.S. General Accounting Office (2001) found little or no difference between the academic achievement of voucher students and that of public school students in Cleveland, Ohio, and Milwaukee, Wisconsin, the two urban school systems with publicly funded voucher programs.

A report released last September compared groups of public school students and voucher students at the beginning of 1st grade and the end of 2nd grade. The public school students' average learning gains over those two years were greater than those of the voucher students in language, reading, and math (Metcalf, 2001).

In a 1998 report, Princeton University researcher Cecilia Rouse compared Milwaukee voucher schools with several of the city's public elementary schools that had reduced class size and provided additional resources in the early grades. The public school students performed as well as the voucher students in math; they significantly outperformed the voucher students in reading.

## Vouchers Hurt Public Schools

Vouchers drain tax dollars from public schools and crowd out funding for crucial reforms that can improve public schools.

As much as $27.6 million that could have gone toward class size reduction, dropout prevention,

Timothy McDonald is the chair of the African American Ministers Leadership Council, a project of the People For the American Way Foundation, and pastor of the First Iconium Baptist Church of Atlanta, Georgia. From Timothy McDonald, "The False Promise of Vouchers," *Educational Leadership*, April 2002, pp. 33–37. Reprinted with permission of the Association for Supervision and Curriculum Development. Copyright © 2002 by ASCD. All rights reserved.

or preschool programs was diverted to vouchers in the first five years of Cleveland's voucher program. Besides the funds for vouchers themselves (a maximum of $2,250 per child), tax dollars went to other expenses such as record keeping and transportation (Oplinger & Willard, 1998). During the voucher program's first year, budgetary pressures forced Cleveland officials to eliminate all-day kindergarten for nonmagnet schools (American Federation of Teachers, 1997).

Last year in Wisconsin, the governor's original budget proposal called for cutting money from the state's successful class size reduction program and spending a similar amount to increase funding for Milwaukee's voucher program (People For the American Way Foundation, 2001). Only a determined grassroots campaign by parents, teachers, and community leaders saved the state's commitment to the class size reduction program, which had demonstrated its effectiveness in narrowing the achievement gap between white and minority students (Molnar, Smith, & Zahorik, 1999, 2000).

Voucher proponents try to downplay public schools' loss of funding, claiming that any loss of per-pupil aid is offset by the money that public schools save because they no longer need to educate voucher students. But per-pupil aid does not only cover an individual student's desk, books, and instructional needs. It also covers the overhead and other fixed costs of operating a public school—teachers, counselors, and other staff; utility costs; maintenance and repairs; and more. Losing a handful of students to vouchers does nothing to change these fixed costs. A financial audit of the Cleveland public schools found that, several years into the voucher program, the public schools were "losing [state aid] without a change in their overall operating costs" (KPMG LLP, 1999, sec. 9, p. 5).

## Vouchers Exclude Many Students

Private schools that participate in voucher programs frequently exclude students who have special education needs, disabilities, behavioral problems, poor academic performance, or the wrong religious affiliation. In other words, under voucher programs, the real "choice" belongs to the private schools, not the poor kids.

**TERM TO NOTE**
School choice

An investigation by the People For the American Way Foundation into the admissions practices of schools that participated in the Milwaukee voucher program in 1998–99 found that many voucher schools imposed unlawful admission requirements on voucher students, charged them unlawful fees, and discouraged parents of voucher students from exercising their statutory right to opt their children out of religious activities (NAACP-Milwaukee Branch & People For the American Way Foundation, 1999).

Besides the factors that prevent or discourage voucher students from entering many private schools, a considerable number of voucher students leave private schools before they graduate. In its fifth year, the Milwaukee voucher program had a student attrition rate of 28 percent (Wisconsin Department of Public Instruction, 2000; Witte, Sterr, & Thorn, 1995).

Voucher schools' inability or unwillingness to serve a variety of students is not exclusive to Milwaukee. In 1998, a federal survey of private schools in large inner cities found that between 70 and 85 percent of schools would "definitely or probably" *not* want to participate in a voucher program if they were required to accept "students with special needs, such as learning disabilities, limited English proficiency, or low achievement" (U.S. Department of Education, 1998, pp. xi, 51).

## Vouchers Go to Many Students Who Don't Need Them

Voucher proponents emphasize the benefits of vouchers for poor families whose children attend public schools. In practice, however, voucher plans direct money to many students who aren't poor or haven't been attending public schools.

Florida's A+ voucher program sets no income caps for students to qualify for vouchers. A study in Ohio found that one in three students participating in the Cleveland program were *already* enrolled in a private school before receiving a voucher (Policy Matters Ohio, 2001). Although the Milwaukee program already serves families that are well above the poverty line, Wisconsin's pro-voucher governor has proposed raising the income caps even higher and permitting families to continue receiving vouchers once they are in the program no matter how high their incomes rise (Legislative Fiscal Bureau, 2001).

## Voucher Programs Decrease Accountability

Over the years, public schools have rightly been urged to strengthen their accountability to the public, parents, and taxpayers. Yet, public schools are already much more accountable than the typical voucher school.

**TERM TO NOTE**
Accountability

Decisions about the governance and operations of private schools eligible for voucher funds are typically made behind closed doors. Voucher schools aren't required to administer state achievement tests to their students. And it has been six years since the last comprehensive evaluation of Milwaukee's voucher schools (People For the American Way Foundation, 2001).

An independent auditor confirmed financial mismanagement of Cleveland's voucher schools and found nearly $2 million in questionable expenses in the first year alone (Petro, 1999). A Wisconsin state audit in 2000 revealed that about 10 percent of Milwaukee's voucher schools "had no accreditation, were not seeking accreditation, and administered no standardized tests" (Wisconsin Legislative Audit Bureau, 2000).

Florida's A+ voucher program also fails to hold participating private schools accountable. Public schools receive a letter grade under the program, but private schools are not graded,

making it impossible to know whether a student who leaves a "failing" public school is entering a better private school.

Florida's McKay Scholarships provide vouchers for students with disabilities, but state officials do not provide adequate oversight. In one instance, the state continued to send voucher payments to W. J. Redmond Academy even though the school had failed a health inspection, many students' records were incomplete, and Redmond officials had neglected to certify that all voucher students were eligible to receive funds (O'Connor, 2001).

When parents choose to pay to send their children to private schools, they do so knowing that these schools operate in a different way. But when the public is *required* to fund private schools, it's only fair to hold these schools accountable to the public for how they spend money, hire staff, and otherwise operate. Voucher supporters want to have it both ways—to operate with public funds but to ignore a variety of public laws and standards.

## We Can Turn Public Schools Around

With nearly 90 percent of all school-age children in the United States attending public schools, we must focus our funding and energy on improving these schools. In the wake of September 11, we have gained a fresh appreciation for public schools and other institutions that instill common values and reflect the diversity and democratic heritage of the United States.

We *can* turn failing public schools around. Many public schools are already showing significant improvement. The Education Trust (2001) recently issued a report identifying 1,320 high-poverty, high-minority public schools in which students were high achievers, "often outperforming predominantly white schools in wealthy communities" (p. 1). Incidentally, more than a dozen high-poverty or high-minority Cleveland public schools were cited in this report. In other words, the public schools that children of color attend can be excellent schools.

Critics complain that turning around a troubled public school takes forever, but experience shows otherwise. The right resources and the right strategies can create positive changes within a matter of months. After-school tutoring and other reforms have been used with success at Rennert Elementary School in Robeson County, North Carolina, for example, where 94 percent of the students qualify for free or reduced-price lunch. Just one year after the school was assigned a state-mandated assistance team to help coordinate improvement strategies, Rennert students' scores in math and reading jumped 10 percent (National Education Association, 2001).

Reducing class size is one strategy that research has proven to make a difference for African American students (Krueger & Whitmore, 2001; Viadero, 1999). Tutorial and other programs that provide extra help are also effective. As Pedro Noguera, an education professor at Harvard, recently observed: "It's not rocket science. In many districts, we know what works and we know what schools need" (Chase, 2001).

So what's the problem? Very often, it's a lack of resources. Class size reduction, tutorial programs, and after-school programs cost money. States must do more to target funding to students who need the most help.

Ohio is one state that has failed to do its homework in this area. From 1991 through 1998, the state appropriated more money for its private schools ($1.1 billion) than it did to refurbish its public schools ($1 billion) (Hawthorne, 1998). Even as Ohio's leaders continue to support voucher funding, they have yet to comply with multiple state supreme court rulings that have struck down Ohio's school funding formula as unconstitutional (Archer, 2000; Sandham, 2002).

Public schools in every city *can* improve—many of them are already improving. Continued progress requires us to keep our eyes on the prize and make our voices and our votes count. We must not allow the false promise of vouchers to distract us from our rightful purpose.

## REFERENCES

American Federation of Teachers. (1997). *The Cleveland voucher program: Who chooses? Who gets chosen? Who pays?* Washington, DC: Author.

Archer, J. (2000, May 17). Ohio high court again overturns finance system. *Education Week,* p. 25.

Chase, R. (2001, November 11). *High hopes for low-performing schools.* Available: www.nea.org/publiced/chase/bc011111.html

Education Trust. (2001, December 12). *First-of-its-kind report identifies thousands of high-poverty and high-minority schools across U.S. performing among top schools in their states.* (News release). Washington, DC: Author. Available: www.edtrust.org/news/12_12_01_dtm.asp

Hawthorne, M. (1998, March 29). State aid to private schools up: Public districts feel slighted. *Cincinnati Enquirer,* p. A1.

KPMG LLP. (1999, September 9). *Cleveland Scholarship and Tutoring Program: Final management study.* Cleveland, OH: Cleveland Municipal School District.

Krueger, A. B., & Whitmore, D. M. (2001, March). *Would smaller classes help close the black-white achievement gap?* (Working Paper No. 451) Princeton, NJ: Princeton University. Available: www.irs.princeton.edu/pubs/pdfs/451.pdf

Legislative Fiscal Bureau. (2001, March). *2001–03 Wisconsin state budget summary of governor's budget recommendations.* Madison: Wisconsin Legislative Audit Bureau.

Metcalf, K. (2001, September). *Education of the Cleveland scholarship program, 1998–2000: Technical report.* Bloomington: Indiana Center for Evaluation, Indiana University.

Molnar, A., Smith, P., & Zahorik, J. (1999, December). *1998–1999 evaluation results of the Student Achievement Guarantee in Education (SAGE) program.* Milwaukee: University of Wisconsin-Milwaukee, Center for Education Research, Analysis, and Innovation.

Molnar, A., Smith, P., & Zahorik, J. (2000, December). *1999–2000 evaluation results of the Student Achievement Guarantee in Education (SAGE) program.* Milwaukee: University of Wisconsin-Milwaukee, Center for Education Research, Analysis, and Innovation.

NAACP-Milwaukee Branch, & People For the American Way Foundation. (1999, August 19). *Milwaukee parental choice program: violations of statutory requirements.* (Legal complaint filed with Wisconsin Superintendent of Public Instruction).

National Education Association. (2001, January). *Priority schools resource guide.* Washington, DC: Author.

O'Connor, L. (2001, October 14). Control limited in state voucher program. *The South Florida Sun-Sentinel,* p. B1.

Oplinger, D., & Willard, D. J. (1998, March 27). Vouchers costing Ohio. *Akron Beacon Journal,* p. A1.

People For the American Way Foundation. (2000). *Voters affirm commitment to public schools and reject vouchers on November 7.* (Editorial memorandum). Washington, DC: Author. Available: www.pfaw. org/issues/education/vouchers_lose.pdf

People For the American Way Foundation. (2001, April). *Punishing success: The governor's proposed education budget in Wisconsin and the SAGE and voucher programs.* Washington, DC: Author.

Petro, J. (1999, January 5). *Petro issues special audit of Cleveland voucher program.* (Press release). Cleveland: Auditor of State, State of Ohio.

Policy Matters Ohio. (2001, September). *Cleveland school vouchers: Where the students come from.* Cleveland, OH: Author.

Rouse, C. E. (1998). Schools and student achievement: More evidence from the Milwaukee parental choice program. *Economic Policy Review, 7*(1): 61–76.

Sandham, J. (2002, January 23). Mediator has tough job in Ohio funding case. *Education Week,* pp. 14, 18.

U.S. Department of Education. (1998). *Barriers, benefits, and costs of using private schools to alleviate overcrowding in public schools. Final report.* Washington, DC: Author.

U.S. General Accounting Office. (2001, August). *School vouchers: Publicly funded programs in Cleveland and Milwaukee.* (GAO-01-914). Washington, DC: Author.

Viadero, D. (1999, May 5). Tenn. class-size study finds long-term benefits. *Education Week,* p. 5.

Walsh, M. (2000, November 15). Voucher initiatives defeated in Calif., Mich. *Education Week,* pp. 14, 18.

Wisconsin Department of Public-Instruction. (2000). *Milwaukee parental school choice program (MPSCP): MPSCP facts and figures for 1999–2000.* Madison: Author. Available: www.dpi.state.wi.us/dpi/dfm/sms/mpcfnf99.html

Wisconsin Legislative Audit Bureau. (2000, February). *Audit summary: Milwaukee Parental Choice program.* Madison: Author.

Witte, J. F., Steer, T. D., & Thorn, C. A. (1995). *Fifth-year report: Milwaukee parental choice program.* Madison: University of Wisconsin-Madison.

Zogby International. (2001, May 23–30). Telephone poll of 1,211 adults conducted for the National School Boards Association.

## POSTNOTE

This article was published just two months before a U.S. Supreme Court ruling was issued permitting school vouchers to be used for religious education by low-income parents. While this ruling will have a profound effect on the educational landscape, it signifies the end of the first real battle rather than the end of the war. Numerous groups of educators and citizens are gearing up for a long struggle against what they see as a violation of our traditional separation of church and state.

The author of this article, clearly a strong opponent of vouchers, marshals considerable evidence to cast doubt on the social and educational value of voucher programs. But consider two points: First, public tax monies going to religious schools is hardly new in this country. During the colonial era and the early years of this nation, taxes regularly went to support religious schools. Even in the nineteenth and early twentieth centuries, our public schools were, de facto, religious schools. There was regular prayer in school. The Christian Bible and the Ten Commandments were mainstays of a child's education. References to God permeated the school day and school functions, such as assemblies and graduation exercises. In addition, in recent years public tax monies, such as Pell Grants, regularly go to religious colleges and universities. There is nothing new here. Second, there are the real and legitimate desires of taxpaying parents. Consider the parents of a poor urban child who have seen first hand the deadening effect of a failing public school on their child. While more financially advantaged Americans in this situation can move to communities with better public schools or purchase a private education for their children, these parents cannot. Nothing burns deeper in the heart of parents than to see their child falling behind, losing self-confidence, and facing a dismal future. There is educational policy, but there is also the issue of justice.

## DISCUSSION QUESTIONS

1. What do you believe are the author's strongest arguments against vouchers?

2. Do you believe the author's contention that more money and energy are needed to turn around failing public schools? Why or why not?

3. If you were the minority parents described in the postnote, what would you want for your child? Why?

# Bear Market

## Henry M. Levin

## 62

The recent entry of for-profit schools into the K–12 arena is an intriguing trend. Their promise is that their endless quest for new customers will drive them to innovate at a faster pace than not-for-profit and public schools. The discipline of market economics supposedly will force for-profit schools to streamline their bureaucracies, retain and reward highly talented administrators and teachers, and raise student achievement on a variety of measures. They will be more responsive to consumers and more accountable to local authorities. In short, they claim to offer a better product at a similar if not lower price. In turn, their siphoning of students will cause not-for-profit and public schools to rethink their approaches to schooling. They will seek to learn from and replicate the more efficient management structures and more effective instructional methods of the for-profits. If all goes according to the free-market theorists' model, introducing the profit motive into education will spark a perpetual discovery process that benefits students, employees, and, let us not forget, investors.

So much for theory. The fact is that we know little about how for-profit schools will operate and how they will affect students and other schools. At least three major questions have yet to be answered satisfyingly:

❯ If schools are a potentially profitable endeavor, then why did entrepreneurs wait so long to enter the market? Is there something unique about schooling that makes it difficult to earn a profit?

❯ Now that we do have for-profit schools, how will they achieve cost savings? Will they bring fundamentally different approaches to education through curricular and technological innovations that will "break the mold"?

❯ Even if they are more effective or less costly, or both, will they earn profits that are comparable to the returns on other investments?

## Why Now?

That for-profit schools have only now become players in the K–12 market is puzzling, given that public schools have been around for two centuries, independent schools for four. Among the 28,000 or so independent schools in the United States, probably no more than a few hundred have gone the for-profit route. Many of these specialize in education for the severely handicapped and charge very high fees, which are usually paid by states and school districts to meet the federal special-education mandates. Only in the past decade have we seen the onset of major efforts to establish for-profit schools for a broad range of students in K–12 education.

**TERM TO NOTE**
Educational Management Organization (EMO)

For the most part, education management organizations (EMOs) such as Advantage Schools and Edison Schools, the two best-known EMOs, have sought to manage charter schools or public schools under contract to school districts. (Note that for-profit firms have always had a significant role in K–12 education by providing various products and services to schools, such as supplies, textbooks, transportation, and food services.) What stopped investors, entrepreneurs, and educators from taking advantage of the profitable opportunities in running

Henry M. Levin is a professor of economics and education and the director of the National Center for the Study of Privatization in Education at Teachers College, Columbia University. From Henry M. Levin, "Bear Market," *Education Next*, Spring 2001. Reprinted with permission of The Hoover Institution, Leland Stanford Junior University.

schools over the past century? In essence, what took so long? Is it possible that few saw potential profits in schooling in the past? Then the question becomes: What has changed to create the opportunities that are perceived today?

One reason that entrepreneurs have been reluctant to enter the schooling market is that they must compete against heavily subsidized public schools, which limits their ability to charge prices that fully cover their costs. Thus, the market has been left to those nonprofit organizations that can raise adequate subsidies to keep tuition low. But that does not explain the existence of private schools that compete very effectively [against] schools in virtually every metropolitan area and whose tuition levels far exceed public-school spending. In my city, New York, elite private schools such as Dalton, Horace Mann, Spence, Brearley, Riverdale Country School, and at least two dozen more levy tuitions in the range of $20,000 a year—exceeding what even the wealthiest New York suburban school districts spend per student. Yet they always have more applicants than openings, a surplus that is maintained in good and bad economic times. Isn't this the kind of niche market that profit-seekers salivate over? But here they are invisible.

The problem for entrepreneurs is that for-profit schools compete at a disadvantage against not only public schools but many nonprofit schools as well. For a variety of reasons, virtually all private schools set tuition below the level that would allow full cost recovery. For instance, I serve on the board of a religious private school that must raise half of its budget, despite a price tag in the $13,000-a-year range for high school. One could argue that this subsidy is necessary to attract an adequate number of students. But this year, its seventh in operation, the school had more than twice as many applications as openings for its freshman class.

Fund raising remains important for such schools, which often provide scholarships to some portion of their students who cannot afford full tuition. In some of the less-expensive independent schools, the fund-raising subsidies are needed to cover operating costs. Moreover, fund-raising often still isn't enough. Many of the nonprofit independent schools are also subsidized with below-market personnel costs, donated facilities, and other payments in kind, benefits that are rarely if ever showered on for-profits.

Further complicating the for-profits' task is the fact that the nonprofits with the highest tuitions also have the highest endowments and most vigorous fund-raising efforts. In conversations with their headmasters, one gets the impression that they see themselves, proudly, as sponsoring activities that are not economically justified by tuition charges. These include extensive community-service programs for students and a much wider range of co-curricular and extracurricular activities and athletic teams than their school enrollments would justify. They also provide a range of amenities whose costs exceed the tuition allotted for them, from very small classes and seminars (ten or fewer students) to guided independent study.

In short, even the most expensive private schools with the most elite clientele fail to cover their costs with tuition. This goes far in explaining why entrepreneurs have shied away from the K–12 market. This is not to say that an individual, for-profit, family-owned school can't survive. I know of a few for-profit schools at the K–12 level and more at the preschool level that appear to be marginally profitable. But much of what appears as profit is due to the family members' hard work for little pay. The salaries they draw on the school understate the value of their time, leaving the impression that the enterprise is profitable.

Whether this can be replicated on a large scale by corporate entities is doubtful. Historically, economic studies have not identified substantial economies of scale in education at school sites or in multi-school endeavors. Perhaps this is for the reason suggested by John Chubb and Terry Moe in *Politics, Markets, and America's Schools* (1990): that the best results are obtained when schools are given great autonomy. A corporate competitor in schooling must establish brand and product identify, which necessitates relatively uniform operations and services from site to site. This puts the need for quality control and similarity from site to site in direct competition with the need to be responsive to differences among particular clients and settings. Moreover, as the economist Richard Rothstein has observed, as corporate entities expand to more and more schools, they are likely to have to rely on standard operating procedures and monitoring to maintain quality control and brand identification. Paradoxically, this is the argument given by states and school districts for their "over-regulation" of public schools—namely, that equity among schools and students requires uniformity that must be secured by mandates, rules, guidelines, and regulations.

## Under New Management

The mandate to cut costs and turn a profit inevitably will dictate some of the for-profits' personnel and instructional practices. Education is a highly labor-intensive activity, with wages usually accounting for 80 percent or more of the school budget. This means that the main cost-cutting opportunities lie in cutting personnel costs by using either cheaper personnel or fewer of them. Thus the for-profits may use more part-time personnel (forgoing staff benefits), less-experienced teachers whose salaries are lower, larger class sizes, or shorter school days. Substituting capital for labor in the form of computers and educational technology may also be possible, although there is little evidence in the education industry that this has been an effective cost-cutting strategy.

For now, though, the differences among the for-profit, non-profit, and public education sectors seem mainly cosmetic. Their approaches to educating children change little from sector to sector. The for-profits generally have adopted curricula that are available commercially to all schools. Many public schools and nonprofit schools have long used similar curricula. Instructional practices also do not seem to differ

very much. Some public, some nonprofit, and some for-profit schools use direct instruction while others use more "progressive" approaches. The three sectors overlap so much in their curricula and instructional practices that it is difficult to distinguish them from one another.

Some of the for-profits rely more heavily on sophisticated use of educational technologies. But so do a large number of public schools. Some also provide tutoring services and extended school days and years. But so do many public schools. Given these similarities, it appears that curriculum and instructional practices vary far more within each sector than they do among the three sectors.

Where the three sectors do seem to diverge is in their personnel practices, professional development, and managerial practices. Given that the growth in for-profit schools has been mainly in contracting with public schools or charter schools to operate individual public schools as EMOs, how much they diverge often depends on state laws and school district contracts. Some states and districts require EMO-managed schools to hire certified teachers or even to retain the existing teacher force. They also may require them to enforce the existing collective bargaining agreements, leaving the tenure policy untouched. In other states, for-profit entities have much more leeway in hiring employees and in designing their contracts.

Where the laws have granted them flexibility, for-profit schools have tended to hire their teachers with less concern than public schools for whether they have met certification requirements. In some states they need not meet conventional certification requirements at all. The for-profit schools prefer to hire for a fixed term, renewing only the contracts of teachers who have been judged effective. They also rely on various versions of merit pay, usually rewarding some teachers for subject specialization and other talents in order to retain valued teachers and to provide incentives for improvement. In some cases, the incentives include

**TERMS TO NOTE**

Certification

Merit pay

more-extensive career ladders for classroom teachers than the public schools offer.

Some for-profits, like Edison Schools, the largest EMO, emphasize strong professional development by providing as much as three weeks of training a year for teaching staff. By contrast, public schools typically provide only three to four days of staff development a year, with little follow-up or assessment of results. In my view, this is an important difference between the two sectors, since strong and cohesive professional-development sessions with subsequent mentoring and assessment is one of the most promising methods for heightening school effectiveness.

**TERMS TO NOTE**
Professional development
Direct instruction

For-profit schools also give their principals more decision-making powers and provide more incentives for making effective decisions, particularly with regard to personnel practices. They expect principals to monitor the selection and hiring process as well as teacher assessment and to retain only those teachers whom they consider highly productive. This flexibility does not, however, carry over to the academic realm. Corporate entities run many of the new for-profit schools, and to establish their brand identity they have sought relative uniformity in instructional practices from site to site. For example, Advantage Schools uses direct instruction in all of its schools, an approach that relies heavily on teacher lectures and drill. Because the use of direct instruction is one of Advantage's selling points, its school principals have no leeway to deviate from this approach. Other firms have selected specific curricula for each learning domain, and all of their schools are required to use these curricula in the same way.

## Attracting Clients

The issue of brand identity raises questions about how for-profit schools will sell themselves in the education market. If their instructional practices don't vary much from those of their public and private competitors, how will they differentiate themselves?

We have too little experience with for-profit schools to answer this question fully. What is clear is that schools will avoid the notion that they are interchangeable, producing similar products and competing on price alone, as the model of perfect competition assumes. Without a voucher system in which parents may supplement the voucher, for-profit schools will be bound by fixed per-pupil allocations, hindering their ability to compete on price. Thus I would expect that they would seek to differentiate themselves from other schools with claims of superior student achievement (difficult to prove in the absence of sophisticated and costly evaluations by third parties) and by using marketing images to persuade parents and school boards that they offer a superior education. If a firm wishes to expand to many schools, then it must have a brand image and at least some evidence that it is succeeding systematically across school sites. The best way to accomplish this is to set unique goals that will appeal to a client niche and claim effectiveness on those goals rather than to compete on similar dimensions with every other school. This is precisely the strategy followed by the middle and upper strata of the nonprofit schools. For example, most private high schools refused even to participate in *U.S. News and World Report's* attempt to rank the nation's best high schools. Likewise, in New York State, a large portion of private schools have sought waivers from the state's requirement that all schools participate in the Regents examinations—for which the state will publicly report the scores.

But, if states and school districts continue to insist on using state standards and tests to judge school performance, then the for-profits will be pushed to compete for contracts and clientele on the basis of a narrower set of criteria. This would give the for-profits, with their more flexible managerial and personnel policies, some advantage in the marketplace. They will be able to hire and maintain a teaching force with the goal of higher test scores in mind, and they will have more flexibility than public schools do to reward or punish their teachers on the basis of test results. For-profit firms are most effective when they focus on tight objectives rather than the normally diffuse activities that we demand from public schools. These narrow goals will also give for-profit schools a powerful incentive to admit and encourage those students whom they expect to do well on achievement tests or who are likely to show the greatest value-added—that is, the greatest improvement in test scores. (There is some reason to believe that it is the lower-middle portion of the student distribution where test scores are most malleable over the short run, as opposed to those students in the least-advantaged or most-advantaged circumstances.) Such policies will pressure the for-profits as well as other schools to "teach to the test" and to provide considerable test practice. If profits are tied to test scores, then the pressure will only build.

There is one area in which costs will most certainly be higher than for public schools: that of marketing and promotion. For-profit schools, especially those with regional and national ambitions, must establish a brand identity for their schools and must also promote themselves intensively to penetrate their markets. Currently this marketing effort is devoted mainly to school districts and charter-school prospects in order to obtain contracts. At the district level, this means considerable lobbying of board members and administrators as well as parents. It also may mean informational retreats at pleasant venues for board members and superintendents and many meetings with stakeholders such as teachers and other unions and parents. Even under a system of vouchers, the emerging competition will require intense marketing to distinguish one EMO's schools from the crowd. All in all, marketing and pro-

motion inevitably will absorb resources that could have gone to instruction.

My observations here are limited by our lack of experience with for-profit education. But there is much to be learned from the case of Chile, where a voucher system has been in place for two decades. In Chile, students are found in four types of schools: elite schools that do not accept vouchers and charge considerably more than the voucher; for-profit voucher schools; nonprofit (usually religious) voucher schools; and municipal schools. Since vouchers were introduced, voucher schools have grown considerably—from only about 15 percent of enrollments in 1981 to about one-third of total enrollments in 1996—and for-profit schools accounted for the majority of the growth. For-profit voucher schools have lowered their costs by hiring part-time teachers (who are often teaching full-time in municipal schools), paying lower salaries, and enlarging class sizes. They devote considerable effort to differentiating themselves in the marketplace, often by choosing English names that lend a patina of prestige. Studies show that after adjusting for student characteristics, the for-profit schools achieve at a slightly lower level in Spanish and mathematics than both the municipal and Catholic schools. Since their costs are lower, however, they are also somewhat more cost-effective. There are no dramatic differences among the three voucher-funded sectors.

Will for-profit education evolve here as it has in Chile? The lack of extensive experience with for-profit schools in the United States means that almost any assertions are speculative. We are going through a period of great experimentation as more and more for-profit firms enter the market to manage schools for the public sector or establish their own schools. Unfortunately, none of the EMOs has been around long enough for us to draw any firm conclusions. And, given their current balance sheets (none has announced profits yet), many may not be around for the long haul.

## POSTNOTE

In the summer of 2002, the Philadelphia public schools hired the Edison Schools, a for-profit education management organization (EMO), to operate twenty of its schools. This controversial move was made in the expectation that Edison could turn around what were considered to be struggling schools. By 2002, approximately ten percent of all charter schools in the United States were for-profit schools. Once the darlings of Wall Street during the 1990s, the stock prices of these publicly traded EMOs have fallen dramatically during the early years of the twenty-first century. Investors are concerned that there may not be the kind of profits in public education that they once thought existed.

Henry Levin explores the pluses and minuses of these for-profit schools, raising good questions about whether they are flashes in the pan or have something substantial and lasting to offer the educational scene. The 2002 Supreme Court ruling that school vouchers do not violate the constitutionality of separation of church and state increases the likelihood that more for-profit schools will emerge and use vouchers to fund their operations. Whether these schools will do a better job than the existing public schools remains to be seen.

## DISCUSSION QUESTIONS

1. What are your views concerning for-profit schools? What do you see as their potential strengths and weaknesses?

2. Would you like to teach in a for-profit school? What do you consider its advantages and disadvantages?

3. With which point in the article do you most agree? Disagree?

## 63

# The Who, What, and Why of Site-Based Management

Jane L. David

S ite-based management may be the most significant reform of the decade—a potential force for empowering educators and communities. Yet no two people agree on what it is, how to do it, or even why to do it.

Kentucky requires virtually every school to have a site-based council with three teachers,

**TERM TO NOTE**

Site-based management

two parents, and the principal, and endows councils with considerable fiscal and policy authority. Maryland and Texas require schools to have school-based decision-making teams, but in contrast to Kentucky, do not specify their composition or legally transfer authority from the district to the school.

In Chicago, state law places significant authority in the hands of local school councils and defines their makeup: six parents, two community representatives, two teachers, and the principal. In Cincinnati, reorganization and downsizing of the central office has shifted considerable responsibility, but no additional legal authority, to school principals.

Colorado governor Roy Romer initiated site-based management in Denver as part of stalled contract negotiations between the school district and the teachers' association and required a business representative on each council. In Memphis, site-based management never got beyond a small pilot phase. In Dade County, Florida, the pilot was expanded but in a much weaker form.

Jane L. David is director of the Bay Area Research Group, Palo Alto, California. From Jane David, "The Who, What, and Why of Site-Based Management." *Educational Leadership*, December 1995/January 1996, pp. 4–9. Reprinted by permission of Jane L. David.

These are only a few examples. According to Ogawa and White (1994), one-third of all school districts had some version of site-based management between 1986 and 1990. Since 1990 at least five states have jumped on the bandwagon. And during the same time, more than 20 states have passed legislation to create charter schools—individual schools that are de facto site-based managed, even though they do not carry that title. All this activity excludes individual schools that have instituted reforms but have not been delegated authority by their district or state, although some of these may be excellent models of democratic decision making (see, for example, Apple and Beane 1995, Wohlstetter and Smyer 1994).

## What Is It?

So what is site-based management? It has almost as many variants as there are places claiming to be "site-based." And they differ on every important dimension—who initiates it, who is involved, what they control, and whether they are accountable to an outside authority. Site-based management may be instituted by state law or by administrative action, by a district, or by a school. It may be linked to an accountability system with consequences tied to student performance, or it may not be.

Most variants of site-based management involve some sort of representative decision-making council at the school, which may share authority with the principal or be merely advisory. Some councils have the power to hire principals, some hire and fire, some do neither. Some can hire other personnel when there are vacancies. Some councils specify that the principal be the chair, others specify that the principal not be the chair.

The composition of site councils also varies tremendously. In addition to teachers, parents, and the principal, they may include classified staff, community members, students, and business representatives. Educators may outnumber non-educators, or vice versa. States or districts may list constituencies who must be represented, or simply leave it to individual schools. Chicago and Kentucky are exceptions in specifying exact membership of the site council—who and how many of each type of constituent.

## Why Do It?

Reasons for initiating site-based management run the gamut, yet virtually all are cloaked in the language of increasing student achievement. To some, site-based management is a governance reform designed to shift the balance of authority among schools, districts, and the state. This tends to be the rationale behind state efforts rather than district reforms, and it is often part of a larger reform agenda that claims to trade school autonomy for accountability to the state.

To others, site-based management is a political reform initiated to broaden the decision-making base, either within the school, the larger community, or both. But democratization of decision making as an end in itself leaves open the question of who should be involved in which decisions.

Site-based management may also be an administrative reform to make management more efficient by decentralizing and deregulating it. Here, too, management efficiency presumably serves the ultimate goal of organization—student learning. Yet another premise of site-based management as educational reform is that the way to enhance student learning is to let education professionals make the important professional decisions.

Further complicating the landscape, there are often underlying motives. Stated purposes may obscure far less lofty aims, such as weakening entrenched and distrusted local school boards, creating the illusion of reform without investing additional resources, putting a positive spin on central office downsizing by calling it decentralization, or simply trying to shift the blame for failure to the school itself.

## Linking Decentralization and Achievement

Although site-based management appears in many guises, at its core is the idea of participatory decision making at the school site. And despite all the variations in rationale, its main stated objective is to enhance student achievement. Participatory decision making and school improvement are presumed to be related, but that's not always the case.

Consider what happens when any group is formed by bringing together people who have never worked as a group, who may have no experience in collaborative decision making, and who may in fact have a history of being adversaries (parents and teachers, for example). To make matters worse, some members may be subject to evaluation by other members (teachers by the principal, most obviously). Why would such a group be expected to improve student learning?

Indeed, groups like these that do function well tend to spend most of their time on issues of discipline, facilities, and extracurricular activities. They limit themselves to these issues for good reason—these are the issues that people are passionate about and have some idea how to tackle. Moreover, these are concerns that parents and teachers share (David 1994).

Curriculum and instruction are much more difficult to deal with, for educators and non-educators alike. And these issues are even more difficult to tackle when states or districts mandate new assessments that require teaching methods that are unfamiliar to many parents and teachers. When there are serious consequences for unsatisfactory student performance—especially teacher or principal dismissal—but a lack of knowledge about how to improve student performance, trust and constructive dialogue are further undermined.

## Who Decides What?

For site-based decisions to be sound, attention must be paid to who decides what. Sound decisions are made by those who are informed about and care about the issues and who know the context in which the decision will be carried out. Otherwise, there is no guarantee that these decisions will be any better than those made by policymakers many steps removed. In fact, school-based decisions could be made by only one person, and that person could be uninformed and insensitive to the context.

Participatory management does not mean that everyone decides everything. Some decisions are best left to the professionals in the school, some to parents, and others to students. Some decisions are appropriately made by representatives of several constituencies, others by a formal schoolwide body. Nor does site-based management mean that all decisions are appropriately made at the school level. Schools belong to larger systems—districts and states—that must provide a strong center if decentralization is to create something other than anarchy (Murphy 1989).

Schools are unlikely to improve unless community members—and particularly parents—participate meaningfully. And in secondary schools, students should be involved as well. Schools are also unlikely to improve unless teachers—the main implementers—shape the direction of change. In general, those who have the strongest personal stake in and the most immediate connection to the school are the ones who should tackle the issues. The challenge is to maximize the likelihood that decisions will be appropriately participatory, informed, and sensitive to the context.

## Internal Elements

Site councils that truly flourish in the school community tend to have a number of characteristics in common, most notably the following.

▶ *A well-thought-out committee structure.* In a well-structured system of council committees, there is a good matchup between the types of decisions to be made and the most appropriate people to debate and resolve those issues. Some committees may be standing, others ad hoc. Some may be composed of teachers, and so defined by naturally existing groups like teams, departments, and grade levels. Some may consist only of parents; other may be representative of all constituencies. Whether the relationship between the committees and the site council is formal (approval) or informal (advisory), the committee structure with overlapping memberships provides a communication network that is critical to an effective council.

▶ *Enabling leadership.* Strong councils are usually led, though not always chaired, by strong principals (and sometimes teachers) who exercise leadership by mobilizing others. They encourage all parties to participate. And they model inquiry and reflection. Such leaders create schoolwide ownership of the improvement agenda so that principal turnover or a change in council membership does not bring efforts to a halt.

▶ *Focus on student learning.* Not all issues have a direct influence on student learning, but strong councils consciously connect non-instructional decisions with conditions that maximize learning opportunities. For example, a decision to invest in classroom telephones to facilitate communication between teachers and parents will also affect students. By linking all issues to teaching and learning, council members don't lose sight of the ultimate goal.

▶ *Focus on adult learning.* There are two points here. First, council members need new skills, assistance, and practice in asking hard questions and gathering evidence about what is and is not working. Second, councils need to appreciate that their constituencies—parents and educators—require access to new knowledge and skills, both to be active decision makers and to change their teaching and learning practices and beliefs.

▶ *Schoolwide perspective.* Functioning councils focus on the collective interests of the parties, devoting their energy to school goals and direction, coordination and communication, and allocation of resources and equity. They do not get caught up in details of management or curriculum, and they do not get waylaid by individual agendas. Naturally most parents will be thinking about their own children's needs, and most teachers will be thinking about their own classrooms, and so they might be defensive. Moreover, everyone may lack confidence in a new process that carries considerable responsibility.

## External Elements

Not many schools are able to create on their own the conditions I have described, particularly when strong enabling leadership is absent. To learn how to do it, most schools require support from their district or state agencies, including the following:

▶ *Long-term commitment.* Councils cannot evolve into effective decision-making bodies at the school site if the pendulum swings from one extreme to the other every two or three years. Site-based management cannot be the reform *du jour* that changes authority and flexibility when the superintendent changes. Sustained commitment is essential. The process is hard work and takes time.

▶ *Curricular guidance.* Schools need a substantive framework within which to make appropriate

choices. Whether that guidance is best communicated in the form of learning goals and standards, curriculum or content guides, or assessments is an open question—as is the way in which choices about such guidance are made. The goal of site-based management is not to let a thousand flowers bloom nor to force every school to reinvent itself from scratch.

In addition, everyone from classroom teachers to other members of committees who diagnose problems must have opportunities to learn new ways of operating, including mediating techniques. School councils must reflect the existing culture. For most schools, if real improvement is to occur, individual beliefs and, ultimately, the school culture will need to change.

▶ *Opportunities for learning and assistance.* Districts can provide resources for the kinds of learning opportunities that adults in schools need to change classroom practices and to function effectively as council and committee members. School councils will necessarily reflect the existing culture. Most councils, but especially those with local conflicts and limited experience in collaborative problem solving, will need assistance and access to facilitation and mediation. For most schools, if site-based management is to lead to improvement, individual beliefs and, ultimately, the culture of the school will need to change.

▶ *Access to information.* Schools must have easy access to the information needed to make decisions, including everything from budget to performance data. A decentralized system can function well only when each unit knows how it is doing. Although schools can gather certain data from students, teachers, and the community, they cannot be expected to have the data collection and analysis capability that a larger organization can support. Moreover, because the system has its own needs for information, the flow must go in both directions.

## Open Questions

Making fundamental changes in systems as complex as state and local school systems raises a number of questions for which there are no pat answers. The solutions simply have to be worked out by those involved. Among these difficult issues are questions of equity, adult learning, decision making, and changing conceptions of teaching and community. In particular:

▶ What policies and supports will ensure that site-based management does not exacerbate resource differences among schools? Schools in poorer neighborhoods tend to have fewer resources and less educated populations. They are at risk of being further disadvantaged under a decentralized system.

▶ How can site-based management create a sense of community in schools that draw from a large geographic area, as do most secondary schools; and in schools in districts with desegregation plans, choice, open enrollment, or magnet schools? Parents and staff at such schools may not have access to transportation or time to participate in school decision making.

▶ New ideas for teacher professional development are emerging, but where are the opportunities for principals, central office staff, and parents to learn new roles and ways to assist site councils?

▶ How should teachers' jobs be redefined to allow time for collaborative decision making and ongoing professional development? Both teachers and the public believe that teachers should devote their time to students, and teachers are finding classroom demands take increasing time and energy.

▶ How can site-based management be structured to balance school autonomy and flexibility with certain centralized operations that require consistency, coordination, and legal constraints? For example, collective bargaining, transportation, and government regulations may all affect class size, schedules, services, and how facilities are used.

▶ What is the best public education analogue to private sector work teams, and where do parents and community members fit in? That is, decentralized private organizations delegate authority to work teams that don't involve the public. But in schools, neither site councils nor groups of teachers are really teams that carry out the work of the organization (teachers typically work in isolation).

▶ Should schools have mandates that require them to involve parents and the community in decisions? What is the likelihood that without such mandates, parents and community members would continue to have little voice in some local schools?

## Risks and Benefits

In theory, the benefits of site-based management overwhelm the costs: the goals of education reform are unlikely to be met in any other way. As public support for public education in general, and reform in particular, dwindles, community members' engagement in their local schools offers the most promise for rebuilding support.

Without a school and community culture that supports ongoing learning, student achievement is unlikely to improve. The challenge is to open avenues for informed conversation and for becoming informed. Ultimate accountability rests on the ability of individuals to influence what is not working (Wiggins 1993). That is certainly far preferable to a state takeover or school closure.

Although the ultimate goal of participatory site-based management is to improve schools in order to improve student performance, the intermediate goals are desired ends in themselves. Involving teachers in decisions about their work must be valued in its own right, as must giving parents and other community members more involvement in their schools.

One risk is that the public will judge site-based management prematurely on the ultimate goals, derailing sound practices whose success is not yet reflected in test scores. When there is more than one desired end and the means to those ends are not clear, it is difficult to assess progress along the way. Therefore, it is critically important to devise new ways of measuring progress for such an undertaking (Bryk et al. 1994).

Another risk, however, is that participants will not judge site-based management in terms of any of its goals—intermediate or ultimate—but simply allow the process to absorb time and energy to no good purpose. Unfortunately, in practice, the potential of site-based management is rarely realized. It can even have deleterious effects, exhausting limited energy and good will in futile exercises. Only with visible progress and results will folks willingly put in the hard work.

The key is to identify and exploit ways to ensure that decisions will be appropriately participatory, informed, and context-sensitive, thereby increasing the likelihood that they will lead to better school practices and stronger instruction. Ultimately, it will be the people who carry out site-based management who determine what it is—and can become. Their success or failure will also help others decide whether it is worthwhile in terms of the human costs it exacts.

Finally, the goal of transforming schools into communities where everyone has a voice goes beyond issues of school reform to the heart of our democratic society. The creation of models of collaboration and participatory decision making for students to witness and become involved in—not only in classrooms but also in their community—ultimately benefits not just the school community but our entire society.

## REFERENCES

Apple, M. W., and J. A. Beane, eds. (1995). *Democratic Schools*. Alexandria, Va.: Association for Supervision and Curriculum Development

Bryk, A. S., et al. (1994). "The State of Chicago School Reform." *Phi Delta Kappan* 76: 74–78.

David, J. L. (1994). *School-Based Decision Making: Linking Decisions to Learning*. Lexington, Ky.: The Prichard Committee for Academic Excellence.

Murphy, J. T. (1989). "The Paradox of Decentralizing Schools: Lessons from Business, Government, and the Catholic Church." *Phi Delta Kappan* 70: 808–812.

Ogawa, R. T., and P. A. White. (1994). "School-Based Management: An Overview." In *School-Based Management: Organizing for High Performance*, edited by S. A. Mohrman, P. Wohlstetter, and Associates. San Francisco: Jossey-Bass.

Wiggins, G. P. (1993). *Assessing Student Performance: Exploring the Purpose and Limits of Testing*. San Francisco: Jossey-Bass.

Wohlstetter, P., and R. Smyer. (1994). "Models of High-Performance Schools." In *School-Based Management: Organizing for High Performance*, edited by S. A. Mohrman, P. Wohlstetter, and Associates. San Francisco: Jossey-Bass.

## POSTNOTE

Like many other educational reforms, site-based management came to education via the business community. During the 1980s and 1990s, many businesses moved away from large, bureaucratic, and centralized decision making to give more decision-making responsibility to the workers on the front line. Workers were empowered to detect and solve problems, without having to "kick the matter upstairs." Businesses found that by decentralizing the decision making, they improved both the quality and the swiftness of the decisions, and employees took more pride in their work.

Since businesses were having such success, why wouldn't the same ideas work to reinvigorate the American educational system and create more of a sense of professionalism among America's teachers? In education, however, site-based management (also known as school-based management and site-based decision making) is having mixed success. Although it is still early in the reform movement, the ultimate impact of site-based management on education remains to be seen.

## DISCUSSION QUESTIONS

1. What differences do you see between the business and education arenas in the implementation of shared decision making?

2. Are any of the schools with which you are familiar engaged in site-based management? If so, what have been their successes and failures?

3. Would you like to be a teacher in a school that employs site-based management? Why or why not?

# Educational Technology

F or much of the past decade, schools have emphasized the acquisition of technology hardware as a major objective. By 2001, it was estimated that there was one instructional computer for every five students in our public schools. Educators have now reached the point where their goal should not be just to acquire technology. Instead, they should ask how technologies should be used to help students reach the higher standards being developed by states and to prepare students for the world they will enter when they leave school.

Although most educators, policymakers, and business leaders believe that technology has the potential to alter dramatically how teachers teach and students learn, there are some who remain skeptical that technology will have a significant impact on education. These skeptics cite as evidence the "hype" that accompanied previous technologies, such as television, that failed to deliver on their promises.

It is clear that if computer and other related technologies are to transform educational practice, much time and effort must go into working with teachers. They need to understand the capabilities of technology and to develop the skills necessary to deliver those capabilities. If this teacher development does not occur, then the latest educational technology, like some earlier ones, will prove to be a bust.

# 64 CLASSIC *The Mad Dash to Compute*

### Jane M. Healy

"I feel as if we're being swept down this enormous river—we don't know where we're going or why, but we're caught in the current. I think we should stop and take a look before it's too late."

This comment about the use of technology in schools was voiced plaintively by an assistant superintendent from Long Island, N.Y. It was typical of many I collected recently in a three-year investigation of our heavily hyped technological revolution.

Having started this saga as a wide-eyed advocate for educational computing, I now must admit that the school official was right. New technologies hold enormous potential for education, but before any more money is wasted, we must pause and ask some pointed questions that have been bypassed in today's climate of competitive technophilia ("My district's hard drives are bigger than yours!").

Educators, who are seen as one of the ripest growth markets in hardware, software and Internet sales, have been carefully targeted by an industry that understandably wants to convince us that its products will solve all our problems. (Did you ever previously see multiple double-page ads in *Education Week* for any educational product? Have you been offered "free" equipment—that eventually demands as much upkeep and fiscal lifeblood as the man-eating plant in "Little Shop of Horrors"?). The advertising's thrust to both educators and parents is that you should invest in as much technology as early as possible or students will be left hopelessly

behind. The parents, failing to appreciate the nonsense inherent in this assumption, in turn put additional pressure on schools to "get with the program."

As educators, we should have the wit to evaluate these pressures, resist public opinion and shun manipulative marketing. It also becomes our obligation to interpret to the public what we know is really good for kids. Yet three major issues are being largely overlooked as we rush to capture the trend. I will call them (1) trade-offs, (2) developmental questions and (3) winners in the long run.

## The Trade-Offs

During my recent research, which involved visits to dozens of elementary and secondary schools across the United States, I was invited to observe the flagship elementary school of a district that prides itself on the scope of its technology budget. Yet I had difficulty finding students using computers. Many expensive machines were sitting idle (and becoming increasingly obsolete) in classrooms where teachers have not learned to incorporate them into daily lessons. ("When they break, I just don't get them repaired," one 1st-grade teacher confided.)

Finally, in the computer lab, I found 32 5th-grade students lined up at two rows of machines and confronted the following scenario: The technology coordinator—technologically adept but with virtually no background in either teaching or curriculum development—explains that this group comes four times a week to practice reading and math skills. Many students are below grade level in basic skills.

I randomly select a position behind Raoul, who was using a math software program. The director, now occupied in fixing a computer that

Jane Healy is an educational psychologist and author of *Endangered Minds, Your Child's Growing Mind* and *Failure to Connect: How Computers Affect Our Children's Minds for Better and Worse.* Reprinted with permission from the April 1999 issue of *The School Administrator* magazine.

eager young fingers have crashed, hastily reminds the students to enter the program at the correct level for their ability, but I begin to suspect something is amiss when Raoul effortlessly solves a few simple addition problems and then happily accepts his reward—a series of smash-and-blast games in which he manages to demolish a sizeable number of aliens before he is electronically corralled into another series of computations. Groaning slightly, he quickly solves these problems and segues expertly into the next space battle.

By the time I move on, Raoul has spent many more minutes zapping aliens than he has in doing math. My teacher's soul cringes at the thought of important learning time squandered. I also wonder if what we are really teaching Raoul is that he should choose easy problems so he can play longer or that the only reason to use his brain even slightly is to be granted—by an automaton over which he has no personal control—some mindless fun as a reward. I wonder who selected this software or if any overall plan dictates the implementation of this expensive gadgetry.

Moreover, this computer lab, like so many others, has been morphed from a music room. In this school system, cutbacks in arts, physical education and even textbooks are used to beef up technology budgets.

The trade-offs inherent in this all-too-typical situation should be troubling to all of us:

▶ *Haste and pressure for electronic glitz.* These should not replace a carefully designed plan based on sound educational practice. Grafting technology onto schools without good curriculum or excellent teaching guarantees failure. First things first.

▶ *Money on hardware, software and networks instead of essential teacher education.* Informed estimates suggest it takes five years of ongoing in-service training before teachers can fully integrate computer uses into lesson plans. They must also have solid technical support so that instructional time is not spent repairing machines.

▶ *Technology coordinators without adequate preparation in education.* Rather, the key instructional decisions should be made by teachers who are adept in linking computer use to significant aspects of curriculum. "The 3rd-graders made T-shirts in computer lab today," one techie boasted during one of my school visits. "Why?" I asked. "Well, we can—and besides, the kids just loved it." If this sort of justification prevails in your schools, don't be surprised if your test scores start to drop!

▶ *Cuts in vital areas used to finance technology purchases.* Computers, which have as yet demonstrated questionable effects on student learning, must not be bought at the expense of proven staples of mental development, such as art, music, drama, debate, physical education, text literacy, manipulatives and hands-on learning aids. One teacher in a Western state told me her district "could be IBM for all the technology we have," yet she was refused money to purchase a set of paperback literature books for her classroom. Why? "The money had all been spent on the machines," she sighed.

▶ *Pie-in-the-sky assumptions.* Don't be misled by claims that computers, instead of proven interventions, will remediate basic skills. Many of today's youngsters need solid, hands-on remediation in reading and math delivered by teachers trained in established programs such as Reading Recovery. Don't forget that those "proven studies" about the impact of electronic learning systems and their cost effectiveness were financed by people with products to sell.

▶ *Installing computers instead of reducing class size.* To my surprise, I found that good technology use is actually more teacher intensive than traditional instruction and works best with smaller classes! Research also is beginning to show the skill/drill software that manages learning for large groups actually may limit students' achievement once the novelty wears off. We need good, objective long-range data before committing money and growing minds to such programs.

▶ *Funding electronic glitz instead of quality early childhood programs.* Again, we must weigh a large expense of unproven value against proven upstream prevention of academic and social problems. Ironically, estimated costs for connecting all classrooms to the Internet also could provide every child with an adequate preschool program.

▶ *Time wasted vs. productive learning.* Without good planning and supervision, youngsters tend to use even the best educational programs for mindless fun rather than meaningful learning. Moreover, if you do not have a district policy on selecting software, implement one today. Poorly selected "edutainment" and drill-and-practice programs actually can depress academic gains, whereas well-implemented simulations and conceptually driven programs may improve learning—if a good teacher is in charge.

## Engaged Learning

Consider a different scenario that I observed at a middle school in a suburban school district. A small group of 12-year-olds eagerly surround a computer terminal but don't complain about the slightly fuzzy image. They are too busy following the action on the screen where a disheveled-looking young man in bicycling clothes stands in a jungle talking earnestly with someone in a bush jacket who appears to be a scientist.

One of the students giggles, pokes another and attempts a whispered comment, but he is rapidly silenced. "Shush, Damon. Don't be such a jerk. We can't hear!" hisses his neighbor.

What has inspired such serious academic purpose among these kids? They and their teacher are involved in directing (along with others around the globe) a three-month bicycle expedition, manned by a team of cyclists and scientists, through the jungles of Central America in search of lost Mayan civilizations. At the moment, they are debating the possibility of sending the team through a difficult, untravelled jungle track to a special site. How fast can they ride? How far? What obstacles will they encounter? What are the odds of success? What plans must be made?

Like others in a new breed of simulations, this activity uses on-line and satellite phone communications to establish real-time links between students around the world and the adventurers. Because students' votes actually determine the course of the journey, they must problem-solve right along with the scientists. To acquire the necessary knowledge, the class also has plunged into a variety of real-life, hands-on learning: history, archaeology, visual arts, math (e.g., Mayans calculated in base 20), science of flora and fauna, Mayan poetry, building a miniature rain forest, reading the daily journals of the adventurers, researching, developing theories and debating about why the civilization collapsed.

This example is only one of many powerful supplements to a well-planned curriculum. New technologies can be used wisely—or they can be a costly impediment to educational quality. As you debate the trade-offs of your technology choices, you might keep these questions in mind:

1. What can this particular technology do that cannot be accomplished by other less expensive or more proven methods?

2. What will we gain—and what will we lose?

3. How can we sell wise educational decisions to a public foolishly buying the message that computers are a magic bullet for education?

## Developmental Questions

A question too rarely considered is what effect extended computer use will have on children's developing bodies and brains. Moreover, it is imperative to ask at what age this technology should really be introduced. My observations have convinced me that normally developing children under age seven are better off without today's computers and software. Technology funds should be first allocated to middle and high schools where computer-assisted learning is much more effective and age-appropriate.

▶ *Physical effects:* Too little is known about technology's physical effects on digitized youngsters, but troubling evidence of problems resulting from computer use include: vision (e.g., nearsightedness), postural and orthopedic complaints (e.g., neck and back problems; carpal tunnel syndrome), the controversial effects of electromagnetic radiation emitted from the backs and sides of machines and even the rare possibility of seizures triggered by some types of visual displays. Administrators should be on top of this.

Nonetheless, I found a woeful disregard in schools of even the basic safety rules mandated for the adult workplace. Clear guidelines exist, and before you consign all your 3rd-graders to laptops you would be wise to check the suggestions out.

▶ *Brain effects:* In terms of what happens to children's cognitive, social and emotional development as a function of computer use, even less is known. The brain is significantly influenced by whatever media we choose for education, and poor choices now may well result in poor thinkers in the next generation.

In my book, *Failure to Connect,* I trace the course of brain development with technology use in mind, and one thing is clear. Computers can either help or hurt the process. For younger children, too much electronic stimulation can become addictive, replacing important experiences during critical periods of development: physical exploration, imaginative play, language, socialization and quiet time for developing attention and inner motivation. For children of any age, improper software choices can disrupt language development, attention, social skills and motivation to use the mind in effortful ways. (The next time you see a classroom of students motivated by computer use, be sure to question whether they are motivated to think and learn—or simply to play with the machines.)

By mid-elementary school, students can start to capitalize on the multimedia and abstract-symbolic capabilities of computers—if an effective teacher is present to guide the learning. For middle and high school students, new technologies can make difficult concepts (e.g., ratio, velocity) more accessible and provide new windows into visual reasoning, creativity and the challenges of research. Yet the first step must still be the filtering process: What is worthwhile in support of the curriculum, and what is merely flashy? Districts that take this job seriously and gear computer use to students' developmental needs are beginning to show real benefits from technology use.

## Winners in the Long Run

"Kids need computers to prepare them for the future."

Like so many advertising slogans, this one bears closer examination. First, learning to use a computer today is a poor guarantee of a student's future, since workplace equipment will have changed dramatically for all but our oldest students. Moreover, because so much current use is harming rather than helping students' brain power and learning habits, the computer "have-nots" today actually may end up as the "haves" when future success is parcelled out.

But even more important is the question of what skills will really prepare today's students for the future. Surely the next decades will be ones of rapid change where old answers don't always work, where employers demand communication and human relations skills as well as the ability to think incisively and imagine creative solutions to unforeseen problems. Many of today's computer applications offer poor preparation for such abilities.

One skill of critical importance in a technological future is symbolic analysis, with reading and writing the common entry point. Yet while cyberspace may be filled with words, "a growing portion of the American population will not be able to use, understand or benefit from those words," contend Daniel Burstein and David Kline in their book, *Road Warriors*. "Some of these people may be digitally literate, in that they feel at home with joysticks and remote controls and are perfectly capable of absorbing the sights and sounds of multimedia entertainment. But if you are not functionally literate, your chances of getting a significant piece of the cyberspace pie are slim, even if you have access to it."

Our future workers also will need other abstract-symbolic skills. As the creation of wealth moves farther and farther away from raw materials and hands-on labor, successful workers will need to synthesize information, judge abstract numbers and acquire multiple-symbol systems in foreign languages, math or the arts; they will also need a familiarity with new digital languages and images. As software improves, computers will doubtless help with such preparation, but the key will continue to lie in the quality of the teachers who plan, mediate and interpret a thoughtful curriculum.

The future also will favor those who have learned how to learn, who can respond flexibly and creatively to challenges and master new skills. At the moment, the computer is a shallow and pedantic companion for such a journey. We should think long and carefully about whether our purpose is to be trendy or to prepare students to be intelligent, reasoning human beings whose skills extend far beyond droid-like button clicking.

If we ourselves cannot think critically about the hard sell vs. the real business of schooling, we can hardly expect our students to do so.

## POSTNOTE

Jane Healy is a deep thinker on the topic of educational technology and its effect on children's learning, earning her article a spot among our Classic selections. In this article, she raises a number of valuable points concerning education's embrace of technology. Two points seem particularly significant: teacher education and trade-offs. Citing research that indicates teachers need five years of in-service training before they can successfully integrate technology into the curriculum, Healy deplores the vast expenditure on hardware and software without concomitant spending on teacher training. The second important point revolves around the question of how else the money might be spent. What are schools not doing in order to buy technology? These are good issues worth thinking about.

## DISCUSSION QUESTIONS

1. What arguments would you state to counter Healy's concerns?

2. In your opinion, is the technology emphasis in schools here to stay or just a fad? Why do you think so?

3. Do you think there is an appropriate age at which to introduce children to computers? How would you address Healy's concern about the potential physical effects of using technology at too young an age?

# Making a Living, Making a Life: Technology Reconsidered

## Neil Postman

I should like to begin by presenting a short poem that I found in a book by Lawrence Cuban that illustrates the history of the relationship between technology and schools. The poem, written by a teacher in the early 1920s, is not very good, but it is instructive and provides a good beginning for this reconsideration of the topic.

> Mr. Edison says
> That the radio will supplant the teacher.
> Already one may learn languages by means of
>     Victrola records.
> The moving picture will visualize
> What the radio fails to get across.
> Teachers will be relegated to the backwoods
> With fire-horses
> And long-haired women.
> Or perhaps shown in museums.
> Education will become a matter
> Of pressing a button.
> Perhaps I can get a position at the switchboard.

I think this poem is worth taking seriously because it describes a few things that are often forgotten. It reminds us, for example, that two things always occur when a new kind of technology is developed. First, the technology is always oversold and frequently envisioned as a panacea; second, businessmen are always interested in exploiting the technology for economic gain. I do not hold that against them; it's what businessmen do. But educators do not always have to accommodate them, and, as the poem's sarcasm suggests, teachers are permitted to be

Neil Postman is chairperson, Department of Culture and Communications, Steinhardt School of Education, New York University, New York, New York. Reprinted with permission. Copyright © 1996 by College Entrance Examination Board. All rights reserved.

skeptical about technology's powers. They are, perhaps, *obliged* to be skeptical.

Another thing the poem tells us is that television, the computer, and their associated technologies do not, by any means, pose an unprecedented challenge to traditional educational practices, including the role of the teacher. Such challenges have presented themselves before. I am not old enough to remember when educators believed that the radio and Victrola would forever change the nature of the classroom. However, I do remember when they thought 16-millimeter film would do so. Then closed-circuit television. Then 8-millimeter film. Then structured, teacher-proof textbooks. Now, of course, the computer, and, if we are to believe Chris Whittle, television again.

In this context, I can't help recalling H. L. Mencken's comment on the educator's quest for panaceas. He said, ". . . there is no sure-cure so idiotic that some superintendent of schools will not swallow it. The aim seems to be to reduce the whole teaching process to a sort of automatic reaction, to discover some master formula . . . [to] take the place of competence and resourcefulness in the teacher." Mencken wrote that in 1918, but the quest for sure cures continues today. There are as many true believers as ever—people who think that our newest technological advances will, at long last, change the structure and even the very purpose of schooling.

At least one of these true believers comes from Arkansas. Late last year, in an address to educators, President Clinton focused his remarks on the great technological changes now taking place. In a remarkable statement, he said, "In the nineteenth century, at most, young Americans needed a high school education to make their way. . . . It was good enough if they could read well and understand basic numbers. In the twenty-first century, our people will have to keep learning all their lives." I call this statement "remarkable" only as a sign of respect. To put it gently, in the nineteenth century, it was also desirable for people to continue learning all their lives; they *had* to because they experienced vast and continuous technological change. I would even say that far more technological change occurred during the nineteenth century than is likely to occur during the twenty-first, despite flamboyant prophecies to the contrary. The nineteenth century gave us telegraphy, photography, the rotary press, the telephone, the typewriter, the phonograph, the transatlantic cable, the electric light, radio waves, movies, the locomotive, the suspension bridge, the steamboat, the X ray, the factory, the revolver, the computer, and the stethoscope, not to mention canned food, the penny press, the modern magazine, the advertising agency, the modern bureaucracy, and even the safety pin. Let us suppose that the president might be willing to concede that the technological challenges of the nineteenth century were as traumatic as any faced by people today.

This does not mean that schools ought not to be doing things that the schools of the nineteenth and twentieth centuries did not do. If, for example, the president wants our schools to concentrate as never before on producing young men and women who, as resourceful, adaptable, questioning, and open-minded students, are not paralyzed by technological change, I would expect him to make an impassioned plea for the humanities, not, as he did, for technical-vocational training. Though educators may not be the smartest people around, we do know that it is mainly through the study of history, philosophy, literature, science, and the arts that people's minds are opened to change and to new possibilities. I might note in passing that just about all the people who invented our new technologies were educated with a heavy concentration in humanistic studies. And, just in case anyone believes that no self-respecting school can carry on without high-tech equipment, it should also be noted that those who invented

our high-tech world were themselves educated exclusively with pen, paper, and books. How did they get so smart, I wonder?

I should make it clear that I have no serious complaint against schools buying computers or spending lavishly on state-of-the-art video. If school systems wish to purchase these rather than pay their teachers more or hire more teachers, and if teachers do not object, I am not inclined to speak against this practice.

I would, however, speak out if such investments distracted educators from providing our youth with a serious form of technology education. By technology education I do not mean instruction in using computers to process information, which strikes me as a rather trivial thing to do for two reasons. First, approximately 35 million people have already learned how to use computers without the benefit of school instruction. If schools do nothing, most of the population will know how to use computers in the next 10 years, just as most of the population learned how to drive cars without school instruction. Second, what we needed to know about cars—which is what we now need to know about computers, television, and other important technologies—is not how to use them, but rather how *they* use us. In the case of cars, what we needed to think about in the early twentieth century was not how to drive them, but what they would do to our air, our landscape, our social relations, our family life, and our cities. I'm afraid we didn't take the combustion engine as seriously as we should have. Similarly, suppose that in 1946 we had started to address significant questions about television. What effects would it have upon our political institutions, our psychic habits, our children, our religious conceptions, our families, our economy? Wouldn't we be better positioned today to control television's massive assault on American culture?

I think we should make technology itself an object of inquiry, not an object of celebration. The idea is that our youth should be more interested in asking questions *about* the computer than in getting answers from it. As for television, using it as an aid to learning is seductive but quite beside the point. The average American youngster clocks 5,000 hours in front of a television set before entering the first grade, 19,000 hours by high school's end, and will have seen approximately 700,000 television commercials by age 20. Television, in other words, is the primary vehicle for communicating social values to our young, not to mention its enormous role in shaping their psychic habits and political biases.

What is the schools' response to this? Did someone actually say, "I have a good idea. Let's spend some money to bring television into the classroom to help the students learn"? You can be assured that television is helping them learn many things without the school's complicity; for example, to value immediate gratification; to believe that consumership is the highest aim in life; to be estranged from the written word; to be impatient with reasoned discourse; to believe that what is not instantly accessible is not worthwhile; to be inured to, if not fascinated by, violence. Yes, television *can* be used to enliven lessons in the classroom. It is not, however, necessary, and in my opinion is not the sort of thing educators need to spend their time thinking about, not when there *are* things worth thinking about. Here are some examples.

Since 1960, our population has increased 41 percent. During that same period, violent crimes have increased 560 percent; illegitimate births have increased 400 percent; divorces have quadrupled; the percentage of children living in single-parent homes has tripled; the teenage suicide rate has increased by more than 200 percent; and, I'm told, a considerable drop in the average SAT scores of high school students has occurred. When teachers were asked in 1940 to identify the most serious problems in schools, they listed talking out of turn, chewing gum, making noise, running in the halls, cutting in line, dress code infractions, and littering. When asked the same question in 1990, they listed drug use, alcohol abuse, pregnancy, suicide, rape, robbery, and assault.

I do not say that schools can fix most of these problems. Some of them were brought on by the technological fury of the past two centuries.

Others result from factors so complex that their origins are difficult to trace. But if schools cannot fix these problems, they can at least *respond* to them. They can acknowledge that these problems exist and embark on a journey to discover what our students need most in a culture stumbling into the twenty-first century. That is to say, we all know that schools cannot remake America, but they can make Americans who have the power and will to undertake the task.

What kind of journey would that be? Not, I fear, a journey into the world of technological wonders. A far more useful journey would take us on an exploration of the human heart, which is more mysterious and more unknown than any other terrain. For it seems to me that we are not suffering in America from a lack of information, and our children in particular are not suffering from technological deprivation. They live in a culture that has 260,000 billboards; 17,000 newspapers; 12,000 periodicals; 27,000 video outlets for renting tapes; 400 million television sets; and well over 500 million radios, not including those in automobiles. There are 40,000 new book titles published every year, and every day in America 41 million photographs are taken. And, just for the record (and thanks to the computer), over 60 billion pieces of advertising junk mail come into our mailboxes every year. Everything from telegraphy and photography in the nineteenth century to the silicon chip in the twentieth has amplified the din of information. From millions of sources all over the globe, through every possible channel and medium—light waves, air waves, ticker tapes, computer banks, telephone wires, television cables, satellites, and printing presses—information pours in. Behind it, in every imaginable form of storage—on paper, on video and audio tape, on disks, film, and silicon chips— is an even greater volume of information waiting to be retrieved. Information has become a form of garbage. It comes indiscriminately, directed at no one in particular, disconnected from usefulness. We are swamped by information, have no control over it, and don't know what to do with it. And we don't know what to do with it because a corresponding loss of meaning, a growing skepticism toward legitimate authority, and a confusing absence of clear moral direction have occurred. We are suffering, if I may put it metaphorically, from a broken heart: a separation of ourselves from any inspiring, life-enhancing narratives or transcendent stories that give meaning to the past, explain the present, and provide guidance for the future.

If there is a single problem that plagues American education at the moment, it is that our children no longer believe, as they once did, in some of the powerful and exhilarating narratives that were the underpinning of American culture. To get an idea of one of these narratives, I suggest we turn away from Bill Gates and pay some attention to Thomas Jefferson, who was among those who wrote the story of our origins. It is a story in which America is brought forth out of revolution, not merely as an experiment in governance, but as part of God's own plan, the story of America as a moral light unto the world. That story provided people with a purpose for learning. As Jefferson saw it, the purpose of school was not to enhance students' economic productivity or to aid them in becoming better consumers. Its purpose was to provide students with the tools with which to protect their liberty and to know when their liberty was threatened. Does anyone take this seriously today?

Does anyone take seriously another great American narrative, the one that was summarized so elegantly in a poem written by Emma Lazarus and that is lodged at the base of the Statue of Liberty? It includes the words, "Give me your tired, your poor, your huddled masses yearning to breathe free." This is the story of America as a nation of many nations, and it provided the schools with a specific imperative: to help make Americans out of the teeming masses; to help the lost and lonely find freedom, peace, and sustenance. Who believes this today? Or the great story—sometimes referred to as the Protestant Ethic—that tells of how self-restraint, discipline, and hard work form the pathway to a fulfilled life. There are still other narratives by which life in America was given form, ideals,

and energy, and which gave the whole enterprise of education a profound purpose.

My point is that the great problem of American education is of a social, moral, and spiritual nature, and has nothing to do with dazzling new technologies. In fact, it has nothing to do with teacher accountability, national standards of assessment, class size, or school financing. These are matters with which we must deal, but they are essentially engineering problems, which, in the end, can be solved by technicians. Far more formidable is the problem of how to mend a broken heart; that is, the problem of finding narratives in which students can believe and that will provide them with transcendent reasons for learning. Without such reasons, schools have no point. They become houses of detention rather than attention no matter how much technology you stuff into them.

I take it as a matter of course that the reason educators are so enthusiastic about technology is that it helps us to evade the central problem we know we must face but that is so difficult we hardly know how to begin. Here's how serious the problem is: It is not enough to say we will teach critical thinking. The question is, about what do we want students to think critically, and for what purpose?

It is not enough to say we want students to be adaptable to change. The question is, to what changes ought they adapt, and what changes ought they resist?

It is not enough to say we want to teach them to be good citizens. The question is, by whose authority do we judge good citizenship?

It is not enough to say we will build our students' self-esteem. The question is, what will they esteem other than self?

It is not even enough to say we will teach them to read. The Germans taught their young to read to become Nazis. The Russians taught their young to read to become communists. Do we have something better in mind? Or have we lost our minds altogether?

I began this sermon by presenting to you an instructive, "bad" poem. I should like to move toward a close by presenting to you an instructive, "good" poem. It was written by Vachel Lindsay of Springfield, Illinois. Lindsay died in 1931, but he knew, even then, what we would need to give to our children. This is the poem.

*Let not young souls be smothered out before*
*They do quaint deeds and fully flaunt their pride.*
*It is the world's one crime its babes grow dull*
*Its poor are ox-like, limp and leaden-eyed.*

*Not that they starve, but starve so dreamlessly*
*Not that they sow, but that they seldom reap*
*Not that they serve, but have no gods to serve.*
*Not that they die, but that they die like sheep.*

In closing, I should like to call your attention to the line that says our children have "no gods to serve," because that speaks to the heart of the matter. The gods of consumership, and economic utility—and, especially, the god of technology—may say something to our young about how to make a living. They are silent on the question of how to make a life. Perhaps someday soon, educators will get together to address that question. Who knows? Maybe the College Board will sponsor such a meeting.

## POSTNOTE

Technology has always been an important topic in education. However, the rapid arrival of the personal computer, CD-ROMs, and the Internet has caught many veteran teachers off guard. The acquisition of new classroom hardware and software is often the result of decisions made from above by school boards and administrators. The interests and skills of today's students, many of whom are used to computer games and have access to the Internet at home, represent pressure from below. In response, teachers are scrambling to become proficient in the new technology and to integrate it into their instruction.

Neil Postman is a long-time student of human communication and education, and an excellent observer of trends in American education. His insights on a variety of topics make his article one of our Classic picks. He offers some wise counsel in this article written for the *College Board Review*. He warns us to keep our heads, not to be carried away with our new toys, not to think ours is the first era to undergo a dramatic technological change. More positively, he calls on us to help students find the "transcendent reasons for learning."

## DISCUSSION QUESTIONS

1. What are Postman's major points about technology and schools?

2. What do you think he meant to convey by quoting the line that our children have "no gods to serve"?

3. Rather than getting rid of new technology, what is Postman suggesting we do?

# 66  Technology Use in Tomorrow's Schools

Barbara Means

Students and teachers have increasing access to almost limitless amounts of information on the World Wide Web. In addition, the trend toward using such general-purpose application packages as word processing, spreadsheet, and database software for school assignments has grown considerably since the 1980s. Nearly 50 percent of teachers in a recent national survey, for example, had required word processing during the previous school year (Becker, 1999). Students also are increasingly involved in building Web pages and multimedia presentations to show their solutions to problems or to demonstrate what they have learned in their research. Educators are using network technology to support collaborations—locally and at great distances—among students, experts, and teachers. The percentage of classrooms participating in network-based collaborations is still relatively small, however.

Despite great strides in incorporating technology into U.S. schools, we still fall short of providing a seamless, convenient, robust, and reliable technology support structure for all students and teachers. Today's desktop computers and Internet usages are not the educational ideal (Roschelle, Hoadley, Pea, Gordin, & Means, in press). Many educators lament the relative paucity of up-to-date computers and network connections in

Barbara Means is codirector of the Center for Technology in Learning, SRI International, 333 Ravenswood Ave., Menlo Park, CA 94025. From Barbara Means, "Technology Use in Tomorrow's Schools," *Educational Leadership*, December 2000/January 2001, pp. 57–61. Reprinted with permission of the Association for Supervision and Curriculum Development. Copyright © 2001 by ASCD. All rights reserved.

**TERMS TO NOTE**
World Wide Web
Word processing
Spreadsheet
Database
Internet

classrooms, but a look into almost any classroom with a sizable number of computers reveals all kinds of problems related to the computers' size, weight, shape, and requirements for multiple cords and wires. Similarly, today's World Wide Web is disorganized, of uneven quality, and overrun with advertising. In too many cases, students and teachers are either not using the technology available to them or are using technology to accomplish tasks that could be done offline more quickly and with less effort extraneous to the learning content (Healy, 1998).

Nevertheless, our experience with the less-than-ideal technological infrastructure available in today's schools suggests important directions for the 21st century. The insights gained from these experiences, coupled with advances in research on human learning and the technological improvements that can be expected in the coming decade, give rise to cautious optimism concerning technology's role in the schools of tomorrow.

## The Roots of Educational Technology

Mastery learning approaches dominated the early days of computer use to teach academic subjects, with skills and subject matter broken down into byte-sized bits for discrete skill practice or knowledge transmission. These efforts to teach content through computers were supplemented by courses in computer literacy and, at the high school level, computer programming.

**TERM TO NOTE**
Mastery learning

In the late 1980s, these practices gave way to an emphasis on incorporating general-purpose technology tools, such as word processors and spreadsheets, into learning in the academic content areas. General office applications became more common in the classroom than software explicitly designed for instructional purposes. The emphasis on adopting general tools for educational purposes received a further boost from the rise of the World Wide Web and search engines for locating Web sites on almost any topic. Such slogans as *connecting the classroom to the world* and *the world at your fingertips* reflect today's emphasis on access to a much broader information base through the Web.

Although classrooms continue to lag behind the business and entertainment sectors in terms of capitalizing on network technologies, the rate of increase in Internet access within U.S. schools during the final decade of the 20th century was phenomenal. In 1990, few U.S. schools had Internet connections, and many of these were low-speed, dial-up modem connections from a single computer. By 1994, the percentage of schools with Internet access was significant—35 percent—and by 1999, the percentage had risen to 95 percent. As with computers, we stopped counting school connections and started looking at the availability of Internet access within individual classrooms.

In 1994, only 3 percent of U.S. classrooms had Internet access. In 1996, President Clinton announced a set of national educational technology goals, including providing Internet access to every classroom in the United States. By 1997, the proportion of connected classrooms had grown to 27 percent. Sixty-three percent of U.S. public school classrooms had Internet access by 1999, according to National Center for Education Statistics data (2000), resulting in part from the E-rate—the telecommunications discount to schools and libraries passed in 1996.

## Technology for Meaningful Learning

As access to technology grows, educators must decide how best to use it. *How People Learn*, a recent report from the National Research Council (Bransford, Brown, & Cocking, 1999), applies principles from research on human learning to issues of education. The report explores the potential of technology to provide the conditions that research indicates are conducive to meaningful learning: real-world contexts for learning; connections to outside experts; visualization and analysis tools; scaffolds for problem solving; and opportunities for feedback, reflection, and revision.

A few examples illustrate how technology can provide these capabilities. The Global Learning and Observations to Benefit the Environment (GLOBE) program helps elementary and secondary school students learn science by involving them in real scientific investigations, such as measuring soil and water quality. Students follow detailed data collection protocols for measuring characteristics of their local atmosphere, soil, and vegetation. Using GLOBE Internet data-entry forms, thousands of students submit data to a central archive, where it is combined with data from other schools to develop visualizations—a data map showing measured values and their geographic locations—that are posted on the Web. The scientists who developed the data collection protocols and depend on the students' data for their research visit classrooms, exchange e-mail with students, and participate with students in scheduled Web chats (Means & Coleman, 2000).

Hands-On Universe, a program of the University of California at Berkeley's Lawrence Hall of Science, gives students the opportunity to use image processing software to investigate images from a network of automated telescopes. Automated telescopes now capture many more images from outer space than professional astronomers have time to analyze. Hands-On Universe enlists students to review images from space and to help search for supernovas and asteroids as they acquire astronomy concepts and research skills. Hands-On Universe lets students use the same kinds of software tools as scientists, albeit with more user-friendly interfaces, to examine and classify downloaded images. Hands-On Universe students have discovered a previously unknown supernova and published their work in a scientific journal.

Teachers have also found advantages in using technology supports for student collaboration within their own schools and classrooms. Knowledge Forum—formerly Computer-Supported Intentional Learning Environments (CSILE)—for example, provides a communal database, with text and graphics capabilities. Students create text and graphics "nodes" about the topic they are studying, labeling their contributions by the kind of thinking represented: "my theory for now" or "what we need to learn about next." Other students can search and comment on these nodes. With teacher support, students can use Knowledge Forum to share information and feedback, to accumulate knowledge over time, and to exercise collaboration skills. The communal hypermedia database provides a record of students' thoughts and electronic conversations over time (Scardamalia & Bereiter, 1996), allowing teachers to browse the database to review their students' emerging understanding of key concepts and their interaction skills (Means & Olson, 1999).

**TERM TO NOTE**

Hypermedia

ThinkerTools software, another visualization and analysis tool, helps middle school students learn about velocity and acceleration. Students begin with what the program developers call "scaffolded inquiry activities"—problems, games, and experiments that help students understand motion, first in one direction and then in two directions. As students progress, they are exposed to more complex simulations, culminating in their learning of the principles underlying Newtonian mechanics. In a carefully controlled study, middle school students who had used ThinkerTools outperformed high school physics students in their ability to apply principles of Newtonian mechanics to real-world situations (White & Frederiksen, 1998).

Although such examples of technology-enhanced learning activities are prominent in the education literature, they do not represent mainstream educational practice in the United States. A national survey of 4,100 teachers found that in the 1997–98 school year, the most commonly assigned use of technology was still word processing—required by nearly 50 percent of the teachers (Becker, 1999). Thirty-five percent of the teachers asked students to use CD-ROMs for research. Internet research or information gathering was the third most common teacher-directed student use of computers. Nearly 30 percent of all the teachers—and more than 70 percent of the teachers with high-speed Internet connections in their classrooms—had their students conduct Internet research (Becker, 1999). Internet assignments had become slightly more common than games and software drills, which 29 percent of the teachers had assigned. Interactive uses of the Internet were relatively infrequent. Only 7 percent of the teachers reported having their students use e-mail three times or more during the school year and even fewer had their students work with students at a distance in cross-classroom projects.

## What's Next?

Despite their relative scarcity, such uses of technology and learning principles in carefully designed instructional activities foretell future innovations that are likely to have the advantage of much more seamless, unobtrusive technology supports. Today's desktop computers and the networks they run on offer a huge array of potential uses—everything from keeping track of student grades to supporting the manipulation of digitized images—but they are bulky, expensive, and awkward to use in a classroom.

Many technology trend watchers believe that the 21st century will see a move away from such strong reliance on general-purpose computing devices toward lower-cost, portable, hand-held devices, often connected through global networks and tailored for specific applications (Norman, 1998). Major equipment manufacturers are investing in wireless technologies, wireless personal area networking has emerged, and the popularity of both hand-held computing devices and cell phones is growing rapidly.

Nowhere is the potential impact of these trends greater than in our nation's schools.

Students could carry and use lightweight, low-cost learning appliances rugged enough to fit in their backpacks as they move from class to class, school to home, or between school-based and community-based learning settings. When used with wireless networks, high-powered servers, and teacher workstations, these low-cost devices are likely to provide more narrow but more effective functionality than today's desktop computers and to be much easier to use. Computing and networking will be taken for granted as part of the school environment. Teacher workstations will be able to exchange information with student devices and with school- or district-level servers. Complex, memory-hogging programs can reside on servers and be pulled down to local computers or appliances on an as-needed basis.

## Tomorrow's Classroom

Given the possibilities of new technologies, what might tomorrow's classroom look like? A MathPad, for example, might be an educational appliance—smaller and lighter than today's hand-held devices, with capability for stylus input, display, and mathematical calculations and graphing. Such devices might feature short-range radio communication capabilities linking the hand-held device to other hand-helds or to another computing device, such as a teacher workstation, a share-board display system, or sensors built into the environment.

Given this emerging technology infrastructure, we can envision such educational activities as the following. Middle school students in an environmental science class monitor local haze using a sun photometer to measure attenuation of sunlight caused by haze, smoke, and smog. Seven small groups of students take their photometer readings at their school's softball field each day at noon, and their readings are automatically sent to their MathPads. The students' MathPads contain a template for displaying the readings of all seven groups, so the students can send their readings to one another.

Upon returning to the classroom, one group transmits the completed template for today's readings to the class's share-board computer, and the teacher begins a class review and discussion of the data on the wall-sized display. The teacher and students call up software that incorporates prompts to help them judge the reasonableness of the measurements the student groups have taken. The teacher plots each group's reading on a graph showing measurements over the last six months as a point of departure for discussing the distinction between accuracy and precision.

The teacher then introduces the next assignment: work in small groups to investigate haze data from their own and other schools. Controlling the display from her workstation, the teacher connects through the Internet to the online Haze Project database and reminds the students of the contents of the database and strategies for navigating the database Web site. To make sure they know how to read the data tables, the teacher asks several comprehension questions, having students submit answers with their MathPads and checking the students' responses on her workstation to make sure no one is lost. She directs students to return to their small groups to explore the data archive before deciding on a research question for a project that will take them several weeks and culminate in presentations for their class and submission of their work to the Haze Project's online student journal. Students may choose to collaborate with students at other schools through e-mail and real-time online discussions using software that allows them to share and manipulate data graphs.

As in today's GLOBE and Hands-on Universe projects, the Haze Project students of tomorrow participate in the real-world context of ongoing scientific investigation. Connections to a larger world become second nature. The students' data and analyses are part of much larger projects with real stakeholders. Students contribute to and learn from a community of investigators. Visualization and analysis tools on the students' MathPads and the teachers' workstation help the students see patterns in their data. Prompts built into the data-recording software scaffold students' efforts to check the reasonableness of the data they have collected. The technology also supports access to similar data sets and conferencing with others involved in the Haze Project, two activities that provide opportunities for reflection, analysis, and revision. The teacher's ability to exchange information with individual student MathPads lets students receive quick feedback on their lines of reasoning and allows the teacher to adjust instruction to meet students' needs.

In terms of the technology itself, a combination of small quantities of expensive equipment (one or a few central workstations for each classroom and a top-notch display facility) and large numbers of inexpensive devices (such as the MathPads themselves) is likely to be more cost-effective than current technology expenditures. The most challenging technical requirement is that of compatibility so that different pieces of equipment can communicate.

## Challenges Ahead

Is this scenario realistic? One could easily predict a very different impact of technology on education. The increasing availability of Web-based alternative learning resources coincides with a decline in public confidence in the efficacy of schools and increasing interest in alternatives, such as voucher programs, charter schools, and homeschooling. Over the next two decades, public schools will likely have to compete for resources and for students—not only with private schools and homeschooling options—but with Internet-based alternatives as well. I doubt that brick-and-mortar schools will become obsolete, if only for their utility as places for students to spend their time, but they will become one among many kinds of organizations offering formally organized, distributed learning.

The increased pressure of competition should stimulate schools to improve. Schools

that incorporate the technology of the future can offer the best combination of traditional face-to-face instruction—role modeling, socialization, and morale building—and projected benefits of learning with new technologies: increased participation in systems of distributed learning that engage broader communities, learning-enhancing representations of concepts and data, a restructuring of teaching and learning roles, and more meaningful assessment practices.

My vision for educational technology use is at least as dependent on improvements in teacher preparation and professional development around pedagogy, content, and assessment practices as it is on technological advances. My vision is technologically feasible—the question is whether our education system, and society in general, will support and promote the policies, resources, and practices needed to make it a reality.

## REFERENCES

Becker, H. J. (1999). *Internet use by teachers: Conditions of professional use and teacher-directed student use.* Irvine, CA: Center for Research on Information Technology and Organizations.

Bransford, J. D., Brown, A. L., & Cocking, R. R. (Eds.). (1999). *How people learn: Brain, mind, experience, and school.* Washington, DC: National Academy Press.

Healy, J. (1998). *Failure to connect: How computers affect our children's minds—for better and worse.* New York: Simon & Schuster.

Means, B., & Coleman, E. (2000). Technology supports for student participation in science investigations. In M. J. Jacobson & R. B. Kozma (Eds.), *Innovations in science and mathematics education* (pp. 287–319). Mahwah, NJ: Erlbaum.

Means, B., & Olson, K. (1999). Technology's role in student-centered classrooms. In H. Walberg & H. Waxman (Eds.), *New directions for teaching practice and research* (pp. 297–319). Berkeley, CA: McCutchan.

National Center for Education Statistics. (2000). *Internet access in U.S. public schools and classrooms: 1994–1999.* (NCES No. 2000086). Washington, DC: U.S. Government Printing Office.

Norman, D. A. (1998). *The invisible computer: Why good products can fail, the personal computer is so complex, and information appliances are the solution.* Cambridge, MA: MIT Press.

Roschelle, J., Hoadley, C., Pea, R., Gordin, D., & Means, B. (in press). Changing how and what children learn in school with computer-based technologies. *The Future of Children.*

Scardamalia, M., & Bereiter, C. (1996, November). Engaging students in a knowledge society. *Educational Leadership, 54*(3), 6–10.

White, B. Y., & Frederiksen, J. R. (1998). Inquiry, modeling, and metacognition: Making science accessible to all students. *Cognition and Science, 16,* 90–91.

*Author's note:* This article is a version of the chapter "Technology in America's Schools: Before and After Y2K," which appeared in the *ASCD Yearbook 2000,* edited by Ron Brandt. Preparation of the chapter was supported in part by National Science Foundation grant CDA-9729384. The opinions expressed are those of the author and do not necessarily reflect the policy or opinions of the Foundation.

## POSTNOTE

Louis Gerstner, Jr., former chairman of IBM, made the following statement at the 1995 National Governors Association meeting: "We need to recognize that our public schools are low-tech institutions in a high-tech society. The same changes that have brought cataclysmic change to every facet of business can improve the way we teach students and teachers." Obviously, Gerstner was not an impartial observer because IBM has strong economic interests in getting schools to use more technology. But is he right? Does technology—in particular, the kind of technology uses described by the author of this article—have the potential to transform how teaching and learning occur?

Pointing to past revolutionary technologies, such as television, that were predicted to change how schools function, skeptics note that their impact was marginal at best. The skeptics conclude that when all the fuss is over, computers and other current technologies will have had limited effects on education. We believe differently, however. No other technology has the power that computers have to put students in control of their own learning. As students learn to use computers, video disks, multimedia materials, electronic networks, and satellite transmissions to access and synthesize information, they gain control of their education and thus of their future.

## DISCUSSION QUESTIONS

1. What strategies could be employed at the local, state, and national levels to speed up the infusion of technology into our schools?

2. What technology skills do you possess that you think will be useful to you as a teacher? What skills do you need to develop?

3. What concerns, if any, do you have regarding the tremendous momentum to incorporate technology in our schools?

# Diversity and Social Issues

The United States is a nation of great diversity: races, cultures, religions, languages, and lifestyles. Although these forms of diversity are part of what makes the United States strong, they nevertheless create challenges. The major challenge is how to recognize and respect these forms of diversity while still maintaining a common culture to which each subgroup can feel welcomed and valued. Early in the twentieth century, American schools tried to create a "melting pot," where group differences were boiled away so that just "Americans" survived. Today, the notion of cultural pluralism has replaced the assimilationist perspective, with the metaphor of a "mosaic" or "quilt" replacing that of the melting pot.

The readings in this section of the book address diversity issues such as multicultural education, immigration and languages, gender issues, inclusion of children with disabilities, and parents' roles in their children's education. Many of these topics are controversial. The viewpoints of both strong proponents and opponents of the various positions are articulated in the articles. As you read the selections, try to sort out your own positions on the issues.

## 67

**CLASSIC** *A Considered Opinion: Diversity, Tragedy, and the Schools*

Diane Ravitch

As U.S. immigration has surged over the past quarter-century, educators have been developing a new response to demographic diversity in the classroom. The public schools have turned away from their traditional emphasis on assimilating newcomers into the national "melting pot." Instead, they have put a new emphasis on multicultural education, deemphasizing the common American culture and teaching children to take pride in their racial, ethnic, and national origins. In the wake of the terrorist attacks on New York City and Washington last September 11, however, the tide may be turning away from multiculturalism. Americans' remarkable display of national unity in the aftermath of the attacks could change the climate in the nation's schools as much as it has the political climate in Washington.

**TERMS TO NOTE**
Melting pot
Multicultural education

Immigration is central to the American experience. Though it is on the rise today, immigration is proportionately smaller now than it was in the first three decades of the 20th century. The census of 2000 found that about 10 percent of the population was foreign-born. In the censuses of 1900, 1910, and 1920, that share was some 14 percent. (Then as now, the nation's black population was about 12 percent.) In those early years of the last century, American society was not certain of its ability to absorb millions of newcomers. The public schools took on the job of educating and preparing them for social, civic, and economic participation in the life of the nation.

What did the public schools in those early years do about their new clientele? First, they taught them to speak, read, and write English—a vital necessity for a successful transition into American society. Because many children served as translators for their parents, these skills were valuable to the entire family in negotiating with employers, shops, and government agencies. The schools also taught habits of good hygiene (a matter of public health), as well as appropriate self-discipline and behavior. More than the three "Rs," schools taught children how to speak correctly, how to behave in a group, how to meet deadlines, and how to dress for different situations (skills needed as much by native-born rural youth as by immigrant children). Certainly, the schools taught foreign-born children about American history (especially about national holidays, the Constitution, the Revolutionary War, and the Civil War), with a strong emphasis on the positive aspects of the American drama.

They also taught children about the "American way of life," the habits, ideals, values, and attitudes (such as the American spirit of individualism) that made their new country special. If one could sum up this education policy, it was one that celebrated America and invited newcomers to become full members of American society.

During the late 1960s and early 1970s, assimilation came to be viewed as an illegitimate, coercive imposition of American ways on unwitting children, both foreign-born and nonwhite. With the rise of the black separatist movement in 1966, black nationalists such as Stokely Carmichael began inveighing against racial integration and advocating community

**TERM TO NOTE**
Assimilation

Diane Ravitch is a nonresident senior fellow in the Brookings Governmental Studies program and research professor at New York University. From Diane Ravitch, "A Considered Opinion: Diversity, Tragedy, and the Schools," *Brookings Review*, Winter 2002. Reprinted with permission of The Brookings Institution.

control of public schools in black neighborhoods. In response, many black educators demanded African-American history, African-American heroes, African-American literature, and African-American celebrations in the public schools. In the 1970s, the white ethnic revival followed the black model, and soon government was funding celebrations of ethnic heritage in the schools. By the mid-1970s, just as immigration was beginning to increase rapidly, the public schools no longer focused on acculturating the children of newcomers to American society. Instead, they encouraged children to appreciate and retain their ethnic and racial origins.

The expectation that the public schools will teach children about their racial and ethnic heritage has created enormous practical problems. First, it has promoted the belief that what is taught in school will vary in response to the particular ethnic makeup of the school. Thus, a predominantly African-American school will learn one set of lessons, while a predominantly Hispanic school will learn yet another, and an ethnically mixed school will learn—what? Second, schools have begun to lose a sense of a distinctive American culture, a culture forged by people from many different backgrounds that is nonetheless a coherent national culture. No state in the nation requires students to read any particular book, poem, or play. Today schools are uncertain about how to teach American history, what to teach as "American" literature, and how to teach world history without omitting any corner of the world (many children learn no world history). Third, the teaching of racial and ethnic pride is itself problematic, as it appears to be a continuation in a new guise of one of the worst aspects of American history.

From our public schools' experiences over the past century, we have learned much about the relative advantages and disadvantages of assimilationism and multiculturalism in the public schools.

Assimilation surely has its strengths. A democratic society must seek to give every young person, whether native-born or newcomer, the knowledge and skills to succeed as an adult. In a political system that relies on the participation of informed citizens, everyone should, at a minimum, learn to speak, read, and write a common language. Those who would sustain our democratic life must understand its history. To maximize their ability to succeed in the future, young people must also learn mathematics and science. Tailoring children's education to the color of their skin, their national origins, or their presumed ethnicity is in some fundamental sense contrary to our nation's founding ideals of democracy, equality, and opportunity.

And yet we know that assimilationism by itself is an inadequate strategy for American public education, for two reasons. First, it ignores the strengths that immigrants have to offer; and second, it presumes that American culture is static, which is surely not true. When immigrants arrive in America, they tend to bring with them, often after an emotionally costly journey, a sense of optimism, a strong family and religious tradition, and a willingness to work hard—values and attitudes that our society respects, but that affluence and media cynicism have eroded among many of our own citizens.

But neither is "celebrating diversity" an adequate strategy for a multiracial, multi-ethnic society like ours. The public schools exist to build an American community, to help both newcomers and native-born children prepare for adulthood as fellow citizens. Strategies that divide children along racial and ethnic lines encourage resentment and alienation rather than mutual respect. The ultimate democratic lesson is human equality, and the schools must teach our children that we are all in the same boat, all members of one society, regardless of race, ethnicity, or place of origin.

We learned that lesson the hardest way possible on September 11, when thousands of people from many countries died together in a single tragedy.

How will America's schools respond in the days ahead? It seems clear that they must make a pact with the children in their care. They must honor the strong and positive values that the children's families bring to America, and in return they must be prepared to give the children access to the best of America's heritage.

America's newcomers did not come to our shores merely to become consumers. They came to share in our democratic heritage and to become possessors of the grand ideas that created and sustained the democratic experiment in this country for more than two centuries. They too have a contribution to make to the evolving story of our nation. Whether they do so will depend in large part on whether our educational system respects them enough to help them become Americans.

The terrible events of this past fall have shown that Americans of all races and ethnic groups share a tremendous sense of national spirit and civic unity. They recognize that, whatever their origins, they share a common destiny as Americans. America's schools should honor that reality.

## POSTNOTE

Diane Ravitch is one of the leading conservative educational thinkers in the United States. Her training as an historian makes her a keen observer of educational trends and an advocate of strengthening student learning in core content subjects. As such, her article is one of our Classic picks.

The tensions Ravitch discusses, between multiculturalism and monoculturalism, between diversity and acculturation, are old and deep in the American schools. Emphasis has shifted back and forth toward one or the other extreme over the years, depending on historical events and, often, the energies of advocates. Currently, because of a huge influx of immigrants into the United States during the 1990s and fueled by the 9/11 attack on our country, the emphasis is shifting toward acculturation and a rebirth of patriotism. Nevertheless, this strikes us as an unnecessary distinction. Our national motto is "E pluribus unum," from the many comes the one. A good school can honor the varied backgrounds of its students and at the same time teach all the requirements and expectations of good citizens. To do less is to miseducate.

## DISCUSSION QUESTIONS

1. How was multiculturalism taught or exhibited in your schooling, and how did students respond to the school's efforts?

2. Have you seen a change in emphasis on either multiculturalism or national acculturation since 9/11?

3. What ideas do you have for dealing with these issues in your classroom?

# Multicultural Education in the New Century

### James A. Banks

## 68

An important goal of multicultural education is to educate citizens who can participate successfully in the workforce and take action in the civic community to help the nation actualize its democratic ideals. These ideals, such as justice, equality and freedom, are set forth in the Declaration of Independence, the U.S. Constitution and the Bill of Rights.

Democratic societies, such as the United States, are works in progress that require citizens who are committed to democratic ideals, who are keenly aware of the gap between a nation's ideals and realities and who are able and willing to take thoughtful action that will help make democratic ideals a reality.

## Distortion by Critics

Although some critics have misrepresented multicultural education and argued it is divisive and will Balkanize the nation, the aim of multicultural education is to unify our nation and to help put in place its ideal of *e pluribus unum*—"out of many, one."

The claim by conservative social commentators that multicultural education will divide the nation assumes that it is now united. However, our nation is deeply divided along racial, ethnic and social-class lines. Multicultural education is trying to help unify a deeply divided nation, not to divide one that is united.

James A. Banks is professor and director of the Center for Multicultural Education, University of Washington, Seattle. He is author of *Educating Citizens in a Multicultural Society*. Reprinted with permission from the May 1999 issue of *The School Administrator* magazine.

Multicultural theorists assume that we cannot unite the nation around its democratic ideals by forcing people from different racial, ethnic and cultural groups to leave their cultures and languages at the schoolhouse door. An important principle of a democratic society is that citizens will voluntarily participate in the commonwealth and that their participation will enrich the nation-state.

When citizens participate in society and bring their cultural strengths to the national civic culture, both they and the nation are enriched. Renato Rosaldo, the Stanford anthropologist, calls this kind of civic participation *cultural citizenship*.

**TERMS TO NOTE**
Multicultural education
Cultural citizenship

We can create an inclusive, democratic and civic national community only when we change the center to make it more inclusive and reflective of the diversity that enriches our nation. This will require that we bring people and groups that are now on the margins of society into the center.

Schools should be model communities that mirror the kind of democratic society we envision. In democratic schools the curriculum reflects the cultures of the diverse groups within society, the languages and dialects that students speak are respected and valued, cooperation rather than competition is fostered among students and students from diverse racial, ethnic and social-class groups are given equal status in the school.

## Major Challenges

Several societal trends present challenges for educating effective citizens in the new century. These trends include the growing ethnic, racial, cultural and language diversity in the United States, caused in part by the largest influx of immigrants to the nation since the beginning of the 20th century.

Unlike in the past, most immigrants are coming from nations in Asia and Latin America. Only a small percentage of the immigrants are coming from European nations. U.S. Census projections indicate that people of color will make up 47.5 percent of the nation's population by 2050. Students of color will make up about 48 percent of the nation's school-age youth by 2020. In 1995, they made up 35 percent of the nation's public school students.

The increasing percentage of school-age youth who speak a first language other than English and the widening gap between the rich and poor also present challenges to educating effective citizens in the new century. In 1990, 14 percent of school-age youth spoke a first language other than English. One in every five was living below the official government poverty line.

## Addressing Diversity

The challenge to school leaders is to find ways to ensure that the rich contributions that diverse groups can make to our nation and the public schools becomes a reality. The cultural and language groups within our nation have values, perspectives and languages that can help the nation solve some of its intractable problems and humanize the lives of all of its citizens. During World War II the lives of many American soldiers were saved because the Navajo language was used in a secret code that perplexed military leaders in Japan. The code contributed to the victory of the Allies in the South Pacific and also was used in the Korean and Vietnam wars.

In order for multicultural education to be implemented in ways that will help actualize effective citizenship education, improve race relations and increase the academic achievement

of students from diverse groups, the field must be viewed broadly and attention must be paid to the research that has accumulated during the last two decades. This research, briefly summarized below, is reviewed extensively in the *Handbook of Research on Multicultural Education*.

Too often multicultural education is conceptualized narrowly to mean adding content about diverse groups to the curriculum or expanding the canon taught in schools. It also should help students to develop more democratic racial and ethnic attitudes and to understand the cultural assumptions that underlie knowledge claims.

Another important dimension of multicultural education is equity pedagogy, in which teachers modify their teaching in ways that will facilitate the academic achievement of students from diverse racial, cultural, language and social-class groups.

**TERM TO NOTE**
Equity pedagogy

## What Research Says

Educational leaders should become familiar with the research evidence about the effects of multicultural education and not be distracted by the critics of multicultural education who disregard or distort this significant body of research.

Research indicates that students come to school with many stereotypes, misconceptions and negative attitudes toward outside racial and ethnic groups. Research also indicates that the use of multicultural textbooks, other teaching materials and cooperative teaching strategies can help students to develop more positive racial attitudes and perceptions.

This research also indicates that these kinds of materials and teaching strategies can result in students choosing more friends from outside racial, ethnic and cultural groups.

Research indicates that teachers can increase the classroom participation and academic achievement of students from different ethnic groups by modifying their instruction so that it draws upon their cultural strengths. In Susan Philips' study, *The Invisible Culture: Communication in Classroom and Community on the Warm Spring Indian Reservation*, American Indian students participated more actively in class discussions when teachers used group-oriented participation structures that were consistent with their community cultures.

Researchers Kathryn Au and Roland G. Tharp, working in the Kamehameha Early Education Program in Honolulu, Hawaii, found that both student participation and standardized achievement test scores increased when they incorporated teaching strategies consistent with the cultures of Native Hawaiian students and used the children's experiences in reading instruction.

Studies summarized by Linda Darling-Hammond, a Stanford University professor and executive director of the National Center for Restructuring Education and Teaching, indicate that the academic achievement of students of color and low-income students increases when they have high-quality teachers who are experts in their content specialization, pedagogy and child development. She points to a significant study by Robert Dreeben, the University of Chicago sociologist. He found that when African American students receive high-quality instruction their reading achievement was as high as that of white students. The quality of instruction, not the race of the students, was the significant variable.

## The Future

School leaders should recognize that the goals of multicultural education are highly consistent with those of the nation's schools: to develop thoughtful citizens who can function effectively in the world of work and in the civic community. Ways must be found for schools to recognize and respect the cultures and languages of students from diverse groups while at the same time working to develop an overarching national culture to which all groups will have allegiance.

This can best be done by bringing groups that are on the margins of society into the center, educating students who have the knowledge, skills and values needed to rethink and change the center so that it is more inclusive and incorporating the research and theory in multicultural education into school reform.

Rethinking and re-imaging our nation in ways that will make it more just and equitable will enrich us all because the fates of all groups are tightly interconnected. Martin Luther King Jr. said, "We will live together as brothers and sisters or die separate and apart as strangers."

## POSTNOTE

James Banks is one of the foremost authorities on multicultural education in the United States, earning him a spot among our Classic articles. Multicultural education is a controversial issue, partly because there is no generally accepted definition. Some people see multicultural education as being divisive, creating separate pockets of different cultures, rather than helping to create a common culture. Others see multicultural education as valuing cultural pluralism, and recognizing that cultural diversity is a valuable resource that should be preserved and extended. James Banks rejects both assimilation and separatism as ultimate goals. He recognizes that each subculture exists as part of an interrelated whole. Multicultural education reaches beyond awareness and understanding of cultural differences to recognize the right of these different cultures to exist and to value that existence.

In addition to valuing cultural diversity, multicultural education is also based on the concept of *social justice,* which seeks to do away with social and economic

**TERM TO NOTE**

Social justice

inequalities for those in our society who have been denied these benefits of a democratic society. African Americans, Native Americans, Asian Americans, Hispanic Americans, women, disabled individuals, people with limited English proficiency, persons with low incomes, members of particular religious groups, and gays are among those groups that have at one time or another been denied social justice. Educators who support multicultural education see establishing social justice for all groups of people who have experienced discrimination as a moral and ethical responsibility. Extending the concept of multicultural education to include a broader population has also contributed to its controversy.

## DISCUSSION QUESTIONS

1. In your own words, what does multicultural education mean?

2. In your opinion, should cultural pluralism be a goal of our society and its schools? Why or why not?

3. What examples of multicultural education can you describe from your own education?

# Multicultural Illiteracy

Sandra Stotsky

The meaning of the word "diversity" has been badly abused in recent decades. American educators have long honored diversity in the only educationally meaningful sense of the word—individual difference.

For generations teachers were trained to look at students as individuals. Each student was supposedly endowed with a different combination of talents, abilities, interests and opinions. There is no question that this way of understanding diversity created strong positive educational outcomes and could continue to do so. Intellectual or social conformity has never been an American trait.

But in an Orwellian transformation of the meaning of the word, diversity has come to mean looking at a student as a representative of a particular demographic category. It now conveys the erroneous notion that, for example, all girls think and learn in one way, all boys in another or that all black students think and learn in one way, all Asians in another, all white students in yet another. To see students as members of a particular racial category or "culture" (to use current educational jargon), rather than as unique individuals, makes all the difference in the world.

Few positive outcomes are possible in an educational system that slots all students into spurious racial categories and then attaches fictitious ways of thinking, learning and knowing to each. The result is not the elimination of stereotypes but the freezing of them.

Sandra Stotsky is the deputy commissioner for Academic Affairs and Planning for the State of Massachusetts and a research associate with the Philosophy of Education Research Center at the Harvard University Graduate School of Education. She is the author of *Losing Our Language: How Multicultural Classroom Instruction Is Undermining Our Children's Ability to Read, Write, and Reason.* Reprinted with permission from the May 1999 issue of *The School Administrator* magazine.

## Classified by Category

We always have had different races and ethnic groups in our schools, although not in the same numbers or kinds in all schools. I grew up in a small Massachusetts town in which the children or grandchildren of early 20th century immigrants were as numerous as the children of those whose families had lived in the town for several hundred years.

As children, we all knew each others' backgrounds. We knew who spoke Italian, Armenian, Greek, Portuguese, Lithuanian, Polish or French Canadian in their home. We knew which families attended the local Catholic church, one of the many Protestant churches in town or the synagogue in a neighboring city. But not one of my teachers, in my presence, ever denigrated our ethnic, linguistic or religious backgrounds. Indeed, what they emphasized was something all our parents wanted them to stress. All of us, we were told repeatedly, were American citizens. And we were individual American citizens, not Lithuanian Americans, Irish Americans and so on, even though our parents may have belonged to the local Lithuanian, Polish or Italian social club or read an Armenian or Polish newspaper. We were not classified into racial or ethnic categories for any purpose.

Yes, there was prejudice in America. Why should this country be different from the others? But we all knew from our families there was even more prejudice elsewhere in the world, especially in those countries from which our families had come. Furthermore, the prejudice here was not just in those families who had been here for generations, it was also in the newcomers.

Every group had its own prejudices toward outsiders, as we all learned through experience, and it didn't bother us much. It was just another one of life's many hurdles to surmount. What was more important was that we all lived under the same set of laws as American citizens. These were ideals, to be sure, not always realities, but they were official ideals with teeth behind them, and we learned that they could be appealed to or drawn on, as women found in the early part of the century in gaining the right to vote, or as court decisions and civil rights legislation showed us in the 1950s and 1960s.

Fortunately for us, our teachers didn't subject us to endless lessons on tolerance and on how to be respectful of each other's "culture." They simply modeled tolerance for us and dealt, briefly, with problematic incidents whenever they arose in school. We were thus able to spend most of our school time on academic matters. Our main responsibility was to go to school every day, to be respectful of our teachers and to do our homework.

It's true we didn't see our home cultures in what we read in school, but we identified with each other as American citizens, something we and our parents were proud to be, despite our country's flaws. We probably would have welcomed attempts at a realistic curriculum that included more information or literature on the many immigrant groups in this country, as well as on the African Americans and Native Americans, but only if it did not end up making it more difficult for us to learn how to read and write English or giving us a warped or dishonest view of our own country and the larger world within which we live.

## Negative Connotations

It is highly ironic that multiculturalism has evolved as an educational philosophy from its original and positive meaning of inclusion to mean something very negative, especially for us. This was one of the major findings of my research on the contents of all the grade 4 and grade 6 readers in six leading basal reading series, pub-

lished between 1993 and 1995, as reported in *Losing Our Language.*

Rather than broadening students' horizons about the ethnic diversity of this country, today's version of multiculturalism has led to the suppression of the stories of most immigrant groups to this country. Overall, the selections in these readers convey the picture of an almost monolithic white world, with none of the real ethnic diversity that can be seen in just the listing of restaurants in a telephone directory for any city in this country. Almost all of the various European ethnic groups I grew up with have been excluded. Instead of the real America, we find a highly shrunken mainstream culture in most series, surrounded by Native Americans, Asian Americans, African Americans and Hispanics, none of whom seem to interact much with each other.

Nor do today's readers give children an informed understanding of the real world within which they live. Nowhere do children read about the first airplane flight, the first transatlantic flight, the first exploration of space, the discovery of penicillin or the polio vaccine or how such inventions as the light bulb, radio, telegraph, steamboat, telephone, sewing machine, phonograph or radar came about. Apparently, accounts of these significant discoveries or inventions have been banished from students' common knowledge because most portray the accomplishments of white males.

But without the stories about the pioneers in science and technology (a few of whom were females, like Marie Curie), both boys and girls are unlikely to acquire a historically accurate timeframe for sequencing the major discoveries that have shaped their life today. The greater loss is that of an educational role model. The current substitutes for these stories in the readers—stories about people who have overcome racism or sexism or physical disabilities—are unlikely to give children insights into the power of intellectual curiosity in sustaining perseverance or the role of intellectual gratification in rewarding this perseverance.

## Wayward Literacy

The most visible problem I found in the readers is at the level of language itself. The kinds of selections now featured in the readers make it almost impossible for children to develop a rich, literate vocabulary in English over the grades. In some series, children must learn a dazzling array of proper nouns, words for the mundane features of daily life, words for ethnic foods in countries around the world and other non-English words, most of which contribute little if anything to the development of their competence in the English language.

For example, consider this paragraph near the end of a story in a grade 4 reader: "In the wee hours of the morning, the family made a circle around Grandma Ida, Beth and Chris. Grandma Ida gave the *tamshi la tutaonana*: 'In this new year let us continue to practice *umoja, kujichagulia, ujima, ujamaa, nia, kuumba* and *imani*. Let us strive to do something that will last as long as the earth turns and water flows.'"

Or consider this sentence in another grade 4 reader: "The whole family sat under wide trees and ate arroz con gandules, pernil, viandas and tostones, ensalada de chayotes y tomates and pasteles."

Or these sentences in a grade 6 reader: "On the *engawa* after dinner, Mr. Ono said to Mitsuo, 'Take Lincoln to the dojo. You are not too tired, are you, Lincoln-kun?'"

Not only are children in this country unlikely to see any of these Swahili, Spanish or Japanese words in any of their textbooks in science, mathematics or history, they are unlikely to see them in any other piece of literature as well. They have wasted their intellectual energy not only learning their meaning but also learning how to pronounce them. It is not clear why these academically useless words, some of which are italicized, some not, are judged to be of importance by contemporary teacher educators.

These educators also seem to think that children should spend a considerable amount of class time engaged in conversations with each other about each other's ethnic cultures and daily lives—in the name of building self-esteem and group identity. But using precious class time for frequent conversations about intellectually barren topics that draw on intellectually limited vocabularies deprives the very students who most need it of opportunities to practice using the lexical building blocks necessary for conceptual growth and analytical thinking.

The present version of multiculturalism may well be largely responsible, through its effects on classroom materials and instruction, for the growing gap between the scores of minority students and other students on the National Assessment of Educational Progress examinations in reading. We need public discussions of the goals that should dominate reading instruction. Do we want teachers absorbed with the development of their children's egos, intent on shaping their feelings about themselves and others in specific ways? Or do we want teachers to concentrate on developing their children's minds, helping them acquire the knowledge, vocabulary and analytical skills that enable them to think for themselves and to choose the kind of personal identity they find most meaningful?

**TERM TO NOTE**
National Assessment of Educational Progress (NAEP)

## POSTNOTE

Raw perception of people and things can quickly overpower us and submerge us in a sea of confusion. The human mind fights back by organizing perceptions into categories and putting labels on those categories: boys, girls, friends, enemies, tall people, short people, conservatives, liberals. However, as soon as we have labeled someone, distortions and mischief tend to set in. Tim with his enormous array of talents is labeled "the ADD [attention deficient disorder] kid." Teresa with all her budding potentialities is "that Hispanic girl." Although we can't live without categories and a method of labeling, we must be constantly vigilant of their limitations and their dangers. Sandra Stotsky's essay points out how, in her lifetime, a system of labeling has changed. She raises serious questions about the education consequences of this change.

## DISCUSSION QUESTIONS

1. State three major points from this essay.

2. What is the difference between the meaning of "diversity" in today's schools and the schools of Stotsky's youth?

3. How do you believe the reality of multiculturalism should be dealt with in our schools?

## 70

# School Reform and Student Diversity

Catherine Minicucci, Paul Berman, Barry McLaughlin, Beverly McLeod, Beryl Nelson, and Kate Woodworth

About one in seven of the nation's 5- to 17-year-olds speaks a home language other than English, and the number of such young people is growing.[1] During the 1980s the number of students considered to be limited English proficient (LEP) grew 2½ times faster than the general school enrollment.[2] LEP students are concentrated in large urban areas in a few states—California, New York, Texas, Florida, Illinois, and New Jersey—and in the rural areas of the Southwest.[3]

**TERM TO NOTE**

Limited English proficient (LEP)

Nearly all language-minority students are also poor, and many are members of racial or ethnic minority groups as well. Most LEP children live in communities beset by poverty and violence and offering limited economic opportunity. LEP children attending public schools frequently do not have access to adequate nutrition, housing, or health and dental care. The misconnections between the school and the community, coupled with the lack of economic opportunity, create an atmosphere of alienation between the home and the school. For their part, schools cannot predict the numbers, literacy levels, or previous school experience of incoming immigrant students.

It should not be surprising, then, that children who come from cultural- and linguistic-minority backgrounds often flounder in American schools. By the time they enter high school, many still lack a solid grounding in reading, writing, mathematics, and science. Moreover, most secondary schools do not offer an academic program in science, math, or social studies that is geared toward LEP students.[4] While dropout rates are not tallied for LEP students per se, it is clear that LEP students in some ethnic groups are dropping out of school at a high rate. The dropout rate for Hispanic immigrants is estimated to be 43%.[5] As young adults, many LEP students are inadequately prepared for higher education or high wage/high skill employment.

Recent reports have called for making the needs of LEP students more central to the national school reform effort. At a time when America seeks to reform its schools so that all students meet high standards, the challenge of educating language-minority students assumes even greater importance. But many schools undergoing restructuring fail to include LEP students in their attempts to revitalize their curriculum and instruction.[6]

There are schools that have made significant breakthroughs in educating LEP students, however.[7] In our study of student diversity, we examined eight such exemplary school reform efforts for language-minority students in grades 4 through 8 in language arts, science, or mathematics.[8] We identified theory-based and practice-proven strategies that effectively teach language arts, mathematics, and science

At the time this article was written, Catherine Minicucci was head of Minicucci Associates, Sacramento, California; Paul Berman was president of BW Associates, Berkeley, California; Barry McLaughlin was director of the National Center for Research on Cultural Diversity and Second Language Learning, University of California, Santa Cruz; Beverly McLeod was a research affiliate at the National Center; Beryl Nelson was senior researcher at BW Associates; and Kate Woodworth was a researcher at BW Associates. Minicucci, Catherine, Paul Berman, Barry McLaughlin, Beverly McLeod, Beryl Nelson, and Kate Woodworth, "School Reform and Student Diversity," *Phi Delta Kappan*, September 1995. Copyright © 1995 by Phi Delta Kappa. Reprinted by permission of authors and publisher.

to students from linguistically and culturally diverse backgrounds.[9]

## Solutions Found in Exemplary Schools

The case studies of eight exemplary schools demonstrate that, while they are becoming literate in English, LEP students can learn the same curriculum in language arts, science, and math as native English speakers. The success of these schools challenges the assumption that students must learn English first, before they learn grade-level science or math. The elements that come together in these schools are 1) a schoolwide vision of excellence that incorporates LEP students and embraces the students' language and culture, 2) the creation of a community of learners engaged in active discovery, and 3) well-designed and carefully executed programs to develop LEP students' skills in English and in their native languages.

While the vision of each exemplary school we studied was unique, they all held high expectations for the learning and personal development of LEP students. The exemplary sites developed a meaningful curriculum that made connections across disciplines, built real-life applications into the curriculum, related the curriculum to student experiences, and emphasized depth of understanding rather than breadth of knowledge. Schools relied on thematic learning that connected science, math, social science, and language arts and validated students' cultural and linguistic backgrounds. Working in teams, teachers developed, assessed, and refined thematic units over a period of years.

The exemplary schools used innovative approaches to help LEP students become independent learners who could take responsibility for their own learning. Teachers understood that they were not the sole sources of information and wisdom, and they acted as facilitators for student learning. The students were the center of classroom activity; they collaborated with their peers and teachers in the processes of inquiry and active discovery. Students understood what was expected of them and viewed each other as resources for learning.

Cooperative learning was used extensively in all eight of the exemplary schools. Cooperative learning strategies are particularly effective with LEP students because they provide opportunities for students to produce language in a setting that is less threatening than speaking before the entire class. Cooperative learning groups promote the development of language related to a subject area, which serves the dual purpose of developing language skills and enhancing understanding of core content.

**TERM TO NOTE**
Cooperative learning

All the schools were "parent friendly" and welcomed parents in innovative ways. The schools were also "family friendly," and some took unusual steps to bring health care, dental care, counseling, and social services onto their campuses to serve the families of students. The schools embraced the cultural and linguistic backgrounds of students by employing bilingual staff members, by communicating with parents in their native language when necessary, by honoring the multicultural quality of the student population, and by ensuring a safe school environment. The value placed on students' culture pervaded the classroom curriculum, whether taught in the student's native language or in sheltered English.

In order to build consensus through broad-based decision making, the exemplary schools developed new governance structures involving teachers, parents, and community members. The teachers in the exemplary schools were treated as professionals, encouraged to learn from one another, and given the time to develop programs. The schools used the findings of educational research to hone their approaches, and they sought assistance from external partners in curriculum development and professional development. In schools with exemplary science programs, external partners played a very important role in adapting innovative science curriculum materials for LEP students.

The exemplary schools created smaller school organizations, such as "families" or "houses," that strengthened the connections among students and teachers alike. Smaller school units set the stage for cross-disciplinary instruction and enhanced teachers' sense of commitment by allowing them to focus on a smaller group of students. One exemplary school kept students together with the same teacher for five years. This continuity offers distinct advantages to students who are learning English. Gaps in student learning between grades taught by different teachers were avoided. Parent involvement was enhanced. LEP students in such long-term "continuum" classes became skilled at cooperative learning, were highly responsible for their own learning tasks, and built a remarkable level of academic self-confidence.

The exemplary schools used time in inventive ways. For the most part, teachers controlled their own daily schedules, and they zealously protected students' time to learn. Several exemplary schools extended the school day and year. This added student learning time and freed time for teacher collaboration and professional development. LEP students making the transition to English instruction need additional time to learn, and the schools met that need through Saturday programs, summer programs, and after-school tutorials.

Exemplary schools paid special attention to the main goal, which is helping students achieve English literacy. The schools used qualified faculty members fluent in the native language of students and trained in second-language learning. Teachers had the flexibility to tailor transitional paths to meet each child's needs. The schools had more than one program path for students to move to English literacy. In these schools native language literacy was universally regarded as a critical foundation for successful attainment of English literacy. The exemplary schools made special academic support (through homework clubs or after-school tutorials) available to LEP students when they were mainstreamed into all-English classes.[10]

The stories of two of these schools will illustrate the dynamic quality of the interplay of school reform, high-quality language development programs, and challenging curriculum for LEP students.

## Inter-American School

Inter-American School is a public school enrolling 650 Chicago students from prekindergarten to eighth grade. It was founded in 1975 by a small group of parents and teachers as a bilingual preschool under the auspices of the Chicago Public Schools. The parents and teachers envisioned a multicultural school in which children would be respected as individuals and their languages and cultures would be respected as well.

Today, the school is a citywide magnet school whose students are 70% Hispanic, 13% African American, and 17% white. The developmental bilingual program at the school has the goal of bilingualism and biliteracy for all students including native speakers of English. At all grade levels, English-dominant and Spanish-dominant students are assigned to classrooms in roughly equal proportions. In prekindergarten, all core subjects are taught in Spanish to all students. Spanish-dominant students take English as a second language, and English-dominant students take Spanish as a second language. An 80/20 ratio of Spanish to English instruction remains through third grade; then English instruction is gradually increased to 50/50 by eighth grade. Students enrolled in fifth and sixth grades at Inter-American School are fully bilingual and biliterate in Spanish and English.

Much of the school's curriculum is integrated across the disciplines and built around themes that reflect the history, culture, and traditions of students. The school emphasizes the study of the Americas and Africa, especially how African history and culture have influenced the Americas. Teachers at each grade level work together to develop their curriculum around themes. For example, fourth-grade teachers use a thematic unit on Mayan civilization to integrate content across the curriculum. In social studies, students study the geographic spread of Mayan civilization, Mayan religion, and Mayan cultural traditions. In science, students study Mayan architecture and agriculture. In language arts, they read and write stories about the Mayans. A volunteer parent taught an art lesson in which students painted Mayan gods. The unit began with a visit to the Field Museum to see an exhibit on Mayan culture, architecture, and religion.

Throughout the year teachers work together intensively in groups that span two grade levels. The teachers at prekindergarten and kindergarten, grades 1 and 2, and so on, plan together, exchange students across grade levels and classrooms, and work together on thematic units.

Like other Chicago schools, Inter-American School has a local school council that sets school policies, hires and evaluates the principal, interviews prospective teachers, and controls the school budget. The professional personnel advisory committee, made up entirely of faculty members, sets priorities and takes responsibility for the instructional program.

## Hanshaw Middle School

Hanshaw Middle School serves 860 sixth-through eighth-graders from a predominantly low-income Latino community in Modesto, California. It opened in the fall of 1991. The Hanshaw student body is roughly 56% Hispanic, 26% white, 11% Asian, and 5% African American. After interviewing 500 families in their homes, the principal and faculty agreed on four principles for the foundation of Hanshaw's program: high expectations for all students, support for the Latino and Chicano experience, a meaning-centered curriculum, and a conscious effort to impart life skills as part of the curriculum. The principal recruited teachers from industry—for example, a former museum director

teaches science, and a former wildlife biologist teaches science. Life skills such as patience, flexibility, integrity, initiative, and effort are taught at the start of each school year. Students are rewarded throughout the year for demonstrating life skills.

Hanshaw is organized into five houses, each named for a campus of the California State University system. Each house is made up of from six to nine teachers, led by a team leader. Teams of two teachers (one for the math/science core and one for the language arts/social studies core) teach groups of 30 to 35 students. All students take two 90-minute core classes, one for math/science and one for language arts/social studies. Each year students visit the college campus their house is named after, meet college students from various ethnic backgrounds, hear lectures, and receive a T-shirt and a "diploma." Students identify strongly with the college campus, which provides them with an alternative to gang affiliation. Teachers within each house make decisions about the school's budget.

The curriculum design decisions that Hanshaw teachers make are based on a simple principle: every lesson or skill must be relevant to the students' lives. Teachers strive to help students know the "why" of an answer or of multiple answers or to help them understand multiple ways of getting to an answer. Teachers build on students' own experiences in thematic instruction. Themes unify instruction across science, math, language arts, and social studies, incorporating topics from the California curriculum frameworks.

Hanshaw offers several programs for LEP students: instruction in Spanish in core curricular areas, sheltered instruction for advanced Spanish-speaking LEP students and students who speak other primary languages, and mainstream English instruction for clusters of LEP students who speak the same first language. When LEP students are considered ready to move to full English instruction, they are clustered together in mainstream classes. Many of the teachers of mainstream classes have special training and credentials in second-language acquisition.

Hanshaw teachers use a constructivist approach to teaching math. A mainstream eighth-grade algebra class we observed included 15 LEP students. The math teacher is

---
**TERM TO NOTE**

Constructivist
---

a former carpenter who had training in second-language acquisition. The spatial math lesson she was conducting challenged students to modify the profile of a building and to graph that profile. Students working in cooperative groups used Lego blocks to re-create the profile in three dimensions. The teacher's role was to set up the challenge and to facilitate the work of cooperative student groups in solving the problem. When students finished the assignment, she asked them to solve it another way. LEP students speaking the same language worked together in both English and their native language in their cooperative groups.

Hanshaw's program is supported by a vigorous relationship with an external partner, Susan Kovalik and Associates from the state of Washington; that partner works with Hanshaw faculty members in intensive summer and weekend retreats. A Kovalik coach assists the school on a monthly basis, designing curriculum, providing instructional coaching, and helping the faculty identify problems and solutions. The school uses both state and federal funds to purchase assistance from Kovalik. Hanshaw also has a comprehensive health and social services center on campus that is staffed by social workers and counselors who are bilingual in Spanish and English.

These two schools provide concrete examples of the broader solutions listed above. Both schools have a schoolwide vision that incorporates high standards for LEP students. Both schools take a number of concrete steps to validate and honor the languages and cultures of their students. Both schools teach challenging academic content to LEP students in their native languages. Both schools use the thematic approach to deliver a meaning-centered curriculum that relates to students' life experiences. And teachers at both schools take responsibility for making decisions about the uses of resources and time.

Exemplary schools, such as Inter-American and Hanshaw, illustrate the way such concepts of school reform as smaller school organizations, protected time for learning, thematic instruction, and teacher collaboration can be harnessed to meet the needs of LEP students. They demonstrate that high-quality LEP programs, which include the development of native language literacy, are certainly compatible with learning science and math through active discovery. The dynamic interplay of greater school autonomy, protected time to learn for smaller groups of students with a small group of teachers, intensive professional development, and development of LEP students' literacy in English and in their native languages holds the promise for success in educating growing numbers of LEP students.

## NOTES

1. General Accounting Office, "Limited English Proficiency: A Growing and Costly Educational Challenge Facing Many School Districts," Report to the Chairman, Committee on Labor and Human Resources, U.S. Senate, Washington, D.C., January 1994; and Diane August and Kenji Hakuta, *Federal Educational Programs for Limited-English-Proficient Students: A Blueprint for the Second Generation* (Stanford, Calif.: Stanford Working Group, 1993).

2. Cynthia A. Chavez, "'State of the Play' in Educational Research on Latino/Hispanic Youth," unpublished manuscript, Rockefeller Foundation, New York, N.Y., May 1991. The phrase "limited English proficient" is used to refer to students whose home language is other than English and who have been determined, using tests of oral English fluency, to require special instruction in order to acquire sufficient English skills to participate in all English instruction.

3. *Numbers and Needs: Ethnic and Linguistic Minorities in the United States,* newsletter published by Dorothy Waggoner, Washington, D.C., May 1992; and Lorraine M. McDonnell and Paul T. Hill, *Newcomers in American Schools: Meeting the Education Needs of Immigrant Youth* (Santa Monica, Calif.: RAND Corporation, 1993).

4. Catherine Minicucci and Laurie Olsen, *Programs for Secondary Limited English Proficient Students: A California*

*Study, Focus #5* (Washington, D.C.: National Clearing-house for Bilingual Education, 1992).

5. *School Success for Limited English Proficient Students: The Challenge and State Response* (Washington, D.C.: Resource Center on Educational Equity, Council of Chief State School Officers, 1990).

6. Laurie Olsen et al., *The Unfinished Journey: Restructuring Schools in a Diverse Society* (San Francisco: California Tomorrow, 1994).

7. See Paul Berman et al., *Meeting the Challenge of Language Diversity,* 5 vols. (Berkeley, Calif.: BW Associates, February 1992).

8. The eight exemplary schools selected after an extensive nationwide search are: Del Norte Heights Elementary School, Ysleta Independent School District (El Paso); Hollibrook Elementary School, Spring Branch Independent School District (Houston); Linda Vista Elementary School, San Diego Unified School District; Inter-American School, Chicago Public Schools; Graham and Parks Alternative School, Cambridge (Mass.) School District; Evelyn Hanshaw Middle School, Modesto (Calif.) City Schools; Horace Mann Middle School, San Francisco Unified School District; and Charles Wiggs Middle School, El Paso Independent School District.

9. *School Reform and Student Diversity,* 3 vols. (Santa Cruz: National Center for Research on Cultural Diversity and Second Language Learning, University of California, in collaboration with BW Associates, September 1995).

10. We conducted focus groups with LEP students who had made the transition to all-English instruction. The students told us that they relied on their bilingual teachers, their older siblings, and their English-speaking peers in learning English and that they benefited from the after-school tutorial opportunities, summer programs, and extracurricular opportunities.

## POSTNOTE

The recent wave of immigration to the United States has had tremendous consequences for our schools. One estimate puts the number of students with limited English proficiency (LEP) at around 3 million, and the numbers are increasing much more rapidly than the overall student enrollment. As these students enter school, most will need to make sense of a new language, a new culture, and possibly new ways of behaving.

The authors of this article studied eight schools with exemplary approaches to working with LEP students. They discovered that the approaches that work for these students are also the approaches that many reformers urge all schools to follow: high expectations for all learners, cross-disciplinary curricula, depth rather than breadth, thematic units, cooperative learning, parental involvement, site-based management, smaller school organizations, and innovative use of time. In other words, what works for "regular" students also works for students with limited English proficiency.

## DISCUSSION QUESTIONS

1. Have you ever traveled or lived in a country where you couldn't speak the language? If so, how did you feel? How did you cope?

2. Were there any aspects of the programs at the Inter-American and Hanshaw schools that particularly appealed to you? Why?

3. Would you like to work with LEP students? Why or why not? If so, what can you do to prepare yourself for success?

**CLASSIC** *Shortchanging Girls and Boys*

Susan McGee Bailey

## 71

Recently gender equity in education has become a hot, or at least a "reasonably warm," topic in education. Higher education institutions across the country are under renewed pressure to provide equal athletic opportunities for female students. The U.S. Supreme Court is considering cases involving the admission of women to all-male, state-supported military institutions. And the continued underrepresentation of women in tenured faculty positions is prompting many donors to withhold contributions to Harvard University's fundraising campaign.

But it is at the elementary and secondary school levels that the shortchanging of girls has been most extensively documented (Wellesley College Center for Research on Women 1992, AAUW 1995, Orenstein 1994, Sadker and Sadker 1994, Thorne 1993, Stein et al. 1993). Twenty-four years after the passage of Title IX—which prohibits discrimination on the basis of sex in any educational programs receiving federal funds—girls and boys are still not on equal footing in our nation's classrooms. Reviews of curricular materials, data on achievement and persistence in science, and research on teacher-to-student and student-to-student interaction patterns all point to school experiences that create significant barriers to girls' education. These factors have fostered widespread discussion and action among parents, educators, and policymakers.

**TERMS TO NOTE**

Gender equity

Title IX

---

Susan McGee Bailey is the Executive Director of the Wellesley Center for Research on Women at Wellesley College, Wellesley, Massachusetts. Susan McGee Bailey, "Shortchanging Girls and Boys," *Educational Leadership*, May 1996, pp. 75–79. Reprinted by permission of the author.

## Barriers to Gender Equitable Education

As the principal author of the 1992 study, *How Schools Shortchange Girls*, I have followed the discussion with considerable interest and mounting concern. The central problem posed in the opening pages of this report continues to be ignored in our discussions of public K–12 education

> [There are] critical aspects of social development that our culture has traditionally assigned to women that are equally important for men. Schools must help girls *and* boys acquire both the relational and the competitive skills needed for full participation in the workforce, family, and community (Wellesley College Center for Research on Women 1992, p. 2).

Too much of the discussion and too many of the proposed remedies rely on simplistic formulations that obscure, rather than address, the complex realities confronting our society.

First among these are the assumptions that 1) gender equity is something "for girls only" and 2) if the situation improves for girls, boys will inevitably lose. These constructions are dangerously narrow and limit boys as well as girls. Gender equity is about enriching classrooms, widening opportunities, and expanding choices for all students.

The notion that helping girls means hurting boys amounts to a defense of a status quo that we all know is serving too few of our students well. Surely it is as important for boys to learn about the contributions of women to our nation as it is for girls to study this information. Surely adolescent pregnancy and parenting are issues for young men as well as young women. And surely boys as well as girls benefit from instructional techniques that encourage cooperation in learning.

A second set of assumptions concerns the single-sex versus coed dichotomy. During discussions of gender equity, rarely does anyone stop to consider that coeducation, as the term is generally used, implies more than merely attending the same institution. It is usually assumed to mean a balanced experience as compared to an exclusive, one-sided, single-sex, all-female or all-male one. Thus the term itself undercuts our ability to achieve genuine coeducation by implying that it already exists.

We would do better to describe U.S. public elementary and secondary education as mixed-sex education rather than as coeducation. Girls and boys are mixed together in our schools, but they are not receiving the same quality or quantity of education—nor are they genuinely learning from and about each other. Our task is to find ways to provide the gender equitable education the term coeducation promises, but does not yet deliver.

## Lessons from All-Girl Schools

It may indeed be easier in an all-girl setting both to value skills, career fields, and avocations generally considered feminine *and* to encourage girls in nontraditional pursuits. Pressures on students from peers, from popular culture, and even from many adults around them all define gender stereotypic behavior as normal, expected, and successful. Particularly for young adolescents, the clarity of these stereotypes can be reassuring; questioning them can be uncomfortable and risky. In a world where being labeled a "girl" is the classic insult for boys, single-sex environments for girls can provide a refuge from put-downs and stereotypes.

But these environments may also send messages that can perpetuate rather than eliminate negative gender stereotyping. Removing girls from classes in order to provide better learning opportunities for them can imply that girls and boys are so different that they must be taught in radically different ways. When all-girl classes are set up specifically in science or math, an underlying, if unintended, message can be that girls are less capable in these subjects. Separating boys from girls in order to better control boys' behavior can indicate that boys are "too wild" to control.

Rather than assuming that we must isolate girls in order to protect them from boys' boisterous, competitive behavior—or that boys will be unduly feminized in settings where girls are valued and comfortable—we must look carefully at why some students and teachers prefer single-sex settings for girls. We must understand the positive aspects of these classrooms in order to begin the difficult task of bringing these positive factors into mixed-sex classes.

In U.S. public schools, this is not only a matter of good sense, but it is a matter of law. Title IX permits single-sex instruction only in very specific situations.[1] In doing so, we will be moving toward genuinely coeducational environments where the achievements, perspectives, and experiences of both girls and boys, women and men, are equally recognized and rewarded whether or not they fall into traditional categories.

## How to Eliminate Barriers

As long as the measures and models of success presented to students follow traditional gender stereotypes and remain grounded in a hierarchy that says paid work is always and absolutely more important and rewarding than unpaid work, that the higher the pay the more valuable the work *and* the worker who does it, we will be unfairly limiting the development of, and the opportunities available to, all our students. Gender equitable education is about eliminating the barriers and stereotypes that limit the options of *both* sexes. To move in this direction, we need to take three major steps.

1. *We must acknowledge the gendered nature of schooling.* Schools are a part of society. Educators cannot single-handedly change the

value structure we ourselves embody, but we can acknowledge and begin to question the ways in which gender influences our schooling. *How Schools Shortchange Girls* points out that the emotions and the power dynamics of sex, race, and social class are all present, but evaded, aspects of our classrooms. We can begin to change this by fostering classroom discussions that explicitly include these issues and that value expressions of feelings as well as recitations of facts.

2. *We must take a careful look at our own practices.* Years ago as a first-year teacher, I was proud of my sensitivity to the needs of my 6th graders. I carefully provided opportunities for boys to take part in class discussions and lead group projects in order to channel their energies in positive ways. I was equally careful to ensure that two very shy, soft-spoken girls never had to be embarrassed by giving book reports in front of the class.

   Only much later did I realize that rather than helping the boys learn cooperative skills, I may merely have reinforced their sense that boys act while girls observe, and that I may have protected the girls from exactly the experiences they needed in order to overcome their initial uncertainties. Further, in protecting the girls, I also deprived the boys of opportunities to learn that both girls and boys can take the risks and garner the rewards of speaking up in class and speaking out on issues.

   One technique that teachers can use to gain a picture of their classes is to develop class projects in which students serve as data collectors. Students are keen observers of the world around them. Having them keep a record of who is taking part in class can serve as a springboard for important discussions. These discussions can raise everyone's awareness of classroom dynamics, dynamics sometimes so ingrained that they have become invisible.

3. *We must learn from all-girl environments about teaching techniques and curricular perspectives that have particular appeal to girls and determine*

*how to use these approaches successfully in mixed-sex classes.* In talking with teachers working in all-girl environments, I hear three frequent suggestions: 1) place less emphasis on competition and speed and more emphasis on working together to ensure that everyone completes and understands the problem or project; 2) place more emphasis on curricular materials that feature girls and women; and 3) increase the focus on practical, real-life applications of mathematics and the sciences.

## Three Practical Suggestions

Teachers can apply these three suggestions in mixed-sex settings. The first is the most difficult. What appears to happen naturally in all-girl settings—for example, girls' working together in an environment where they feel empowered to set the pace—must be deliberately fostered in settings where a different style has been the norm. Girls and their teachers speak of all-girl classes as places where fewer students shout out answers and interrupt one another. Teachers indicate that they deliberately work to ensure that all girls take some active part in class activities. If teachers can directly address these factors in an all-girl setting, surely we can begin to address them in mixed-sex settings.

Further, teachers must experiment with instructions and with reward systems that will encourage students to value a thorough understanding of a task as well as a quick answer, and of group success as well as individual performance. In doing so, we will be encouraging strengths many girls have developed and helping boys acquire skills that they need.

The second suggestion is also not without difficulties when transported to mixed-sex settings. As television producers have discovered, girls may watch programs with male characters, but programs featuring girls are less likely to attract or hold boys' interests. But schools are places where students come to learn. Boys *and* girls need to learn to appreciate and value the accomplishments of women and women's groups who have succeeded in traditionally male fields: Shirley Chisholm, Indira Gandhi, Sally Ride, the Women's Campaign Fund, as well as those whose success has been in traditionally female areas of employment and avocation: Jane Addams, Mary McLeod Bethune, the Visiting Nurses Association.

In *Natural Allies, Women's Associations in American History*, Anne Firor Scott notes that "by the 1930s the landscape was covered with libraries, schools, colleges, kindergartens, museums, health clinics, houses of refuge, school lunch programs, parks, playgrounds, all of which owed their existence to one or several women's societies" (1991, p. 3). Our students—male and female—need to learn more of this work if they are to grow into adults who can carry on activities vital to our survival as a viable, humane society.

The third factor is perhaps the least problematic. Although girls may be most enthusiastic about pursuing science when they see it as relevant to daily life, boys will surely not be less interested when presented with more relevance! For teachers to develop new lesson plans and materials in the sciences, however, will require increased support from school administrators and school boards for professional development, new materials and equipment, and perhaps a reorganization of class time.

Operation Smart, an after-school informal science program for girls developed by Girls, Inc., is just one example of new relevant science programs. A unit on water pollution, for example, offers middle school and junior high school girls an opportunity to study the effects of pollution in their own communities and to gain an understanding of the value of scientific knowledge and procedures in improving living conditions (Palmer 1994).

Mixed-sex classes can easily adapt such projects, and many have. Last year my nieces, both middle school students in mixed-sex classes in Mystic, Connecticut, eagerly showed me their science projects. Sarah's, done with her close friend Caitlin, contained several different pieces of cloth, each of which had been put through a series of trials: burned, washed, stretched, and frozen. "We thought the synthetic pieces of cloth would be stronger, but they weren't! Now we know natural material is very tough."

Aidan, a year older, collected samples of river water at points varying in distance from the mouth of the Mystic River where it joins the salt water of Fisher's Island Sound. Expecting that the water would be less salty the farther away it was from the Sound, she was surprised to find that her graph was not a straight line: a very salty sample appeared at a point quite far upriver. Trying to figure out what might account for this became the most interesting aspect of the project. For both Sarah and Aidan, science is about their own questions, not out of a book or in a laboratory and it is certainly not a boys-only activity!

## Moving Beyond Stereotypes

As we move into a new century, we must leave behind our boys-only and girls-only assumptions and stereotypes. On any given measure of achievement or skill, we can find greater similarity between the average score of girls as a group and the average score of boys as a group than we can find when comparing among individual girls or among individual boys. We must no longer allow stereotypic assumptions to guide our expectations or obscure the reality that empathy, cooperation, and competition are all important skills—and are important for all our students.

## NOTE

1. Under Title IX, portions of elementary and secondary school classes dealing with human sexuality and instruction in sports that involve bodily contact may, but do not have to be, separated by sex. (Title IX Rules and Regulations of the Educational Amendments of 1972, section 86.34)

## REFERENCES

Orenstein, P. (1994). *SchoolGirls: Young Women, Self-Esteem, and the Confidence Gap.* New York: Doubleday.

Palmer, L. (1994). *The World of Water: Environmental Science for Teens.* New York: Girls Incorporated.

Sadker, D., and M. Sadker, (1994). *Failing at Fairness: How America's Schools Cheat Girls.* New York: C. Scribner's Sons.

Scott, A. F. (1991). *Natural Allies: Women's Associations in American History.* Urbana, Ill.: University of Illinois Press.

Stein, N., N. Marshall, and L. Tropp. (1993). *Secrets in Public: Sexual Harassment in Our Schools.* Wellesley, Mass.: The Wellesley College Center for Research on Women.

Thorne, B. (1993). *Gender Play: Girls and Boys in School.* New Brunswick, N.J.: Rutgers University Press.

Wellesley College Center for Research on Women. (1992). *The AAUW Report: How Schools Shortchange Girls.* Washington, D.C.: American Association of University Women Educational Foundation; reprint ed., (1995). New York: Marlowe and Company.

## POSTNOTE

Susan Bailey has been one of the national leaders for gender equity in education, making her article one of our Classic selections. This article raises a number of hotly debated issues. Many educators agree with Bailey's contention that certain practical steps can and should be taken to increase gender equity in our schools. Other scholars, though, have sharply criticized the body of research on which these arguments rest, debating both the methodologies and the conclusions. Indeed, some studies claim that boys, who have much higher dropout rates and significantly poorer achievement scores than girls, are the ones being shortchanged by our schools.

Bailey's reference to findings from single-sex schools that can be applied to mixed-sex schools raises yet another issue. Research on single-sex schools by Anthony Bryk and his colleagues demonstrates rather conclusively that girls flourish more academically in a girls-only setting. Why, then, is there not more interest in expanding single-sex education, particularly during the tumultuous preadolescent and adolescent years? From a historical perspective, coeducation or mixed-sex education is an innovation. If we are unhappy with the performance of girls and/or boys in our mixed-sex system, should we consider abandoning this innovation?

## DISCUSSION QUESTIONS

1. What suggestions from single-sex schools does Bailey want to apply to mixed-sex schools?

2. What are your views on the value of single-sex education in middle schools and high schools?

3. Which group, girls or boys, do you believe is shortchanged the most in schools today?

## 72

# *Clearing the Hurdles of Inclusion*

### Sandy Merritt

Many general education teachers are frightened by the prospect of including students with disabilities in the general classroom because they have no formal training in dealing with the challenges that these students face. Yes, inclusion can be a frightening endeavor. Nevertheless, for me, a 1st grade teacher of 29 years, inclusion has provided some of the best experiences of my career.

## What Inclusion Is—and Isn't

Underlying inclusion is the premise that students should be educated with their peers in the least-restrictive environment for as much of the day as possible. In many cases, this environment is the general education classroom for at least part of the day. The intent, however, is not to drop the student in general education without providing needed support. The individualized education program (IEP) should note and make available everything the student needs to make this placement successful—including support, services, and the time recommended for each support and service. For example, a student may require the aid of a teaching assistant in the classroom for at least part of the day.

**TERMS TO NOTE**
Inclusion
Least restrictive environment (LRE)
Individualized education program (IEP)

Sandy Merritt is a first grade/Reading Recovery teacher at Center Point–Urbana Elementary School, Center Point, IA 52213. She also facilitates the inclusion resource team at Grant Wood Area Education Agency, Cedar Rapids, IA. From Sandy Merritt, "Clearing the Hurdles of Inclusion," *Educational Leadership*, November 2001, pp. 67–70. Reprinted with permission of the Association for Supervision and Curriculum Development. Copyright © 2001 by ASCD. All rights reserved.

Inclusion does not mean that the student cannot be taken from the room for instruction if the IEP team deems it necessary. If it is not in the best interest of all students in the classroom for the special education student to remain there, the team can and should make changes in the student's placement. There is not one recipe for the inclusion of special education students. Because inclusion is individualized, it will look different for every student.

## A Step Toward Inclusion

Neither my undergraduate training nor my staff development courses prepared me for teaching in an inclusive classroom. My life changed five years ago when my principal attended one of our 1st grade team meetings to tell us about two girls who were fully included in one of our kindergarten classrooms; she told us that she hoped to fully include them into 1st grade the following year. She then asked for a volunteer to work with the students.

After volunteering, I spent the rest of that year and summer attending workshops, reading, meeting the girls' parents, sitting in on weekly kindergarten team meetings, and visiting the students in their classroom so that I could get to know them. Because one of the girls used a wheelchair, the IEP team and I also looked at my classroom to see which adaptations we would need to make for her. In addition, a full-time teacher associate was assigned to my room to help.

**TERM TO NOTE**
Adaptation

## The First Year

By the start of the next school year I had begun to wonder what I had gotten myself into. I was convinced that I didn't know enough. What would I do if faced with a problem? How could I possibly teach these students how to read? What if I couldn't even communicate with them?

## Kim

Kim[1] had multiple disabilities resulting from low muscle tone. She could use her hands, but small motor activities were difficult for her. She often used a wheelchair, although she also got around well by crawling. In fact, the IEP team and I had already decided that we would leave her wheelchair in the hall and allow her to crawl around the classroom. She came to the classroom that year able to make about seven utterances that represented words. She could not use sign language effectively because of poor hand control; however, she was able to point and had her own versions of some signs to communicate her needs. Her academic performance was well below grade level, but it was difficult to determine how much she really understood because she could not communicate her cognitive abilities easily.

From the first day of school, I saw how determined and stubborn Kim was and how much she desired to learn and to be like everyone else. She had a bench that was easier for her to climb on and that provided more stability than a chair. She didn't want to sit on the bench, however, and, when given the choice, would choose a chair like those her classmates used. Her occupational therapist and I decided to provide her with an adapted classroom chair; she sat in it happily for the rest of the year, and we removed the bench from the classroom.

It took me a month to understand some of her signs. It was frustrating for both of us when Kim pointed and squealed to request something, and I had no idea what she was trying to convey. I felt helpless, but she never gave up on me. Fortunately, her teacher associate, who had been with her for two years, also helped me understand her.

[1]All names have been changed.

Kim put me in my place several times throughout our year together. For example, I falsely assumed early in the year that Kim would not be able to complete an alphabet recognition assessment with the other children. In fact, I was wrong about her abilities. I learned that Kim was as capable of learning as my other students and that I could demonstrate my respect by holding higher expectations for her. I decided that her curriculum ought to look like that of any other 1st grader until it became clear that she required a particular adaptation.

As the year progressed, Kim began to read emergent-level books and expanded her vocabulary to include a few more words. She even learned to form short sentences. Every day we read an ABC book together containing words that she could articulate. One day while reading, she pointed to the word *baby*—a word she knew well—but repeatedly said the word *Deon* instead. I discovered that she had just learned how to say her brother's name the night before and wanted to share the new word with me— and I was deeply touched.

I longed for Kim to succeed in writing as well as speaking. We struggled together, but writing with a pencil continued to be difficult for her. It was painful to concede defeat and admit that she was not going to be able to use a pencil to write. Eventually, we accepted the setback and turned our attention to the keyboard instead. With time, Kim successfully used the computer for writing activities.

## Sara

Sara had fetal alcohol syndrome. She had a short attention span and found it difficult to remember information. She needed adult help to remain focused and to accomplish a task. In addition, she perseverated—that is, she repeated what others said and did (picking up inappropriate words from other children on the playground and repeating them endlessly in the classroom, for example) and didn't understand

**TERM TO NOTE**
Fetal alcohol syndrome

that sometimes her speech and behavior were inappropriate. Nevertheless, she was able to care for herself most of the time without assistance.

Sara was a happy child who usually got along with others, yet often got lost in the crowd. She rarely spoke unless I initiated a conversation, and even then her responses were brief. She was content to exist on the periphery of the class, quietly observing, for about the first month of school. She was afraid to walk down the hall by herself and always took my hand as I walked her to the outside door. She relied on a classroom friend to walk with her to recess. Gradually, she overcame that fear and one day took off down the hall by herself with a great big smile.

Sara's academic performance was well below grade level; her cognitive development was delayed by two to three years. Although she loved to be read to, Sara had difficulty reading. She struggled to remember vocabulary words from day to day. I could see the frustration in her eyes when she couldn't recall a word that she had known the day before. She would make progress for a while and then plateau for a week or more. She required much reinforcement and review. We had to spend several days on each book, but she too learned to read emergent-level books by the end of the year.

Her writing skills also took some time to develop. She progressed slowly from filling a page with straight lines to eventually writing a few readable sentences. I will always remember the day that I helped Sara write her first "book." Yes, it was simple—one sentence to a page and only four pages long—but the words flowed from page to page. She was thrilled to be able to read her "book" to several other teachers.

Sara's and Kim's classmates accepted and supported them. The other students included the girls in everything we did. It was heartwarming to see the students respond to the girls' individual needs. Someone would hold a chair steady so that Kim could get on it. When they worked in small groups, teammates managed to find suitable jobs for Kim and Sara. The girls weren't the only ones who benefited from their inclusion in the classroom; the other students in my classroom that year learned acceptance, tolerance, and the meaning of community. I learned that I didn't have to shoulder the whole responsibility for the girls' inclusion experience because a team of professionals stood ready and eager to assist me. I met with that team weekly to discuss problems, plan accommodations, and celebrate successes. I also learned that checking for understanding helps all students; that accommodations made for one child can benefit others as well; that the little victories count; and that every student deserves the chance to be in a general education classroom for at least part of the day.

## The Second Year

As my first year of inclusion drew to a close, I went to my principal and volunteered to work with special education students the following year. Once again, a special education student was placed in my room.

### Rob

Rob had been diagnosed with Pervasive Developmental Delay (PDD), a high-functioning level of autism. PDD presented me with a new set of symptoms to learn about and new challenges to work through. A teacher associate came to the room to work with him for two hours a day, and we focused on tempering Rob's need for routine and helping him develop social skills. Rob's need for routine frightened me because no two days are ever exactly alike in a developmentally appropriate primary classroom like mine. Initially, I made a pictorial schedule for Rob, and that was enough for him on most days. He often feared new people, objects, and experiences, so I had to introduce them carefully. Once I understood his anxiety, I tried to prepare him for novelty as much as possible. For example, we found that breaking a new task into smaller parts made it easier for Rob to accept it and feel successful.

**TERM TO NOTE**

Autism

Rob would often refuse to try new or difficult tasks. For example, one day we were reading a story; Rob was reading well until he came to a page full of text. He stopped and said that he couldn't go on. I agreed to read part of the section if he would read part of it. He tried the next page by himself, and when he finished the story, he turned to me with a big smile on his face and said, "I am a really good reader, aren't I?"

Rob had difficulty interacting positively with peers. He had a hard time sharing and playing fairly; he would often get mad and stomp off, shout at other students, or hit them. With time, training, and practice using appropriate social behaviors, Rob made tremendous improvements and learned to control his temper most of the time. He sought friendships. It was rewarding for me to see him go to recess arm in arm with a classmate, something that probably would not have happened in a pullout program. His parents were proud and amazed; they had not dreamed he could accomplish as much as he did.

## Suggestions for Successful Inclusion

My own experience has taught me that even a teacher with no special education experience can make inclusion work. There are no magic formulas for success—simply using good teacher sense is the best advice that I can offer. I approach all my students with the same high expectations, believing that just because a student has an individualized education program does not mean that he or she cannot learn. Following are suggestions for teachers faced with an inclusive classroom environment.

### The Planning Stage

▶ Meet the student and his or her family and learn about his or her disabilities as early as possible.

▶ Attend team meetings regarding the student before the placement to gain insight into the student's abilities and the accommodations that need to be made.

▶ Attend individualized education program meetings.

▶ Resolve physical accessibility problems during the summer.

▶ Schedule a meeting at the end of the preceding year with the classroom and special education teachers to discuss the student's progress.

### The Implementation Stage

▶ Discover and emphasize what the student can do.

▶ Be patient and take time to build a trusting relationship with the student.

▶ Rely on your instincts as a professional educator to make curriculum decisions that concern the student.

▶ Accept that you will make mistakes. We all make them, and we can learn from them.

▶ Begin early to build a classroom community. Treat every student as a worthy member of that community.

▶ Involve parents in the student's education; update them regularly on the student's progress. Listen to their hopes and dreams for the student, which are primarily that their child will fit in and make friends.

▶ Schedule regular team meetings for all those who work with the student.

▶ Start with the least-restrictive classroom environment possible and make accommodations as needs arise.

▶ Give the student the same opportunities that other students have. He or she should get to be the special helper, reader or author of the day, and so on. Make accommodations when necessary to include the student and make him or her feel special.

▶ Treat the student fairly, but avoid favoritism. In most cases, the student's disability does not warrant special treatment. For example, he or she should have to take turns just as everyone else does.

▶ Be involved in the individualized education program development process because the program mandates the level of support that the student receives; teacher input is crucial.

## Lessons Learned

When inclusion comes your way, you have two options: You can complain and convince yourself that you will have a bad year, or you can embrace inclusion and learn something new. After four terrific years of teaching in an inclusive environment, I feel confident that I am a better teacher now.

## POSTNOTE

This first-grade teacher's experiences with inclusion provide us with many insights. Ms. Merritt reveals how her preconceived notions of what particular children with disabilities were capable of achieving were dramatically altered. She also reveals how other students accepted and supported those with disabilities. The teacher plays a critical role in achieving this acceptance by the way she communicates expectations and provides opportunities for special education students to be integrated into classroom activities. The attitude with which a teacher approaches inclusion plays a huge part in whether or not the special education students, the teacher, and the other students succeed in having a productive, engaging class.

## DISCUSSION QUESTIONS

1. Have you had any experiences working with children with disabilities? If so, describe the circumstances and your successes/failures. If you haven't worked with children with disabilities, are you planning on getting this experience? If so, how?

2. How do you feel about collaborative teaching with a special education teacher? (If you are a special education teacher, how do you feel about collaborative teaching with a regular education teacher?) What concerns, if any, do you have about the experience?

3. Which of the three children (Kim, Sara, Rob) described in the article do you think would have presented you with the greatest challenge? Why?

## 73

# "Our School Doesn't Offer Inclusion" and Other Legal Blunders

Paula Kluth, Richard A. Villa, and Jacqueline S. Thousand

I n 1975, Congress passed the Education for All Handicapped Children Act (Public Law 94-142), guaranteeing for the first time that all students with disabilities would receive a public education. The law, whose name changed in subsequent reauthorizations in 1990 and 1997 to the Individuals with Disabilities Education Act (Public Law 101-476; Public Law 105-17), set the stage for inclusive schooling, ruling that every child is eligible to receive a free and appropriate public education and to learn in the least restrictive environment possible. Specifically, the law ensures

**TERMS TO NOTE**
Education for All Handicapped Children Act (PL94-142)

Individuals with Disabilities Education Act (IDEA)

Least restrictive environment

Inclusion

> that to the maximum extent appropriate, children with disabilities, including children in public or private institutions and other care facilities, are educated with children who are not disabled. (Individuals with Disabilities Education Act, 20 U.S.C. § 1412 [a][5])

In 1994, the U.S. Department of Education's Office of Special Education Programs issued policy guidelines stating that school districts cannot use the lack of adequate personnel or resources as

Paula Kluth is an assistant professor in the Department of Teaching and Leadership, Syracuse University, Syracuse, NY. Richard A. Villa is president, Bayridge Consortium, San Marcos, CA. Jacqueline S. Thousand is a professor in the College of Education, California State University–San Marcos. From Paula Kluth, Richard A. Villa, and Jacqueline S. Thousand, "Our School Doesn't Offer Inclusion and Other Legal Blunders," *Educational Leadership*, December 2001/January 2002, pp. 24–27.

an excuse for failing to make a free and appropriate education available, in the least restrictive environment, to students with disabilities.

Schools have taken much time to implement the law. Although many schools and districts have been educating students with disabilities in inclusive settings for years, families often still have to fight to get their children into general education classrooms and inclusive environments.

An analysis of U.S. Department of Education reports found that in the dozen years between 1977 and 1990, placements of students with disabilities changed little. By 1990, for example, only 1.2 percent more students with disabilities were in general education classes and resource room environments: 69.2 percent in 1990 compared with 68 percent in 1977. Placements of students with disabilities in separate classes declined by only 0.5 percent: 24.8 percent in 1990 compared with 25.3 percent in 1977. And, students with disabilities educated in separate public schools or other separate facilities declined by only 1.3 percent: 5.4 percent of students with disabilities in 1990 compared with 6.7 percent of students with disabilities in 1977 (Karagiannis, Stainback, & Stainback, 1996).

More recently, the National Council on Disability (2000) released similar findings. Investigators discovered that every state was out of compliance with the requirements of the Individuals with Disabilities Education Act and that U.S. officials are not enforcing compliance. Even today, schools sometimes place a student in a self-contained classroom as soon as they see that the student is labeled as having a disability. Some students enter self-contained classrooms as soon as they begin kindergarten and never have an opportunity to experience regular education. When families of students with disabilities move to a different district, the new school sometimes moves the student out of general education environments and into segregated classrooms.

In some cases, districts may be moving slowly toward inclusive education, trying to make a smooth transition by gradually introducing teachers and students to change—but moving slowly cannot be an excuse for stalling when a learner with a disability comes to school requiring an inclusive placement.

Clearly, more than 25 years after the law came into effect, many educators and administrators still do not understand the law or how to implement it. Three common misunderstandings still determine decisions about students with disabilities in U.S. schools.

### "Our School Doesn't Offer Inclusion"

We often hear teachers and families talking about inclusion as if it were a policy that schools can choose to adopt or reject. For example, we recently met a teacher who told us that her school "did inclusion, but it didn't work," so the school "went back to the old way." Similarly, a parent explained that she wanted her child to have an inclusive education, but her neighborhood school doesn't "have inclusion."

Special education is not a program or a place, and inclusive schooling is not a policy that schools can dismiss outright. Since 1975, federal courts have clarified the intent of the law in favor of the inclusion of students with disabilities in general education (Osborne, 1996; Villa & Thousand, 2000a, 2000b). A student with a disability should be educated in the school he or she would attend if not identified as having a disability. The school must devise an individualized education program that provides the learner with the supports and services that the student needs to receive an education in the least restrictive environment possible.

**TERM TO NOTE**
Individualized education program (IEP)

The standard for denying a student access to inclusion is high. The law clearly states that students with disabilities may be removed from the regular education environment only

> when the nature or severity of the disability is such that education in regular classes with the use of supplementary aids and services cannot be achieved satisfactorily. (Individuals with Disabilities Education Act, 20 U.S.C. § 1412 [a][5])

If schools can successfully educate a student with disabilities in general education settings with peers who do not have disabilities, then the student's school must provide that experience.

### "She Is Too Disabled to Be Educated in a Regular Classroom"

A special education teacher recently told us that she was interested in inclusive schooling and that she decided to "try" it with one of her students. Patricia, a young student with Down's syndrome, began 1st grade in September, but the school moved her back to a special education classroom by November. The teacher told us how difficult the decision had been and explained why educators had changed Patricia's placement: "The kids really liked her and she loved 1st grade, but she just wasn't catching on with the reading. She couldn't keep up with the other kids."

Many families and teachers have the common misperception that students with disabilities cannot receive an inclusive education because their skills are not "close" enough to those of students without disabilities. Students with disabilities, however, do not need to keep up with students without disabilities to be educated in inclusive classrooms; they do not need to engage in the curriculum in the same way that students without disabilities do; and they do not need to practice the same skills that students without disabilities practice. Learners need not fulfill any prerequisites to participate in inclusive education.

For instance, a middle-school social studies class is involved in a lesson on the U.S. Constitution. During the unit, the class writes its own constitution and bill of rights and reenacts the Constitutional Convention. Malcolm, a student with significant disabilities, participates in all these activities even though he cannot speak and is just beginning to read. During the lesson, Malcolm works with a peer and a speech and language therapist to contribute one line to the class bill of rights; the pair uses Malcolm's augmentative communication device to write the sentence. Malcolm also participates in the dramatic interpretation of the Constitutional Convention. At the Convention, students acting as different Convention participants drift around the classroom introducing themselves to others. Because he cannot speak, Malcolm—acting as George Mason—shares a little bit about himself by handing out his "business card" to other members of the delegation. Other students are expected to submit three-page reports at the end of the unit, but Malcolm will submit a shorter report, a few sentences, which he will write using his communication device. His teacher will assess Malcolm's grade on the basis of his report and participation in the class activities, his demonstration of new skills related to programming his communication device, and his social interactions with others during the Constitutional Convention exercise.

The Constitutional Convention example illustrates how students with disabilities can participate in general education without engaging in the same ways or having the same skills and abilities that others in the class may have. In addition, this example highlights ways in which students with disabilities can work on individual skills and goals within the context of general education lessons. Most important, his teachers designed and put in place the supports and adaptations that Malcolm needed for success. Malcolm did not have to display all the skills and abilities of other students to participate. Instead,

Malcolm's teachers created a context in which Malcolm could demonstrate competence.

For Malcolm to be successful in his classroom, his teachers need to provide him with a range of "supplemental supports, aids, and services," one of the law's requirements (Individuals with Disabilities Education Act, 20 U.S.C. § 1412 [a][5]). Supports, aids, and services might include a piece of assistive technology, use of an education consultant, instruction from a therapist, support from a paraprofessional, peer tutors, different seating or environmental supports, modified assignments, adapted materials (such as large-print books, graphic organizers, or color-coded assignment books), curriculum that is differentiated to meet the needs of the learner, time for teachers' collaborative planning, coteaching, training for school personnel, or any number of other strategies, methods, and approaches. Schools do not need to provide every support available, but they must provide those required by the student with disabilities.

> **TERMS TO NOTE**
>
> Assistive technology
> Paraprofessional
> Coteaching

Families do not have to prove to the school that a student with disabilities can function in the general classroom. In *Oberti v. Board of Education of the Borough of Clementon School District* (1993), for example, a U.S. circuit court determined that the neighborhood school of Raphael Oberti, a student with Down's syndrome, had not supplied him with the supports and resources he needed to be successful in an inclusive classroom. The judge also ruled that the school had failed to provide appropriate training for his educators and support staff. The court placed the burden of proof for compliance with the law's inclusion requirements squarely on the school district and the state instead of on the family. In other words, the school had to show why this student *could not* be educated in general education with aids and services, and his family did not have to prove why he *could.* The federal judge who decided the case stated, "Inclusion is a right, not a special privilege for a select few."

## "We Offer Special Programs Instead of Inclusion"

A few years ago, one of us went to a neighborhood school to vote. To get to the ballot machines, voters had to walk down a long hallway to a classroom marked *Autistic Center*. Knowing that the district had been providing inclusive education to many students with disabilities, we were surprised to learn that although students with mild disabilities were in general education classrooms, others were still in "special programs." The teacher in the Autistic Center was responsible for educating all the district's students who were diagnosed with autism—eight learners, ages 6 to 14.

Across the United States, many school districts still operate programs for discrete groups of students. Separate programs and classrooms exist for students identified with certain labels—emotional disabilities, for example—and for students with perceived levels of need, such as severe or profound disabilities. In many cases, students enter these self-contained settings without an opportunity to receive an education in a general classroom with the appropriate aids and services.

In 1983, the *Roncker v. Walter* case challenged the assignment of students to disability-specific programs and schools. The ruling favored inclusive, not segregated, placement and established a *principle of portability*. The judge in the case stated,

> It is not enough for a district to simply claim that a segregated program is superior. In a case where the segregated facility is considered superior, the court should determine whether the services which make the placement superior could be feasibly provided in a nonsegregated setting (i.e., regular class). If they can, the placement in the segregated school would be inappropriate under the act (IDEA). (*Roncker v. Walter*, 1983, at 1063)

The *Roncker* court found that placement decisions must be determined on an individual basis. School districts that automatically place students in a predetermined type of school solely on the basis of their disability or perceived level of functioning rather than on the basis of their education needs clearly violate federal laws.

## Benefits of Understanding the Law

Implementation of the law is still in its infancy, and educators are still learning about how the law affects students in their classrooms. Reviewing the intent and language of the Individuals with Disabilities Education Act will help administrators shape districtwide or school-based policies and procedures; evaluate the ways in which programs are labeled and implemented; and make more informed decisions about student assessment, placement, and service delivery. Administrators should also consider the following questions:

▶ Are all students in the least restrictive environment?

▶ Are we providing students with disabilities with the necessary supplemental supports, aids, and services?

▶ Do teachers and administrators understand their responsibilities under the Individuals with Disabilities Education Act?

▶ Do teachers and administrators talk about inclusive education as if it were a choice that can be made by a school or by a teacher?

▶ Do school personnel require additional training?

School district leaders and school principals who understand the federal law can avoid lawsuits, enhance education experiences for students with and without disabilities, and move toward the development of school communities that are egalitarian, just, and democratic for all.

## REFERENCES

Education for All Handicapped Children Act of 1975, Public Law 94–142 (1975).

Individuals with Disabilities Education Act, 20 U.S.C. § 1400 *et seq.* (1997).

Karagiannis, A., Stainback, S., & Stainback, W. (1996). Historical overview of inclusion. In S. Stainback & W. Stainback (Eds.), *Inclusion: A guide for educators* (pp. 17–28). Baltimore: Brookes.

National Council on Disability. (2000, January 25). *Back to school on civil rights.* (NCD #00-283). Washington, DC: Author.

*Oberti v. Board of Education of the Borough of Clementon School District,* 995 F.2d 1204 (3rd Cir. 1993).

Osborne, A. G. (1996). *Legal issues in special education.* Needham Heights, MA: Allyn & Bacon.

*Roncker v. Walter,* 700 F.2d 1058 (6th Cir. 1983), *cert. denied,* 464 U.S. 864 (1983).

Villa, R., & Thousand, J. (Eds.). (2000a). *Restructuring for caring and effective education.* Baltimore: Brookes.

Villa, R. & Thousand, J. (2000b). Setting the context: History of and rationales for inclusive schooling. In R. Villa & J. Thousand (Eds.), *Restructuring for caring and effective education: Piecing the puzzle together* (pp. 7–37). Baltimore: Brookes.

## POSTNOTE

Working successfully with children with disabilities is one of the most challenging tasks facing beginning teachers. About 5.7 million students, 13 percent of the total public school population, receive federal aid for their disabilities, so it is likely that you will have students with disabilities in your classroom. It is important that you approach instruction for these children as you would for other students: expect diversity, expect a range of abilities, and look for the particular strengths and learning profiles of each student. If you are a regular education teacher, work with the special education teachers in your school to coordinate instruction and services for your students with disabilities. If you are a special education teacher, you will be expected to work closely with regular education teachers to provide the least restrictive environment for these children and the best instruction possible. Only by working closely together can regular and special education teachers ensure that "no child is left behind."

## DISCUSSION QUESTIONS

1. What concerns, if any, do you have about teaching children with disabilities? What can you do to address those concerns?

2. Is full inclusion a good idea? What limitations, if any, do you see in its implementation?

3. How would you go about ensuring that your regular education students are accepting and helpful to any students with disabilities who might be in your class?

# 74

# *The Parent Trap*

## Tom Loveless

A new kind of revolution of rising expectations is sweeping the United States. It is a revolution fomented by reformers who believe that setting higher expectations in the schools is the key to improving academic performance. There is bipartisan political enthusiasm for the creation of tough new learning standards. Just about everyone wants to end social promoting, the practice of passing a student on to the next grade regardless of whether he or she has learned anything. Reformers poke, prod, cajole, and coax schools to embrace lofty academic expectations which, they believe, schools would not adopt on their own. They are confident that such heightened expectations will yield dramatic increases in student achievement.

**TERMS TO NOTE**

Standards

Social promotion

In focusing on the schools, however, reformers are taking for granted one of the most powerful influences on the quality of American education: the American parent. They assume that parents will do whatever is necessary to raise children's levels of achievement. But will they? Do parents really consider classroom learning the most important aspect of their children's education? What are they willing to give up so that their children will learn more? Will family life change as academic achievement assumes a more prominent role in education? Will political support for reform remain firm if parents recoil from the everyday costs?

There are indications that many parents have trouble accepting the fact that improving education is not a pain-free exercise. In Virginia, when tough new statewide tests revealed earlier this year that only 6.5 percent of the schools met state standards, many parents (and others) responded with cries of anger and disbelief. Their anger was directed not at the schools but at the standards. There are other signs that parents' commitment to academic excellence is not very deep. A 1996 Gallup Poll asked: "Which one of the following would you prefer of an oldest child—that the child get A grades or that he or she make average grades and be active in extracurricular activities?" Only 33 percent of public school parents answered that they would prefer A grades, while 56 percent preferred average grades combined with extracurricular activities. (Among private school parents, the breakdown was almost the same, 34 percent to 55 percent.)

The importance of nonacademic activities in teenagers' lives is thoroughly documented in *Beyond the Classroom* (1996), a study of how American teens spend their out-of-school time, the portion of their weekly schedule that (in theory at least) parents directly control. Three nonacademic categories dominate, according to Temple University psychologist Laurence Steinberg: extracurricular activities, primarily sports, consuming 10 to 15 hours; part-time employment, 15 to 20 hours; and a host of social activities, including dating, going to the movies, partying, and just hanging out with friends, 20 to 25 hours. The national average for time spent on homework is four hours per week, not surprising given the few waking hours that remain after the whirlwind of nonacademic pursuits.

This distribution of teens' time represents a huge drag on academic learning. More than

Tom Loveless is a senior fellow in the Governance Studies Program and director of the Brown Center on Education Policy at the Brookings Institution in Washington, DC. From Tom Loveless, "The Parent Trap," *The Wilson Quarterly*, Autumn 1999. Reprinted with permission of Tom Loveless.

one-third of the teens with part-time jobs told Steinberg they take easier classes to keep up their grades. Nearly 40 percent of students who participate in school-sponsored activities, usually sports, reported that they are frequently too tired to study. More than one-third of students said they get through the school day by "goofing off with friends," and an equal number reported spending five or more hours a week "partying." And these self-reports probably underestimate the problem.

The big story here is that teenagers' time is structured around the pursuit of a "well-rounded" life. American families might value academic achievement, but not if it intrudes on the rituals of teen existence, especially part-time employment, sports, and a busy social calendar. This stands in stark contrast to the situation in other nations. In Europe and most Asian countries, it is assumed that the central purpose of childhood is to learn. Part-time employment of teenagers is rare, sports are noticeably subordinate to a student's academic responsibilities, and although there is plenty of socializing, it is usually in conjunction with studying or working with others on academic projects. The American student's four hours per week of homework is equal to what students in the rest of the industrialized world complete every day.

Significant cultural differences also appear in how parents judge their children's academic performance. A study by James Stigler of the University of California, Los Angeles, and Harold Stevenson of the University of Michigan, Ann Arbor, asked several hundred mothers from the United States, Japan, and China about the school performance of their fifth-grade children. More than 50 percent of the American mothers pronounced themselves very satisfied with their children's schoolwork, as opposed to only five percent of the Asian mothers. On tests measuring what these same children actually knew, however, the American students scored far below their Chinese and Japanese counterparts. When asked to explain their children's poor performance, the American mothers cited a lack of inborn ability. When the Japanese and Chinese children failed, their parents blamed the kids for not working hard enough.

American parents see academic achievement as a product of intrinsic ability rather than hard work, as just one of many attributes they want children to possess, and as something their own kids are accomplishing anyway. These beliefs, along with widespread peer pressure against academic excellence (who wants to be a "geek"?), an unrelenting strain of anti-intellectualism in American culture, and the weak academic demands of schools, combine to dampen the importance of academics for American youth and their parents.

We need not let educators off the hook, but parents bear some responsibility both for the lax standards in today's schools and for students' mediocre achievement. Parents appear more willing to embrace academic excellence in the abstract than to organize their family's daily life in order to achieve it. They enthusiastically support attempts to change schools in general but are ambivalent when it comes to schools they actually know.

Polls show that parents believe their children's schools have higher standards and are of significantly better quality than the nation's schools in general. This phenomenon—the idea that "I'm OK, but you're not"—also shows up in surveys on health care (my doctor is great, but the nation's health care stinks), Congress (my representative is terrific, but Congress is terrible), and the status of the American family (mine is in fine shape, but families in general are going to hell in a hand basket).

Such complacency undermines meaningful school reform. Raising the level of achievement is hard work. Unless children can actually learn more math, science, literature, and history without breaking a sweat, then the prospects for reforms that ask children and parents for more —more time, more homework, more effort— are not very good. We don't hear much about what today's educational reforms may require of families.

Indeed, when it comes to the subject of parents, the rhetoric seldom gets beyond calls for more "parent involvement" or for "empowering" parents. Reforms that grant parents control over where their children go to school, a favorite of the Right, or that offer parents a stake in governing local school affairs, a favorite of the Left, may prove to be valuable public policies for other reasons, but they have not yet convinced skeptics that they will significantly increase student achievement.

In Chicago, an experiment that involved creating parent-dominated school "site councils" to oversee individual schools produced a few renaissance stories, but also tales of schools engulfed in petty squabbling. As vouchers and charter schools become more widespread, will parents actually take advantage of the opportunities to improve the education of their children? Buried in the national comparisons of private and public schools is an interesting and relevant anomaly. Despite well-publicized research showing that private schools outperform public schools on achievement tests, more students transfer from private to public school than vice versa at the beginning of high school, precisely the time when one's academic accomplishments really start to matter in terms of college and employment. The desire to keep extracurricular activities close to home and to keep their children close to neighborhood kids appears to weigh heavily in parents' choices.

**TERMS TO NOTE**
Vouchers
Charter schools

Another reason to doubt that empowered parents will wholeheartedly insist on higher achievement can be found in the history of American schooling. Schools have always attended to the convenience of parents, and, as a result, cultivating the mind has simply occupied one place among many on a long list of purposes for the school. At the beginning of the 19th century, education came within the province of the family. Children learned reading at home, along with basic arithmetic and minimal geography, science, and history. Farming dictated the tempo of family life. Older students only attended school during the winter months, when their labor wasn't needed in the fields. At other times, even toddlers were sent to school, crowding classrooms with students from three to 20 years of age.

Later in the century, as fathers and mothers abandoned the farm for the factory and intermittently relocated in search of work, the modern public school began to evolve. One of its functions was custodial, providing a place for children to spend the day while busy parents earned a living. The magnitude of the change is staggering. As late as 1870, American students attended school only an average of 78 of 132 scheduled days; today's students spend more than 160 days in the classroom, and the modern school calendar runs to 180 days. More than 90 percent of school-age children now attend high school. At the beginning of the century, less than 10 percent did.

But the school's power is limited. Its monopoly over children's daylight hours never led to the recognition of intellectual activities as the most important pursuits of adolescents, either outside or inside school. Why do parents allow two-thirds of today's teenagers to work? After-school jobs are considered good for young people, teaching them a sense of responsibility and the value of a dollar. Most Americans think it's fine if teenagers spend 20 hours a week flipping hamburgers instead of studying calculus or the history of ancient Rome.

The development of young minds also finds competition in the school curriculum itself. For example, the federal government has funded vocational education since 1917. Americans have always expected schools to teach students the difference between right and wrong and the fundamental elements of citizenship. In the last three decades, schools have also taken on therapeutic tasks, spending untold time and resources on sex education, psychological counseling, drug and alcohol programs, diversity training, guidance on topics such as teen parenting, sexual harassment, and a host of other initiatives that have little to do with sharpening the intellect.

Some analysts maintain that parents don't support such diversions from academic learning, that these programs are nothing more than the faddish whims of professional educators. If so, parents have been awfully quiet about it. A more reasonable explanation is that, with parents busily working at two or more jobs, with many of these topics awkward for parents to discuss, and with parental authority showing its own signs of weakening throughout society, parents now look to schools to provide instruction that they once delivered themselves.

Schools are acting more like parents, and implementing real academic standards will probably force parents to act more like schools. They will need to stay informed about test scores and closely monitor their children's progress. Parents of students who fall short of standards must be prepared for drastic changes in family life. Summers will be for summer school, afternoons and weekends for tutoring. This will cost money and impinge upon family time. Struggling high school students will be forced to spend less time on sports, to forgo part-time jobs, and to keep socializing to a minimum.

No one knows how parents will react to such changes. Higher standards are overwhelmingly supported in public opinion polls, but what will happen when they begin to pinch? In 1997, hundreds of parents in an affluent suburb of Detroit refused to let their children take a high school proficiency test, arguing that the nine-hour exam was too long and that it would unfairly label children who performed poorly. In Portland, Oregon, the school district invited the parents of 3,500 youngsters who had failed statewide proficiency exams to send the children to a summer school session set up at great expense and amid much hoopla; only 1,359 kids were enrolled. Every state has its share of stories. The elimination of social promotion presents the biggest test. Will the parents of children who are compelled to repeat, say, third or fourth grade, continue to support high standards? Or will they dedicate themselves to the defeat and removal of standards? In districts that see huge

numbers of students facing mandatory summer school or failing to win promotion to the next grade, will parents push to water down tests and lower passing scores?

Some years ago, I came face to face with some of these implications when I taught sixth grade in a special program for exceptionally gifted, high-achieving youngsters, students approximately two years above grade level in all subjects. The curriculum was accelerated to the eighth- and ninth-grade levels, and I taught all academic subjects. Students applied for admission to the program, and my fellow teachers and I stressed that it wasn't for everyone. Parents seeking an education emphasizing creativity or the arts were advised to look elsewhere. An extremely bright student who hated doing homework would also have had a difficult time.

Getting to know the parents of my students was one of the most satisfying aspects of my job. They were actively involved in the school and indispensable to organizing field trips, raising money for computers, putting on plays, and doing anything else that enhanced their children's education. If ever a group supported lofty standards, this was it. But dealing with parents was not all sweetness and light. Grading policies drew the most complaints. One upset parent threatened a lawsuit because I gave a zero to a student who cheated on a test. During a three-hour, late-night phone call, an angry mother repeatedly told me that I would suffer eternal damnation because her son had received grades disqualifying him for admission to an honors program.

Complaints were also voiced because I didn't accept late homework—"We had friends over last night and Johnny simply didn't have time to do his history," one father explained in a note—or because I wouldn't excuse absences for family ski trips or a student's "R&AMPR day" of TV soap operas and game shows. And these complaints came despite the fact that enrollment in the program was by choice, the school's reputation for academic rigor well known, and the policies on these issues crystal clear.

Such conflicts go with the territory. Anyone who teaches—and sticks to the principles making the career a serious undertaking in the first place—will experience occasional problems with parents. The usual conflicts stem from the different yet overlapping roles that parents and teachers play in a child's life. Both are concerned with the same individual's welfare, but their roles are not interchangeable. Parents are infinitely more important to a child's upbringing, but the teacher is usually the most significant nonfamily adult presence in the child's life and, ideally, is more objective about the child's interactions with the larger world. Teachers pursue goals established by society rather than the family. They must be warm and understanding, but they must also make decisions serving the best interests of 30 or more people who have much to accomplish every day in the same small space.

The differentiation of parent and teacher roles, which strengthened schools and families in the 19th century, may be at the bottom of many parents' unrealistic perceptions of their children's school experiences. Just as reformers are probably right that the demand for high educational standards must come from outside the schools, the imposition of academic burdens on children probably must come from outside families.

There is some evidence that parents intuitively understand this. In a recent study by the Public Agenda Foundation that examined how parents view their role in education, parents said that the most significant contribution they can make is to send children to school who are respectful, hard working, and well behaved. They do not want a bigger say in how schools are run. Nor do they want to decide curricular content or methods of instruction. They trust educators who have earned their trust, and they want schools to do their job as schools so that parents can do their job as parents.

These seem like reasonable sentiments. But in the same study, parents also admit that they absolutely hate fighting kids to get them to do their homework. They gauge how things are going at school primarily by how happy their children seem and nearly 90 percent believe that as long as children try hard, they should never feel bad about themselves because of poor grades. These attitudes are potentially in conflict with more rigorous learning standards. If social promotion ends, many children will be held back in a grade despite their having tried hard. And these children will be unhappy. Other children will not get the acceptable grades they once did. A lot of people are going to be very unhappy.

Higher standards and the end of social promotion now enjoy tremendous popular support. But the true test will come when words become deeds. Until now, raising expectations in education has been portrayed as cost-free. It isn't. Schools and students and parents will bear the costs. If parents are not willing to do so, few of the ambitious changes American reformers are now so eagerly pursuing will make much difference.

## POSTNOTE

One of the verities of American education is that, in general, the intensity of parents' interest in their children's academic progress erodes from kindergarten through high school graduation. One clear indicator of this is the attendance of parents at "Back to School Night" and parents' meetings. Typically, the kindergarten and first-grade teachers encounter a full house of eager parents, anxious to hear what is in store for Jack and how Jill is doing so far. By the late years of high school, attendance drops off dramatically, since parents by then have a pretty good fix on their teenagers' academic performance, and most stay home to watch television. Except, that is, for parents who have high ambitions for their children, who sometimes can be too interested! Over the course of a P–12 education, parents seem to come to terms with their children's academic performance and capabilities and their focus shifts to their general happiness and social adjustment. As the author suggests, this makes parents an uncertain ally in serious academic reform, particularly at the high school level, where much of the reform movement is focused.

## DISCUSSION QUESTIONS

1. How would you describe your parents' level of interest in your P–12 academic performance? Were your parents typical?

2. What is the author's major point about parents and efforts to reform schools?

3. What do you believe are the consequences of the author's contention that parents have a complacent attitude toward American education?

# Glossary

**Note: Boldfaced terms that appear within definitions can be found elsewhere in the glossary.**

**Abstinence-only**  Sexual education programs that teach the benefits of abstaining from sexual activity until marriage or adulthood as the safest and most healthy alternative.

**Abstinence-plus**  Sexual education programs that emphasize delaying sexual activity, but also urge the use of condoms and other contraceptives for protected sexual activity.

**Academic freedom**  The freedom of teachers to teach about an issue or to use a source without fear of penalty, reprisal, or harassment.

**Academic learning time**  Time spent by students performing academic tasks with a high success rate.

**Academies**  A type of academic secondary school popular during the early national period, which stressed the classics as a preparation for college.

**Acceptable use policy (AUP)**  A statement of rules governing student use of school computers, especially regarding access to the Internet.

**Accountability movement**  Reform movement in the 1970s embracing the idea that schools and educators should be required to demonstrate what they are accomplishing and should be held responsible for student achievement and learning.

**Achievement gap**  Differences in educational achievement between students of different socioeconomic or racial and ethnic groups.

**Adaptation**  Changes in instruction or materials made to meet the needs of learners with disabilities.

**Aesthetic**  Appreciative of or responsive to the beautiful.

**American Federation of Teachers (AFT)**  The nation's second-largest teacher's association or union. Founded in 1916, it is affiliated with the AFL-CIO, the nation's largest union.

**Artifacts**  Products of civilization that show human workmanship or modification.

**Assessment**  The process of determining students' learning progress.

**Assimilation**  The absorption of an individual or a group into the cultural tradition of a population or another group.

**Assistive technology**  The array of devices and services that help people with disabilities to perform better in their daily lives. Such devices include motorized chairs, remote control units that turn appliances on and off, computers, and speech synthesizers.

**At risk**  A term used to describe conditions, for example, poverty, poor health, or learning disabilities, that put children in danger of not succeeding in school.

**Attendance-zoned school**  School to which children are assigned because they are of mandatory school age and live within the school's designated neighborhood boundaries.

**Autism**  A developmental disorder characterized by self-absorption, repetitive behaviors, and problems with social and language skills.

**Back-to-basics movement**  A theme in education reform during the late 1970s and early 1980s that called for more emphasis on traditional subject matter such as reading, writing, arithmetic, and history. It also included the teaching of basic morality and called for more orderly and disciplined student behavior.

**Behavioral psychology**  A branch of psychology dealing with human action that seeks generalizations of people's behavior in society.

**Behaviorism (behaviorist)**  The psychological theory that all human behavior is shaped by environmental events or conditions. Behaviorists are people who follow or practice behaviorism.

**Benefit maximization**  An ethical principle suggesting that individuals should choose the course of action that will make people generally better off.

**Bilingual education**  A variety of approaches to educating students who speak a primary language other than English.

**Block grants** Federal aid to states or localities that comes with only minimal federal restrictions on how the funds should be spent (as opposed to categorical aid, which restricts federal funds to specified uses or categories of use).

**Block scheduling** An approach to class scheduling in which students take fewer classes each school day, but spend more time in each class.

***Brown v. Board of Education of Topeka*** U.S. Supreme Court ruling in 1954 holding that segregated schools are inherently unequal.

**Buckley Amendment** An act passed by Congress in 1974, the real name of which is the Family Educational Rights and Privacy Act. It stipulates that students have the right to see the files kept on them by colleges and universities, and that parents should be allowed to see school files kept on their children.

**Busing** The controversial practice of transporting children to different schools in an attempt to achieve racial desegregation.

**CD-ROM** An acronym for Compact Disc–Read Only Memory, a type of computer disk that stores several hundreds megabytes of data and is currently used for many kinds of multimedia software.

**Carnegie Forum (on Education and the Economy)** A program of the Carnegie Corporation of New York that was created to draw attention to the link between economic growth and the skills and abilities of the people who contribute to that growth, as well as to help develop education policies to meet economic challenges. In 1986 the Forum's Task Force on Teaching as a Profession issued *A Nation Prepared: Teachers for the 21st Century*, a report that called for establishing a national board for professional teaching standards.

**Carnegie unit** A measure of clock time used to award high school credits toward graduation.

**Certification** Recognition by a profession that one of its practitioners has met certain standards. Often used as a synonym for *licensure*, which is governmental approval to perform certain work, such as teaching.

**Channel One** A controversial commercial program that delivers ten minutes of high-quality news programming directly to public school classrooms free of cost in exchange for two minutes of advertising.

**Chapter 1** *See* **Title I.**

**Character** The sum of an individual's enduring habits, which largely determines how one responds to life's challenges and events.

**Character education** Efforts by the home, the school, the religious community, and the individual student to help the student know, love, and do the good, and, in the process, to forge good qualities such as courage, respect, and responsibility.

**Charter school** School in which the educators, often joined by members of the local community, have made a special contract, or charter, with the school district. Usually the charter allows the school a great deal of independence in its operation.

**Citizenship education** A curriculum that includes teaching the basic characteristics and responsibilities of good citizenship, including neighborliness, politeness, helpfulness, and respect.

**Civil Rights Act of 1964** Established that discrimination on the basis of race, color, or national origin is illegal in any program or activity receiving federal funding.

**Class size** The number of students in a particular classroom, usually under the direction of an individual teacher.

**Classical humanism** Renaissance philosophy centered on human values and exalting humans' free will and their superiority to the rest of nature.

**Classicism** The philosophy, originally rooted in the thoughts of the Greek philosophers, that humans are neither inherently good nor bad, but in need of conscious efforts to rise above their limited natural state.

**Collective bargaining** A procedure for reaching agreements and resolving conflicts between employers and employees; in education, it covers the teacher's contract and work conditions.

**Common curriculum** A curriculum in which there is agreement about what students ought to know and be able to do and, often, about the age or grade at which they should be able to accomplish these goals.

**Common school** Public elementary schools that are open to children of all races, nationalities, and classes. During the nineteenth century, the common school became the embodiment of universal education.

**Competency-based testing** Assessment strategy aimed at gauging the acquisition of particular learnings.

**Comprehensive high school** The predominant form of secondary education in the United States in the twentieth century. It provides both a preparation for college and a vocational education for students not going to college.

**Compulsory education** The practice of requiring school attendance by law.

**Computer literacy** Basic knowledge of and skills in the use of computer technology; considered an essential element of contemporary education.

**Conant Report** A study of the American comprehensive high school written by James B. Conant, a former president of Harvard University.

**Conservation, concept of** Demonstrated through Jean Piaget's famous demonstration of pouring water from a narrow container into a wider one and then posing the question to children of various ages, "Is this more water, less water, or the same amount of water?" Used to show the importance of providing children with **developmentally appropriate** learning experiences.

**Constructivism** A theory, based on research from cognitive psychology, that people learn by constructing their own knowledge through an active learning process, rather than by simply absorbing knowledge directly from another source.

**Cooperative learning** An educational strategy, composed of a set of instructional methods, in which students work in small, mixed-ability groups to master the material and to ensure that all group members reach the learning goals.

**Core knowledge** *See* **Cultural literacy.**

**Core knowledge sequence** A curriculum based on a strong, specific elementary core of studies as a prerequisite for excellence and fairness in education; intended to be the basis for about 50 percent of a school's curriculum. The Core Knowledge Foundation is directed by E. D. Hirsch, Jr., of the University of Virginia.

**Cosmopolitan** Social values that are determined by modern voices from across the world.

**Cosmos** An orderly, harmonious universe.

**Coteaching** A situation in which two teachers, often a special education teacher and a general education teacher, teach the same class together.

**Council for Exceptional Children** A national organization of individuals concerned about the education of children with disabilities or gifts. The organization promotes research, public policies, and programs that champion the rights of exceptional individuals.

**Creative thinking skills** The set of skills involving creative processes as means of analysis and decision making.

**Criterion-referenced testing** Assessment in which an individual's performance is evaluated against a set of preestablished objectives or standards (for comparison, *see* **norm-referenced testing**).

**Critical thinking** A general instructional approach intended to help students evaluate the worth of ideas, opinions, or evidence before making a decision or judgment.

**Cultural citizenship** Citizens participating in society by bringing their cultural strengths to the national civic culture.

**Cultural literacy** Being aware of the central ideas, stories, scientific knowledge, events, and personalities of a culture; a concept that led to the **core knowledge curriculum.**

**Cultural milieu** The characteristics of a particular culture, particularly the characteristics that determine one's value or success. For instance, the self-made person is valued in a highly competitive culture such as that of the United States. The cultural milieu is strongly promulgated by the mass media.

**Cultural pluralism** An approach to the diversity of individuals that calls for understanding and appreciation of differences.

**Curriculum** All the organized and intended experiences of the student for which the school accepts responsibility.

**Curriculum standards** *See* **Standards movement.**

**Dame schools** Schools run by housewives during the early colonial period.

**Database** A software program that organizes and stores complex sets of information in the form of records that can be sorted according to different criteria.

**Decentralization** The practice of diffusing the authority and decision making of a central individual or agency and allocating these responsibilities and privileges among others. As a restructuring approach in education, decentralization is intended to achieve more responsive and flexible management and decision making; **site-based decision making** is an example.

**Desegregation** The practice of eliminating **segregation;** that is, bringing together students of different racial, ethnic, and socioeconomic levels.

**Developmentally appropriate** The term used to describe learning tasks appropriate to the child's level of intellectual development.

**Dewey, John** American philosopher, educator, and author (1859–1952) who taught that learning by doing should form the basis of educational practice.

**Didactic instruction**  A lecture approach to teaching that emphasizes compliant behavior on the part of the student while the teacher dispenses information.

**Didactic philosophy**  The view that teachers should be masters of particular subject areas and that their role is to transmit their knowledge to students. Under this philosophy, teaching methods include lectures and recitations. Students are expected to memorize facts and concepts and practice skills until mastery has been achieved. (For comparison, *see* **constructivism**.)

**Differentiation**  A variety of techniques used to adapt instruction to the individual ability levels and learning styles of each student in the classroom.

**Dimensions of learning model**  Developed by Robert Marzano, this model outlines five dimensions of **higher-order thinking skills** or learning.

**Direct instruction**  Instruction in which the teacher explains the intended purpose and presents the content in a clear, orderly way.

**Directive teaching**  Instructional method in which the teacher leads the students through the learning process rather than allowing learning to be student-led.

**Disaggregated data**  Usually statistical information which has been broken down into smaller parts.

**Distance learning**  The use of technology to link students and teachers who are separated in terms of location.

**Domain-specific knowledge**  Knowledge that is specialized to a particular subject or application.

**Due process**  The deliberative process that protects a person's constitutional right to receive fair and equal protection under the law.

**Early childhood education**  Programs that concentrate on educating young children (usually up to age eight). Early childhood education has become an important priority in helping children from disadvantaged backgrounds achieve educational parity with other children.

**Edison Project**  Experiment in entrepreneurial education begun in 1992 that seeks to establish partnerships with the public schools to create schools with a common curriculum and greater use of technology, among other characteristics. Now called the Edison Schools.

**Educable mentally retarded (EMR)**  A classification of individuals who are mentally retarded but capable of learning basic skills and information.

**Education for All Handicapped Children Act (PL94-142)**  1975 federal law that established the right of all students with disabilities to a free appropriate public education.

**Education Management Organization (EMO)**  A private company that contracts with a school district to operate one or more public schools.

**Educational Testing Service (ETS)**  A nonprofit organization, located in Princeton, New Jersey, that develops educational tests like the SAT.

**Effective schools**  Schools characterized by explicit academic goals for children, frequent evaluation of performance, maximum time on learning tasks and with a focus on order and discipline in the classroom.

**Empathy**  The capacity to participate in another's feelings or ideas.

**English as a second language (ESL)**  Method of teaching English to non-English speakers.

**Epistemic knowledge**  Representational or symbolic knowledge; the understanding that explicit concepts and domains connect or correspond. Such knowledge is demonstrated by the use of manipulatives such as blocks in teaching mathematics.

**Equal Access Act of 1984**  Statute making it unlawful for any public secondary school receiving federal funds to discriminate against any students who want to conduct a meeting on school premises during "noninstructional time" (before and after regular school hours) if other student groups (such as clubs) are allowed to use school facilities during these times.

**Equal educational opportunity**  The legal principle that all children should have equal chances to develop their abilities and aptitudes to the fullest extent regardless of family background, social class, or individual differences.

**Equal respect**  An ethical principle suggesting that our actions acknowledge the equal worth of humans (i.e., the Golden Rule).

**Equity pedagogy**  Teachers modifying their teaching in ways that will facilitate the academic achievement of students from diverse racial, cultural, language, and social-class groups.

**Ethics**  A branch of philosophy that emphasizes values that relate to "good" and "bad" behavior; examining morality; and rules of conduct. Proponents believe that an educated person must have these values and that all children should be taught them.

**Eurocentrism**  Term used to describe the heavy focus in school curricula on European history and contributions to Western civilization and the effective exclusion from instruction of the history and advances of other peoples.

**"Evaded" curriculum**  A term coined to describe issues central to students' lives that are addressed briefly, if at all, in most schools; examples include teenage pregnancy and sexually transmitted disease.

**Excellence movement**  Education reform movement of the mid-1980s, in which greater academic rigor and higher standards were required of both students and teachers.

**Extended school year**  Provision of education programs beyond the minimum number of school days mandated by law. Often referred to as "summer school."

**Extrinsic motivation**  Rewards or motivation that are external to an activity itself, such as grades, gold stars, and prizes.

**Fair use doctrine**  A legal principle defining specific, limited ways in which copyrighted material can be used without permission from the author.

**Family Educational Rights and Privacy Act (1974)**  *See* **Buckley Amendment.**

**Fetal Alcohol Syndrome (FAS)**  A disorder caused by a mother's consumption of alcohol during pregnancy, which can lead to retardation and delayed growth in the child.

**Formal curriculum**  Subjects taught in school and the instructional approaches used to transmit this knowledge.

**Formative assessment**  *See* **Formative evaluation.**

**Formative evaluation**  Evaluation used as a means of identifying a particular point of difficulty and prescribing areas in need of further work or development. Applied in developmental or implementation stages.

**Fourteenth Amendment**  Requires that there be no law "respecting the establishment of religion or prohibiting the free exercise thereof." Relevant case law has been applied to keep public schools neutral in matters of religion.

**Frontal teaching**  Traditional teaching method, now much criticized, in which the teacher's primary instructional method is lecturing in front of the classroom.

**Full-day kindergarten**  An extension of the standard initial three- or four-hour introductory educational program for four- to six-year-old children to a full six- to eight-hour program.

**Full-service schools**  Schools where the educational, health, psychological, and social requirements of students and their families are addressed by coordinating the services of professionals from these various disciplines at the school site.

**Gender equity**  Treating males and females equally in terms of opportunities to learn and expectations for achievement. Avoids gender bias or stereotyping.

**Globalization**  The recent move toward heightened connection among nations and people around the world, fed by technology, free markets, and the free flow of information.

**Goals 2000**  *See* **National Education Goals.**

**Group investigation**  Form of cooperative learning in which students work in small groups using cooperative inquiry, group discussion, and projects.

**Guided Reflection Protocol**  Method developed to aid teachers, alone or with colleagues, to think about their teaching practice.

**Head Start**  A federally funded compensatory education program, in existence since the mid-1960s, that provides additional educational services to young children suffering the effects of poverty.

**Heuristic learning**  Educational method in which the student is encouraged to learn independently through extensive and reflective trial-and-error investigation.

**Hidden curriculum**  *See* **Informal curriculum.**

**High-stakes tests**  The use of standardized test scores as a major determinant of significant educational outcomes, such as graduation, admission, or promotion.

**Higher-order thinking skills**  Skills involving critical analysis of a problem or situation; the ability to apply one's whole range of knowledge and cognitive skills to problem evaluation and decision making. To do so involves moving beyond such skills as memorization and demonstration to application and conceptual understanding.

**HIV [human immunodeficiency virus]**  An infection of the blood predisposing the individual to death from AIDS.

**Holistic scoring** Grading a student's work as a whole, considering achievement in all relevant skill areas; the opposite of analytic scoring, which involves grading work according to specific, quantifiable achievement criteria.

**Home schooling** A movement that allows parents to keep their children out of regular public or private school and to educate them in the home.

**Hypermedia** A framework for creating interconnected, weblike assemblages of content in a computer application or network. Hypermedia can be thought of as interlinked **multimedia** that the user can explore in a nonlinear manner, following embedded links from one piece of content (text, graphics, video, sound) to another.

**Ideology** The integrated assertions, theories, and aims that constitute a sociopolitical program.

**Inclusion** The commitment to educate each child, to the maximum extent appropriate, in the regular school and classroom, rather than moving children with disabilities to separate classes or institutions.

**Individualized education program/plan (IEP)** A management tool required for every student covered by the provisions of the **Individuals with Disabilities Education Act.** It must indicate a student's current level of performance, short- and long-term instructional objectives, services to be provided, and criteria and schedules for evaluation of progress.

**Individuals with Disabilities Education Act (IDEA)** Federal law passed in 1990, extending and expanding the provisions of the Education for All Handicapped Children Act of 1975.

**Informal curriculum** The teaching and learning that occur in school but are not part of the formal, or explicit, curriculum; also called the *hidden curriculum.*

*in loco parentis* The responsibility of the teacher to function "in the place of the parent" when a student is in school.

**Inquiry** An education method that confronts the learner with an issue or problem and guides the learner toward a solution.

**Inservice training** Training provided by a school or school district to improve the skills and competencies of its professional staff, particularly teachers.

**Intelligence** According to classical theory, a single and general human capacity to think and solve problems.

**Internet** A worldwide computer network that can be accessed by individuals to communicate with others and to retrieve various kinds of information stored electronically in many locations throughout the world.

**Interstate New Teacher Assessment and Support Consortium (INTASC)** A project sponsored by the Council of Chief State School Officers that is identifying standards for what beginning teachers should know and be able to do.

**Intrinsic motivation** Motivation that comes from the satisfaction of doing something, in contrast to **extrinsic motivation,** which comes from the reward received for doing something.

**Invented spelling** Child's attempt to express in symbols (letters) the group of sounds that make up a word.

**Iowa Test of Basic Skills** A series of standardized achievement tests that measure learning in reading, mathematics, language, and word study skills in grades K–9.

**IQ** Intelligence quotient, a measure of an individual's general intelligence.

**Jigsaw teaching** Form of cooperative learning in which each student on a team becomes "expert" on one topic by working with members from other teams assigned the same topic. On return to the home team, each expert teaches the group, and all students are assessed on all aspects of the topic.

**Kohlberg's moral dilemma discussions** Values education methodology involving presentation of moral dilemmas as catalysts for student discussions and the development of moral reasoning.

**Learning criteria** Specific statements of what students should know and be able to do after having completed a learning experience.

**Learning disability (LD)** A disability classification referring to a disorder in basic psychological processing that affects the individual's ability to listen, think, speak, read, write, spell, or do mathematical calculations. A learning disability is not primarily the result of visual, hearing, or motor disabilities; of mental retardation; of emotional disturbance; or of environmental, cultural, or economic disadvantage.

**Learning style** Characteristic way a student learns, including such factors as the way an individual processes information, preference for competition or cooperation, and preferred environmental conditions such as lighting or noise level.

**Least restrictive environment (LRE)** A requirement of the **Individuals with Disabilities Act** that students with disabilities should participate in regular education programs to the extent appropriate.

**Lemon test** A set of three requirements, established by the Supreme Court ruling in the case *Lemon v. Kurtzman,* that limits government action or legislation with respect to religion in the schools. Government action must not 1) have a religious purpose, 2) have the primary effect of either enhancing or inhibiting religion, and 3) create "excessive entanglement" between church and state.

**Liberal education** A broadly-based education that teaches people to think for themselves rather than follow a particular orthodoxy.

**Licensure (Licensing)** Governmental approval to perform certain work, such as teaching.

**Limited English Proficient (LEP)** Term for students whose native language is not English and who have difficulty understanding and using English.

**Linear thinking** The process of thinking through a concept or idea from start to finish by using step-by-step reasoning to reach a logical conclusion.

**Local area network (LAN)** A method of connecting computers within a relatively small area to allow people to work together and share information. Especially useful for fostering communication among classrooms within a school.

**Magnet schools** Alternative schools that provide instruction in specified areas such as the fine arts, for specific groups such as the gifted and talented, or using specific teaching styles such as open classrooms. In many cases, magnet schools are established as a method of promoting voluntary desegregation in schools.

**Mainstreaming** The practice of placing special education students in general education classes for at least part of the school day, while also providing additional services, programs, or classes as needed.

**Mastery learning** An instructional approach that requires students to achieve specific objectives before moving on to new material.

*McGuffey Readers* A six-volume series of textbooks, written by William Holmes McGuffey, that sold over 100 million copies during the nineteenth century. The books contained poetry, moral teachings,

and writings of statesmen and religious leaders, as well as grammar teaching.

**Median** A statistical term meaning the midpoint of a set of scores; that is, the point on either side of which half the scores occur.

**Melting pot** A metaphor and historical theory that suggests that although America takes in a wide variety of peoples (races, creeds, nationalities, and classes), the process of living in this country and being an American melts away differences so that all peoples blend together.

**Merit pay** The system of paying teachers according to the quality of their performance, usually by means of a bonus given for meeting specific goals.

**Metacognitive thinking** The process of monitoring one's own thinking.

**Metaknowledge** "Knowing what you know"; awareness of what knowledge one possesses.

**Mixed-ability (or heterogeneous) grouping** A placement approach in which students of different abilities are grouped together. Rooted in the belief that peer supervision, peer teaching, and group learning are effective means of educating all students, this approach is the opposite of **tracking** or ability grouping.

**Mnemonics** Techniques for improving the memory, such as creating an acronym of the phrase or information to be learned.

**Modern** A vague term, but usually refers to the time period after World War II.

**Moral leadership** Guiding or setting examples in matters of **ethics, character,** and right or wrong.

**Multicultural education** An approach to education intended to recognize cultural diversity and foster the cultural enrichment of all children and youth.

**Multiculturalism** A concept or situation in which individuals understand, respect, and participate in aspects (such as sports, food, customs, music, and language) of many different cultures.

**Multimedia** The combination of various media, such as text, graphics, video, music, voice narration, and manipulative objects; today, the term is often applied to computerized applications that incorporate two or more media.

**Multiple intelligence (MI) theory** A theory of human intelligence advanced by Howard Gardner, which suggests that humans have the psychobiological potential to solve problems or to fashion products that are valued in at least one cultural context. Gardner's research indicates at least eight separate faculties.

*A Nation at Risk: The Imperative for Educational Reform* A highly influential 1983 national commission report calling for extensive education reform, including more academic course requirements, more stringent college entrance requirements, upgraded and updated textbooks, and longer school days and years.

**National Assessment of Education Progress (NAEP)** A congressionally-mandated survey of American students that is the primary source on educational achievement, and has become known as "the nation's report card."

**National Board for Professional Teaching Standards (NBPTS)** A professional agency that is setting voluntary standards for what experienced teachers should know and be able to do in more than thirty different teaching areas.

**National Child Abuse Prevention and Treatment Act of 1974** Federal law that defines child abuse and neglect as "the physical or mental injury, sexual abuse or exploitation, negligent treatment, or maltreatment of a child under the age of eighteen, or the age specified by the child protection law of the state in question, by a person who is responsible for the child's welfare."

**National Commission on Teaching and America's Future** Blue-ribbon panel that in 1996 released the report *What Matters Most: Teaching for America's Future*. The report emphasized the importance of high-quality teaching and recommended the National Board certification of 105,000 teachers by the year 2006.

**National Council for Accreditation of Teacher Education (NCATE)** Nationally recognized organization awarding voluntary accreditation to college-level teacher education programs. Approximately 500 colleges and universities in the United States are accredited through NCATE.

**National Education Association (NEA)** The nation's largest teachers' association, founded in 1857 and having a membership of over 2.2 million educators.

**National Education Goals** Goals for U.S. education, established by the president and the fifty state governors in 1990.

*New England Primer* An illustrated book of religious texts and other readings that was the most famous basic school text for the period between 1690 and 1790.

**New math** A mathematics curriculum popular in the 1960s that focused on teaching students to understand the structure of the discipline of mathematics rather than on teaching computation techniques.

**Norming** The process of establishing norms for standardized tests, based on reviews of norm groups and their scores. Most tests are renormed approximately every seven years; the trend has been to raise norms on subsequent evaluations, so that increasingly higher performance has been required to reach the 50th percentile (or normal performance).

**Norm-referenced testing** Assessment in which an individual's performance is evaluated against what is typical of others in his or her peer group (i.e., norm*s*) (for comparison, *see* **criterion-referenced testing**).

**OERI** The Office of Educational Research and Improvement, a division of the U.S. Department of Education up until 2003.

**Old Deluder Act** A Massachusetts law passed in 1647 that strengthened an earlier law that required parents to educate their children by requiring citizens to support schools, which would in turn enable children to thwart the snares of Satan by their ability to read God's word in the Bible.

**Oldfield schools** An early form of community schools in rural areas, usually built in abandoned, worn-out fields and supported by parents' contributions and tuition payments.

**Paideia** From the Greek *pais,* meaning "the upbringing of a child"; used as the equivalent of the Latin *humanitas* (from which came "the humanities"), signifying the general learning that should be the possession of all human beings.

**Pantheism** The belief that there are many gods and that they inhabit all reality.

**Paraprofessional** A trained aide who assists a professional, such as a teacher's aide.

**Pedagogy** The art or profession of teaching.

**Peer coaching** A method by which teachers help one another learn new teaching strategies and material. It often involves release time to allow teachers to visit one another's classes as they start to use new programs, such as **cooperative learning.**

**Performance-based tests** Tests that require students to actually perform, as by writing or drawing, to demonstrate the skill being measured.

**Personalism** An approach to life that focuses on the satisfaction of individual desires.

**Philosophy**  The love or search for wisdom; the quest for basic principles to understand the meaning of life. Western philosophy traditionally contains five branches of philosophy: metaphysics, ethics, aesthetics, epistemology, and logic.

**Phonics**  An instructional strategy used to teach letter-sound relationships to beginning readers by having them sound out words.

**Politically correct (PC)**  A term coined to describe thinking that is politically popular. Taken to extreme, such thinking is so euphemistic and generalized as to be opinionless.

**Portfolio**  A collection of a person's work. For students, portfolios are being used as a relatively new form of authentic assessment. They can contain a great range of work, from paper and pen work to sculpture.

**Portfolio assessment**  A means of assessment based on a collection of a person's work. For students, portfolios may contain a great range of work, from paper and pen work to sculpture.

**Positivism**  A philosophy asserting a radical distinction between facts, which can be scientifically proven, and values, which positivism holds are mere expressions of feelings, not objective truth. Positivism provides the philosophical underpinnings for moral **relativism.**

**Postmodern**  Somewhat imprecise term, usually denoting the period that began during the latter third of the twentieth century, characterized by the heavy social influence of mass media, technology, new social and sexual mores, and a change in the traditional roles of men and women.

**Pragmatism**  Belief that one tests truth by its practical consequences. Therefore, truth is relative.

**Presage characteristics**  Characteristics of teachers resulting from formative experiences, training, and individual properties such as intelligence and personality.

**Private venture schools**  Schools run by individuals or corporations, which theoretically can generate a profit.

**Privatization**  A movement in which public schools are run by private, often for-profit, organizations.

**Problem-solving skills**  Skills involving the application of knowledge and information to solving a given problem, for example, definition, analysis, comparison/contrast, and sequencing; synonymous with **higher-order thinking skills.**

**Process criteria**  Learning criteria used for grading and reporting in which teachers take into account effort, work habits, classroom quizzes, homework, class participation, or attendance. (For comparison, *see* **product criteria** and **progress criteria.**)

**Product criteria**  Learning criteria used for grading and reporting in which teachers base their grades or reports exclusively on final examination scores, overall assessments, or other culminating demonstrations of learning. (For comparison, *see* **process criteria** and **progress criteria.**)

**Professional development**  Continuous advances in teacher's knowledge and skills; lifelong learning.

**Professional development schools**  Innovative public schools formed through partnerships between professional education programs and P–12 schools. Their mission is professional preparation of candidates, faculty development, inquiry directed at the improvement of practice, and enhanced student learning.

**Professionalization of teaching**  The movement toward establishing or recognizing teaching as a profession, not merely an application of skills toward a particular task. This movement supports such practices as **site-based decision making** and other efforts that give teachers more authority and control over educating students.

**Progress criteria**  Highly individualized learning criteria used for grading and reporting in which teachers look at how far students have come rather than where they are. (For comparison, *see* **process criteria** and **product criteria.**)

**Progressive school**  A school that focuses on students' personal and social development. *See* **progressivism.**

**Progressivism (progressive ideals)**  An educational philosophy that embraces largely unstructured educational programs, focusing on implicit teaching and individualized instruction.

**Provincial**  Social values that are determined by local traditions and mores.

**Pull-out groups**  Groups of students who periodically leave the regular classroom for special education services. For instance, students with hearing impairments may attend regular sessions of instruction in sign language.

**Readiness**  A judgment that a student is capable of learning a specific topic or skill.

**Reciprocal teaching**  An instructional procedure designed to teach students cognitive strategies that might lead to improved reading comprehension. Examples include summarization, question generation, clarification, and prediction, supported through dialogue between teacher and students and the attempt to gain meaning from the text.

**Reflection**　An inner process in which the individual thinks back on events, attempting to see them in a more objective matter with a view toward improvement.

**Regression analysis**　A statistical approach that allows judgment regarding the impact of one variable independent of the effects of other variables.

**Relativism**　The theory that all truth is relative to the individual and to the time or place in which he or she acts.

**Romanticism**　A nineteenth-century philosophical movement celebrating all that is natural and disparaging all that is artificial. In education, this philosophy leads to a focus on the child's natural instincts and interests.

**Sabbatical**　A study leave granted to selected teachers, usually after a number of years of service.

**Saxon Math Program**　A traditional skills-based approach for teaching mathematics developed by John Saxon; it emphasizes repetition of mathematical operations.

**School choice**　Allowing parents to select alternative educational programs for their children, either within a given school or among different schools.

**School culture**　The prevailing mores, values, and rituals that permeate a school.

**School within a school**　In large schools, the establishment of "houses" of teachers and 100 to 400 students who spend much of their time together.

**Scientific creationism**　A theory of world creation, based on the Book of Genesis, that some Christians have proposed as a counterbalance to the teaching of evolution in science classes.

**Scientism**　An exaggerated trust in the efficacy of the methods of natural science to explain social or psychological phenomena, to solve pressing human problems, or to provide a comprehensive unified picture of the meaning of the **cosmos.**

**SCORE**　Acronym for the essential goals in Strong, Silver, and Robinson's model of student engagement: *Success, Curiosity, Originality,* and *Relationships,* resulting in *Energy* to complete tasks and work productively.

**Secularism**　An educational approach that ignores religious and spiritual perspectives in favor of a scientific and totally human perspective, excluding, too, the role of religious motivation in his-

torical events (e.g., the movement to free slaves in nineteenth-century America).

**Segregation**　The act of separating people according to such characteristics as race, ethnicity, or **socioeconomic status.** In education, the fact that most students attend schools in the areas in which they live means that student populations will be homogeneous and thus segregated; **desegregation** is achieved when student populations are mixed.

**Self-actualization**　The status of having achieved one's potential through one's own efforts. Providing opportunities for self-actualization greatly promotes self-esteem.

**Self-fulfilling prophecy**　Students' behavior that comes about as a result of teachers' expectations that the students will behave in a certain way. Teachers expect students to behave in a certain way, they communicate those expectations by both overt and subtle means, and students respond by behaving in the way expected.

**Sexism**　Discriminatory attitudes and actions against a particular gender group, especially women.

**Sexual harassment**　Acts directed against an individual of the opposite sex that are intended to humiliate, intimidate, or oppress. Sexual harassment includes making comments of a sexual nature, propositioning, touching, making unwelcome sexual advances, or making one's successful employment or education contingent upon accepting or tolerating such harassment.

**Sexually-transmitted diseases (STDs)**　Bacteria and infectious syndromes, including syphilis, gonorrhea, chlamydia, trichomonas, bacterial vaginosis, and pelvic inflammatory disease.

**Site-based management**　*See* **Site- or school-based decision making.**

**Site- or school-based decision making**　A school reform effort to decentralize, allowing decisions to be made and budgets to be established at the school-building level, where most of the changes need to occur. Usually teachers become involved in the decision-making process. Also known as *site-based management* or *school-based management.*

**Skepticism**　An attitude of doubt or a disposition to incredulity either in general or toward a particular object.

**Social justice**　The concept of doing away with social and economic inequalities for those in our society who have been denied these benefits of a democratic society.

**Social learning theory** The part of psychology that deals with human learning in social situations, including attitudes, motivations, and behavior.

**Social promotion** The practice of promoting students to the next grade whether or not they have accomplished the goals of their current grade.

**Socialization** The general process of social learning whereby the child learns the many things he or she must know to become an acceptable member of society.

**Socioeconomic status** The status one occupies on the basis of social and economic factors such as income level, educational level, occupation, area of residence, family background, and the like.

**Socratic instruction** A method of teaching in which the teacher asks questions and leads the student through responses and discussion to an understanding of the information being taught.

**Split-brain theory** Theory suggesting that certain intellectual capacities and functions are controlled by the left hemisphere of the brain and others by the right hemisphere.

**Spreadsheet** Computer software used to calculate and analyze numerical data.

*Sputnik 1* The Soviet rocket launched into space in 1957 that threatened American security and thus stimulated educational reform.

**Standard** Exemplary performance that serves as a benchmark.

**Standardized tests** Tests given to large groups of students under uniform, or standard, conditions and scored according to uniform procedures.

**Standards-based education** *See* **Standard** and **Standards movement.**

**Standards-based reform** *See* **Standards movement.**

**Standards movement** Efforts at the local, state, and federal level to make clear exactly what students need to know and be able to do and, therefore, what schools need to teach. Implicit in the standards movement is an attempt to increase the academic achievement of students.

**Summative assessment** *See* **Summative evaluation.**

**Summative evaluation** Evaluation used to assess the adequacy or outcome of a program after the program has been fully developed and implemented.

**Tao** A Chinese term used by C. S. Lewis that combines the wisdom of many cultures to identify a universal path to becoming a good person.

**Teach for America** An alternative teacher education and placement program for college graduates who have not taken an undergraduate teacher preparation program. After training, recruits are placed in urban or rural schools and make a two-year commitment to stay in teaching.

**Teacher competencies** The characteristics that make a teacher qualified to do the job, including various areas of subject-matter expertise and a wide range of personality variables. Some school reform proposals urge that teachers undergo periodic assessment of their competencies to maintain licensure or earn incentives.

**Teacher empowerment** The process of giving teachers (or of teachers taking) greater control over their professional lives and how they deliver their educational services.

**Teaching for understanding** An educational approach in which the goal is to enable students to explain information in their own words and use it effectively in school and nonschool settings. This approach fosters the development of **critical thinking** or **problem-solving skills** through the direct application of knowledge and information.

**Teaching portfolio** Collection of such items as research papers, pupil evaluations, teaching units, and videocassettes of lessons to reflect the quality of a teacher's teaching. Portfolios can be used to illustrate to employers the teacher's expertise or to obtain national board certification.

**Tenure** A legal right that confers continuing employment on teachers, protecting them from dismissal without adequate cause.

**TIMSS** The Third International Mathematics and Science Study, which is the largest and most extensive international study of academic achievement in mathematics and science ever undertaken.

*Tinker v. Des Moines Independent Community School District* The 1969 decision in which the Supreme Court held that the schools cannot prohibit students' expression of opinions when the expression does not materially and substantially interfere with the requirements of appropriate discipline in the schools; to do so would violate the First Amendment of the Constitution.

**Title I (Chapter 1)** Part of the 1965 Elementary and Secondary Education Act that delivers federal funds to local school districts and schools for the education of students from low-income families. It also supplements the educational services provided to low-achieving students in those districts.

**Title IX** A provision of the 1972 federal Education Amendment Act that prohibits discrimination on the basis of sex for any educational program or activity receiving federal financial assistance.

**Tracking**   The homogeneous grouping of students for learning tasks on the basis of some measure(s) of their abilities.

**Traditional school**   A school that seeks to transmit to its students the best knowledge, skills, and values in society.

**Transfer of learning**   Connection or application of learned material to future knowledge or skill acquisition.

**Values clarification**   A values education methodology advocating the presentation of values to students free from imposed value judgments. Students should then be allowed freedom to choose their own values.

**Voucher programs**   A type of **school choice** plan that gives parents a receipt or written statement that they can exchange for the schooling they feel is most desirable for their child. The school, in turn, can cash in its received vouchers for the money to pay teachers and buy resources.

**White flight**   A response to public school racial integration efforts in which white citizens move out of the central city into the suburbs so their children can attend neighborhood schools with a lower percentage of minority students.

**Whole language**   A progressive approach to the teaching of reading that emphasizes the integration of language arts skills and knowledge across the curriculum.

**Word processing**   Computer software used for writing.

**World Wide Web**   An interconnected collection of individual information, opinion, and entertainment sites available on the Internet.

# Index

# *Article Review Form*

Feel free to photocopy this page and use it to help you review each article you read in this edition of *Kaleidoscope*.

Name: _____ Date: _____ Article no.: _____

**In your own words, briefly state the main idea of the article.**

_____

_____

_____

_____

**With what points or arguments made by the author(s) do you agree or disagree?**
*Agree:*

_____

_____

_____

*Disagree:*

_____

_____

_____

**What did you learn from the article that you think is (1) important, (2) interesting, and (3) unclear?**

(1) _____

(2) _____

(3) _____

**List any new terms or concepts you found in the article, and briefly define them.**

_____

_____

_____

_____

# Student Response Form

We'd like to make this book as useful as we can for readers, and your views are vital to our task. What did you think about the selection of articles in this tenth edition of *Kaleidoscope*? Your comments on the form below will help us revise the book for the next edition. You can use a scale of 1 to 5 to "grade" the articles you've read:

5—Excellent   4—Good   3—Average   2—Below average   1—Poor

Please mail the completed form to College Marketing, Houghton Mifflin Company, 222 Berkeley Street, Boston, MA 02116-3764.

**Grade    Author/Title**

_____ 1. Csikszentmihalyi & McCormack, *The Influence of Teachers*

_____ 2. Hole & McEntee, *Reflection Is at the Heart of Practice*

_____ 3. Fried, *The Heart of the Matter*

_____ 4. Ducharme, *The Great Teacher Question: Beyond Competencies*

_____ 5. Haberman, *Selecting "Star" Teachers for Children and Youth in Urban Poverty*

_____ 6. Wise, *Creating a High-Quality Teaching Force*

_____ 7. Wolf, *Developing an Effective Teaching Portfolio*

_____ 8. Ness, *Lessons of a First-Year Teacher*

_____ 9. Houghton, *Finding Allies: Sustaining Teachers' Health and Well-Being*

_____ 10. Metzger, *Calling in the Cosmos*

_____ 11. Crowley, *Letter from a Teacher*

_____ 12. Barr, *Who Is This Child?*

_____ 13. Edelman, *Leaving No Child Behind*

_____ 14. Eitzen, *Problem Students: The Sociocultural Roots*

_____ 15. Woods, *Hostile Hallways*

_____ 16. Wasicsko & Ross, *How to Create Discipline Problems*

_____ 17. Cates, Markell, & Bettenhausen, *At Risk for Abuse: A Teacher's Guide for Recognizing and Reporting Child Neglect and Abuse*

_____ 18. Strong, Silver, & Robinson, *What Do Students Want (and What Really Motivates Them)?*

_____ 19. Barth, *The Culture Builder*

_____ 20. Elkind, *The Cosmopolitan School*

_____ 21. Cuban, *A Tale of Two Schools*

_____ 22. Cohen, *Schools Our Teachers Deserve*

**Grade    Author/Title**

_____ 23. Wasley, *Small Classes, Small Schools: The Time Is Now*

_____ 24. Finders & Lewis, *Why Some Parents Don't Come to School*

_____ 25. Hofferth & Jankuniene, *Life After School*

_____ 26. Lines, *Home Schooling Comes of Age*

_____ 27. Peddiwell, *The Saber-Tooth Curriculum*

_____ 28. Thompson, *The Authentic Standards Movement and Its Evil Twin*

_____ 29. Adler, *The Paideia Proposal: Rediscovering the Essence of Education*

_____ 30. Hirsch, *Seeking Breadth and Depth in the Curriculum*

_____ 31. Glasser, *The Quality School Curriculum*

_____ 32. Nord, *The Relevance of Religion to the Curriculum*

_____ 33. Noddings, *Teaching Themes of Care*

_____ 34. Ryan, *Mining the Values in the Curriculum*

_____ 35. Kirby, *What Does the Research Say About Sexuality Education?*

_____ 36. Haycock, *Closing the Achievement Gap*

_____ 37. Dodd, *Engaging Students: What I Learned Along the Way*

_____ 38. Clifford, *Students Need Challenge, Not Easy Success*

_____ 39. Perkins, *The Many Faces of Constructivism*

_____ 40. Guskey, *Making the Grade: What Benefits Students?*

_____ 41. Johnson & Johnson, *Making Cooperative Learning Work*

_____ 42. Cooper, *Homework for All—in Moderation*

_____ 43. Stiggins, *Assessment Crisis: The Absence of Assessment FOR Learning*

| Grade | Author/Title |
|---|---|
| _____ | 44. Tomlinson, *Mapping a Route Toward Differentiated Instruction* |
| _____ | 45. Hardiman, *Connecting Brain Research with Dimensions of Learning* |
| _____ | 46. Dewey, *My Pedagogic Creed* |
| _____ | 47. Hutchins, *The Basis of Education* |
| _____ | 48. Rogers, *Personal Thoughts on Teaching and Learning* |
| _____ | 49. Hirsch, *Romancing the Child* |
| _____ | 50. Boyer, *The Educated Person* |
| _____ | 51. Carper, *The Changing Landscape of U.S. Education* |
| _____ | 52. Glickman, *Dichotomizing Education: Why No One Wins and America Loses* |
| _____ | 53. Strike, *The Ethics of Teaching* |
| _____ | 54. McDaniel, *The Teacher's Ten Commandments: School Law in the Classroom* |
| _____ | 55. Lickona, *The Return of Character Education* |
| _____ | 56. Darling-Hammond, *What Matters Most: A Competent Teacher for Every Child* |
| _____ | 57. Eisner, *The Kind of Schools We Need* |
| _____ | 58. Raywid, *Accountability: What's Worth Measuring?* |

| Grade | Author/Title |
|---|---|
| _____ | 59. Miles, *Putting Money Where It Matters* |
| _____ | 60. Viteritti, *Coming Around on School Choice* |
| _____ | 61. McDonald, *The False Promise of Vouchers* |
| _____ | 62. Levin, *Bear Market* |
| _____ | 63. David, *The Who, What, and Why of Site-Based Management* |
| _____ | 64. Healy, *The Mad Dash to Compute* |
| _____ | 65. Postman, *Making a Living, Making a Life: Technology Reconsidered* |
| _____ | 66. Means, *Technology Use in Tomorrow's Schools* |
| _____ | 67. Ravitch, *A Considered Opinion: Diversity, Tragedy, and the Schools* |
| _____ | 68. Banks, *Multicultural Education in the New Century* |
| _____ | 69. Stotsky, *Multicultural Illiteracy* |
| _____ | 70. Minicucci, Berman, McLaughlin, McLeod, Nelson, & Woodworth, *School Reform and Student Diversity* |
| _____ | 71. Bailey, *Shortchanging Girls and Boys* |
| _____ | 72. Merritt, *Clearing the Hurdles of Inclusion* |
| _____ | 73. Kluth, Villa, & Thousand, *"Our School Doesn't Offer Inclusion" and Other Legal Blunders* |
| _____ | 74. Loveless, *The Parent Trap* |

Title of course in which you used this book: _____

Name of your school: _____

Your name (optional): _____

Suggestions for next edition (topics, types of articles, specific selections—any ideas you'd like to share with us):

_____

_____

_____

_____

_____